W9-CEV-920

Sixth Edition

Volume II: Since 1865
Chapters 17–32

NATION OF NATIONS

A Narrative History of the American Republic

James West Davidson

Brian DeLay
University of Colorado

Christine Leigh Heyrman
University of Delaware

Mark H. Lytle
Bard College

Michael B. Stoff
University of Texas, Austin

Here is not merely a nation but a teeming nation of nations
Walt Whitman

McGraw-Hill
Higher Education

Boston   Burr Ridge, IL   Dubuque, IA   New York   San Francisco   St. Louis
Bangkok   Bogotá   Caracas   Kuala Lumpur   Lisbon   London   Madrid   Mexico City
Milan   Montreal   New Delhi   Santiago   Seoul   Singapore   Sydney   Taipei   Toronto

The McGraw-Hill Companies

McGraw-Hill
Higher Education

NATION OF NATIONS: A NARRATIVE HISTORY OF THE AMERICAN REPUBLIC,
VOLUME II: SINCE 1865

Published by McGraw-Hill, a business unit of The McGraw-Hill Companies, Inc., 1221 Avenue of the
Americas, New York, NY 10020. Copyright © 2008 by The McGraw-Hill Companies, Inc. All rights
reserved. No part of this publication may be reproduced or distributed in any form or by any means, or
stored in a database or retrieval system, without the prior written consent of The McGraw-Hill Companies,
Inc., including, but not limited to, any network or other electronic storage or transmission, or
broadcast for distance learning.

Some ancillaries, including electronic and print components, may not be available to customers outside
the United States.

1 2 3 4 5 6 7 8 9 0 DOW/DOW 0 9 8

ISBN: 978-0-07-333016-7
MHID: 0-07-333016-7

Vice president and editor-in-chief: *Michael Ryan*   Manuscript editor: *Stacey Sawyer*
Publisher: *Lisa Moore*   Art director: *Jeanne M. Schreiber*
Sponsoring editor: *Jon-David Hague*   Design manager: *Violeta Díaz*
Development editors: *Barbara Conover,*   Cover designer: *Laurie Entringer*
 Nicole Caddigan-Bridge   Interior designer: *Kiera Pohl*
Editorial coordinator: *Sora Lisa Kim*   Art manager: *Robin Mouat*
Marketing manager: *Pamela Cooper*   Photo research coordinator: *Nora Agbayani*
Marketing Specialist: *Clare Cashen*   Photo researcher: *PhotoSearch, Inc.*
Media Project Manager: *Jessalyn Clark*   Illustrators: *Mapping Specialists, Patti Isaacs*
Production editor: *Mel Valentín*   Production supervisor: *Richard DeVitto*
Production assistant: *Rachel J. Castillo*

The text was set in 10/12 ITC Galliard Std Roman by Aptara-York, and printed on acid-free 45#
Publisher's Matte Plus by R.R. Donnelley & Sons.

Cover image: Selma to Montgomery March (1965). Photograph © James H. Karales. Used by permission Estate of James Karales.

Page 244-45 From Charles A. Johnson, *Frontier Camp Meeting*, pp. 43 and 47, copyright 1955, 1985.
SMU Press. Reprinted with permission; **435** "Resources of the Union and the Confederacy, 1861",
Adapted from THE CIVIL WAR DAY BY DAY by E.B. Long, copyright © 1971 by E.B. Long. Used
by permission of Doubleday, a division of Random House, Inc.; **506** "Spending on Education in the
South before and after Disfranchisement", Robert A. Margo, Disfranchisement, School Finance, and
the Economics of Segregated Schools in the U.S. South, 1890–1910 (New York: Garland Press, 1985).
Table 1-1; **718** Charles P. Kindleberg, "Declining World Trade, 1929–1933", *The World in Depression,
1929–1939* (revised ed., 1986) p. 170. copyright © 1986. The Regents of the University of California;
831 Levy, Frank. Figure 6.1, "Major U.S. Migration Flows in the late 1940s and 1950s." In *Dollars and
Dreams: The Changing American Income Distribution.* © 1987 Russell Sage Foundation, 112 East 64th
St., New York, NY 10021. Reprinted with Permission.

Because this page cannot legibly accommodate all acknowledgements for copyrighted material, credits
appear at the end of the book, and constitute an extension of this copyright page.

Library of Congress Cataloging-in-Publication Data
Nation of nations : a history of the American Republic / James West Davidson . . . [et al.].
—6th ed.
    p. cm.
Includes bibliographical references and index.
ISBN-13: 978-0-07-340684-8 (alk. paper)
ISBN-10: 0-07-340684-8 (alk. paper)
 1. United States—History—Textbooks. 2. United States—History—Sources. I. Davidson,
James West.
E178.1.N346 2007
973—dc22   2007042451

Contents in Brief

Contents

Chapter 17
Reconstructing the Union
1865–1877

Chapter 18
The New South and the
Trans-Mississippi West
1870–1914

Chapter 19
The New Industrial Order
1870–1914

Chapter 22

The Progressive Era 1890–1920

Chapter 23

The United States and the Collapse of the Old World Order 1901–1920

Chapter 24

The New Era 1920–1929

Chapter 25

The Great Depression and the New Deal 1929–1939

Chapter 26
America's Rise to Globalism
1927–1945

Chapter 31
The Conservative Challenge
1976–1992

Chapter 32

Nation of Nations in a Global Community 1980–2007

List of Maps and Charts

Preface to the Sixth Edition

This revision is the most comprehensive one undertaken since the book was conceived more than two decades ago. Our touchstone remains the same—that all good history begins with a good story. But the shape of that story continues to change, enriched by stimulating recent scholarship. We have sought to place the history of this "nation of nations"—Walt Whitman's phrase—within a broader context of communities and environments, from the earliest peopling of the continent to our ongoing complex relationship with its resources. *Nation of Nations* has always been characterized by our attention to a global perspective, and we have made an even stronger effort to establish both continental and international frameworks for such topics as the trans-Atlantic communities created in the wake of first contact between Europe, Africa, and the Americas; the economic and cultural systems created by the spread of slavery and plantation agricultures; the dispersion of democratic and industrial revolutions and a consumer culture in the eighteenth and nineteenth centuries; the imperial and colonial conflicts of the late nineteenth and twentieth centuries; and the tightly linked information networks and global terrorism of the twenty-first century.

The addition of a new author to the *Nation of Nations* team, Brian DeLay of the University of Colorado, sparks our continued effort to incorporate perspectives that are both continental and global. DeLay's transnational study of how native peoples shaped the era of the U.S.-Mexican War, *The War of a Thousand Deserts* (2008), takes just such a continental perspective, integrating Indians and their politics into the narrative of both nation's histories during the first half of the nineteenth century. Especially in Volume I, *Nation of Nations* provides expanded coverage of the dynamics of white-Indian relations, and greater emphasis on the southwestern and western United States than in previous editions.

While adding to our scholarship, we have also streamlined and trimmed our existing narrative, maintaining sensitivity to length and the oft mentioned demands of "too much material and too little time."

Changes to the Sixth Edition

New Features:

- **Chapter Outlines:** For quick and easy reference, brief outlines appear at the beginning of each chapter, mapping out the organization and objectives of the reading material.

- *After the Fact in Brief:* In addition to the longer essays, every chapter of the text now includes a shorter feature, *After the Fact in Brief,* showcasing the variety of evidence historians consult when piecing together the past. Beyond the traditional primary sources, such evidence can include cartoons, maps, material culture—everything from a grisly skull pendant (Chapter 2) to a starched collar (Chapter 19) or an atomic blaster ring (Chapter 27).

- **Global conclusions:** Each chapter ends with a thematic conclusion that steps back to place events in American history in a continental or global context.

- **Map program:** All of the maps have been completely redesigned and updated to provide an exceptional visual presentation and clarity that supports the narrative.

The following list represents a few of the many instances of new and expanded coverage:

- **Chapter 18** includes discussion of both the Southern and the Western ties to international markets and the scramble for colonies rich in natural resources.

Just as the North became increasingly focused on using the South and West as sources of raw materials, European nations were engaged in their own imperialistic search for raw materials.

- **Chapter 20** notes the rise of urban environments worldwide, from Germany to Tokyo. It puts the flood of "new immigrants" to the United States in perspective, noting, for example, that before 1900 two of every three emigrating Italians booked passage not for the United States but for South America.

- **Chapter 22** links the Progressive movement in the United States with progressive reform across the industrialized world, some of it preceding efforts in America by many decades. This chapter also includes discussion of women's suffrage movements across the globe.

- **Chapter 24** includes a new section which compares and contrasts the positions of Booker T. Washington, Marcus Garvey, the Harlem Renaissance, and W. E. B. Du Bois. New material on the Great Flood of 1927 discusses the environmental effects of deforestation, the devastation for African Americans in the Mississippi Delta, and the first piece of legislation to give the government responsibility for controlling such disasters.

- **Chapter 29** includes new material highlighting the link between the American civil rights movement and third world nationalist movements in Africa.

- Vietnam coverage in revamped **Chapter 30** now takes the narrative from the escalation of the 1960s through the fall of Saigon within a single chapter. A revised discussion of the identity and value politics movements highlights the interconnections and overlaps among Latino and Native American movements, feminism, and the consumer and environmental movements. The narrative makes clearer how domestic policy and foreign policy both undermined the consensus politics of the 1950s. This chapter compares protests on American campuses with student movements in Europe, the "Prague Spring" in Czechoslovakia, and the lionizing of radicals like Mao Zedong, Che Guevara, and Ho Chi Minh.

- **Chapter 31** has been thoroughly revised to reflect recent scholarship on the Reagan presidency. The Carter presidency is presented as a part of the conservative trend in American politics and society. New scholarship on evangelical Christians and the Moral Majority places Conservative Christian politics in a broader context. A section on Technoburbs explores the new computer-generated information and medical technology systems that created new lifestyles, jobs, and communities during the 1980s.

- **The epilogue from the fifth edition is incorporated into a single final chapter,** taking the narrative from 1992 to the present, including more recent developments in the war on terror, the Iraq War, the disaster caused by Hurricane Katrina, and the domestic policies of the Bush administration.

Information about Supplements

For Students

Online Learning Center The Online Learning Center, at www.mhhe.com/davidsonnation6, provides them a wide range of tools that will help students test their understanding of the book. It includes chapter overviews, interactive maps, quizzes, and primary source indexes.

Primary Source Investigator Now Available Online.

McGraw-Hill's Primary Source Investigator (PSI), now available online at www.mhhe.com/psi, is designed to support and enrich the text discussion in *Nation of Nations*. PSI gives instructors and students access to more than 650 primary and secondary sources including documents, images, maps, and videos. Students can use these resources to formulate and defend their arguments as well as further their understanding of the topics discussed in each chapter. All assets are indexed alphabetically as well as by type, subject, place, and time period, allowing students and instructors to locate resources quickly and easily.

- **Online Reader:** The Online Reader gives students an opportunity to try their hand at historical analysis. Based on sources found in PSI, the reader's modules ask students to evaluate sources and formulate their own interpretations and analysis.
- **Writing Guide:** The online Writing Guide offers both general assistance for writing college papers, as well as specific tips for history papers. Topics include research, paragraph and argument creation, a comparison of style guides, information on plagiarism and source citation, and much more.

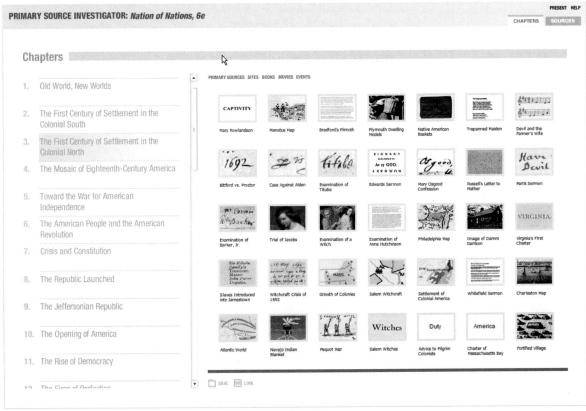

For the Instructor

Online Learning Center for Instructors The Online Learning Center located at www.mhhe.com/davidsonnation6 includes the computerized test bank and power point presentations. The annotated Faculty Guide provides a list of themes, lecture strategies, and easy reference to all learning assets, both in the text and on PSI. Each chapter is accompanied by a rich list of resources, including PowerPoint slides, image bank, outline maps, book maps, and test bank questions, all keyed to the chapter. Resources are organized within chapters by A-Heads to streamline lecture and assignment preparation. Icons allow users to quickly differentiate between text and PSI sources.

Classroom Performance System (CPS) The Classroom Performance System brings ultimate interactivity to *Nation of Nations*. CPS is a wireless response system that gives you immediate feedback from every student in the class. With CPS you can ask subjective and objective questions during your lecture, prompting every student to respond with their individual, wireless response pad, and providing you with instant results. A complete CPS Tutorial is available at www.einstruction.com.

Acknowledgments

We are grateful to the many reviewers who generously offered comments and suggestions at various stages in our development of this manuscript. Our thanks go to:

Keith J. Alexander
Jefferson Community College,
Indiana-Purdue University

Jonathan M. Atkins
Berry College

Mario A.J. Bennekin
Georgia Perimeter College

Jamie Bronstein
New Mexico State University

Kathleen S. Carter
High Point University

Douglas W. Dodd
CSU Bakersfield

Hal Friedman
Henry Ford Community College

David J. Gerleman
George Mason University,
Marymount University

Reid Holland
Midlands Technical College

Carol A. Keller
San Antonio College

Andrew S. Moore
Saint Anselm College

Robert Olwell
University of Texas at Austin

Jaako Puisto
California State University, Stanislaus

Jonathan Rees
Colorado State University–Pueblo

Philip Rubio
Duke University

Mark Meltzer Sawin
Eastern Mennonite University

John E. Semonche
UNC–Chapel Hill

Steven Schultz
Mesa State College

Michael Shepherd
Mid-South Community College

Susan Strauss
Santa Fe Community College

Richard A. Straw
Radford University

Paul D. Travis
Texas Women's University

Paul Toro
Alamo Community College

Richard A. Voeltz
Cameron University

David White
McHenry County College

William Woodward
Seattle Pacific University

One acknowledgment we can never make too often is to the work of our co-author, colleague, and friend, William E. Gienapp. Bill traveled with us on this journey from the book's earliest conception up until his untimely passing in 2003. His insight, erudition and good humor made him a pleasure to work with, and his contribution to the book will endure no matter how many new revisions appear. We would like also to thank Bill's wife, Erica Gienapp, for her unstinting assistance over the years, as she provided suggestions for new illustrations, patient reminders about misplaced modifiers, and substantive contributions to the text. Our families have continued to lend their encouragement but in particular our new member of the team, Brian DeLay, would like to thank his wife, Diliana Angelova, for her support. And as always, we appreciate any suggestions, corrections, or comments from our readers.

James West Davidson
Brian DeLay
Christine Leigh Heyrman
Mark H. Lytle
Michael B. Stoff

Additional Features

Chapter Table of Contents

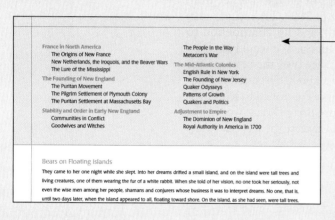

Bears on Floating Islands

They came to her one night while she slept. Into her dreams drifted a small island, and on the island were tall trees and living creatures, one of them wearing the fur of a white rabbit. When she told of her vision, no one took her seriously, not even the wise men among her people, shamans and conjurers whose business it was to interpret dreams. No one, that is, until two days later, when the island appeared to all, floating toward shore. On the island, as she had seen, were tall trees,

Brief outlines appear at the beginning of each chapter, mapping out the organization and chapter reading objectives.

After the Fact

Each chapter in the text includes a brief essay presenting the detective work and research strategies used by historians as they go about reconstructing the past. A wide variety of methods are showcased, from demographic analysis to the deconstruction of cartoons and songs to the exploration of material culture, films, diaries, murals, and statues. The topics under discussion include skull pendants, starched collars, Indian blankets, the Cuyahoga river fire, Ku Klux Klan costumes, minie balls and repeating rifles, phonographs, Scopes trial songs, and the "Great Wall" mural of Tujunga Wash. In addition to these brief features, eight longer essays examine topics in more detail, including the relationship between Thomas Jefferson and Sally Hemings, the causes of the New York draft riots, the demise of the bison and the decision to drop two atomic bombs on Japan.

AFTER THE FACT in Brief
"His Master's Voice"

Assessing the Technologies of Imperialism

How do historians measure the reach and influence of imperialism? Clearly technology played an important role in the conquests of the "Great Powers," most obviously the technology of force, including rifles, explosives, battleships with cannons and armor-plated hulls. But in subduing native peoples, western nations also depended on less blunt instruments such as trade (of goods eagerly desired) and religion (which preached a salvation-embracing western culture along with the westerners' god). Imperialism's reach was also extended by another force, which might be referred to as the technology of culture.

When Edison invented the phonograph in 1877, few people would have thought of it as a weapon of conquest. Instead, it was considered an instrument of entertainment and a civilizing force. But when Americans and Europeans brought the machine with them to less technologically advanced societies, native peoples were awestruck by the sounds it made and sometimes cowed by those who controlled it. These white men, it appeared, had the power to conjure up the voices of invisible speakers and summon music from thin air. The RCA Victrola Company for many years used the painting of a dog sitting attentively in front of an old-fashioned phonograph, with the slogan, "His Master's Voice." Historians have come to see Edison's talking machine as one element (can you think of others?) of the technology of culture that helped make the Great Powers masters.

Daily Lives

DAILY LIVES Play Ball

crowd goes wild, cheering their favorites. So many magnificent athletes trained to win, looking all the more formidable in their heavily padded gear. Which team will carry the day? A great deal is at stake for both players and spectators—honor, wealth, perhaps even life itself. The outcome hangs on the arc of a ball.

The Super Bowl? The World Series? Good guesses, because those present-day athletic spectacles bear striking resemblances to the scene described above: the beginning of a ball game in pre-Columbian Mesoamerica. Those contests, with all their accompanying fanfare, consumed the attention of both elites and commoners for many centuries.

It was the Olmecs who got the ball rolling (and flying) around 1500 B.C.E. In the main plazas of their cities, they built ornate stone ballcourts for teams to compete and celebrated star athletes with towering stone sculptures. Even as civilizations rose and fell in Mesoamerica, the passion for playing ball, following the games, and gambling on their outcome not only endured but even spread to the Hohokam in the American Southwest. Archaeological digs have revealed that nearly every city built by the Maya, Toltecs, and Aztecs boasted its own ball court: the most impressive were larger than present-day football fields, painted in vivid colors, and decorated with intricately carved birds, jaguars, and skeletal heads. Renowned players inspired artists to paint murals or to fashion clay figurines depicting ballplayers in full

athletic regalia—kneepads, gloves, and belts festooned with images of their gods or skeletal heads.

In most cultures, the rules of the game dictated that players could use only their hips, buttocks, or knees to bounce the ball against the parallel walls of the court and the alley lying between. And after about A.D. 800, the game became even more challenging: teams earned the most points by shooting hoops—that is, by sending the ball through a stone ring set in the center of the side walls. No mean feat, since players could not use their hands or feet, and the impact of a flying ball—about six pounds of solid rubber—could inflict serious and even fatal injuries.

But it was the ritual significance of these competitions that made for greater danger. In the Southwest, ball games often figured as friendly rivalries, festive occasions intended to strengthen military or trading alliances among neighboring peoples. In Mesoamerica, however, the games typically celebrated military conquests: during postgame rituals, the captain of the losing team—a captive taken in war—was beheaded with an obsidian knife by the winning captain. That practice seems to have stemmed from the religious significance invested in the ball games, which both the winning players and spectators understood as a religious ceremony celebrating their main deity, the Sun, an orb greater than any other celestial body, and encouraging the soil's fertility with a sacrifice of human blood.

Heavy padding protects the internal organs of this Aztec ball player from being injured by the heavy, dangerous rubber ball; the player's head dress is a culture painted brilliant Mayan blue.

The band strikes up—trumpets blaring, drums pounding, flutes trilling. Dancers whirl and gymnasts cavort. Then the players parade into the stadium, and the

Each chapter contains an essay focusing on the lives of ordinary Americans. Topics like food, fashion, and entertainment establish a greater context for each time period in history.

Marginal Headings

Succinct notes in the margins highlight key terms and concepts

The Los Angeles riots of 1992 revealed divisions in the city's multicultural communities of African Americans, Latinos, and Asian Americans.

candidate. Although the situation of African Americans had improved vastly compared with their position in the 1950s, race still mattered—as the case of Rodney King, a black motorist, showed.

Rodney King and the Los Angeles Riots

In 1991 Los Angeles police arrested King for speeding and drunken driving. As he lay on the ground, the four white officers proceeded to beat him with nightsticks more than 50 times. When blacks complained about such brutality at the hands of largely white police, public officials often dismissed their complaints. This case was different. A man in a nearby apartment videotaped the beating, which the news media repeatedly broadcast to the entire nation. But the following year, an all-white suburban jury acquitted the officers, concluding that King had been threatening and that the officers had acted within their authority.

The verdict enraged the African American community in Los Angeles, where widespread riots erupted for three days, making the violence the worst civil disturbance in Los Angeles history. By the time police and the National Guard restored order, nearly 2,000 people had been injured, 40 people had died, over 4,500 fires burned, and $500 million of property had been looted, damaged, or destroyed.

Complexity of the Riots

At first glance the riot appeared to be much like the one that had decimated Watts, a poor area of Los Angeles, in 1965 (see page 863). Poor African Americans had lashed out in frustration at white racism. In fact, the 1992 riots were multiracial in character,

Chapter Summary

A bulleted summary reinforces each chapter's main points

Chapter Summary

During the eighteenth century, Spain, France, and Great Britain competed for power and influence in North America. Native peoples too played off these shifting alliances, as their cultures were disrupted by epidemics, European settlement, and the arrival of new plants, animals, and technologies. British North Americans grew increasingly diverse, which made the prospect of any future colonial political union appear remote.

• Differences became more pronounced among whites because of the immigration of larger numbers of non-English settlers, the spread of settlement to the backcountry, and the growth of major seaports.

• Although disorder was not uncommon either on the frontier or in cities, the most serious social and political conflict drew its strength from sectional controversies between East and West.

• The South became more embattled, too, as a result of the massive importation of slaves directly from Africa during the

first half of the eighteenth century and a rising tide of black resistance to slavery.

• After about 1750 the growth of a native-born population strengthened black communal and family life.

• Religious conflict among colonials was intensified by the spread of Enlightenment ideas and the influence of the first Great Awakening.

• Despite their many differences, a majority of white colonials took pride in their common English ancestry and in belonging to a powerful empire.

• Although the British colonies seemed reluctant in 1754 to unite politically to protect themselves against their French rivals, the looming war for empire eventually created a situation in which British colonials would begin to think themselves better off united and independent.

Additional Readings

Annotated references to both classic studies and recent scholarship encourage further pursuit of the topics and events covered in the chapter.

Additional Reading

Understanding the effects of ethnic and racial diversity is essential to appreciating the dynamism of eighteenth-century colonial society. Some vivid accounts include Bernard Bailyn, *Voyagers to the West* (1986), and Bernard Bailyn and Philip Morgan, eds., *Strangers within the Realm* (1991). Philip Morgan's *Slave Counterpoint* (1998) offers a state-of-the-art overview of African American cultures in the early South. For mounting class, ethnic, and racial tensions in American seaports, consult Jill Lepore, *New York Burning* (2005), and Gary Nash, *The Urban Crucible* (1979).

Nancy Shoemaker, *A Strange Likeness* (2004) and James M. Merrell, *Into the American Woods* (1999), are two compelling

accounts of how Indians and white Americans came to perceive one another as different peoples. For the expansion of colonial settlement into the eighteenth-century backcountry, begin with Eric Hinderaker and Peter C. Mancall, *At the Edge of Empire* (2003), and Rachel Klein, *The Unification of a Slave State* (1990). Among the best studies of religion in eighteenth-century society are Rhys Isaac, *The Transformation of Virginia, 1740–1790* (1982); Patricia Bonomi, *Under the Cope of Heaven* (1986); and George Marsden, *Jonathan Edwards* (2003).

For a fuller list of readings, see the Bibliography at www.mhhe.com/davidsonnation6.

Significant Events

A chronology at the end of each chapter gives a brief list of important dates and events.

Significant Events

1790	Slater's textile mill opens
1793	Eli Whitney invents the cotton gin
1798	Whitney begins work on a system of interchangeable parts
1807	Fulton's *Clermont* begins regular steamboat service on the Hudson River
1810	*Fletcher v. Peck*
1810–1820	Cotton boom begins in the South
1811	First steamboat trip from Pittsburgh to New Orleans
1816	Second Bank of the United States chartered; protective tariff enacted
1819	*Dartmouth College v. Woodward; McCulloch v. Maryland*
1819–1823	Panic and depression
1820	Lowell mills established
1824	*Gibbons v. Ogden*
1825	Erie Canal opened
1825–1850	Canal era
1830	Baltimore and Ohio Railroad begins passenger service
1834	National Trades' Union founded
1837	Panic
1839–1843	Depression
1844	Samuel F. B. Morse sends first intercity telegraphic message
1847	Rotary printing press invented

About the Authors

James West Davidson   received his Ph.D. from Yale University. A historian who has pursued a full-time writing career, he is the author of numerous books, among them *After the Fact: The Art of Historical Detection* (with Mark H. Lytle), *The Logic of Millennial Thought: Eighteenth-Century New England*, and *Great Heart: The History of a Labrador Adventure* (with John Rugge). He is co-editor with Michael Stoff of the *Oxford New Narratives in American History*, in which his own most recent book appears: *'They Say': Ida B. Wells and the Reconstruction of Race* (2007).

Brian DeLay   is Assistant Professor of History at the University of Colorado, where he has taught since receiving his Ph.D. from Harvard University. He has published articles in the *American Historical Review* and the *Journal of the Early Republic*. His book *The War of a Thousand Deserts: How Indians Shaped the Era of the U.S.–Mexican War* will be published by Yale University Press in 2008.

Christine Leigh Heyrman   is the Robert W. and Shirley P. Grimble Professor of American History at the University of Delaware. She received a Ph.D. in American Studies from Yale University and is the author of *Commerce and Culture: The Maritime Communities of Colonial Massachusetts, 1690–1750*. Her book *Southern Cross: The Beginnings of the Bible Belt* was awarded the Bancroft Prize in 1998.

Mark H. Lytle,   a Ph.D. from Yale University, is Professor of History and Chair of the Environmental Studies Program at Bard College. He has served two years as Mary Ball Washington Professor of American History at University College, Dublin, in Ireland. His publications include *The Origins of the Iranian-American Alliance, 1941–1953*, *After the Fact: The Art of Historical Detection* (with James West Davidson), *America's Uncivil Wars: The Sixties Era from Elvis to the Fall of Richard Nixon*, and most recently, *The Gentle Subversive: Rachel Carson, Silent Spring, and the Rise of the Environmental Movement*. He is also co-editor of a joint issue of the journals *Diplomatic History* and *Environmental History* dedicated to the field of environmental diplomacy.

Michael B. Stoff   is Associate Professor of History and Director of the Plan II Honors Program at the University of Texas at Austin. The recipient of a Ph.D. from Yale University, he has been honored many times for his teaching, most recently with election to the Academy of Distinguished Teachers. He is the author of *Oil, War, and American Security: The Search for a National Policy on Foreign Oil, 1941–1947*, co-editor (with Jonathan Fanton and R. Hall Williams) of *The Manhattan Project: A Documentary Introduction to the Atomic Age*, and series co-editor (with James West Davidson) of the *Oxford New Narratives in American History*. He is currently working on a narrative of the bombing of Nagasaki.

Introduction

History is both a discipline of rigor, bound by rules and scholarly methods, and something more: the unique, compelling, even strange way in which we humans define ourselves. We are all the sum of the tales of thousands of people, great and small, whose actions have etched their lines upon us. History supplies our very identity—a sense of the social groups to which we belong, whether family, ethnic group, race, class, or gender. It reveals to us the foundations of our deepest religious beliefs and traces the roots of our economic and political systems. It explores how we celebrate and grieve, how we sing the songs we sing, how we weather the illnesses to which time and chance subject us. It commands our attention for all these good reasons and for no good reason at all, other than a fascination with the way the myriad tales play out. Strange that we should come to care about a host of men and women so many centuries gone, some with names eminent and familiar, others unknown but for a chance scrap of information left behind in an obscure letter.

Yet we do care. We care about Sir Humphrey Gilbert, "devoured and swallowed up of the Sea" one black Atlantic night in 1583; we care about George Washington at Kips Bay, red with fury as he takes a riding crop to his retreating soldiers. We care about Octave Johnson, a slave fleeing through Louisiana swamps trying to decide whether to stand and fight the approaching hounds or take his chances with the bayou alligators; we care about Clara Barton, her nurse's skirts so heavy with blood from the wounded, that she must wring them out before tending to the next soldier. We are drawn to the fate of Chinese laborers, chipping away at the Sierras' looming granite; of a Georgian named Tom Watson seeking to forge a colorblind political alliance; and of desperate immigrant mothers, kerosene lamps in hand, storming Brooklyn butcher shops that had again raised prices. We follow, with a mix of awe and amusement, the fortunes of the quirky Henry Ford ("Everybody wants to be somewhere he ain't"), turning out identical automobiles, insisting his factory workers wear identical expressions ("Fordization of the Face"). We trace the career of young Thurgood Marshall, crisscrossing the South in his own "little old beat-up '29 Ford," typing legal briefs in the back seat, trying to get black teachers to sue for equal pay, hoping to get his people somewhere they weren't. The list could go on and on, spilling out as it did in Walt Whitman's *Leaves of Grass:* "A southerner soon as a northerner, a planter nonchalant and hospitable, / A Yankee bound my own way . . . a Hoosier, a Badger, a Buckeye, a Louisianian or Georgian . . . " Whitman embraced and celebrated them all, inseparable strands of what made him an American and what made him human:

> In all people I see myself, none more and not one a barleycorn less; And the good or bad I say of myself, I say of them.

To encompass so expansive an America, Whitman turned to poetry; historians have traditionally chosen *narrative* as their means of giving life to the past. That mode of explanation permits them to interweave the strands of economic, political, and social history in a coherent chronological framework. By choosing narrative, historians affirm the multicausal nature of historical explanation—the insistence that events be portrayed in context. By choosing narrative, they are also acknowledging that, although long-term economic and social trends shape societies in significant ways, events often take on a logic (or an illogic) of their own, jostling one another, being deflected by unpredictable personal decisions, sudden deaths, natural catastrophes, and chance. There are literary reasons, too, for preferring a narrative approach, because it supplies a dramatic force usually missing from more structural analyses of the past.

In some ways, surveys such as this text are the natural antithesis of narrative history. They strive, by definition, to be comprehensive: to furnish a broad, orderly exposition of their chosen field. Yet to cover so much ground in so limited a space necessarily deprives readers of the context of more detailed accounts. Then, too, the resurgence of social history—with its concern for class and race, patterns of rural and urban life, the spread of market and industrial economies—lends itself to more analytic, less chronological treatments. The challenge facing historians is to incorporate these areas of research without losing the story's narrative drive or the chronological flow that orients readers to the more familiar events of our past.

In the end, the best tale recognizes that the political and the social aspects of the tale are intimately intertwined. It is impossible to separate the marketplace of boom and bust or the vectors of a flu pandemic from the corridors of political maneuvering and the pomp of a presidential inauguration. The primary question of this narrative—how the fledgling, often tumultuous confederation of these United States managed to transform itself into an enduring republic—must grapple with the environmental effects of deforestation or global warming as well as with minimum wages or wars in the Persian Gulf.

In order to survive, a republic must resolve conflicts between citizens of different geographic regions and economic classes, of diverse racial and ethnic origins, of competing religions and ideologies. The resolution of these conflicts has produced tragic consequences, perhaps, as often as noble, ones. But tragic or noble the destiny of these states cannot be understood without comprehending both the social and the political dimensions of the story.

ICELAND

NORWAY

SWEDEN

FINLAND

RUSSIA

UNITED KINGDOM

IRELAND

DENMARK

EST.
LATVIA
LITH.
RUSS.
BELARUS

NETH.
BELG.
LUX.
FRANCE
GERMANY
POLAND
UKRAINE

SWITZ.
CZECH.
SLOVAK.
AUSTRIA
HUNG.
MOLDOVA

SLOVN.
CRO.
ROM.

ITALY
BOS. SERB.
BULG.
MONT.
ALB.
MACE.

KAZAKHSTAN

MONGOLIA

N. KOREA

SPAIN

PORTUGAL

GREECE

TURKEY

GEORGIA
ARMENIA
AZERB.

UZBEKISTAN
KYRGYZSTAN

TURKMENISTAN
TAJIKISTAN

CHINA

S. KOREA

JAPAN

Canary
Islands

MOROCCO

TUNISIA

SYRIA
LEBANON
ISRAEL
IRAQ

IRAN

AFGHANISTAN

PAKISTAN

NEPAL
BHUTAN

TAIWAN

Tropic of Cancer

WESTERN
SAHARA

ALGERIA

LIBYA

EGYPT

JORDAN

KUWAIT

SAUDI
ARABIA

QATAR
U.A.E.

INDIA

HONG KONG

MYANMAR
LAOS

PACIFIC OCEAN

MAURITANIA

MALI

NIGER

CHAD

SUDAN

ERITREA

YEMEN

OMAN

BANGLADESH

THAILAND

VIETNAM

PHILIPPINES

SENEGAL

BURKINA
FASO

NIGERIA

DJIBOUTI

CAMBODIA

SSAU

GUINEA

IVORY
COAST

GHANA

BENIN

CAMEROON

CENTRAL
AFRICAN REP.

ETHIOPIA

SRI LANKA

BRUNEI

RRA LEONE

LIBERIA

TOGO

EQUATORIAL GUINEA

GABON

SOMALIA

UGANDA

MALAYSIA

SAO TOME AND PRINCIPE

CONGO

DEMOCRATIC
REPUBLIC
OF THE
CONGO

KENYA

RWANDA

INDIAN OCEAN

INDONESIA

PAPUA
NEW
GUINEA

Solomon
Islands

EAST TIMOR

BURUNDI

SEYCHELLES

TANZANIA

ANGOLA

ZAMBIA

MALAWI

MADAGASCAR

MAURITIUS

Vanuatu

New Caledonia
(Fr.)

SOUTH
ATLANTIC
OCEAN

NAMIBIA

ZIMBABWE

BOTSWANA

MOZAMBIQUE

RÉUNION

AUSTRALIA

Tropic of Capricorn

SWAZILAND

SOUTH
AFRICA

LESOTHO

Tasmania

NEW ZEALAND

Abbreviations

ALB.	ALBANIA
AZERB.	AZERBAIJAN
BELG.	BELGIUM
BOS.	BOSNIA-HERZEGOVINA
BULG.	BULGARIA
CRO.	CROATIA
CZECH.	CZECH REPUBLIC
EST.	ESTONIA
HUNG.	HUNGARY
LITH.	LITHUANIA
LUX.	LUXEMBOURG
MACE.	MACEDONIA
MONT.	MONTENEGRO
NETH.	NETHERLANDS
ROM.	ROMANIA
RUSS.	RUSSIA
SERB.	SERBIA
SLOVAK.	SLOVAKIA
SLOVN.	SLOVENIA
SWITZ.	SWITZERLAND
U.A.E.	UNITED ARAB EMIRATES

Arctic Circle

Antarctic Circle

Vancouver
Island

Puget Sound

• Seattle

Olympia ★

WASHINGTON

CASCADE RANGE

Portland •

★ Salem

Columbia R.

OREGON

Great Falls •

Missouri R.

Helena ★

MONTANA

R O C K Y

NORTH
DAKOTA

★ Bismarck

Farg

• Boise

IDAHO

Snake R.

SOUTH
DAKOTA

★ Pierre

BLACK
HILLS

Sio
Fa

SIERRA

Sacramento R.

Carson
City ★

NEVADA

Great
Salt
Lake

Salt Lake
City •

UTAH

WYOMING

M O U N T A I N S

Cheyenne ★

NEBRASKA

Linc

San
Francisco •

★ Sacramento

San Joaquin R.

NEVADA

CALIFORNIA

Las
Vegas •

Colorado R.

Denver ★

COLORADO

KANSAS

Arkansas R.

Wichita

Los Angeles •

ARIZONA

Santa Fe ★

• Albuquerque

OKLAHOM

Oklahoma
City

San Diego •

PACIFIC
OCEAN

★ Phoenix

NEW
MEXICO

TEXAS

Austin

RUSSIA

ARCTIC OCEAN

BROOKS RANGE

Bering Strait

Yukon R.

ALASKA

CANADA

ALASKA RANGE

Bering
Sea

• Anchorage

Juneau ★

Gulf of Alaska

ALEUTIAN ISLANDS

0   250   500 miles

0   250   500 kilometers

San Antonio •

Rio Grande

Kauai

Niihau

Oahu

Honolulu ★

Molokai

Lanai

Maui

Kahoolawe

HAWAII

PACIFIC
OCEAN

Hawaii

0   50   100 miles

0   50 100 kilometers

M E X I C O

Lake
Winnipegosis

CANADA

MAINE

Augusta

Burlington
Montpelier
Portland

VERMONT
Concord
NEW
HAMPSHIRE

Manchester

Albany
MASSACHUSETTS
Boston

NEW
YORK
Providence

Hartford
RHODE ISLAND

CONNECTICUT

Lake Nipigon

Lake of
the Woods

Lake Superior

NESOTA

St. Paul
nneapolis

WISCONSIN

MICHIGAN

Lake Huron

Lake Ontario

Buffalo

PENNSYLVANIA

New York
Newark

Milwaukee
Madison

Lansing

Detroit

Lake Erie

Harrisburg
Pittsburgh

Trenton

Philadelphia

NEW JERSEY

IOWA

Chicago

Cleveland

OHIO

Wheeling

Baltimore

Dover
DELAWARE

Annapolis

Des Moines

ILLINOIS

INDIANA

Columbus

W.
VA.

Washington,
D.C.

MARYLAND

naha

Kansas
City

Springfield

Indianapolis

Cincinnati

Charleston

Richmond

Norfolk

St. Louis

Frankfort

Louisville

VIRGINIA

peka
Jefferson
City

KENTUCKY

Raleigh

ATLANTIC
OCEAN

MISSOURI

Nashville

NORTH CAROLINA

Charlotte

ARKANSAS

TENNESSEE

Columbia

Memphis

SOUTH
CAROLINA

Atlanta

Little
Rock

Birmingham

Charleston

0   150   300 miles

ALABAMA

GEORGIA

0   150   300 kilometers

MISSISSIPPI

Montgomery

Land Elevation

Jackson

Feet   Meters

LOUISIANA

Over 13,000   Over 3,000

Tallahassee

6,560-13,000   2,000-3,000

Baton Rouge

3,280-6,560   1,000-2,000

New Orleans

660-3,280   2001-1,000

FLORIDA

0-660   0-200

uston

Below sea level   Below sea level

Gulf of Mexico

Lake
Okeechobee

B A H A M A S

ATLANTIC OCEAN

Miami

San Juan

PUERTO
RICO

Caribbean Sea

0   50   100 miles

0   50   100 kilometers

CUBA

APPALACHIAN MOUNTAINS

NATION OF NATIONS

A Narrative History of the American Republic

Volume II: Since 1865
Chapters 17–32

lived. While heavily Irish, industrial laborers in iron foundries and railroad shops did not work alongside African Americans. Athough hostile to blacks, they aimed their anger more directly at the Republican party. Rather than roaming throughout the city as many common laborers did, industrial workers concentrated on their own neighborhoods, from which they tried to remove all reminders of Republican authority, particularly draft officials, policemen, and soldiers. Although many policemen were not Republicans, the Metropolitan Police had been created by the Republican party in 1857, and its members had been particularly zealous in arresting individuals suspected of disloyalty.

In the end, no single grievance can explain New York's draft riots. Hostility to Republican employers, Protestant reformers, and authorities merged with antiblack racism, fears of job competition, and economic marginality. By itself, opposition to the draft did not produce the escalating violence and extraordinary destruction. But when that inflammatory issue sparked an avalanche of protest, it provided an outlet for more deeply rooted grievances. The result was the most serious civil disturbance of the war.

Bibliography   Iver Bernstein, *The New York City Draft Riots* (1990), does an admirable job of placing the riots within the context of changing class relations and work patterns. Adrian Cook, *The Armies of the Streets* (1974), presents a more straightforward narrative, but it has been superseded by the magisterial study of Barnet Schecter, *The Devil's Own Work* (2005), which sets a gripping account of the riots within the larger context of political, class, ethnic and racial rivalries in the decades preceding the riot, and looks at the riot's consequences for Reconstruction in the decades following the war.

CHAPTER 17
Reconstructing the Union
1865~1877

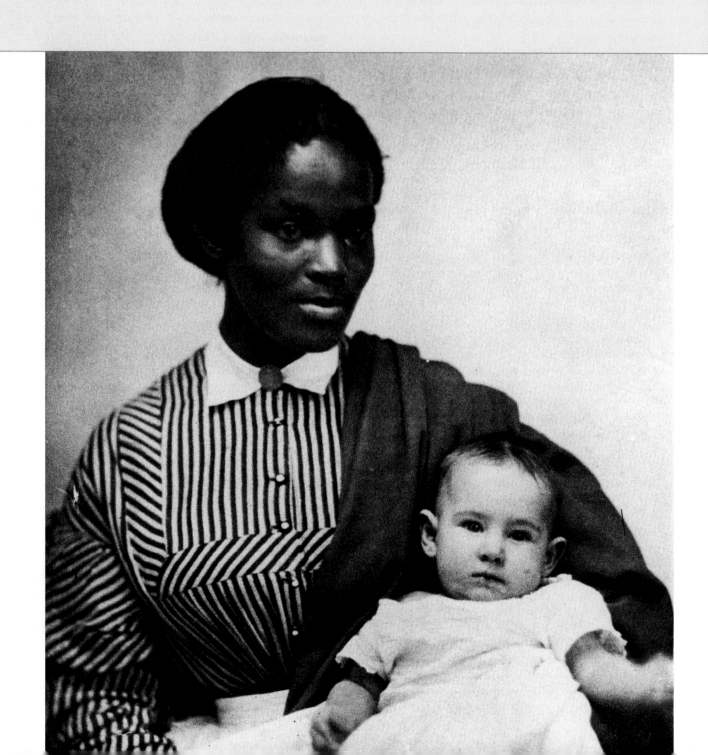

A Secret Sale at Davis Bend

Joseph Davis had had enough. Well on in years and financially ruined by the war, he decided to quit farming. In November 1866, he sold his Mississippi plantations Hurricane and Brierfield to Benjamin Montgomery and his sons. The sale of southern plantations was common enough after the war, but this transaction was bound to attract attention, since Joseph Davis was the elder brother of Jefferson Davis. Indeed, before the war the Confederate president had operated Brierfield as his own plantation, although his brother retained legal title to it. In truth, the sale was so unusual that the parties involved agreed to keep it secret, since the Montgomerys were black, and Mississippi law prohibited African Americans from owning land.

Though a slave, Montgomery had been the business manager of the two Davis plantations before the war. He had also operated a store on Hurricane Plantation for white as well as black customers with his own line of credit in New Orleans. In 1863 Montgomery fled to the North, but when the war was over, he returned to Davis Bend, where the federal government was leasing plots of the land on confiscated plantations, including Hurricane and Brierfield, to black farmers. Montgomery quickly emerged as the leader of the African American community at the Bend.

Then, in 1866, President Andrew Johnson pardoned Joseph Davis and restored his lands. By then Davis was over 80 years old and lacked the will and stamina to rebuild. Yet unlike many ex-slaveholders, he still felt bound by obligations to his former slaves. He was convinced that with proper encouragement African Americans could succeed economically in freedom. Only when the law prohibiting African Americans from owning land was overturned in 1867 did Davis publicly confirm the sale to his former slave.

For his part, Montgomery undertook to create a model society at Davis Bend based on mutual cooperation. He rented land to black farmers, hired others to work his own fields, sold supplies on credit, and ginned and marketed the crops. To the growing African American community, he preached the gospel of hard work, self-reliance, and education.

Various difficulties dogged these black farmers, including the destruction caused by the war, several disastrous floods, insects, droughts, and declining cotton prices. Yet before long, cotton production exceeded that of the prewar years, and in 1870 the black families at Davis Bend produced 2,500 bales. The Montgomerys eventually acquired another plantation and

A black nursemaid holds a baby entrusted to her care in this daguerrotype taken around 1865. After emancipation, freedmen often sought jobs in urban areas, including domestic work for women. But the abolition of slavery inevitably changed relationships as African Americans sought their rights as free citizens and white southerners strove to come to terms with the changed social order.

A Visit from the Old Mistress, *by Winslow Homer, captures the conflicting, often awkward, emotions felt by both races after the war.*

owned 5,500 acres, which made them reputedly the third largest planters in the state. They won national and international awards for the quality of their cotton. Their success demonstrated what African Americans, given a fair chance, might accomplish.

The experiences of Benjamin Montgomery during the years after 1865 were not those of most black southerners, who did not own land or have a powerful white benefactor. Yet Montgomery's dream of economic independence was shared by all African Americans. As one black veteran noted, "Every colored man will be a slave, and feel himself a slave until he can raise him own bale of cotton and put him own mark upon it and say dis is mine!" Blacks could not gain effective freedom simply through a proclamation of emancipation. They needed economic power, including their own land that no one could unfairly take away.

For nearly two centuries the laws had prevented slaves from possessing such economic power. If those conditions were to be overturned, black Americans needed political power too. Thus the Republic would have to be reconstructed to give African Americans political power that they had been previously denied.

War, in its blunt way, had roughed out the contours of a solution, but only in broad terms. Clearly, African Americans would no longer be enslaved. The North, with its industrial might, would be the driving force in the nation's economy and retain the dominant political voice. But beyond that, the outlines of a reconstructed Republic remained vague. Would African Americans receive effective power? How would the North and the South readjust their economic and political relations? These questions lay at the heart of the problem of Reconstruction.

Presidential Reconstruction

Throughout the war Abraham Lincoln had considered Reconstruction his responsibility. Elected with less than 40 percent of the popular vote in 1860, he was acutely aware that once the states of the Confederacy were restored to the Union, the Republicans would be weakened unless they ceased to be a sectional party. By a generous peace, Lincoln hoped to attract former Whigs in the South, who supported many of the Republicans' economic policies, and build up a southern wing of the party.

Lincoln's 10 Percent Plan

Lincoln outlined his program in a Proclamation of **Amnesty** and Reconstruction issued in December 1863. When a minimum of 10 percent of the qualified voters from 1860 took a **loyalty oath** to the Union, they could organize a state government. The new state constitution had to be republican in form, abolish slavery, and provide for black education, but Lincoln did not insist that high-ranking Confederate leaders be barred from public life.

Lincoln indicated that he would be generous in granting pardons and did not rule out compensation for slave property. Moreover, while he privately suggested permitting some black men to vote in the disloyal states, "as for instance, the very intelligent and especially those who have fought gallantly in our ranks," he did not demand social or political equality for black Americans, and he recognized pro-Union governments in Louisiana, Arkansas, and Tennessee that allowed only white men to vote.

The Radical Republicans found Lincoln's approach much too lenient. Strongly antislavery, Radical members of Congress had led the struggle to make emancipation a war aim. Now they were in the forefront in advocating rights for the freed people. Lincoln argued that the executive branch should bear the responsibility for restoring proper relations with the former Confederate states. The Radicals, on the other hand, believed that it was the duty of Congress to set the terms under which states would regain their rights in the Union. Though the Radicals often disagreed on other matters, they were united in a determination to readmit southern states only after slavery had been ended, black rights protected, and the power of the planter class destroyed.

Under the direction of Senator Benjamin Wade of Ohio and Representative Henry Winter Davis of Maryland, Congress formulated a much stricter plan of Reconstruction. It proposed that Confederate states be ruled temporarily by a military governor, required half the white adult males to take an oath of allegiance before drafting a new state constitution, and restricted political power to the hard-core Unionists in each state. When the Wade-Davis bill passed on the final day of the 1864 congressional session, Lincoln exercised his right of a **pocket veto.** Still, his own program could not succeed without the assistance of Congress, which refused to seat Unionist representatives who had been elected from Louisiana or Arkansas. As the war drew to a close, Lincoln appeared ready to make concessions to the Radicals. At his final cabinet meeting, he approved placing the defeated South temporarily under military rule. But only a few days later Booth's bullet found its mark, and Lincoln's final approach to Reconstruction would never be known.

The Mood of the South

In the wake of defeat, the immediate reaction among white southerners was one of shock, despair, and hopelessness. Some former Confederates, of course, were openly antagonistic. A North Carolina innkeeper remarked bitterly that Yankees had stolen his slaves, burned his house, and killed all his sons, leaving him only one privilege: "To hate 'em. I git up at half-past four in the morning, and sit up till twelve at night, to hate 'em." Most Confederate soldiers were less defiant, having had their fill of war. Even among hostile civilians the feeling was widespread that the South must accept northern terms.

Radical Republicans

Wade-Davis Bill

The mood of white southerners at the end of the war was mixed. Many, like the veteran caricatured here by northern cartoonist Thomas Nast, remained hostile. Others, like Texas captain Samuel Foster, came to believe that the institution of slavery "had been abused" and that men "who actually owned and held slaves up to this time,—have now changed in their opinions regarding slavery . . . to see that for a man to have property in man was wrong, and that the 'Declaration of Independence' meant more than they had ever been able to see before."

This psychological moment was critical. To prevent a resurgence of resistance, the president needed to lay out clearly what white southerners had to do to regain their old status in the Union. Any wavering on the peace terms could only increase the likelihood of resistance. Perhaps even a clear and firm policy would not have been enough. But with Lincoln's death, the executive power came to rest in far less capable hands.

Johnson's Program of Reconstruction

Johnson's Character and Values

Andrew Johnson, the new president, had been born in North Carolina and eventually moved to Tennessee, where he worked as a tailor. Barely able to read and write when he married, he rose to political power by portraying himself as the champion of the people against the wealthy planter class. "Some day I will show the stuck-up aristocrats who is running the country," he vowed as he began his political career. He had not opposed slavery before the war—in fact, he hoped to disperse slave ownership more widely in southern society. Although he accepted emancipation as one consequence of the war, Johnson remained a confirmed racist. "Damn the negroes," he said during the war, "I am fighting these traitorous aristocrats, their masters."

Because Johnson disliked the planter class, Republican Radicals in Congress expected him to uphold their views on Reconstruction. In fact, the new president did speak of trying Confederate leaders and breaking up planters' estates. Unlike most Republicans, however, Johnson strongly supported states' rights. Furthermore, his prickly personality made conflict between the president and Congress inevitable. Scarred by his humble origins, Johnson remained an outsider throughout his life. When challenged or criticized, he became tactless and inflexible, alienating even those who sought to work with him.

Johnson's Program

Johnson moved quickly to return the southern states to their place in the Union. He prescribed a loyalty oath that white southerners would have to take to regain their civil and political rights and to have their property, except for slaves, restored. Excluded were high Confederate officials and those with property worth over $20,000, who had to apply for individual pardons. Johnson announced that once a state had drafted a new constitution and elected state officers and members of Congress, he would revoke martial law and recognize the new state government. Suffrage was limited to white citizens who had taken the loyalty oath. This plan was similar to Lincoln's, though more lenient. Only informally did Johnson ask that the southern states renounce their ordinances of secession, repudiate the Confederate debt, and ratify the proposed Thirteenth Amendment abolishing slavery.

The Failure of Johnson's Program

Southern Defiance

The southern delegates who met to construct new governments were in no frame of mind to follow Johnson's recommendations. Several states merely repealed instead of repudiating their ordinances of secession, rejected the Thirteenth Amendment, or refused to repudiate the Confederate debt.

Nor did the new governments allow African Americans any political rights or make any effective provisions for black education. In addition, each state passed a series of laws, often modeled on its old slave code, that applied only to African Americans. These **black codes** did grant African Americans some rights that had not been enjoyed by slaves. They legalized marriages performed under slavery and allowed black southerners to hold and sell property and to sue and be sued in state courts. Yet their primary purpose was to keep African Americans as propertyless agricultural laborers with inferior legal rights. The new **freedmen,** or **freedpeople,** could not serve on juries, testify against whites, or work as they pleased. South Carolina forbade blacks to engage in anything other than agricultural labor without a special license; Mississippi prohibited them from buying or renting farmland. Most states ominously provided that black people who were vagrants could be arrested and hired out to landowners. Many northerners were incensed by the restrictive black codes.

Black Codes

Elections in the South

Southern voters under Johnson's plan also defiantly elected prominent Confederate military and political leaders to office, headed by Alexander Stephens, the vice president of the Confederacy, who was elected senator from Georgia. At this point, Johnson could have called for new elections or admitted that a different program of Reconstruction was needed. Instead he caved in. For all his harsh rhetoric, he shrank from the prospect of social upheaval, and he found it enormously gratifying when upper-class planters praised his conduct and requested pardons. As the lines of ex-Confederates waiting to see him lengthened, he began issuing special pardons almost as fast as they could be printed. In the next two years he pardoned some 13,500 former rebels.

In private, Johnson warned southerners against a reckless course. Publicly he put on a bold face, announcing that Reconstruction had been successfully completed. But many members of Congress were deeply alarmed.

Johnson's Break with Congress

The new Congress was by no means of one mind. A small number of Democrats and a few conservative Republicans backed the president's program. At the other end of the spectrum, a larger group of Radical Republicans, led by Thaddeus Stevens, Charles Sumner, Benjamin Wade, and others, was bent on remaking southern society in the image of the North. Reconstruction must "revolutionize Southern institutions, habits, and manners," insisted Representative Stevens, "... or all our blood and treasure have been spent in vain." Unlike Johnson, Radicals championed civil and political rights for African Americans and believed that the only way to maintain loyal governments and develop a Republican party in the South was to give black men the ballot.

As a minority, the Radicals could accomplish nothing without the aid of the moderate Republicans, the largest bloc in Congress. Led by William Pitt Fessenden and Lyman Trumbull, the moderates hoped to avoid a clash with the president, and they had no desire to foster social revolution or promote racial equality in the South. But they wanted to keep Confederate leaders from reassuming power, and they were convinced that the former slaves needed federal protection. Otherwise, Trumbull declared, the freedpeople would "be tyrannized over, abused, and virtually reenslaved."

Moderates agreed that the new southern governments were too harsh toward African Americans, but they feared that too great an emphasis on black civil rights would alienate northern voters.

In December 1865, when southern representatives to Congress appeared in Washington, a majority in Congress voted to exclude them. Congress also appointed a joint committee, chaired by Senator Fessenden, to look into how to implement Reconstruction. The split with the president became clearer when Congress passed a bill extending the life of the Freedmen's Bureau. Created in March 1865, the bureau provided emergency food, clothing, and medical care to war refugees (including white southerners) and took charge of settling freedpeople on abandoned lands. The new bill gave the bureau the added responsibilities of supervising special courts to resolve disputes involving freedpeople and establishing schools for black southerners. Although this bill passed with near unanimous Republican support, Johnson vetoed it. Congress failed to override his veto.

Johnson's Vetoes

Johnson also vetoed a civil rights bill designed to overturn the most severe provisions of the black codes. The law made African Americans citizens of the United States and granted them the right to own property, make contracts, and have access to courts as parties and witnesses. For most Republicans Johnson's action was the last straw, and in April 1866 Congress overrode his veto, the first major legislation in American history to be enacted over a presidential veto. Congress then approved a slightly revised Freedmen's Bureau bill in July and promptly overrode the president's veto. Johnson's refusal to compromise drove the moderates into the arms of the Radicals.

Thaddeus Stevens, Radical leader in the House

The Fourteenth Amendment

To prevent unrepentant Confederates from taking over the reconstructed state governments and denying African Americans basic freedoms, the Joint Committee on Reconstruction proposed an amendment to the Constitution, which passed both houses of Congress with the necessary two-thirds vote in June 1866. The amendment, coupled with the Freedmen's Bureau and civil rights bills, represented the moderates' terms for Reconstruction.

Provisions of the Amendment

The Fourteenth Amendment put a number of matters beyond the control of the president. The amendment guaranteed repayment of the national war debt and prohibited repayment of the Confederate debt. To counteract the president's wholesale pardons, it disqualified prominent Confederates from holding office and provided that only Congress by a two-thirds vote could remove this penalty. Because moderates, fearful of the reaction of white northerners, balked at giving the vote to African Americans, the amendment merely gave Congress the right to reduce the representation of any state that did not have impartial male suffrage. The practical effect of this provision, which Radicals labeled a "swindle," was to allow northern states to restrict suffrage to whites if they wished, since unlike southern states they had few African Americans and thus would not be penalized.

The amendment's most important provision, Section 1, defined an American citizen as anyone born in the United States or naturalized, thereby automatically making African Americans citizens. Section 1 also prohibited states from abridging "the privileges or immunities" of citizens, depriving "any person of life, liberty, or property, without due process of law," or denying "any person . . . equal protection of the laws." The framers of the amendment probably intended to prohibit laws that applied to one race only, such as the black codes, or that made certain acts felonies when committed by black but not white people, or that decreed different penalties for the same crime when committed by white and black lawbreakers. The framers probably did not intend to prevent African Americans from being excluded from juries or to forbid segregation (the legal separation of the races) in schools and public places.

This politician is literally "waving the bloody shirt"— using the bitter memories of the Civil War to rouse voters to side with Republicans.

Nevertheless, Johnson denounced the proposed amendment and urged southern states not to ratify it. Ironically, of the seceded states only the president's own state ratified the amendment, and Congress readmitted Tennessee with no further restrictions. The telegram sent to Congress by a longtime foe of Johnson announcing Tennessee's approval ended, "Give my respects to the dead dog in the White House." The amendment was ratified in 1868.

The Elections of 1866

When Congress blocked his policies, Johnson undertook a speaking tour of the East and Midwest in the fall of 1866 to drum up popular support. But the president found it difficult to convince northern audiences that white southerners were fully repentant. News that summer of major race riots in Memphis and New Orleans heightened northern concern. Forty-six African Americans died when white mobs invaded the black section of Memphis, burning homes, churches, and schoolhouses. About the same number were killed in New Orleans when whites attacked both black and white delegates to a convention supporting black suffrage. "The negroes now know, to their sorrow, that it is best not to arouse the fury of the white man," boasted one Memphis newspaper. When the president encountered hostile audiences during his northern

Antiblack Riots

campaign, he only made matters worse by trading insults and ranting that the Radicals were traitors. Even supporters found his performance humiliating.

Not to be outdone, the Radicals vilified Johnson as a traitor aiming to turn the country over to rebels and Copperheads. Resorting to the tactic of "waving the **bloody shirt**," they appealed to voters by reviving bitter memories of the war. In a classic example of such rhetoric, Governor Oliver Morton of Indiana proclaimed that "every bounty jumper, every deserter, every sneak who ran away from the draft" was a Democrat; everyone "who murdered Union prisoners. . . . In short, the Democratic party may be described as a common sewer."

Voters soundly repudiated Johnson, as the Republicans won more than a two-thirds majority in both houses of Congress, every northern gubernatorial contest, and control of every northern legislature. The Radicals had reached the height of their power.

Repudiation of Johnson

Congressional Reconstruction

With a clear mandate in hand, congressional Republicans passed their own program of Reconstruction, beginning with the first Reconstruction Act in March 1867. Like all later pieces of Reconstruction legislation, it was repassed over Johnson's veto.

Placing the 10 unreconstructed states under military commanders, the act directed officials to include black adult males as voters but not former Confederates barred from holding office under the Fourteenth Amendment. State conventions would frame constitutions that provided for black suffrage and that disqualified prominent ex-Confederates from office. The first state legislatures to meet under the new constitution were required to ratify the Fourteenth Amendment. Once these steps were completed and Congress approved the new state constitution, a state could send representatives to Congress.

White southerners found these requirements so obnoxious that officials took no steps to register voters. Congress then enacted a second Reconstruction Act, also in March, ordering the local military commanders to put the machinery of Reconstruction into motion. Johnson's efforts to limit the power of military commanders produced a third act, passed in July, that upheld their superiority in all matters. When elections were held to ratify the new state constitutions, white southerners boycotted them in large numbers. Undaunted, Congress passed the fourth Reconstruction Act (March 1868), which required ratification of the constitution by only a majority of those voting rather than those who were registered.

Resistance of Southern Whites

By June 1868 Congress had readmitted the representatives of seven states. Georgia's state legislature expelled its black members once it had been readmitted, granting seats to those barred by Congress from holding office. Congress ordered the military commander to reverse these actions, and Georgia was then admitted a second time in July 1870. Texas, Virginia, and Mississippi did not complete the process until 1869.

Post-Emancipation Societies in the Americas

With the exception of Haiti's revolution (1791–1804), the United States was the only society in the Americas in which the destruction of slavery was accomplished by violence. But the United States, uniquely among these societies, enfranchised former slaves almost immediately after the emancipation. Thus in the United States former masters and slaves battled for control of the state in ways that did not occur in other post-emancipation societies. In most of the Caribbean, property requirements for voting left the planters in political control. Jamaica, for example, with a population of 500,000 in the 1860s, had only 3,000 voters.

Moreover, in reaction to political efforts to mobilize disfranchised black peasants, Jamaican planters dissolved the assembly and reverted to being a Crown colony governed from London. Of the sugar islands, all but Barbados adopted the same policy, thereby blocking the potential for any future black peasant democracy. Nor did any of these societies have the counterparts of the Radical Republicans, a group of outsiders with political power that promoted the fundamental transformation of the

The Southern States During Reconstruction

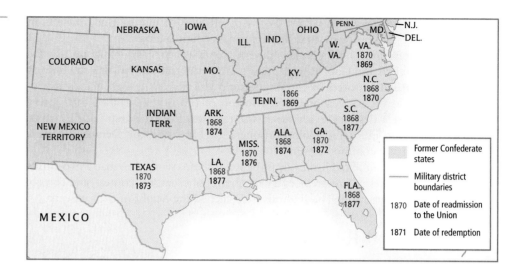

post-emancipation South. These comparisons highlight the radicalism of Reconstruction in the United States, which alone saw an effort to forge an interracial democracy.

The Land Issue

Blacks' Desire for Land

While the political process of Reconstruction proceeded, Congress confronted the question of whether land should be given to former slaves to foster economic independence. At a meeting with Secretary of War Edwin Stanton near the end of the war, African American leaders declared, "The way we can best take care of ourselves is to have land, and till it by our own labor." During the war, the Second Confiscation Act of 1862 had authorized the government to seize and sell the property, including land, of supporters of the rebellion. In June 1866, however, President Johnson ruled that confiscation laws applied only to wartime.

Congress debated land confiscation off and on from December 1865 until early 1867. Thaddeus Stevens, a leading Radical in the House, advocated confiscating 394 million acres of land from about 70,000 of what he termed the "chief rebels" in the South, who made up less than 5 percent of the South's white families. He proposed to give 40 acres to every adult male freedperson and then sell the remaining land, which would amount to nine-tenths of the total, to pay off the public debt, compensate loyal southerners for losses they suffered during the war, and fund Union veterans' pensions. Land, he insisted, would be far more valuable to African Americans than the right to vote.

Failure of Land Redistribution

But in the end Congress rejected all proposals. Given Americans' strong belief in self-reliance, little sympathy existed for the idea that government should support any group. In addition, land redistribution represented an attack on property rights, another cherished American value. By 1867 land reform was dead.

Few freedpeople acquired land after the war, a development that severely limited African Americans' economic independence and left them vulnerable to white coercion. It is doubtful, however, that this decision was the basic cause of the failure of Reconstruction. In the face of white hostility and institutionalized racism, African Americans probably would have been no more successful in protecting their property than they were in maintaining the right to vote.

Impeachment

Tenure of Office Act

Throughout 1867 Congress routinely overrode Johnson's vetoes. Still, the president had other ways of undercutting congressional Reconstruction. He interpreted the new laws as narrowly as possible and removed military commanders who vigorously enforced them. Congress responded by restricting Johnson's power to issue orders to military commanders in the South. It also passed the Tenure of Office Act, which forbade Johnson to remove any member of the cabinet without the Senate's consent. The intention of this law was to prevent him from firing Secretary of War Edwin Stanton, the only Radical in the cabinet.

When Johnson tried to dismiss Stanton in February 1868, the determined secretary of war barricaded himself in his office (where he remained night and day for about two months). Angrily, the House of Representatives approved articles of impeachment. The articles focused on the violation of the Tenure of Office Act, but the charge with the most substance was that Johnson had conspired to systematically obstruct Reconstruction legislation. In the trial before the Senate, his lawyers argued that a president could be impeached only for an indictable crime, which Johnson clearly had not committed. The Radicals countered that impeachment applied to political offenses and not merely criminal acts. In May 1868 the Senate voted 36 to 19 to convict, one vote short of the two-thirds majority needed. The seven Republicans who joined the Democrats in voting for acquittal were uneasy about using impeachment as a political weapon.

Johnson Acquitted

Reconstruction in the South

The refusal of Congress to convict Johnson sent a clear signal: the power of the Radicals in Congress was waning. Increasingly the success or failure of Reconstruction hinged on developments not in Congress but in the southern states themselves. Power there rested with the new Republican parties, representing a coalition of black and white southerners and transplanted northerners.

Black Office Holding

Almost from the beginning of Reconstruction, African Americans had lobbied for the right to vote. After they received the **franchise,** black men constituted as much as 80 percent of the Republican voters in the South. They steadfastly opposed the Democratic party with its appeal to white supremacy.

Throughout Reconstruction, African Americans never held office in proportion to their voting strength. No African American was ever elected governor, and only in South Carolina, where more than 60 percent of the population was black, did they control even one house of the legislature. During Reconstruction between 15 and 20 percent of the state officers and 6 percent of members of Congress (2 senators and 15 representatives) were black. Only in South Carolina did black officeholders approach their proportion of the population.

Blacks who held office generally came from the top levels of African American society. Among state and federal officeholders, perhaps four-fifths were literate, and more than a quarter had been free before the war, both marks of distinction in the black community. Their occupations also set them apart: two-fifths were professionals (mostly clergy), and of the third who were farmers, nearly all owned land. Among black members of Congress, all but three had a secondary school education, and four had gone to college. In their political and social values, African American leaders were more conservative than the rural black population was, and they showed little interest in land reform.

Background of Black Political Leaders

Hiram Revels, a minister and educator, became the first African American to serve in the U.S. Senate, representing Mississippi. Later he served as president of Alcorn University.

White Republicans in the South

Black citizens were a majority of the voters only in South Carolina, Mississippi, and Louisiana. Thus in most of the South the Republican party had to secure white votes to stay in power. Opponents scornfully labeled white southerners who allied with the Republican party **scalawags,** yet an estimated quarter of white southerners at one time voted Republican. Although the party appealed to some wealthy planters, they were outnumbered by Unionists from the upland counties and hill areas who were largely yeoman farmers. Such voters were attracted by Republican promises to rebuild the South, restore prosperity, create public schools, and open isolated areas to the market with railroads.

The other group of white Republicans in the South was known as **carpetbaggers.** Originally from the North, they allegedly had arrived with all their worldly possessions stuffed in a carpetbag, ready to plunder the defeated South. Some did, but northerners moved south for a variety of reasons. Those in political office were especially well educated. Though carpetbaggers made up only a small percentage of Republican voters, they controlled almost a third of the offices. More than half of all southern Republican governors and nearly half of Republican members of Congress were originally northerners.

Divisions Among Southern Republicans

The Republican party in the South had difficulty maintaining unity. Scalawags were especially susceptible to the race issue and social pressure. "Even my own kinspeople have turned the cold shoulder to me because I hold office under a Republican administration," testified a Mississippi white Republican. As black southerners pressed for greater recognition and a greater share of the offices, white southerners increasingly defected to the Democrats. Carpetbaggers were less sensitive to race, although most felt that their black allies should be content with minor offices. The friction between scalawags and carpetbaggers, which grew out of their rivalry for party honors, was particularly intense.

The New State Governments

New State Constitutions

The new southern state constitutions enacted several reforms. They put in place fairer systems of legislative representation, allowed voters to elect many officials who before had been appointed, and abolished property requirements for officeholding. In South Carolina, for the first time, voters were allowed to vote for the president, governor, and other state officers. (Previously, presidential electors as well as the governor had been chosen by the South Carolina legislature.) The Radical state governments also assumed some responsibility for social welfare and established the first statewide systems of public schools in the South.

Race and Social Equality

All the new constitutions proclaimed the principle of equality and granted black adult males the right to vote. On social relations they were much more cautious. No state outlawed segregation, and South Carolina and Louisiana were the only states that required integration in public schools (a mandate that was almost universally ignored).

Economic Issues and Corruption

The war left the southern economy in ruins, and problems of economic reconstruction were as difficult as those of politics. The new Republican governments encouraged industrial development by providing subsidies, loans, and even temporary exemptions from taxes. These governments also largely rebuilt the southern railroad system, often offering lavish aid to railroad corporations. The investments in the South helped double its manufacturing establishments in the two decades after 1860. Yet the harsh reality was that the South steadily slipped further behind the booming industrial economy of the North. Between 1854 and 1879, 7,000 miles of railroad track were laid in the South, but in the same period 45,000 miles were constructed in the rest of the nation.

Corruption

The expansion of government services offered temptations for corruption. In many southern states, officials regularly received bribes and kickbacks for their award of railroad charters, franchises, and other contracts. By 1872 the debts of the 11 states of the Confederacy had increased by $132 million, largely because of railroad grants and new social services such as schools. The tax rate grew as expenditures went up, so that by the 1870s it was four times the rate of 1860.

THE FIFTEENTH AMENDMENT.

CELEBRATED MAY 19TH 1870.

From the beginning of Reconstruction, African Americans demanded the right to vote as free citizens. The Fifteenth Amendment, ratified in 1870, secured that right for black males. In New York, black citizens paraded in support of Ulysses S. Grant for president. Parades played a central role in campaigning: this parade exhibits the usual banners, flags, costumes, and a band. Blacks in both the North and the South voted solidly for the Republican party as the party of Lincoln and emancipation, although white violence in the South increasingly reduced black turnout.

Corruption, however, was not only a southern problem: the decline in morality affected the entire nation. During these years in New York City alone, the Democratic Tweed Ring stole more money than all the Radical Republican governments in the South combined. Moreover, corruption in the South was hardly limited to Republicans. Many Democrats and white business leaders participated in the looting. "Everybody is demoralizing down here. Corruption is the fashion," reported Louisiana governor Henry Warmoth.

Corruption in Radical governments existed, but southern whites exaggerated its extent for partisan purposes. Conservatives just as bitterly opposed honest Radical regimes as they did corrupt ones. In the eyes of most white southerners, the real crime of the Radical governments was that they allowed black citizens to hold some offices and tried to protect the civil rights of African Americans. Race was the conservatives' greatest weapon. And it would prove the most effective means to undermine Republican power in the South.

SAML. DOVE wishes to know of the whereabouts of his mother, Areno, his sisters Maria, Neziah, and Peggy, and his brother Edmond, who were owned by Geo. Dove, of Rockingham county, Shenandoah Valley, Va. Sold in Richmond, after which Saml. and Edmond were taken to Nashville, Tenn., by Joe Mick; Areno was left at the Eagle Tavern, Richmond
Respectfully yours,
SAML. DOVE.
Utica, New York, Aug. 5, 1865–3m

A Tennessee newspaper advertisement seeking a family, 1865.

Black Aspirations

Emancipation came to slaves in different ways and at different times. For some it arrived during the war when Union soldiers entered an area; for others it came some time after the Confederacy's collapse, when Union troops or officials announced that they were free. Whatever the timing, freedom meant a host of precious blessings to people who had been in bondage all their lives.

Experiencing Freedom

The first impulse was to think of freedom as a contrast to slavery. Emancipation immediately released slaves from the most oppressive aspects of bondage—the whippings, the breakup of families, the sexual exploitation. Freedom also meant movement, the right to travel without a pass or white permission. Above all, freedom meant that African Americans' labor would be for their own benefit. One Arkansas freedman, who earned his first dollar working on a railroad, recalled that when he was paid, "I felt like the richest man in the world."

Changing Employment

Freedom included finding a new place to work. Changing jobs was one concrete way to break the psychological ties of slavery. Even planters with reputations for kindness sometimes saw their former hands depart. The cook who left a South Carolina family even though they offered her higher wages than her new job explained, "I must go. If I stays here I'll never know I'm free."

Importance of Names

Symbolically, freedom meant having a full name, and African Americans now adopted last names. More than a few took the last name of some prominent individual; more common was to take the name of the first master in the family's oral history as far back as it could be recalled. Most, however, retained their first name, especially if the name had been given to them by their parents (as most often had been the case among slaves). It had been their form of identity in bondage, and for those separated from their family it was the only link with their parents. Whatever name they took, it was important to black Americans that they make the decision themselves without white interference.

The Black Family

Upholding the Family

African Americans also sought to strengthen the family in freedom. Because slave marriages had not been recognized as legal, thousands of former slaves insisted on being married again by proper authorities, even though a ceremony was not required by law. Blacks who had been forcibly separated in slavery and later remarried confronted the dilemma of which spouse to take. Laura Spicer, whose husband had been sold away in slavery, received a series of wrenching letters from him after the war. He had thought her dead, had remarried, and had a new family. "You know it never was our wishes to be separated from each other, and it never was our fault. I had rather anything to had happened to me most than ever have been parted from you and the children," he wrote. "As I am, I do not know which I love best, you or Anna." Declining to return, he closed, "Laura, truly, I have got another wife, and I am very sorry. . . ."

Like white husbands, black husbands deemed themselves the head of the family and acted legally for their wives. They often insisted that their wives would not work in the fields as they had in slavery, a decision that had major economic repercussions for agricultural labor. In negotiating contracts, a father also demanded the right to control his children and their labor. All these changes were designed to insulate the black family from white control.

The Schoolhouse and the Church

Black Education

In freedom, the schoolhouse and the black church became essential institutions in the black community. Next to ownership of land, African Americans saw education as the best hope for advancement. At first, northern churches and missionaries, working with the Freedmen's Bureau, set up black schools in the South. Tuition represented 10 percent or more of a laborer's monthly wages. Yet these schools were full. Many parents sent their children by day and attended classes themselves at night. Eventually, the Bureau schools were replaced by the new public school systems, which by 1876 enrolled 40 percent of African American children.

Black adults had good reasons for seeking literacy. They wanted to be able to read the Bible, to defend their newly gained civil and political rights, and to protect themselves from being cheated. One elderly Louisiana freedman explained that giving children an education was better than giving them a fortune, "because if you left them even $500, some man having more education than they had would come along and cheat them out of it all."

Teachers in the Freedmen's Bureau schools were primarily northern middle-class white women sent south by northern missionary societies. "I feel that it is a precious privilege," Esther Douglass wrote, "to be allowed to do something for these poor people." Many saw themselves as peacetime soldiers, struggling to make emancipation a reality. Indeed, on more than one occasion, hostile white southerners destroyed black schools and threatened and even murdered white teachers. Then there were the everyday challenges: low pay, dilapidated buildings, lack of sufficient books, classes of 100 or more children, and irregular attendance. Meanwhile, the Freedmen's Bureau undertook to train black teachers, and by 1869 most of the 3,000 teachers in freedmen's schools were black.

Teachers in Black Schools

Before the war, most slaves had attended white churches or services supervised by whites. Once free, African Americans quickly established their own congregations led by black preachers. In the first year of freedom, the Methodist Church South lost fully half of its black members. By 1870 the Negro Baptist Church had increased its membership threefold when compared to the membership in 1850, and the African Methodist Episcopal Church expanded at an even greater rate.

Independent Black Churches

Black churches were so important because they were the only major organizations in the African American community controlled by blacks. Black ministers were respected leaders, and many of the black men elected to office during Reconstruction were preachers. As it had in slavery, religion offered African Americans a place of refuge in a hostile white world and provided them with hope, comfort, and a means of self-identification.

New Working Conditions

As a largely propertyless class, blacks in the postwar South had no choice but to work for white landowners. Except for paying wages, whites wanted to retain the old system of labor, including close supervision, gang labor, and physical punishment. Determined to remove all emblems of servitude, African Americans refused to work under these conditions, and they demanded time off to devote to their own interests. Convinced that working at one's own pace was part of freedom, they simply would not work as long or as hard as they had in slavery. Because of shorter hours and the withdrawal of children and women from the fields, work output declined by an estimated 35 percent in freedom. Blacks also refused to live in the old slave quarters located near the master's house. Instead, they erected cabins on distant parts of the plantation. Wages at first were $5 or $6 a month plus provisions and a cabin; by 1867, they had risen to an average of $10 a month.

These changes eventually led to the rise of sharecropping. Under this arrangement African American families farmed separate plots of land and then at the end of the year split the crop with the white landowner. Sharecropping had higher status and offered greater personal freedom than being a wage laborer. "I am not working for wages," one black farmer declared in defending his right to leave the plantation at will, "but am part owner of the crop and as [such,] I have all the rights that you or any other man has." Although black per capita agricultural income increased 40 percent in freedom,

Sharecropping

On the plantations of the Old South, slaves had lived in cabins along a central path in the shadow of the white master's "big house." These quarters were the center of their community, where marriages and other festivals were celebrated and family life went on. But with the coming of emancipation, freedpeople looked to leave the old quarters, which stood as a symbol of bondage and of close white supervision. African Americans either built new housing or dismantled their old cabins and hauled them to the plots of land they rented as tenants or sharecroppers. Moving enabled them to live on the land they farmed, just as white farmers and tenants did.

Like slave cabins, most sharecroppers' dwellings were one story high, about 16 feet square, and usually built of logs

chinked with mud. The few windows had shutters to protect against the weather;

glass was rare. Though the inside walls normally lacked plaster or sheeting, they

Chimneys on sharecroppers' cabins were often tilted deliberately so that they could be pushed away from the house quickly if they caught fire.

sharecropping was a harshly exploitative system in which black families often sank into perpetual debt.

The Freedmen's Bureau

The task of supervising the transition from slavery to freedom on southern plantations fell to the Freedmen's Bureau, a unique experiment in social policy supported by the federal

After living for years in a society where teaching slaves to read and write was usually illegal, freedpeople viewed literacy as a key to securing their newfound freedom. Blacks were not merely "anxious to learn," a school official in Virginia reported, they were "crazy to learn."

were given a coat of whitewash annually to brighten the dark interior.

The main room served as kitchen and dining room, parlor, bathing area, and the parents' bedroom. To one side might be a homemade drop-leaf table (essential because of cramped space), which served as a kitchen work counter and a dining table. The other side of the room had a few plain beds, their slats or rope bottoms supporting corn shuck or straw mattresses. The social center of the room was the fireplace, the only source of heat and the main source of light after dark. Pots and pans were hung on the wall near the fireplace, and the mother and daughters did the cooking stooped over an open fire. In the summer, cooking was done outdoors.

The cabin's chimney was made of small logs notched together and covered with several layers of clay to protect it from the heat. Sometimes its height was extended by empty flour barrels. A taller chimney drew better, which kept smoke from blowing back down into the house and kept sparks away from the roof. After the evening meal the family gathered around the fireplace, the children to play with homemade dolls and toys, the mother to sew, and the father perhaps to play the fiddle. At bedtime a trapdoor in the ceiling offered access up a ladder to the loft beneath the gabled roof, where older children slept, usually on pallets on the floor, as had been the case in slavery.

Gradually, as black sharecroppers scraped together some savings, they improved their homes. By the end of the century, frame dwellings were more common, and many older log cabins had been covered with wood siding. The newer homes were generally larger, with wood floors, and often had attached rooms such as a porch or kitchen. In addition, windows had glass panes, roofs were covered with shingles instead of planking, and stone and brick chimneys were less unusual.

Without question, the cabins of black sharecroppers provided more space than the slave quarters had, and certainly more freedom and privacy. Still, they lacked many of the comforts that most white Americans took for granted. Such housing reflected the continuing status of black sharecroppers as poverty-stricken laborers in a caste system based on race.

government. Assigned the task of protecting freedpeople's economic rights, approximately 550 local agents supervised and regulated working conditions in southern agriculture after the war. The racial attitudes of Bureau agents varied widely, as did their commitment and competence. Then, too, they had to depend on the army to enforce their decisions.

Most agents encouraged or required written contracts between white planters and black laborers, specifying not only wages but also the conditions of employment. Although agents sometimes intervened to protect freedpeople from unfair treatment, they also provided important help to planters. They insisted that black laborers not desert at harvest time; they arrested those who violated their contracts or refused to sign new ones at the beginning of the year; and they preached the gospel of work and the need to be orderly and respectful. Given such attitudes, freedpeople increasingly complained that Bureau agents were mere tools of the planter class. "They are, in fact, the planters' guards, and nothing else," claimed the New Orleans *Tribune*, a black newspaper.

The primary means of enforcing working conditions were the Freedmen's Courts, which Congress created in 1866 to avoid the discrimination African Americans received in state courts. These new courts functioned as military tribunals, and often the agent was the entire court. The sympathy black laborers received varied from state to state.

But in 1869, with the Bureau's work scarcely under way, Congress decided to shut it down, and by 1872 it had gone out of business. Despite its mixed record, it was the most effective agency in protecting blacks' civil and political rights. Its disbanding signaled the beginning of the northern retreat from Reconstruction.

Bureau's Mixed Record

End of the Bureau

Planters and a New Way of Life

Planters and other white southerners faced emancipation with dread. "All the traditions and habits of both races had been suddenly overthrown," a Tennessee planter recalled, "and neither knew just what to do, or how to accommodate themselves to the new situation."

The old ideal of a paternalistic planter, which required a facade of black subservience and affection, gave way to an emphasis on strictly economic relationships. Mary

Planters' New Values

Jones, a Georgia slaveholder before the war who did more for her workers than the law required, lost all patience when two workers accused her of trickery and hauled her before a Freedmen's Bureau agent, with whom she won her case. Upon returning home, she announced to the assembled freedpeople that "I have considered them friends and treated them as such but now they were only laborers under contract, and only the law would rule between us." Only with time did planters develop new norms and standards to judge black behavior. What in 1865 had seemed insolence was viewed by the 1870s as the normal attitude of freedom.

Slavery had been a complex institution that welded black and white southerners together in intimate relationships. After the war, however, planters increasingly embraced the ideology of segregation. Because emancipation significantly reduced the social distance between the races, white southerners sought psychological separation and kept dealings with African Americans to a minimum. By the time Reconstruction ended, white planters had developed a new way of life based on the institutions of sharecropping and segregation and undergirded by a militant white supremacy.

Although most planters kept their land, they did not regain the economic prosperity of the prewar years. Rice plantations, unsuitable to tenant farming, largely disappeared after the war. In addition, southern cotton growers faced increased competition from new areas such as India, Egypt, and Brazil. Cotton prices began a long decline, and by 1880 the value of southern farms had slid 33 percent below the level of 1860.

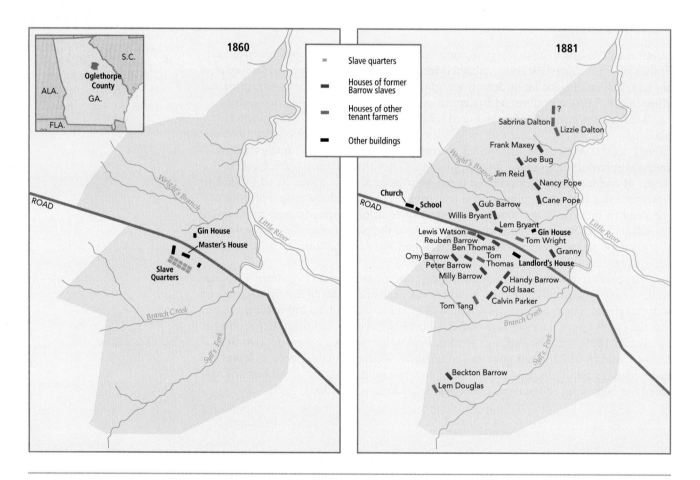

A Georgia Plantation after the War   *After emancipation, sharecropping became the dominant form of agricultural labor in the South. Black families no longer lived in the old slave quarters but dispersed to separate plots of land that they farmed themselves. At the end of the year each sharecropper turned over part of the crop to the white landowner.*

The Abandonment of Reconstruction

On Christmas Day 1875, a white acquaintance approached Charles Caldwell on the streets of Clinton, Mississippi, and invited him into Chilton's store to have a drink to celebrate the holiday. A former slave, Caldwell was a state senator and the leader of the Republican party in Hinds County, Mississippi. But the black leader's fearlessness made him a marked man. Only two months earlier, he had been forced to flee the county to escape a white mob angry about a Republican barbecue he and his fellow Republicans had organized. For four days the mob hunted down and killed nearly 40 Republican leaders for presuming to hold a political meeting. Despite that hostility, Caldwell had returned to vote in the November state election. Even more boldly, he had led a black militia company through the streets to help quell the disturbances. Now, as Caldwell and his "friend" raised their glasses in a holiday toast, a gunshot exploded through the window. Caldwell collapsed, mortally wounded from a bullet to the back of his head. He was taken outside, where his assassins riddled his body with bullets.

Charles Caldwell shared the fate of more than a few southern black Republicans. Southern whites used violence, terror, and political assassination to challenge the federal government's commitment to Reconstruction. If northerners had boldly countered such terrorism, Reconstruction might have ended differently. But in the years following President Johnson's impeachment trial in 1868, the influence of Radical Republicans steadily waned. The Republican party was being drained of the crusading idealism that had stamped its early years.

The Election of Grant

Immensely popular after the war, Ulysses S. Grant was the natural choice of Republicans to run for president in 1868. Although Grant was elected, Republicans were shocked that despite his great military stature, his popular margin was only 300,000 votes. An estimated 450,000 black Republican votes had been cast in the South, which meant that a majority of whites casting ballots had voted Democratic. The 1868 election helped convince Republican leaders that an amendment securing black suffrage throughout the nation was necessary.

Lucy Stone, a major figure in the women's rights movement.

Fifteenth Amendment

In February 1869 Congress sent the Fifteenth Amendment to the states for ratification. It forbade any state to deny the right to vote on grounds of race, color, or previous condition of servitude. Some Radicals had hoped to forbid literacy or property requirements to protect blacks further. Others wanted a simple declaration that all adult male citizens had the right to vote. But the moderates in the party were aware that many northerners were increasingly worried about the number of immigrants who were again entering the country and wanted to be able to restrict their voting. As a result, the final amendment left loopholes that eventually allowed southern states to **disfranchise** African Americans. The amendment was ratified in March 1870, aided by the votes of the four southern states that had not completed the process of Reconstruction and thus were also required to endorse this amendment before being readmitted to Congress.

Proponents of women's suffrage were gravely disappointed when Congress refused to prohibit voting discrimination on the basis of sex as well as race. The Women's Loyal League, led by Elizabeth Cady Stanton and Susan B. Anthony, had pressed for first the Fourteenth and then the Fifteenth Amendment to recognize women's public role. But even most Radicals, contending that black rights had to be ensured first, were unwilling to back women's suffrage. The Fifteenth Amendment ruptured the feminist movement. Although disappointed that women were not included in its provisions, Lucy Stone and the American Woman Suffrage Association urged ratification. Stanton and Anthony, however, broke with their former allies among the Radicals, denounced the amendment, and organized the National Woman Suffrage Association to work for passage of a new amendment giving women the ballot. The division hampered the women's rights movement for decades to come.

Women's Suffrage Rejected

The Grant Administration

Ulysses Grant was ill at ease with the political process. His simple, quiet manner, while superb for commanding armies, did not serve him as well in public life, and his well-known resolution withered when he was uncertain of his goal. Also, he lacked the moral commitment to make Reconstruction succeed.

Corruption under Grant

A series of scandals wracked Grant's presidency. Although Grant did not profit personally, he remained loyal to his friends and displayed little zeal to root out wrong-doing. His relatives were implicated in a scheme to corner the gold market, and his private secretary escaped conviction for stealing federal whiskey revenues only because Grant interceded on his behalf. His secretary of war resigned to avoid impeachment.

Nor was Congress immune from the lowered tone of public life. In such a climate ruthless state machines, led by men who favored the status quo, came to dominate the party. Office and power became ends in themselves, and party leaders worked in close cooperation with northern industrial interests. The few Radicals still active in public life increasingly repudiated Grant and the Republican governments in the South. Congress in 1872 passed an amnesty act, removing the restrictions of the Fourteenth Amendment on officeholding except for about 200 to 300 ex-Confederate leaders.

As corruption in both the North and the South worsened, reformers became more interested in cleaning up government than in protecting blacks' rights. These liberal Republicans opposed the continued presence of the army in the South, denounced the corruption of southern governments as well as the national government, and advocated free trade and civil service reform. In 1872 they broke with the Republican party and nominated for president Horace Greeley, the editor of the New York *Tribune*. A onetime Radical, Greeley had become disillusioned with Reconstruction and urged a restoration of home rule in the South as well as adoption of civil service reform. Democrats decided to back the Liberal Republican ticket. The Republicans renominated Grant, who, despite the defection of a number of prominent Radicals, won an easy victory with 56 percent of the popular vote.

Grant swings from a trapeze while supporting a number of associates accused of corruption. Among those holding on are Secretary of the Navy George M. Robeson (top center), who was accused of accepting bribes for awarding navy contracts; Secretary of War William W. Belknap (top right), who was forced to resign for selling Indian post traderships; and the president's private secretary, Orville Babcock (bottom right), who was implicated in the Whiskey Ring scandal. Although not personally involved in the scandals during his administration, Grant was reluctant to dismiss supporters accused of wrongdoing from office.

Growing Northern Disillusionment

Civil Rights Act of 1875

During Grant's second term, Congress passed the Civil Rights Act of 1875, the last major piece of Reconstruction legislation. This law prohibited racial discrimination in all public accommodations, transportation, places of amusement, and juries. At the same time, Congress rejected a ban on segregation in public schools, which was almost universally practiced in the North as well as the South. Although some railroads, streetcars, and public accommodations in both sections were desegregated after the bill passed, the federal government made little attempt to enforce the law, and it was ignored throughout most of the South. In 1883 the Supreme Court struck down its provisions except the one relating to juries.

Despite passage of the Civil Rights Act, many northerners were growing disillusioned with Reconstruction. They were repelled by the corruption of the southern governments, they were tired of the violence and disorder in the South, and they had little faith in black Americans. "We have tried this long enough," remarked one influential northern Republican of Reconstruction. "Now let the South alone."

As the agony of the war became more distant, the Panic of 1873 diverted public attention from Reconstruction to economic issues. In the severe depression that followed over the next four years, some 3 million people found themselves out of work. Congress became caught up in the question of whether printing greenbacks would help the economy prosper. Battered by the panic and the corruption issue, the Republicans lost a shocking 77 seats in Congress in the 1874 elections, and along with them control of the House of Representatives for the first time since 1861. "The truth is our people are tired out with the worn out cry of 'Southern outrages'!!" one Republican concluded. "Hard times and heavy taxes make them wish the 'ever lasting nigger' were in hell or Africa." Republicans spoke more and more about cutting loose the unpopular southern governments.

Depression and Democratic Resurgence

The Triumph of White Supremacy

As northern commitment to Reconstruction waned, southern Democrats set out to overthrow the remaining Radical governments. White Republicans already in the South felt heavy pressure to desert their party. In Mississippi one party member justified his decision to leave on the grounds that otherwise he would have "to live a life of social oblivion" and his children would have no future.

To poor white southerners who lacked social standing, the Democratic appeal to racial solidarity offered great comfort. As one explained, "I may be poor and my manners may be crude, but . . . because I am a white man, I have a right to be treated with respect by Negroes. . . . That I am poor is not as important as that I am a white man; and no Negro is ever going to forget that he is not a white man." The large landowners and other wealthy groups that led southern Democrats objected less to black southerners voting. These well-to-do leaders did not face social and economic competition from African Americans, and in any case, they were confident that if outside influences were removed, they could control the black vote.

Democrats also resorted to economic pressure to undermine Republican power. In heavily black counties, white observers at the polls took down the names of black residents who cast Republican ballots and published them in local newspapers. Planters were urged to discharge black tenants who persisted in voting Republican. But terror and violence provided the most effective means to overthrow the Radical regimes. A number of paramilitary organizations broke up Republican meetings, terrorized white and black Republicans, assassinated Republican leaders, and prevented black

This campaign badge from 1868 made the sentiments of white Democrats clear.

Racism

Minstrels, Carnivals, and Ghosts

Uncovering the Cultural Roots of a KKK "Performance"

The costumes of Ku Klux Klan night riders—pointed hoods and white sheets—have become a staple of history books. In fact, not all the KKK wore costumes, and those who did sported a variety of outfits. But why use such outlandish, often elaborate disguises? To hide the identity of members, according to some accounts, or to terrorize freedpeople into thinking they were being menaced by Confederate ghosts. But clearly African Americans knew these were living, mortal enemies. Though simpler masks would have hidden identities, the guns that they brandished were far more frightening than any "ghostly" robes.

One historian has suggested that the KKK performances took their cues from traditions already a part of American popular culture: the costumes of Mardi Gras and similar carnivals, as well as the humorous sketches of minstrel shows. In behaving like minstrel performers or carnival revelers, KKK members may have had other audiences in mind. Northerners who read accounts of their doings could be lulled into thinking that the repressive night rides were just humorous pranks, not a threat to Radical rule. For southern Democrats, KKK rituals provided a way to reassert a sense of white supremacy.

Klansmen might have been defeated in war, but their theatrical night rides helped overturn the social order of Reconstruction, just as carousers at carnivals disrupted the night. The ritual garb provided more innocent cover for a campaign of intimidation that often turned deadly.

citizens from voting. The most famous was the Ku Klux Klan, founded in 1866 in Tennessee. It and similar groups functioned as unofficial arms of the Democratic party.

Congress finally moved to break the power of the Klan with the Force Act of 1870 and the Ku Klux Klan Act of 1871. These laws made it a felony to interfere with the right to vote; they also authorized use of the army and suspension of the writ of habeas corpus. The Grant administration eventually suspended the writ of habeas corpus in nine South Carolina counties and arrested hundreds of suspected Klan members throughout the South. Although these actions weakened the Klan, terrorist organizations continued to operate underground.

Mississippi Plan

Then in 1875 Democrats inaugurated what became known as the Mississippi Plan, the decision to use as much violence as necessary to carry the state election. Several local papers trumpeted, "Carry the election peaceably if we can, forcibly if we must." When Republican governor Adelbert Ames requested federal troops to stop the violence, Grant's advisers warned that sending troops to Mississippi would cost the party the Ohio election. In the end the administration told Ames to depend on his own forces. Bolstered by terrorism, the Democrats swept the election in Mississippi. Violence and intimidation prevented as many as 60,000 black and white Republicans from voting, converting the normal Republican majority into a Democratic majority of 30,000. Mississippi had been "redeemed."

The Disputed Election of 1876

With Republicans on the defensive across the nation, the 1876 presidential election was crucial to the final overthrow of Reconstruction. The Republicans nominated Ohio governor Rutherford B. Hayes to oppose Samuel Tilden of New York. Once again, violence prevented many Republican votes, this time an estimated quarter of a million, from being cast in the South. Tilden had a clear majority of 250,000 in the popular vote, but the outcome in the Electoral College was in doubt because both parties claimed South Carolina, Florida, and Louisiana, the only reconstructed states still in Republican hands. Hayes needed all three states to be elected, for even without them, Tilden had amassed 184 electoral votes, one short of a majority. Republican canvassing boards in power disqualified enough Democratic votes to give each state to Hayes.

To arbitrate the disputed returns, Congress established a 15-member electoral commission: 5 members each from the Senate, the House, and the Supreme Court. By a straight party vote of 8–7, the commission awarded the disputed electoral votes—and the presidency—to Hayes.

When angry Democrats threatened a filibuster to prevent the electoral votes from being counted, key Republicans met with southern Democrats on February 26 at the Wormley Hotel in Washington. There they reached an informal understanding, later known as the Compromise of 1877. Hayes's supporters agreed to withdraw federal troops from the South and not oppose the new Democratic state governments. For their part, southern Democrats dropped their opposition to Hayes's election and pledged to respect the rights of African Americans.

Compromise of 1877

Without federal support, the Republican governments in South Carolina and Louisiana promptly collapsed, and Democrats took control of the remaining states of the Confederacy. By 1877, the entire South was in the hands of the **Redeemers,** as they called themselves. Reconstruction and Republican rule had come to an end.

Redeemers Take Control

The Failure of Reconstruction

Reconstruction failed for a multitude of reasons. The reforming impulse that had created the Republican party in the 1850s had been battered and worn down by the war. The new materialism of industrial America inspired in many Americans a jaded cynicism about the corruption of the age and a desire to forget uncomfortable issues. In the South, African American voters and leaders inevitably lacked a certain amount of education and experience; elsewhere, Republicans were divided over policies and options.

Yet beyond these obstacles, the sad fact remains that the ideals of Reconstruction were most clearly defeated by the deep-seated racism that permeated American life. Racism was why the white South so unrelentingly resisted Reconstruction. Racism was why most white northerners had little interest in black rights except as a means to preserve the Union or to safeguard the Republic. Racism was why northerners were willing to write off Reconstruction and with it the welfare of African Americans. While Congress might pass a constitutional amendment abolishing slavery, it could not overturn at a stroke the social habits of two centuries.

Certainly the political equations of power, in the long term, had been changed. The North had fought fiercely during the war to preserve the Union. In doing so, it had secured the power to dominate the

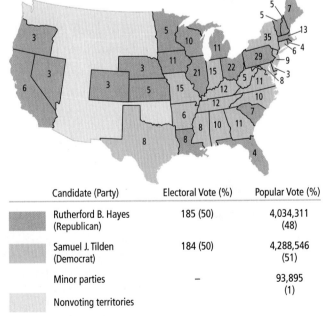

Candidate (Party)	Electoral Vote (%)	Popular Vote (%)
Rutherford B. Hayes (Republican)	185 (50)	4,034,311 (48)
Samuel J. Tilden (Democrat)	184 (50)	4,288,546 (51)
Minor parties	–	93,895 (1)
Nonvoting territories		

Election of 1876

Benjamin Montgomery, together with his sons, purchased Jefferson Davis's plantation along the Mississippi River after the war. A former slave, Montgomery pursued the dream of black economic independence by renting land to black farmers at Davis Bend.

economic and political destiny of the nation. With the overthrow of Reconstruction, the white South had won back some of the power it had lost in 1865. But even with white supremacy triumphant, African Americans did not return to the social position they had occupied before the war. They were no longer slaves, and black southerners who walked dusty roads in search of family members, sent their children to school, or worshiped in churches they controlled knew what a momentous change emancipation was. Even under the exploitative sharecropping system, black income rose significantly in freedom. Then, too, the Fourteenth Amendment principles of "equal protection" and "due process of law" had been written into the Constitution. These guarantees would be available for later generations to use in championing once again the Radicals' goal of racial equality.

End of the Davis Bend Experiment

But this was a struggle left to future reformers. For the time being, the clear trend was away from change or hope—especially for former slaves like Benjamin Montgomery and his sons, the owners of the old Davis plantations in Mississippi. In the 1870s bad crops, lower cotton prices, and falling land values undermined the Montgomerys' financial position, and in 1875 Jefferson Davis sued to have the sale of Brierfield invalidated. A lower court ruled against him, since he had never received legal title to the plantation. Davis appealed to the state supreme court, which, following the overthrow of Mississippi's Radical government, had a white conservative majority. In a politically motivated decision, the court awarded Brierfield to Davis in 1878, and the Montgomerys lost Hurricane as well.

A Wider World

The waning days of Reconstruction were filled with such ironies: of governments "redeemed" by violence and Supreme Court decisions using Fourteenth Amendment rights to protect giant corporations rather than individual African Americans. Increasingly, the industrial North focused on the economic task of integrating the South and West into the Union. Northern factories sought southern and western raw materials (cotton, timber, cattle, and minerals) to produce goods to sell in national and international markets.

This trend was global in scope. During the coming decades European nations also scrambled to acquire natural resources and markets. In the onrushing age of imperialism, Western nations would seek to dominate newly acquired colonies in Africa and Asia. There would be gold rushes in South Africa as well as in the United States, vast cattle ranches in Argentina and Canada as well as across the American Great Plains. Farmers would open up lands in New Zealand and Australia as well as in Oklahoma and Wyoming. And just as racism replaced slavery as the central justification for white supremacy in the South, it promoted the campaigns against Indians and Hispanics in the West and in a belief in "inferior races" to be swept aside by imperialists all across the world. The ideal of a truly diverse and democratic society remained largely unsought and unfulfilled.

Significant Events

1863	Lincoln outlines Reconstruction program
1864	Lincoln vetoes Wade-Davis bill; Louisiana, Arkansas, and Tennessee establish governments under Lincoln's plan
1865–1866	Black codes enacted
1865	Freedmen's Bureau established; Johnson becomes president; presidential Reconstruction completed; Congress excludes representatives of Johnson's governments; Thirteenth Amendment ratified; Joint Committee on Reconstruction established
1866	Civil rights bill passed over Johnson's veto; Memphis and New Orleans riots; Ku Klux Klan organized; Republicans win decisive victory in congressional elections
1867	Congressional Reconstruction enacted; Tenure of Office Act
1868	Johnson impeached but acquitted; Fourteenth Amendment ratified; Grant elected president
1870	Fifteenth Amendment ratified; Force Act passed
1871	Ku Klux Klan Act
1872	General Amnesty Act; Freedmen's Bureau closes down; Liberal Republican revolt
1873–1877	Panic and depression
1875	Civil Rights Act; Mississippi Plan
1876	Disputed Hayes-Tilden election
1877	Compromise of 1877; Hayes declared winner of electoral vote; last Republican governments in South fall

Chapter Summary

Presidents Abraham Lincoln and Andrew Johnson and the Republican-dominated Congress each developed a program of Reconstruction to restore the Confederate states to the Union.

- Lincoln's 10 percent plan required that 10 percent of qualified voters from 1860 swear an oath of loyalty to begin organizing state government.

- Following Lincoln's assassination, Andrew Johnson changed Lincoln's terms and lessened Reconstruction's requirements.

- The more radical Congress repudiated Johnson's state governments and enacted its own program of Reconstruction, which included the principle of black suffrage.

  —Congress passed the Fourteenth and Fifteenth Amendments and also extended the life of the Freedmen's Bureau, a unique experiment in social welfare.
  —Congress rejected land reform, however, which would have provided the freedpeople with a greater economic stake.

  —The effort to remove Johnson from office through impeachment failed.

- The Radical governments in the South, led by black and white southerners and transplanted northerners, compiled a mixed record on matters such as racial equality, education, economic issues, and corruption.

- Reconstruction was a time of both joy and frustration for former slaves.

  —Former slaves took steps to reunite their families and establish black-controlled churches.
  —They evidenced a widespread desire for land and education.
  —Black resistance to the old system of labor led to the adoption of sharecropping.
  —The Freedmen's Bureau fostered these new working arrangements and also the beginnings of black education in the South.

- Northern public opinion became disillusioned with Reconstruction during the presidency of Ulysses S. Grant.

- Southern whites used violence, economic coercion, and racism to overthrow the Republican state governments.

- In 1877 Republican leaders agreed to end Reconstruction in exchange for Rutherford B. Hayes's election as president.

- Racism played a key role in the eventual failure of Reconstruction.

Additional Reading

Historians' views of Reconstruction have dramatically changed over the past half century. Modern studies offer a more sympathetic assessment of Reconstruction and the experience of African Americans. Indicative of this trend is Eric Foner, *Reconstruction* (1988), and his briefer treatment (with photographic essays by Joshua Brown) *Forever Free: the Story of Emancipation and Reconstruction* (2005). Michael Les Benedict treats the clash between Andrew Johnson and Congress in *The Impeachment and Trial of Andrew Johnson* (1973). Political affairs in the South during Reconstruction are examined in Dan T. Carter, *When the War Was Over* (1985), and Thomas Holt, *Black over White* (1977), an imaginative study of black political leadership in South Carolina. Hans Trefousse, *Thaddeus Stevens: Nineteenth-Century Egalitarian* (1997), provides a sympathetic reassessment of the influential Radical Republican.

Leon Litwack, *Been in the Storm So Long* (1979), sensitively analyzes the transition of enslaved African Americans to freedom. Heather Andrea Williams, *Self-Taught: African American Education in Slavery and Freedom* (2005), illustrates the black drive for literacy and education. James L. Roark, *Masters without Slaves* (1977), discusses former slaveholders' adjustment to the end of slavery. The dialectic of black-white relations is charted from the antebellum years through Reconstruction and beyond in Steven Hahn, *A Nation under Our Feet: Black Political Struggles in the Rural South from Slavery to the Great Migration* (2003). Two excellent studies of changing labor relations in southern agriculture are Julie Saville, *The Work of Reconstruction* (1995), and John C. Rodrigue, *Reconstruction in the Cane Fields* (2001). For contrasting views of the Freedman's Bureau see George R. Bentley, *A History of the Freedman's Bureau* (1955)—favorable—and Donald Nieman, *To Set the Law in Motion* (1979)—more critical. "William Gillette, *Retreat from Reconstruction, 1869–1879* (1980) focuses on national politics and the end of Reconstruction, while Michael Perman, *The Road to Redemption* (1984), looks at developments in the South."

For a fuller list of readings, see the Bibliography at www.mhhe.com/davidsonnation6.

CHAPTER 18
The New South &
The Trans-Mississippi West
1870~1914

"Come West"

The news spread across the South during the late 1870s. Perhaps a man came around with a handbill telling of cheap land, or a letter might arrive from friends or relatives and be read aloud at church. The news spread in different ways, but in the end, it always spelled Kansas.

Few black farmers had been that far west themselves. More than a few knew that the abolitionist Old John Brown had made his home in Kansas before coming east to raid Harpers Ferry. Black folks, it seemed, might be able to live more freely in Kansas. "You can buy land at from a dollar and a half to two dollars an acre," wrote one settler to his friend in Louisiana. There was another distinct advantage: "They do not kill Negroes here for voting."

In 1878 such prospects excited hundreds of black families already stretched to their limits by hardship and violence. With Rutherford Hayes president, Reconstruction was at an end. Southern state governments had been "redeemed" by conservative whites, and the future seemed uncertain. "COME WEST," concluded The Colored Citizen, a newspaper in Topeka. "COME TO KANSAS." St. Louis learned of these rumblings in the first raw days of March 1879, as steamers from downriver began unloading freedpeople in large numbers. Some came with belongings and money; others, with only the clothes on their backs. By the end of 1879, more than 20,000 had arrived. With the weather still cold, they sought shelter beneath tarpaulins along the river levee, built fires, and got out frying pans to cook meals.

When the crowds overwhelmed the wharves and temporary shelters, the city's black churches banded together to house the "refugees," feed them, and help them continue toward Kansas. Repeated rumors that rail passage would not be free failed to shake their hopes. "We's like de chilun ob Israel when dey was led from out o' bondage by Moses," one explained, referring to the Bible's tale of exodus from Egypt. So the "Exodusters," as they became known, pressed westward. In the end, more black emigrants settled in growing towns like Topeka, Lincoln, and Kansas City. Men worked as hired hands; women took in laundry. With luck, couples made $350 a year, saved a bit for a home, and put down roots.

The host of Exodusters who poured into Kansas were part of a human flood westward. It had many sources—played-out farms of New England and the South, crowded cities, all of Europe. In 1879, as African Americans traveled up the Mississippi

African Americans wait on a levee, as many Exodusters did in moving to Kansas in 1879 and 1880. Often traveling with few resources, the journey was uncertain. In the foreground a young child sleeps on the only bedding available.

to St. Louis, 1,000 white emigrants arrived in Kansas every week. Special trains brought settlers to the plains, all eager to start anew. During the 1880s the number of Kansans jumped from a million to a million and a half. Other western states experienced similar booms.

The optimism of boomers black and white could not mask the serious strains in the rapidly expanding nation, especially in the South and the trans-Mississippi West. As largely agricultural regions, they struggled to find their place in the new age of industry emerging from Reconstruction. In the South, despite a strong push to industrialize, the continuing dominance of white supremacy undercut economic growth, encouraging the scourge of sharecropping and farm tenancy and spawning a system of racial violence and caste to replace slavery. For its part, the booming West began to realize at least some of the dreams of antebellum reformers: for free homesteads in Kansas and beyond, for a railroad that spanned the continent, for land-grant colleges to educate its people. Yet the West, too, built a society based on racial violence and caste.

Relations Between the South, West, and Northeast

Much as the national markets emerging after the War of 1812 drew the lands beyond the Appalachian Mountains into their economic orbit, the industrial economy emerging after the Civil War incorporated the South and the trans-Mississippi region as well. By the end of the nineteenth century, both the South and West had assumed their place as suppliers of raw materials, providers of foodstuffs, and consumers of finished goods. A nation of "regional nations" was thus knit together in the last third of the nineteenth century. Not all southerners and westerners were happy with the result. As we shall see in Chapter 21, their frustrations mounted as the Northeast enriched itself at their expense and the powers in Washington ignored their plight.

The Southern Burden

Inequities between the agricultural South and the industrial North infuriated Henry Grady, the editor of the *Atlanta Constitution*. Grady often liked to tell the story of the poor cotton farmer buried in a pine coffin in the pine woods of Georgia. Except the coffin hadn't been made in Georgia but in Cincinnati. The nails in the coffin had been forged in Pittsburgh, though an iron mine lay near the Georgia cemetery. Even the farmer's cotton coat was made in New York and his trousers in Chicago. The "South didn't furnish a thing on earth for that funeral but the corpse and the hole in the ground!" fumed Grady. The irony of the story was the tragedy of the South. The region had human and natural resources aplenty but, alas, few factories to manufacture the goods it needed.

The Gospel of a "New South"

In the 1880s Grady campaigned to bring about a "New South" of bustling industry, cities, and commerce. The business class and its values would displace the old planter class as southerners raced "to out-Yankee the Yankee." Grady and other publicists recognized the South's potential. Extending from Delaware south to Florida and west to Texas, the region took in a third of the nation's total area. It held a third of its arable farmlands, vast tracts of lumber, and rich deposits of coal, iron, oil, and fertilizers. To overcome the destruction of the Civil War and the loss of slaveholding wealth, apostles of the New South campaigned to catch up with the industrial North. Yet well into the twentieth century, Grady's New South remained the poorest section of the country—largely decentralized, rural, and agricultural. And the South suffered as well the burden of an unwieldy labor system that was often unskilled, usually underpaid, and always divided along lines of race.

Agriculture in the New South

A Cotton-Dominated Economy

For all the talk of industry, the economy of the postwar South remained agricultural, tied to crops like tobacco, rice, sugar, and especially cotton. By using fertilizers, planters were able to introduce cotton into areas once considered marginal. The number of acres planted in cotton more than doubled between 1870 and 1900. Some southern farmers sought prosperity in crops other than cotton. George Washington Carver, of Alabama's Tuskegee Institute (see page 607), persuaded many poor black farmers to plant peanuts. But most southern soils were too acidic and the spring rains too heavy for other legumes and grains to flourish. Parasites and diseases plagued cattle herds. Work animals like mules were raised more cheaply in other regions. Try as southerners might to diversify, cotton still dominated their economy.

From 1880 to 1900 world demand for cotton grew slowly, and prices fell. As farms in other parts of the country were becoming larger and more efficient and were tended by fewer workers per acre, southern farms decreased in size. This decrease reflected the breakup of large plantations, but it also resulted from a high birthrate. Across the country, the number of children born per mother was dropping, but in the South, large families remained common because more children meant more farmhands. Each year, fewer acres of land were available for each person to cultivate. Even though the southern economy kept pace with national growth, **per capita income** fell behind.

After the Civil War, African Americans marked their freedom by ending field labor for most women and children. The women instead played a vital role in the domestic economy. Home garden plots supplemented the family food supply.

Tenancy and Sharecropping

To freedpeople across the South, the end of slavery brought hopes of economic independence. Surely John Solomon Lewis was one such hopeful soul. After the Civil War Lewis rented land to grow cotton in Tensas Parish, Louisiana. A depression in the 1870s dashed his dreams. "I was in debt," Lewis explained, "and the man I rented land from said every year I must rent again to pay the other year, and so I rents and rents and each year I gets deeper and deeper in debt."

The dream of economic independence was rooted in a theory of landholding called the "agricultural ladder," in vogue after the Civil War. According to this theory, any poor man could work his way up, rung by rung, until he finally owned his own land. Each rung in the agricultural ladder brought greater autonomy and—with it—the chance to achieve self-sufficiency and independence. At the bottom was the hired hand, who worked for wages on someone else's farm. On the next rung, the sharecropper was paid no wages but instead received a share of the proceeds when the owner sold the harvest, about half minus whatever debts had been incurred. The tenant, higher still, rented a parcel of land, had his own tools and work animals, and owned the crop itself. As rent, the tenant turned over part of the harvest, usually a quarter of the cotton crop and a third of any grains, to the landowner. Through ruthless penny-pinching, the tenant eventually could purchase land and rise finally to the status of independent farmer.

Agricultural Ladder

In practice, harsh realities overwhelmed theory, as John Solomon Lewis and other poor farmers—black and white—learned. The South's best land remained in the hands of large plantation owners. Few freedpeople or poor whites ever had enough money to acquire property. The problem lay in a ruinous system of credit. The harvest,

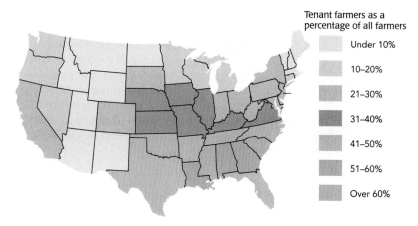

Tenant farmers as a percentage of all farmers

Under 10%

10–20%

21–30%

31–40%

41–50%

51–60%

Over 60%

Tenant Farmers, 1900
Tenant farming dominated southern agriculture after the Civil War. But notice that by 1900 it also accounted for much of the farm labor in the trans-Mississippi West, where low crop prices, high costs, and severe environmental conditions forced independent farmers into tenancy.

Debt Peonage in India, Egypt, and Brazil

whether produced by croppers or tenants or even small, independent farmers, was rarely enough for the worker to make ends meet, let alone to pay off debts and move up the agricultural ladder. Most farmers had to borrow money in the spring just to buy seeds, tools, or necessities such as food and clothing. Usually the only source of supplies and credit was the country store.

When John Solomon Lewis and other tenants entered the store, they saw two prices: one for cash and one for credit. The credit price might be as much as 60 percent higher. Creditors justified the difference on the grounds that high interest rates protected them against the high numbers of unpaid loans. As security for the loan, independent farmers mortgaged their land and soon slipped into tenancy as debts mounted and creditors foreclosed on their farms. The only asset tenants had was the crop they owned or the share they received. So they put up a mortgage or **lien** on the crop. The lien gave the shopkeeper first claim on the crop until the debt was paid.

Across the South, sharecropping and crop liens reduced many farmers to virtual slavery by shackling them to perpetual debt. Year after year, they rented or worked the land and borrowed against their future returns until they found themselves so deeply in debt that they could never escape. This economic dependence, known as **debt peonage,** turned the agricultural ladder into an agricultural slide, robbing small farmers of their land and sending them to the bottom rungs of tenancy, sharecropping, and migrant-farm work. By the 1880s three of every four African American farmers in the black belt states of Mississippi, Alabama, and Georgia were croppers. Twenty years later, a majority of southern white farmers had fallen into sharecropping. Few had the freedom to move up. The landlord or shopkeeper (often the same person) could insist that tenants grow only cash crops such as cotton rather than produce they could eat. Most landlords also required that cotton be ginned, baled, and marketed through their mills—at rates they controlled.

The slide of sharecroppers and tenants into debt peonage occurred elsewhere in the cotton-growing world. In India, Egypt, and Brazil agricultural laborers gave up **subsistence farming** to raise cotton as a cash crop during the American Civil War, when the North prevented southern cotton from being exported. New railroad and telegraph lines built in these growing regions helped make the export of cotton more efficient and profitable. But when prices fell, growers borrowed to make ends meet, as in the American South. In India moneylenders charged interest as high as 24 percent annually on such debts; in Egypt, sometimes 60 percent. In the mid-1870s, the pressures on cotton growers led them to revolt in India and Brazil, attacking money lenders, destroying land records, and refusing to pay taxes. As we shall see in Chapter 21, in the 1890s, American farmers rose up too.

Southern Industry

The crusade for a New South did bring change. From 1869 to 1909, industrial production grew faster than the national rate. So did productivity for southern workers. A boom in railroad building after 1879 furnished the region with good transportation. In two areas, cotton textiles and tobacco, southern advances were striking. With cotton fiber and cheap labor close at hand, 400 cotton mills were humming by 1900, when they employed almost 100,000 workers.

Boom in Textiles

Most new textile workers were poor white southerners escaping competition from black farm laborers or fleeing the hardscrabble life of the mountains. Entire families worked in the mills. Older men had the most trouble adjusting. They lacked the experience,

This girl had been working in a cotton mill in Whitnel, North Carolina, for about a year, sometimes on the night shift. She made 48 cents a day. When asked how old she was, she hesitated, then said, "I don't remember." But then she added, confidentially, "I'm not old enough to work, but do just the same."

temperament, and dexterity to tend spindles and looms in cramped mills. Only over time, as farm folk adapted to the tedious rhythm of factories, did southerners become competitive with workers from other regions of the United States and western Europe.

Tobacco and Cigarettes

The tobacco industry also thrived in the New South. Before the Civil War, American tastes had run to cigars, snuff, and chewing tobacco. In 1876, James Bonsack, an 18-year-old Virginian, invented a machine to roll cigarettes. That was just the device Washington Duke and his son James needed to boost the fortunes of their growing tobacco business. Cigarettes suited the new urban market in the North, "clean, quick, and potent" according to one observer.

Between 1860 and 1900, the annual rate of tobacco consumption nearly quadrupled. Americans spent more money on tobacco than on clothes or shoes. The sudden interest in smoking offered southerners a rare opportunity to control a national market. But the factories were so hot, the stench of tobacco so strong, and the work so exhausting that native-born white southerners generally refused the jobs. Duke solved the labor problem by hiring Jewish immigrants, experts in making cigars, to train black southerners in the techniques of tobacco work. Then he promoted cigarettes in a national advertising campaign, using gimmicks like collectible picture cards. By the 1890s his American Tobacco Company led the industry.

Timber and Steel

The realities of southern economic life were more accurately reflected in lumber and steel than in tobacco and textiles. After the Civil War, the South possessed more than 60 percent of the nation's timber resources. With soaring demand from towns and cities across the nation, lumber and turpentine became the South's chief industries and employers.

If anything, however, aggressive lumbering left the South far poorer. Corruption of state officials and a relaxed federal timber policy allowed northerners and foreigners to acquire huge forest tracts at artificially low prices. The timber was then sold as raw

This railroad served a lumber mill. The lumber industry in the South exploited large stands of timber, but overcutting led to erosion and tended to impoverish the region.

lumber rather than as more profitable finished products such as cedar shingles or the coffins Henry Grady liked to mention.

Overcutting added little to local economies. Logging camps were isolated and temporary. Visitors described the lumberjacks as "single, homeless, and possession-less." Once loggers leveled the forests around their camps, they moved on to other sites. Most sawmills operated for only a few years before the owners followed the loggers to a new area. Thus loggers and millers had little time to put down roots and invest their cash in the community.

Environmental Costs

The environmental costs were high. In the South, as elsewhere, overcutting and other logging practices stripped hillsides bare. As spring rains eroded soil and unleashed floods, forests lost their capacity for self-renewal. By 1901 a Georgian complained that "from most of the visible land the timber is entirely gone." With it went the golden eagles, the peregrine falcons, and other native species.

Turpentine mills, logging, and lumber milling provided young black southerners with their greatest source of employment. Occasionally an African American rose to be a supervisor, though most supervisors were white. Southerners often blamed these workers, not the operators or the horrid working conditions and low pay, for the industry's high turnover rates and low morale among workers. As one critic complained, "The sawmill negro is rather shiftless and is not inclined to stay in any one location and consequently there is little incentive on the part of the owner or operator to carry on welfare work in any extensive manner." In fact, most black workers left the mills in search of higher wages or to sharecrop in order to marry and support families.

Birmingham Steel

The iron and steel industry most disappointed promoters of the New South. The availability of coke as a fuel made Chattanooga, Tennessee, and Birmingham, Alabama, major centers for foundries. By the 1890s the Tennessee Coal, Iron, and Railway Company (TCI) of Birmingham was turning out iron pipe for gas, water, and sewer lines vital to cities. Unfortunately Birmingham's iron deposits were ill-suited for the kinds of steel in demand. In 1907 the financially strapped TCI was sold to the giant U.S. Steel Corporation, controlled by northern interests.

The pattern of lost opportunity was repeated in other southern industries— mining, chemical fertilizers, cottonseed oil, and railroads. Under the campaign for a New South, all grew dramatically in employment and value, but not enough to end poverty or industrialize the region.

The Sources of Southern Poverty

Why did poverty persist in the New South? Surely, as many southerners claimed, the South became something of a colonial economy controlled by business interests in

New York or Pittsburgh rather than Atlanta or New Orleans. Raw materials such as minerals, timber, and cotton were shipped to other regions, which earned larger profits by turning them into finished goods.

Three other factors also contributed to the region's poverty. First, the South began to industrialize later than the Northeast. Northern workers produced more not because they were more energetic or disciplined but because they were more experienced.

Late Start in Industrializing

Second, the South commanded only a small technological community to guide its industrial development. Northern engineers and mechanics seldom followed northern capital into the region. Few people were available to adapt modern technology to southern conditions or to teach southerners how to do it themselves.

Education might have overcome the problem by upgrading the region's workforce. But no region in the nation spent less on schooling than did the South. Southern leaders, drawn from the ranks of the upper class, cared little about educating ordinary white residents and openly resisted educating black southerners. And the region's low wages encouraged educated workers to leave the South for higher pay. Few southern states invested in technical colleges and engineering schools, and so none could match those of the North.

Undereducated Labor

Lack of education aggravated a third source of southern poverty: the isolation of its labor force. In 1900 agriculture still dominated the southern economy. It required unskilled, low-paid sharecroppers and wage laborers. Southerners feared that outsiders, with their new ways, might spread discontent among workers. So southern states discouraged social services and opportunities that might have attracted human and financial resources. The South remained poor because it received too little, not too much, outside investment.

The Isolated Southern Labor Market

Life in the New South

Life in the New South was a constant struggle to balance love of the hell-raising life with the equally powerful pull of heavenly Christian piety. Divided in its soul, the South was also divided by race. Even after the Civil War ended slavery, some 90 percent of African Americans continued to live in the rural South. Without slavery, however, southerners lost the system of social control that had defined race relations. Over time they substituted a new system of racial separation, called **segregation,** that eased but never eliminated white fear of African Americans.

Rural Life

Pleasure, piety, race—all divided southern life, in town and country alike. And life separated along lines of gender as well, especially in the rural areas where most southerners lived.

Southern males found one source of pleasure in hunting. Hunting offered men welcome relief from heavy farm work. For rural people a successful hunt could also add meat and fish to a scanty diet. And through hunting many boys found a path to manhood. Seeing his father and brothers return with wild turkeys, young Edward McIlhenny longed for "the time when I would be old enough to hunt this bird."

Hunting

The thrill of illicit pleasure also drew many southern men to events of violence and chance, including cockfighting. They valued combative birds and were convinced that their champions fought more boldly than did northern bantams. Gambling doubtless heightened the thrills. Such sport offended churchgoing southerners by its cruelty and wantonness. They condemned as sinful "the beer garden, the base ball, the low theater, the dog fight and cock fight and the ring for the pugilist and brute."

Many southern customs involved no such disorderly behavior. Work-sharing festivals such as house raisings, log rollings, quiltings, and road work gave isolated farm folk the chance to break their daily routine, to socialize, and to work for a common good. These events, too, generally segregated along gender lines. Men did the heavy chores

Farm Entertainments

and competed in contests of physical prowess. Women shared more domestic tasks such as cooking, quilting, and sewing. Community gatherings also offered young southerners a relaxed place for courtship. In one courting game, the young man who found a rare red ear of corn could have the rare treat of kissing "the lady of his choice."

Town

For rural folk, a trip to town brought special excitement, along with a bit of danger. Saturdays, court days, and holidays drew people from far and wide. Once again, there were male and female domains. For men the saloon, the blacksmith shop, or the storefront was a place to do business and to let off steam. Few men went to town without participating in social drinking in the local saloon, but when men turned to roam the streets, the threat of brawling and violence drove most women away.

Court week, when a district judge arrived to mete out justice, drew the biggest crowds. Some people came to settle disputes; most came to enjoy the spectacle or do some business. Peddlers and entertainers worked the crowds with magic tricks, patent medicines, and other wares. Town also offered a chance to attend the theater or a traveling circus.

The Church

At the center of southern life stood the church as a great stabilizer and custodian of social order. "When one joined the Methodist church," a southern woman remembered, "he was expected to give up all such things as cards, dancing, theatres, in fact all so called worldly amusements." Many devout southerners pursued these ideals, although such restraint asked more of people than many were willing to show, except perhaps on Sunday.

Rural Religion

Congregations were often so small and isolated that they could attract a preacher only once or twice a month. The pious counted on the Sunday sermon to steer them from sin. In town, a sermon might last 30 to 45 minutes, but in the country, a preacher could go on for two hours or more, whipping up his congregation until "even the little children wept."

By 1870 southern churches were segregated by race. Indeed, the black church was the only institution controlled by African Americans after slavery and thus a principal source of leadership and identity in addition to comfort (see pages 482–483). Within churches both black and white, congregations were segregated by gender, too. As a boy entered manhood, he moved from the female to the male section. Yet churches were, at

For Baptists in the South, both white and black, the ceremony of adult baptism included total immersion, often in a nearby river. The ritual symbolized the waters of newfound faith washing away sins that had been forgiven by God's free grace. Here, a black congregation looks on, some holding umbrellas to protect against the sun.

base, female domains. Considered guardians of virtue, more women were members, attended services, and ran church activities.

Church was a place to socialize as well as worship. Many of the young went simply to meet those of the opposite sex. Church picnics and all-day sings brought as many as 30 or 40 young people together for hours of eating, talk, services, and hymn singing. Still, these occasions could not match the fervor of a weeklong camp meeting. In the late summer or early fall, town and countryside emptied as folks set up tents in shady groves and listened to two or three ministers preach day and night in the largest event of the year. The camp meeting refired faith while celebrating traditional values of home and family.

Segregation

Nothing challenged tradition in the South more than race. With the abolition of slavery and the end of Reconstruction, white northerners and southerners achieved sectional harmony by sacrificing the rights of black citizens. During the 1880s, Redeemer governments moved to formalize a system of segregation or racial separation. Redeemers were Democratic politicians who came to power in southern states to end the Republican rule established during Reconstruction. They were eager to reap the benefits of economic expansion and to attract the business classes—bankers, railroad promoters, industrial operators. As their part of the bargain, the Redeemers assured anxious northerners that Redeemer rule would not mean political disfranchisement of the freedpeople. That part of the bargain they would not keep.

Pressure to reach a new racial accommodation in the South increased as more African Americans moved into southern towns and cities, competing for jobs with poor whites. One way to preserve the social and economic superiority of white southerners, poor as well as rich, was to separate blacks as an inferior caste. But federal laws designed to enforce the Civil Rights Act of 1866 and the Fourteenth Amendment with its promise of equal protection for all under law stood in the way. In effect, these laws established social equality for all races in public gathering places such as hotels, theaters, and railroads.

In 1883, however, the Supreme Court ruled (in the *Civil Rights Cases*) that hotels and railroads were not "public" institutions because private individuals owned them. The Fourteenth Amendment was thus limited to protecting citizens from violations of their civil rights by states, not by private individuals. The national policy of **laissez faire** in race relations could not have been made any clearer.

Within 20 years every southern state had enacted segregation as law. The earliest laws legalized segregation in trains and other such public conveyances where blacks and whites were likely to mingle. Soon a complex web of "Jim Crow" statutes had drawn an indelible color line separating the races in prisons, parks, hotels, restaurants, hospitals, and virtually all public gathering places except streets and stores. (The term *Jim Crow*, used to denote a policy of segregation, originated in a song of the same name sung in minstrel shows of the day.)

Jim Crow Laws

In 1892, Homer Adolph Plessy, an African American, agreed to test a Louisiana law requiring segregated railroad facilities by sitting in the all-white section of a local train. He was promptly arrested, and slowly the case of *Plessy v. Ferguson* worked its way up to the Supreme Court. In 1896, the Court ruled that segregation did not constitute discrimination as long as accommodations for both races were "separate but equal." Justice John Marshall Harlan (ironically from a former slaveholding family) issued the lone dissent: separate, whether equal or not, was always a "badge of servitude" and a violation of the "color-blind" Constitution. The doctrine of separate but equal none the less became part of the fabric of American law and governed race relations for more than half a century to come. When coupled with a growing campaign in the 1890s to disfranchise black voters across the South (see pages 605–606), segregation provided a formidable barrier to African American progress.

Plessy v. Ferguson

A long line of African American voters waits to cast ballots in Caddo Parish, Louisiana, in 1897. Clearly, interest in voting remained high among black citizens. Two years later Louisiana followed the lead of other Southern states in disfranchising most of its black voters (as well as many poor whites).

By the turn of the century segregation was firmly in place, stifling economic competition between the races and reducing African Americans to second-class citizenship. Many kinds of employment, such as work in the textile mills, went largely to whites. Skilled and professional black workers generally served black clients. African Americans were barred from juries and usually received far stiffer penalties than whites for the same crimes.

As Jim Crow laws became entrenched, so did stifling social custom. Black southerners always addressed white southerners as Mister, Miss, and Ma'am—even those of lower status. But white southerners called black southerners by their first names or more simply Sister or Boy, no matter their age or profession. Any African American who crossed the color line risked violence. Some were tarred and feathered, others whipped and beaten, and many lynched. Of the 187 lynchings averaged each year of the 1890s, some 80 percent occurred in the South. The victims were almost always African Americans.

Spending on Education in the South before and after Disfranchisement *With disfranchisement and segregation, education was separate, but hardly equal, for blacks and whites. In these states, after blacks were disfranchised, spending on white students rose while spending on black students decreased.*

[*Source:* Data from Robert A. Margo, *Disfranchisement, School Finance, and the Economics of Segregated Schools in the U.S. South, 1890–1910* (New York: Garland Press, 1985), table I-1.]

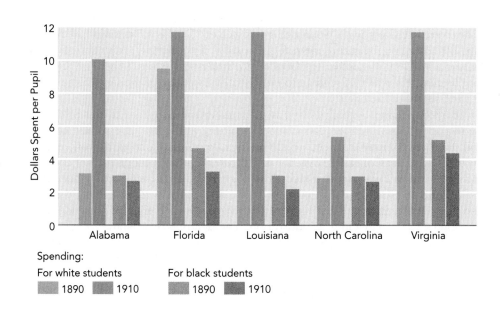

Spending:

For white students   For black students
1890   1910   1890   1910

Western Frontiers

The black Exodusters flooding into Kansas in the 1870s and 1880s were only part of the vast migration west. Looking beyond the Mississippi in the 1840s and 1850s, white "overlanders" had set their sights on California and Oregon and the promise of land. They headed across the Mississippi River, pushing the frontier of Anglo settlement to the edge of the continent.

The overlanders went west in search of opportunity and "free" land. They found opportunity elusive to those without money or power. They also found Indians—perhaps as many as 360,000—and "Hispanos," settlers of Spanish descent, who hardly considered the land free for use by Anglos.

The overlanders discovered as well that the West was not one region but many, each governed by a different ecology. And its frontiers moved in many directions, not just from east to west. Before the Civil War, the frontier for easterners had moved beyond the Mississippi to the timberlands of Missouri but skipped over the Great Plains, as the overlanders settled in California and Oregon. But another frontier then pushed east from the Pacific coast, following miners into the Sierra Nevada. For Texans, the frontier moved from south to north as cattle ranchers sought new grazing land, as had the ancestors of the Spanish rancheros of the Southwest. And for American Indians, these constantly shifting frontiers shaped and reshaped their ways of life.

Moving Frontiers

Western Landscapes

Whatever perspective one adopts, the West is above all a place of varied landscapes. Early travelers from the United States labeled the vast region beyond the Mississippi the "Great American Desert." Most of the land between the 98th meridian and the lush lowlands of the West Coast receives less than 20 inches of rain a year, making what came to be known as the Great Plains a treeless expanse of prairie grass and dunes. Infrequent stands of timber cluster along river bottoms, and wood for housing and fences is scarce. Overlanders of the 1840s and 1850s compared its vast windy spaces to the oceans: a "sea of grass" stretching to the horizon and crossed by "prairie schooners."

Dry Territory West of the 98th Meridian

But the plains are only part of the trans-Mississippi West. And even they can be divided. The Great Plains west of the 98th meridian are semiarid, but the eastern Prairie

Eyedazzlers and Beads

Material Culture and Global Patterns of Trade

The ordinary objects used in everyday life—material culture—have significance for historians beyond their obvious functions. The Navajo blanket shown here is known as an "eyedazzler;" and, as its name suggests, the blanket was meant to do more than keep its user warm. Such blankets also show us how global influences, in this case the market economy, shaped Indian life and art.

Eyedazzlers became popular during what is known as the "transitional period" in Navajo textile making, roughly from 1868 to 1890, when the market for such blankets was shifting from natives to tourists. International trade and the demands of non-Indian consumers led Navajo weavers to redesign their blankets. They employed the brightly colored thread of European dye makers with the geometric designs typical of Mexican *serapes* (patterns themselves derived from the Moorish artisans of Spain). The eyedazzlers eventually disappeared, however, as market tastes changed from the dyed fabrics of European manufacturers to the natural colors of earlier Navajo weavers. Consumers found these blankets more appealing because they seemed more "primitive" and were easier to clean.

The global reach of material culture extended in the opposite direction as well. Nineteenth-century traders sold millions of tiny glass beads to Indians for their embroidery, and Indians had their own strong preferences in terms of style and color. Bead supplies came from skilled glassmakers as far away as

Venice, Italy. For Indians and Europeans alike, material culture was global in significance.

Plains are favored with good soil and abundant rain. Beyond the plains the jagged peaks of the Rocky Mountains stretch from Alaska to New Mexico. And west of the mountains lies the Great Basin of Utah, Nevada, and eastern California, where temperatures climb above 100 degrees. Near the coast rise the Sierra Nevada and Cascades, rich in minerals and lumber and sloping to the temperate shores and fertile valleys of the Pacific.

Easterners who watched the wagons roll west liked to conjure up the image of a "trackless wilderness." In truth, even in the 1840s, the Great Plains and mountain frontier comprised a complex web of cultures and environments in which Spanish, Anglo-American, and Indian cultures penetrated one another and often produced swift change.

One example is the horse, introduced into North America by the colonial Spanish. By the eighteenth century horses were grazing on prairie grass across the Great Plains. By the nineteenth century the Comanche, Cheyenne, Apache, and other tribes had become master riders and hunters who could shoot their arrows with deadly accuracy at a full gallop. The new mobility of the Plains Indians far extended the area in which they could hunt buffalo, which soon became a staple of their existence. Their lives shifted from settled, village-centered agriculture to nomadic hunting.

Indian Peoples and the Western Environment

Some whites embraced the myth of the Indian as "noble savage" who lived in perfect harmony with the natural world. To be sure, Plains Indians were inventive in using scarce resources. Cottonwood bark fed horses in winter, and the buffalo supplied not only meat but also bones for tools, fat for cosmetics, sinews for thread, even dung for fuel. Yet Indians could not help but shape their ecosystems. Plains Indians hunted buffalo by stampeding herds over cliffs, which often led to waste. They irrigated crops and set fires to improve vegetation and game. By the mid–nineteenth century some tribes had become so enmeshed in trade with whites that they overtrapped their own hunting grounds.

Ecosystems, in turn, shaped Indian cultures. Although big-game hunting was common among many western tribes, the nomadic buffalo culture of the Great Plains Indians was hardly representative. In the lush forests and mountain ranges of the Pacific Northwest, Yuroks, Chinook, and other tribes hunted bear, moose, elk, and deer. Along the rocky coast they took whales, seals, and a variety of fish from the ocean. The early Hohokams and later the Pima and other tribes in New Mexico and Arizona developed irrigation to allow farming of beans, squash, and corn in the arid climate.

Despite their diversity, Indian peoples shared certain values. Most tribes were small extended kinship groups of 300 to 500 people in which the well-being of all outweighed the needs of each member. Although some tribes were better off than others, the gap between rich and poor within tribes was seldom large. Such small material differences often promoted communal decision making. The Cheyenne, for example, employed a council of 44 to advise the chief.

Indians also shared a reverence for nature, whatever their actual impact on the natural world. They believed human beings were part of an interconnected world of animals, plants, and other natural elements. All had souls of their own but were bound together, as if by contract, to live in balance through the ceremonial life of the tribe and the customs related to plants and animals. The Taos of New Mexico thought that each spring the pregnant earth issued new life. Whites were mystified by the explanation of one chief for why his people refused to farm: "You ask me to plow the ground! Shall I take a knife and tear my mother's bosom? . . . You ask me to cut grass and make hay and sell it, and be rich like white men! But how dare I cut off my mother's hair?"

Regard for the land endowed special places with religious meaning often indecipherable to whites. Where the Sioux saw in the Black Hills the sacred home of Wakan Tanka—the burial place of the dead and the site of their vision quests—whites saw grass for grazing and gold for the taking. From such contrasting views came conflict.

Variety of Indian Cultures

The cultures of western Indians were remarkably varied, ranging from the nomadic Plains tribes to the more settled peoples of the northwest coast who lived off the sea. This Sioux woman gathers firewood; the photograph was taken by Edward Curtis, who spent many years recording the faces and lives of native peoples of the West.

Whites and the Western Environment: Competing Visions

William Gilpin, a
Western Booster

As discoveries of gold and silver lured whites into Indian territory, many whites adopted the decidedly un-Indian outlook of Missouri politician William Gilpin. Only a lack of vision prevented the opening of the West for exploitation, Gilpin told an Independence, Missouri, audience in 1849. What were most needed were cheap lands and a railroad linking the two coasts "like ears on a human head." Distance, climate, topography, and even the Indians were mere obstacles.

By 1868 a generous Congress had granted western settlers their two greatest wishes: free land under the Homestead Act of 1862 and a transcontinental railroad. As

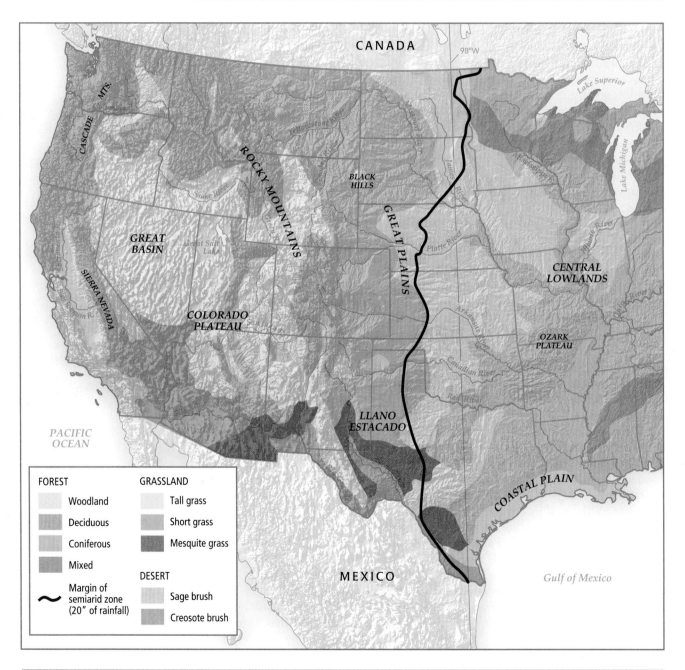

FOREST
- Woodland
- Deciduous
- Coniferous
- Mixed
- ~ Margin of semiarid zone (20″ of rainfall)

GRASSLAND
- Tall grass
- Short grass
- Mesquite grass

DESERT
- Sage brush
- Creosote brush

Natural Environment of the West   *With the exception of Oregon and Washington in the Pacific Northwest, few areas west of the 20-inch rainfall line receive enough annual precipitation to support agriculture without irrigation. Consequently, water has been the key to growth and development in the area west of the 98th meridian, which encompasses more than half the land area of the continental United States. The dominance of short grasses and coniferous (evergreen) trees reflects the rainfall patterns.*

the new governor of Colorado, Gilpin crowed about the region's limitless resources. One day, he believed, the West would support more than a billion people. Scarce rainfall and water did not daunt him, for in his eyes the West was an Eden-like garden, not "the great American Desert." Once the land had been planted, Gilpin assured listeners, the rains would develop naturally. He subscribed to the popular notion that "rain follows the plow," a myth sustained by an unusually wet cycle from 1878 to 1886. When the dry weather returned in the late 1880s, not rain but hardship followed farmers who moved west.

Unlike the visionary Gilpin, John Wesley Powell knew something about water and farming. After losing an arm in the Civil War, geologist Powell went west. In 1869 and 1871 he led scientific expeditions down the Green and Colorado rivers through the Grand Canyon. After navigating the swirling rapids that blocked his way, he returned to warn Congress that developing the West required more scientific planning. Much of the region had not even been mapped or its resources identified.

John Wesley Powell

In 1880 Powell became director of the recently formed U.S. Geological Survey. He, too, had a vision of the West, but one based on the limits of its environment. The key was water, not land. In the water-rich East, the English legal tradition of river rights prevailed. Whoever owned the banks of a river or stream controlled as much water as they might take, regardless of the consequence for those downstream. Such a practice in the water-starved West, Powell recognized, would enrich the small number with access while spelling ruin for the rest.

Water as a Key Resource

The alternative was to treat water as community property. The practice would benefit many rather than a privileged few. To that end Powell suggested that the federal government establish political boundaries defined by watersheds and regulate the distribution of the scarce resource. But his scientific realism could not overcome the popular vision of the West as a limitless American Eden. Powerful interests ensured that development occurred with the same helter-skelter, laissez-faire credo that was shaping the East. The first to feel the effects of this unrestrained expansion would be the Indian and Latino residents of the region.

The War for the West

So marginal did federal officials consider the Great Plains that they left the lands to the Indians. By the end of the Civil War, some two-thirds of all Indian peoples lived on the Great Plains. But even before the war, a series of gold and silver discoveries beginning in 1848 signaled the first serious interest by white settlers in the arid and semiarid lands beyond the Mississippi.

To open more land to white settlement and to protect the Indians from white settlers, federal officials introduced in 1851 a policy of "concentration." They pressed tribes to sign treaties limiting the boundaries of their hunting grounds to "reservations"— the Sioux to the Dakotas, the Crows to Montana, the Cheyenne to the foothills of Colorado—where they would be taught to farm.

Policy of Concentration

Such treaties often claimed that their provisions would last "as long as waters run," but time after time, land-hungry pioneers broke the promises of their government by squatting on Indian lands and demanding federal protection. The government, in turn, forced more restrictive agreements on the western tribes. This cycle of promises made and broken continued, until a full-scale war for the West raged between whites and Indians.

Contact and Conflict

The policy of concentration began in the Pacific Northwest and produced some of the earliest clashes between whites and Indians. In an oft-repeated pattern, Indian resistance led to war and war to Indian defeat. In the 1850s, as territorial governor Isaac Stevens was browbeating local tribes into giving up millions of acres in Washington Territory, a

The Battle of the Little Big Horn: An Indian View   *This 1898 watercolor by one of the Indian participants portrays the aftermath of the Battle of the Little Big Horn, June 25–26, 1876, in which an army unit under the command of General George Armstrong Custer was surrounded and wiped out by Sioux and Cheyenne warriors. This grisly painting shows Indians on horseback riding over the corpses of Custer and his men. Custer can be seen lying at left center, dressed in yellow buckskin with his hat beside him. The four standing men at center are Sitting Bull, Rain-in-the-Face, Crazy Horse, and Kicking Bear (the artist). At lower right, Indian women begin preparations for a ceremony to honor the returning warriors.*

gold strike flooded the Indian homelands with miners. The tribes fought them off, only to be crushed and forced onto reservations.

In similar fashion, by 1862 the lands of the Santee Sioux had been whittled down to a strip 10 miles wide and 150 miles long along the Minnesota River. Lashing out in frustration, the tribe attacked several undefended white settlements along the Minnesota frontier. In response, General John Pope arrived in St. Paul declaring his intention to wipe out the Sioux. "They are to be treated as maniacs or wild beasts and by no means as people," he instructed his officers. When Pope's forces captured 1,800 Sioux, white Minnesotans were outraged that President Lincoln ordered only 38 hanged.

Chivington Massacre

The campaign under General Pope was the opening of a guerrilla war that continued on and off for some 30 years. The conflict gained momentum in 1864, when Governor John Evans of Colorado sought to end all land treaties with Indian peoples in eastern Colorado. In November, a force of 700 Colorado volunteers under Colonel John Chivington fell upon a band of friendly Cheyenne gathered at Sand Creek under army protection. Chief Black Kettle raised an American flag to signal friendship, but Chivington would have none of it. "Kill and scalp all, big and little," he told his men. The troops massacred at least 150, including children holding white flags of truce and mothers with babies in their arms. A joint congressional investigation later condemned Chivington. A year later in 1865 virtually all Plains Indians joined in the First Sioux War to drive whites from their lands.

Among the soldiers who fought the Plains Indians were African American veterans of the Civil War. In 1866 two regiments of black soldiers formed the Ninth and Tenth

Calvary under the command of white officers. Their Indian foes dubbed them "buffalo soldiers," reflecting the similarity they saw between the hair of African Americans and that of the buffalo. It was also a sign of hard-won respect. The buffalo soldiers fought Indians across the West for more than 20 years. But they also subdued bandits, cattle thieves, and gunmen—from the rugged country of Big Bend to the badlands of South Dakota. And they helped to foster white settlement by laying the foundations for posts such as Fort Sill in Oklahoma and by locating water, wood, and grasslands for eager homesteaders.

White settlement undermined tribal cultures in several ways. Diseases introduced by settlers, including smallpox, measles, and cholera, killed more Indians than combat. Liquor furnished by white traders entrapped many a brave in a deadly cycle of alcoholism. Trading posts altered traditional ways of life with metal pots and pans, traps, coffee, and sugar but furnished no employment and thus few ways for their Indian customers to pay for these goods. Across the West mines, crops, grazing herds, and fences disturbed native hunting and farming lands.

On the Great Plains the railroad disrupted the migratory patterns of the buffalo and thus the patterns of the hunt on which the Plains Indians depended. When buffalo robes became popular in the East in the 1870s and hides became a source of leather for industrial belts, commercial companies hired professional hunters, who could kill bison at the rate of 100 an hour. Military commanders promoted the butchery as a way of undermining Indian resistance. And even Indians were caught up in the scramble for profit from commercial trading. By 1883 bison had nearly disappeared from the plains (see Historians Reconstruct the Past, "Where Have All the Bison Gone?" on pages 532–535). With them went a way of life that left the Plains Indians more vulnerable to white expansion.

Custer's Last Stand—and the Indians'

The Sioux War ended in 1868 with the signing of the Treaty of Fort Laramie. It established two large Indian reservations, one in Oklahoma and the other in the Dakota Badlands. Only six years later, however, in the summer of 1874, Colonel George Armstrong Custer led an expedition into *Paha Sapa,* the sacred Black Hills of the Sioux. In doing so, he disregarded the treaty of 1868. Custer, a Civil War veteran, already had a reputation as a "squaw killer" for his cruel warfare against Indians in western Kansas. To open the Black Hills to whites, his expedition spread rumors of gold "from the grass roots down." Prospectors poured into Indian country. When negotiations for a new treaty failed, President Grant ordered all "hostiles" in the area rounded up and driven onto the reservations.

Led by a young war chief named Crazy Horse and medicine man Sitting Bull, the worried Cheyenne allied with the Sioux for the first time. Against them marched several army columns, including Custer's Seventh Cavalry, a force of about 600 troops. Custer, eager for glory, arrived at the Little Big Horn River a day earlier than the other columns. Hearing of a native village nearby, he attacked, only to discover that he had stumbled onto an encampment of more than 12,000 Sioux and Cheyenne extending for almost 3 miles. From a deep ravine Crazy Horse charged Custer, killing him and some 250 soldiers.

As he led the attack, Crazy Horse yelled "It is a good day to die!"—the traditional war cry. He spoke more truth than he knew. Although Custer had been killed, railroads stood ready to extend their lines, prospectors to make fortunes, and soldiers to protect them. By late summer the Sioux were forced to split into small bands to evade the army. Sitting Bull barely escaped to Canada; Crazy Horse and 800 other men, women, and children surrendered in 1876 after a winter of suffering and starvation.

The battles along the Platte and upper Missouri rivers did not end the war between whites and Indians, but never again would it reach such proportions nor would Indians win many victories like that of the Little Big Horn. Even peaceful tribes like the Nez Percé of Idaho found no security once whites began to hunger for their land. The Nez

Le Sabre Indian School, Montana   *After the end of the Indian wars of the late nineteenth century, government authorities and private philanthropists tried in many ways to encourage Indians to assimilate into mainstream white American society. One of the most ambitious, and controversial, was a series of boarding schools for Indian children, where white teachers worked to teach them the ways of the English-speaking world. Most such schools were for boys, but some—such as this school in Montana, run by Catholic nuns—were created for girls.*

Percé had become breeders of livestock, rich in horses and cattle that they grazed in the meadows west of the Snake River canyon. Their livestock business did not prevent the government from trying to force them onto a small reservation in 1877.

Chief Joseph

Rather than see his people humiliated, Chief Joseph led almost 600 Nez Percé toward Canada, pursued by the U.S. Army. In just 75 days they traveled more than 1,300 miles. Every time the army closed to attack, Chief Joseph and his warriors drove them off. But before the Nez Percé could reach the border, they were forced to surrender. Chief Joseph's words still ring with eloquence: "Hear me, my chiefs, I am tired; my heart is sick and sad. From where the sun now stands I will fight no more forever." The government then shipped the defeated tribe to the bleak Indian Country of Oklahoma. There disease and starvation finished the destruction begun by the army.

Killing with Kindness

Over these same years Indians saw their legal sovereignty being whittled away sometimes even with good intentions in mind. Originally, federal authorities had treated various tribes as autonomous nations within the United States, with whom treaties could be made. That tribal status began shrinking in 1831, when the Supreme Court declared Indians "domestic dependent nations." Although the United States continued to negotiate treaties with the tribes, government officials began treating Indians as wards, regarding them as inept children. In 1869 President Grant created the Board

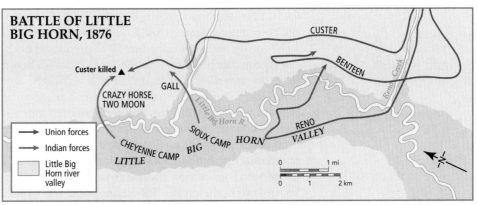

The Indian Frontier   *As conflict erupted between Indian and white cultures in the West, the government sought increasingly to concentrate tribes on reservations. Resistance to the reservation concept helped unite the Sioux and Cheyenne, traditionally enemies, in the Dakotas during the 1870s. Along the Little Big Horn River, the impetuous Custer underestimated the strength of his Indian opponents and attacked before the supporting troops of Reno and Benteen were in a position to aid him.*

of Indian Commissioners, whose members were chosen by Protestant churches to help settle conflicts with local tribes and to spread Christian values and white styles of living. Finally, in 1871, Congress abandoned the treaty system altogether and with it the legal core of Indian autonomy.

Some whites and Indians spoke out against the tragedy taking place on the Great Plains. In the 1870s, Susette La Fleche, daughter of an Omaha chief, lectured eastern   La Fleche and Jackson audiences about the mistreatment of Indian peoples and inspired reformers to action. Similarly moved, the poet Helen Hunt Jackson lobbied for Indian rights and against government policy. In 1881, she published *A Century of Dishonor*. The best-selling exposé detailed government fraud and corruption in Indian affairs, as well as the many treaties broken by the United States.

Reformers began pressing for assimilation of Indians into white society, ironically as the only means of preserving Indians in a society that seemed bent on destroying them. The Women's National Indian Association, created in 1874, and the later Indian Rights Association, joined by Helen Hunt Jackson, sought to end the Indian way of life by suppressing communal activities, reeducating Indian children, and establishing individual homesteads.

Reformers also recognized that the policy of concentrating Indians on reservations had failed. Deprived of their traditional lands and culture, reservation tribes became dependent on government aid. In any case, whites who coveted Indian lands were quick to violate treaty terms. With a mix of good intentions and unbridled greed, Congress **Dawes Act** adopted the Dawes Severalty Act in 1887. It ended reservation policy by permitting the president to distribute land to Indians who had severed their attachments to their tribes. The goals of the policy were simple: to draw Indians into white society as farmers and small property owners and (less high-mindedly) to bring Indian lands legally into the marketplace.

In practice, the Dawes Act was more destructive than any blow struck by the army. It undermined the communal structure on which Indian tribal life was based. Lands held by tribes would now be parceled out to individuals: 160 acres to the head of a family and 80 acres to single adults or orphans. But as John Wesley Powell had warned, small homestead farms in the West could not support a family—white or Indian—unless the farms were irrigated. Most Indians, moreover, had no experience with farming, managing money, or other white ways.

The sponsors of the Dawes Act, knowing that whites might swindle Indians out of their private holdings, arranged for the government to hold title to the land for 25 years. That arrangement did not stop unscrupulous speculators from "leasing" lands. Furthermore, all reservation lands not allocated to Indians were opened to non-Indian homesteaders. In 1881, Indians held more than 155 million acres of land. By 1890 the figure had dropped to 104 million and by 1900 to just under 78 million.

Against such a dismal future, some Indians sought solace in the past. In 1890 a religious revival swept the Indian nations when word came from the Nevada desert that a humble Paiute named Wovoka had received revelations from the Great Spirit. Wovoka preached that if his followers adopted his mystical rituals and lived together in love and harmony, the Indian dead would come back to life, whites would be driven from the land, and game would be thick again. As the rituals spread, alarmed settlers referred to the shuffling and chanting as the "Ghost Dance." The army moved to stop **Wounded Knee** the proceedings among the Sioux for fear of another uprising. At Wounded Knee in South Dakota the cavalry fell on one band and with blazing machine guns killed some 146 men, women, and children.

Wounded Knee was a final act of violence against an independent Indian way of life. After 1890 the battle was over assimilation, not extinction. The system of markets, rail networks, and extractive industries was linking the Far West with the rest of the nation. Free-roaming bison were being replaced by herded cattle and sheep, nomadic tribes by prairie sodbusters, and sacred hunting grounds by gold fields. Reformers relied on education, citizenship, and allotments to move Indians from their communal lives into white society. Many Indians were equally determined to preserve their tribal ways and separateness as a people.

Borderlands

The coming of the railroad in the 1880s and 1890s brought wrenching changes to the Southwest as well, especially to the states and territories along the old border with

Western cities attracted ethnically diverse populations. This chili stand in San Antonio served the city's large Latino population.

Mexico. But here there was a twist. As new markets and industries sprang up, new settlers poured in not only from the east but also from the south, across the Mexican border. Indians such as the Navajo and the Apache thus faced the hostility of new-comers—Anglos and Mexicans alike—as well as of Hispanos, those settlers of Spanish descent long in the region. Before the Mexican War of 1846, the Spanish governors of northern Mexico had offered bounties for Indian scalps.

Like Indians, Hispanos discovered that they had either to accommodate or to resist the flood of new Anglos. The elite, or Ricos, often aligned themselves with Anglos against their countryfolk to protect their status and property. Others, including Juan José Herrera, resisted the newcomers. When Anglo cattle ranchers began forcing Hispanos off their lands near Las Vegas, New Mexico, Herrera assembled a band of masked nightriders known as Las Gorras Blancas (the White Caps). In 1889 and 1890 as many as 700 White Caps burned Anglo fences, haystacks, and occasionally barns and houses. Herrera's followers also set thousands of railroad ties afire when the Atchison, Topeka and Santa Fe Railroad refused to raise the low wages it paid Hispano workers.

New Anglos frequently fought Hispanos. But it was western lawyers and politicians, using legal tactics, who deprived Hispanos of most of their property. Thomas Catron, an ambitious New Mexico lawyer, squeezed out many Hispanos by contesting land titles so aggressively that his holdings grew to 3 million acres. In those areas of New Mexico and California where they remained a majority, Hispanos continued to play a role in public life. During the early 1890s Herrera and his allies formed a "People's Party," swept local elections, and managed to defeat a bid by Catron to represent the territory in Congress.

With the railroads came more white settlers as well as Mexican laborers from south of the border. Just as the southern economy depended on African American labor, the Southwest grew on the labor of Mexicans. Mexican immigrants worked mostly as contract and seasonal laborers for railroads and large farms. Many of them settled in the growing cities along the rail lines: El Paso, Albuquerque, Tucson, Phoenix, and Los Angeles. They lived in segregated barrios, Spanish towns where their cultural traditions persisted. But by the late nineteenth century, most Hispanics, whether in barrios or on farms and ranches, had been excluded from power.

Yet to focus on cities alone would distort the experience of most southwesterners of Spanish descent, such as those who lived in the small villages of northern New Mexico and southern Colorado. In those areas emerged a pattern of adaptation and resistance to Anglo penetration. As the market economy advanced, Hispanic villagers turned to migratory labor to adapt. Women continued to work in the old villages, whereas

Juan José Herrera and the White Caps

Mexican Immigrants

Formation of Regional Communities

men traveled from job to job in mining, in farming, and on the railroads. The resulting network of villages and migrant workers furnished a base from which Hispanics could seek employment and a haven to which they could return. This "regional community" allowed for both the preservation of the communal life of the old Hispanic village and an entry into the new world of market capitalism that was transforming the West.

Ethno-Racial Identity in the New West

The New West met the Old South in the diamond-shaped Blackland Prairie of central Texas. Before the Civil War, King Cotton had thrived in its rich soil. Afterward, Texas became the leading cotton-producing state in the country. Having embraced the slave system of the Old South, Texas also adopted the New South's system of segregation, with its racial separation, restrictions on black voting, and biracial labor force of African Americans and poor whites.

Yet Texas was also part of the borderlands of the American West, where the Anglo culture of European Americans met the Latino culture of Mexicans and Mexican Americans. Many Mexicanos had lived in Texas since before the 1840s, when it had been part of Mexico. In the late nineteenth and early twentieth centuries, more newcomers crossed the Rio Grande in search of work.

Between 1890 and 1910, the Spanish-speaking population of the Southwest nearly doubled. In central Texas, the presence of this large and growing force of Mexicano laborers complicated racial matters. The black-and-white poles of European and African Americans that had defined identity in the Old South were now replaced by a new racial triad of black, white, and brown that negotiated identity and status among themselves.

A New Racial Triad

Like African Americans, Mexican Americans and Mexican immigrants in Texas were separated from Anglos by a color line and considered inferior by most whites. Unlike African Americans, however, Texans of Mexican descent sometimes found themselves swinging between the white world of privilege and the black world of disadvantage. In 1914, for example, Mexicans gained status by joining Anglos in the Land League, a radical organization of Texas renters dedicated to land reform. Its secretary, frustrated over the reluctance of whites to sign on, extolled the virtues of Mexican members: "Mexican tenants not only join the League but will starve before they will submit to a higher rent than the League and the law says is just."

And whites could lose status, as had the many Texans who sank into landlessness and poverty on the eve of World War I. White landowners disdained them as "white trash" and a "white scourge," found them to be more expensive tenants, and thus were more likely to rent to what they now regarded as "hard-working" Mexican Americans and Mexican immigrants. As small white operators lost their farms and ranches to large corporations, they saw the social distance shrink between themselves and black and brown laborers, sharecroppers, and tenants. By the 1920s, a multiracial labor force of landless wage earners worked on giant ranches and farms across the Southwest. In Texas, the labor force was triracial, but in California it also included Asian Americans, and, elsewhere, American Indians. Thus racial identity in the New West would be more complicated and, for Mexicans and Mexican Americans, more fluid.

Boom and Bust in the West

Opportunity in the New West lay in land and resources, but wealth also accumulated in the towns and cities. Each time speculative fever hit a region, new communities sprouted to serve those who rushed in to grab gold or other riches. The western boom began in mining—with the California gold rush of 1849 and the rise of San Francisco (see page 393). In the decades that followed, new hordes threw up towns in Park City in Utah, Tombstone in Arizona, and other promising sites. All too often, busts followed booms, transforming boom towns into ghost towns.

Mining Sets a Pattern

The gold and silver strikes of the 1840s and 1850s set a pattern followed by other booms. Stories of easy riches attracted single prospectors with their shovels and wash pans. Almost all were male, and nearly half were foreign born. Someone entering the local saloon could expect to hear English, an Irish brogue, German, French, Spanish, Chinese, Italian, Hawaiian, and various Indian dialects. Muddy mining camps sprang up in which a prospector could register a claim, get provisions, bathe, and buy a drink or a companion.

Prostitution flourished openly in mining towns (as it did in cattle towns). Such makeshift communities provided ideal conditions: large numbers of rootless men, few women, and money enough to buy any favor. In the booming towns of Gold Hill and Virginia City near the Comstock Lode of Nevada, men outnumbered women 2 to 1 in 1875. Almost 1 woman in 12 was a prostitute. Usually prostitutes were young, in their teens and 20s. They walked the streets and plied their trade in one-room shacks called "cribs." If young and in demand, they worked in dance halls, saloons, and brothels. Pay varied by race, with Anglos at the top, followed by African Americans, Mexicans, and Indians. All told, as many as 50,000 women plied this trade in the trans-Mississippi West before the turn of the century.

Prostitution

Blasting away with pressurized water jets, miners loosen gold-bearing gravel. Such techniques damaged the environment in the rush to exploit western resources. The artist, Mrs. Jonas Brown, lived in Idaho City during the height of its gold rush.

A far more profitable source of revenue came from outfitting these boom societies with the equipment they needed. Such sales siphoned riches into the pockets of store owners and other suppliers. Once the quick profits were gone, a period of consolidation brought more order to towns destined to remain. Police departments replaced vigilantes. Brothels, saloons, and gambling dens were limited to certain districts. Larger scale came to regional businesses. In the mine fields, that meant corporations with the capital for hydraulic water jets to blast ore loose and for the heavy equipment needed to crush rock and extract silver and gold from deeper veins.

Environmental Costs of Mining

In their quest for profit, such operations often led to environmental disaster. With each snow melt and rain, the gravel from hydraulic mining worked its way down into river systems. The resulting floods, mudslides, and dirty streams threatened the livelihood of farmers in the valleys below. Outside Sacramento, 39,000 acres of farmland lay under the debris by the 1890s, and another 14,000 acres were nearly ruined. Meanwhile, underground mining consumed so much timber that one observer called the Comstock Lode in Nevada "tomb of the forest of the Sierras." In Butte, Montana, the smoke from sulfur-belching smelters turned the air so black that by the 1880s townsfolk had trouble seeing even in daylight.

In corporate mining operations, paid laborers replaced the independent prospectors of earlier days. As miners sought better wages and working conditions, shorter hours, and the right to unionize, management fought back. In Coeur d'Alene, Idaho, troops crushed a strike in 1892, killing seven miners. The miners then created the Western Federation of Miners. In the decade after 1893 the union attracted some 50,000 members and gained a reputation for militancy. In a common cycle, the rowdy mining frontier of small-scale prospectors was integrated into the industrial system of wage labor, large-scale resource extraction, and high-finance capital.

The Transcontinental Railroad

As William Gilpin predicted in 1849, the development of the West awaited the railroads. Before the Central and Union Pacific railroads were joined to span the continent in 1869, travel across the West was slow and dusty. Vast distances and sparse population gave entrepreneurs little chance to follow the eastern practice of building local railroads from city to city.

Railroad Land Grants

In 1862 Congress granted the Central Pacific Railroad the right to build the western link of the transcontinental railroad eastward from Sacramento. To the Union Pacific Corporation fell responsibility for the section from Omaha westward. Generous loans and gifts of federal and state lands made the venture wildly profitable. For every mile of track completed, the rail companies received between 200 and 400 square miles of land—some 45 million acres by the time the route was completed. Fraudulent stock practices, corrupt accounting, and wholesale bribery (involving a vice president of the United States and at least two members of Congress) swelled profits even more. More than 75 western railroads eventually benefited from such government generosity, as did millions of ordinary Americans and the entire national economy.

General Grenville Dodge, an army engineer on leave to the Union Pacific, recruited his immense labor force from Civil War veterans as well as Irish and other European immigrants. He drove them with ruthless army discipline, completing as much as 10 miles of track in a single day. Charles Crocker of the Central Pacific had no similar source of cheap labor in California. Worse yet, he faced the formidable task of cutting through the Sierra Nevada. When his partner Leland Stanford suggested importing workers from China, Crocker dismissed him with a laugh—at first. But it was some 10,000 Chinese laborers who accomplished the feat. With wheelbarrows, picks, shovels, and baskets they inched eastward, building trestles like the one at Secrettown and chipping away at the Sierras' looming granite walls. On the worst stretches they averaged only eight inches a day.

Once Chinese crews broke into the flat country of the desert basin, the two railroads raced to claim as much federal land as possible. In the resulting scramble, the two

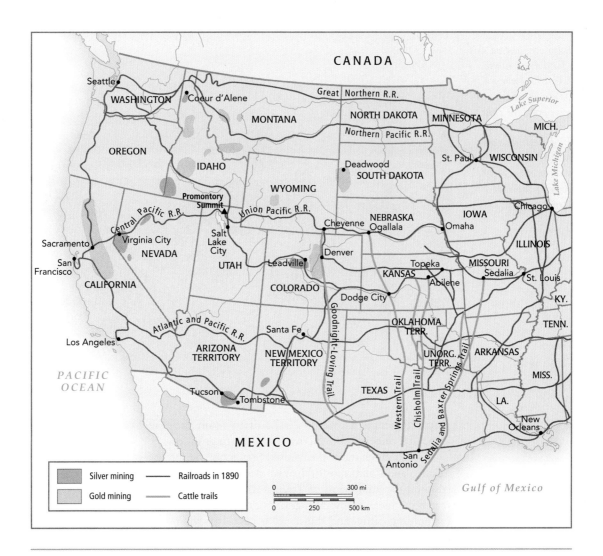

The Mining and Cattle Frontiers   *In the vast spaces of the West, railroads, cattle trails, and gold mining usually preceded the arrival of enough settlers to establish towns and cities. The railroads forged a crucial link between the region's natural resources and urban markets in the East and in Europe, but by transecting the plains they also disrupted the migratory patterns of the buffalo herds, undermining Plains Indian cultures while opening the land to cattle grazing and farming.*

sides passed each other, laying more than 200 miles of parallel track before the government ordered them to join. On May 10, 1869, at Promontory Summit, Utah, a silver hammer pounded a gold spike into the last tie. East and West were finally linked by rail. Travel time across the continent was slashed from months to little more than a week.

The rail companies recognized early the strategic value of their enterprise. If a key to profiting from the gold rush was supplying miners, one way to prosper from the West was to control transportation. Just by threatening to bypass a town, a railroad could extract concessions on rights-of-way, taxes, and loans. That coercion was one reason why westerners developed such mixed feelings—gratitude for the transportation, rage at the bullying—toward the railroads.

Cattle Kingdom

Westerners realized that railroads were crucial components of the cattle industry. Cow towns such as Abilene, Denver, and Cheyenne flourished in the growing cattle kingdom. By 1860, some 5 million longhorn cattle were wandering the grassy plains of

Clara Williamson painted this herd on the long drive north from Texas. Cowboys normally worked in pairs, opposite each other, as shown here; the chuck wagon can be seen at the rear of the train. So strenuous was the work that each cowboy brought with him about eight horses so that fresh mounts would be always available.

Texas. Ranchers allowed their herds to roam the unbroken or "open" range freely, identified only by a distinctive brand on their hides.

Cattle ranching in the United States had begun in Texas and California, largely by Tejanos and Californios of Spanish descent. Anglo Americans who came to Texas readily adopted the equipment of Tejanos: the tough mustangs and broncos (horses suited to managing mean-spirited longhorns), the branding iron for marking the herds, the corral for holding cattle, and the riata, or lariat, for roping. The cowboys also wore Mexican chaps, spurs, and broad-brimmed sombreros, or "hats that provide shade." In Texas, at least a third of all cowboys were Mexicans and black freedmen after the Civil War, the rest largely Confederate veterans. And sometimes rivalries developed among them. One Mexican *corrido,* or ballad, boasted of a herd of 500 steers that could not be corralled by 30 Anglo cowboys, when suddenly five Mexican *vaqueros* arrived: *"Esos cinco mexicanos al momento los echaron / y los trienta americanos se quedaron azorados."* ("Those five Mexicans in a moment put in the steers / and the 30 Americans were left astonished.")

In 1866, as rail lines swept west, Texas ranchers began driving their herds north to railheads for shipment to market. These "long drives" lasted two to three months and sometimes covered more than 1,000 miles. When early routes to Sedalia, Missouri, proved unfriendly, ranchers scouted alternative paths. The Chisholm Trail led from San Antonio to Abilene and Ellsworth in Kansas. More westerly routes soon ran to Dodge City and even Denver and Cheyenne.

Home on the Range

Because cattle grazed on the open range, early ranches were primitive. Most had a house for the family, a bunkhouse for the hired hands, and about 30 to 40 acres of grazing land per animal. Women were scarce in the masculine world of the cattle kingdom. Most were ranchers' wives, strong and resourceful women who cooked, nursed the sick, and helped run the ranch. Some women ranched themselves. When Helen Wiser Stewart of Nevada learned in July 1884 that her husband had been murdered, she took over the ranch, buying and selling cattle, managing the hands, and tending to family and crops.

Farmers looking for their own homesteads soon became rivals to the cattle ranchers. The "nesters," as ranchers disdainfully called them, fenced off their lands, thus shrinking the open range. Vast grants to the railroads also limited the area of free land, and ranchers intent on breeding heavier cattle with more tender beef began to fence in their stock to prevent them from mixing with inferior strays. Before long, farmers and ranchers found themselves locked in deadly "range wars" over grazing and water rights. Farmers usually won.

Conflicts also arose between cattle ranchers and herders of another animal introduced by the Mexicans—sheep. Cattle ranchers had particular contempt for the sheep raiser and the "woolies." Sheep cropped grasses so short that they ruined land for cattle grazing. To protect the range they saw as their own from the "hooved locust," cattle ranchers attacked shepherds and their flocks. On one occasion enraged cattle ranchers clubbed 8,000 sheep to death along the Green River in Wyoming. The feuds often burst into range wars, some more violent than those between farmers and ranchers.

A Boom and Bust Cycle

The cattle boom that began with the first long drive of 1866 reached its peak from 1880 to 1885. Ranchers came to expect profits of 25 to 40 percent a year. Millions of dollars poured into the West from eastern and foreign interests eager to cash in on soaring cattle prices. Ranching corporations extended the open range from Texas into Wyoming and Montana.

As in most booms, a bust often followed. High profits soon swelled the size of the herds and led to overproduction. Increased competition from cattle producers in Canada and Argentina caused beef prices to fall. And nature imposed its own limits. On the plains, nutritious buffalo and gamma grasses were eaten to the nub, only to be replaced by unpalatable species. When overgrazing combined with drought, as in New Mexico in the 1880s and 1890s, the results could be disastrous. In all these regions, as vegetation changed, erosion increased, further weakening the ecosystem. In 1870, 5 acres of plains land were needed to feed a steer. By the mid-1880s, 50 acres were required.

Increasing Erosion

There was, moreover, simply not enough grass along the trails to support the millions of head on their way to market. And diseases such as "Texas fever" sometimes wiped out entire herds. Then in 1886 and 1887 came two of the coldest winters in recorded history. The winds brought blizzards that drove wandering herds up against fences, where they froze or starved to death. Summer heat and drought then scorched the grasslands and dried up waterholes. In the Dakotas, Montana, Colorado, and Wyoming, losses ran as high as 90 percent.

By the 1890s the open range and the long drives had largely vanished. What prevailed were the larger cattle corporations such as the King Ranch of Texas. Only the large corporations had enough capital to acquire and fence vast grazing lands, hire ranchers to manage herds, and pay for feed during winter months. As for the cowboys, most became wage laborers employed by the ranching corporations. Like mining, cattle ranching was becoming a corporate industrial enterprise, succumbing to the eastern pattern of economic concentration and labor specialization.

The Final Frontier

In the 1860s they had come in a trickle; in the 1870s they came in a torrent. They were farmers from the East and Midwest, black freedpeople from the rural South, and peasant-born immigrants from Europe. What bound them together was a craving for land. They had read railroad and steamship advertisements and heard stories from friends about millions of free acres west of the 98th meridian. Hardier strands of wheat like the "Turkey Red" from Russia, improved machinery, and new farming methods made it possible to raise crops in what once had been the "Great American Desert." The number of farms in the United States jumped from some 2 million on the eve of the Civil War to almost 6 million in 1900.

A Rush for Land

The desire for land was so intense that in the spring of 1889 nearly 100,000 people made their way by wagon, horseback, carriage, mule, even on bicycles and on foot to a line near present-day Oklahoma City, in the center of land once reserved for the Indians. These were "Boomers," gathered for the last great land rush in the trans-Mississippi West. At noon on April 22, 1889, the Boomers raced across the line to claim some 2 million acres of Indian territory just opened for settlement. Beyond the line lay the "Sooners"—those who had jumped the gun and hidden in gullies and thickets, ready to leap out an instant after noon to claim their stake in prosperity.

Even as the hopefuls lined up in Oklahoma, thousands of other settlers were abandoning their farms to escape mounting debts. The dream of the West as a garden paradise was already being shaken by harsh weather, overproduction, and competition from abroad. Wheat sold for $1.60 a bushel during the Civil War. It fell to 49 cents in the 1890s.

Farming on the Plains

Farmers looking to plow the plains faced a daunting task. Under the Homestead Act (1862), government land could be bought for $1.25 an acre or claimed free if a homesteader worked it for 5 years. But the best parcels—near a railroad line, with access to eastern markets—were owned by the railroads themselves or by speculators and sold for much more, around $25 an acre.

Once land was acquired, expenses only mounted. Sturdy steel-tipped plows and spring-toothed harrows, which turned over sun-baked prairie soil and left a blanket of dust to reduce evaporation, were needed for **dry farming** in parched climates. Newly developed threshers, combines, and harvesters brought in the crop, and powerful steam tractors pulled the heavy equipment. For such machinery, along with horses, seed, and other farm tools, the average farmer spent $1,200, a small fortune in 1880. (Bigger operators invested 10 or 20 times that total.) If their land abutted a ranch, farmers also had to erect fences to keep cattle from trampling fields. Lacking wood, they found the answer in barbed wire, first marketed by Illinois farmer Joseph Glidden in 1874. Crop yields of wheat increased tenfold as a result of these innovations.

Tracts of 160 acres granted under the Homestead Act might be enough for eastern farms, but in the drier West more land was needed to produce the same harvest. Farms of more than 1,000 acres, known as "bonanza farms," were most common in the wheat lands of the northern plains. A steam tractor working a bonanza farm could plow, harrow, and seed up to 50 acres a day—20 times more than a single person could do without machinery. Against such competition, small-scale farmers could scarcely survive. Like the southerners, many westerners became tenants on land owned by someone else. Bonanza farmers hired as many as 250 laborers to work each 10,000 acres in return for room, board, and 50 cents a day in wages.

A Plains Existence

For poor farm families, life on the plains meant sod houses or dugouts carved from hillsides for protection against the wind. Tough, root-bound sod was cut into bricks a foot wide and three feet long and laid edgewise to create walls. Sod bricks covered rafters for a roof. The average house was seldom more than 18 by 24 feet, and in severe weather it had to accommodate animals as well as people. One door and often a single window provided light and air. The thick walls kept the house warm in winter and cool in summer, but a heavy, soaking rain or snow could bring the roof down or drip mud and water into the living area. Armies of flies, gnats, mosquitoes, and fleas attacked inhabitants as soon as they moved in. Katherine Gibson of the Dakota territories went to light her stove one cold morning only to be attacked by a rattlesnake and its offspring.

The heaviest burdens fell to women like Gibson. With stores and supplies scarce, they spent long days over hot tubs preparing tallow wax for candles or soaking ashes and boiling lye with grease and pork rinds to make soap. In the early years of settlement wool was in such short supply that resourceful women used hair from wolves and other wild animals to make cloth. Buttons had to be fashioned from old wooden spoons.

Nature added its hardships. In summer, searing winds blasted the plains for weeks. Grasses grew so dry that a single spark could ignite thousands of acres. Farmers in the Southwest lived in dread of stinging centipedes and scorpions that inhabited wall cracks. From Missouri to Oregon, nothing spelled disaster like locusts. They descended without warning in swarms 100 miles long. Beating against houses like hailstones, they stripped all vegetation, including the bark of trees. Winter held special horrors. Blizzards swept the plains, piling snow to the rooftops and halting all travel. Settlers might awaken to find their food frozen and snow on their beds. Weeks would pass before farm families saw an outsider.

Even out on the plains in sod huts, farmers cherished the culture they could bring from distant places. This family proudly displays the pump organ they imported from the East.

In the face of such hardships many westerners found comfort in religion. Indians turned to traditional spiritualism and Hispanics to the Catholic church as a means of coping with nature and change. Though Catholics and Jews came west, evangelical Protestants dominated the Anglo frontier in the mining towns and in other western communities. Worship offered an emotional outlet and some intellectual stimulation as well as a means of preserving old values and sustaining hope. In the West, as in the rural South, circuit riders compensated for the shortage of preachers, while camp meetings offered the chance to socialize. Both brought contact with a world beyond the prairie. In many communities it was the churches that first instilled order on public life, addressing problems such as the need for schools or charity for the poor.

The Comfort of Religion

The Urban Frontier

Not all westerners lived in isolation. By 1890 the percentage of those in cities of 10,000 or more was greater than in any other section of the country except the Northeast.

Out on the treeless plains the Indians had adjusted to scarcity of food, water, and other necessities by adopting a nomadic way of life. Their small kinship groups moved each season to wherever nature supplied the food they needed. Such mobility discouraged families from acquiring many possessions. Tools and housing had to be light and portable. Even tribes that raised crops on which to live often moved with the seasons.

Unlike the Indians, farmers, ranchers, and townspeople rooted themselves to a single place. What the surrounding countryside could not supply had to be brought from afar, generally at

Like southern women, women in the West played an essential role in the family economy. There was time for fun, too: this woman has found a rather remarkable way to feed her cat.

great effort and expense. For those on the isolated prairie, keeping food on the table was nearly impossible in some seasons. Something as simple as finding water suitable for drinking or cooking became a problem in the West, where the choice might be between "the strong alkaline water of the Rio Grande or the purchase of melted manufactured ice (shipped by rail) at its great cost."

Gardening, generally a woman's responsibility, brought variety to the diet and color to the yard. The legume family

Usually unruly, often chaotic and unplanned, western cities were mostly the products of history, geography, technology, and commerce rather than the carefully drawn plans of men and women.

Some western cities—San Antonio, El Paso, and Los Angeles—were old Spanish towns whose growth had been sparked by the westward march of Anglo migrants, the northward push of Mexican immigrants, and the spread of railroad lines. Other cities profited from their location near commercial routes, such as Portland near the Columbia River in western Oregon. Still others, such as Wichita, Kansas, arose to serve the cattle and mining booms of the West. And as technology freed people from the need to produce their own food and clothing, westerners turned to the business of supplying goods and services, enterprises that required the labor of more densely populated cities.

Most newer cities had wide streets and large blocks. Whereas the streets of eastern cities measured 30 to 60 feet across, street widths of 80 feet or more were typical in the West. Streets had to be broad enough to allow ox-drawn wagons to turn, but they also reflected the big plans of town promoters. "Every town in the West," marveled one European, "is laid out on a plan as vast as though it were destined, at no distant future, to contain a million of inhabitants."

Denver Denver, Colorado, was typical. Founded in 1859, Denver exploded with the discovery of gold at the mouth of Cherry Creek. The town catered largely to miners with a mix of supply stores, saloons, gambling parlors, and brothels. As it grew, so did its reputation for violence. "A city of demons," said one disgusted visitor, where "a man's life is of no more worth than a dog's." Until the early 1860s, when the city hired its first police force, vigilante committees kept the peace with "the rope and the revolver."

In the 1870s Denver embarked on a new phase of growth. The completion of the Denver Pacific and Kansas Pacific railroads made it the leading city on the eastern slope of the Rocky Mountains. Its economy diversified, and its population soared from about 5,000 in 1870 to more than 100,000 by 1890, when its population ranked behind only Los Angeles and Omaha among western cities.

Like much of the urban West, Denver grew outward rather than upward, spreading across the open landscape. Such sprawling patterns of growth produced a city with sharply divided districts for business, government, and industry. Workers lived in one section of town; managers, owners, and other wealthier citizens in another.

Development was so rapid that Denver struggled to keep up with itself. By 1900, the city contained 800 miles of streets, but only 24 of them were paved. A British of peas and beans, in particular, provided needed protein. Flowers were much prized but seldom survived the wind, heat, and droughts. To prepare for the lean winter months, women stocked their cellars and made wild fruits into leathery cakes eaten to ward off the scurvy that resulted from vitamin deficiency.

Until rail lines made the shipment of goods cheaper and until Sears, Roebuck "wishbooks" brought mail order to the frontier, a woman's kitchen was modest. One miner's wife in Montana during the 1870s considered her kitchen "well-furnished" with two kettles, a cast iron skillet, and a coffeepot. A kitchen cupboard might be little more than a box nailed to a log.

Without doctors, women learned how to take care of themselves. Whiskey and patent medicines were often more dangerous than the disease, but they were used to treat a range of ills from frostbite to snakebite and from sore throats to burns and rheumatism. Cobwebs could bandage small wounds; turpentine served as a disinfectant. Mosquitoes were repelled with a paste of vinegar and salt. Most parents thought the laxative castor oil could cure almost any childhood malady. Some women adapted remedies used on their farm animals. Sarah Olds, a Nevada homesteader whose family was plagued by fleas and lice, recalled that "we all took baths with plenty of sheep dip in the water. . . . I had no disinfectant . . . so I boiled all our clothing in sheep dip and kerosene."

Gradually, as the market system penetrated the West, families had less need to improvise in matters of diet and medicine. Through catalogs they might order spices like white pepper or poultry seasoning and appliances like grinders for real coffee. If a local stagecoach passed by the house, a woman might send her eggs and butter to town to be exchanged for needed store-bought goods like thread and needles.

observer marveled at "how [Denver's] future vast proportions seem to exist already in the minds of its projectors. Instead of its new streets and buildings being huddled as with us in our urban beginnings, they are placed here and there at suitable points, with confidence that the connecting links will soon be established." So, too, with the rest of the urban West, where human imagination began to transform the natural landscape.

The West and the World Economy

The ceaseless search for resources led all manner of people—and their money—west, including foreign investors. As raw materials flowed out of the region, capital flowed in, mostly from the East and from Europe. Foreign investments varied from industry to industry but generally came in two forms: direct stock purchases and loans to western corporations and individuals. The great open-range cattle boom of the 1870s and 1880s, for example, brought an estimated $45 million into the western livestock industry from Great Britain alone. The Scottish-owned Prairie Cattle Company owned nearly 8000 square miles of western cattle land in three huge tracts. By 1887, Congress had become so alarmed at foreign ownership that it enacted the Alien Land Law, which prohibited the purchase of any land in western territories by foreign corporations or by individuals who did not intend to become citizens. Capital-hungry westerners ignored it.

Like southerners, westerners rarely consumed what they took from the ground. In most instances, they located the resources, extracted them, and sent them outside the region to be turned into finished products. Only when manufactured goods returned to the West did westerners finally consume them.

But westerners were more than consumers. They were part of a worldwide network of production and trade. Between 1865 and 1915, world population increased by more than 50 percent, and demand mushroomed. Better and cheaper transportation allowed westerners to supply raw materials and agricultural goods to places they knew only as exotic names on a map.

Global reach came at a cost, however. Decisions made elsewhere—in London and Paris, in Tokyo and Buenos Aires—now determined what westerners charged and how much they made. A bumper crop in Europe could drive down grain prices so sharply that debt-ridden farmers lost their land. And the effect in Europe was just as devastating, squeezing peasant farmers out and sending many of them to the Great Plains, where they increased the rivalry for land and profits.

Packaging and Exporting the "Wild West"

No one linked the West to the wider world and shaped perceptions of the region more than William F. ("Buffalo Bill") Cody. Already a well-known scout for the frontier army and a buffalo hunter for hungry railroad crews, Cody garnered added fame when Edward Judson, writing under the pen name "Ned Buntline," published a series of novels in the 1870s based loosely on Cody's life. In them, the dashing Buffalo Bill fought desperadoes and Indians, saved distressed damsels, and brought order to the wild frontier. He became an icon of a mythic West: where opportunity was there for the taking, where good always triumphed over evil, where all Indians hunted bison and lived in tepees, and where romance and adventure obscured the realities of Anglo conquest, unchecked exploitation, and growing corporate control.

Buffalo Bill Cody's Wild West Show

Trading on his fame and a flair for showmanship, Cody packaged the West in 1883, when he created the "Wild West, Rocky Mountain, and Prairie Exhibition" and took it on tour. Rope-twirling, gun-slinging cowboys, savage-looking Indians, and Annie

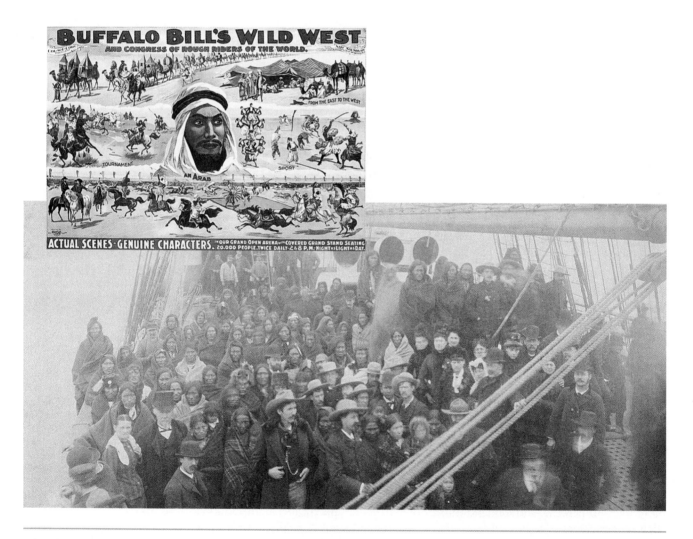

This photograph of Buffalo Bill Cody (standing in front with his hand resting on a rope) and the cast of his Wild West was taken on a cross-Atlantic voyage to England in 1887. By the 1880s, when Cody created the show, Americans were already longing for the "vanishing frontier." Buffalo Bill provided it for them, complete with mythical stereotypes that reinforced the image of a savage land in need of taming but also as an Eden of boundless opportunity and adventure. The reach of such fantasies was truly global, and cultural exchange flowed in both directions, as the poster for the grand opening of the Wild West's new amphitheater suggests. Note the Arabs and cowboys on horseback and exotic camels. Note, too, the use of new technology—electric spotlighting—which allowed for a second, evening show by making "night as light as day."

Oakley, as celebrated for her beauty as for her pinpoint aim, entertained audiences as large as 40,000 or more in giant, open-air theaters. They reenacted famous frontier events, including Custer's Last Stand, and performed daring feats of marksmanship, horseback riding, and calf-roping. Cody even hired Sitting Bull, the most famous Indian in America, to stare glumly at gawking ticket holders.

Marginalized as a people, Indians were now typecast and commercialized as a commodity and packaged along with other stereotypes of the American West, including, of course, the sturdy, brave cowboy of legend. Yet the show also broke stereotypes that spoke to Cody's own reformist impulses—for women's rights in the graceful, gun-toting Annie Oakley and for the preservation of Indian life in its remnant representatives whooping and galloping across the arena.

The popularity of Buffalo Bill's Wild West show soon extended overseas. Cody's troupe, animals and all, circled the globe by steamship, train, and wagon. The photograph here shows them embarking for London from New York in 1887, but they played to audiences as far away as Outer Mongolia. Queen Victoria saw them twice. Indeed, for many Europeans the "Wild West" of Buffalo Bill Cody was America itself.

The South and the West in Sum

Examining the census records of 1890, the superintendent of the census noted that landed settlements stretched so far that "there can hardly be said to be a frontier line." One after another, territories became states: Nebraska in 1867; Colorado in 1876; North Dakota, South Dakota, Montana, and Washington in 1889; Wyoming in 1890; Utah in 1896; Oklahoma in 1907; and New Mexico and Arizona in 1912. A new West was emerging as a mosaic of ethnicities, races, cultures, and climates but with the shared identity of a single region.

That sense of a regional identity was heightened for both westerners and southerners because so many of them felt isolated from the mainstream of industrial America. Ironically, it was not their isolation from northern industry but their links to it that marginalized them. The campaign for a New South to out-Yankee the industrial Yankee could not overcome the low wages and high fertility rates of an older South. The promoters of the West had greater success in adapting large-scale industry and investment to mining, cattle ranching, and farming. Still, they too confronted the limits of their region, whose resources were not endless and whose rainfall did not follow the plow. Like easterners, westerners found that large corporations with near-monopoly control over markets and transportation bred inequality, corrupt politics, and resentment.

In the end, it was not simply the disappearance of the frontier within the United States that was at work. Across the world frontiers were being pushed back and eradicated as the rest of the industrialized world scrambled for colonies rich in natural resources and potential for markets. Miners combed the hills of California for gold in 1849, as they did two years later in Victoria, Australia. In South Africa, the rush was for diamonds discovered along the Vaal and Orange Rivers and gold near present-day Johannesburg. In Canada, Argentina, Australia, and New Zealand, farmers and cattle ranchers moved steadily toward establishing the larger commercial farms seen in the American West.

In their cities and on their farms, deep in their mineshafts, and atop their towering forests, southerners and westerners were thus being linked to the world economy. Cotton picked by sharecroppers in the Mississippi Delta might end up in the petticoats of royalty. Longhorn cattle that grazed on the prairies of Texas fed the cities of Europe. Timber from the piney woods of Georgia or the redwood forests of the

Pacific Northwest could find its way into the coffins of Mexico City's dead or the hulls of British schooners. And **racialism**—the widely accepted practice of categorizing people according to race—justified exploitation elsewhere in the world just as it was used to thwart southern black sharecroppers or Indians driven from their land by prospectors, cowhands, and sodbusters. So it was that coolie laborers died by the thousands in India clearing jungles for tea plantations owned by British firms, while black miners labored in South Africa for Dutch diamond companies and Chinese workers in Australia for European investors, only to be excluded from mainstream society wherever they worked.

The small cotton growers in India, Egypt, and Brazil who faced plummeting prices were just as baffled by market economics as cotton farmers in the American South who found themselves deep in debt to merchants. One British official, traveling into a remote cotton-growing region of India, reported that growers found "some difficulty in realizing . . . that, by means of the Electric Telegraph, the throbbings of the pulse of the Home markets communicate themselves instantly to Hingunghat and other trade centres throughout the country." Throughout the world, he might have added. Indeed it was the "pulse of Home markets" worldwide that controlled the fortunes of those in the cotton fields of India and the United States. A global industrial system increasingly determined interest rates, prices, and wages in ways that affected ordinary folk everywhere.

Significant Events

1849–1859	Gold and silver strikes open western mining frontier
1862	Homestead Act; Minnesota Sioux uprising begins Plains Indian wars
1864	Chivington massacre
1866	Drive to Sedalia, Missouri, launches cattle boom
1869	Completion of first transcontinental railroad; Powell explores the Grand Canyon
1872–1874	The great buffalo slaughter
1874	Black Hills gold rush; barbed wire patented
1876	Battle of Little Big Horn; Nez Percé resist relocation
1877	Crazy Horse surrenders
1879	Height of Exoduster migration to Kansas
1880	Bonsack cigarette-rolling machine invented
1883	*Civil Rights Cases*
1886–1887	Severe winter and drought cycle in the West
1887	Dawes Severalty Act
1889	Oklahoma opened to settlement
1890	Ghost Dance Indian religious revival; Wounded Knee
1892	Union violence at Coeur d'Alene, Idaho; Wyoming range wars
1896	*Plessy v. Ferguson* upholds separate but equal doctrine

Chapter Summary

In the years after the Civil War, both the South and the West became more closely linked to the industrial Northeast.

- Despite differences in geography and history, the South and the West shared many features.

  —Both became sources of agricultural goods and raw materials that fed urban and industrial growth in the northeastern and north central states.

  —Both were racially divided societies in which whites often used violence to assert their dominance.

  —Both looked beyond their regions for the human and financial resources needed to boost their economies.

  —Southerners embraced the philosophy of the "New South" that industrialization would bring prosperity.

- The South nonetheless remained wedded to agriculture, especially cotton, and to a system of labor that exploited poor whites and blacks.

  —Important in the South were the *crop-lien system,* which shackled poor southerners to the land through debt, and *Jim Crow segregation,* which kept blacks and whites apart.

- White westerners too exploited people of other races and ethnicities through settlement, conquest, and capture.

  —By 1890, the emergence of the Ghost Dance and the closing of the frontier signaled that Indians must adapt to life within the boundaries set by white culture despite their efforts at resistance.

  —Latinos were increasingly subjected to similar exploitation but resisted and adapted more effectively to the intrusions of white culture and market economy.

  —In a pattern that became typical for western mining, ranching, and agriculture, small operators first grabbed quick profits and then were followed by large corporations that increased both the scale and the wealth of these industries.

Additional Reading

The themes of change and continuity have characterized interpretations of southern history after Reconstruction. For years C. Vann Woodward's classic *The Origins of the New South* (1951) dominated thinking about the region with its powerful argument for a changing South. Edward Ayers, *The Promise of the New South* (1992), offers a fresh, comprehensive synthesis that sees both change and continuity. Gavin Wright, *Old South, New South* (1986), destroys the myth of the southern colonial economy. Ted Ownby, *Subduing Satan* (1990), provides a valuable discussion of southern social life, especially the role of religion. On the issue of race relations see Joel Williamson, *The Crucible of Race: Black-White Relations in the South since Emancipation* (1984).

The contours of western history were first mapped by Fredrick Jackson Turner in his famous address "The Significance of the Frontier in American History" (1893) but have been substantially reshaped by Richard White, *"It's Your Own Misfortune and None of My Own": A New History of the American West* (1992); Patricia Limerick, *A Legacy of Conquest: The Unbroken Past of the American West* (1987); Gregory Nobles, *American Frontier: Cultural Encounter and Continental Conquest* (1997); and Donald Worster, *Rivers of Empire* (1985). Each describes the history of the West less as a traditional saga of frontier triumphs than as an analysis of how the region and its resources have been exploited by various peoples and cultures. For a beautifully written and superbly researched study of the Great Plains as a contested zone among environment, animals, and people, see Elliott West's *The Contested Plains: Indians, Goldseekers, and the Rush to Colorado* (1998). On John Wesley Powell and his seminal role in the West, see Donald Worster, *A River Running West: The Life of John Wesley Powell* (2001). Sarah Deutsch, *No Separate Refuge: Culture, Class, and Gender on an Anglo-Hispanic Frontier in the American Southwest, 1880–1940* (1987), develops the concept of regional community to depict the interpenetration of cultures and their impact on gender in New Mexico and Colorado, and Robert M. Utley offers an excellent survey of American Indians in *The Indian Frontier of the American West 1846–1890* (1984). On the growing literature of ethno-racial identity in the West, see Neil Foley, *White Scourge: Mexicans, Blacks, and Poor Whites in Texas Cotton Culture* (1997), and David Gutiérrez, *Walls and Mirrors: Mexican Americans, Mexican Immigrants, and the Politics of Ethnicity* (1995). For an excellent account of the African American experience in shaping the West, see Quintard Taylor, *In Search of the Racial Frontier: African Americans in the American West, 1528–1990* (1998).

For a fuller list of readings, see the Bibliography at www.mhhe.com/davidsonnation6.

Historians Reconstruct the Past

Where Have All the Bison Gone?

Between 1872 and 1874 the great American bison—staple of Plains-Indian life and an increasingly profitable source of commercial coats and robes—nearly became extinct in the American West. For years people believed that the steep decline was the result of white hunters decimating the herds. But by combining tools from various disciplines—meteorology, ecology, dendrology, animal husbandry, and old-fashioned history—historians offer a more complex and intriguing answer to the important question of where all the bison have gone. Why does that question matter for understanding the history of the Great Plains and its people?

Hunting Bison

In late summer of 1875 a herd of great American bison—the largest animals in North America—grazed lazily along a shallow creek bed. Summering on the highlands of the southern plains, they fed on the mid and tall grasses of early spring and the late-sprouting short grasses of summer. They groomed, played, and mated before beginning their slow trek down to the river bottoms, where naturally cured short grasses and cottonwood bark nourished them during the winter months.

So the cycle had spun for thousands of years. But on this day in 1875 the bison of this herd began mysteriously to die.

One by one, they dropped to the ground as if swatted by a huge, invisible hand. Those at the herd's edges went first. Occasionally the animals gathered about a carcass and sniffed at the warm blood. Or they raised their heads to scent the wind for trouble. With the poorest eyesight on the plains, the bison could see little—certainly not the puff of smoke that appeared downwind as each new bison staggered and fell.

The hunter lay perfectly still. No need to move—his powerful .50-caliber Sharps rifle could drop a "shaggy" at 600 feet. No need for horses—they would only spook the herd. The man lay quietly downwind, ideally firing one, maybe two rounds a minute, keeping the pace of killing slow and steady. With care, a good hunter might bag as many as a hundred bison a day. And Tom Nixon was a good hunter, a professional in it for profit.

On this day in 1875, legend has it, Nixon killed 120 bison in 40 minutes. The barrel of his Sharps grew so hot that his bullets wobbled in flight. He forgot about the slow and steady kill, forgot even about his rifle, which was ruined in the hunt. That day he was out for a record, and he got it. The season was as profitable as the day. From September 15 to October 20, Nixon killed 2,127 bison.

The buffalo robe of a Hidatsa warrior. Kiowa Indians kept calendars on buffalo skin robes, which historians have used to help estimate bison populations.

Other hunters fared well too. A buffalo robe fetched as much as $5 in the East. Operating in bands of three or four—a shooter, two skinners, and a cook—professional hunters wreaked havoc with the southern herd of the Great Plains in the 1870s. And within a decade, the northern herd had nearly vanished. By some counts, the 30 million bison that roamed the plains in the early nineteenth century shrank to 5,000 by the mid-1880s.

The Questions   Where had all the bison gone? Popular historical accounts have focused almost entirely on the gun-toting white hunters of legend and the smoke-belching railroad: symbols of a market economy penetrating the West. Without doubt, the market economy played a role in eliminating the vast herds. As far back as the 1830s and 1840s, fur trappers and traders were eating buffalo meat; so too were the railroad crews who extended tracks west. More to the point, the new rail lines provided easy transport of bulky robes and skins to the East. Railroad companies also brought whole trainloads of tourists to shoot at the herd from open windows or atop the cars. In all, the great hunts brought about 10 million bison hides to market.

Ten million is an immense number. But even conservative estimates have suggested that 30 million buffalo had been roaming the plains. What other factors can account for the precipitous drop?

Understanding the fate of the bison herds has required historians to analyze the entire ecology of the plains, of which the bison were an integral part. In many ways, the decades of the 1870s and 1880s represent the end of a process begun much earlier. In reconstructing that process, historians have assembled evidence ranging from traditional accounts of traders and trappers to Indian oral traditions, agricultural census data for livestock, and meteorology reports. They have even found ingenious ways to evaluate the rings of trees and pollen sediment.

One piece of the bison puzzle appears in the 1850s, nearly 20 years before the great white hunts. Starving Indians began to appear across the central and southern plains. Traders reported that the Cheyenne were eating their treasured horses, and other tribes were raiding Mexico for stock. Historians are also able to catch a glimpse of these hard times in the painted robe calendars of the Kiowa. The calendars show the sign for "few or no bison" for four successive years beginning in 1849.

Contemporaries blamed white emigrants headed overland to the Pacific coast. But the pressures of overland migration alone were not enough to bring the Indians to starvation. From accounts in their diaries and letters, overlanders themselves admitted to being poor hunters of bison. Few recorded ever killing more than a handful at a time. More puzzling, many overlanders reported seeing the "blanched skulls and bones" of bison in the early 1840s, *before* the height of the overland migration. Most puzzling, bison were disappearing first from the western portion of the central plains, where whites were most scarce.

Here, in the western plains, was precisely where Indians were plentiful. Since the seventeenth century, Indian peoples had been lured to the bison-rich plains. The bison became a staple of Indian life, providing a "grocery store on the hoof," hides for clothing and shelter, and a source of powerful religious symbols. Most Plains Indians followed the herds for their subsistence, but as the commercial trade in buffalo robes grew in the 1870s, tribes such as the Blackfeet were being drawn into the hunt for profit. In the first half of the nineteenth century, moreover, new Indian peoples had come

This Blackfoot robe records the history of one warrior's exploits. It also shows the importance in plains culture of the horse, which competed with the bison for food, especially during the winter. Dozens of horseshoes record animals stolen from enemies.

two- to five-year-old bison cows for their tender meat and their thinner, more easily processed hides. The death of these cows, the most fertile members of the herd, sharply reduced the number of new births.

Biotic Invasions and Climate Changes

Yet more was at work on the plains than the onslaught of hunters, white or Indian. A broader biotic invasion was under way. Incoming whites and Indians carried animals with them. Indians brought tens of thousands of horses, while the Pacific-bound overlanders brought oxen, cattle, mules, and sheep. These ungulates carried diseases new to the plains—brucellosis, tuberculosis, and a variety of parasites. Later in the century, bison in refuges were found to be riddled with these deadly ailments. The new species also competed for grazing land. So overlanders and Indians were weakening the herds less through slaughter than by occupying the *habitats* of the bison and consuming their food.

Then, beginning in the late 1840s, two decades of unusually heavy rainfall were followed by years of drought. Scientists can deduce these conditions using the science of dendrochronology, which focuses on reading tree rings to provide clues about the weather of a particular era. Around 1850 tree rings began to shrink, indicating the onset of a cycle with more frequent droughts. As highland springs and creeks dried up and summer short grasses grew poorly, more bison began to disappear.

Earlier cycles of drought had led to the virtual disappearance of bison from the plains. No bison bones appear, for example, at archaeological levels that match pollen data indicating droughts between 5,000 and 2,500 B.C.E. and 500 to 1300 C.E. Thereafter a cycle of above-average rainfall and cooler weather created a more hospitable climate for bison. Unusually abundant rains in the early nineteenth century allowed the herds to grow much larger than normal, as Indian

to the plains, pushed by the westward advance of European Americans and by hostile tribes from the Great Lakes region. The Indian population in the central plains grew from perhaps 8,000 in 1820 to as many as 20,000 in the 1850s.

For a time, the competition between tribes actually helped protect the bison. Warring groups created buffer zones between them. These contested spaces served as refuges for bison, because hunting could be conducted only sporadically for fear of enemy attack. But after 1840 Indian diplomacy brought peace among many rival tribes. The bison began to disappear as Indians stepped up the hunt across the former buffer zones of the western range. They especially favored

By comparing the rings from this pine tree taken from the Grand Canyon, historians can date the years of its growth. The widest ring, indicating the wettest year, was 1767.

In contrast, 1754 was extremely dry.

calendars also noted. When drought set in, the herds started to shrink.

In the end, the bison were brought low not by one factor but by many. Drought, Indian population increases, and Indian market hunting weakened the great herds. The disturbances created by overlanders and their animals, the appearance of new bovine diseases, and the increased competition for grazing land only made matters worse. By the time the great white hunts began, the bison, though still numerous, were already in crisis.

Bibliography   Mari Sandoz, *The Buffalo Hunters: The Story of the Hide Men* (1954), provides a vivid description of white hunters in the 1870s and 1880s. Dan Flores sets that traditional tale in a broader context in his pathbreaking article "Bison Ecology and Bison Diplomacy: The Southern Plains from 1800 to 1840," *Journal of American History* (September 1991): 465–485. Flores focuses on the southern plains, but more recently, Elliott West has come to similar conclusions in *The Way to the West: Essays on the Central Plains* (1995), which includes a broader discussion of the interplay of climate, animals, plants, and people in the region. Most recently Andrew C. Isenberg has addressed the issue over a broad chronological framework in *The Destruction of the Bison: An Ecological History, 1750–1920* (2000).

CHAPTER 19
The New Industrial Order
1870~1914

Brooklyn Bridge under construction, c. 1876.

Waiting for Their Brains

It was so dark, Robert Ferguson could not see his own feet. Inching along the railroad tracks, he suddenly pitched forward and felt his breath taken away as the ground vanished beneath him. To his dismay, he found himself wedged between two railroad ties, his legs dangling in the air. Scrambling back to solid ground, he retreated along the tracks to the railroad car, where he sat meekly until dawn.

Ferguson, a Scot visiting America in 1866, had been in Memphis only two days earlier, ready to take the "Great Southern Mail Route" east some 850 miles to Washington. Things had gone badly from the start. About 50 miles outside of town, a broken river bridge forced him to take a ferry. He spent the next 10 miles bumping along in a mule-drawn truck before learning that the rail line did not resume for another 40 miles. Disheartened, he decided to return to Memphis to try again.

The train to Memphis arrived six hours late, dawdled its way home, and then, barely three miles from the city, derailed in the middle of the night. When a few passengers decided to hike the remaining distance into town, Ferguson tagged along. It was then that he had fallen between the tracks onto a flimsy, high river bridge. Ferguson had trouble managing the trestle even in daylight.

Before he finally reached Washington, the Scot faced six more days of difficult travel. One line ended, and passengers and freight would be forced onto another because rail gauges—the width of the track—differed from line to line. Or a bridge was out, or there was no bridge at all. Trains had no meals "on board" or any sleeping cars. "It was certainly what the Americans would call 'hard travelling,'" Ferguson huffed; "—they do not make use of the word 'rough,' because roughness may be expected as a natural condition in a new country."

Cross-country travel proved so rough that it inspired even an American to fantasy. In 1859, the *Southern Literary Messenger* carried the first of several installments describing Miss Jane Delaware Peyton's trip to Washington, D.C., from Rasselas, Oregon, in 2029, 170 years in the future. Elegant trains whisked her from one end of the country to the other in only 8 days at unimaginable speeds of 60 miles an hour. While this "immense velocity" presented no physical problems, Miss Peyton

Painting of Henry Bessemer's Steel Plant, opened in Sheffield, England, in 1859.

had to guard against "Tourbilliere," an all-too-common mental disorder of the future. After 10 or more hours on a speeding train, quick-witted passengers found perception accelerating but memory lapsing. "The mind loses an idea almost as soon as it has been formed," Miss Peyton reported. The only cure was to stop and let the mind catch up to its changing surroundings. So every few days Miss Peyton and her fellow travelers disembarked from their train to sit quietly at a depot until their symptoms subsided. Such persons were said to be "waiting for their brains."

By the 1880s, some of our writer's fantasies had come true, as T. S. Hudson discovered in 1882 when he launched a self-proclaimed "Scamper through America." Hudson, another British tourist, did not cross the continent in quite 8 days, but it took him just 60 days to go from England to San Francisco and back. And he booked his rail ticket from a single agent in Boston. Such centralization would have been unthinkable in 1859, when a transcontinental railroad was still a decade from completion.

Hudson rode in Pullman "Palace" cars with luxury sleeping quarters and a full breakfast of coffee, iced milk, eggs, "game in their season," and fresh fruits. Newly installed air brakes made trains safer and their stops smoother. Bridges appeared where none had been before, including a "magnificent" span over the Mississippi at St. Louis. Hudson also found himself in the midst of a communications revolution. Traveling across the plains, he was struck by the number of telephone poles along the route.

What made America in the 1880s so different from just a few decades earlier was not the speed and comfort of travel or the wonders of the new technology. The true marvel was the emerging industrial order that underlay those technologies and made them possible. Because this order was essentially in place by the beginning of the twentieth century, we tend to take its existence for granted. Yet its growth in scale, scope, and complexity was at first slow and required innovations in many different areas of society to achieve its effects.

The process of industrialization began in the United States at least three decades before the Civil War, with small factories producing light consumer goods such as clothing, shoes, and furniture. Much of the economy remained local. Only after the 1850s did the industrial economy develop a set of interlocking systems that allowed larger factories, using more and bigger machines, to produce goods with greater efficiency and market them on a national and international scale.

The transformation, remarkable as it was, brought pain along with progress. The demand for natural resources led to virgin forests being cut down and open-pit mines spewing hazardous runoffs. Factory-lined rivers of the Northeast were left toxic with industrial wastes. In 1882, the year Hudson scampered by rail across America, an average of 675 people were killed on the job every week. Like most people, workers scrambled—sometimes literally—to adjust. Few Americans anywhere had time to "wait for their brains" to catch up to the dizzying pace of change.

An Industrial Transformation

The Development of Industrial Systems

The new industrial order can best be understood as a web of complex industrial systems woven together in the second half of the nineteenth century. By "industrial system," historians mean a set of orderly arrangements or processes—whether of extraction, production, transportation, distribution, or finance—organized to make

The magnificent steel arches of the Eads Bridge, the engineering marvel that awed T. S. Hudson, spanning the Mississippi River at St. Louis. The center arch, under which the paddle-wheel steamer is sailing, is some 524 feet in length. The adjoining arches are each 500 feet long. The whole structure is supported by limestone piers sunk deeply into the bedrock of the river. The bridge took more than 7 years to build, cost $10 million, and opened amid great fanfare on July 4, 1874. The steel came from the mills of Andrew Carnegie.

the whole industrial order function smoothly. Look, for example, at the industrial systems required to build the bridge across the Mississippi that T. S. Hudson so admired. When James B. Eads constructed its soaring arches in 1874, he needed steel, most likely made from iron ore mined in northern Michigan. Giant steam shovels scooped up the ore and loaded whole freight cars in a few strokes. A transportation system—railroads, boats, and other carriers—probably moved the ore to Pittsburgh, where the factory system furnished the labor and machinery to finish the steel. The capital to create such factories came from a system of finance that linked investment banks and stock markets to entrepreneurs in need of money. Only with a national network of industrial systems could the Eads bridge be built and a new age of industry arise.

Natural Resources and Industrial Technology

The earliest European settlers had marveled at the "merchantable commodities" of America, from the glittering silver mines of the Spanish empire to the continent's hardwood forests. What set the new industrial economy apart from that older America were the scale and efficiency of using such natural resources. New technologies made it possible to exploit them in ways undreamed of only decades earlier.

Bessemer Process

Steel, for example, had been made from iron and carbon alloyed with other metals and forged into swords as far back as the Middle Ages. In the 1850s, inventors in England and America discovered a cheaper way—called the Bessemer process after its British developer—to convert large quantities of iron into steel. By the late 1870s, the price of steel had dropped by more than half. Steel was lighter than iron, could support 20 times as much weight, and lasted 20 years instead of 3. Steel tracks soon carried most rail traffic; steel girders replaced old cast-iron building frames; steel cables supported new suspension bridges.

Petroleum Industry

Industrial technology made some natural resources more valuable. New distilling methods transformed a thick, smelly liquid called petroleum into kerosene for lighting lamps, oil for lubricating machinery, and paraffin for making candles. Beginning in 1859, new drilling techniques began to tap vast pools of petroleum below the surface. About the same time, Frenchman Etienne Lenoir constructed the first practical internal combustion engine. After 1900, new vehicles like the gasoline-powered carriage turned the oil business into a major industry.

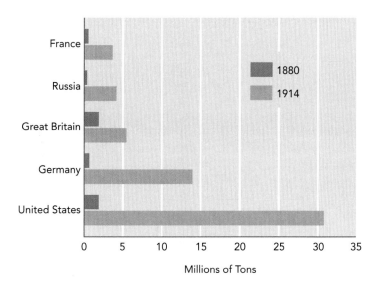

Steel Production, 1880 and 1914 *While steel production jumped in western industrial nations from 1880 to 1914, it skyrocketed in the United States because of rich resources, cheap labor, and aggressive management.*

Environmental Costs

The vast scale of these operations used equally vast amounts of resources and produced huge quantities of waste. Coal mining, logging, and the industrial toxins of factories led to only the most obvious forms of environmental degradation—scarred land, vanishing forests, contaminated waters. As giant water cannons blasted away hillsides in search of gold in California, rock and gravel washed into rivers, raising their beds and threatening populations downstream with floods. Some industrialists did succeed in limiting pollution, often to turn a profit as much as to protect the environment. Chicago meat packers stretched their imaginations to use every conceivable part of the animals that came into their plants. Straight-length bones were turned into cutlery, hoofs and feet into glue and oil, fat into oleomargarine.

Systematic Invention

Industrial technology rested on invention. For sheer inventiveness, the 40 years following the Civil War have rarely been matched in American history. Between 1790 and 1860, 36,000 **patents** on new inventions were registered with the government. Over the next three decades, the U.S. Patent Office granted more than half a million, as the process of invention became systematized. Small-scale inventors were replaced by orderly "invention factories"—forerunners of expensive research labs.

Edison's Contributions

No one did more to bring system, order, and profitability to invention than Thomas Alva Edison. In 1868, at the age of 21, Edison went to work for a New York brokerage house and promptly improved the design of the company's stock tickers. A $40,000 bonus (worth perhaps $400,000 in current dollars) allowed him to become an independent inventor. For the next five years, Edison patented a new invention almost every five months.

Edison was determined to bring system and order to the process of invention. Only then could breakthroughs come in a steady and profitable stream. He moved 15 of his workers to Menlo Park, New Jersey, where in 1876 he created perhaps his greatest invention—an "invention factory." Like a manufacturer, Edison subdivided the work among gifted inventors, engineers, toolmakers, and others.

The Spread of an Electrical Power System

This orderly bureaucracy soon evolved into the Edison Electric Light Company. Its ambitious owner aimed at more than perfecting his new electric light bulb. Edison wanted to create a unified electrical power system—central stations to generate electric current, wired to users, all powering millions of small bulbs in homes and businesses. To launch his enterprise, Edison won the backing of several large banking houses by lighting up the Wall Street district in 1882. It was like "writing

Thomas Edison, unkempt and wrinkled, in his research lab

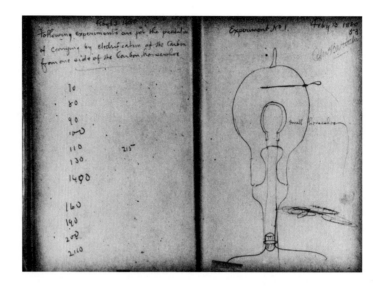

Edison's Notebook   *This page from one of Thomas Edison's notebooks shows sketches of and notes on some of his early experiments with an incandescent lamp—what we know as an electric lightbulb. Edison was not only the most celebrated inventor of his day, but by the early twentieth century one of the greatest popular heroes in American life in a time when scientific and technological progress was considered the defining feature of the age.*

by daylight," recorded one reporter. Soon Edison power plants sprang up in major cities across the country.

Electricity was more flexible than earlier sources of energy. Factories no longer had to be built near rivers and falls to make use of water power. Before the end of the century, electricity was running automatic looms, trolley cars, subways, and factory machinery. Electricity not only revolutionized industry; it also worked in the homes of ordinary citizens. The electric motor, developed commercially by George Westinghouse and Nikola Tesla in 1886, powered everything from sewing machines to Edison's "gramophone," later known as the record player.

George Eastman revolutionized photography by making the consumer a part of his inventive system. In the process, he democratized picture taking, once the province of the skilled professional, by inventing a camera that anyone could use at a price ($25) many could afford. In 1888 Eastman marketed the "Kodak" camera. The small black box weighed just over two pounds and contained a strip of celluloid film that replaced hundreds of pounds of photography equipment. After 100 snaps of the shutter, the owner simply sent the camera back to Eastman's Rochester factory, along with a $10 fee, then waited for the developed photos and a reloaded camera to return by mail. "You press the button—we do the rest" was Eastman Kodak's apt slogan. So successful was he that Eastman had to fight off competitors for legal control of his patents. In a pattern that has held ever since, other inventors faced similar court battles.

Transportation and Communication

The Problem of Scale   Abundant resources and new inventions remained worthless to industry until they could be moved to processing plants, factories, and offices. But distance was daunting. Where 100 miles of railroad track would do for shipping goods in Germany and England, 1,000 miles was necessary in America.

Nonetheless, by 1870 an efficient transportation system created an integrated national market and tied the United States into an emerging international economy. By the 1870s railroads crisscrossed the country, and steam-powered ships (introduced before the Civil War) were pushing barges down rivers and carrying passengers and freight across the oceans. The time of transatlantic travel was cut in half, to about 10 days. Eventually the rail and water transportation systems fused. By 1900 railroad companies owned nearly all the country's domestic steamship lines.

A thriving industrial nation also required effective communication. Information was a precious commodity, as essential to industry as were resources or technology. In the early 1840s, it took newspapers as many as 10 days to reach Indiana from New York and 3 months to arrive by ship in San Francisco. In 1844 Samuel Morse succeeded in sending the first message over an electrical wire between cities. By 1861 the Western Union Company had strung 76,000 miles of telegraph lines across the country. If a bank collapsed in Chicago, bankers in Dallas knew of it that day. Railroads could keep traffic unsnarled through the dots and dashes of Morse's code. By the turn of the century a million miles of telegraph wire handled some 63 million messages a year, not to mention those flashing across underwater cables to China, Japan, Africa, and South America.

A second innovation in communication, the telephone, vastly improved on the telegraph. Alexander Graham Bell, a Scottish immigrant, was teaching the deaf when he began experimenting with ways to transmit speech electrically. In 1876, he transmitted his famous first words to a young assistant: "Mr. Watson, come here! I want you." No longer did messages require a telegraph office, the unwieldy Morse code, and couriers to deliver them.

President Rutherford B. Hayes installed the first telephone in the White House in 1878, when the instrument was still a curiosity. The same year, the city of New Haven, Connecticut, opened the first telephone exchange in America. By 1900 there were 1.5 million of Bell's machines in America. The telephone patent proved to be the most valuable ever granted. In the scramble for profits, the Bell Telephone Company battled challenges from competitors and suits from rivals who claimed that their contributions were worth a share of the rights.

Along with other innovations in communication (see Daily Lives, "The Rise of Information Systems," next page), telephones modernized offices and eased business transactions. In 1915 the American Telephone and Telegraph Company opened the first transcontinental line. A business executive in New York now could speak personally to an associate in San Francisco. When commercial rates dropped after the turn of the century, the telephone became part of a social revolution. Like the railroad and the telegraph, it compressed distances and reduced differences across the country, tying the nation together through another network of communication.

Telegraph

Telephone

A young Alexander Graham Bell with an early version of his "speaking telegraph."

Finance Capital

As industry grew, so did the demand for investment capital—the money spent on land, buildings, and machinery. The scale of industry required more funds than ever. Between 1870 and 1900, the number of workers in an average iron and steel firm grew from 100 to 400, and the capital invested jumped to nearly $1 million, about seven times what it had been in 1870.

Where did the money come from? For the first three-quarters of the nineteenth century, investment capital came mostly from the savings of firms. In the last half of the century "capital deepening"—a process essential for industrialization—took place. Simply put, as national wealth increased, people began to save and invest more of their money, which meant that more funds could be loaned out.

Savings and investment grew more attractive with the development of a complex network of financial institutions. Commercial and savings banks, investment houses, and insurance companies gave savers new opportunities to channel money to industry.

Sources of Capital

In 1877, a year after its invention, advertisements were already touting Alexander Graham Bell's "speaking telegraph": "Conversation can easily be carried on after slight practice and occasional repetition of a word or sentence. . . . [A]fter a few trials the ear becomes accustomed to the peculiar sound."

It was not so for everyone. Some people had great difficulty understanding the strange sounds. Others reported terrifying "stage fright" that left them speechless. Still others had no idea how to greet callers. Bell answered with a chipper "Ahoy!" Operators at the first public telephone exchange used the old-fashioned "What is wanted?" But it was Thomas Edison's melodious "Hello" (derived from "Halloo," the traditional call to bring hounds to the chase) that won out by 1880.

At first Bell's electrical toys could be rented only in pairs by individuals who wanted to connect two places. In 1877 the advantages of such direct communication led to the first intercity hookup, between New York and Boston. Before the turn of the century, the Bell-organized American Telephone and Telegraph

Systems of finance and communications intersected at Wall Street, New York, where the nation's most important investment banks and markets were located. The Great Blizzard of 1888 buried the district with snow and also shadowed in white the crisscrossing "blizzard" of wires needed for the communications networks.

The New York Stock Exchange, in existence since 1792, linked eager investors with money-hungry firms. By the end of the nineteenth century, the stock market had established itself as the basic means of making capital available to industry.

The Corporation

For those business leaders with the skill to knit the industrial pieces together, large profits awaited. This was the era of the "robber barons," entrepreneurs who bulled their way to success at the expense of competitors and employees. To be sure, sheer ruthlessness went a long way in the fortune-building game. "Law? Who cares about law!" railroad magnate Cornelius Vanderbilt once boasted. "Hain't I got the power?"

But to survive in the long term, business leaders could not depend on ruthlessness alone. They had to have ingenuity, an eye for detail, and the gift of foresight. The growing scale of enterprise and need for capital led them to adapt an old device, the corporation, to new needs. Corporations had existed since colonial times, when governments granted charters of incorporation to organizations that ran public facilities such as turnpikes, canals, and banks. After the Civil War the modern corporation came into use for raising money and protecting business holdings.

Advantages of the Corporation

The corporation had several advantages over more traditional forms of ownership: the single owner and the partnership. A corporation could raise large sums quickly by selling "stock certificates," or shares in its business. It could also outlive its owners (or stockholders) because it required no legal reorganization if one of the owners died. It limited liability because owners were no longer personally responsible

Company had combined more than 100 local telephone companies to furnish business and government with long-distance service. When rates dropped after 1900, telephones found their way into ordinary American homes.

The telephone revolutionized communications, cutting time and obliterating distances. It also liberated social relations by freeing people from the nineteenth-century convention of addressing only those to whom they had been properly introduced. And it acted as a great social leveler. Almost overnight, telephone operators (called "hello girls") began connecting people of different locales and classes who might never have spoken to each other at all, let alone as peers.

During the first half of the nineteenth century, information had traveled mostly through the mails. In 1844 Samuel F. B. Morse sent the first intercity message across electrical wires, thereby achieving instantaneous communication. But the telegraph had drawbacks. Instantaneous communication was hardly direct. Messages had to be taken to a telegraph office, where trained clerks could translate them into Morse code, an unwieldy system of dots and dashes. Only then could they be transmitted by electrical impulse. When they arrived at the receiving station, messages were recast into understandable language, then carried by hand to their precise destination.

Another device that increased business efficiency was the typewriter. C. Latham Sholes, a Milwaukee printer and editor, had been tinkering with an automatic numbering machine when a friend suggested he develop a mechanical letter-writing device. In 1868 he patented the "Type-Writer." By the early twentieth century the typewriter had taken its modern shape—a keyboard with upper- and lowercase letters and a carriage that allowed typists to see the output.

The need for speed and efficiency in the office led to other breakthroughs. Carbon paper, designed for making a typewritten copy along with the original, was patented in 1872. In 1890 Alfred Dick invented the mimeograph to reproduce many copies of a single document cheaply, a communications boon not only to businesses but also to churches, reform organizations, and political groups. Communications, like the rest of the new industrial order, were steadily becoming more orderly and efficient, permitting the rapid distribution of information to those people who desired it.

for corporate debts. And it separated owners from day-to-day management of the company. A growing web of highly skilled professional managers could now operate complex businesses. So clear were these advantages that before the turn of the century, corporations were making two-thirds of all manufactured products in the United States.

An International Pool of Labor

Last, but hardly least important for the new industrial order, was a pool of labor. In the United States the demand for workers far outstripped what native-born citizens could supply. In 1860 it took about 4.3 million workers to run all the factories, mills, and shops in the United States. By 1900 there were approximately 20 million workers in industrial and associated enterprises.

In part, the United States relied on a vast global network to fill its need for workers. In Europe as well as Latin America, Asia, Africa, and the Middle East, seasonal migrations provided a rich source of workers for many nations, including the United States. Beginning in the 1870s, for example, rural laborers and tenant farmers from the Mezzogiorno in Italy traveled throughout Europe seeking wage work in construction during the building season, which stretched from spring through early fall. Mechanization, poverty, oppression, and ambition pushed many of these rural laborers from farms into industrial cities and soon to other continents once steamships made transoceanic travel easier.

To draw these workers to the United States, industrialists advertised in newspapers, distributed pamphlets, and sent agents fanning out across the globe. Between 1870 and

Global Labor Network

Occupational Distribution, 1880 and 1920 *Between 1880 and 1920, management and industrial work—employing white- and blue-collar workers—grew at the expense of farm work.*

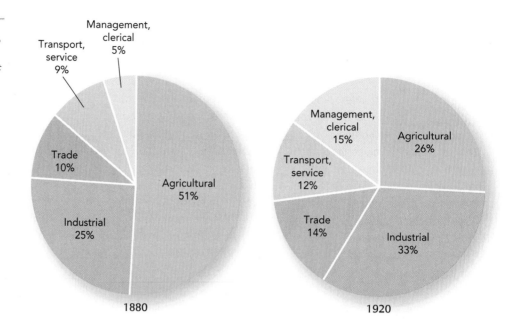

1890, more than 8 million immigrants arrived in the United States, another 14 million by 1914. Some came from Asia and Latin America, but most came from Europe and settled in industrial cities. Like migratory laborers elsewhere, they hoped to find work, fatten their purses, and go home. According to one estimate, between 25 and 60 percent of all immigrants returned to their homelands from the United States during these years.

Migration Chains

In the United States as in other countries, immigrants relied on well-defined migration chains of family and friends to get jobs. A brother might find work with other Slavs in the mines of Pennsylvania; or the daughter of Greek parents, in a New England textile mill filled with relatives. Labor contractors also served as a funnel to industry. Tough and savvy immigrants themselves, they met newcomers at the docks and train stations with contracts to work in local factories, mines, and other industries. For their trouble they took a fee or a slice of the new workers' wages. Among Italians they were known as *padrones;* among Mexicans, as *enganchistas.* By the end of the nineteenth century such contractors controlled two-thirds of the labor in New York.

Mexicans, too, formed part of this transnational labor pool, streaming across the border especially after the Mexican Revolution in 1910. But even earlier, seasonal migration of Mexican laborers to plant and pick crops from Texas to California was common enough to spawn cross-border family networks. "Come! Come! Come over," a Mexican migrant remembered being told by family friends. Mexican laborers also helped build the transcontinental railroad and, after the turn of the century, moved farther north for jobs in the tanneries, meatpacking plants, foundries, and rail yards of Chicago, St. Louis, and other centers of industry.

Domestic Sources

Rural Americans—some 11 million between 1865 and 1920—provided a home-grown source of labor, similar in the roots and patterns of their movements to migrants from abroad. Driven from the farm by machines and bad times or the desire for a new life, they moved first to small, then to larger, cities in search of work. Most lacked the skills for high-paying jobs. But unlike their foreign counterparts, they spoke English, many could read and write, and few thought of returning home. In iron and steel cities as well as in coal-mining towns, the better industrial jobs and supervisory positions often went to them. Other rural migrants found work in retail stores or offices and slowly entered the new urban middle class of white-collar workers.

Most African Americans continued to work the fields of the South. About 300,000 moved to northern cities between 1870 and 1910, perhaps more to southern cities. Between 1880 and 1910, the black urban population across the South jumped, more than doubling in industrial cities such as Birmingham. In some instances, black migrants were escaping domineering fathers; in others, seeking the excitement of the city; and in still others, following a husband or fleeing the prejudices of the Old South. These migrants too relied on family migration chains in their journey, sometimes traveling in groups, sometimes alone. On occasion, they brought siblings or spouses and children, often one by one, after they had found work.

In one way or another, all these black migrants came in search of opportunity, and all faced the burden of continued discrimination when they arrived. Newer industries such as textile manufacturing and railroad shop work refused to hire African Americans, but some businesses, like Andrew Carnegie's steel mills in Pittsburgh, employed blacks as janitors and wage laborers. Women found jobs as domestic servants and laundresses. Still, by 1890 less than 10 percent of black laborers worked in industry.

Chicago laborer

Railroad Time

Railroads: America's First Big Business

The system was a mess: any good railroad executive knew as much. Along the tracks that spanned the country, each town—each rail station—set its clocks separately by the sun. In 1882, the year T. S. Hudson scampered across America, New York and Boston were 11 minutes and 45 seconds apart. Stations often had several clocks showing the time on different rail lines, along with one displaying "local mean time." In 1883, without consulting anyone, the railroad companies solved the problem by dividing the country into four zones, each an hour apart. One Chicago newspaper compared the feat to Joshua's making the sun stand still. Cities and towns soon adjusted, but Congress did not get around to making the division official until 1918.

At the center of the new industrial systems lay the railroads, moving people and freight, spreading communications, reinventing time, ultimately tying the nation together. Railroads also stimulated economic growth, simply because the sheer building of them required so many resources—coal, wood, glass, rubber, brass, and by the 1880s 75 percent of all U.S. steel. By lowering transportation costs, railroads allowed manufacturers to reduce prices, attract more buyers, and increase business. Perhaps most important, as America's first big business they devised new techniques of management, soon adopted by other companies.

A Managerial Revolution

To the men who ran them, railroads provided a challenge in organization and finance. In the 1850s the Pepperell textile mills of Maine, one of the largest industrial enterprises in America, employed about 800 workers. By the early 1880s the Pennsylvania Railroad had nearly 50,000 people on its payroll. From setting schedules and rates to determining costs and profits, such size required a level of coordination unknown in earlier businesses.

The so-called trunk lines pioneered new systems of management. Scores of early companies had serviced local networks of cities and communities, often with less than 50 miles of track. During the 1850s longer trunk lines emerged east of the Mississippi to connect the shorter branches, or "feeder" lines. By the outbreak of the Civil War, four great trunk lines linked the eastern seaboard with the Great Lakes and western rivers. After the war, trunk lines grew in the South and West.

Pioneering Trunk Lines

The operations of large lines spawned a new managerial elite, beneath owners but with wide authority over operations. Cautious by nature, they preferred to negotiate and administer rather than compete. In the 1850s, Daniel McCallum, superintendent of the New York and Erie Railroad, laid the foundation for this system by drawing up the first table of organization for an American company. A tree trunk with roots

The New Managers

Collaring Respectability

Visible Signs of an Urban Middle Class

By the 1880s Troy, New York, bore the nickname "Collar City," because Troy was the home of the booming collar-and-cuff industry. Looking back at the late nineteenth century, we can see detachable collars and cuffs not simply as matter of changing fashion; we can tell much more if we examine who was wearing them and why.

The market for detachable collars and cuffs grew as the urban middle class emerged. Each day a man could affix a clean collar and set of cuffs to his shirt without having to wash the entire shirt. The savings thus afforded by fresh collars and cuffs meant money in the pocket, of course, but the white-collared shirts also set their middle-class wearers apart from their working-class counterparts, whose grimy, blue-denim shirts signified that they labored by the sweat of their brows.

As distinguished from such "blue-collar workers," these "white-collar workers" were "brainworkers"—doctors, lawyers, business managers, and even clerks, who used their heads rather than their hands.

represented the president and board of directors; five branches constituted the main operating divisions; leaves stood for the local agents, train crews, and other workers. Information moved up and down the trunk so that managers could get daily reports to and from the separate parts.

By the turn of the century, these managerial techniques had spread to other industries. Local superintendents were responsible for daily activities. Central offices served as corporate nerve centers, housing divisions for purchases, production, transportation, sales, and accounting. As a new class of middle managers imposed new order on business operations, executives, managers, and workers operated in increasingly precise and coordinated ways.

Competition and Consolidation

Although managers made operations more systematic, the struggle among railroad companies to dominate the industry was anything but precise and rational. In the 1870s and 1880s the pain of railroad progress began to tell.

In addition to large start-up costs, railroads were saddled with enormous fixed costs—land, equipment, debts. These remained constant regardless of the volume of traffic. Beginning in the 1860s, railroads constructed more lines in hopes of increasing traffic and thus revenues. Soon the railroads had overbuilt. With so much extra capacity, railroad owners schemed to win new accounts. They gave free passes to favored shippers, promised them free sidings at their plants, offered free land to lure businesses to their territory.

The most savage and costly competition came over the rates charged for shipping goods. Managers lowered rates for freight that was shipped in bulk, on long hauls, or on return routes (since the cars were empty anyway). They used "rebates"—secret discounts to preferred customers—to drop prices below the posted rates of competitors (and then recouped the losses by overcharging small shippers like farmers). When the economy plunged or a weak line sought to improve its position, rate wars broke out. By 1880, 65 lines had declared bankruptcy.

Cooperation worked better than competition. During the 1870s railroad managers created regional federations to pool traffic, set prices, and divide profits among members. Pooling—informal agreements among competing companies to act together—was designed to remove the competition that led to rate wars. Without the force of law, however, pools failed. Members broke ranks by cutting prices in hopes of quick gain. In the end, rate wars died down only when weaker lines failed or stronger ones bought up competitors.

Pooling

The Challenge of Finance

Earlier in the nineteenth century, many railroads relied on state governments for financial help. Backers also looked to counties, cities, and towns for bonds and other forms of aid. People living near the ends of rail lines, who stood to gain from construction, were persuaded to take railroad stock in exchange for land or labor. In the 1850s and 1860s western promoters went to Washington for help and returned with $65 million in loans to six western railroads and some 131 million acres of land.

Federal aid helped to build only part of the nation's railroads. Most of the money came from private investors. The New York **Stock Exchange** expanded rapidly as railroad corporations began to trade their stocks and bonds. Large investment banks

New Ways of Raising Money

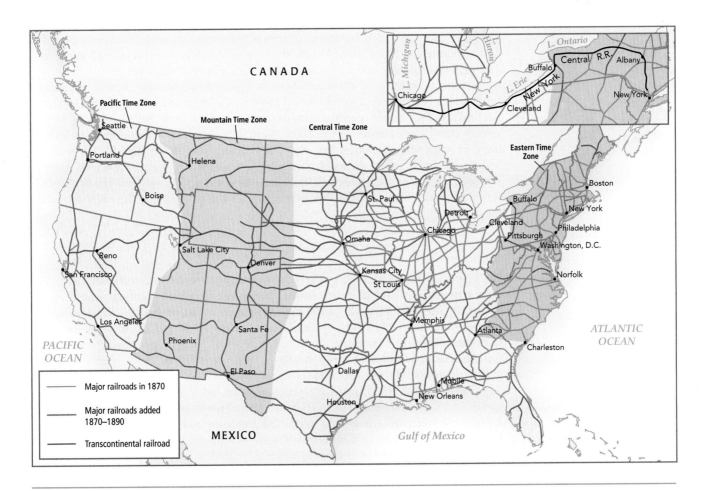

Railroads, 1870–1890 *By 1890, the railroad network stretched from one end of the country to the other, with more miles of track than in all of Europe. New York and Chicago, linked by the New York Central trunk line, became the new commercial axes.*

developed financial networks to track down money at home and abroad. By 1898 a third of the assets of American life insurance companies had gone into railroads, while Europeans owned nearly a third of all American railroad stocks.

Because investment bankers played such large roles in funding railroads, they found themselves advising companies about their business affairs. If a company fell into bankruptcy, bankers sometimes served as the "receivers" who oversaw the property until financial health returned. By absorbing smaller lines into larger ones, eliminating rebates, and stabilizing rates, the bankers helped reduce competition and impose order and centralization. In the process, they often came to control the companies they counseled.

By 1900, the new industrial systems had transformed American railroads. Some 200,000 miles of track were in operation, 80 percent of it owned by only six groups of railroads. Time zones coordinated schedules; standardized track made cross-country freighting easier. Soon passengers were traveling 16 billion miles a year. To that traffic could be added farm goods, raw materials, and factory-finished products. Everything moved with a new regularity that allowed businesses to plan and prosper.

The Growth of Big Business

In 1865, 26-year-old John D. Rockefeller sat stone-faced in the office of his Cleveland oil refinery, about to conclude the biggest deal of his life. Rockefeller's business was flourishing, but not his partnership with Maurice Clark. The two had fallen out over how quickly to expand. Rockefeller was eager to grow fast; the cautious Clark was not. They dissolved their partnership and agreed to bid for the company. Bidding opened at $500, rocketed to $72,500, and abruptly stopped. "The business is yours," said Clark. The men shook hands and a thin smile crept across Rockefeller's face.

Twenty years later, Rockefeller's Standard Oil Company controlled 90 percent of the nation's refining capacity and an oil empire that stretched well beyond Cleveland. Around the clock, trains sped Standard executives to New York, Philadelphia, and other eastern cities. The railroads were a fitting form of transportation for Rockefeller's company; in many ways they were the key to his oil empire. They carried his oil products and discounted his rates, giving him the edge to squeeze out rivals. And they pioneered the business systems on which Rockefeller was building. As we shall see with other American firms, Standard Oil was improving on the practices of the railroads to do bigger and bigger business.

Strategies of Growth

But first a great riddle had to be solved: How to grow and still control the ravages of competition? In Michigan in the 1860s, salt producers found themselves fighting for their existence. The presence of too many salt makers had begun an endless round of price-cutting that was driving them all out of business. Seeing salvation in combination, they drew together in the nation's first pool. In 1869 they formed the Michigan Salt Association. They voluntarily agreed to divide production, assign markets, and set prices—at double the previous rate.

Horizontal Growth

Competition often plagued salt processing and other manufacturers of **consumer goods** because their start-up costs were low. **Horizontal combination**—joining loosely together with rivals that produced the same goods or services—had saved Michigan salt producers. The railroads were among the first big businesses to employ pools. By the 1880s there was a whiskey pool, a cordage pool, and countless others. Such informal arrangements ultimately proved unenforceable and therefore unsatisfactory. (After 1890 they were also considered illegal restraints on trade.) But other forms of horizontal growth, such as formal mergers, spread in the wake of an economic panic in the 1890s.

Some makers of consumer products worried less about direct competition and concentrated on boosting efficiency and sales. They adopted a growth strategy called **vertical integration,** in which one company gained control of two or more stages of a business operation. A fully integrated manufacturing company, for example, possessed its own raw materials, transportation facilities, factories, and marketing outlets.

Vertical Integration

Gustavus Swift, a New England butcher, saw the advantages of such integration when he arrived in Chicago in the mid-1870s. Aware of the demand for fresh beef in the East, he acquired new refrigerated railcars to ship meat from western slaughterhouses and a network of ice-cooled warehouses in eastern cities to store it. By 1885 he had created the first national meatpacking enterprise, Swift and Company. Swift moved upward, closer to consumers, by putting together a fleet of wagons to distribute his beef to retailers. He moved down toward raw materials, extending and coordinating the purchase of cattle at the Chicago stockyards. By the 1890s Swift and Company was a fully integrated, vertically organized corporation operating on a nationwide scale. Soon Swift, Armour and Company, and three other integrated giants—together called the "Big Five"—controlled 90 percent of the beef shipped across state lines.

Vertical growth generally brought producers of consumer goods closer to the marketplace. For them, profit came from high-volume sales. The Singer Sewing Machine Company and the McCormick Harvester Company created their own retail sales arms. Manufacturers began furnishing ordinary consumers with technical information, credit, and repair services in an effort to expand sales. Advertising expenditures grew, to some $90 million by 1900, to identify markets, shape buying habits, and drum up business.

Carnegie Integrates Steel

Industrialization encouraged vertical integration in heavy industry but more often downward, toward reliable sources of raw materials. These firms made heavy machinery and materials—called **producer goods**—for big users like railroads and factory builders. Their markets were easily identified and changed little. For them, profits lay in securing limited raw materials and in holding down costs.

Andrew Carnegie led the way in steel. A Scottish immigrant, he worked his way up from bobbin boy in a textile factory to expert telegrapher to superintendent of the western division of the Pennsylvania Railroad at the age of 24. A string of wise investments paid off handsomely. He owned a share of the first sleeping car, the first iron railroad bridge, a locomotive factory, and finally an iron factory that became the nucleus of his steel empire.

In 1872, on a trip to England, Carnegie chanced to see the new Bessemer process for making steel. Awestruck by its fiery display, he rushed home to build the biggest steel mill in the world. The J. Edgar Thomson Mills (shrewdly named in honor of the president of the Pennsylvania Railroad) opened in 1875, in the midst of a severe depression. Over the next 25 years, Carnegie added mills at Homestead and elsewhere in Pennsylvania and moved from railroad building to city building. He supplied steel for the Brooklyn Bridge, New York City's elevated railway, and the Washington Monument.

Bessemer Process

Carnegie succeeded, in part, by taking advantage of the boom-and-bust business cycle. He jumped in during hard times, building and buying when equipment and businesses were cheap. But he also found skilled managers who employed the administrative techniques of the railroads. And Carnegie knew how to compete. He scrapped machinery, workers, even a new mill to keep costs down and undersell competitors.

Keys to Carnegie's Success

The final key to Carnegie's success was expansion. His empire spread horizontally by purchasing rival steel mills and constructing new ones. It spread vertically, buying up sources of supply, transportation, and eventually sales. Controlling such an integrated system, Carnegie could ensure a steady flow of materials from mine to mill and market as well as a steady stream of profits. In 1900 his company turned out more steel than Great Britain and netted him $40 million.

Carnegie steel furnaces, Braddock, Pennsylvania, on the banks of the Monongahela River were opened in 1875 as part of the J. Edgar Thomson Steel Works. Its giant Bessemer converters were capable of producing as much as 225 tons of steel rails a day, many of which went into the construction of the Pennsylvania Railroad line.

Integration of the kind Carnegie employed expressed the logic of the new industrial age. More and more, the industrial activities of society were being linked together in one giant, interconnected process.

Rockefeller and the Great Standard Oil Trust

John D. Rockefeller began his career as a refiner of petroleum and soon accomplished in oil what Carnegie achieved in steel. And he went further, developing an innovative business structure—the trust—that promised greater control than even Carnegie's integrated system. At first Rockefeller grew horizontally by buying out or joining competing oil refiners. To cut costs, he expanded vertically, with oil pipelines, warehouses, and barrel factories. By 1870, when he and five partners formed the Standard Oil Company of Ohio, his high-caliber, low-cost products could compete with any other.

Rockefeller's Methods of Expansion

Because the oil refining business was a jungle of competitive firms, Rockefeller proceeded to twist arms. He bribed rivals, spied on them, created phony companies, and slashed prices. His decisive edge came from the railroads. Desperate for business, they granted Standard Oil not only rebates on shipping rates but also "drawbacks," a fee railroaders paid Standard for petroleum products shipped by a rival. Within a decade Standard dominated the oil business with a vertically integrated empire that stretched from drilling to selling.

Throughout the 1870s Rockefeller kept his empire stitched together through informal pools and other business combinations. But they were weak and afforded him too little control. He could try to expand further, except that corporations were restricted by state law. In Rockefeller's home state of Ohio, for example, corporations could not own plants in other states or own stock in out-of-state companies.

The Trust

In 1879 Samuel C. T. Dodd, chief counsel of Standard Oil, came up with a solution, the "trust." Under the trust, the stockholders of corporations surrendered their shares "in trust" to a central board of directors with the power to control all property. In exchange, stockholders received certificates of trust that paid hefty dividends. Because it did not literally own other companies, the trust violated no state law.

In 1882 the Standard Oil Company of Ohio formed the country's first great trust. It brought Rockefeller what he sought so fiercely—centralized management of the oil industry. Other businesses soon created trusts of their own—in meatpacking, wire-making, and farm machinery, for example. Just as quickly, trusts became notorious for crushing rivals and fixing prices.

The Mergers of J. Pierpont Morgan

The trust was only a stepping-stone to an even more effective means of avoiding competition, managing people, and controlling business: the corporate merger. The idea of two corporations merging—one buying out or pooling with another—remained impossible until 1889, when New Jersey began to permit corporations to own other corporations.

In 1890, the need to find a substitute for the trust grew urgent. Congress outlawed trusts under the Sherman Antitrust Act (page 555). The Sherman Act specifically banned business from "restraining trade" by setting prices, dividing markets, or engaging in other unfair practices. The ever-inventive Samuel Dodd came up with a new idea, the "holding company," a corporation of corporations that had the power to hold shares of other companies. Many industries converted their trusts into holding companies, including Standard Oil, which moved to New Jersey in 1899.

The Holding Company

Two years later came the biggest corporate merger of the era, created by a financial wizard named J. Pierpont Morgan. His orderly mind detested the chaotic competition that threatened his profits. "I like a little competition," Morgan used to say, "but I like combination more." After the Civil War he had taken over his father's powerful investment bank. For the next 50 years, the House of Morgan played a part in consolidating almost every major industry in the country.

Morgan's greatest triumph came in steel, where for years Carnegie had refused to combine with rivals. In January 1901, with the threat of a colossal steel war looming,

Morgan convinced Carnegie to put a price tag on his company. When a messenger brought back the scrawled reply—more than $400 million—Morgan merely nodded and said, "I accept this price." He then bought Carnegie's eight largest competitors and announced the formation of the United States Steel Corporation.

U.S. Steel gobbled up more than 200 manufacturing and transportation companies, 1,000 miles of railways, and the whole Mesabi iron range of Minnesota. The mammoth holding company produced nearly two-thirds of all American steel. Its value of $1.4 billion exceeded the national debt and made it the country's first billion-dollar corporation.

The Merger Movement

What Morgan helped to create in steel was rapidly coming to pass in other industries. A wave of mergers swept through American business after the depression of 1893. As the economy plunged, cutthroat competition bled businesses until they were eager to sell out. Giants sprouted almost overnight. By 1904, in each of 50 industries one firm came to account for 60 percent or more of the total output.

Corporate Defenders

The Gospel of Wealth

As Andrew Carnegie's empire grew, his conscience turned troubled. Preaching a "gospel of wealth," he urged the rich to act as stewards for the poor, "doing for them better than they would or could do for themselves." He devoted his time to philanthropy by creating foundations and endowing libraries and universities with some $350 million in contributions.

Defenders of the new corporate order were less troubled than Carnegie was about the rough-and-tumble world of big business. They justified the system by stressing the opportunity created for individuals by economic growth. Through frugality, acquisitiveness, and discipline—the sources of cherished American individualism—anyone could rise, as did Andrew Carnegie.

Social Darwinism

When most ordinary citizens failed to follow in Carnegie's footsteps, defenders blamed the individual. Financial failures were lazy, ignorant, or morally depraved, they said. British philosopher Herbert Spencer added the weight of science by applying Charles Darwin's theories of evolution where naturalist Darwin had never intended—to society. Spencer maintained that in society, as in biology, only the "fittest" survived. The competitive social jungle doomed the unfit to poverty and rewarded the most fit with property and privilege.

Spencer's American apostle, William Graham Sumner, argued that competition was natural and had to proceed without any interference, including government regulation. Millionaires were simply the "product of natural selection." Such "social Darwinism" found strong support among turn-of-the-century business leaders. The philosophy of ruthless competition certified their success even as they worked to destroy the very competition it celebrated.

Corporate Critics

Andrew Carnegie invoked the gospel of wealth to justify his millions, but a group of radical critics looked on his libraries and foundations as desperate attempts to buy peace of mind. For all the contemporary celebrations of wealth and big business, they saw the new industrial order as exploitative, divisive, and immoral. It was built on the backs of ordinary "toilers," whose labors profited the few Carnegies of the world.

Henry George, a journalist and self-taught economist, began his critique with a simple question. How could poverty exist when industrial progress had created such wealth? George pointed to greedy landowners who bought property when it was cheap and then held it until the forces of society—labor, technology, and speculation on nearby sites—had increased its value. They reaped most of the rewards, despite the hard work of others. In his best-selling book *Progress and Poverty* (1879), George proposed a single tax on these "unearned" profits to end monopoly landholding. With all other taxes abolished, income would be slowly redistributed. "Single-tax" clubs sprang up throughout the country, and George nearly won the race for mayor of New York in 1886.

The journalist Edward Bellamy tapped the same popular resentment against the inequalities of industrial capitalism. In his best-selling novel *Looking Backward* (1888) Julian West, a fictional Bostonian, falls asleep in 1887 and awakens Rip Van Winkle–like in the year 2000. In place of the competitive, class-ridden society of the nineteenth century is an orderly utopia managed by a benevolent government trust. "Fraternal co-operation," shared abundance, and "nationalism," which puts the interests of the community above those of the individual, are the guiding principles. By 1892, Bellamy's philosophy had spawned over 160 clubs in 27 states with followers demanding redistribution of wealth, civil service reform, and nationalization of railroads and utilities.

DESIGN FOR A TABLET IN ANTIQUE BRASS TO BE PLACED IN THE CHICAGO UNIVERSITY

This drawing is from a 1905 edition of Collier's *magazine, famous for exposing corporate abuses. Here it mocks John D. Rockefeller, head of the Standard Oil Company, as the new God of the industrial age by parodying the Protestant doxology of thanks: "Praise God from whom all blessings flow, Praise him all creatures here below!"*

Less popular but equally hostile to capitalism was the Socialist Labor party, formed in 1877. Under Daniel De Leon, a West Indian immigrant, it stressed class conflict and called for a revolution to give workers control over production. De Leon refused to compromise his radical beliefs, and advocates of **socialism** ended up attracting more intellectuals than workers. Some immigrants found its class consciousness appealing, but most rejected its radicalism and rigidity. A few party members, bent on gaining greater support, revolted and in 1901 founded the more successful Socialist Party of America. Workers were beginning to organize their own responses to industrialism.

By the mid-1880s, in response to the growing criticism of big business, several states in the South and West enacted laws limiting the size of corporations. But these laws proved all too easy to evade when states such as New Jersey and Delaware eased their rules to allow corporations to grow nationwide.

In 1890, the public clamor against **trusts** finally forced Congress to act. The Sherman Antitrust Act relied on the only constitutional authority the federal government had over business: its right to regulate interstate commerce. The act outlawed "every contract, combination in the form of trust or otherwise, or conspiracy, in restraint of trade or commerce." The United States stood practically alone among industrialized nations in regulating such business combinations.

Its language was purposefully vague, but the Sherman Antitrust Act did give the government the power to break up trusts and other big businesses. So high was the regard for the rights of private property, however, that few in Congress expected the government to exercise that power or the courts to uphold it. They were right. Before 1901, the Justice Department filed only 14 antitrust suits against big businesses, virtually none of them successful. And in 1895, the Supreme Court dealt the law a major blow by severely limiting antitrust when it ruled against the government in its suit against the E. C. Knight Company, which controlled over 90 percent of sugar refining in the country. *United States v. E. C. Knight Co.* held that businesses involved in manufacturing (as

Socialist Labor Party

Sherman Antitrust Act

United States v. E. C. Knight Co.

Boom and Bust Business Cycle, 1865–1900
Between 1865 and 1900, industrialization produced great economic growth but also wild swings of prosperity and depression. During booms, productivity soared and near-full employment existed. But the rising number of industrial workers meant high unemployment during deep busts.

opposed to "trade or commerce") lay outside the authority of the Sherman Act. The ruling thus excluded most firms other than transportation companies that carried goods across state lines. Not until after the turn of the century would the law be used to bust a trust.

The Costs of Doing Business

The heated debates between the critics and defenders of industrial capitalism made clear that the changes in American society were two-edged. Big businesses certainly helped to order or rationalize production, increase national wealth, and tie the country together. Yet they also concentrated power, corrupted politics, and made the gap between rich and poor more apparent than ever. In 1890, the richest 9 percent of Americans held nearly three-quarters of all wealth in the United States. But by 1900, one American in eight (nearly 10 million people) lived below the poverty line.

The Boom-and-Bust Cycle

More to the point, the practices of big business subjected the economy to enormous disruptions. The banking system could not always keep pace with the demand for capital, and businesses failed to distribute enough profits to sustain the purchasing power of workers. The supply of goods periodically outstripped the demand for them, and then the wrenching cycle of boom and bust set in. Three severe depressions— 1873–1879, 1882–1885, and 1893–1897—rocked the economy in the last third of the nineteenth century. With hard times came fierce competition as managers searched frantically for ways to cut costs, and the industrial barons earned their reputations for ruthlessness.

The Workers' World

At seven in the morning, Sadie Frowne sat at her sewing machine in a Brooklyn garment factory. The boss, a man she barely knew, dropped a pile of unfinished skirts next to her. She pushed one under the needle and began to rock her foot quickly on the pedal that powered her machine. Sometimes Sadie pushed the fabric too hastily, and the needle pierced her finger. "The machines go like mad all day because the faster you work the more money you get," Sadie explained of the world of industrial work in 1902.

A sweatshop boss bellows at a seamstress.

The cramped sweatshops, the vast steel mills, the dank tunnels of the coal fields— all demanded workers and required them to work in new ways. Farmers or peasants who had once timed themselves by the movement of the sun now lived by the clock and labored in the twilight of gaslit factories. Instead of being self-employed, they had to deal with supervisors and were paid by the piece or hour. Not the seasons but the relentless cycle of machines set their pace. Increasingly, workers bore the brunt of depressions, faced periodic unemployment, and toiled under dangerous conditions as they struggled to bring the new industrial processes under their control.

Industrial Work

In 1881, the Pittsburgh Bessemer Steel Company opened its new mill in Homestead, Pennsylvania. Nearly 400 men and boys went to work in its 60 acres of sheds. They kept the mill going around the clock by working in two shifts: 12 hours a day the first week, 12 hours a night the next. In the furnace room, some men fainted from the heat, while the vibration and screeching of machinery deafened others. There were no breaks, even for lunch. "Home is just the place where I eat and sleep," said a steel-worker. "I live in the mills."

Few industrial workers labored under conditions quite so harsh, but the Homestead mill reflected the common characteristics of industrial work: the use of machines for mass production; the division of labor into intricately organized, menial tasks; and the dictatorship of the clock. At the turn of the century, two-thirds of all industrial work came from large-scale mills.

Pattern of Industrial Work

Under such conditions labor paid dearly for industrial progress. By 1900, most of those earning wages in industry worked 6 days a week, 10 hours a day. They held jobs that required more machines and fewer skills. Repetition of small chores replaced fine craftwork. In the 1880s, for example, almost all the 40 different steps that had gone into making a pair of shoes by hand could be performed by a novice, or "green hand," with a few days of instruction at a simple machine.

With machines also came danger. Tending furnaces in a steel mill or plucking to-bacco from cigarette-rolling machines was tedious. If a worker became bored or tired, disaster could strike. Each year from 1880 to 1900 industrial mishaps killed an average of 35,000 wage earners and injured over 500,000. Workers could expect no payment

Industrial Accidents

West Lynn Machine Shop
This machine tool shop in West Lynn, Massachusetts, photographed in the mid-1890s, suggests something of the growing scale of factory enterprise in the late nineteenth century—and also of the extraordinary dangers workers in these early manufacturing shops faced.

Workers fortunate enough to bring food used a "lunch pail" like the one at left.

from employers or the government for death or injury. Accidents were assumed to be workers' own fault.

Industrial workers rarely saw an owner. The foreman or supervisor exercised complete authority over the unskilled in his section, hiring and firing them, even setting their wages. Skilled workers had greater freedom, yet they too felt the pinch of technology and organization. By the 1880s, carpenters were finding that machine-made doors were replacing the ones they once constructed at the site. Painters no longer mixed their own paints. "I regard my people," said one manager, "as I regard my machinery. So long as they can do my work for what I choose to pay them, I keep getting out of them all I can."

Higher productivity and profits were the aims, and for Frederick W. Taylor, efficiency was the way to achieve them. During the 1870s and 1880s, Taylor undertook careful time-and-motion studies of workers' movements in the steel industry. He set up standard procedures and offered pay incentives for beating his production quotas. On one occasion, he designed 15 ore shovels, each for a separate task. One hundred forty men were soon doing the work of 600. By the early twentieth century "Taylorism" was a full-blown philosophy, complete with its own professional society.

Taylorism

For all the high ideals of Taylorism, ordinary laborers refused to perform as cogs in a vast industrial machine. In a variety of ways, they worked to maintain control. Many European immigrants continued to observe the numerous saints' days and other religious holidays of their homelands, regardless of factory rules. When the pressure of six-day weeks became too stifling, workers took an unauthorized "blue Monday" off. Or they slowed down to reduce the grueling pace. Or they simply walked off the job. Come spring and warm weather, factories reported turnover rates of 200 to 300 percent.

Worker Citizens

For some laborers, seizing control of work was more than a matter of survival or self-respect. Many workers regarded themselves as citizens of a democratic republic. They expected to earn a "competence"—enough money to support and educate their families and enough time to stay abreast of current affairs. Few but highly skilled workers could realize such democratic dreams. More and more, labor was being managed as another part of an integrated system of industry.

Children, Women, and African Americans

In the mines of Pennsylvania, nimble-fingered eight- and nine-year-olds snatched bits of slate from amid the chunks of coal. In Illinois glass factories, quick-footed "dog boys" dashed with trays of red-hot bottles to the cooling ovens. By 1900, the industrial labor force included some 1.7 million children, more than double the number 30 years earlier. Parents often had no choice. As one union leader observed, "Absolute necessity compels the father . . . to take the child into the mine to assist him in winning bread for the family." On average, children worked 60 hours a week and carried home paychecks a third the size of those of adult males.

Women had always labored on family farms, but by 1870 one in four nonagricultural workers was female. In general they earned one-half of what men did. Nearly all were single and young, anywhere from their mid-teens to their mid-20s. Most lived in boardinghouses or at home with their parents. Usually they contributed their wages to the family kitty. Once married, they took on a life of full-time housework and child rearing.

Only 5 percent of married women held jobs outside the home in 1900. Married black women (in need of income because of the low wages paid to their husbands) were four times more likely than married whites to work away from home. Domestic service was by far the most common occupation for these women. But industrialization inevitably pushed women into new jobs. Mainly they worked in industries considered extensions of housework: food processing, textiles and clothing, and cigar making. And many women actually preferred factory labor, with its long

Injured boy from the mills.

hours and dirty conditions, to being a live-in servant, where they were at work over six days a week and on call 24 hours a day.

New methods of management and marketing opened positions for white-collar women as "typewriters," "telephone girls," bookkeepers, and secretaries. On rare occasions women entered the professions, though law and medical schools still regarded them as unwelcome invaders. Such discrimination drove ambitious, educated women into nursing, teaching, and library work. Their growing presence soon "feminized" these professions, pushing men upward into managerial slots or out entirely.

Even more than women, African American men faced discrimination in the workplace. They were paid less than whites and given menial jobs. Their greatest opportunities in industry often came as strikebreakers to replace white workers. Once a strike ended, however, black workers were replaced and hated by the white regulars whose jobs they had taken. The service trades furnished the largest single source of jobs. Waiting on whites in restaurants or on railroads lay within the boundaries set by prevailing prejudice. Craftworkers and a sprinkling of black professionals could usually be found in cities. After the turn of the century, black-owned businesses thrived in the growing black neighborhoods of the North and South.

The American Dream of Success

Whatever their separate experiences, working-class Americans did improve their overall lot. Though the gap between the very rich and the poor widened, most wage earners made some gains. Between 1860 and 1890 real daily wages—pay in terms of buying power—climbed some 50 percent, more the result of gradually falling prices than of increases in pay. And after 1890, the number of hours on the job began a slow decline.

Yet most unskilled and semiskilled workers in factories continued to receive low pay. In 1890, an unskilled laborer could expect about $1.50 for a 10-hour day; a skilled one, perhaps twice that amount. It took about $600 to make ends meet, but most manufacturing workers made under $500 a year. Native-born white Americans tended to earn more than immigrants, those who spoke English more than those who did not, men more than women, and all others more than African Americans, Latinos, and Asians.

Rising Real Wages

Clerks' jobs, traditionally held by men, came to be filled by women as growing industrial networks created more managerial jobs for men. In this typical office, male managers literally oversee female clerks.

Social Mobility

Few workers repeated the rags-to-riches rise of Andrew Carnegie. But some did rise despite periodic unemployment and ruthless wage cuts. About one-quarter of the manual laborers in one study entered the lower middle class in their own lifetimes. More often such unskilled workers climbed in financial status within their own class. Most workers, seeing some improvement, believed in the American dream of success, even if they did not fully share in it.

The Systems of Labor

Putting in more hours to save a few pennies, walking out in exhaustion or disgust, slowing down on the job—in these ways individual workers coped with industrial America. Sporadic and unorganized, such actions stood little chance of bringing the new industrial order under the control of labor. For ordinary workers to begin to shape industrialization they had to combine, as businesses did. They needed to combine horizontally—organizing not just locally but on a national scale. And they needed to integrate vertically by coordinating action across a wide range of jobs and skills, as Andrew Carnegie coordinated the production of steel. Unions were the workers' systematic response to industrialization.

Early Unions

In the United States **unions** began forming before the Civil War. Skilled craftworkers—carpenters, iron molders, cigar makers—joined together to protect themselves against the growing power of management. Railroad "brotherhoods" also furnished insurance for those hurt or killed on the accident-plagued lines. Largely local and exclusively male, these early craft unions remained weak and unconnected to each other as well as to the growing mass of unskilled workers.

National Labor Union

After the Civil War, a group of craft unions, brotherhoods, and reformers united skilled and unskilled workers in a nationwide organization. The National Labor Union (NLU) hailed the virtues of a simpler America, when workers controlled their workday, earned a decent living, and had time to be good citizens. NLU leaders attacked the wage system as unfair and enslaving and urged workers to manage their own factories. By the early 1870s, NLU ranks had swelled to more than 600,000.

The NLU pressed energetically for the eight-hour workday, the most popular labor demand of the era. Workers saw it as a way not merely of limiting their time on the job but of limiting the power of employers over their lives. "Eight hours for work; eight hours for rest; eight hours for what we will!" proclaimed a banner at one labor rally. Despite the popularity of the issue, the NLU wilted during the depression of 1873.

The Knights of Labor

More successful was a national union born in secrecy. In 1869 Uriah Stephens and nine Philadelphia garment cutters founded the Noble and Holy Order of the Knights of Labor. They draped themselves in ritual and regalia to deepen their sense of solidarity and met in secret to evade hostile owners. The Knights remained small and fraternal for a decade. Their strongly Protestant tone repelled Catholics, who made up almost half the workforce in many industries.

Terence Powderly

In 1879 the Knights elected Terence V. Powderly as their Grand Master Workman. Handsome, dynamic, Irish, and Catholic, Powderly threw off the Knights' secrecy, dropped their rituals, and opened their ranks. He called for "one big union" to embrace the "toiling millions"—skilled and unskilled, men and women, natives and immigrants, all religions, all races. By 1886, membership had leaped to over 700,000, including nearly 30,000 African Americans and 3,000 women.

Like the NLU, the radical Knights of Labor looked to abolish the wage system. In its place they wanted to construct a cooperative economy of worker-owned mines, factories, and railroads. The Knights set up more than 140 cooperative workshops, where workers shared decisions and profits, and sponsored some 200 political candidates, who enjoyed only sporadic success. To tame the new industrial order, they supported the eight-hour workday and the regulation of trusts. Underlying this program was a moral vision of society. If people only renounced greed, laziness, and dishonesty, Powderly argued, corruption and class division would disappear, and democracy would flourish. To reform citizens, the Knights promoted the prohibition of child and convict labor and the abolition of liquor.

It was one thing to proclaim a national union, quite another to coordinate the activities of so many members. Powderly soon found locals resorting to strikes and violence, actions he condemned. In the mid-1880s, such stoppages wrung concessions from the western railroads, but the organization soon became associated with unsuccessful strikes and violent extremists. Even its impressive gains against railroads were wiped out when the Texas and Pacific Railroad broke a strike by local Knights. By 1890 the Knights of Labor, symbol of organized labor's resistance to industrial capitalism, teetered near extinction.

The American Federation of Labor

The Knights' position as the premier union in the nation was taken by the rival American Federation of Labor (AFL). The AFL reflected the practicality of its leader, Samuel Gompers. Born in a London tenement, the son of a Jewish cigar maker, Gompers had immigrated in 1863 with his family to New York's Lower East Side. Unlike the visionary Powderly, Gompers preached accommodation, not resistance. He urged his followers to accept capitalism and the wage system. What he wanted was "pure and simple unionism"—a worker organization that bargained for higher wages, fewer hours, improved safety, more benefits.

Samuel Gompers

Gompers chose to organize highly skilled craftworkers because they were difficult to replace. He bargained with employers and used strikes and boycotts only as last resorts. With the Cigar Makers' Union as his base, Gompers helped create the first national federation of craft unions in 1881. In 1886, it was reorganized as the American Federation of Labor. Twenty-five labor groups joined, representing nearly 140,000 skilled workers.

Here was labor's answer to the corporation and the trust: a horizontal organization trying to minimize competition among skilled workers. Gompers fought off radicals and allied himself with whatever candidate supported labor. Stressing gradual, concrete gains, he made the AFL the most powerful union in the country. By 1901 it had more than a million members, almost a third of all skilled workers in America.

Failure of Organized Labor

Despite the success of the AFL, the laboring classes did not organize themselves as systematically as did the barons of industrial America. For one thing, Gompers and the AFL were less interested in vertical integration that combined skilled and unskilled workers and had little inclination to include women and African Americans. For another, workers themselves were separated by language and culture, divided along lines of race and gender, and fearful of retaliation by management. A strong strain of individualism made many workers regard any collective action as un-American. And so they often resisted unionization. In 1900, union membership comprised less than 10 percent of industrial workers.

The Limits of Industrial Systems

It was the vagaries of the marketplace and stubbornness of owners that in the end broke the labor movement and set the limits of industrial systems for workers. As managers increased their control over the workplace, workers often found themselves at the mercy of the new industrial order. Even in boom times, one in three workers was out of a job at least three or four months a year. The word *unemployment* dates from the late nineteenth century.

In this painting by Robert Koehler, entitled The Strike *(1886), labor confronts management in a strike that may soon turn bloody. One worker reaches for a stone as an anxious mother and her children look on.*

Spontaneous Protests

When a worker's pay dropped and frustration mounted, when a mother worked all night and fell asleep during the day while caring for her children, when food prices suddenly jumped—anger might boil over into protest. "A mob of 1,000 people, with women in the lead, marched through the Jewish quarter of Williamsburg last evening and wrecked half a dozen butcher shops," reported the *New York Times* in 1902. In the late nineteenth century a wave of labor activism swept the nation. More often than mobs, it was strikes and boycotts that challenged the authority of employers and gave evidence of working-class identity and discontent.

Most strikes broke out spontaneously, organized by informal leaders in a factory. "Malvina Fourtune and her brother Henry Fourtune it was them who started the strike," declared a company informer in Chicopee, Massachusetts. "They go from house to house and tells the people to keep up the strike." Thousands of rallies and organized strikes were staged as well, often on behalf of the eight-hour workday, in good times and bad, by union and nonunion workers alike.

Molly Maguires

Some workers resorted to terrorism to resist the new industrial order. In the coalfields of Pennsylvania, Irish miners organized a secret society called the Molly Maguires, named for an earlier group of protesters in Ireland who had disguised themselves as women and roamed the Irish countryside beating and sometimes killing tyrannical landlords. The American Mollys founded their society in 1866. For the next decade the small but dedicated band resorted to intimidation, arson, and murder to combat the horrid working conditions of coal miners. In 1876, 20 Mollys were brought to trial and a year later executed for 16 murders. For most Americans, justice was served, despite the questionable legality of the trial—and in its wake, the secret society vanished. But for those who had joined the Mollys, violence was a long-established tradition, imported from Ireland and employed as both a form of protest and a means of achieving "retributive justice" against oppressors.

Great Railroad Strike

In 1877, in the midst of a deep depression, the country's first nationwide strike opened an era of confrontation between labor and management. When the Baltimore and Ohio Railroad cut wages by 20 percent, a crew in Martinsburg, West Virginia, seized the local depot and blocked the line. President Hayes sent federal troops to enforce a court order ending the strike, but instead two-thirds of the nation's tracks were shut down in sympathy. The novel tactic suggested a growing sense of solidarity among workers. The country ground to a halt.

When owners brought in strikebreakers, workers torched rail yards, smashed engines and cars, and tore up track. Local police, state militia, and federal troops finally quashed the strike after 12 bloody days. The "Great Railroad Strike" of 1877 left 100 people dead and more than $10 million worth of railroad property in rubble. It signaled the rising power and unity of labor and sparked fears, as one newspaper warned, that "this may be the beginning of a great civil war in this country, between labor and capital."

Molly Maguires warning note: ". . . if you don't leave this place right away, you will be a dead man."

The Civil War between North and South was still fresh in the minds of Atlantans when 3,000 laundresses struck for higher wages in 1881. Over 98 percent of the city's domestic workers were black women, just a decade and a half out of slavery. Pitiful wages already had led many of them to employ informal strategies to protest. They took unauthorized breaks, pretended to be sick, or "pantoted" (stole) leftovers from the kitchens of their white employers. Washerwomen were among the most privileged domestics because they neither worked nor lived with their employers. Instead they labored together in common spaces in their neighborhoods, where they built social and political networks. In 1881 they formed the Washing Society and threatened to leave much of the city without clean clothes unless their demands for higher wages were met. Though little resulted from the strike, it nonetheless showed the growing appeal of organized protest against economic inequality and laid the groundwork for later civil rights protests.

Laundresses Strike

In 1886, tension between labor and capital exploded in the "Great Upheaval"—a series of strikes, boycotts, and rallies. One of the most violent episodes occurred at Haymarket Square in Chicago. A group of anarchists was protesting the recent killing of workers by police at the McCormick Harvester Company. As rain drenched the small crowd, police ordered everyone out of the square. Suddenly a bomb exploded. One officer was killed; 6 others were mortally wounded. Armed with billy clubs and pistols, police opened fire. The crowd fired back. Nearly 70 policemen were injured, and at least 4 civilians died.

Haymarket Square Riot

Conservatives charged that radicals were responsible for the "Haymarket Massacre." Though the bomb thrower was never identified and no evidence connecting the accused to the bombing was ever presented, a jury found eight anarchists guilty of conspiracy to commit murder. Four were hanged, one killed himself, and three remained in jail until they were pardoned by Governor John Peter Altgeld in 1893. He considered their conviction a miscarriage of justice, but ordinary citizens who had supported labor grew fearful of what newspapers called its "Samson-like power." Cities enlarged their police forces, and states built more National Guard armories on the borders of working-class neighborhoods.

Management Strikes

The strikes, rallies, and boycotts of 1886 were followed by a second surge of labor activism in 1892. In the remote silver mines of Coeur d'Alene, Idaho, at the Carnegie

Government troops were often called in to help management quell strikes. In the Pullman Strike of 1894, U.S. Regulars "give the butt" to angry laborers in this drawing by Frederick Remington.

"GIVING THE BUTT"—THE WAY THE "REGULAR" INFANTRY TACKLES A MOB.

steel mill in Homestead, Pennsylvania, in the coal mines near Tracy City, Tennessee, strikes flared, only to be crushed by management. Often state and federal troops joined company guards and private detectives from the Pinkerton agency to fight workers.

The broadest confrontation between labor and management took place two years later. A terrible depression had shaken the economy for almost a year when George Pullman, owner of the Palace Car factory and inventor of the plush railroad car, laid off workers, cut wages (but kept rents high on company-owned housing), and refused to discuss grievances. In 1894 workers struck and managed to convince the new American Railway Union to support them by boycotting all trains that used Pullman cars. Quickly the strike spread to 27 states and territories.

Anxious railroad owners appealed to President Grover Cleveland for federal help. On the slim pretext that the strike obstructed mail delivery (strikers had actually been willing to handle mail trains without Pullman cars), Cleveland secured a court order halting the strike. He then called several thousand special deputies into Chicago to enforce it. In the rioting that followed, 12 people died and scores were arrested. But the strike was crushed.

Management Weapons

In all labor disputes the central issue was the power to shape the new industrial systems. Employers always enjoyed the advantage. They hired and fired workers, set the terms of employment, and ruled the workplace. They fought unions with "yellow dog" contracts that forced workers to refuse to join. Blacklists circulated the names of labor agitators. Lockouts kept protesting workers from plants, and company spies infiltrated their organizations. With a growing pool of labor, employers could replace strikers and break strikes.

Management could also count on local, state, and federal authorities for troops to break strikes. In addition, businesses used a powerful new legal weapon, the **injunction.** These court orders prohibited certain actions, including strikes, by barring workers from interfering with their employer's business.

It was just such an order that had brought federal deputies into the Pullman strike and put Eugene Debs, head of the American Railway Union, behind bars. The Indiana-born Debs, a former locomotive fireman and early labor organizer, received a six-month jail sentence for violating the court injunction. After his release, he abandoned the Democratic party to become the foremost Socialist leader in America.

Pullman Strike

In a matter of only 30 or 40 years, the new industrial order transformed the landscape of America. It left its mark elsewhere in the world, too. British railroad mileage grew to some 20,000 miles by the 1870s, while Germany and France built even larger systems. Japan began constructing its network in the 1870s, at first with the help of hundreds of engineers from the United States and Great Britain and in the 1880s with newly trained Japanese engineers. Other nonindustrial countries followed, especially those rich in raw materials and agricultural commodities, such as South Africa, Mexico, Argentina, and Egypt. In India, the British built the fourth-longest railway system in the world. None outstripped the United States, however. By 1915, its rail network was longer than the next seven largest systems combined.

With remarkable speed, global networks of communication and transportation were set into place. Underwater telegraph cables were laid from the United States to Europe in 1866, to Australia in 1871 and 1872, to Latin America in 1872 and 1873, and to West Africa by 1886. The completion of the Suez Canal in 1869 (the same year a golden spike connected the last link in the transcontinental railroad) hastened the switch from sail-power to steam-driven ships, by slicing thousands of miles from the journey between Europe and Asia. By the dawn of the new century the average size of steam freighters had jumped to 7,500 tons, up from only 200 tons in 1850. Wheat from the United States and India, wool from Australia, and beef from Argentina poured into Europe, while Europe sent textiles, railroad equipment, coal, and machinery to Asia and the Americas.

Such changes might have seemed effortless to someone such as T. S. Hudson, scampering across the rails of America in 1882. But as these networks tied together national economies, swings in the business cycle produced global consequences. When an Austrian bank failed in 1873, depression soon reached the United States. In the mid-1880s and again in the mid-1890s, recessions drove prices down and unemployment up all across the industrialized world. Industrial workers bore the brunt of the burden, but in Europe they had greater success in unionizing, especially after anticombination laws forbidding strikes were abolished in the decades following 1850. By 1900 British unions had signed up 2 million workers, twice the number of members in either the United States or Germany. As strikes became more common and labor unions more powerful, industrializing nations passed social legislation that included the first social security systems and health insurance. Despite such laws, in the new industrial order material progress walked hand in hand with social pain and upheaval.

Significant Events

1859	First oil well drilled near Titusville, Pennsylvania
1866	National Labor Union founded
1869	Knights of Labor created
1870	John D. Rockefeller incorporates Standard Oil Company of Ohio
1873	Carnegie Steel Company founded; Panic of 1873

1874	Massachusetts enacts first 10-hour workday law for women
1876	Alexander Graham Bell invents telephone
1877	Railroad wage cuts lead to violent strikes
1879	Edison develops incandescent light bulb; Henry George's *Progress and Poverty* published
1882	Rockefeller's Standard Oil Company becomes nation's first trust
1883	Railroads establish standard time zones
1886	American Federation of Labor organized; Haymarket Square bombing
1892	Homestead Steel stike; General Electric opens first research and development department
1894	Pullman strike
1901	U.S. Steel Corporation becomes nation's first billion-dollar company

Chapter Summary

In the last third of the nineteenth century, a new industrial order reshaped the United States.

- New systems—of resource development, technology, invention, transportation, communications, finance, corporate management, and labor—boosted industrial growth and productivity.

- Businesses grew big, expanding vertically and horizontally to curb costs and competition and to increase control and efficiency.

- Industrialization came at a price.

  —Workers found their power, job satisfaction, and free time reduced as their numbers in factories mushroomed.
  —The environment was degraded.
  —A vicious cycle of boom and bust afflicted the economy.

- Workers both resisted and accommodated the new industrial order.

  —Some resisted through informal mechanisms such as slowdowns, absenteeism, and quitting and through spontaneous and more formal ones, including radical unions like the Knights of Labor.
  —Other workers were more accommodating, accepting low-paying jobs and layoffs and creating "pure-and-simple" unions, such as the American Federation of Labor, that accepted the prevailing system of private ownership and wage labor while bargaining for better wages and working conditions.

- The benefits of industrialization were equally undeniable.

  —Life improved materially for many Americans.
  —The real wages of even industrial workers climbed.

- The United States rocketed from fourth place among industrial nations in 1860 to first by 1890.

Additional Reading

For a useful introduction to the period, see Edward C. Kirkland, *Industry Comes of Age: Business, Labor, and Public Policy, 1860–1897* (1967). Mechanization and its impact are the focus of Siegfried Giedion's classic *Mechanization Takes Command* (1948). The best overview of American labor is American Social History Project, *Who Built America? Working People and the Nation's Economy, Politics, Culture, & Society,* Volume Two: *From the Gilded Age to the Present* (1992). Herbert Gutman, *Work, Culture, and Society in Industrializing America: Essays in American Working-Class History* (1976), explores the development of working-class communities in the nineteenth century, especially the role of ethnicity in creating a working-class culture. David Montgomery offers a broad look at the impact of industrialization on American labor in *The Fall of the House of Labor: The Workplace, the State, and American Labor Activism, 1865–1925* (1987), and Leon Fink, *Workingmen's Democracy: The Knights of Labor and American Politics* (1983), examines early efforts of the Knights of Labor to challenge corporate capitalism by organizing workers and socializing them into a labor culture. Alice Kessler-Harris, *Out to Work: A History of Wage-Earning Women in the United States* (1982), surveys female wage earners and their effect on American culture, family life, and values. Kevin Kenny, *Making Sense of the Molly Maguires* (1998), is a superb study not only of the mysterious Mollys and their tragic end but of immigration, working-class violence, and the history of the Irish in America.

No book did more to set the idea of big business as ruthless robber barons than Matthew Josephson, *The Robber Barons: The Great American Capitalists, 1861–1901* (1934). Ron Chernow's *Titan: The Life of John D. Rockefeller, Sr.* (1998) and Jean Strouse's definitive *Morgan: American Financier* (1999) help to debunk the image of business leaders as "Robber Barons," without minimizing their ruthlessness. David Nasaw's *Andrew Carnegie* (2006) gives us the most human portrait of the legendary steel baron. Business historian Alfred D. Chandler Jr.'s *Strategy and Structure: Chapters in the History of American Industrial Enterprise* (1962) and *The Visible Hand: The Managerial Revolution in American Business* (1977) are seminal accounts of business organization and management that stress the adaptations of business structures and the emergence of a new class of managers. For a comparative view of the rise of big business in the United States, Great Britain, and Germany, see his *Scale and Scope* (1988).

For a fuller list of readings, see the Bibliography at www.mhhe.com/davidsonnation6.

CHAPTER 20
The Rise of an Urban Order
1870~1914

THE CITY OF NEW YORK.

NEW YORK, PUBLISHED BY CURRIER & IVES, 115 NASSAU ST.

A Day in the Life of Boss Plunkitt

Graziano's bootblack stand was jammed with people milling about, looking for help. Above the crowd, enthroned like an Irish king, sat George Washington Plunkitt, ward boss of Manhattan's Fifteenth Assembly District. There to help, Plunkitt asked little in return, only votes on election day. Plunkitt understood the close relationship between help and votes. "There's got to be in every ward," another boss explained, "somebody that any bloke can come to—no matter what he's done—and get help. *Help, you understand; none of your law and justice, but help.*" Plunkitt knew the reverse to be true as well: to maintain power, political bosses had to be able to count on the support of those they helped.

For years Plunkitt had been a leader of Tammany Hall, the Democratic party organization that ruled New York City politics from 1850 to 1930. Much of Plunkitt's daily routine was taken up with helping. One typical day began when a bartender roused him at two in the morning to get a friend out of jail. Plunkitt succeeded but didn't return to bed until after three. Howling fire sirens woke him at six. Before dawn he was assisting burned-out tenants with food, clothing, and shelter. Only at midnight did he crawl into bed, after a day of helping all he could.

Such relentless effort helped Plunkitt as well. Born poor to Irish immigrants, he died a millionaire in 1924. His pluck and practicality would have made him the envy of any industrialist. As with the Carnegies and Rockefellers, fierce ambition fueled his rise from butcher boy to political boss. City politics was his way out of the slums in a world that favored the rich, the educated, and the well-established.

In the late nineteenth century the needs of rapidly growing cities gave political bosses such as George Washington Plunkitt their chance. "I seen my opportunities and I took 'em," Plunkitt used to say. Every city contract and bond issue, every tax assessment, every charter for a new business offered Plunkitt and his cronies an opportunity to line their pockets. Money made from defrauding the public was known as "boodle," or honest graft. ("Black" graft came from vice and extortion.) How much boodle bosses collected depended on how well their organization managed to elect sympathetic officials. That explained why Plunkitt spent so much time helping his constituents.

This bird's-eye view of New York City by printmakers Nathaniel Currier (1813–1888) and James Merritt Ives (1824–1895) was published in 1876. It shows several points of interest including what was then called "the New York and Brooklyn Bridge" linking Manhattan and Long Island. The Brooklyn Bridge was still being built in 1876 but is seen here as completed on the right-hand side of the map.

Realist painters like George Bellows, who were scorned by critics as the "Ashcan School," captured the grittiness and vibrancy of teeming urban life. Cliff Dwellers *makes dramatic use of light and shadow, relying on line, mass, and color to achieve its naturalism.*

Plunkitt's New York was the first great city in history to be ruled by ordinary people in an organized and continuing way. Bosses and their cronies came from the streets and saloons, the slums and tenements, the firehouses and funeral homes. Many of their families had only recently arrived in America. While the Irish of Tammany Hall ran New York, Germans governed St. Louis, Scandinavians Minneapolis, and Jews San Francisco.

In an earlier age political leadership had been drawn from the ranks of the wealthy and native-born. America had been an agrarian republic where personal relationships were grounded in small communities. By the late nineteenth century, the country was in the midst of an urban explosion. Industrial cities of unparalleled size and diversity were transforming American life. They lured people from all over the globe, created tensions between natives and newcomers, reshaped the social order. For Plunkitt, as for so many Americans, a new urban age was dawning. The golden door of opportunity opened onto the city.

A New Urban Age

The modern city was the product of industrialization. Cities contained the great investment banks, the smoky mills and dingy sweatshops, the spreading railroad yards, the grimy tenements and sparkling mansions, the new department stores and skyscrapers. People came from places as near as the countryside and as far as Russia, Armenia, China, and Japan. By the end of the nineteenth century America had entered a new urban age, with tens of millions of "urbanites," an urban landscape, and a growing urban culture.

The Urban Explosion

During the 50 years after the Civil War, the population of the United States nearly tripled—from roughly 33 million to 92 million. Yet the number of people living in American cities increased nearly sevenfold. In 1860, only one American in six lived in a city with a population of 8,000 or more; in 1900, one in three did. By 1910 nearly half the nation lived in cities large and small.

Cities grew in every region of the country, some faster than others. In the Northeast and upper Midwest early industrialization created more cities than in the West and the South, although those regions contained big cities as well. Atlanta, Nashville, and later Dallas and Houston boomed under the influence of railroads. Los Angeles had barely 6,000 people in 1870; by 1900, with a population of 100,000, it trailed only San Francisco among large cities on the Pacific coast.

Large urban centers dominated whole regions and tied the country together in a complex urban network. New York, the nation's banker, printer, and chief marketplace, ruled the East. Smaller cities operated within narrower spheres of influence and often specialized. Milwaukee was famous for its beer, Tulsa for oil, and Hershey, Pennsylvania, for chocolate.

Cities even shaped the natural environment hundreds of miles beyond their limits. Chicago became not only the gateway to the West but also a powerful agent of ecological change. As its lines of commerce and industry radiated outward, the city transformed the ecosystems of the West. Wheat to feed Chicago's millions replaced sheltering prairie grasses. Great stands of white pine in Wisconsin vanished, only to reappear in the furniture and frames of Chicago houses or as fence rails shipped to prairie farms.

Ecological Impact on the Regions around Them

The Great Global Migration

Between 1820 and 1920, some 60 million people left farms and villages for cities across the globe. They formed part of a migrating pool of labor, moving from country to country in search of work. Beginning in the 1870s, the use of oceangoing, steam-powered ships made it possible for migrating laborers to seek work across continents.

Several factors conspired to push people out of Europe. Mushrooming populations, aided by scientific breakthroughs and advances in technology, gave the emigrants a powerful push out. The end of the Napoleonic Wars in 1815 launched a cycle of baby booms that continued at 20-year intervals for the rest of the century. Improved diet and sanitation, aided by Louis Pasteur's discovery that bacteria cause infection and disease, reduced deaths. Meanwhile machinery cut the need for farm workers. In 1896 one man in a wheat field could do what had taken 18 men just 60 years earlier. Surplus farm workers formed a ragtag army of migrants both in America and in Europe.

Push and Pull Factors

Other factors pulled immigrants to industrialized countries, including the United States. The prospect of factory work for better pay and fewer hours lured especially the young to cities. Labor agents combed Europe, pulling immigrants to the United States with often false promises of high-paying jobs and unimagined riches. "They told me that in America the streets were paved with gold," reported one immigrant. "When I got here, I found the streets were not paved with gold, they were not paved at all, and they expected me to pave them." In America, young farm women spearheaded the migration. Mechanization and the rise of commercial agriculture made them less valuable in the fields, while mass-produced goods from mail-order houses made them less useful at home.

Asia sent comparatively fewer newcomers to the United States, Canada, and other industrializing nations hungry for workers, but Asian immigrants followed migration patterns similar to those of the workers leaving Europe and for similar reasons. In China, for example, several factors combined to push some 370,000 people out of the country and into the United States and Hawaii between 1850 and 1882. Defeats in the Opium Wars (1839–1842) and the Anglo-Chinese War (1856–1860) forced the Chinese to pay large **indemnities** to Great Britain and to limit the duties charged on foreign imports.

Chinese Immigrants

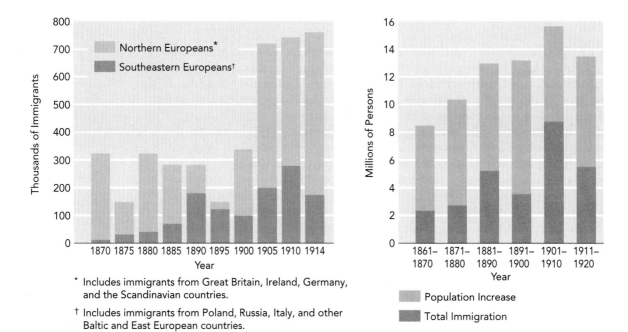

Immigration and Population, 1860–1920   *Between 1860 and 1920, immigration increased dramatically as the sources of immigrants shifted from northern Europe to southeastern Europe. Despite fears to the contrary, the proportion of newcomers as a percentage of population increases did not show nearly the same jump.*

When the Chinese government raised taxes to make up the difference, small landowners unable to afford them lost their farms, tenants unable to pay higher rents lost their plots, and peasants who had turned their homes into centers of small industry lost income. They simply could not compete with the now-cheaper manufactured goods from the West. In Japan and other Asian nations, similar forces of push and pull sparked migration into the United States, including some 400,000 Japanese between 1885 and 1924.

The "New" Immigration   Earlier in the century, European immigrants had come to the United States from northern and western Europe. In the 1880s, **"new" immigrants** from southern and eastern Europe began to arrive. Some, like Russian and Polish Jews, were fleeing religious and political persecution. Others left to evade famine or diseases such as cholera, which swept across southern Italy in 1887. But most came for the same reasons as migrants from the countryside—a job, more money, a fresh start.

Ambitious, hardy, and resourceful, immigrants found themselves tested every step of the way to America. They left behind the comfort of family, friends, and old ways. The price of one-way passage by steamship—about $50 in 1904—was far too expensive for most to bring relatives, at least at first. And the trip was dangerous even before immigrants stepped on board a ship. They traveled for weeks, stealing across heavily guarded borders, just to reach a port such as Le Havre in France.

It took one to two weeks to cross the Atlantic aboard steam-powered ships. Immigrants spent most of the time belowdecks in cramped, filthy compartments called **steerage.** Most arrived at New York's Castle Garden or the newer facility on nearby Ellis Island, opened in 1892. If coming from Asia, they landed at Angel Island in San Francisco Bay. Sometimes they were held in the facility for weeks. As one Chinese newcomer gazed out on San Francisco Bay, he scribbled a poem on the gray walls:

> Why do I have to languish in this jail?
> It is because my country is weak and my family poor.
> My parents wait in vain for news;
> My wife and child, wrapped in their quilt, sigh with loneliness.

By the 1890s, a flood of Southern and Eastern European immigrants were streaming into the new receiving centre of Ellis Island in New York harbor, while the relatively fewer Asian immigrants who arrived (most were barred from entry by the Chinese Exclusion Act of 1882) came through Angel Island in San Francisco Bay. The rapid rise in immigration ignited nativist fears that immigrants were taking over the country. In the 1870s cartoon pictured here, Irish and Chinese immigrants in their native dress literally gobble up Uncle Sam.

Immigrants then had to pass a medical examination, have their names recorded by customs officials, and pay an entry tax. At any point, they could be detained or shipped home.

Immigrants arrived in staggering numbers—over 6 million between 1877 and 1890, some 30 million by 1920. By 1900 they made up nearly 15 percent of the population. Most were young, between the ages of 15 and 40. Few spoke English or had skills or much education. Unlike earlier arrivals, who were mostly Protestant, these new immigrants worshiped in Catholic, Greek, or Russian Orthodox churches and Jewish synagogues. Almost two-thirds were men. A large number came to make money for buying land or starting businesses back home. Some changed their minds and sent for relatives, but those returning were common enough to be labeled "birds of passage."

Jews were an exception. Russian Jews escaped from Europe by the tens of thousands after the assassination of Czar Alexander II in 1881 rekindled anti-Semitic "pogroms," or riots. Between 1880 and 1914, a third of eastern Europe's Jews left. They made up 10 percent of all immigration to the United States during those years. Almost all stayed and brought their families, often one by one. They had few choices. As one Jewish immigrant wrote of his Russian homeland, "Am I not despised? Am I not urged to leave? . . . Do I not rise daily with the fear lest the hungry mob attack me?"

Immigrant Profile

Chin Shee was 21-years-old and bound for San Francisco at the time this boarding pass was issued in Hong Kong in 1911.

The Shape of the City

In colonial days, Benjamin Franklin could walk from one end of Boston to the other in an hour. Only Franklin's adopted home, Philadelphia, spilled into suburbs. Over

Growth of New Orleans to 1900   *Streetcars helped cities spread beyond business districts while still functioning as organic wholes. By 1900, streetcar lines in New Orleans reached all the way to Audubon Park and Tulane University, bringing these once-distant points within the reach of city dwellers and creating "streetcar suburbs."*

Patterns of Settlement

the years these colonial "walking cities" developed ringed patterns of settlement. Merchants, professionals, and the upper classes lived near their shops and offices in the city center. As one walked outward, the income and status of the residents declined.

Cities of the late nineteenth century still exhibited this ringed pattern, except that industrialization had reversed the order of settlement and increased urban sprawl. As the middle and upper classes moved out of a growing industrial core, the poor, some immigrants, African Americans, and lower-class laborers filled the void. They took over old factories and brownstones, shanties and cellars. By sheer weight of numbers they transformed these areas into the slums of the central city.

Curled around the slums was the "zone of emergence," an income-graded band of those "emerging" from poverty. It contained second-generation city dwellers, factory workers, skilled laborers, and professional mechanics. They lived in progressively better tenements and neater row houses as the distance from center city increased. Poverty no longer imprisoned them, but they could still slip back in hard times.

Farther out was the suburban fringe, home to the new class of white-collar managers and executives. They lived in larger houses with individual lots on neat, tree-lined streets. The very wealthy still maintained mansions on fashionable city avenues, but by the 1870s and 1880s, they too began to keep suburban homes.

Urban Transport

For all their differences, the circles of settlement held together as a part of a massive and interdependent whole. One reason was an evolving system of urban transportation. Civic leaders came to understand that the modern city could not survive, much less grow, without improved transportation. San Francisco installed trolley cars pulled by steam-driven cables. It worked so well in San Francisco that Chicago, Seattle, and other hilly cities installed cable systems in the 1880s. Some cities experimented with elevated trestles to carry steam locomotives; others, with cable lines high above crowded streets. But none of the breakthroughs quite did the trick. Cables remained slow and unreliable; the elevated railways, or "els," were dirty, ugly, and noisy.

Electricity rescued city travelers. In 1888 Frank Julian Sprague, a naval engineer who had once worked for Thomas Edison, installed the first electric trolley line in Richmond, Virginia. Electrified streetcars were soon speeding along at 12 miles an hour, twice as fast as horses. By 1902 electricity drove nearly all city railways.

Role of Electricity

Sprague's innovations also meant that "subways" could be built without having to worry about tunnels filled with a steam engine's smoke and soot. Between 1895 and 1897 Boston built the first underground electric line. New York followed in 1904 with a subway that ran from City Hall on the southern tip of Manhattan north to Harlem. Once considered too far afield, Harlem soon became dotted with new apartment and tenement developments. When the white middle class of New York refused to move so far uptown, Philip A. Peyton convinced landlords to allow his Afro-American Realty Company to handle the properties. Within a decade Harlem had become the black capital of America.

The rich had long been able to keep homes outside city limits, traveling to and fro in private carriages. New systems of mass transit freed the middle class and even the poor to live miles from work. For a nickel or two, anyone could ride from central shopping and business districts to the suburban fringes and back. A network of moving vehicles held the segmented and sprawling city together and widened its reach out to "streetcar suburbs."

Bridges and Skyscrapers

Because cities often grew along rivers and harbors, their separate parts sometimes had to be joined over water. The principles of building large river bridges had already been worked out by the railroads. It remained for a German immigrant and his son, John and Washington Roebling, to make the bridge a symbol of urban growth.

The Brooklyn Bridge, linking New York City with Brooklyn, took 13 years to complete. It cost $15 million and 20 lives, including that of designer John. When it opened in 1883, it stretched more than a mile across the East River, with passage broad enough for a footpath, two double carriage lanes, and two railroad lines. Its arches were cut like giant cathedral windows, and its supporting cables hung, said an awestruck observer, "like divine messages from above." Soon other suspension bridges were spanning the railroad yards in St. Louis and the bay at Galveston, Texas.

Even as late as 1880 church steeples dominated the urban landscape. They towered over squat factories and office buildings. But growing congestion and the increasing value of land pushed architects to search for ways to make buildings taller. In place of thick walls of brick that restricted factory floor space, builders used cast iron columns. The new "cloudscrapers" were strong, durable, and fire-resistant. Their open floors were ideal for warehouses and also for office buildings and department stores.

Steel, tougher in tension and compression, turned cloudscrapers into skyscrapers. William LeBaron Jenney first used steel in his 10-story Home Insurance Building (1885) in Chicago. By the end of the century steel frames and girders raised buildings to 30 stories or more. New York City's triangular Flatiron building

Flatiron Building, New York City

(at right), named for its shape, used the new technology to project an angular yet remarkably delicate elegance. In Chicago, Daniel Burnham's Reliance Building (1890) relied so heavily on new plate glass windows that contemporaries called it "a glass tower fifteen stories high."

It was no accident that many of the new skyscrapers arose in Chicago, for the city had burned nearly to the ground in 1871. The "Chicago school" of architects helped rebuild it. The young maverick Louis H. Sullivan promised a new urban profile in which the skyscraper would be "every inch a proud and soaring thing." In the Wainwright Building (1890) in St. Louis and the Carson, Pirie, and Scott department store (1889–1904) in Chicago, Sullivan produced towering structures that symbolized the modern industrial city.

Architects did not create the towering landscapes of modern industrial cities without help. Soaring skyscrapers were of little value without an efficient, safe means of transporting people aloft. In 1861, Elisha Graves Otis developed a trustworthy, fast elevator. By the 1890s, new electric elevators were whisking people to the tops of towering buildings in seconds. The elevator extended the city upward, just as the streetcar extended it outward, and in the process both transformed the physical and social space of urban America.

Slum and Tenement

Far below the skyscrapers lay the slums and tenements of the inner city. In cramped rooms and sunless hallways, along narrow alleys and in flooded basements lived the city's poor. They often worked there, too, in "sweaters' shops" where as many as 18 people labored and slept in foul two-room flats.

In New York, whose slums were the nation's worst, crime thrived in places called "Bandit's Roost" and "Hell's Kitchen." Bands of young toughs with names like the

Perils of the Slum Neighborhood

"Dumbbell" tenements were designed to use every inch of available space in the standard 25-by-200-foot city lot while providing ventilation and reducing the spread of disease.

"Sewer Rats" and the "Rock Gang" stalked the streets in search of thrills and easy money. Gambling, prostitution, and alcoholism all claimed their victims most readily in the slums. The poor usually turned to such crime in despair. A 20-year-old prostitute supporting a sickly mother and four brothers and sisters made no apologies: "Let God Almighty judge who's to blame most, I that was driven, or them that drove me to the pass I'm in."

The poor diets of slum dwellers left them vulnerable to disease, but it was their close quarters and often filthy surroundings that raised their rates of infection to epidemic levels. Cholera, typhoid, and an outbreak of yellow fever in Memphis in the 1870s killed tens of thousands. Tuberculosis was deadlier still. As late as 1900, among infectious diseases it ranked behind only influenza and pneumonia *combined* as a killer. Slum children—all city children—were most vulnerable. Almost a quarter of children born in American cities in 1890 never lived to see their first birthday.

The installation of new sewage and water purification systems helped. The modern flush toilet came into use only after the turn of the century. Until then people relied on water closets and communal privies. Some catered to as many as 800. All too often cities dumped waste into old private vaults or rivers used for drinking water. In 1881 an exasperated mayor of Cleveland called the Cuyahoga River "an open sewer through the center of the city."

Slum housing was often more dangerous than the water. The tubercle bacillus flourished in musty, windowless tenements. In 1879 New York enacted a new housing law requiring a window in all bedrooms of new **tenements.** Architect James E. Ware won a competition with a design that contained an indentation on both sides of the building. When two tenements abutted each other, the indentations formed a narrow shaft for air and light. From above, the buildings looked like giant dumbbells. Up to 16 families lived on a floor, with only two toilets in the hall.

Originally hailed as an innovation, Ware's dumbbell tenement spread over such cities as Cleveland, Cincinnati, and Boston "like a scab," said an unhappy reformer. Ordinary blocks contained 10 such tenements and housed as many as 4,000 people. The airshafts became giant silos for trash. They blocked what little light had entered and, worse still, carried fires from one story to the next. When the New York housing commission met in 1900, it concluded that conditions were worse than when reformers had started 33 years earlier.

Running and Reforming the City

Every new arrival to the city brought dreams and altogether too many needs. Schools and houses had to be built, streets paved, garbage collected, sewers dug, fires fought, utility lines laid. Running the city became a full-time job, and a new breed of professional politician rose to the task. So, too, did a new breed of reformer, determined to help the needy cope with the ravages of urban life.

Weaknesses of City Governments

The need for change was clear. Many city charters dating from the eighteenth century included a cumbersome system of checks and balances. Mayors vetoed city councils; councils ignored mayors. Jealous state legislatures allowed cities only the most limited and unpopular taxes, such as those on property. But to the cities more than the states fell responsibility for providing services. Municipal government grew into a tangle of little governments—fragmented, scattered, at odds with one another. By 1890, Chicago had 11 branches of government, each with its own regulations and taxing authority. Just as such decentralization paralyzed city governments, the traditional sources of political leadership evaporated. The middle and upper classes were being drawn into business and moving to the suburbs. As immigrants and rural newcomers flocked to factories and tenements, the structures of urban government strained to adapt.

Boss Rule

"Why must there be a boss," journalist Lincoln Steffens asked Boss Richard Croker of New York, "when we've got a mayor—and a city council?" "That's why," Croker broke in. "It's because we've got a mayor and a council and judges—*and*—a hundred other men to deal with." The boss was right. He and his system furnished cities with the centralization, authority, and services they sorely needed.

Bosses ruled through the **political machine.** Often, like New York's Tammany Hall, machines dated back to the late eighteenth and early nineteenth centuries. They began as fraternal and charitable organizations. Over the years they became centers of political power. In New York the machine was Democratic; in Philadelphia, Republican. Some were less centralized, as in Chicago; some less ethnically mixed, like Detroit's. Machines could be found even in rural areas. In Duval County, Texas, for instance, the Spanish-speaking Anglo boss Archie Parr molded a powerful alliance with Mexican American landowners.

In an age of enterprise, the political machine operated similarly to a corporation. Like a corporate executive, the boss looked on politics as a business. His office might be a saloon, a funeral home, or, like George Washington Plunkitt's, a shoeshine stand. His managers were party activists, connected in a corporate-style chain of command. Local committeemen reported to district captains, captains to district leaders, district leaders to the boss or bosses who directed the machine.

The stock in trade of the machine was simple: a Christmas turkey, a load of coal for the winter, jobs for the unemployed, English language classes for the recently arrived. Bosses sponsored fun, too—sports teams, glee clubs, balls and barbecues with bands playing and drink flowing. This system, rough and uneven as it was, served as a form of public welfare at a time when private charity could not cope with the crush of demand. To the unskilled, the boss doled out jobs in public construction. For bright, ambitious young men, he had places in city offices or in the party. These positions represented the first steps into the middle class.

A Crude Welfare System

In return, citizens were expected to show their gratitude at the ballot box. Sometimes the grateful were not enough, so bosses turned elsewhere. "Little Bob" Davies of Jersey City mobilized the "graveyard vote." He drew names from tombstones to pad lists of registered voters and hired "repeaters" to vote under the phony names. When reformers introduced the Australian (secret) ballot in the 1880s to prevent fraud, bosses pulled the "Tasmanian dodge" by premarking election tickets. Failing that, they dumped whole ballot boxes into the river or drove unpersuaded voters from the polls with hired thugs.

Rewards, Costs, and Accomplishments

Why did bosses go to such lengths? Some simply loved the game of politics. More often bosses loved money. Their ability to get it was limited only by their ingenuity or the occasional success of reform. The record for brassiness must go to Boss William Tweed. During his reign in the 1860s and 1870s, Tweed swindled the city of New York out of a fortune. His masterpiece was a chunky three-story courthouse in lower Manhattan originally budgeted at $250,000. When Tweed was through, the city had spent more than $13 million, over 60 percent of which ended up in the pockets of Tweed and his cronies. They got kickbacks from favored contractors; they padded

The Sawdust Trail, *painted by George Bellows in 1916, depicts one of the revival meetings of William Ashley ("Billy") Sunday in Philadelphia. Sunday, a hard-drinking professional baseball player turned evangelist, began his religious revivals in the 1890s and drew thousands. Here, Sunday leans down from the platform to shake the hand of an admirer. In the foreground, a swooning woman, overcome with a sense of her sins, is carried away.*

bills, inflated costs, and even hired nonexistent employees whose salaries they kept for themselves. Tweed died in prison, but with such profits to be made, it was small wonder that bosses rivaled the pharaohs of Egypt as builders.

In their fashion bosses played a vital role in the industrial city. Rising from the bottom ranks, they guided immigrants into American life and helped some of the underprivileged up from poverty. They changed the urban landscape with massive construction programs and modernized city government by uniting it and making it more effective. Choosing the aldermen, municipal judges, mayors, and administrative officials, bosses exerted new control to provide the contracts and franchises to run cities. Such accomplishments fostered the notion that government could be called on to help the needy. The welfare state, still decades away, had some of its roots here.

The toll was often outrageous. Inflated taxes, extorted revenue, and unpunished vice and crime were only the obvious costs. A woman whose family enjoyed Plunkitt's Christmas turkey might be widowed by her husband's accident in a dangerous sweatshop kept open by timely bribes. Filthy buildings might claim her children, as corrupt inspectors ignored serious violations. Buying votes and selling favors, bosses turned democracy into a petty business—as much a "business," said Plunkitt, "as the grocery or dry-goods or the drug business." Yet they were the forerunners of the new breed of full-time, professional politicians who would soon govern the cities and the nation as well.

Nativism, Revivals, and the Social Gospel

Urban blight and the condition of the poor inspired social as well as political activism, especially within churches. Not all of it was positive. The popular Congregationalist minister Josiah Strong concluded that the city was "a menace to society." Along with anxious economists and social workers, he held immigrants responsible for everything from corruption to unemployment and urged restrictions on their entry into the country.

In the 1880s and 1890s, two depressions sharpened such anxieties. Nativism, a defensive and fearful nationalism, peaked as Americans blamed their economic woes on foreigners and foreign competition. New organizations like the Immigration Restriction League attacked Catholics and the foreign-born for subverting democracy, taking jobs, and polarizing society. Already the victims of racial prejudice, the Chinese were an easy target. In 1882 Congress enacted the Chinese Exclusion Act. It banned the entry of Chinese laborers and represented an important step in the drive to restrict immigration. In 1897 the first bill requiring literacy tests for immigrants passed Congress, but President Grover Cleveland vetoed it.

Some clergy took their missions to the slums to bridge the gap between the middle class and the poor. Beginning in 1870 Dwight Lyman Moody, a 300-pound former shoe salesman, won armies of lowly converts with revivals in Boston, Chicago, and other cities. Evangelists helped to found American branches of the British Young Men's Christian Association and the Salvation Army. By the end of the century the Salvation Army had grown to 700 corps staffed by some 3,000 officers. They ministered to the needy with food, music, shelter, and simple good fellowship.

A small group of ministers rejected the old ethos that weak character explained sin and that society would be perfected only as individual sinners were converted. They spread a new "Social Gospel" that focused on improving the conditions of society in order to save individuals. In *Applied Christianity* (1886), the influential Washington Gladden preached that the church must be responsible for correcting social injustices, including dangerous working conditions and unfair labor practices.

The Social Settlement Movement

Church-sponsored programs sometimes repelled the immigrant poor when they saw them as thinly disguised missionary efforts. Not all were. Many urban church programs, such as A. B. Simpson's in New York City, served body and soul successfully and without heavy-handed evangelizing.

Immigrants and other slum dwellers were more receptive to a bold experiment called the **settlement house.** Often situated in the worst slums, these early community centers were run by middle-class women and men to help the poor and foreign-born. At the turn of the century there were more than 100 of them, the most famous being Jane Addams's Hull House in Chicago. When Hull House opened in 1889, it occupied a crumbling mansion on South Halstead Street. Slowly it grew to a dozen buildings over more than a city block. In 1898 the Catholic church sponsored its first settlement house in New York, and in 1900 Bronson House opened its doors to the Latino community in Los Angeles.

High purposes inspired settlement workers. They left comfortable middle-class homes to live in settlement houses and dedicated themselves (like the "early Christians," said one) to service and sacrifice. Teaching immigrants American ways and creating a community spirit would foster "right living through social relations." But immigrants were also urged to preserve their heritages through festivals, parades, and museums. Like political bosses, settlement reformers furnished help, from day nurseries to English

The Settlement House

language and cooking classes to playgrounds and libraries. Armed with statistics and personal experiences, they also lobbied for social legislation to improve housing, women's working conditions, and public schools.

City Life

City life reflected the stratified nature of American society in the late nineteenth century. Every city had its tenements and slums but also its fashionable avenues for the rich, who constituted barely 1 percent of the population but owned a fourth of all wealth. In between tenement and mansion lived the broad middle of urban society—educated professionals, white-collar clerks and salespeople, shopkeepers, corporate managers and executives, public employees, and their families. They composed nearly a third of the population and owned about half the nation's wealth. With more money and more leisure time, their power and influence were growing.

Urban Social Stratification

In the impersonal city of the late nineteenth century, class distinctions continued to be based on wealth and income. But no longer were dress and manners enough to distinguish one class from another. Such differences were more often reflected by where people lived, what they bought, which organizations they joined, and how they spent their time.

The Immigrant in the City

When the ship put into port, the first thing an immigrant was likely to see was a city. Perhaps it was Boston or New York or Galveston, Texas, where an overflow of Jewish immigrants was directed after the turn of the century. Enough of the newcomers traveled inland so that by 1900 three-quarters of the residents of Minnesota and Wisconsin and nearly two-thirds in Utah had at least one foreign-born parent.* But some 70 percent of all immigrants, exhausted physically and financially, settled in cities.

Ethnic Neighborhoods

Cities developed well-defined mosaics of ethnic communities, because immigrants usually clustered on the basis of Old World families, villages, or provinces. But these neighborhoods were constantly changing. As many as half the residents moved out every 10 years, often because of better-paying jobs or more family members who worked. Though one nationality usually dominated a neighborhood, there were always others.

Adapting to America

Ethnic communities served as havens from the strangeness of American society and as springboards to a new life. From the moment they stepped off the boat, newcomers felt pressed to learn English, don American clothes, and drop their "greenhorn" ways. Yet in their neighborhoods they also found comrades who spoke their language, theaters that performed their plays and music, restaurants that served their food. Houses of worship were always at the center of neighborhood life, often reflecting the practices of individual towns or provinces. Foreign-language newspapers reported events from both the Old World and the New in a native tongue first-generation immigrants could understand. Meanwhile, immigrant aid societies furnished assistance with housing and jobs and sponsored insurance programs, English classes, and even baseball teams.

Sometimes immigrants combined the old and new in creative adaptations. Italians developed a pidgin dialect called "Italglish." It permitted them to communicate quickly with Americans and to absorb American customs. So the Fourth of July became "Il Forte Gelato" (literally "The Great Freeze"), a play on the sound of the words. Other immigrant groups invented similar idioms, like Chuco, a dialect that developed among border Mexicans in El Paso.

---

*Mormons serving as missionaries in Europe and Great Britain especially swelled Utah's population with converts.

The backgrounds and cultural values of immigrants often influenced the jobs they took. Because Chinese men did not scorn washing or ironing, more than 7,500 of them could be found in San Francisco laundries by 1880. Sewing ladies' garments seemed unmanly to many native-born Americans but not to Russian and Italian tailors. Slavs tended to be physically robust and valued steady income over education. They worked in the mines for better pay than in factories and pulled their children from school to send them to work.

On the whole, immigrants married later and had more children than the native-born. Greeks and eastern European Jews prearranged marriages according to tradition. They imported "picture brides," betrothed by mail with a photograph. After marriage men ruled the household, but women managed it. Although child-rearing practices varied, immigrants resisted the relative permissiveness of American parents. Youngsters were expected to contribute like little adults to the welfare of the family.

Family Life

In these "family economies" of working-class immigrants, key decisions—over whether and whom to marry, over work and education, over when to leave home—were made on the basis of collective rather than individual needs. Though boys were more likely to work outside the home than girls, daughters in immigrant families went to work at an early age so sons could continue their education. It was customary for one daughter to remain unmarried so she could care for younger siblings or aged parents.

The Chinese were an exception to the pattern. The ban on the immigration of Chinese laborers in the 1880s (see page 579) had frozen the sex ratio of Chinese communities into a curious imbalance. Like other immigrants, most Chinese newcomers had been single men. In the wake of the ban, those in the United States could not bring over their wives and families. Nor by law in 13 states could they marry whites. With few women, Chinese communities suffered from high rates of prostitution, large numbers of gangs and secret societies, and low birth totals. When the San Francisco earthquake and fire destroyed birth records in 1906, resourceful Chinese immigrants created "paper sons" (and less often "paper daughters") by forging American birth certificates and claiming their China-born children as American citizens.

Special Situation of the Chinese

Caught between past and present, immigrants from all countries clung to tradition and acculturated slowly. Their children adjusted more quickly. They soon spoke English like natives, married whomever they pleased, and worked their way out of old neighborhoods. Yet the process was not easy. Children faced heartrending clashes with parents and rejection from peers. Sara Smolinsky, the immigrant heroine of

Acculturation

Entertainment in immigrant neighborhoods often resulted in a cross-fertilization of cultures. The New Cathay Boys Club Band, a marching band of Chinese Americans (shown here), was formed in San Francisco's Chinatown in 1911. It was inspired by the Columbia Park Boys Band of Italians from nearby North Beach and played American music only.

Anzia Yezierska's novel *Bread Givers* (1925), broke away from her tyrannical family, only to discover a terrible isolation: "I can't live in the old world and I'm yet too green for the new."

Urban Middle-Class Life

The Home as Status Symbol and Haven

Life and leisure for the urban middle class revolved around home and family. By the turn of the century just over a third of middle-class urbanites owned their homes. Often two or three stories, made of brick or brownstone, these houses were a measure of their owners' social standing. The plush furniture, heavy drapes, antiques, and curios all signaled status and refinement.

Such homes, usually on their own lots, served as havens to protect and nourish the family. Seventeenth-century notions of children as inherently sinful had given way to more modern theories about the shaping influence of environment. Calm and orderly households with nurturing mothers would launch children on the right course. "A clean, fresh, and well-ordered house," stipulated a domestic adviser in 1883, "exercises over its inmates a moral, no less than physical influence, and has a direct tendency to make members of the family sober, peaceable, and considerate of the feelings and happiness of each other."

A woman was judged by the state of her home. The typical homemaker prepared elaborate meals, cleaned, laundered, and sewed. Each task took time. Baking bread alone required several hours, and in 1890, four of five loaves were still made at home. Perhaps 25 percent of urban households had live-in servants to help with the work. They were on call about 100 hours a week, were off just one evening and part of Sunday, and averaged $2 to $5 a week in salary.

By the 1890s a host of new consumer products eased the burdens of housework. Brand names trumpeted a new age of commercially prepared food—Campbell's soup, Quaker oats, Pillsbury flour, Jell-O, and Cracker Jacks, to name a few. New appliances such as "self-working" washers offered mechanical assistance, but shredded shirts and aching arms testified to how far short mechanization still fell.

Toward the end of the century, Saturday became less of a workday and more of a family day. Sunday mornings remained a time for church, still an important center of family life. Afternoons had a more secular flavor. There were shopping trips (city stores often stayed open) and visits to lakes, zoos, and amusement parks (usually built at the end of trolley lines to attract more riders). Outside institutions of all kinds—fraternal organizations, uplift groups, athletic teams, and church groups—were becoming part of middle-class urban family life.

Newly developed "electroplating," which deposited a thin layer of silver or gold over less expensive material, allowed manufacturers to sell wares previously reserved for the wealthy to middle-class consumers. Pictured here are a silver- and gold-plated card receiver and a calling card, once part of the courtly culture of elites and by the 1880s found in more and more middle-class homes. This "downward mobility" of manners and material culture allowed the middle class to ape the conventions of their social superiors, in this case by using calling cards to reinforce social networks and to serve as social barriers should personal contact be unwanted.

At Home
Wednesdays, July nineteenth and twenty-sixth, at Eighteen Liberty Street, Montpelier.

Victorianism and the Pursuit of Virtue

Middle-class life reflected a code of behavior called Victorianism, named for Britain's long-reigning Queen Victoria (1837–1901). It emerged in the 1830s and 1840s as part of an effort to tame the turbulent urban-industrial society developing in Europe.

Victorianism dictated that personal conduct be based on orderly behavior and disciplined moralism. It stressed sobriety, industriousness, self-control, and sexual modesty and taught that demeanor, particularly proper manners, was the backbone of society. It strictly divided the gender roles of men and women, especially in the realm of sexuality. According to its rules, women were "pure vessels" devoid of sexual desire, men wild beasts unable to tame their lust. A woman's job was to control the "lower natures" of her husband by withholding sex except for procreation.

Women's fashion mirrored Victorian values. Strenuously laced corsets ("an instrument of torture," one woman called them) pushed breasts up, stomachs in, and rear ends out. Internal organs pressed unnaturally against one another; ribs occasionally cracked; uteruses sagged. Fainting spells and headaches were all too common. But the resulting wasplike figure accentuated the image of women as child bearers. Ankle-length skirts were draped over bustles, hoops, and petticoats to make hips look larger and suggest fertility. Such elegant dress symbolized wealth, status, and modesty. It also set off middle- and upper-class women from those below, whose plain clothes signaled lives of drudgery and want.

When working-class Americans failed to follow Victorian guidelines, reformers helped them pursue virtue. It seemed natural to Frances Willard that women, who cared for the moral and physical well-being of their families, should lead the charge. She resigned her position as dean of women at Northwestern University and in 1879 became the second president of the newly founded Woman's Christian Temperance Union (WCTU, organized in 1874). The very title of the organization, stressing the singular "woman," spoke for the unity of women. Under Willard's leadership, the organization grew by the 1890s to 150,000 members, all of them women and most of them middle-class and white. By the turn of the century it was the largest women's organization in the world.

Initially the WCTU focused on **temperance**—the movement, begun in the 1820s, to stamp out the sale of alcoholic beverages and to end drunkenness. For these women, the campaign seemed not merely a way to reform society but also a way to protect their homes and families from abuse at the hands of drunken husbands and fathers. And in attacking the saloon, Willard also sought to spread democracy by storming these all-male bastions, where political bosses conducted so much political business and where women were refused entry. Soon, under the slogan of "Do Everything," the WCTU was also promoting suffrage for women, prison reform, better working conditions, and an end to prostitution. Just as important, it offered talented, committed women an opportunity to move out of their homes and churches and into the public arena of lobbying and politics.

Anthony Comstock crusaded with equal vigor against what he saw as moral pollution, ranging from pornography and gambling to the use of nude art models. In 1873 President Ulysses S. Grant signed the so-called Comstock Law, a statute banning from the mails all materials "designed to incite lust." Two days later Comstock went to work as a special agent for the Post Office. In his 41-year career, he claimed to have made more than 3,000 arrests and destroyed 160 tons of vice-ridden books and photographs.

Victorian crusaders like Comstock were not simply missionaries of a stuffy morality. They were apostles of a middle-class creed of social control and discipline who responded to growing alcoholism, venereal disease, gambling debts, prostitution, and unwanted pregnancies. No doubt they overreacted in warning that the road to ruin lay behind the door of every saloon, pool hall, or bedroom. Yet the new urban environment did indeed reflect the disorder of a rapidly industrializing society.

The insistence with which moralists warned against "impropriety" suggests that many people did not heed their advice. Three-quarters of women surveyed toward the turn of the century reported that they enjoyed sex. The growing variety of contraceptives—including spermicidal douches, sheaths made of animal intestines, rubber condoms, and forerunners of the diaphragm—testified to the desire for pregnancy-free intercourse. Abortion, too, was prevalent. According to one estimate, a third of all pregnancies were aborted, usually with the aid of a midwife. (By the 1880s abortion had been made illegal in most states, following the lead of the first antiabortion statute in England in 1803.) Despite Victorian marriage manuals, middle-class Americans became more conscious of sexuality as an emotional dimension of a satisfying union.

Woman's Christian Temperance Union

Comstock Law

Contraceptives and Abortion

Challenges to Convention

A few bold men and women openly challenged conventions of gender and propriety. Victoria Woodhull, publisher of *Woodhull & Claflin's Weekly,* divorced her husband, ran for president in 1872 on the Equal Rights party ticket, and pressed the case for sexual freedom. "I am a free lover!" she shouted to a riotous audience in New York. Although Woodhull made a strong public case for sexual freedom, in private she believed in strict monogamy and romantic love for herself.

The same cosmopolitan conditions that provided protection for Woodhull's unorthodox beliefs also made possible the growth of self-conscious communities of homosexual men and women. Earlier in the century, Americans had idealized romantic friendships among members of the same sex, without necessarily attributing sexual overtones to those friendships. But for friendships with an explicitly sexual dimension, the anonymity of large cities provided new meeting grounds. Single factory workers and clerks, living in furnished rooms rather than with their families in small towns and on farms, were freer to seek others who shared their sexual orientation. Homosexual men and women began forming social networks: on the streets where they regularly met or at specific restaurants and clubs, which, to avoid controversy, sometimes passed themselves off as athletic associations or chess clubs.

Only toward the end of the century did physicians begin to notice homosexual behavior, usually to condemn it as a disease or an inherited infirmity. Indeed, not until the turn of the century did the term *homosexual* come into existence. Certainly homosexual love itself was not new. But for the first time in the United States, the conditions of urban life allowed gay men and lesbians to define themselves in terms of a larger, self-conscious community, even if they were stoutly condemned by Victorian morality.

Educational reformers in the 1870s pushed elementary schools to include drawing as a required subject. Their goal was not to turn out gifted artists but to train students in the practical skills needed in an industrial society. Winslow Homer's portrait of a teacher by her blackboard shows the geometric shapes behind practical design.

City Culture

"We cannot all live in cities," reformer Horace Greeley lamented just after the Civil War, "yet nearly all seemed determined to do so." Economic opportunity drew people to the teeming industrial city. But so, too, did a vibrant urban culture, boasting temples of entertainment, electrified trolleys and lights, the best schools, stores and restaurants, the biggest newspapers, and virtually every museum, library, art gallery, bookshop, and orchestra in America.

Public Education in an Urban Industrial World

Those at the bottom and in the middle ranks of city life found one path to success in public education. Although the campaign for public education began in the Jacksonian era, it did not make real headway until after the Civil War, when industrial cities began to mushroom. As late as 1870 half the children in the country received no formal education at all, and one American in five could not read.

Between 1870 and 1900, an educational awakening occurred. As more and more businesses required workers who could read, write, and figure sums, attendance in public schools more than doubled. The length of the school term rose from 132 to 144 days. Illiteracy fell by half. At the turn of the century, nearly all the states outside the South had enacted mandatory education laws. Almost three of every four school-age children were enrolled. Even so, the average American adult still attended school for only about five years, and less than 10 percent of those eligible ever went to high school.

The average school day started early, but by noon most girls were released under the assumption that they needed less formal education. Curricula stressed the fundamentals of reading, writing, and arithmetic. Courses in manual training, science, and physical education were added as the demand for technical knowledge grew and opportunities to exercise shrank. Students learned by memorization, sitting in silent study with hands clasped or standing erect while they repeated phrases and sums. Few schools encouraged creative thinking. "Don't stop to think," barked a Chicago teacher to a class of terrified youngsters in the 1890s, "tell me what you know!"

A rigid social philosophy underlay the harsh routine. In an age of industrialization, massive immigration, and rapid change, schools taught conformity and values as much as facts and figures. Teachers acted as drillmasters, shaping their charges for the sake of society. "Teachers and books are better security than handcuffs and policemen," wrote a New Jersey college professor in 1879. In *McGuffey's Reader*, a standard textbook used in grammar schools throughout the nineteenth century, students learned not only how to read but also how to behave. Hard work, Christian ethics, and obedience to authority would lead boys to heroic command, girls to blissful motherhood, and society to harmonious progress.

As Reconstruction faded, so did the impressive start made in black education. Most of the first generation of former slaves had been illiterate. So eager were they to learn that by the end of the century nearly half of all African Americans could read. But discrimination soon took its toll. For nearly 100 years after the Civil War, the doctrine of "separate but equal," upheld by the Supreme Court in *Plessy v. Ferguson* (1896), kept black and white students apart but scarcely equal (see page 505). By 1882 public schools in a half dozen southern states were segregated by law, the rest by practice. Underfunded and ill-equipped, black schools served dirt-poor families whose every member had to work. In fact, only about a third of the South's black children attended and rarely for the entire school year.

Like African Americans, immigrants saw education as a way of getting ahead. Some educators saw it as a means of Americanizing newcomers. They assumed that immigrant and native-born children would learn the same lessons in the same language and turn out the same way. Only toward the end of the century, as immigration mounted, did eastern cities begin to offer night classes that taught English, along with civics lessons for foreigners. When public education proved inadequate, immigrants established their own schools. Catholics, for example, started an elaborate expansion of their parochial schools in 1884.

By the 1880s educational reforms were helping schools respond to the needs of an urban society. Opened first in St. Louis in 1873, American versions of innovative German "kindergartens" put four- to six-year-olds in orderly classrooms while parents went off to work. **Normal schools** multiplied to provide teachers with more professional training. By 1900 almost one teacher in five had a professional degree. In the new industrial age, science and manual training supplemented more conventional subjects in order to supply industry with better-educated workers. And vocational education reduced the influence of unions. Now less dependent on a system of apprenticeship controlled by labor, new workers were also less subject to being recruited into unions.

Higher Learning and the Rise of the Professional

As American society grew more organized, mechanized, and complex, the need for managerial, technical, and literary skills brought greater respect for college education. The Morrill Act of 1862 generated a dozen new state colleges and universities, eight mechanical and agricultural colleges, and six black colleges. Private charity added more. Railroad barons like Johns Hopkins and Leland Stanford used parts of their fortunes to

Educational Values and Conformity

Educational Discrimination

Educational Reforms

Higher Education

Forbidden Fruit?

Decoding a Mural Celebrating Women

Why on Earth would the American Impressionist Mary Cassatt paint a mural of women picking apples, in entirely unsuitable clothing no less? The painting was featured in the Gallery of Honor in the Women's Building at the Chicago World's Columbian Exposition. The answer to that question tells us much about changing conceptions of gender in late nineteenth-century America.

We can find one clue to the riddle in the mural's title: *Young Women Plucking the Fruits of Knowledge or Science.* Traditionally, the apple had always been identified as the fruit on the tree of knowledge in the Garden of Eden. According to the Bible, that fruit was forbidden: when it was eaten by Eve, who shared it with Adam, the result was original sin.

Cassatt stood the story of Eve on its head. In doing so, she suggested that the place of women in society was changing. No longer bound by cultural conventions against the dangers of educated and potentially "uppity" women, a new generation of educated females was to be justly celebrated for its achievements in science, the arts, and the professions. (The Women's Building, in fact, was designed by architect Sophia Hayden, whose first name, appropriately, was Greek for *wisdom*.) Cassatt's mural—as well as Hayden's career—heralded a new woman, one more educated than her predecessors and capable of passing formerly forbidden knowledge to the young girls who followed.

found colleges named after them (Hopkins in 1873, Stanford in 1890). The number of colleges and universities nearly doubled between 1870 and 1910, though less than 5 percent of college-age Americans enrolled in them.

Black Colleges

A practical impulse inspired the founding of several black colleges. In the late nineteenth century, few institutions mixed races. Church groups and private foundations, such as the Peabody and Slater funds (supported by white donors from the North), underwrote black colleges such as Fisk and Howard Universities during Reconstruction and, later, colleges such as Livingstone and Spelman. By 1900, a total of 700 black students were enrolled. About 2000 had graduated. Through hard work and persistence, some even received degrees from institutions normally reserved for whites.

Professional Schools

In keeping with the new emphasis on practical training, professional schools multiplied to provide training beyond a college degree. American universities adopted the German model requiring young scholars to perform research as part of their training. The number of law and medical schools more than doubled between 1870 and 1900; medical students almost tripled. Ten percent of them were women, though their numbers shrank as the medical profession became more organized and exclusive.

Professionals of all kinds—in law, medicine, engineering, business, academics—swelled the ranks of the middle class. Slowly they were becoming a new force in urban America, replacing the ministers and gentleman freeholders of an earlier day as community leaders.

Higher Education for Women

Before the Civil War women could attend only three private colleges. After the war they had new ones all their own, among them Smith (1871), Wellesley (1875), and Bryn Mawr (1885). Many land-grant colleges, chartered to serve all people, admitted women from the start. By 1910 some 40 percent of college students were women, almost double the 1870 figure. Only one college in five refused to accept them.

Potent myths continued to make college life hard for women. As Dr. Edward Clarke of the Harvard Medical School told thousands of students in *Sex in Education* (1873), the rigors of a college education could lead the "weaker sex" to physical or mental collapse, infertility, and early death. Women's colleges therefore included a strict program of physical activity to keep students healthy. Many also offered an array of courses in "domestic science"—cooking, sewing, and other such skills—to counter the claim that higher education would be of no value to women.

College students, together with office workers and female athletes, became role models for ambitious young women. These "new women," impatient with custom, cast off Victorian restrictions. Fewer of them married, and more were self-supporting. They shed their corsets and bustles and donned lighter, more comfortable clothing, including "shirtwaist" blouses (styled after men's shirts) and lower-heeled shoes. Robust and active, they could be found ice-skating in the winter, riding bicycles in the fall and spring, playing golf and tennis in the summer.

A Culture of Consumption

The city spawned a new material culture built around consumption. As standards of living rose, American industries began providing "ready-made" clothing to replace garments that had once been made at home. Similarly, food and furniture were mass-produced in greater quantities. The city became a giant marketplace for these goods, where new patterns of mass consumption took hold. Radiating outward to more rural areas, this urban consumer culture helped to level American society. Increasingly, city businesses sold the same goods to farmer and clerk, rich and poor, native-born and immigrant.

Well-made, inexpensive merchandise in standard sizes and shapes found outlets in new palaces of consumption called "department stores" because they displayed their goods in separate sections or departments. The idea was imported from France, where shopping arcades had been built as early as the 1860s. Unlike the small exclusive shops of Europe, department stores were palatial, public, and filled with inviting displays of furniture, housewares, and clothing.

Department Stores

The French writer Emile Zola claimed that department stores "democratized luxury." Anyone could enter free of charge, handle the most elegant and expensive goods, and buy whatever they could afford. When consumers found goods too pricey, department stores pioneered layaway plans with deferred payments. Free delivery and free returns or exchanges were available to all, not just the favored customers of exclusive fashion makers. The department store also educated people by displaying what "proper" families owned and the correct names for things like women's wear and parlor furniture. This process of socialization was taking place not only in cities but in towns and villages across America. Mass consumption was giving rise to a mass culture.

"Chain stores" (a term coined in America) spread the culture of consumption without frills. They catered to the working class, who could not afford department stores, and operated on a cash-and-carry basis. Owners kept their costs down by buying in volume to fill the small stores in growing neighborhood chains. Founded in 1859, the Great Atlantic and Pacific Tea Company was the first of the chain stores. By 1876 its 76 branch stores had added groceries to its original line of teas.

Chain Stores and Mail-Order Houses

Far from department and chain stores, rural Americans joined the community of consumers by mail. In 1872, Aaron Montgomery Ward sent his first price sheet to farmers from a livery stable loft in Chicago. Ward eliminated the intermediary and promised savings of 40 percent on fans, needles, trunks, harnesses, and scores of other goods. By 1884, his catalog boasted 10,000 items, each illustrated by a woodcut. Similarly, Richard W. Sears and Alvah C. Roebuck built a $500 million mail-order business by 1907. Schoolrooms that had no encyclopedia used a Ward's or Sears' catalog instead. Children were drilled in reading and spelling from them. When asked the source of the Ten Commandments, one farm boy replied that they came from Sears, Roebuck.

Leisure

As mechanization slowly reduced the number of hours on the job, factory workers found themselves with more free time. So did the middle class, with free weekends, evenings, and vacations. A new, stricter division between work and leisure developed. City dwellers turned their free time into a consumer item that often reflected differences in class, gender, and ethnicity.

Sports and Class Distinctions

Sports, for example, had been a traditional form of recreation for the rich. They continued to play polo, golf, and the newly imported English game of tennis. Croquet had more middle-class appeal because it required less skill and special equipment. Perhaps as important, croquet could be enjoyed in mixed company, like the new craze of bicycling. Bicycles evolved from unstable contraptions with large front wheels into "safety" bikes with equal-sized wheels, a dropped middle bar, pneumatic tires, and coaster brakes. A good one cost about $100, far beyond the reach of a factory worker but within the grasp of a mechanic or a well-paid clerk. On Sunday afternoons city parks became crowded with cyclists. Women also rode the new safety bikes, although social convention forbade them to ride alone. But cycling broke down conventions too. It required looser garments, freeing women from corsets. Lady cyclists demonstrated that they were hardly too frail for physical exertion.

Spectator Sports for the Urban Masses

Organized spectator sports attracted crowds from every walk of life. Baseball overshadowed all others. For city dwellers with dull work, tight quarters, and isolated lives, baseball offered the chance to join thousands of others for an exciting outdoor spectacle.

Artist Edward Shinn's Sixth Avenue Shoppers *shows a nighttime scene in the city's shopping district. In an era of more flexible gender roles, Shinn nonetheless captures a traditional division of gender with the women (at left) crowded around shopping stalls and men (at right) hunched over a cockfight.*

By the 1890s it was attracting crowds of 60,000. Baseball began to take its modern form in 1869, when the first professional team, the Cincinnati Red Stockings, appeared. Slowly the game evolved: umpires began to call balls and strikes, the overhand replaced the underhand pitch, and fielders put on gloves. Teams from eight cities formed the National League of Professional Baseball Clubs in 1876, followed by the American League in 1901. League players were distinctly working class. At first, teams featured a few black players. When African Americans were barred in the 1880s, black professionals formed their own team, the Cuban Giants of Long Island, New York, looking to play anyone they could. Their name was chosen with care. In an age of racial separation, the all-black team hoped to increase its chances of playing white teams by calling itself "Cuban."

Horse racing, bicycle tournaments, and other sports of speed and violence helped to break the monotony, frustration, and routine of the industrial city. In 1869, without pads or helmets, Rutgers beat Princeton in the first intercollegiate football match. By the 1890s the service academies and state universities fielded teams. Despite protests against rising death tolls (18 players died in 1905), football soon attracted crowds of 50,000 or more. Beginning in 1891 when Dr. James Naismith nailed a peach basket to the gymnasium wall at the YMCA Training School in Springfield, Massachusetts, "basketball" became the indoor interlude between the outdoor sports of spring and fall.

Bare-knuckled prizefighting, illegal in some states, took place secretly in saloons and commercial gyms. In the rough-and-tumble world of the industrial city, the ring gave

This lithograph is from an 1894 poster for the Barnum & Bailey Circus. It depicts a menagerie tent in which exotic animals are displayed side by side with "Strange and Savage Tribes," thus collapsing the boundaries between animals and human beings. Much smaller than the Big Top, menagerie tents allowed Euro-American patrons to examine animals and humans up close. The Barnum show presented its first "ethnological congress" of "native" peoples in 1886, as the United States began its drive for empire abroad. The human specimens were meant to give Americans a glimpse of foreign cultures and to be instructive. "Even the best informed and most intellectual had something to learn," boasted a circus route book.

It looked like a palace or some high-toned concert hall. Patrons walked through a richly ornamented arched gateway to gold-domed, marble ticket booths. Ushers guided them through a stately lobby cushioned with velvet carpets. The house seats were thick and comfortable and positioned well back from the stage. Thousands of electrical fixtures set the place aglow. When the lights dimmed, the audience sank into polite silence as the show began.

Benjamin Franklin Keith, who had worked in circuses, tent shows, and dime museums, opened the New Theatre in Boston in 1894. Seeing housewives with children as a source of new profits, resourceful theater owners such as Keith had cleaned up the bawdy variety acts of saloons and music halls, borrowed the animal and acrobat acts from circuses and Wild West shows and the comedy acts of minstrel shows, and moved them to plusher surroundings. They called the new shows "vaudeville," after the French "pièces de vaudeville" developed at eighteenth-century street fairs.

Balconies at vaudeville shows, like this one depicted by Charles Dana Gibson, attracted a wide variety of customers. Most seats cost $1, and theater owners scheduled performances from morning until night.

Boxing

young men from the streets the chance to stand out from the crowd and to prove their masculinity. "Sporting clubs" of German, Irish, and African American boxers sprouted up in cities along the East Coast. *The National Police Gazette* and other magazines followed the bouts with sensational stories chronicling matches in detail. When the sport adopted the Marquis of Queensbury rules in the 1880s, including the use of gloves, boxing gained new respectability and appeal. Soon boxing, like other sports, was being commercialized with professional bouts, large purses, and championship titles.

City Entertainment at Home and on the Road

City entertainment, like city life, divided along lines of class. For the wealthy and middle class there were symphonies, operas, and theater. Highbrow productions of Shakespearean plays catered to the aspirations of the American upper class for culture and European refinement. Popular melodramas gave their largely middle-class audiences the chance to ignore the ambiguities of modern life, if only for an evening. They booed villains and cheered heroes, all the while marveling at the tricky stage mechanics that made ice floes move and players float heavenward. By 1900, people were bringing their entertainment home, snapping up new phonograph recordings at the rate of 3 million a year.

Workingmen found a haven from the drudgery of factory, mill, and mine in the saloon. It was an all-male preserve—a workingmen's club—where one could drink and talk free from Victorian finger-wagging. Rougher saloons offered fulfillment of still more illicit desires in the form of prostitutes, gambling, and drugs. Young working women found escape alone or on dates at vaudeville shows (above), dance halls, and the new amusement parks with their mechanical "thrill rides." In the all-black gaming houses and honky-tonks of St. Louis and New Orleans, the syncopated rhythms of African American composer Scott Joplin's "Maple Leaf Rag" (1899) and other ragtime tunes heralded the coming of jazz.

For anywhere from a dime to two dollars, a customer could see up to nine acts—singers, jugglers, acrobats, magicians, trained animals, and comics. The mix of performers reflected the urban tempo and new urban tastes. Skits often drew on the experience of immigrants, and early comedy teams had names like "The Sport and the Jew" and "Two Funny Sauerkrauts." "Continuous shows" ran one after another, from early morning until late at night.

Saloon music halls had catered to a rowdy all-male, working-class clientele. Vaudeville was aimed at middle-class and wealthier working-class families who could no longer afford "legitimate" theater and light opera. Keith worked diligently to make each of his theaters "homelike." Backstage he tacked signs warning performers not to say "slob" or "son-of-a-gun" or "hully-gee' . . . ." Within a few years Keith was producing the kind of show, as one comedian put it, "to which any child could bring his parents."

The audience, too, was instructed on proper behavior. No liquor was served. No cigars or cigarettes were permitted. Printed notices directed patrons to "kindly avoid the stamping of feet and pounding of canes on the floor. Please don't talk during acts, ..."

Enjoying its heyday from 1890 to 1920, vaudeville became big business. Nearly one in five city dwellers went to a show once every seven days. Headliners earned $1,000 a week, theaters $20,000. Owners such as Keith and Edward Albee merged their operations into gigantic circuits. By the time of Keith's death in 1914, the Keith-Albee circuit had built an empire of 29 theaters in more than seven cities.

Vaudeville became middle-class mass entertainment. Moderate and moral, it furnished cheap recreation that also reinforced genteel values. Skits encouraged audiences to pursue success through hard work. An emerging star system made American heroes out of performers like Will Rogers and George M. Cohan and American models out of Fanny Brice and Mae West. Ethnic comics defused tensions among immigrants with spoofs that exaggerated stereotypes and stressed the common foibles of all humanity. And theatergoers learned how to behave. Order and decorum replaced the boisterous atmosphere of saloons and music halls. Vaudeville audiences adopted the middle-class ideal of behavior—passive and polite.

As much as any form of entertainment, the traveling circus embodied the changes of the new urban, industrial world. Moving outward from their bases in large cities, circuses rode the new rail system across the country (after the first transcontinental tour in 1869) and with the advent of steamships crisscrossed the globe. The largest, the mammoth New York–based Barnum and Bailey Circus, carried dozens of gilded show wagons, hundreds of animals, tons of equipment, and sometimes thousands of performers, work hands, and animal tenders.

With factory-like precision, circus workers erected and dismantled small tent cities in hours, moved them across vast spaces in days or weeks, and performed as many as three shows daily. Under huge canvas "big tops," they drew audiences from every class, ethnicity, and race, sometimes numbering in the tens of thousands.

Circuses were popular entertainment and big businesses, but they also were disseminators of culture that both supported and subverted social conventions. When owners reassured customers that their scantily clad dancers came from respectable Victorian families or their muscular lady acrobats prized the Victorian ideals of family, motherhood, and domesticity, they winked slyly because they knew that the very appearance of these women, let alone their talents, defied the Victorian ideal of dainty and demure femininity. When in 1886 Barnum & Bailey displayed exotic peoples and animals in the first "Ethnological Congress" ever to accompany a traveling circus, patrons saw living embodiments of "strange and savage tribes" from Africa, the Middle East, and Asia. These displays opened American eyes to a wider world while reinforcing prevailing notions of white supremacy.

As the United States was embarking on a quest for empire (see Chapter 21), circuses trumpeted national expansion with celebrations of American might and exceptionalism. To audiences at home, reenactments of famous battles abroad brought faraway places near and made abstract principles of foreign policy real. To foreign audiences, those same reenactments trumpeted the rise of a new world power.

Traveling Circuses

Industrialization ignited the growth of cities not just in the United States but all over the world. Great Britain, the birthplace of the Industrial Revolution, became the world's first country in which by 1851 over half its people lived in towns and cities. Fifty years later, London's population had more than doubled, from 2.7 million to 6.6 million. By 1914, on the eve of World War I, eight of every ten Britons lived in cities, as did six of ten Germans and nearly five of ten French. Growing cities spilled over into nearby towns and villages, obliterating the open spaces between them whether in the English Midlands, the Ruhr Valley of Germany, or the environs of Tokyo.

Just as European immigrants poured into cities across the United States, newcomers from Europe, Asia, and the Middle East flowed into South America, Australia, and the Caribbean. Before 1900 two of every three emigrating Italians booked passage not for the United States but for Brazil or Argentina. Chinese immigrants harvested sugar cane in Cuba, built railroads and opened restaurants in Peru, and launched businesses in Trinidad. By 1920 Sao Paulo, the largest city in Brazil, was exploding with Asian immigrants, and Brazil boasted the world's largest Japanese population outside Japan itself.

The hubbub, the overcrowding, and the corruption of cities such as Boss Plunkitt's Manhattan were reflected elsewhere in the world. Before the arrival of mass transit British urban workers were forced to live within walking distance of factories, in dingy row houses beset by the overflow from privies and garbage in the streets. A deadly cholera epidemic in 1848 spurred a campaign to install iron pipes and drains to provide running water and sewers throughout major cities. About the same time Paris underwent a radical renovation in which workers tore down the city's medieval fortress walls, widened major streets into boulevards, and set aside land for green parks. Borrowing innovations from the United States, Europeans adopted horse-drawn streetcars and, later, electric trolleys. With an intracity transportation network in place, the old "walking cities" of Europe, like those in the United States, added suburbs, partially easing the crush of earlier crowding.

The world over, industrial cities transformed both the urban landscape and the daily lives of city dwellers. Critics damned the city's crime and corruption; defenders celebrated its vibrancy and diversity. No matter how they felt, Americans had to find ways to make that new industrial order work for them.

Significant Events

1869	Cincinnati Red Stockings become first professional baseball team
1870	Elevated railroad begins operation in New York City
1872	William "Boss" Tweed convicted of defrauding city of New York
1873	Comstock Law enacted
1874	Women's Christian Temperance Union founded
1875	Dwight Moody begins urban evangelical revivals
1876	Johns Hopkins University opens nation's first graduate school
1882	Chinese Exclusion Act

1883   Brooklyn Bridge opens
1885   Home Life Insurance Building, world's first skyscraper, built in Chicago; first all-black professional baseball team, the Cuban Giants, organized
1888   Nation's first electric trolley line begins operation in Richmond, Virginia
1889   Hull House opens in Chicago
1892   Ellis Island opens as a receiving station for immigrants
1894   Immigration Restriction League organized
1897   Boston opens nation's first subway station

Chapter Summary

The modern city was the product of industrialization, lying at the center of the new integrated systems of transportation, communications, manufacturing, marketing, and finance.

- Fed by a great global migration of laborers, cities began to grow and to assume their modern shape of ringed residential patterns around central business districts and strict divisions among different classes, races, and ethnic groups.

- The challenge for the political system was to find within its democratic traditions a way to bring order out of the seeming chaos of unchecked urban growth.

- The urban boss and the urban political machine met the needs of cities for centralized authority but at a terrible cost

in corruption, while social settlement houses, the Salvation Army, and the Social Gospel churches represented only start at coping with the problems of poverty and urban blight.

- As cities grew, the middle-class code of behavior—called Victorianism—spread, teaching the values of sobriety, hard work, self-control, and modesty that served the needs of new industrial society for efficiency and order and the middle-class need for protection against the turbulence of city life.

- Yet for all the emphasis on skills, discipline, and order, the vibrancy of city culture remained attractive, drawing millions in search of education, entertainment, and opportunity and radiating outward to almost every corner of the country.

Additional Reading

The best treatment of the rise of cities is Howard B. Chudacoff, *The Evolution of American Urban Society* (rev. ed., 1981). John Stilgoe, *Borderland: The Origins of the American Suburb, 1820–1929* (1988), chronicles the growth of suburban America. William Cronon, *Nature's Metropolis: Chicago and the Great West* (1991), looks at Chicago as part of the ecological landscape. In *Boss Cox's Cincinnati: Urban Politics in the Progressive Era* (1968), Zane Miller reassesses the urban political machine, and Paul Boyer explores efforts at controlling city life in *Urban Masses and Moral Order in America, 1820–1920* (1978). John F. Kasson, *Rudeness & Civility: Manners in Nineteenth-Century Urban America* (1990), and Lawrence Levine, *Highbrow/Lowbrow: The Emergence of Cultural Hierarchy in America* (1988), investigate the emerging urban culture. For a penetrating examination of traveling circuses as conduits for cultural exchanges, see Janet M. Davis's *The Circus Age: Culture and Society under the American Big Top* (2002).

Marcus Lee Hanson's classic *The Atlantic Migration, 1607–1860* (1940) began the shift in immigration history away from the national and toward a more global perspective. For richly detailed comparative examinations of the immigrant experience, see Roger Daniels, *Coming to America: A History*

of Immigration and Ethnicity in American Life (1990), and Ronald Takaki, *A Different Mirror: A History of Multicultural America* (1993). Susan A. Glenn, *Daughters of the Shtetl: Life and Labor in the Immigrant Generation* (1990), throws light on the issue of gender by probing the lives and labor of immigrant women, with particular attention to the shaping effect of Old World Jewish culture. Virginia Yans-McLaughlin, ed., *Immigration Reconsidered: History, Sociology, and Politics* (1990), offers a collection of penetrating essays that places American immigration in its international context. In *New Spirits: Americans in the Gilded Age, 1865–1905* (2006), Rebecca Edwards revises the traditional portrait of the "Gilded Age" by emphasizing the anxieties and optimism of ordinary people, many of them city dwellers, in what she regards as the birth of modern America. Helen Lefkowitz Horowitz's *Rereading Sex: Battles over Sexual Knowledge and Suppression in Nineteenth-Century America* (2002) explores the contradictions of Victorian thinking about all manner of sexual matters, including contraception, abortion, pornography, and free speech.

For a fuller list of readings, see the Bibliography at www.mhhe.com/davidsonnation6.

CHAPTER 21
The Political System under Strain at Home and Abroad
1877~1900

"The World United at Chicago"

On May 1, 1893, nearly half a million people jostled into a dramatic plaza fronted on either side by gleaming white buildings overlooking a sparkling lagoon. Named the Court of Honor, the plaza was the center of a strange ornamental city that was at once awesome and entirely imaginary. At one end stood a building whose magnificent white dome exceeded even the height of the capitol in Washington. Unlike the marble-built capitol, however, this building was all surface: a stucco shell plastered onto a steel frame and then sprayed with white oil paint to make it glisten. Beyond the Court of Honor stretched thoroughfares encompassing over 200 colonnaded buildings, piers, islands, and watercourses. Located five miles south of Chicago's central business district, this city of the imagination proclaimed itself the "World's Columbian Exposition" in honor of the 400th anniversary of Columbus's voyage to America.

President Grover Cleveland opened the world's fair in a way that symbolized the nation's industrial transformation. He pressed a telegrapher's key. Instantly electric current set 7,000 feet of shafting into motion—motion that in turn unfurled flags, set fountains pumping, and lit 10,000 electric bulbs. The lights played over an array of exhibition buildings soon known far and wide as the "White City."

One English visitor dismissed the displays within as little more than "the contents of a great dry goods store mixed up with the contents of museums." In a sense he was right. Visitors paraded by an unending collection of typewriters, pins, watches, agricultural machinery, cedar canoes, and refrigerators, to say nothing of a map of the United States fashioned entirely out of pickles. But this riot of mechanical marvels, gewgaws, and bric-a-brac was symbolic too of the nation's industrial transformation. The fair resembled nothing so much as a tangible version of the new mail-order catalogs whose pages were now introducing the goods of the city to the hinterlands.

The connections made by the fair were international as well. This event was the *World's* Columbian Exposition, with exhibits from 36 nations. Germany's famous manufacturer of armaments, Krupp, had its own separate building. It housed a 120-ton rifled gun. Easily within the range of its gunsights was a replica of the U.S. battleship *Illinois,* whose own bristling

In 1893 the World's Columbian Exposition set the night ablaze with a towering searchlight visible 60 miles away. Here the beam spotlights the fair's theme, "The World United," just as the giant exhibition halls highlighted the way the new industrial order was reshaping the globe.

World's Columbian
Exposition

turrets stood just offshore of the exposition, on Lake Michigan. At the fair's amusement park, visitors encountered exotic cultures—and not just temples, huts, and totems, but exhibits in the living flesh. The Arabian village featured Saharan camels, veiled ladies, and elders in turbans. Nearby, Irish peasants boiled potatoes over turf fires while Samoan men threw axes.

Like all such fairs, the Columbian Exposition created a fantasy. Beyond its boundaries, the new industrial order was showing signs of strain. Early in 1893 the Philadelphia and Reading Railroad had gone bankrupt, setting off a financial panic. By the end of the year, nearly 500 banks and 15,000 businesses had failed. Although millions of tourists continued to marvel at the fair's wonders, crowds of worried and unemployed workers also gathered elsewhere in Chicago. On Labor Day, Governor John Altgeld of Illinois told a crowd that the government was powerless to soften the "suffering and distress" brought by this latest economic downturn.

Strains on the
Political System

In truth, the political system was ill equipped to cope with the economic and social revolutions reshaping America. The executive branch remained weak, while members of Congress and the courts found themselves easily swayed by the financial interests of the industrial class. The crises of the 1890s strained the political order and forced it to confront such inequities.

International Consequences

The political system also had to take into account developments abroad. Industrialization had sent American businesses around the world in search of raw materials and new markets. As that search intensified, many influential Americans argued that the United States needed to compete with European nations in acquiring territory overseas. By the end of the century, the nation's political system had taken its first steps toward modernization, including a major political realignment at home and a growing empire abroad. The changes launched the United States into the twentieth century and an era of prosperity and global power.

The Politics of Paralysis

During the 1880s and 1890s, as the American political system came under strain, Moisei Ostrogorski was traveling across the United States. Part of a flood of foreign observers, the Russian political scientist had come to see the new democratic experiment in action. His verdict was as blunt as it was widely shared: "the constituted authorities are unequal to their duty." It seemed that the glorious experiment had fallen victim to greed, indifference, and political mediocrity.

In fact, there were deeper problems: a great gulf between rich and poor; a wrenching cycle of boom and bust; the unmet needs of African Americans, Indians, and women. Politics was the traditional medium of resolution, but it was grinding into a dangerous stalemate.

Political Stalemate

From 1877 to 1897 American politics rested on a delicate balance of power that left neither Republicans nor Democrats in control. Republicans inhabited the White House for 12 years; Democrats, for 8. Margins of victory in presidential elections were paper thin. No president could count on having a majority of his party in both houses of Congress for his entire term. Usually Republicans controlled the Senate and Democrats the House of Representatives.

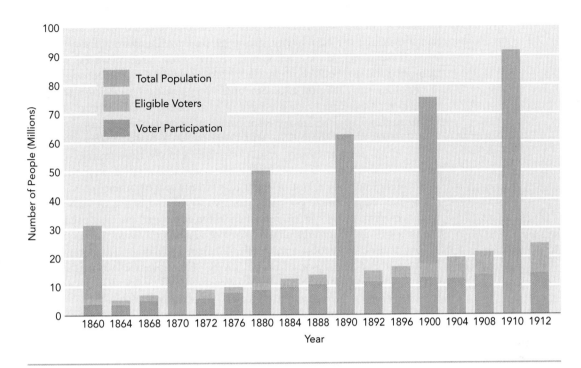

The Voting Public, 1860–1912   *Between 1860 and 1910 the population and the number of eligible voters increased nearly threefold. As reforms of the early twentieth century reduced the power of political machines and parties, the percentage of voter participation actually declined.*

With elections so tight, both parties worked hard to turn out the vote. Brass bands, parades, cheering crowds of flag-wavers were "the order of the day and night from end to end of the country," reported a British visitor. In cities party workers handed out leaflets and pinned campaign buttons on anyone who passed. When Election Day arrived, stores and businesses shut down. At political clubs and corner saloons men lined up to get voting orders (along with free drinks) from ward bosses. In the countryside, fields went untended as farmers took their families to town, cast their ballots, and bet on the outcome.

An average of nearly 80 percent of eligible voters turned out for presidential elections between 1860 and 1900, a figure higher than at any time since. New party discipline and organization helped to turn out the vote, but it is also true that in this era the electorate made up a smaller percentage of the population. Only one American in four qualified to vote, and only one in five actually voted in presidential elections from 1876 to 1892. Most voters were white males. Women could vote in national elections only in a few western states, and beginning in the 1880s, the South erected barriers that eventually disfranchised many African American voters.

Voter Turnout

Party loyalty rarely wavered. In every election, 16 states could be counted on to vote Republican and 14 Democratic (the latter mainly in the South). In only six states—the most important being New York and Ohio—were the results in doubt. National victories often hung on their returns.

The Parties

What inspired such loyalty? While Republicans and Democrats shared broad values, they also had major differences. Both parties supported business and condemned radicalism, and neither offered embattled workers or farmers much help. Democrats believed in states' rights and limited government, while Republicans favored federal activism to foster economic growth. The stronghold of Democrats lay in the South, where they reminded voters that they had led the states of the Old Confederacy, "redeemed" them from Republican Reconstruction, and championed white supremacy. Republicans dominated the North with strong support from industry and business. They, too, invoked memories of the Civil War to secure votes, black as well as white. "Not every Democrat was a rebel," they chanted, "but every rebel was a Democrat."

Ethnic and
Religious Factors

Ethnicity and religion also cemented voter loyalty. Republicans relied on old-stock Protestants, who feared new immigrants and put their faith in promoting pious behavior throughout society. In the Republican party, they found support for immigration restriction, prohibition, and English-only schools. In the North, the Democratic party attracted urban political machines, their immigrant voters, and the working poor. Often Catholic, these voters saw salvation in following their own religious rituals, not in dictating the conduct of others.

Region, religion, and ethnicity thus bound voters to each party, but outside the two-party system, reformers often fashioned political organizations of their own. Some groups aligned themselves behind issues rather than parties. Opponents of alcohol created the Woman's Christian Temperance Union (1874) and the Anti-Saloon League (1893). Champions of women's rights joined the National Woman Suffrage Association (1890), a reunion of two branches of the women's suffrage movement that had split in 1869.

Like these political organizations, third political parties also crystallized around an issue or a group. Advocates of temperance rallied to the Prohibition party (1869). Those who sought inflation of the currency formed the Greenback party (1874). Angry farmers in the West and South created the Populist, or People's, party (1892). All drew supporters from both conventional parties, but as largely single-interest groups they mobilized minorities, not majorities.

The Issues

In the halls of Congress, attention focused on well-worn issues: veterans' benefits, appointments, tariffs, and money. The presidency had been weakened by the impeachment of Andrew Johnson, the scandals of Ulysses S. Grant, and the contested victory of Rutherford B. Hayes in 1876. So Congress enjoyed the initiative in making policy. Time after time, legislators squandered it amid electioneering and party infighting or simply were swamped by the ever-increasing flood of proposed legislation.

Some divisive issues were the bitter legacy of the Civil War. Republicans and Democrats waved the symbolic "bloody shirt," each tarring the other with responsibility for the war. The politics of the Civil War also surfaced in the lobbying efforts of veterans. The Grand Army of the Republic, an organization of more than 400,000 Union soldiers, petitioned Congress for pensions to make up for poor wartime pay and to support the widows and orphans of fallen comrades. By the turn of the century Union army veterans and their families were receiving $157 million annually. It was one of the largest public assistance programs in American history, which at its peak accounted for nearly half of the federal budget. It was also one of the first government programs to offer benefits to African Americans and laid the foundations of the modern welfare state.

More important than veterans' benefits was the campaign for a new method of staffing federal offices. From barely 53,000 employees at the end of the Civil War, the federal government had grown to 166,000 by the early 1890s. Far more of these new jobs required special skills. But dismantling the reigning **spoils system** proved difficult for politicians who had rewarded faithful supporters with government jobs regardless of their qualifications. Reacting to the scandals of the Grant administration, a group of independents formed the National Civil Service Reform League in 1881. The league promoted the British model of civil service based on examination and merit. But in Congress neither party was willing to take action when it held power (and thus controlled patronage).

"For three months processions, usually with brass bands, flags, badges, crowds of cheering spectators, are the order of the day and night from end to end of the country," commented a British observer. Here, Denver Republicans lead a nighttime parade to celebrate the election of Benjamin Harrison in the presidential contest of 1888.

One July morning in 1881, a frustrated office seeker named Charles Guiteau unwittingly broke the log jam. As President James Garfield hurried to catch a train, Guiteau jumped from the shadows and shot him twice. Garfield's death finally produced reform. In 1883 the Civil Service Act, or Pendleton Act, created a bipartisan civil service commission to administer competitive examinations for some federal jobs. By 1896 almost half of all federal workers came under civil service jurisdiction.

Pendleton Act

The protective tariff also stirred emotions in Congress. Since 1812, tariffs, or taxes on imported goods, had been used to shield "infant industries" in the United States from foreign competition. But by the 1880s many American industries had grown into strapping adults, no longer in need of such protection. Worse still, tariff revenues had created a budget surplus so large that it could undermine prosperity by depriving the economy of money for investment in employment and productivity.

As promoters of business, Republicans usually championed tariffs and were joined by industrialists, westerners who sold protected raw materials like wool and timber, and even many workers, who believed that the tariff safeguarded their jobs and their wages. Democrats, with their strength in the agricultural South, sought to reduce tariffs in order to lower the prices that farmers and other consumers paid for manufactured goods.

In 1890, when Republicans controlled the House, Congress enacted the McKinley Tariff, named for its sponsor, Ohio senator William McKinley. It raised tariff rates so high that they threatened to choke off all manufactured imports. It also contained a novel twist to appease reductionists. A "reciprocity" clause allowed the president to lower rates if other countries did the same. It was not enough to soothe opponents, who helped to drive McKinley and other Republicans from office in the elections of 1890. For the next two decades and more, a national tug-of-war would be waged over the tariff.

McKinley Tariff

In this cartoon, Uncle Sam sits securely behind a locked door, protected by the soon-to-be-enacted Dingley Tariff bill (1897) from the riotous clamor of foreigners seeking entry into U.S. markets. Whenever reformers tried to reduce tariffs, political support for protection made the task nearly impossible. In 1882 Congress created a commission to consider lowering tariffs, but it was quickly captured by the interests who stood to gain most from high tariffs. Complained one senator: "There was a representative of the wool growers on the commission; . . . of the iron interest . . . of the sugar interest. . . . And those interests were very carefully looked out for."

Gold, Silver, and Greenbacks

Just as divisive was the issue of currency. For most of the nineteenth century, currency was backed by both gold and silver. The need for more money during the Civil War had led Congress to issue "greenbacks"—currency printed on paper with a green back and not convertible to gold or silver. For the next decade and a half Americans argued over whether to print more such paper money or take it out of circulation. Farmers and other debtors favored printing greenbacks as a way of inflating prices and thus reducing their debts. For the opposite reasons, bankers and creditors stood for "sound money" backed by gold. Fear of **inflation** led Congress first to reduce the number of greenbacks and then in 1879 to make all remaining paper money convertible into gold.

Crime of '73

A more heated battle was developing over silver-backed money. By the early 1870s so little silver was being used that Congress officially stopped coining it in 1873, touching off a steep economic slide as the supply of money contracted. With it came charges that a conspiracy of bankers had been responsible for "demonetizing" silver and wrecking the economy in what was widely referred to as the "Crime of '73." In truth, the money supply was inadequate. By the late nineteenth century, the supply of goods had expanded more rapidly than the amount of money in circulation. As the demand for money grew, pressure to raise interest rates, the charges for borrowing, grew as well. So, too, did deflation, or falling prices, as too little money chased too many goods. All added to economic instability and increased calls for enlarging the money supply.

Bland-Allison Act

In 1878 the Bland-Allison Act inaugurated a limited form of silver coinage. But pressure for unlimited coinage of silver—coining all silver presented at U.S. mints—mounted as silver production quadrupled between 1870 and 1890. In 1890 pressure for silver peaked in the Sherman Silver Purchase Act. It obligated the government to buy 4.5 million ounces of silver every month. Paper tender called "treasury notes," redeemable in either gold or silver, would pay for it. The compromise satisfied both sides only temporarily.

The White House from Hayes to Harrison

From the 1870s through the 1890s a string of nearly anonymous presidents presided over the country. Not all were mere caretakers. Some tried to energize the office, but Congress continued to dominate Washington.

Republican Rutherford B. Hayes was the first of the "Ohio dynasty," which included three presidents from 1876 to 1900. He moved quickly to end Reconstruction, but his pursuit of civil service reform ended only in splitting his party. Hayes left office after a single term, happy to be "out of a scrape." In 1880, Republican James Garfield, another Ohioan, spent his first hundred days in the White House besieged by office hunters. After Garfield's assassination only six months into his term, Chester A. Arthur, the "spoilsman's spoilsman," became president. To everyone's surprise, the dapper Arthur turned out to be an honest president. He broke with machine politicians, worked to lower the tariff, warmly endorsed the new Civil Service Act, and reduced the federal surplus by beginning construction of a modern navy. Such evenhandedness left him little chance for renomination from divided party leaders.

The Dirty Election of 1884

The election of 1884 was one of the dirtiest ever recorded. Senator James G. Blaine fought off charges of corrupt dealings with the railroads, while Democrat Grover Cleveland, the former governor of New York, admitted to fathering an illegitimate child. In the last week of the race a New York minister labeled the Democrats the party of "Rum, Romanism, and Rebellion" (alcohol, Catholicism, and the Civil War). In reaction the Irish Catholic vote swung strongly to Cleveland and with it New York and the election.

Cleveland was the first Democrat elected to the White House since James Buchanan in 1856, and he was more active than many of his predecessors. He pleased reformers by expanding the civil service, and his devotion to gold-backed currency, economy, and efficiency earned him praise from business. He supported the growth of federal power by endorsing a new federal regulatory agency created by the Interstate Commerce Act (1887), new agricultural research, and federal arbitration of labor disputes.

Cleveland's presidential activism nonetheless remained limited. He vetoed two of every three bills brought to him, more than twice the number of all his predecessors. Toward the end of his term, embarrassed by the large federal surplus, Cleveland finally reasserted himself by attacking the tariff, but to no avail. The Republican-controlled Senate blocked his attempt to lower it.

In 1888 Republicans nominated a sturdy defender of tariffs, Benjamin Harrison, the grandson of President William Henry Harrison. President Cleveland won a **plurality** of the popular vote but lost in the Electoral College. The "human iceberg" (as Harrison's colleagues called him) worked hard, rarely delegated management, and turned the White House into a well-regulated office. He helped to shape the Sherman Silver Purchase Act (1890), kept up with the McKinley Tariff (1890), and accepted the Sherman Antitrust Act (1890) to limit the power and size of big businesses. At the end of Harrison's term in 1893, Congress had completed its most productive session of the era, including the first billion-dollar peacetime budget.

A Chinese laborer, holding his queue of long hair in hand, proudly displays patches in support of the 1888 Democratic presidential candidate, Grover Cleveland, and his running mate, Allen B. Thurman. Cleveland and Thurman lost to Benjamin Harrison and Levi P. Morton, a wealthy New York banker. After his victory, Harrison, a pious Presbyterian, grabbed the hand of Senator Matthew Quay and crowed, "Providence has given us the victory." "Providence hadn't a damn thing to do with it," Quay said later, irked that Harrison seemed to have no idea how many Republicans "were compelled to approach the gates of the penitentiary to make him President."

Ferment in the States and Cities

Despite its growing expenditures and more legislation, most people expected little from the federal government. Few newspapers even bothered to send correspondents to Washington. Public pressure to curb the excesses of the new industrial order mounted closer to home, in state and city governments. Experimental and often effective, state programs began to grapple with the problems of corporate power, discriminatory shipping rates, political corruption, and urban decay.

Starting in 1869 with Massachusetts, states established commissions to investigate and regulate industry, especially railroads, America's first big business. By the turn of the century, almost two-thirds of the states had them. These weak commissions gathered and publicized information on shipping rates and business practices and furnished advice about public policy. On the West Coast and in the Midwest, state legislatures empowered commissions to end rebates and monitor freight rates. Illinois in 1870 became the first of several states to define railroads as public highways subject to regulation, including setting maximum rates.

 State Commissions

Concern over political corruption and urban blight led reformers to hold state municipal conventions to discuss solutions to urban problems. Iowa held the first in 1877. Philadelphia sponsored a national conference on good city government in 1894. A year later reformers founded the National Municipal League. It soon had more than 200 branches. Its model city charter advanced such farsighted reforms as separate city and state elections, limited contracts for utilities, and more authority for mayors. Meanwhile cities and states in the Midwest enacted laws closing stores on Sundays, prohibiting the sale of alcohol, and making English the language of public

National Municipal League

schools—all in an effort to standardize social behavior and control the habits of new immigrants.

The Revolt of the Farmers

In 1890, the politics of stalemate cracked as the patience of farmers across the South and the western plains reached an end. Beginning in the 1880s, a sharp depression drove down agricultural prices and forced thousands from their land. But farmers suffered from a great deal more, including heavy mortgages, widespread poverty, and railroad rates that sometimes discriminated against them. In 1890 their resentment boiled over. An agrarian revolt—called **Populism**—swept across the political landscape and helped break the political stalemate of the previous 20 years.

The Harvest of Discontent

The revolt of the farmers stirred first on the southern frontier, spread eastward from Texas through the rest of the Old Confederacy, then moved west across the plains. Farmers blamed their troubles on obvious inequalities: manufacturers protected by the tariff, railroads with sky-high shipping rates, wealthy bankers who held their mounting debts, expensive intermediaries who stored and processed their commodities—all seemed to profit at their expense.

Targets of Farm Anger

The true picture was fuzzier. The tariff protected industrial goods but also supported some farm commodities such as wool and sugar. Railroad rates, however high, actually fell from 1865 to 1890. And while mortgages were heavy, most were short, no more than four years. Farmers often refinanced them and used the money to buy more land and machinery, thus increasing their debts. Millers and operators of grain elevators or storage silos earned handsome profits, yet every year more of them came under state regulation.

In hard times, of course, none of this mattered. And in the South many poor farmers seemed condemned forever to hard times. Credit lay at the root of their problem, because most southern farmers had to borrow money to plant and harvest their crops. The inequities of sharecropping and the crop-lien system (pages 499–500) forced them into debt. When the prices for their crops fell, they borrowed still more, stretching the financial resources of the South beyond their meager limits. Within a few years after the Civil War, Massachusetts' banks had five times as much money as all the banks of the Old Confederacy.

Beginning in the 1870s, nearly 100,000 debt-ridden farmers a year picked up stakes across the Deep South and fled to Texas to escape this ruinous system of credit, only to find it waiting for them. Others stood and fought, as one pamphlet exhorted in 1889, "not with glittering musket, flaming sword and deadly cannon, but with the silent, potent and all-powerful ballot."

Mary Shelley's novel of a man-made monster who turns against its creator strikes the theme for this 1874 cartoon titled "The American Frankenstein." Here, the railroad is a monstrous creation that crushes the common people in its path. It carries the symbols of wealth and might—a cloak of ermine and a club of capital. "Agriculture, commerce, and manufacture are all in my power," the monster bellows in the caption. Figures of authority, like the policeman at the lower right, can only snap to attention and salute.

The Origins of the Farmers' Alliance

Before farmers could vote together, they had to get together. Life on the farm was harsh, drab, and isolated. Such conditions shocked Oliver Hudson Kelley as he traveled across the South after the Civil War. In 1867 the young government clerk founded the Patrons of Husbandry to brighten the lives of farmers and broaden their horizons. Local chapters, called "granges," brought a dozen or so farmers and their families together to pray, sing, and learn new farming techniques. The Grangers sponsored fairs, picnics, dances, lectures—anything to break the bleakness of farm life. By 1875 there were 800,000 members in 20,000 locals, most in the Midwest, South, and Southwest.

Patrons of Husbandry

At first the Grangers swore off politics. But in a pattern often repeated, socializing led to economic and then political action. Pooling their money to buy supplies and equipment to store and market their crops, Grangers could avoid the high charges of intermediaries. By the early 1870s they also were lobbying midwestern legislatures to adopt "Granger laws" regulating rates charged by railroads, grain elevator operators, and other intermediaries.

Eight "Granger cases" came before the Supreme Court in the 1870s to test the new regulatory measures. *Munn v. Illinois* (1877) upheld the right of Illinois to regulate private property (in this case, the giant elevators for storing grain) as long as it was "devoted to a public use." Later decisions allowed state regulation of railroads, but only within state lines. Congress responded in 1887 by creating the Interstate Commerce Commission, a federal agency that could regulate commerce across state boundaries. In practice, it had little power, but it was a key step toward establishing the public right to oversee private companies.

Granger Cases

Slumping prices in the 1870s and 1880s bred new farm organizations. Slowly they blended into what the press called the "Alliance Movement." The Southern Alliance, formed in Texas in 1875, spread rapidly after Dr. Charles W. Macune took command in 1886. A doctor and lawyer as well as a farmer, Macune planned to expand the state's network of local chapters, or suballiances, into a national network of state Alliance Exchanges. Like the Grangers, the exchanges pooled their resources in cooperatively owned enterprises for buying and selling, milling and storing, banking and manufacturing.

Southern Alliance

For a brief period, between 1886 and 1892, the Alliance cooperatives grew to more than a million members throughout the South and challenged accepted ways of doing business. Macune claimed that his new Texas Exchange saved members 40 percent on plows and 30 percent on wagons. But most Alliance cooperatives were managed by farmers without the time or experience to succeed. Usually opposed by irate local merchants, the ventures eventually failed.

Although the Southern Alliance admitted no African Americans, it encouraged them to organize. A small group of black and white Texans founded the Colored Farmers' National Alliance and Cooperative Union in 1886. By 1891 a quarter of a million farmers had joined. Its operations were largely secret, because public action often brought swift retaliation from white supremacists. When the Colored Farmers' Alliance organized a strike of black cotton pickers near Memphis in 1891, white mobs hunted down and lynched 15 strikers. The murders went unpunished, and the Colored Alliance began to founder.

Colored Farmers' Alliance

The Alliance Peaks

Farmer cooperation reached northward to the states of the Midwest and Great Plains in the National Farmers' Alliance, created in 1880. In June 1890 Kansas organizers formed the first People's party to compete with Democrats and Republicans. Meanwhile the Southern Alliance changed its name to the National Farmers' Alliance and Industrial Union, incorporated the strong Northern Alliances in the Dakotas and Kansas, and made the movement truly national.

The key to Alliance success was not organization but leadership, both at the top and in the middle. Alliance lecturers fanned out across the South and the Great Plains, organizing suballiances and teaching new members about finance and cooperative businesses. At least one-quarter of Alliance members were women. The Alliance movement continued the old Grange practice of sponsoring family-oriented activities, such as songfests, parades, picnics, and even burial services. Although Alliance members remained sharply divided over woman suffrage, more than a few women became speakers and organizers. "Wimmin is everywhere," noted one observer of the Alliance. The comment seemed to apply literally to Alliance member Mary Elizabeth Lease, who in the summer of 1890 alone gave 160 speeches.

Ocala Demands

In 1890, members of the Alliance met in Ocala, Florida, and issued the "Ocala Demands." The manifesto reflected their deep distrust of "the money power"—large corporations and banks whose financial power gave them the ability to manipulate the "free" market. The Ocala Demands called on government to correct such abuses by reducing tariffs, abolishing national banks, regulating railroads, and coining silver money freely. The platform also demanded a federal income tax and the popular election of senators to make government more responsive to the public.

The most innovative feature of the platform came from Charles Macune. His "subtreasury system" would have required the federal government to furnish warehouses for harvested crops and low-interest loans to tide farmers over until prices rose. Under such a system farmers would no longer have had to sell in a glutted market, as they did under the crop-lien system. And they could have exerted control over the money supply, expanding it simply by borrowing at harvest time.

In the elections of 1890 the old parties faced hostile farmers across the nation. In the South, the Alliance continued to work within the Democratic party and elected 4 governors, won 8 legislatures, and sent 44 members of Congress and 3 senators to Washington. In the Great Plains, Alliance candidates drew farmers from the Republican party. Newly created farmer parties elected 5 representatives and 2 senators in Kansas and South Dakota and took over both houses of the Nebraska legislature.

In the West especially, Alliance organizers began to dream of a national third party that would be free from the corporate influence, sectionalism, and racial tensions that split Republicans and Democrats. In their minds, it would be a party not just of farmers but also of the downtrodden and the "toilers," including industrial workers.

The People's Party

In February 1892, as the presidential election year opened, a convention of 900 labor, feminist, farm, and other reform delegates (100 of them black) met in St. Louis. They founded the People's, or Populist, party and called for another convention to nominate a presidential ticket. Initially southern Populists held back, clinging to their strategy of working within the Democratic party. But when newly elected Democrats failed to support Alliance programs, southern leaders such as Tom Watson of Georgia abandoned the Democrats and began recruiting black and white farmers for the Populists. Although he was a wealthy farmer, Watson sympathized with the poor of both races.

The national convention of Populists met in Omaha, Nebraska, on Independence Day, 1892. Their impassioned platform promised to return government "to the hands of 'the plain people.'" More conservative southern Populists succeeded in blocking a plank for woman suffrage, though western Populists joined the campaign that would win women the right to vote in Colorado in 1893. Planks advocated the subtreasury plan, unlimited coinage of silver and expansion of the money supply, direct election of senators, an income tax, and government ownership of railroads, telegraph, and telephone. To attract wage earners the party endorsed the eight-hour workday, restriction of immigration, and a ban on the use of Pinkerton detectives in labor disputes—for the Pinkertons had engaged in a savage gun battle with strikers that year at Andrew Carnegie's Homestead steel plant. Delegates rallied behind the old greenbacker and Union general James B. Weaver, carefully balancing their presidential nomination with a one-legged Confederate veteran as his running mate.

The Election of 1892

The Populists enlivened the otherwise dull campaign of 1892, as Democrat Grover Cleveland and Republican incumbent Benjamin Harrison refought the election of 1888. This time, however, Cleveland won, and for the first session since the Civil War, Democrats gained control of both houses of Congress. The Populists, too, enjoyed success. Weaver polled over a million votes, the first third-party candidate to do so. Populists elected 3 governors, 5 senators, 10 representatives, and nearly 1,500 members of state legislatures.

Despite these victories, the election revealed dangerous weaknesses in the People's party. Across the nation thousands of voters did change political affiliations, but most often from the Republicans to the Democrats, not to the Populists. No doubt a Democratic party campaign of intimidation and repression hurt the People's party in the South, where white conservatives had been appalled by Tom Watson's open courtship of black southerners. ("You are kept apart that you may be separately fleeced of your earnings," Watson had told his racially mixed audiences.) In the North, Populists failed to win over labor and most city dwellers. Both were more concerned with family budgets than with the problems of farmers and the downtrodden.

The darker side of Populism also put off many Americans. Its rhetoric was often violent; it spoke ominously of conspiracies and stridently in favor of immigration restriction. In fact, in 1892 the Alliance lost members, an omen of defeats to come. But for the present, the People's party had demonstrated two conflicting truths. It showed how far from the needs of many ordinary Americans the two parties had drifted and how difficult it would be to break their power.

Long-Term Weaknesses of the Populists

The Rise of Jim Crow Politics

In 1892, despite the stumping of Populists like Tom Watson, African Americans cast their ballots for Republicans, when they were permitted to vote freely. But increasingly, their voting rights were being curtailed across the South.

As the nineteenth century drew to a close, a long-standing **racialism**—categorizing people on the basis of race—deepened. The arrival of "new" immigrants from eastern and southern Europe and the acquisition of new overseas colonies highlighted differences among races and helped encourage prejudices that stridently justified segregation and other forms of racial control (see pages 505–506). In the South racialism was enlisted into a political purpose—preventing an alliance of poor blacks and whites that might topple white conservative Democrats. The white supremacy campaign, on the face of it directed at African Americans, also had a broader target in the world of politics: rebellion from below, whether black or white.

Mississippi, whose Democrats had led the move to "redeem" their state from Republican Reconstruction, in 1890 took the lead in disfranchising African Americans. A new state constitution required voters to pay a poll tax and pass a literacy test, requirements that eliminated the great majority of black voters. Conservative Democrats favored the plan because it also reduced voting among poor whites, who were most likely to join opposition parties. Before the new constitution went into effect, Mississippi contained more than 250,000 eligible voters, black and white. By 1892, after its adoption, there were fewer than 77,000.

Disfranchisement

Soon an all-white combination of conservatives and "reformers"—those disgusted by frequent election-stealing with blocs of black votes—passed disfranchisement laws across the South. In 1898, the Supreme Court upheld these laws in *Williams v. Mississippi,* ruling that they were valid because they did not discriminate solely against African Americans. The decision dealt a mortal blow to the Republican Party in the South for generations because much of its support in the region came from African Americans. By 1908 campaigns to limit voting had won in every southern state.

The disfranchisement campaign succeeded in achieving its broad aim of splitting rebellious whites from blacks, as the tragic fate of Tom Watson demonstrated. Only a dozen years after his biracial campaign of 1892, Watson was promoting black disfranchisement and white supremacy in Georgia. Like other southern Populists, Watson returned to the Democratic party still hoping to help poor whites. But under the increased atmosphere of intolerance, only by playing a powerful race card could he hope to win election. "What does civilization owe the negro?" he asked bitterly. "Nothing! Nothing!! NOTHING!!!"

To mount a successful campaign for disfranchisement, white conservatives inflamed racial passions. They staged "White Supremacy Jubilees" and peppered newspaper editorials with complaints of "bumptious" and "impudent" African Americans. The lynchings of blacks peaked during the 1890s, averaging over a hundred a year for the decade. Most took place in the South. White mobs in cities such as Atlanta and New Orleans terrorized blacks for days in the newly heightened atmosphere of tension.

The African American Response

Ida B. Wells

African Americans worked out their own responses to the climate of intolerance. Ida B. Wells, a black woman born into slavery, turned her talents into a nationwide campaign against lynching when a friend, Thomas Moss, and two of his partners in the People's Grocery were brutally murdered in Memphis after a fight with a white competitor in 1892. Wells meticulously documented the murders of African Americans across the South, demonstrating an astounding 200 percent increase between 1882 and 1892. Wells turned antilynching into a personal crusade. She spent much of her time educating Americans about the use of lynching and other forms of mob violence as devices for terrorizing African Americans in the absence of slavery. Black men like Thomas Moss, who might want to start black-owned businesses or alter race relations in the South, were particular targets because they threatened the prevailing racial and economic hierarchy in the South. Though her lobbying failed to produce a federal antilynching law, Wells did help organize black women, eventually into the National Association of Colored Women in 1896. The organization supported wide-ranging reforms, including in education, housing, and health care, and, of course, antilynching.

Booker T. Washington

Wells's campaign focused on mob violence, but another former slave, Booker T. Washington, stressed instead the need for accepting the framework for race relations and working within it. "I love the South," Washington reassured an audience of white

In keeping with Booker T. Washington's emphasis on vocational training, the Tuskegee Institute, opened in Alabama in 1881, was training 1,400 students in 30 trades by 1900. Academic subjects received attention, too, as evidenced by this photograph of a history class (segregated by gender) learning about Captain John Smith and Pocahontas.

and black southerners in Atlanta in 1895. He conceded that white prejudice against blacks existed throughout the region but nonetheless counseled African Americans to accept what was offered them and work for their economic betterment through manual labor. Every laborer who learned a trade, every farmer who tilled the land could increase his or her savings. And those earnings amounted to "a little green ballot" that "no one will throw out or refuse to count." Toward that end, Washington organized the Tuskegee Institute in 1881 and created a curriculum stressing vocational skills for farming, manual trades, and industrial work.

Many white Americans hailed Washington's "Atlanta Compromise," for it struck the note of patient humility they were eager to hear. For African Americans, it made the best of a bad situation. Washington, an astute politician, discovered that philanthropists across the nation hoped to make Tuskegee an example of their generosity. He was the honored guest of Andrew Carnegie at his imposing Skibo Castle. California railroad magnate Collis Huntington became his friend, as did other business executives eager to discuss "public and social questions."

Atlanta Compromise

Washington always preached accommodation to the racial caste system. He accepted segregation (as long as separate facilities were equal) and qualifications on voting (if they applied to white citizens as well). Above all Washington sought economic self-improvement for common black folk in fields and factories. In 1900 he organized the National Negro Business League to help establish African Americans in business as the leaders of their people. The rapid growth of local chapters (320 by 1907) extended his influence across the country.

In the "Solid South" (as well as an openly racist North) it was Washington's restrained approach that set the agenda for most African Americans. The ferment of the early 1890s, among black Populists and white, was replaced by a lily-white Democratic party that dominated the region but remained in the minority on the national level.

The New Realignment

On May 5, 1893, only four days after President Grover Cleveland opened the World's Columbian Exposition in Chicago, a wave of bankruptcies engulfed the nation. Overexpansion had once again set in motion the boom-and-bust business cycle, ruining major firms and driving stock prices to all-time lows. By the time the exposition's gleaming White City shut its doors in October, nearly 200,000 workers had lost their jobs in Chicago alone. Millions across the nation shared that fate, in what became the worst depression to that date in the history of the Republic.

The sharp contrast between the White City and the nation's economic misery demonstrated the inability of the political system to smooth out the economy's cycle of boom and bust. The new industrial order that had linked Americans economically had brought prosperity in the 1880s. But in 1893, the price of interdependence became obvious, as a downturn in one sector of the economy quickly affected others. With no way to control the swings in the business cycle, depression came on a scale as large as that of the booming prosperity. Out of it emerged a new realignment that left the Republican party in control of national politics for decades to come.

The Depression of 1893

Railroad baron and descendant of two presidents Charles Francis Adams Jr. called the depression a "convulsion," but the country experienced it as crushing idleness. In August 1893, unemployment stood at 1 million; by the middle of 1894, it was 3 million. At the end of the year nearly one worker in five was out of a job.

Working and middle-class families took in boarders, laundry, and sewing to make ends meet. With so many fathers and husbands unemployed, more and more wives and children left home to work. In the 1890s the number of laboring women actually increased, from 4 million to 5.3 million, but mainly in the exploitative fields of domestic and clerical work. In the South, where half the nation's working children were employed, child labor rose by

Charles Dana Gibson, the Massachusetts-born illustrator famous for his portraits of well-bred young women in the 1890s, tackles a different subject in this ink drawing, a bread line of mixed classes during the depression of 1893.

160 percent in textile mills during the decade. Concern for the young became so acute that middle-class women created the League for the Protection of the Family in 1896. Among other things it advocated compulsory education to keep children out of factories and mines.

The federal government had no program at all to combat the effects of the depression. "While the people should patriotically and cheerfully support their Government," President Cleveland had said at his inauguration, "its functions do not include the support of the people." The states offered little more. Relief, like poverty, was considered a private matter. The burden fell on local charities, benevolent societies, churches, labor unions, and ward bosses. In city after city, citizens organized relief committees to distribute bread and clothing until their meager resources gave out.

Others were less charitable. As the popular preacher Henry Ward Beecher told his congregation, "No man in this land suffers from poverty unless it be more than his fault—unless it be his sin." But the scale of hardship was so great, its targets so random, that anyone could be thrown out of work—an industrious neighbor, a factory foreman with 20 years on the job, a bank president. Older attitudes about personal guilt and responsibility for poverty began to give way to new ideas about its social origins and the obligation of public agencies to help.

The Rumblings of Unrest

Even before the depression, rumblings of unrest had begun to roll across the country. The Great Railroad Strike of 1877 had ignited nearly two decades of labor strife (see pages 561–563). After 1893 discontent mounted as employers cut employees' wages, laid employees off, and closed factories. During the first year of the depression, 1,400 strikes sent more than half a million workers from their jobs.

Uneasy business executives and politicians saw radicalism and the possibility of revolution in every strike. But the depression of 1893 had unleashed a more elemental force: simple discontent. In the spring of 1894, it focused on government inaction. On Easter Sunday, "General" Jacob Coxey, a 39-year-old Populist and factory owner, launched the "Tramps' March on Washington" from Massillon, Ohio. His "Commonweal Army of Christ"—some 500 men, women, and children—descended on Washington at the end of April to offer "a petition with boots on" for a federal program of public works. President Cleveland's staff tightened security around the White House as other "armies" of unemployed mobilized: an 800-person contingent left from Los Angeles; a San Francisco battalion of 600 swelled to 1,500 by the time it reached Iowa.

Coxey's Army

On May 1, Coxey's troops, armed with "clubs of peace," massed at the foot of the Capitol. When Coxey entered the Capitol grounds, 100 mounted police routed the demonstrators and arrested the general for trespassing on the grass. Nothing came of the protest, other than to signal a growing demand for federal action.

President Cleveland blamed the Sherman Silver Purchase Act of 1890 for shaking business confidence by forcing the government to use its shrinking reserves of gold to purchase (though not coin) silver. Repeal of the act, Cleveland believed, was the way to build gold reserves, restore confidence, and achieve recovery. After bitter debate, Congress complied.

But repeal of silver purchases brought no economic revival. In the short run abandoning silver hurt the economy by shrinking the money supply just when expansion might have stimulated it by providing needed credit. As panic and unemployment spread, Cleveland's popularity wilted. Democrats were buried in the congressional elections of 1894. Dropping moralistic reforms and stressing national activism, Republicans won control of both the House and the Senate. With the Democrats now confined

William Jennings Bryan made the first of his three presidential bids in 1896, when he ran on both the Democratic and Populist tickets. Passionate in his convictions and devoted to the plain people, the "Great Commoner" is depicted in this hostile cartoon as a Populist snake devouring the Democratic party.

to the South, the politics of stalemate was over. All that remained for the Republican party was to capture the White House in 1896.

The Battle of the Standards

The campaign of 1896 quickly became known as the "battle of the standards"—a reference to the burning question of whether gold alone or gold and silver should become the monetary standard. Most Republicans saw gold as the stable base for building business confidence and economic prosperity. They adopted a platform calling for "sound money" supported by gold alone. Their candidate, Governor William McKinley of Ohio, cautiously supported the gold plank and firmly believed in high tariffs to protect American industry.

Silverites, on the other hand, campaigned for "free and independent" coinage of silver, in which the Treasury freely minted all the silver presented to it, independent of other nations. The supply of money would increase, prices would rise, and the economy would revive—or so their theory held. But the free silver movement was more than a monetary theory. It was a symbolic protest of region and class—of the agricultural South and West against the commercial Northeast, of debt-ridden farm folk against industrialists and financiers.

Rejecting Cleveland's gold wing of the party, silverites controlled the Democratic national convention from the start. They paraded with silver banners, wore silver buttons, and wrote a plank into the platform calling for free and unlimited coinage of the metal. The high point came when William Jennings Bryan of Nebraska stepped to the lectern, threw back his head, and offered himself to "a cause as holy as the cause of liberty— the cause of humanity." The crowd was in a near frenzy as he reached the dramatic climax and spread his arms in mock crucifixion: "You shall not crucify mankind upon a cross of gold." The next day the convention nominated him for the presidency.

Populists were in a quandary. They expected the Democrats to stick with Cleveland and gold, sending unhappy silverites headlong into their camp. Instead, the Democrats stole their thunder. "If we fuse [with the Democrats] we are sunk," complained one Populist. "If we don't fuse, all the silver men we have will leave us for the more powerful Democrats." At a bitter convention, fusionists nominated Bryan for president. The best antifusionists could do was drop the Democrats' vice presidential candidate in favor of the fiery agrarian rebel from Georgia, Tom Watson.

Free Silver

"Cross of Gold" Speech

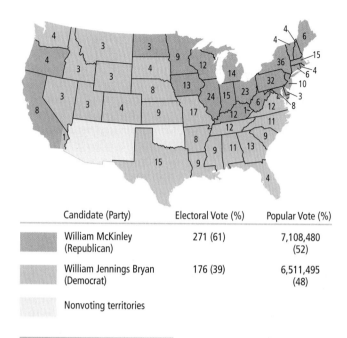

Candidate (Party)	Electoral Vote (%)	Popular Vote (%)
William McKinley (Republican)	271 (61)	7,108,480 (52)
William Jennings Bryan (Democrat)	176 (39)	6,511,495 (48)
Nonvoting territories		

Election of 1896

Republican Coalition

Bryan knew he faced an uphill battle. Adopting a more active style that would be imitated in future campaigns, he traveled 18,000 miles by train, gave as many as 30 speeches a day, and reached perhaps 3 million people in 27 states. The nomination of the People's party actually did more harm than good by labeling Bryan a Populist (which he was not) and a radical (which he definitely was not). Devoted to the "plain people," the Great Commoner spoke for rural America and Jeffersonian values: small farmers, small towns, small government.

McKinley knew he could not compete with Bryan's barnstorming, so he contented himself with sedate speeches from his front porch in Canton, Ohio. There thousands of his supporters flocked regularly to hear him promise a "full dinner pail" for everyone. The folksy appearance of the campaign belied its reality. From the beginning, it had been engineered by Marcus Alonzo Hanna, a talented Ohio industrialist. Hanna relied on modern techniques of organization and marketing. He advertised McKinley, said Theodore Roosevelt, "as if he were patent medicine." Hanna also saturated the country with millions of leaflets, along with 1,400 speakers attacking free trade and free silver.

When the votes were counted, McKinley emerged victorious, the first president since Ulysses Grant to win a majority of the popular vote. Indeed, both candidates tallied more votes than did any of their predecessors. The election also proved to be one of the most critical in the Republic's history.* Over the previous three decades, political life had been characterized by vibrant campaigns, slim party margins, high voter turnout, and low-profile presidents. The election of 1896 signaled a new era of dwindling party loyalties, stronger presidents, and Republican rule.

McKinley's victory, moreover, broke the political stalemate and forged a powerful coalition that dominated politics for the next 30 years. It rested on the industrial cities of the Northeast and Midwest and combined old support from business, farmers, and Union army veterans with broader backing from industrial wage earners. The Democrats controlled little but the South. And the Populists vanished, but not before leaving a compound legacy: as a catalyst for political realignment, a cry for federal action from the South and West, and a prelude to a new age of reform.

McKinley in the White House

In William McKinley, Republicans found a skillful chief with a national agenda and personal charm. He cultivated news reporters, openly walked the streets of Washington, and courted the public with handshakes and flowers from his own lapel. Firmly but delicately, he curbed the power of old-time state bosses. When need be, he prodded Congress to action. In all these ways, he foreshadowed "modern" presidents, who would act as party leaders rather than as executive caretakers.

Fortune at first smiled on McKinley. When he entered the White House, the economy had already begun its recovery. Factory orders were slowly increasing, and unemployment dropped. Farm prices climbed. New discoveries of gold in Alaska and South Africa expanded the supply of money without causing "gold bugs" to panic that currency was being destabilized by silver.

Freed from the burdens of the economic crisis, McKinley called a special session of Congress to revise the tariff. In 1897 the Dingley Tariff raised protective rates still

---

*Five elections, in addition to the contest of 1896, are often cited as critical shifts in voter allegiance and party alignments: the Federalist defeat of 1800, Andrew Jackson's rise in 1828, Lincoln's Republican triumph of 1860, Al Smith's Democratic loss in 1928, and—perhaps—Ronald Reagan's conservative tide of 1980.

higher but allowed tariffs to come down if other nations lowered theirs. McKinley also sought a solution for resolving railroad strikes, like the earlier Pullman conflict, before they turned violent. The Erdman Act of 1898 set up machinery for government mediation. McKinley even began laying plans for stronger regulation of trusts.

But affairs overseas competed for his attention. The same expansive forces that had transformed the United States were also causing Americans to look increasingly beyond their borders. McKinley found himself facing a crisis with Spain that would force the nation to decide whether a democratic, industrial republic should also become an imperial nation. Regulation—and a true age of reform—would await the next century.

Visions of Empire

The crisis with Spain was only the affair of the moment that turned American attention abroad. Underlying the conflict were larger forces linking the destiny of the United States with international events. By the 1890s, southern farmers were exporting half their cotton crop to factories worldwide, while western wheat farmers earned some 30 to 40 percent of their income from markets abroad. John D. Rockefeller's Standard Oil Company shipped about two-thirds of its refined products overseas, and Cyrus McCormick supplied Russian farmers with the reaper.

More than these growing commercial ties turned American heads overseas. Since the 1840s expansionists had spoken of a Manifest Destiny to overspread the North American continent from the Atlantic to the Pacific. Between 1880 and 1914, Western nations gobbled up large chunks of Asia and Africa. In 1878, less than 10 percent of Africa lay under European rule. By 1900, nearly the entire continent was controlled by Europeans. In Asia, British influence radiated outward from its stronghold in India, while France ruled Indochina (present-day Vietnam, Cambodia, and Laos). Armed with new, rapid-firing machine guns and the drug quinine to control deadly malaria, western soldiers, merchants, and missionaries established a new age of imperialism, sometimes through outright conquest and occupation, as in India and Indochina, sometimes by forging strong ties of trade and commerce, as in Latin America.

The results of European technological superiority could be devastating for native populations. In 1898 at the Battle of Omdurman, a small Anglo-Egyptian contingent under the command of British General Horatio Kitchener faced 40,000 Sudanese. The Anglo-Egyptian force was armed with machine guns and artillery, the Sudanese with little more than muskets and spears. When the smoke cleared hours later, 11,000 Sudanese had been shredded to pieces, whereas only 48 British had lost their lives.

An 1896 Republican campaign poster features presidential hopeful William McKinley atop a giant gold coin engraved with the words "sound money" and supported by workers and businessmen alike. The poster promises domestic prosperity and respect overseas. The links between prosperity and empire as well as commerce and civilization were made not only in McKinley's campaign but also by later presidents.

European Expansion Worldwide

The scramble for empire was well under way by the time the Americans, Germans, and Japanese entered the fray in the late nineteenth century. Spain and Portugal still clung to the remnants of their colonial empires, dating from the fifteenth and sixteenth centuries. In the early nineteenth century, England, France, and Russia accelerated their drive to control foreign peoples and lands. But the late nineteenth century became the new age of **imperialism** because the technology of arms and the networks of communication, transportation, and commerce brought the prospect of effective, truly global empires within much closer reach. Some Americans still cast covetous eyes north toward Canada and south toward Mexico and Cuba. More often they dreamed of empire in more distant lands in Asia and Latin America, less through traditional territorial conquest than by opening the doors of trade to foreign markets and resources. Such visions of empire, however, soon brought the United States into conflict with old imperial powers—Great Britain, France, Belgium, and Spain—and with newcomers Germany and Japan. All had imperial visions of their own.

The speed and efficiency with which Europeans expanded prompted many Americans to argue for this European-style imperialism of conquest and possession.

"His Master's Voice"

Assessing the Technologies of Imperialism

How do historians measure the reach and influence of imperialism? Clearly technology played an important role in the conquests of the "Great Powers," most obviously the technology of force, including rifles, explosives, battleships with cannons and armor-plated hulls. But in subduing native peoples, western nations also depended on less blunt instruments such as trade (of goods eagerly desired) and religion (which preached a salvation-embracing western culture along with the westerners' god). Imperialism's reach was also extended by another force, which might be referred to as the technology of culture.

When Edison invented the phonograph in 1877, few people would have thought of it as a weapon of conquest. Instead, it was considered an instrument of entertainment and a civilizing force. But when Americans and Europeans brought the machine with them to less technologically advanced societies, native peoples were awestruck by the sounds it made and sometimes cowed by those who controlled it. These white men, it appeared, had the power to conjure up the voices of invisible speakers and summon music from thin air. The RCA Victrola Company for many years used the painting of a dog sitting attentively in front of an old-fashioned phonograph, with the slogan, "His Master's Voice." Historians have come to see Edison's talking machine as one element (can you think of others?) of the technology of culture that helped make the Great Powers masters.

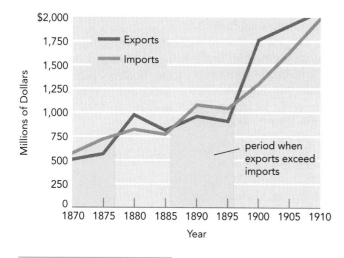

But other Americans preferred a more indirect imperialism: one that exported products, ideas, and influence. To them, this American imperialism seemed somehow purer, for without naked conquest Americans could be portrayed as bearers of long-cherished values: democracy, free-enterprise capitalism, and Protestant Christianity.

While Americans tried to justify imperial control in the name of such values, social, economic, and political forces were drawing them rapidly into the imperial race. The growth of industrial networks linked them to international markets as never before, whether they were Arkansas sharecroppers dependent on world cotton prices or Pittsburgh steelworkers whose jobs were made possible by orders for Singer sewing machines for Europe, China, and the Hawaiian Islands.

Balance of U.S. Imports and Exports, 1870–1910 *After the depression of 1893, both imports and exports rose sharply, suggesting one reason why the age of imperialism was so closely linked with the emerging global industrial economy.*

The Shapers of American Imperialism

Although the climate for expansion and imperialism was present at the end of the nineteenth century, the small farmer or steelworker was little concerned with how the United States advanced its goals abroad. An elite group—Christian missionaries, intellectuals, business leaders, and commercial farmers—joined navy careerists to shape a more active American imperialism.

Without a strong navy, imperialism of any sort was out of the question. By 1880 the once-proud Civil War fleet of more than 600 warships was rotting from neglect.

The U.S. Navy ranked twelfth in the world, behind Denmark and Chile. The United States had a coastal fleet but no functional fleet to protect its interests overseas. Discontented navy officers now combined with trade-hungry business leaders to lobby Congress for a modern navy.

Alfred Thayer Mahan, a Navy captain and later admiral, formulated their ideas into a widely accepted theory of **navalism**. In *The Influence of Sea Power upon History* (1890), Mahan argued that great nations were seafaring powers that relied on foreign trade for wealth and might. In times of overproduction and depression, as had occurred repeatedly in the United States after the Civil War, overseas markets assumed even greater importance. The only way to protect foreign markets, Mahan reasoned, was with large cruisers and battleships. Operating far from American shores, these ships would need coaling stations and other resupply facilities throughout the world.

Mahan Calls for a Strong Navy

Mahan's logic was so persuasive and the profits to be reaped from foreign trade were so great that in the 1880s Congress launched a program to rebuild the old wood-and-sail navy with steam vessels made of steel. By 1900, the U.S. Navy ranked third in the world. With a modern navy, the country had the means to become an imperial power.

Protestant missionaries provided a spiritual rationale for imperialism that complemented Mahan's military and economic arguments. As devout Americans sought to convert "heathen" unbelievers in the faraway lands of China, the Middle East, and the western Pacific, they encountered people whose cultural differences often made them unreceptive to the Christian message. Many missionaries believed that natives first had to become Western in culture before turning Christian in belief. They introduced Western goods, schools, and systems of government administration—any "civilizing medium," as one minister remarked when he invited the Singer Company to bring its famous sewing machines to China. Yet most missionaries were not territorial imperialists. They opposed outright military or political intervention.

Missionaries

From scholars, academics, and scientists came racial theories to justify European and American expansion. Charles Darwin's *On the Origin of Species* (1859) had popularized the notion that among animal species, the fittest survived through a process of natural selection. Social Darwinists such as Herbert Spencer in England and William Graham Sumner in the United States argued that the same laws of survival governed the social order. By natural as well as divine law, the fittest people (those descended from Anglo-Saxon and Teutonic stock, said Spencer and Sumner) would assert their dominion over "lesser peoples" of the world.

Social Darwinism

Perhaps more compelling than either religious or racial motives for American expansion was the need for trade. The business cycle of boom and bust reminded Americans of the unpredictability of their economy. In hard times, people sought salvation wherever they could, and one obvious road to recovery lay in markets abroad. Entrepreneurs such as Minor Keith and his Tropical Fruit Company (later the mammoth United Fruit Company) had already constructed a railroad in Costa Rica and begun importing bananas from Central America. In Cuba and Hawaii, American planters were reaping harvests of sugarcane, pineapples, and other commercial crops to be processed and sold in domestic and foreign markets. By 1900, the Singer Sewing Machine Company was sending some 60,000 sales agents across the globe to hawk the virtues of their "iron tailor." It is no wonder, then, that as American companies extended their investments abroad and the depression of 1893 deepened at home, the National Association of Manufacturers insisted that the "expansion of our foreign trade is [the] only promise of relief."

Commercial Factors

No one had done more to initiate the idea of a "new Empire" for the United States than William Henry Seward, secretary of state (1861–1869) under Lincoln and Andrew Johnson. Seward believed that "empire has . . . made its way constantly westward . . . until the tides of the renewed and decaying civilizations of the world meet on the shores of the Pacific Ocean." The United States must thus be prepared to win

William Henry Seward

Imperialist Expansion, 1900　*A comparison of Africa in 1878 (inset) and 1900 shows how quickly Europeans extended their colonial empires. Often resource-poor countries like Japan and England saw colonies as a way to acquire raw materials, such as South African diamonds and tin from Southeast Asia. Closer scrutiny shows that four of the most rapidly industrializing countries—Germany, Japan, Russia, and the United States—had few if any overseas possessions, even in 1900. And while China appears to be undivided, all the major powers were eagerly establishing spheres of influence there.*

supremacy in the Far East—not by planting colonies or sending troops but by pursuing trade. The idea that a commercial empire could be gained by demanding equal access to foreign markets was what made Seward's strategy truly revolutionary.

While he pursued ties to Japan, Korea, and China, Seward promoted a transcontinental railroad at home and a canal across Central America. Link by link, he was trying to connect eastern factories to western ports in the United States and, from there, to markets and resources in Asia. In pursuit of these goals Seward made two acquisitions in 1867: Midway Island in the Pacific and Alaska. Unimportant by itself,

Acquisition of Midway and Alaska

Missionaries often viewed the Chinese as uncivilized "heathen" whose souls needed saving and whose culture needed civilizing. This cartoon, published around 1900, pokes fun at the common stereotype by suggesting what the Chinese must think of American "heathen." "Contributions Received Here to Save the Foreign Devils," reads the sign of the Chinese "preacher," who laments the uncivilized behavior of corrupt American city governments, feuding backwoodsmen, rioting laborers, and mobs tormenting Chinese and black Americans.

the value of Midway lay as a way station to Asia not far from Hawaii, where missionary planters were already establishing an American presence. Critics called Alaska "Seward's Folly," but he paid only about 2 cents an acre for a mineral-rich territory twice the size of Texas.

Seward's conviction that the future of the United States lay in the Pacific and Asia produced little in his lifetime. But it flourished in the 1890s, when Mahan provided the naval theory necessary to make the leap and the vanishing American frontier supplied an economic rationale for extending Manifest Destiny beyond the nation's continental borders. In the 1880s, Secretary of State James G. Blaine had already began to look for ways to expand American trade and influence southward into Central and South America, where Great Britain had interests of its own to protect.

Looking to Latin America

Blaine launched a campaign to cancel the Clayton-Bulwer Treaty (1850), which shared with Great Britain rights to any canal built in Central America. At the same time, he tried to shift imports to Central America from British to U.S. goods by proposing a Pan-American Union to reduce tariffs and other trade barriers in the Americas. When Latin American nations balked at lowering their tariffs, Blaine threatened to ban any export to the United States of the products of their generally single-crop economies.

Blaine's Pan-American Union

With Latin America dependent on such exports, only three nations—Colombia, Haiti, and Venezuela—had the will to resist joining the union.

The Venezuelan Boundary Dispute

Gold, with its capacity to muddy the waters from which it was panned, stirred trouble in the jungles of Venezuela. In the 1880s, prospectors unearthed a 32-pound nugget along the border between Venezuela and British Guiana, setting off a boundary dispute between Britain and Venezuela. In 1895, President Cleveland intervened, insisting on the right of the United States to mediate the dispute under the Monroe Doctrine. Great Britain and the United States rattled their sabers at each other but neither could afford war. The British finally accepted an American mediated settlement in 1897. Anglo-American tensions eased in the wake of the crisis.

The two countries reached a new peak of friendship with a treaty concluded by Secretary of State John Hay and British ambassador Julian Paunceforte in 1901. The Hay-Paunceforte Treaty ceded British interest in building a canal across the Central American isthmus and required the United States to leave such a canal open to ships of all nations. The campaign begun years earlier by James Blaine to pave the way for a U.S.-owned canal had finally come to an end.

Reprise in the Pacific

If American expansionists wanted to extend trade across the Pacific to China, Hawaii was the crucial link. It afforded a fine naval base and a way station along the route to Asia. In 1893, American sugar planters overthrew the recently enthroned Queen Liliuokalani, a Hawaiian nationalist eager to rid the island of American influence. Their success was ensured when a contingent of U.S. marines arrived ashore on the pretext of protecting American lives.

Sugar was the key to Hawaii's English- and American-dominated plantations. Polynesians were culturally ill suited to the backbreaking labor that sugar cultivation demanded. Planters filled their labor needs by recruiting Japanese workers like this one.

Eager to avoid the McKinley Tariff's new tax on sugar imported into the United States, planters lobbied for the annexation of Hawaii, but President Cleveland refused. He was no foe of expansion but was, as his secretary of state noted, "unalterably opposed to stealing territory, or of annexing people against their consent, and the people of Hawaii do not favor annexation." The idea of incorporating the nonwhite population also troubled Cleveland. For a time, matters stood at a stalemate.

The Imperial Moment

Cuba in Revolt

In 1895, after almost 15 years of planning from exile in the United States, José Martí returned to Cuba to renew the colony's struggle for independence from Spain. With cries of "Cuba libre," Martí and his rebels cut railroad lines, destroyed sugar mills, and set fire to the cane fields. Within a year, rebel forces controlled more than half the island. But even as they fought the Spanish, the rebels worried about the United States. Their island, just 90 miles off the coast of Florida, had long been a target of American expansionists and business interests. Martí had no illusions. "I have lived in the bowels of the monster," he explained of his exile in the United States, "and I know it."

The Spanish struck back at Martí and his followers with brutal force. Governor-General Valeriano Weyler herded half a million Cubans from their homes into fortified camps where filth, disease, and starvation killed perhaps 200,000. Outside these "reconcentration" camps, Weyler chased the rebels across the countryside, polluting drinking water, killing farm animals, burning crops.

The revolt in Cuba was only the first round in a struggle that would eventually end in a war between the United States and Spain. By the time it was over, the Spanish-American War would leave Spain defeated and banished from the Western Hemisphere, Cuba free of Spanish rule, and the United States with new colonial possessions in the Pacific and the Caribbean. The knotty problem of what to do with them soon became the subject of a national debate. For better or worse, America's imperial moment had arrived.

Mounting Tensions

President Cleveland had little sympathy for the Cuban revolt, but Republican expansionists such as Theodore Roosevelt and Massachusetts senator Henry Cabot Lodge wanted to recognize Cuban independence—a step that if taken would likely provoke war with Spain. William McKinley, however, was only a moderate expansionist. As president, he lobbied Spain only privately to stop cracking down on the rebels and destroying American-owned property. With over $50 million invested in Cuban sugar and an annual trade of over $100 million, American business interests had much to lose in a war with Spain.

In October 1897, Spain promised to remove the much-despised Weyler, end the reconcentration policy, and offer Cuba greater autonomy. The shift encouraged McKinley to resist pressure at home for more hostile action. But leaders of the Spanish army in Cuba had no desire to compromise. Although Weyler was removed, the military renewed efforts to quash the rebellion. Early in 1898, McKinley dispatched the battleship *Maine* to show that the United States meant to protect its interests and its citizens.

An investigation years later concluded that the sinking of the Maine *resulted from a spontaneous explosion aboard ship, but at the time fervent patriots turned the event into a call for war and, as can be seen in the lower right corner, memorabilia, here in the form of a button carrying the famous rallying cry, "Remember the Maine." The peaceful arrival of the* Maine *in Havana harbor is depicted on the upper-left-hand corner of the painting, the grisly aftermath of the explosion in the large painting.*

Early on February 3, 1874, a fleet of chunky monitors, steam frigates, and sloops lumbered out of Key West at a slow 4.5 knots. It was the largest assembly of American naval power since the Civil War. To the officers watching from shore, the fleet was an embarrassment. "Two modern vessels of war would have done us up in 30 minutes," a future admiral observed.

In the era after the Civil War technology transformed the navies of Europe. Compound engines, improved armor plating, self-propelled torpedoes, and large rifled guns revolutionized naval warfare. The U.S. Navy, in contrast, sailed into the past. With 3,000 miles of ocean as protection and no colonies to defend, a large blue-water fleet seemed unnecessary. Even steamships seemed impractical because the United States had no coaling stations in foreign waters to fuel them. By 1878 the navy had just

Passengers on riverboats and yachts saluted the new steel-hulled, steam-powered American fleet as it made its way triumphantly up the Hudson River after naval victories in the Spanish-American War. Within a few years, these modern ships would be obsolete due to the international arms race which forced rapid innovation in naval design.

6,000 sailors, the smallest force since the presidency of Andrew Jackson.

In 1873, as the U.S. Navy fell into disrepair, the British launched the *Devastation,*

The de Lôme Letter

Then in February 1898 the State Department received a stolen copy of a letter to Cuba sent by the Spanish minister in Washington, Enrique Dupuy de Lôme. So did William Randolph Hearst, a pioneer of sensationalist, or **yellow, journalism,** who was eager for war with Spain. "WORST INSULT TO THE UNITED STATES IN ITS HISTORY," screamed the headline of Hearst's *New York Journal*. What had de Lôme actually written? After referring to McKinley as a "would-be politician," the letter admitted that Spain had no intention of changing policy in Cuba. The Spanish planned to crush the rebels. Red-faced Spanish officials recalled de Lôme, but most Americans now believed that Spain had deceived the United States.

Sinking of the *Maine*

On February 15, 1898, as the USS *Maine* lay peacefully at anchor in the Havana harbor, explosions ripped through its hull. Within minutes the ship sank to the bottom, killing some 260 American sailors. Much later, an official investigation concluded that the explosion was the result of spontaneous combustion in a coal bunker aboard ship. Most Americans at the time, however, inflamed by hysterical news accounts, concluded that Spanish agents had sabotaged the ship. McKinley sought a diplomatic solution but also a $50 million appropriation "to get ready for war."

Pressures for war proved too great to resist, and on April 11, McKinley asked Congress to authorize "forceful intervention" in Cuba. Nine days later Congress recognized Cuban independence, insisted on the withdrawal of Spanish forces, and gave the president authority to use military force. In a flush of idealism, legislators also

Teller Amendment

adopted the Teller Amendment, renouncing any aim to annex Cuba. Certainly both idealism and moral outrage led many Americans down the path to war. But in the end, the "splendid little war" (as Secretary of State Hay called it) resulted from less lofty ambitions—empire, trade, glory.

a single-masted, steam-driven vessel with heavy armor and powerful twin turrets. A forerunner of the modern battleship, it could steam across the Atlantic and back without stopping for coal. Less than a decade later, a British fleet smashed Alexandria, Egypt, whose fortifications were sturdier than those of American ports.

The battle convinced Congress that the American coast was no longer safe. In 1883 it appropriated $1.3 million for four modern, steel-hulled vessels—three cruisers, each 3,000 to 4,500 tons, and the 1,500-ton dispatch boat *Dolphin.* These early "protected" cruisers (so named for the armored deck built over boilers, engines, and other machinery) were an odd mix of old and new. The three had full sail rigs yet were completely electrified and contained watertight compartments and double bottoms.

The naval program that began as a halfhearted effort had become a major commitment by the turn of the century. The fleet included additional protected cruisers, larger armored cruisers, and its first full-sized battleships—the *Indiana, Massachusetts,* and *Oregon,* each displacing more than 10,000 tons. (Soon after 1900, giant battleships were displacing 20,000 tons; on the eve of World War I they reached more than 30,000 tons.) With five more first-class battleships commissioned by 1896, the U.S. Navy rose to fifth place in the world. The prestige of naval service had risen, too, and with it the number of sailors: nearly 10,000 in uniform.

The new navy, unlike the civilian world, was not a democratic culture. Privileges of rank were everywhere apparent. Commanders lived in wood-paneled luxury and dined on specially prepared cuisine, capped by coffee, brandy, and cigars. The crew ate salted meats, beans, and potatoes. Officers had private quarters, while enlisted men, so the saying went, lived under the place where they slept and slept under the place where they ate. At night the tables and benches used for dining in the common quarters were stowed between overhead beams from which hammocks were hung.

In 1907 President Theodore Roosevelt decided to put American naval power on display. He sent 16 battleships on a 46,000-mile, 14-month world tour. Ironically, the Great White Fleet (named for the gleaming white hulls of its ships) was already out of date. In 1906 Great Britain had commissioned the *Dreadnought,* a warship whose new guns rendered all others, including the U.S. navy, virtually obsolete—but not for long. The United States would match the British, for it had joined a naval arms race that would help to lead the world down the path to the carnage of World War I.

The Imperial War

For the 5,462 men who died, there was little splendid about the Spanish-American War. Only 379 gave their lives in battle. The rest suffered from accidents, disease, and the mismanagement of an unprepared army. As war began, the American force totaled only 30,000, none of whom had been trained for fighting in tropical climates. The sudden expansion to 60,000 troops and 200,000 volunteers overtaxed the army's graft-ridden supply system. Rather than tropical uniforms, some troops were issued winter woolens, and some fed on rations that were diseased, rotten, or even lethally spoiled. Others found themselves fighting with weapons from the Civil War.

The navy fared better. Decisions in the 1880s to modernize the fleet now paid off handsomely. (See "Daily Lives: The New Navy") Naval battles largely determined the outcome of the war. As soon as war was declared, Admiral George Dewey ordered his Asiatic battle squadron from China to the Philippines. Just before dawn on May 1, he began shelling the Spanish ships in Manila Bay. Five hours later the entire Spanish squadron lay at the bottom of the bay. Three hundred eighty-one Spaniards were killed but only one American died, a ship's engineer who succumbed to a heart attack. Dewey had no plans to follow up his stunning victory with an invasion. His fleet carried no marines with which to take the city of Manila. So ill-prepared was President McKinley for war, let alone victory, that only after learning of Dewey's success did he order 11,000 American troops to the Philippines.

Halfway around the globe, another Spanish fleet had slipped into Santiago harbor in Cuba just before the arrival of the U.S. Navy. The navy, under Admiral William

Dewey at Manila

Sampson, blockaded the island, expecting the Spanish to flee under the cover of darkness. Instead, on July 3, the Spanish fleet made a desperate daylight dash for the open seas. So startled were the Americans that several of their ships nearly collided as they rushed to attack their exposed foes. All seven Spanish ships were sunk, with 474 casualties. Only one American was killed and one wounded. With Cuba now cut off from Spain, the war was virtually won.

War in Cuba

Few Americans had heard of the Philippine Islands; fewer still could locate them on a globe. McKinley himself followed news from the Pacific front on an old textbook map. But most Americans knew that Cuba lay barely 90 miles off the Florida coast.

Before the outbreak of hostilities, Tampa, Florida, was a sleepy coastal town with a single railroad line. But when it became the port of embarkation for the Cuban expeditionary force, some 17,000 troops arrived in the spring of 1898 alone. Tampa's overtaxed facilities soon broke down, spawning disease, tension, and finally racial violence. President McKinley had authorized the army to raise five volunteer regiments of black soldiers. By the time war was declared, over 8,000 African Americans had signed up, half of them stationed around segregated Tampa. They found that although they could sail off to die freeing the peasants of Cuba, they were forbidden from buying a soda at the local drugstore. "Is America any better than Spain?" one dismayed black chaplain wondered. After drunken white troops shot at a black child, black troops in Tampa rioted. Three white and 27 black Americans were wounded in the melee.

Matters were scarcely less chaotic as 17,000 disorganized troops and hundreds of reporters finally scrambled aboard ship early in June 1898. There they sat for

Racial Tensions

Black veterans of the western Indian wars along with volunteers, segregated and commanded by white officers, made up almost a quarter of the American force that invaded Cuba. Members of the Tenth Cavalry, shown here, were clearly in no mood to be subjected to the harassment they and other black troops encountered around Tampa. Later the Tenth Cavalry supported a charge by Colonel Teddy Roosevelt's Rough Riders at the battle of San Juan Hill.

a week, until sailing on June 14 for Santiago and battle. By June 30, the Americans had landed to challenge some 24,000 Spanish, many equipped with modern rifles. The following day 7,000 Americans—including the black soldiers of the Ninth and Tenth Cavalry regiments—stormed up heavily fortified San Juan and nearby Kettle hills.

Among them Lieutenant Colonel Theodore Roosevelt thrilled at the experience of battle. He had raised a cavalry troop of cowboys and college polo players, originally called "Teddy's Texas Tarantulas." By the time they arrived in Cuba, the volunteers were answering to the nickname "Rough Riders." As they charged toward the high ground, Roosevelt yelled: "Gentlemen, the Almighty God and the just cause are with you. Gentlemen, charge!" The withering fire drowned out his shrill, squeaky voice, so he repeated the call to his troops. Charge they did and conquer the enemy, though the battle cost more than 1,500 American casualties. (See "After the Fact," pages 628–631.)

The Rough Riders

Without a fleet for cover or way to escape, the Spanish garrison surrendered on July 17. In the Philippines, a similar brief battle preceded the American capture of Manila on August 13. The "splendid little war" was over in less than four months.

Peace and the Debate over Empire

Conquering Cuba and the Philippines proved easier than deciding what to do with the islands. The Teller Amendment had renounced any American claim to Cuba. But clearly the United States had not freed the island to see chaos reign or American business and military interests excluded. And what of the Philippines—and Spanish Puerto

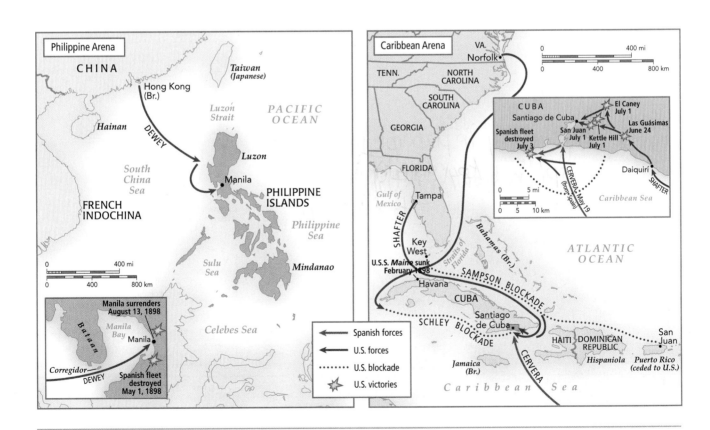

The Spanish-American War   *Had the Spanish-American War depended largely on ground forces, the ill-prepared U.S. Army might have fared poorly. But the key to success, in both Cuba and the Philippines, was naval warfare, in which the recently modernized American fleet had a critical edge. Proximity to Cuba also gave the United States an advantage in delivering troops and supplies and in maintaining a naval blockade that isolated Spanish forces.*

Rico, which American forces had taken without a struggle? Powerful public and congressional sentiment pushed McKinley to claim empire as the fruits of victory.

The president himself favored such a course. The battle in the Pacific highlighted the need for naval bases and coaling stations. "To maintain our flag in the Philippines, we must raise our flag in Hawaii," the New York *Sun* insisted. On July 7, McKinley signed a joint congressional resolution annexing Hawaii, as planters wanted for nearly a decade.

Annexing Hawaii

The Philippines presented a more difficult problem. Filipinos greeted the American forces as liberators, not new colonizers. The popular leader of the rebel forces fighting Spain, Emilio Aguinaldo, had returned to the islands on an American ship. But to the rebels' dismay, McKinley insisted that the islands were under American authority until the peace treaty settled matters.

Aguinaldo

Such a settlement, McKinley knew, would have to include American control of the Philippines. He had no intention of leaving Spain in charge or of seeing the islands fall to other European rivals. American military advisers warned that without control of the entire island of Luzon, its capital, Manila, would be indefensible as the naval base McKinley wanted. Nor, McKinley felt certain, were the Filipinos capable of self-government. Aguinaldo and his rebels thought otherwise, and in June Aguinaldo declared himself president of a new Philippine republic.

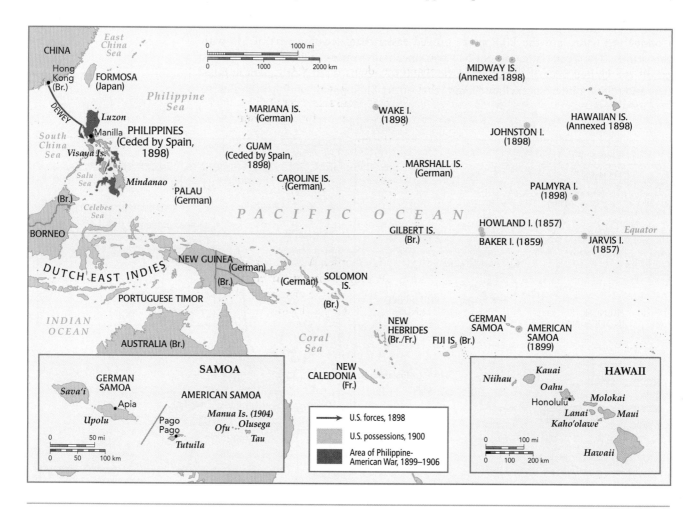

The United States in the Pacific   *In the late nineteenth century both Germany and the United States emerged as major naval powers and as contestants for influence and commerce in China. The island groups of the central and southwest Pacific, though of little economic value, had potential strategic significance as bases and coaling stations along the routes to Asia. Rivalry (as in the case of Samoa) sometimes threatened to erupt into open conflict. Control of Hawaii, Midway, Samoa, Guam, and the Philippines gave the United States a string of strategic stepping-stones to the Orient.*

Many influential Americans—former president Grover Cleveland, steel baron Andrew Carnegie, novelist Mark Twain—opposed annexation of the Philippines. Yet even these anti-imperialists favored expansion, if only in the form of trade that would benefit the nation without the costs of maintaining the Philippines as a colony. Annexation would mire the United States too deeply in the quicksands of Asian politics, many business leaders argued. More important, a large, costly fleet would be necessary to defend the islands. To the imperialists that was precisely the point: a large fleet was crucial to the interests of a powerful commercial nation.

Anti-Imperialists

Racial ideas shaped both sides of the argument. Imperialists believed that the racial inferiority of nonwhites made occupation of the Philippines necessary, and they were ready to assume the "White Man's Burden" by governing the islands. Filipinos, they said, would gradually be taught the virtues of Western civilization, Christianity, democracy, and self-rule. (In fact, most Filipinos were already Catholic after many years under Spanish rule.) Anti-imperialists, on the other hand, feared racial intermixing and the possibility of Filipino and other Asian workers flooding the American labor market. They also maintained that dark-skinned people would never develop the capacity for self-government. An American government in the Philippines could be sustained only at the point of bayonets—yet the U.S. Constitution made no provision for governing people without representation or equal rights. Such a precedent abroad, the anti-imperialists warned, might one day threaten American liberties at home.

The Role of Race

Still, when the Senate debated the Treaty of Paris ending the Spanish-American War in 1898, the imperialists had the support of the president, most of Congress, and the majority of public opinion. Even a sturdy anti-imperialist such as William Jennings Bryan, defeated by McKinley in 1896, endorsed the treaty. In it Spain surrendered title to Cuba, ceded Puerto Rico and Guam to the United States, and in return for $20 million turned over the Philippines as well.

Eager to see war ended, Bryan and other anti-imperialists believed that once the United States possessed the Philippines, it could free them. The imperialists had other notions. Having acquired an empire and a modern navy to protect it, the United States could now assert its new status as one of the world's great powers.

From Colonial War to Colonial Rule

Acquiring an empire was one thing, managing it quite another. As the Senate debated annexation of the Philippines in Washington, rebels fought with an American patrol outside of Manila. The few Americans who paid attention to the ensuing clash called it the "Filipino insurrection," but to those who fought, it was a brutal war. When it ended more than three years later, nearly 5,000 Americans, 25,000 rebels, and perhaps as many as 200,000 civilians lay dead.

Filipino Insurrection

Racial antagonism spurred some of the most savage fighting. American soldiers dismissed Filipinos as nearly subhuman. Their armed resistance to American occupation often transformed the frustrations of ordinary troops into brutality and torture. To avenge a rebel attack, one American officer swore he would turn the surrounding countryside into a "howling wilderness." Before long the American force was resorting to a garrison strategy of herding Filipinos into concentration camps while destroying their villages and crops. The policy was embarrassingly reminiscent of the tactics of "Butcher" Weyler in Cuba. Only after the Americans captured Aguinaldo himself, in 1902, did the war end.

In contrast to the bitter guerrilla war, the United States ruled the Philippines with relative benevolence. Under William Howard Taft, the first civilian governor, the Americans built schools, roads, sewers, and factories and instituted modern farming techniques. The aim, said Taft, was to prepare the island territory for independence, and in keeping with it, he granted great authority to local officials. These advances—social, economic, and political—benefited the Filipino elite and thus

The American decision to occupy the Philippines rather than give it independence compelled Filipino nationalists to fight U.S. troops, as they had already been fighting the Spanish since 1896. Forces like the ones pictured at the right were tenacious enough to require more than 70,000 Americans (left) to put down the rebellion. Sporadic, bloody guerrilla fighting continued until 1902, and other incidents persisted until 1906.

earned their support. Decades later, on July 4, 1946, the Philippines were finally granted independence.

Puerto Rico

The United States played a similar role in Puerto Rico. As in the Philippines, executive authority resided in a governor appointed by the U.S. president. Under the Foraker Act of 1900, Puerto Ricans received a voice in their government as well as a nonvoting representative in the U.S. House of Representatives. All the same, many Puerto Ricans chafed at the idea of such second-class citizenship. Some favored eventual admission to the United States as a state; others advocated independence—a division of opinion that persists today.

An Open Door in China

Like a reciprocal equation, interest in Asia drove the United States to annex the Philippines, and annexation of the Philippines only whetted American interest in Asia. The possibility of markets in China—whether for Christian souls or consumer goods—proved irresistible.

Both the British, who dominated China's export trade, and the Americans, who wanted to, worried that China might soon be carved up by other powers. Japan had defeated China in 1895, encouraging Russia, Germany, and France to join in demanding trade concessions. Each nation sought to establish an Asian **sphere of influence** in which its commercial and military interests reigned. Often such spheres resulted in restrictions against rival powers. Since Britain and the United States wanted the benefits of trade rather than actual colonies, they tried to limit foreign demands while leaving China open to all commerce.

The Open-Door Notes

In 1899, at the urging of the British, Secretary of State Hay circulated the first of two "open-door" notes among the imperial powers. He did not ask them to give up their spheres of influence in China, only to keep them open to free trade with other nations. The United States could hardly have enforced even so modest a proposal, for it lacked the military might to prevent the partitioning of China. Still, Japan and most of the European powers agreed in broad outline with Hay's policy out of fear that the Americans might tip the delicate balance by siding with a rival. Hay seized on the tepid response and brashly announced that the open door in China was international policy.

Unrest soon threatened to close the door. Chinese nationalists, known to Westerners as Boxers for their clenched-fist symbol, formed secret societies to drive out the *fon kwei*, or foreign devils. Encouraged by the Chinese empress, Boxers murdered hundreds of Christian missionaries and their followers and set siege to foreign diplomats and citizens at the British Embassy in Beijing. European nations quickly dispatched troops to quell the uprising and free the diplomats, while President McKinley sent 2,500 Americans to join the march to the capital city. Along the way, the angry foreign armies plundered the countryside and killed civilians before reaching Beijing and breaking the siege.

Boxer Rebellion

Hay feared that once in control of Beijing the conquerors might never leave. So he sent a second open-door note in 1900, this time asking foreign powers to respect China's territorial and administrative integrity. They endorsed the proposal in principle only. In fact, the open-door notes together amounted to little more than an announcement of American desires to maintain political stability and commercial trade in Asia. Yet they reflected a fundamental purpose to which the United States dedicated itself across the globe: to open closed markets and to keep open those markets that other empires had yet to close. The new American empire would have its share of colonies, but in Asia as elsewhere it would be built primarily on trade.

To expansionists such as Alfred Thayer Mahan, Theodore Roosevelt, and John Hay, American interests would be secure only when they had been established worldwide, a course of action they believed to be blessed by divine providence. "We will not renounce our part in the mission of the race, trustee under God of the civilization of the world," declared Senator Albert Beveridge. But to one French diplomat, more accustomed to wheeling and dealing in the corridors of international power, it seemed that the Americans had tempted fate. With a whiff of Old World cynicism or perhaps a prophet's eye, he remarked, "The United States is seated at the table where the great game is played, and it cannot leave it."

Sense of Mission

In the end, the Chicago World's Fair of 1893 proved an apt reflection of the world at home and abroad. Though the fair showed off its exhibits within gleaming white buildings, at the same time the political system cracked under the strain of a depression. As the Fair gathered exhibits from all over the globe, the scramble for resources and markets culminated in an age of imperialism. National greatness walked hand in hand with empire, it seemed—whether reflected in the plaster buildings of the White City or the German guns on exhibit. Employing the gendered language of the day, the German historian Heinrich von Treitschke proclaimed, "Every virile people has established colonial power." The United States joined the rush somewhat late, trailing behind the French, British, Germans, and Dutch in part because it was still extracting raw materials from its own "colonial" regions in the defeated South and the booming West.

As in the United States, European imperialists sometimes justified their rule over nonwhite peoples in Darwinian fashion. "The path of progress is strewn with the wreck . . . of inferior races," proclaimed one English professor in 1900. British poet Rudyard Kipling even suggested that Europeans were making a noble sacrifice on behalf of their colonial subjects. "Take up the White Man's Burden," he exhorted his fellow Britons in 1899. "Send forth the best ye breed— / Go bind your sons to exile / To serve your captives' need."

European critics, like those in the United States, rejected imperialism on the grounds that it delivered few economic benefits, compromised the moral standing of the colonizers, and distracted the public from undertaking much needed reforms at home. Just as Populists in the United States called on "toilers" to band together and on government to play a more active role in managing the excesses of the new industrial order, radicals in Europe such as the German-born Karl Marx exhorted "workers of the world" to unite and "throw off your chains" by abandoning capitalism and embracing socialism.

Significant Events

1850	Clayton-Bulwer Treaty
1867	Patrons of Husbandry ("Grange") founded; Alaska acquired
1869	Prohibition party founded; Massachusetts establishes first state regulatory commission
1874	Greenback party organized; Women's Christian Temperance Union formed
1875	First Farmers' Alliance organized
1877	*Munn v. Illinois* establishes the right of states to regulate private property in the public interest
1881	President James Garfield assassinated; Chester Arthur sworn in; Booker T. Washington founds Tuskegee Normal and Industrial Institute in Alabama
1887	Interstate Commerce Commission created
1889	First Pan-American Congress
1890	Sherman Antitrust Act; Wyoming enters the Union as the first state to give women the vote; Sherman Silver Purchase Act; Mahan's *The Influence of Sea Power upon History, 1660–1793* published
1892	Populist party formed; Grover Cleveland elected president
1893	Panic of 1893; Anti-Saloon League created
1894	Coxey's Army marches on Washington to demand public works for unemployed
1896	William McKinley elected president
1898	Sinking of the *USS Maine;* war with Spain; Dewey captures the Philippines; Treaty of Paris; Hawaii formally annexed
1899	First open-door notes
1899–1902	Philippine war
1900	Boxer Rebellion; Foraker Act establishes civil government in Puerto Rico

Chapter Summary

The end of the nineteenth century witnessed a crisis arising out of years of political stalemate at home as well as the realization of dreams of empire abroad.

- Republicans and Democrats ground politics into near-gridlock over the well-worn issues of regional conflict, tariff, and monetary reform.

- Discontented Americans often fashioned political instruments of their own, whether for woman suffrage, temperance, monetary change, antilynching and civil rights, or farm issues.

- The political deadlock finally came to an end in the turbulent 1890s, when depression-spawned labor strife and a revolt of farmers produced the People's, or Populist, party and a political realignment that left the Republicans in control of national politics.

- By the 1890s, too, the tradition of Manifest Destiny combined powerfully with the needs of the new industrial order for raw materials and markets and the closing of the American frontier to produce a powerful drive toward empire, which rested on these two principles of American foreign policy:

  —The old Monroe Doctrine (1823), which warned European powers to stay out of the Americas.

  —The newer open-door notes of Secretary of State John Hay (1899–1900), which stressed the importance of equal commercial access to the markets of Asia.

- Most Americans favored an overseas empire for the United States but disagreed over whether it should be territorial or commercial.

- In the end America's overseas empire was both territorial and commercial. A victory in the Spanish-American War (1898) capped an era of territorial and commercial expansion by furnishing colonial possessions in the Caribbean and the Pacific and at the same time providing more stepping-stones to the markets of Asia.

Additional Reading

Sean Dennis Cashman, *America in the Gilded Age: From the Death of Lincoln to the Rise of Theodore Roosevelt* (1984), is a good overview of the era, as is Heather Richardson, *West From Appomattox: The Reconstruction of America After the Civil War* (2007). The importance of the presidential politics of the Gilded Age is stressed in H. Wayne Morgan, *From Hayes to McKinley: National Party Politics, 1877–1896* (1969), but for the importance of ethnicity and religion see Paul Kleppner, *The Cross of Culture: A Social Analysis of Midwestern Politics, 1850–1900* (1970). Republican Party politics from the age of Lincoln to the election of George W. Bush receives detailed coverage in Lewis L. Gould's *Grand Old Party: A History of the Republicans* (2003). John Hicks's classic *The Populist Revolt* (1931) emphasizes poverty as the driving force behind Populism, while Lawrence Goodwyn portrays the Populists as crusaders for radical democratic change in *Democratic Promise: The Populist Movement in America* (1976). Also useful is Robert C. McMath, Jr., *American Populism: A Social History, 1877–1898* (1993). Michael Kazin stresses William Jennings Bryan's religious moorings and liberal instincts in *A Godly Hero: The Life of William Jennings Bryan* (2006). Charles Hoffman, *The Depression of the Nineties: An Economic History* (1970), furnishes a lucid account of the economy and the depression of 1893. On the spread of segregation in the post-Reconstruction South, see C. Vann Woodward's classic *The Strange Career of Jim Crow* (3rd rev. ed., 1974). Woodward focuses on changes in the law, while John Cell, *The Highest Stage of White Supremacy* (1982), points to the role of the city. Contrasting approaches to race relations can be seen in Louis Harlan's two-volume biography, *Booker T. Washington* (1972 and 1983), and David Levering Lewis, *W.E.B. DuBois: Biography of a Race* (1993). James West Davidson uses Ida B. Wells to provide a cultural portrait of the first generation of freed African Americans during these years in *'They Say': Ida B. Wells and the Reconstruction of Race* (2007).

For a conventional view of the rise of the welfare state in the 1930s, see Harold Wilensky and Charles N. Lebeaux, *Industrial Society and Social Welfare* (1958). A revision of those views can be found in Theda Skocpol's *Protecting Soldiers and Mothers: The Political Origins of Social Policy in the United States* (1994), which stresses the nineteenth-century origins of the welfare state and the interplay between the state and nongovernmental political groups.

For broad interpretive views of American foreign policy, see Michael Hunt, *Ideology and American Foreign Policy* (1984); John Dobson, *America's Ascent: The United States Becomes a Great Power, 1880–1914* (1978); and Walter LaFeber, *The American Age* (1989). A. G. Hopkins, ed., *Global History: Interactions Between the Universal and the Local* (2006), provides useful cultural perspectives on a variety of topics. LaFeber contains a rich bibliography, and his *Inevitable Revolutions* (3rd ed., 1993) is good on Central America. Michael Hunt, *The Making of a Special Relationship: The United States and China to 1914* (1983), is excellent on Sino-American relations. On the role of missionaries, especially women, see Jane Hunter's *The Gospel of Gentility: American Women Missionaries in Turn-of-the-Century China* (1984). For the Spanish-American War and the rise of the new American empire, see Ivan Musicant, *Empire by Default: The Spanish-American War and the Dawn of the American Century* (1998). Brian McAlister Linn's *The Philippine War* (2000) presents a thorough and well-researched account. For the Philippines, see Stanley Karnow, *In Our Image* (1989).

For a fuller list of readings, see the Bibliography at www.mhhe.com/davidsonnation6.

Historians Reconstruct the Past

Engendering the Spanish-American War

For many years, historians have examined foreign policy through the traditional lenses of diplomacy, commerce, imperial ambition, national mission, and national security. Such perspectives are not likely to go out of fashion, but recently cultural historians have begun to use new categories of analysis, particularly race and gender, to understand how foreign policy is made and carried out. Though gender may seem far-fetched in penetrating the complexities of diplomacy and military action, it can add new insights into the reasons why the United States declared war against Spain in 1898. Examining how conceptions of manliness and femininity shaped decisions to go to war also tells us much about American society in the turbulent 1890s. How did manliness and femininity influence American participation in the Spanish-American War?

The San Juan Charge

"What, are you cowards?" The shrill voice could barely be heard above the gunfire, but for the man who possessed it, the only sounds that mattered would be the cries of Spanish troops surrendering on the San Juan Heights. For the second time Lieutenant Colonel Theodore Roosevelt was assaulting a hill during the soggy Cuban summer of 1898. The first attack had only just ended, with Roosevelt and his "Texas Tarantulas" (recently dubbed the "Rough Riders") helping to overrun what the Americans called Kettle Hill. The colonel had been easy to spot: he was the only man on horseback. But Roosevelt had his reasons for the daring display, as he explained later: "It is always hard to get men to start when they can not see whether their comrades are going." And perhaps there was another reason: it showed manly grit to defy death.

The second charge was aimed at nearby San Juan Hill, this time on foot. With a pistol recovered from the sunken battleship *Maine* and a pair of eyeglasses in each of his ten custom-made pockets, Roosevelt stormed the Spanish entrenchment—practically alone, as it turned out. Bubbling with excitement, he had neglected to give the order to attack. A hundred yards into the assault, he realized what had happened and returned to rally his men. Finally they charged and, this time conquered.

Roosevelt's triumph during the Spanish-American War gave him a legendary, career-launching victory and the manly glory he had pursued since childhood. The sickly, bespectacled boy became a man, proving his courage, honor, and character in the way he thought best, in war. "San Juan," he recalled years later, "was the great day of my life."

Why War?

For many Americans, especially those born after the Civil War or too young to have fought in it, the Spanish-American War was the grand moment when their country became a great power and they a new generation of war heroes. But why did the United States go to war with Spain in 1898?

Historians have offered many explanations. Some stress the commercial rewards expected from newly acquired markets overseas. Others view the war as the global extension of the nation's "manifest destiny" to overspread the continent. Still others emphasize a geostrategic push for coaling stations in the Pacific to fuel a growing navy and for the islands in the Caribbean to block European imperialism. Humanitarian concern for the Cubans, a mission of Christian uplift for "lesser breeds," the glory of empire, political advantage at home and the spread of democracy abroad, revenge for the sinking of the *Maine,* frantic war cries from overheated journalists—all these factors enter into the historical calculus, depending on which historian is doing the math.

Yet the motives are so varied, the drums of war beating from so many quarters, historians have had difficulty tying the multiple causes into a coherent purpose. Is there a common thread among those who wanted war with Spain? Recent work has pointed to the broad-based political culture of shared values, institutions, and assumptions as the source of American belligerency. Within that political culture, some historians have highlighted gender as key.

It may seem implausible to look for the sources of the Spanish-American War in the cultural roles assigned to men and women. Gender, after all, deals with the identity of individuals, whereas the study of international relations lies in the realm of sovereign nations. But the evidence pointing toward the role of gender in this war is intriguing, to say the least.

Gendered Cartoons

Political cartoons offer a graphic clue. William Randolph Hearst's *New York Journal* took the lead in howling for war. A surprising number of cartoons in Hearst's papers, and later in others, relied on then-popular images of masculinity and femininity to make their case. In one drawing, a determined Uncle Sam spoils for a fight as he rips his jacket from his chest. "Off comes his coat—now look out!" reads the caption. In another, Sam looks down from behind a cannon at an aristocrat labeled "Spain." The Spaniard holds a bloody sword and a burning torch. At his feet lie a ravaged mother ("Cuba") and her child. "Peace—But Quit That!" says Sam. In yet another cartoon, President McKinley, who had his doubts about fighting the Spanish, is depicted as an "Old Woman" trying to "Sweep Back the Sea" of congressional support for war. Finally, Secretary of State John Sherman wags his finger in disapproval at a diminutive Alfonso XIII, the boy-king of Spain, who stands near a shackled prisoner, a beheaded statuette, and a cage filled with Americans.

In these and other political cartoons, we find notions of masculinity and femininity at the center of the message. Resolute males stand ready to fight or to rebuke those who break the codes of chivalry. Men opposing war or indecisive about it, such as McKinley, are dressed as women. The Spanish, on the other hand, are reduced to puny figures, like the petulant Alfonso, or are made out to be bloodthirsty violators of helpless womanhood. True men, the cartoons seem to be saying, go to war to protect the principles of chivalry and the women who embody them; dishonorable, cowardly men ravage women or become them.

Gendered Words

Words, too—in the halls of Congress, in boardrooms, on street cosrners, on the pages of newspapers—furnish more evidence. The country must take up arms, thundered Representative James R. Mann of Illinois—not because of some "fancied slight" or "commercial wrong" or lust for empire but "because it has become necessary to fight if we would uphold our manhood." When the

This detail from the popular painting by W. G. Read captured the Rough Riders' legendary charge—manly, courageous, romantic, and all wrong, as the more accurate painting by Frederic Remington (bottom) shows. Only Roosevelt rode. The Rough Riders ran up the hill on foot—literally for their lives—to avoid being hit by rifle fire.

Maine was sunk, Senator Richard R. Kenny of Delaware exploded over the insult: "American manhood and American chivalry give back the answer that innocent blood shall be avenged." Some urged arbitration to resolve the matter, but Senator George Perkins rejected it as unmanly: "Men do not arbitrate questions of honor," he insisted.

Such language, some historians have concluded, reflected a larger "crisis of manhood" imperiling American politics at the end of the nineteenth century. More than one observer of the political scene, they point out, worried that the creature comforts of the industrial age were making men "sluggish" and "soft," particularly upper- and middle-class men who were the source of political leadership. Worse still, the hot pursuit of money and things was corroding the manly sense of honor, integrity, and valor that contemporaries believed to be essential for good government and the basis of leadership in politics.

"Off comes his coat—now look out!"

Threats to Masculinity

As if these dangers were not enough, the rise of the "New Woman" threatened to emasculate men as women charged into the all-male preserve of politics. Woman activists laid claim to the right to vote and asserted the superiority of feminine virtue, which was needed to temper the corrupt "male" influence dominating the political system. Alice Stone Blackwell, editor of the pro-suffrage *Woman's Journal,* put it bluntly: "Assuming for the sake of argument that this war is . . . utterly inexcusable . . . it is a Congress of men that has declared it." Morality and intelligence rather than manliness, these women maintained, should be the touchstones of politics.

The depression of 1893 only aggravated this sense of crisis. Men lost their jobs, their self-respect, and with them their independence and vitality. In a Darwinian world of killing competition—in other words, the world as Americans

of the late nineteenth century conceived it—the loss of male vigor could spell disaster at home and abroad.

Resolution

Whatever else it did, the Spanish-American War offered a resolution to this crisis of manhood. The war furnished an opportunity for action in the tradition of the legendary father figures who fought in the American Revolution and the Civil War and thereby set the mold for political leadership. The war would toughen American men for survival in the realm of domestic politics as well as in the rough-and-tumble world of great imperial powers. At the same time, rescuing the Cubans from Spanish oppression would restore the heroic sense of honor believed to be so vital to leadership. In the process, the "New Woman" would be defanged. Women would resume their "proper" roles as nurturers who respected their men and raised their sons to be the next generation of brave, honorable males.

Undoubtedly, such gendered rhetoric is arresting. Whether it serves to tie together the various explanations for war and empire is another matter. Establishing the identity of a single individual is complicated enough, for character is shaped by many factors, including gender, race, ethnicity, religion, class,

"Peace—But Quit That."

"Another Old Woman Tries to Sweep Back the Sea."

twentieth-century America, see Gail Bederman's *Manliness and Civilization: A Cultural History of Gender and Race in the United States, 1880–1917* (1995). The myriad interpretations of the Spanish-American War are summarized in Luis Perez Jr.'s *The War of 1898: The United States and Cuba in History and Historiography* (1998). For his part, Perez stresses the largely ignored role of the Cuban *insurrectos,* who he feels were close to winning Cuban independence when the United States intervened to ensure that it controlled Cuba's future. Lewis L. Gould's *The Spanish-American War and President McKinley* (1982) tells the story from the presidential vantage point, while Theodore Roosevelt's *The Rough Riders* (1899) offers TR's own inflated recollections of his role in the Cuban campaign.

and education. National identity and the actions that derive from it are more complex still, and the actions of real people in the real world are perhaps thorniest of all. Even a staunch booster of war and manly vigor like Theodore Roosevelt was capable as president of pursuing the "unmanly" path of arbitration to end the Russo-Japanese War in 1905.

To say that gender shaped policy, is different from saying that gender created policy. Even so, constructions of gender did play a role in the Spanish-American War, if only in their widespread use by those who sold the country on war and by those who fought it.

Bibliography   Gender has become an increasingly important category of analysis for historians, even for those of American foreign policy. We draw heavily here on the innovative and provocative work of Kristin L. Hoganson, *Fighting for American Manhood: How Gender Politics Provoked the Spanish-American and Philippine-American Wars* (1998). For a broader view of the impact of gender on late-nineteenth- and early-

"Secretary Sherman Talks to the Boy-King."

CHAPTER 22
The Progressive Era
1890~1920

By 1900 a wave of corporate mergers led muckraking reformers to use imagery like this grasping octopus, by George Luks, to drama-tize the evils of monopoly. Progressives sought to counter the new powers of industrial society by invigorating government.

Burned Alive in the City

Quitting time, March 25, 1911. The long day was about to end at the Triangle Shirtwaist Company near the lower end of Manhattan. The deafening whir of some 1,500 sewing machines would soon be silenced as hundreds of workers—mostly young immigrant women—were set free.

To some, quitting time seemed like an emancipation. Twelve-hour days in stifling, crowded workrooms, weekly paychecks of only $3 to $15, fines for the tiniest mistakes, deductions for needle and thread, even for electricity, made the young seamstresses angry. Two years earlier, their frustration had boiled over into an industrywide strike for better wages and working conditions. Despite a union victory, the only change visible at Triangle was that every morning the doors were locked to keep workers in and union organizers out.

The fire broke out in the lofts as the workers were leaving their machines. In minutes the top stories were ablaze. Terrified seamstresses groped through the black smoke, only to find exits locked or clogged with bodies. All but one of the few working fire escapes collapsed. When the fire trucks arrived, horrified firefighters discovered that their ladders could not reach the top stories. "Spectators saw again and again pitiable companionships formed in the instant of death—girls who placed their arms around each other as they leaped," read one news story. Their bodies hit the sidewalk with a sickening thud or were spiked on the iron guard rails.

One hundred forty-six people died, most of them young immigrant women. In far-off Russia and Poland, news of the disaster sent families into spasms of grief. "Most of these old parents had an idea of America as one big town," explained one immigrant. "Each of them was almost sure that their daughter was a victim of that terrible catastrophe."

A few days later 80,000 New Yorkers joined the silent funeral procession snaking slowly up Fifth Avenue in the rain. A quarter of a million watched. At the Metropolitan Opera House, union leader Rose Schneiderman told a rally, "This is not the first time that girls have been burned alive in the city. Every year thousands of us are maimed." A special state commission investigated the tragedy. Over the next four years its recommendations produced 56 state laws regulating fire safety, hours, machinery, and home work. They amounted to the most far-reaching labor code in the country.

In 1911 the fiery deaths of 146 people at the Triangle Shirtwaist Company shocked the nation. Firefighters arrived within minutes, but their ladders could not reach the top stories. Trapped by locked doors, those who failed to escape perished within or leaped to their deaths on the streets below. Following the horrifying episode, New York enacted the most ambitious labor code in the country.

The Triangle fire shocked the nation and underscored a widespread fear: modern industrial society had created profound strains, widespread misery, and deep class divisions. Men, women, and children worked around the clock in unsafe factories for wages that barely supported them. Corporations grew to unimagined size, bought and sold legislators, dictated the terms of their own profit. In cities across America, tenement-bred diseases took innocent lives. Criminals threatened people and property, while saloons tied the working poor to dishonest political bosses. Even among the middle class, inflation was shrinking wallets at the rate of 3 percent a year. "It was a world of greed," concluded one garment worker; "the human being didn't mean anything."

But human beings did mean something to followers of an influential reform movement sweeping the country. Progressivism emerged as a political force in the mid-1890s and continued to shape politics through World War I. The movement sprang from many impulses, mixing a liberal concern for the poor and working class with conservative efforts to stabilize business and avoid social chaos. But liberal or conservative, most progressives shared a desire to soften the harsher aspects of industrialization, urbanization, and immigration.

Progressivism thus began in the cities, where the wellspring of misery was fullest, political corruption deepest, and social division clearest. It was organized by an angry, idealistic middle class and percolated up from neighborhoods to city halls, state capitals, and, finally, Washington. Though usually pursued through politics, the goals of progressives were broadly social—to create a "good society" where people could live decently, harmoniously, and prosperously, along middle-class lines.

Unlike past reformers, progressives saw government as a protector, not an oppressor. Only government possessed the resources for the broad-based reforms they sought. Progressivism spawned the modern activist state, with its capacity to regulate the economy and manage society. And because American society had become so interdependent, progressivism became the first nationwide reform movement. No political party monopolized it; no single group controlled it. It flowered in the presidencies of Republican Theodore Roosevelt and Democrat Woodrow Wilson. In 1912 it even gave birth to its own party, the Progressive, or "Bull Moose," party. But by then progressivism had filtered well beyond politics into every realm of American life.

The Roots of Progressive Reform

Families turned from their homes; an army of unemployed on the roads; hunger, strikes, and bloody violence across the country—the wrenching depression of 1893 forced Americans to take a hard look at their new industrial order. They found common complaints that cut across lines of class, religion, and ethnicity. If streetcar companies raised fares while service deteriorated, if food processors doctored their canned goods with harmful additives, if politicians skimmed money from the public till, everyone suffered.

Aims of Progressives

The result was not a coherent progressive movement but a set of loosely connected goals. Some progressives fought to make government itself efficient and honest. Others called for greater regulation of business and a more orderly economy. Some sought social justice for the poor and working classes; others, social welfare to protect children, women, and consumers. Still other progressives looked to purify society by outlawing alcohol and drugs, stamping out prostitution and slums, and restricting the flood of new immigrants. And all tried to make business and government more responsive to the democratic will of the people.

Paternalistic by nature, progressives often imposed their solutions, no matter what the less "enlightened" poor or oppressed saw as their own best interests. Then, too, reformers acted partly out of nostalgia. In a rapidly changing world, they wanted to redeem such traditional American values as democracy, opportunity for the individual, and the spirit of public service. Yet if the ends of progressives were traditional, their means were distinctly modern. They used the systems and methods of the new industrial order—the latest techniques of organization, management, and science—to fight its excesses and soften its impact.

The Progressive System of Beliefs

Progressives were moderate modernizers—reformers, not revolutionaries. They accepted the American system as sound, only in need of adjustment. Many drew on the increasingly popular Darwinian theories of evolution to buttress this gradual approach to change. With its notion of slowly changing species, evolution undermined the acceptance of fixed principles that had guided social thought in the Victorian era. Progressives saw an evolving landscape and ever-shifting values. They denied the old Calvinist doctrine of inborn sinfulness and instead saw people as having a greater potential for good than for evil.

Yet progressives had seen the mean side of industrialism and somehow had to explain the existence of evil and wrongdoing. Most agreed that they were "largely, if not wholly, products of society or environment." People went wrong, wrote one progressive, because of "what happens to them." By changing what happened, the human potential for good could be released. As reformer Jane Addams explained, "what has been called 'the extraordinary pliability of human nature'" made it "impossible to set any bounds to the moral capabilities which might unfold under ideal civic and educational conditions."

With an eye to results, progressives asked not "Is it true?" but "Does it work?" Philosopher Charles Peirce called this new way of thinking **pragmatism.** William James, the Harvard psychologist, became its most famous popularizer. For James, pragmatism meant "looking towards last things, fruits, consequences, facts."

Pragmatism

The Pragmatic Approach

Pragmatism led educators, social scientists, and lawyers to adopt new approaches to reform. John Dewey, the master educator of the progressive era, believed that environment shaped the patterns of human thought. Instead of demanding mindless memorization of abstract and unconnected facts, Dewey tried to "make each one of our schools an embryonic community life." At his School of Pedagogy, founded in 1896 with his wife, Alice, he let students unbolt their desks from the floor, move about, and learn by doing so they could train for real life.

Psychologist John B. Watson believed that human behavior could be shaped at will. "Give me a dozen healthy infants," he wrote, ". . . and my own specified world to bring them up in, and I'll guarantee to take any one at random and train him to become any specialist I might select, doctor, lawyer, artist, merchant, chief, and yes, even beggarman and thief." **Behaviorism** swept the social sciences and later advertising, where Watson himself eventually landed.

Behaviorism

John Dewey, progressive philosopher and educator

Lawyers and legal theorists applied their own blend of pragmatism and behaviorism. Justice Oliver Wendell Holmes Jr., appointed to the Supreme Court in 1902, rejected the idea that the traditions of law were constant and universal. "Long ago I decided I was not God," said Holmes. Law was a living organism to be interpreted according to experience and the needs of a changing society.

Sociological Jurisprudence

This environmental view of the law, known as **sociological jurisprudence,** found a skilled practitioner in Louis Brandeis. Shaken by the brutal suppression of the Homestead steel strike of 1892, Brandeis quit his corporate practice and proclaimed himself the "people's lawyer." The law must "guide by the light of reason," he wrote, by which he meant bringing everyday life to bear in any court case. Whereas older court opinions had been based largely on legal precedent, progressives asked courts to look at the world around them and realize that society had undergone changes so fundamental that many precedents of the past no longer applied. Past and present must stand on equal footing in interpreting the law, they said.

Brandeis Brief

Brandeis had a chance to test his practical principles when laundry owner Curt Muller challenged an Oregon law that limited his laundresses to working 10 hours a day. Brandeis defended the statute before the Supreme Court in 1908. His famous legal brief in *Muller v. Oregon* contained 102 pages describing the damaging effects of long hours on working women and only 15 pages of legal precedents. The Supreme Court upheld Oregon's right to limit the working hours of laborers and thus legitimized the "Brandeis Brief."

The Progressive Method

Seeing the nation riven by conflict, progressives tried to restore a sense of community through the ideal of a single public interest. Christian ethics were the guide, to be applied after using the latest scientific methods in gathering and analyzing data about a social problem. The modern corporation furnished an appealing model for organization. Like corporate executives, progressives relied on careful management, coordinated systems, and specialized bureaucracies to carry out reforms.

Between 1902 and 1912 a new breed of journalists investigated wrongdoers, named them in print, and described their misdeeds in vivid detail. Most exposés began as articles in mass-circulation magazines. *McClure's* magazine stirred controversy and boosted circulation when it sent reporter Lincoln Steffens to uncover the crooked ties between business and politics. Steffens's "Tweed Days in St. Louis" appeared in the October 1902 issue of *McClure's* and was followed in the November issue by Ida M. Tarbell's *History of the Standard Oil Company,* another stinging, well-researched indictment. Soon a full-blown literature of exposure was covering every ill from unsafe food to child labor.

Muckrakers

A disgusted Theodore Roosevelt thought the new reporters had gone too far and called them "muckrakers," after the man who raked up filth in the seventeenth-century classic *Pilgrim's Progress.* Still, by documenting dishonesty and blight, muckrakers not only aroused people but also educated them. No broad reform movement of American institutions would have taken place without them.

Voluntary Organizations

To solve the problems that muckrakers exposed, progressives stressed volunteerism, civic responsibility, and collective action. They drew on the organizational impulse that seemed everywhere to be bringing people together in new interest groups. Between 1890 and 1920 nearly 400 organizations were founded, many to combat the ills of industrial society. Some, like the National Consumers' League, grew out of efforts to promote general causes—in this case protecting consumers and workers from exploitation. Others, such as the National Tuberculosis Association, aimed at a specific problem.

When voluntary action failed, progressives looked to government to protect the public welfare. They mistrusted legislators, who might be controlled by corporate interests or political machines. So they strengthened the executive branch by increasing the power of individual mayors, governors, and presidents. Then they watched those executives carefully.

Professionals

Progressives also drew on the expertise of the newly professionalized middle class. Confident, cosmopolitan professionals—doctors, engineers, psychiatrists, city planners—mounted campaigns to stamp out sexually transmitted disease and dysentery, to reform prisons and asylums, and to beautify cities. At all levels—local, state, federal—new agencies and commissions staffed by impartial experts began to investigate and regulate lobbyists, insurance and railroad companies, public health, even government itself.

The Search for the Good Society

If progressivism ended in politics, it began with social reform: the need to reach out, to do something to bring the "good society" a step closer. Ellen Richards had just such ends in mind in 1890 when she opened the New England Kitchen in downtown Boston. Richards, a chemist and home economist, designed the Kitchen to sell cheap, wholesome food to the working poor.

The New England Kitchen promoted social as well as nutritional reform. Women freed from the drudgery of cooking could seek gainful employment. And as a "household experiment station" and center for dietary information, the Kitchen tried to educate the poor and Americanize immigrants by showing them how the middle class prepared meals. According to philanthropist Pauline Shaw, it was also a "rival to the saloon." A common belief was that poor diets fostered drinking, especially among the poor and working classes.

In the end, the New England Kitchen served more as an inexpensive eatery for middle-class working women and students than as a resource for the poor or an agency of Americanization. Still, Ellen Richards's experiment reflected a pattern typical of progressive social reform: the mix of professionalism with uplift of the needy, socially conscious women entering the public arena, the hope of creating a better world along middle-class lines.

Pattern of Reform

Poverty in a New Light

During the 1890s crime reporter and photographer Jacob Riis launched a campaign to introduce middle-class audiences to urban poverty. Writing in vivid detail in *How the*

Jacob Riis, the Danish-born reporter and photographer, stalked the streets of New York, meticulously recording the squalor in which many slum-dwellers lived. Here we have a Riis photograph of a cramped tenement on Bayard Street, where for "5 cents a spot" a lodger could find a place to sleep for the night. The room, Riis wrote in How the Other Half Lives, *was "not thirteen feet either way" and housed "twelve men and women, two or three in bunks in a sort of alcove, the rest on the floor." What originally had been a lifeless engraving in the first edition of the book appeared as this sharp photograph in later editions, adding detail and poignancy to its sleepy-eyed subjects.*

Other Half Lives (1890), Riis brought readers into the teeming tenement. Accompanying the text were shocking photos of poverty-stricken Americans—Riis's "other half." He also used slide shows to publicize their plight. His pictures of slum life appeared artless, merely recording the desperate poverty before the camera. But Riis used them to tell a moralistic story, much the way the earlier English novelist Charles Dickens had used his melodramatic tales to attack the abuses of industrialism in England. People began to see poverty in a new, more sympathetic light, the result less of flawed individuals than of environment.

Social Work

A new profession—social work—proceeded from this new view of poverty. Social work developed out of the old settlement house movement (see pages 579–580). Like the physicians from whom they drew inspiration, social workers studied hard data to diagnose the problems of their "clients." Unlike nineteenth-century philanthropists, the new social workers refused to do things to or for people. Instead they worked with their clients, enlisting their help to solve their own problems. A social worker's "differential casework" attempted to treat individuals case by case, each according to the way the client had been shaped by environment.

In reality poverty was but a single symptom of many personal and social ills. Most progressives continued to see it as a by-product of political and corporate greed, slum neighborhoods, and "institutions of vice" such as the saloon. Less clear to them was how deeply rooted poverty had become.

Expanding the "Woman's Sphere"

Progressive social reform attracted a great many women seeking what Jane Addams called "the larger life" of public affairs. In the late nineteenth century, women found that protecting their traditional sphere of home and family forced them to move beyond it. Bringing up children, making meals, keeping house, and caring for the sick now involved community decisions about schools, public health, and countless other matters.

Women's Organizations

In the nineteenth century, many middle- and upper-middle-class women received their first taste of public life from women's organizations, including mothers' clubs, temperance societies, and church groups. By the turn of the century, some 500 women's clubs boasted over 160,000 members. Through the General Federation of Women's Clubs, they funded libraries and hospitals and supported schools, settlement houses,

"The Awakening," a 1915 cartoon, offers a more graphic and emotion-laden map of woman suffrage than the one on page 640. Here, a torch-bearing woman in classical dress carries the franchise from western states, where woman suffrage has already been enacted, to the eastern states, where desperate women eagerly reach out. A poem by suffragist Alice Duer Miller, later collected in Are Women People? *(1915), appears below the map. The title of Miller's book became a slogan of the woman suffrage movement.*

compulsory education, and child labor laws. Eventually they moved beyond the concerns of home and family to endorse such controversial causes as woman suffrage, unionization, and the fight against lynching.

New Woman

The dawn of the century saw the rise of a new generation of women. Longer lived, better educated, and less often married than their mothers, they were also willing to pursue careers for fulfillment. Usually they turned to professions that involved their traditional role of nurturers—nursing, library work, teaching, and settlement house work.

Custom and prejudice still restricted these new women. The faculty at the Massachusetts Institute of Technology, for example, refused to allow Ellen Richards to pursue a doctorate. Instead they hired her to run the gender-segregated "Woman's Laboratory" for training public school teachers. At the turn of the century, only about 1500 women lawyers practiced in the whole country, and in 1910 women made up barely 6 percent of licensed physicians. That figure rapidly declined as male-dominated medical associations grew in power and discouraged the entry of women.

Margaret Sanger and Birth Control

Margaret Sanger sought to free women from the bonds of chronic pregnancy. Sanger, a visiting nurse on the Lower East Side of New York, had seen too many poor women overburdened with children, pregnant year after year, with no hope of escaping the cycle. The consequences were sometimes deadly but always crippling. "Women cannot be on equal footing with men until they have complete control over their reproductive functions," she argued.

The insight came as a revelation one summer evening in 1912 when Sanger was called to the home of a distraught immigrant family on Grand Street. Sadie Sachs, mother of three, had nearly died a year earlier from a self-induced abortion. In an effort to terminate another pregnancy, she had accidentally killed herself. Sanger vowed that night "to do something to change the destiny of mothers whose miseries were as vast as the sky." She became a crusader for what she called "birth control." By distributing information on contraception, she hoped to free women from unwanted pregnancies and the fate of Sadie Sachs.

Single or married, militant or moderate, professional or lay, white or black, more and more middle-class urban women thus became "social housekeepers." From their own homes they turned to the homes of their neighbors and from there to all of society.

Social Welfare

In the "bigger family of the city," as one woman reformer called it, settlement house workers soon concluded that private acts of charity would have to be supplemented by government action to make real progress. Laws had to be passed and agencies created to promote social welfare, including improved housing, workplaces, parks, and playgrounds; the abolition of child labor; and the enactment of eight-hour-day laws for working women.

By 1910 the more than 400 settlement houses across the nation had organized into a loose affiliation, with settlement workers ready to help shape government policy. Often it was women who led the way. Julia Lathrop, a Vassar College graduate, spent 20 years at Jane Addams's Hull House before becoming the first head of the new federal Children's Bureau in 1912. By then two-thirds of the states had adopted some legislation limiting child labor, although loopholes exempted countless youngsters from coverage. Under Lathrop's leadership, Congress was persuaded to pass the Keating-Owen Act (1916), forbidding goods manufactured by children from crossing state lines.*

Keating-Owen Act

---

*The Supreme Court struck down the law in 1918 as an improper regulation of local labor; nonetheless, the law focused greater attention on the abuses of child labor.

In Macon County, Illinois, officials provided newly enfranchised women voters with their own ballot box.

Florence Kelley, who had also worked at Hull House, spearheaded a similar campaign in Illinois to protect women workers by limiting their workday to eight hours. As general secretary of the National Consumers' League, she also organized boycotts of companies that treated employees inhumanely. Eventually most states enacted laws restricting the number of hours women could work.

Woman Suffrage

No one had ever seen pickets in front of the White House before, let alone picketing women. But starting on January 10, 1917, from ten in the morning until half past five in the evening, there they stood stiff and silent at the front gates, six days a week, rain or shine. The "Silent Sentinels," as they called themselves, let their banners speak for them. One quoted the words of Inez Milholland. Only a year earlier, she had collapsed at a suffrage rally in Los Angeles as she rose to speak in favor of granting women the right to vote. "Mr. President," she had said with her dying breath, "how long must women wait for liberty?"

Ever since the conference for women's rights held at Seneca Falls in 1848, women reformers had pressed for the right to vote on the grounds of equal opportunity and simple justice. Progressives embraced woman suffrage by stressing what they saw as the practical results: reducing political corruption, protecting the home, and increasing the voting power of native-born whites. The "purer sensibilities" of women—an ideal held by Victorians and progressives alike—would help cleanse the political process of selfishness and corruption, while their sheer numbers would keep the political balance tilted away from immigrant newcomers.

The suffrage movement benefited, too, from new leadership. In 1900 Carrie Chapman Catt became president of the National American Woman Suffrage Association, founded by Susan B. Anthony in 1890. Politically astute and a skilled organizer, Catt mapped a grassroots strategy of education and persuasion from state to state. She called it "the winning plan." As the map below shows, victories came first in the West, where women and men had already forged a more equal partnership to overcome the hardships of frontier life. By 1914, 10 western states (and Kansas) had granted women the vote in state elections, as Illinois had in presidential elections.

Militant Suffragists

The slow pace of progress drove some suffragists to militancy. The shift began in England after 1900, when Emmeline Pankhurst, her daughters Christabel and Sylvia,

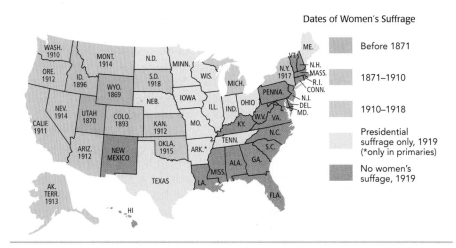

Woman Suffrage *Western states were the first to grant women the right to vote. Sparsely populated and more egalitarian than the rest of the nation, the West was used to women participating fully in settlement and work. Other sections of the country, notably the Midwest, granted women partial suffrage that included voting for school boards and taxes. Suffragists encountered the most intractable resistance in the South, where rigid codes of social conduct elevated women symbolically but shackled them practically.*

along with their followers, chained themselves to the visitors' gallery in the House of Commons and slashed paintings in museums. When those tactics failed, they invaded the time-honored bastion of British manhood—the golf course—and scrawled "VOTES FOR WOMEN" in acid on the greens. They smashed the windows of department stores, broke up political meetings, even burned the houses of members of Parliament. British authorities threw many of the protesters in jail, Emmeline Pankhurst included. When the women went on hunger strikes, wardens tied them down, held open their mouths with wooden clamps, and fed them by force.

Among the British suffragists was a small American with large, determined eyes. In 1907, barely out of her teens, Alice Paul had gone to England to join the suffrage crusade. When asked why she had enlisted, she recalled her Quaker upbringing. "One of their principles . . . is equality of the sexes," she explained. Paul marched arm-in-arm with British suffragists and more than once was imprisoned and refused to eat. In 1910, she returned to the United States and brought the aggressive tactics with her. Three years later, in 1913, Paul organized 5,000 women to parade in protest at President Woodrow Wilson's inauguration. Wilson himself was not convinced that woman suffrage was a good idea and favored a state-by-state approach to the issue. Half a million people watched as a near riot ensued. Paul and other suffragists were hauled to jail, stripped naked, and thrown into cells with prostitutes.

In 1914, Paul broke with the more moderate National American Woman Suffrage Association and formed the Congressional Union, dedicated to enacting national woman suffrage at any cost through a constitutional amendment. She allied her organization with western women voters in the militant National Woman's party in 1917. It was also Paul who organized the Silent Sentinels at the White House, when the president refused to see any more delegations of women urging a constitutional amendment. She was arrested at the gates of the White House and dragged off to a cell block in the Washington jail, where she and others refused to eat. Prison officials declared her insane, but a public outcry soon led to her release.

Such repression only widened public support for woman suffrage. So did the contributions of women to World War I at home and abroad (see Chapter 23). In the wake of the war, Great Britain granted women (over age thirty) the right to vote in 1918, Germany and Austria in 1919, and the United States in 1920 through the Nineteenth Amendment. Overnight the number of eligible voters in the country doubled.

Nineteenth Amendment

Controlling the Masses

"Observe immigrants," wrote one American in 1912. "You are struck by the fact that from ten to twenty percent are hirsute, low-browed, big-faced persons of obviously low mentality. . . . They clearly belong in skins, in wattled huts at the close of the Ice Age." The writer was neither an uneducated fanatic nor a stern opponent of change. He was Professor Edward A. Ross, a progressive from Madison, Wisconsin, who prided himself on his scientific study of sociology.

Faced with the chaos and corruption of urban life, more than a few progressives feared they were losing control of their country. Saloons and dance halls lured youngsters and impoverished laborers; prostitutes walked the streets; vulgar amusements pandered to the uneducated. Strange Old World cultures clashed with "all-American" customs, and ethnic groups jostled uneasily. The city challenged middle-class reformers to convert this riot of diversity into a more uniform society. To maintain control progressives sometimes moved beyond education and regulation and sought restrictive laws to control the masses.

Stemming the Immigrant Tide

A rising tide of immigrants from southern and eastern Europe especially troubled native-born Americans, including reformers anxious over the changing ethnic complexion of the country. In northern cities progressives often succeeded in reducing immigrant voting power by increasing residency requirements.

On a sunny May morning in 1903, 45,000 people poured through the gates of Luna Park at Coney Island, just south of Brooklyn. What they saw on opening day amazed them: "a storybook land of trellises, columns, domes, minarets, lagoons, and lofty aerial flights." Barkers beckoned them into a Venetian city, a Japanese garden, and a bustling Asian Indian celebration. They could hop aboard the "Switchback" Railroad, a forerunner of the roller coaster, or careen on flat-bottomed boats down a steep incline into the "Shoot-the-Chutes" lagoon. Those who spent their days in crowded tenements rolling cigars or sleeping nights in stuffy apartments might well blink in awe as a quarter of a million electric lights, strung like glittering pearls across the buildings, turned night into enchanted day.

Gondolas in Venice Canal, Venice, California

The Venice Amusement Park in California was meant to conjure up Venice, Italy, complete with a network of canals and gondolas. The founders dubbed Venice Park "the Coney Island of the Pacific."

Eugenics

A new science called "eugenics" lent respectability to the idea that newcomers were biologically inferior. Eugenicists believed that heredity largely shaped human behavior, and they therefore advocated selective breeding for human improvement. By 1914 more magazine articles discussed eugenics than slums, tenements, and living standards combined. In *The Passing of the Great Race* (1916), upper-crust New Yorker and amateur zoologist Madison Grant helped popularize the notion that the "lesser breeds" threatened to "mongrelize" America. So powerful was the pull of eugenics that it captured the support of some progressives, including birth-control advocate Margaret Sanger.

Americanization

Most progressives, however, believed in the shaping impact of environment and so favored either assimilating immigrants into American society or restricting their entry into the country. Jane Addams, for one, stressed the cultural "gifts" immigrants brought with them: folk rituals, dances, music, and handicrafts. With characteristic paternalism, she and other reformers hoped to "Americanize" the foreign-born (the term was newly coined) by teaching them middle-class ways. Education was one key. Progressive educator Peter Roberts, for example, developed a lesson plan for the Young Men's Christian Association that taught immigrants to dress, tip, buy groceries, and vote.

Literacy Test

Less-tolerant citizens sought to restrict immigration as a way of reasserting control and achieving social harmony. Though white, Protestant, and American-born, these **nativists** were only occasionally progressives themselves, but they did employ progressive methods of organization, investigation, education, and legislation. The first solid victory for restrictionists came in 1882, when they succeeded in barring the entry of Chinese laborers into the country. After the turn of the century, restrictionists gained strength as the tidal wave of eastern and southern European immigrants crested. Active since the 1890s, the Immigration Restriction League pressed Congress in 1907 to require a literacy test for admission into the United States. Presidents Taft and Wilson vetoed it in 1913 and 1915, but Congress overrode Wilson's second veto in 1917, when war fever raised defensive nationalism to a new peak.

Coney Island was but one of a host of similar parks that popped up across the country at the turn of the century. Soaring urban populations, increases in leisure time, more spending money, and new trolley systems that made for cheap excursions from the city led to the opening of Boston's Paragon Park, Cleveland's Euclid Beach, Atlanta's Ponce de Leon Park, and Los Angeles's Venice Beach.

All traded in entertainment, but of a sort new to city dwellers. Earlier Victorian reformers had promoted two models of public entertainment: the spacious city park and the grand public exposition. Both were meant to instruct as well as amuse. Their planners hoped to reduce urban disorder by raising public taste and refining public conduct. When

it opened in 1858, New York City's Central Park became a model pastoral retreat in the midst of the city. Its rustic paths, tranquil lakes, and woodsy views were designed as respites from the chaos of urban life. Some amusement parks, like Venice Beach's, mimicked the neoclassical European style of the World's Columbian Exposition (see pages 595–596).

But it did not escape the amusement park operators that people wanted to have fun. At the Columbian Exposition, the amusements section, a mile-long strip of theaters, restaurants, sideshows, and rides, had lured more people than did the free public exhibits. As one owner put it, parks were in the business of "amusing the million." Coney Island's

Luna Park drew 5 million paying customers in a single season.

Jostling with crowds, eating ice cream and hot dogs, riding Shoot-the-Chutes, young working men and working women, single, in couples, or married, and even the newest immigrant could feel gloriously free and independent, gloriously American. A sense of solidarity drew the mostly working-class crowds together, and the zaniness of the setting loosened social restraints. The Victorian values of sober industry, thrift, and orderly conduct could hardly compete with the democratic abandon and gaiety of the new amusement parks. The parks heralded the rise of mass culture, invading public space with the private dreams of ordinary people.

The Curse of Demon Rum

Tied closely to concern over immigrants was an attack on saloons. Part of a broader crusade to clean up cities, the antisaloon campaign drew strength from the century-old drive to lessen the consumption of alcohol. Women made up a disproportionate number of alcohol reformers. The temperance movement reflected their growing campaign to storm male domains—in this case the saloon—and to contain male violence, particularly the wife and child abuse associated with drinking.

By 1900 the dangers of an alcoholic republic seemed all too real. Alcohol consumption had risen to an annual rate of more than two gallons per person. Over half of Boston and Chicago visited a bar at least once a day. Often political bosses owned saloons or conducted their business there. To alcohol reformers, taverns and saloons thus seemed at the center of many social problems—gambling and prostitution, political corruption, drug trafficking, unemployment, and poverty. Few reformers recognized the complex cycle of social decay that produced such problems, fewer still the role of saloons as "workingmen's clubs." The saloon was often the only place to cash a check, find out about jobs, eat a cheap meal, or take a bath.

Reformers considered a national ban on drinking unrealistic and intrusive. Instead they concentrated on prohibiting the sale of alcohol at local and state levels and attacked businesses that profited from it. Led by the Anti-Saloon League (1893), a massive publicity campaign bombarded citizens with pamphlets and advertisements. Doctors cited scientific evidence linking alcohol to cirrhosis, heart disease, and insanity. Social workers connected alcohol consumption with the deterioration of the family; employers, to accidents on the job and lost efficiency.

Anti-Saloon League

By 1917 three out of four Americans lived in "dry" counties. Nearly two-thirds of the states had adopted laws outlawing the manufacture and sale of alcohol. Not all progressives were prohibitionists, but the many who were sighed with relief at having taken the profit out of human pain and corruption.

The "Inebriate's Express," loaded with drunken riders, is heading straight for hell. This detail from a chromolithograph, published around 1900, was typical of Victorian-era responses to the problems posed by alcohol. To the all-seeing eye of the omnipotent God, faith, hope, charity, and the Bible are sufficient to cure the problems of drinking.

Prostitution

In 1910, the Chicago Vice Commission estimated that 5,000 full-time and 10,000 occasional prostitutes plied their trade in the city. Other cities, small and large, reported similar numbers. An unlikely group of reformers united to fight this vice: feminists who wanted husbands to be as chaste as their wives, public health officials worried about the spread of sexually transmitted disease, and immigration restrictionists who regarded the growth of prostitution as yet another sign of corrupt newcomers. Progressives condemned prostitution but saw the problem in economic and environmental terms. "Poverty causes prostitution," concluded the Illinois Vice Commission in 1916. On average, prostitutes earned five times the income of factory workers.

Some reformers saw more active agents at work. Rumors spread of a vast and profitable "white slave trade." Men armed with hypodermic needles were said to be lurking about streetcars, amusement parks, and dance halls in search of young women. Although the average female rider of the streetcar was hardly in danger of abduction, in every city there could be found cribs with locked doors where women were held captive and forced into prostitution. By conservative estimates they made up some 10 percent of all prostitutes.

As real abuses blended with sensationalism, Congress passed the Mann Act (1910), prohibiting the interstate transport of women for immoral purposes. By 1918 reformers succeeded in banning previously tolerated **red-light districts** in most cities. Once again, progressives went after those businesses that, like the liquor trade, made money from misery.

"For Whites Only"

Most progressives paid little attention to the misery suffered by African Americans. The 1890s had been a low point for black citizens, most of whom still lived in the South. Across the region, the lynching of African Americans increased dramatically, as did restrictions on black voting and the use of segregated facilities to separate whites from blacks. Signs decreeing "For Whites Only" appeared on drinking fountains and restrooms and in other public places.

A few progressives, such as muckraker Ray Stannard Baker and settlement-house worker Lillian Wald, decried racial discrimination, but most ignored it—or used it to their political advantage. Throughout the South, white progressives and even old-guard politicians, including Senator Ben Tillman of South Carolina and Governor James K. Vardaman of Mississippi, used the rhetoric of reform to support white supremacy. Such "reformers" won office by promising to disfranchise African Americans in order to break the power of corrupt political machines that rested on the black vote, much as northern machines marshaled the immigrant vote.

In the face of such discrimination, African Americans fought back. After the turn of the century, black critics in the North rejected the cautious accommodation of Booker T. Washington's "Atlanta Compromise," which counseled African Americans to accept segregation and work their way up the economic ladder (see pages 606–607). W. E. B. Du Bois, a professor at Atlanta University, leveled the most stinging attack in *The Souls of Black Folk* (1903). Du Bois saw no benefit for African Americans in sacrificing intellectual growth for narrow vocational training. Nor would he accept the South's

W. E. B. Du Bois

Taking a Chance on His Pleasures

Biography along the Fault Lines of American Culture

Black boxing champ Jack Johnson did not take sass from anyone, black or white. Americans sat up and took notice in 1910 when Johnson beat former heavyweight champion Jim Jeffries. Billed as the "Hope of the White Race," Jeffries turned out to be little more than a punching bag for Johnson. "JEFFRIES MASTERED BY GRINNING, JEERING NEGRO," lamented the *San Francisco Chronicle.*

Johnson's turbulent career has fascinated historians just as it did contemporaries, though for different reasons. Can we use an individual life—an atypical life, no doubt—to illuminate American society? Precisely because Johnson was *not* conventional, his performance in and out of the ring exposed culture fault lines. In a segregated society, not only did he beat—and taunt—white opponents, Johnson used his celebrity to violate racial conventions. He paraded his sexuality. He consorted with white women. He drank hard and drove fast. "I always take a chance on my pleasures," he boasted. Johnson knew what he wanted; he knew what was forbidden. Trespassing boundaries was one way of declaring independence, not merely in pursuit of equality but defiant superiority.

Hounded by the authorities, Johnson was eventually convicted by a white jury of violating the Mann Act for transporting a woman across state lines for sexual purposes. In the end Johnson became more than a symbol of racial rebellion. By pushing the boundaries of celebrity, he also exposed the limits of tolerance in a Progressive culture that was finding all kinds of pleasure—whether in amusement parks, dance halls, saloons, or sports arenas—both desirable and disturbing at the same time.

Jack Johnson

discriminatory caste system. A better future would come only if black citizens struggled politically to achieve suffrage and equal rights.

Instead of exhorting African Americans to pull themselves up slowly from the bottom, Du Bois called on the "talented tenth," a cultured black vanguard, to blaze a trail of protest against segregation, **disfranchisement,** and discrimination. In 1905 he founded the Niagara Movement for political and economic equality, and in 1909 a coalition of blacks and white reformers transformed the Niagara Movement into the National Association for the Advancement of Colored People. As with other progressive organizations, its membership was largely limited to the middle class. It worked to extend the principles of tolerance and equal opportunity in a color-blind fashion by mounting legal challenges to the Jim–Crow system of segregation and bigotry. By 1914, the NAACP had some 6,000 members in 50 branches throughout the country. Accommodation was giving way to new combative organizations and new forms of protest.

NAACP

The Politics of Municipal and State Reform

Reform the system. In the end, so many urban problems seemed to come back to the premise that government had to be overhauled. Jane Addams learned as much outside the doors of her beloved Hull House in Chicago, where garbage piled up in the streets. Off to city hall she and her co-workers went to protest—700 times in one summer during the 1890s. In Chicago, as elsewhere, corrupt city bosses had made garbage collection a plum to be awarded to the company that paid them the most for it.

In desperation, Addams herself submitted a bid for garbage removal in the ward. When it was thrown out on a technicality, she won an appointment as garbage inspector. For almost a year she dogged collection carts, but boss politics kept things dirty. So Addams ran candidates in 1896 and 1898 against local ward boss Johnny Powers. They lost, but Addams kept up the fight for honest government and social reform—at city hall, in the Illinois legislature, and finally in Washington. Politics turned out to be the only way to clean things up.

Jane Addams founded her settlement at Hull House in Chicago because she was convinced, like many progressives, that reform must be practical, arising out of the needs of individuals within a community. As Addams continued her campaigns, she also looked beyond the local neighborhood to reform political structures of municipal and state governments.

The Reformation of the Cities

For middle-class reformers, the urban battleground furnished the first test of political reform. And a series of colorful and independent mayors demonstrated that cities could be run humanely without changing the structure of government.

In Detroit, shoe magnate Hazen Pingree turned the mayor's office into an instrument of reform when elected in 1889. By the end of his fourth term, Detroit had new parks and public baths, fairer taxes, ownership of the local light plant, and a work-relief program for victims of the depression of 1893. In 1901, Cleveland mayor Tom Johnson launched a similar reform campaign. Before he was through, municipal franchises had been limited to a fraction of their previous 99-year terms and the city ran the utility company. By 1915 nearly two out of three cities in the nation had copied some form of this "gas and water socialism" to control the runaway prices of utility companies.

Tragedy dramatized the need to alter the very structure of government. On a hot summer night in 1900 a tidal wave from the Gulf of Mexico smashed the port city of Galveston, Texas. Floods killed one of every six residents. The municipal government sank into confusion and political wrangling. In reaction business leaders won approval of a new charter that replaced the mayor and city council with a powerful commission. Each of five commissioners controlled a municipal department, and together they ran the city. By 1920 nearly 400 cities had adopted the plan. Expert commissioners enhanced efficiency and helped to check party rule in municipal government.

City-Manager Plan

In other cities, elected officials appointed an outside expert, or "city manager," to run things. The first was hired in Staunton, Virginia, in 1908. Within a decade, 45 cities had them. At lower levels experts took charge of services: engineers oversaw utilities; accountants, finances; doctors and nurses, public health; specially trained firefighters and police, the safety of citizens. Broad civic reforms attempted to break the corrupt alliance between companies doing business with the city and the bosses who controlled the wards. Citywide elections replaced the old ward system, and civil service laws helped create a nonpartisan bureaucracy based on merit. Political machines and ethnic voters lost power, while city government gained efficiency.

Progressivism in the States

"Whenever we try to do anything, we run up against the charter," complained the reform mayor of Schenectady, New York. Charters granted by state governments defined the powers of cities. The rural interests that generally dominated state legislatures rarely gave cities adequate authority to levy taxes, set voting requirements, draw up budgets, or legislate reforms. State legislatures, too, found themselves under the influence of business interests, party machines, and county courthouse rings. Reformers therefore tried to place their candidates where they could do some good—in the governors' mansions.

State progressivism enjoyed its greatest success in the Midwest, under the leadership of Robert La Follette of Wisconsin. A mainstream Republican until a party boss offered him a bribe in a railroad case, La Follette turned about and pledged to break "the power of this corrupt influence." In 1900 he won the governorship of Wisconsin as an uncommonly independent Republican.

Over the next six years "Battle Bob" La Follette made Wisconsin, in the words of Theodore Roosevelt, "the laboratory of democracy." La Follette's **Wisconsin idea** produced the most comprehensive set of state reforms in American history. There were new laws regulating railroads, controlling corruption, and expanding the civil service. His direct primary weakened the hold of party bosses by transferring nominations from the backrooms of party conventions and caucuses to the voters at large. Among La Follette's notable "firsts" were a state income tax, a state commission to oversee factory safety and sanitation, and a Legislative Reference Bureau at the University of Wisconsin. University-trained experts poured into state government.

Other states copied the Wisconsin idea or hatched their own programs of reform. By 1916 all but three had direct primary laws. To cut the power of party organizations and make officeholders directly responsible to the public, progressives worked for three additional reforms: initiative (voter introduction of legislation), referendum (voter enactment or repeal of laws), and recall (voter-initiated removal of elected officials). By 1912 a dozen states had adopted initiative and referendum, and seven, recall. A year later the Seventeenth Amendment to the Constitution permitted the direct election of senators, previously selected by state legislatures.

Almost every state established regulatory commissions with the power to hold public hearings and to examine company books and question officials. Some could set maximum prices and rates. Yet it was not always easy to define, let alone serve, the "public good." All too often commissioners found themselves refereeing battles within industries—between carriers and shippers, for example—rather than between what progressives called "the interests" and "the people." Regulators had to rely on the advice of experts drawn from the business community itself. Many commissions thus became "captured" by the industries they regulated.

Social welfare received special attention from the states. The lack of workers' compensation for injury, illness, or death on the job had long drawn fire from reformers and labor leaders. American courts still operated on the common-law assumption that employees accepted the risks of work. Workers or their families could collect damages only if they proved employer negligence. Most accident victims received nothing. In 1902 Maryland finally adopted the first workers' compensation act. By 1916, most states required insurance for factory accidents and over half had employer liability laws. Thirteen states also provided pensions for widows with dependent children.

Despite the progressive attack on machine politics, political bosses survived, in part by adapting the climate of reform to the needs of their working-class constituents. After the Triangle fire of 1911, for example, it was Tammany Democrats Robert F. Wagner and Alfred E. Smith who led the fight for a new labor code to govern conditions in the workplace. This working-class "urban liberalism" also found advocates among women's associations, especially those concerned with mothers, children, and working women. The Federation of Women's Clubs led the fight for mothers' pensions (a forerunner of

On the state level, progressives made their greatest impact in Wisconsin, where Robert La Follette led the fight to regulate railroads, control corruption, and expand the civil service. In trying to do an end run around political party bosses, he used his publication, La Follette's Magazine, *to reach ordinary Americans directly.*

aid to dependent children). When in 1912 the National Consumers' League and other women's groups succeeded in establishing the Children's Bureau, it was the first federal welfare agency and the only female-run national bureau in the world. At a time when women lacked the vote, they nonetheless sowed the seeds of the welfare state as they helped to make urban liberalism a powerful instrument of social reform.

Progressivism Goes to Washington

On September 6, 1901, at the Pan-American Exposition in Buffalo, New York, Leon Czolgosz stood nervously in line. He was waiting among well-wishers to meet President William McKinley. Unemployed and bent on murder, Czolgosz shuffled toward McKinley. As the president reached out, Czolgosz fired two bullets into his chest. McKinley slumped into a chair. Eight days later the president was dead. The mantle of power passed to Theodore Roosevelt. At 42 he was the youngest president ever to hold office.

Roosevelt's entry into the White House was a political accident, as he himself acknowledged. Party leaders had seen the weak office of vice president as a way of removing him from power, but the tragedy in Buffalo foiled their plans. "It is a dreadful thing to come into the presidency this way," Roosevelt remarked, "but it would be a far worse thing to be morbid about it." Surely progressivism would have come to Washington without Theodore Roosevelt, and while there he was never its most daring advocate. In many ways he was quite conservative. He saw reform as a way to avoid more radical change. Yet without Roosevelt, progressivism would have had neither the broad popular appeal nor the buoyancy he gave it.

TR

TR, as so many Americans called him, was the scion of seven generations of wealthy, aristocratic New Yorkers. A sickly boy, he built his body through rigorous exercise, sharpened his mind through constant study, and pursued a life so strenuous that few

Bullnecked and barrel-chested, Theodore Roosevelt was "pure act," said Henry Adams. TR may have had the attention span of a golden retriever, as one critic charged, but he also embodied the great virtues of his day—honesty, hard work, constancy, courage, and, while in power, self-control.

could keep up. He learned to ride and shoot, roped cattle in the Dakota Badlands, mastered judo, and later in life climbed the Matterhorn, hunted African game, and explored the Amazon.

In 1880, driven by an urge to lead and serve, Roosevelt won election to the New York State Assembly. In rapid succession he became a civil service commissioner in Washington, New York City police commissioner, assistant secretary of the navy, and the Rough Rider hero of the Spanish-American War. At the age of 40 he won election as reform governor of New York and two years later as vice president. Through it all, TR remained a solid Republican, personally flamboyant but committed to mild change only.

To the Executive Mansion (he renamed it the "White House"), Roosevelt brought a passion for order, a commitment to the public, and a sense of presidential possibilities. Most presidents believed the Constitution set specific limits on their power. Roosevelt thought that the president could do anything not expressly forbidden in the document. Recognizing the value of publicity, he gave reporters the first press room in the White House and favored them with all the stories they wanted. He was the first president to ride in an automobile, fly in an airplane, and dive in a submarine—and everyone knew it.

To dramatize racial injustice, Roosevelt invited black educator Booker T. Washington to lunch at the White House in 1901. White southern journalists called such mingling with African Americans treason, but for Roosevelt the gesture served both principle and politics. His lunch with Washington was part of a "black and tan" strategy to build a biracial coalition among southern Republicans. He denounced lynching and appointed black southerners to important federal offices in Mississippi and South Carolina.

Sensing the limits of political feasibility, Roosevelt went no further. Perhaps his own narrowness when it came to race stopped him too. In 1906, when Atlanta exploded in a race riot that left 12 people dead, he said nothing. Later that year he discharged "without honor" three entire companies of African American troops because some of the soldiers were unjustly charged with having "shot up" Brownsville, Texas. All lost their pensions, including six winners of the Medal of Honor. The act stained Roosevelt's record. (Congress acknowledged the wrong in 1972 by granting the soldiers honorable discharges.)

Brownsville Incident

A Square Deal

Philosophy of the
Square Deal

By temperament, Roosevelt was not inclined to follow McKinley's cautious course. He had more energetic actions in mind. He accepted growth—whether of business, labor, or government—as natural. In the pluralistic system he envisioned, big labor would counterbalance big capital, big farm organizations would offset big food processors, and so on. Standing astride them all, mediating when needed, was a big government that could ensure fair results for all. Later, as he campaigned for a second term in 1904, Roosevelt named this program the "Square Deal."

Anthracite Coal Strike

In a precedent-breaking display of presidential initiative, Roosevelt in 1902 intervened in a strike that idled 140,000 miners and paralyzed the anthracite (hard) coal industry. As winter approached, public frustration with the mine owners mounted. They refused even to recognize the miners' union, let alone negotiate worker demands for higher wages and fewer hours. Roosevelt summoned both sides to the White House. John A. Mitchell, the young president of the United Mine Workers, agreed to arbitration, but management balked. Roosevelt leaked word to Wall Street that the army would take over the mines if the owners did not yield.

Seldom had a president acted so boldly, and never on behalf of strikers. In late October 1902 the owners settled by granting miners a 10 percent wage hike and a nine-hour day in return for increases in coal prices and no recognition of the union. Roosevelt was equally prepared to intervene on the side of management, as he did when he sent federal troops to end strikes in Arizona in 1903 and Colorado in 1904. His aim was to establish a vigorous presidency ready to deal squarely with all sides.

Roosevelt especially needed to confront the issue of economic concentration. Financial power had become consolidated in giant **trusts** following a wave of mergers at the end of the century. As large firms swallowed smaller ones, Americans feared that monopoly would destroy individual enterprise and free competition. A series of government investigations revealed a rash of corporate abuses—rebates, collusion, **"watered" stock,** payoffs to government officials. The conservative courts showed

U.S. v. E. C. Knight

little willingness to break up the giants or blunt their power. In *United States v. E. C. Knight* (1895), the Supreme Court had crippled the Sherman Antitrust Act by ruling that the federal law applied only to **interstate commerce** and not to manufacturing. The decision left the American Sugar Refining Company in control of 98 percent of the nation's sugar-making factories.

In his first State of the Union message, Roosevelt told Congress that he did not oppose business concentration. As he saw it, large corporations were not only inevitable but capable of producing more at lower prices than were smaller operations. He wanted to regulate, not destroy, them, to make them fairer and more efficient. Only then would the economic order be humanized, its victims protected, and class violence avoided. Like individuals, trusts had to be held to strict standards of morality. Conduct, not size, was the yardstick TR used to measure "good" and "bad" trusts.

With a progressive's faith in the power of publicity and a regulator's need for the facts, Roosevelt moved immediately to strengthen the federal power of investigation. He called for the creation of a Department of Commerce with a Bureau of Corporations that could force companies to hand over their records. Congressional conservatives shuddered at the prospect of putting corporate books on display. Finally, in 1903, after Roosevelt charged that John D. Rockefeller was orchestrating the opposition, Congress enacted the legislation and provided the Justice Department with additional staff to prosecute antitrust cases.

Northern Securities

In 1902, to demonstrate the power of government, Roosevelt had Attorney General Philander Knox file an antitrust suit against the Northern Securities Company. The mammoth holding company virtually monopolized railroads in the Northwest. Worse still, it had bloated its stock with worthless certificates. Here, clearly, was a symbol of the "bad trust." J. P. Morgan, one of the company's founders, rushed to the White House. "Send your man [the attorney general] to my man [Morgan's lawyer] and they can fix it up," he told Roosevelt and Knox. "We don't want to fix it up," replied the attorney general. "We want to stop it." In the end the Supreme Court ordered the company to dissolve in 1904. Ultimately, the Roosevelt administration brought suit against 44 giants, including the Standard Oil Company, the American Tobacco Company, and the Du Pont Corporation.

Railroad Regulation

Despite his reputation for trustbusting, Roosevelt always preferred regulation. The problems of the railroads, for example, were newly underscored by a recent round of consolidation that had contributed to higher freight rates. Roosevelt pressed Congress to strengthen the weak Interstate Commerce Commission (ICC) (see page 603). In 1903 Congress enacted the Elkins Act, which gave the ICC power to end rebates. Even the railroads supported the act because it saved them from the costly practice of granting special fee reductions to large shippers.

By the election of 1904 the president's boldness had won him broad popular support. He trounced his two rivals, Democrat Alton B. Parker, a jurist from New York, and Eugene V. Debs of the Socialist party. No longer was he a "political accident," Roosevelt boasted.

Conservatives in his own party opposed Roosevelt's meddling in the private sector. But progressives, goaded by Robert La Follette, demanded still more regulation of the railroads, in particular a controversial proposal for making public the value of all rail property. In 1906, the president finally reached a compromise typical of his restrained approach to reform. The Hepburn Railway Act allowed the ICC to set ceilings on rates and to regulate sleeping car companies, ferries, bridges, and terminals. La Follette did not obtain the provision to disclose company value he wanted, but the Hepburn Act drew Roosevelt nearer to his goal of continuous regulation of business.

Bad Food and Pristine Wilds

Extending the umbrella of federal protection to consumers, Roosevelt belatedly threw his weight behind two campaigns for healthy foods and drugs. In 1905 Samuel Hopkins Adams of *Collier's Weekly* wrote that in its patent medicines "Gullible America" would get "huge quantities of alcohol, an appalling amount of opiates and narcotics," and worse—axle grease, acid, glue. Adams sent the samples he had collected to Harvey Wiley, chief chemist at the Agriculture Department. Wiley's "Poison Squad" produced scientific evidence of Adams's charges.

Patent medicines made wild curative claims. These promised to restore hair and end dandruff with extracts from the yucca plant, long used by Indians of the Southwest for medicinal and non-medicinal purposes.

The appearance of Upton Sinclair's *The Jungle* in 1906 spurred Congress to act. Sinclair intended to recruit people to socialism by exposing the plight of workers in the meatpacking industry. His novel contained a brief but vivid description of the slaughter of cattle infected with tuberculosis, of meat covered with rat dung, and of men falling into cooking vats and being served to the public as "Durham's Pure Leaf Lard." Readers paid scant attention to the workers, but their stomachs turned at what they might be eating for breakfast. The Pure Food and Drug Act of 1906 sailed through Congress, and the Meat Inspection Act soon followed.

Conservation Through Planned Management

Roosevelt had come late to the consumer cause, but on conservation he led the nation. An outdoors enthusiast, he galvanized public concern over the reckless use of natural resources. His chief forester, Gifford Pinchot, persuaded him that planned management under federal guidance was needed to protect the natural domain. Cutting trees must be synchronized with tree plantings, oil needed to be pumped from the ground under controlled conditions, and so on.

In the western states water was the problem, as U.S. Geological Survey director John Welsey Powell had noted years earlier (see pages 510–511). Economic growth, even survival, depended on it. Two visions of what to do about Powell's water-starved West emerged. One emphasized the conservation of water (and other scarce resources) through planned use; the other, preservation of resources in a pristine state. Supporters of conservation pointed to the economic benefits flowing from planned water use: bringing marginal land into production, luring settlers into a region that was land-rich and people-poor, implanting agriculture and industry on an unimagined scale.

Conservation versus Preservation

The Sierra Club, founded by naturalist John Muir, believed in the importance of preserving wilderness in its natural state. "In God's wildness," Muir wrote in 1890, "lies the hope of the world—the great fresh unblighted, unredeemed wilderness." Muir helped persuade President Theodore Roosevelt to double the number of national parks. Here, some Sierra Club members lounge at the base of a giant redwood in Big Basin in 1905.

Advocates of preservation pointed to the ecological costs of developing a region whose scarce water could be drained or contaminated and whose natural environment was thus ill-suited for agriculture and industry.

As fragmented local and state water policies sparked controversy, violence, and waste, many progressives campaigned for a federal program to replace the chaotic web of rules. Democratic senator Frederick Newlands of Nevada introduced the Reclamation Act of 1902 to set aside proceeds from the sale of public lands for irrigation projects. The Reclamation Act signaled a progressive step toward the conservationist goal of rational resource development.

John Muir and Preservation

Conservation often conflicted with the more radical vision of preservationists, led by naturalist and wilderness philosopher John Muir. Muir founded the Sierra Club in 1892 in hopes of maintaining such natural wonders as the Hetch-Hetchy valley in Yosemite National Park in a state "forever wild" to benefit future generations. Many conservationists saw such valleys only as sites for dams and reservoirs to manage and control water. Controversy flared after 1900, when San Francisco announced plans to create a reservoir in the Hetch-Hetchy valley. Could a dam be built in a national park? For 13 years Muir waged a publicity campaign against the reservoir and its "devotees of ravaging commercialism." Pinchot enthusiastically backed San Francisco's claim. Roosevelt, torn by his friendship with Muir, did so less loudly. Not until 1913 did President Woodrow Wilson finally decide the issue in favor of San Francisco by authorizing the construction of the O'Shaughnessy Dam. Construction had won over preservation.

Roosevelt nonetheless advanced many of Muir's goals. Over the protests of cattle and timber interests, he added nearly 200 million acres to government forest reserves; placed coal and mineral lands, oil reserves, and water-power sites in the public domain; and enlarged the national park system. When Congress balked, he reserved another 17 million acres of forest before the legislators could pass a bill limiting him. Like a good progressive, he sent hundreds of experts to work applying science, education, and technology to environmental problems.

In truth, Roosevelt's reform record was still modest when he announced in 1908 that he would not run for another term. Yet by reinvigorating the presidency and the executive branch, TR opened the way to even more thorough reforms. The conservative business community was well aware of that possibility, as was Roosevelt himself, when he turned the presidency over to his successor, William Howard Taft.

The Troubled Taft

On March 4, 1909, as snow swirled outside the White House, William Howard Taft readied himself for his inauguration. Over breakfast with Roosevelt, he warmed in the glow of recent Republican victories. Taft had beaten Democrat William Jennings Bryan in the "Great Commoner's" third and last bid for the presidency. Republicans had retained control of Congress, as well as a host of northern legislatures. Reform was at high tide, and Taft was eager to continue the Roosevelt program.

William Howard Taft—big, good-natured, and modest— was reluctant to run for the presidency in 1908. At the outset of the campaign, President Roosevelt sent him pointed advice: "Photographs on horseback, yes, tennis, no, and golf is fatal." But Taft played anyway. He loved golf despite its reputation as a "dude's game."

"Will," as Roosevelt called Taft, was his handpicked successor. A distinguished jurist and public servant, the first American governor-general of the Philippines, and Roosevelt's secretary of war, Taft had great administrative skill and personal charm. But he disliked the political maneuvering of Washington and preferred conciliation to confrontation. Even Roosevelt had doubts. "He's all right," TR had told a reporter on inauguration day. "But he's weak. They'll get around him. They'll"—and here Roosevelt pushed the reporter with his shoulder—"lean against him."

Trouble began early when progressives in the House moved to curb the near-dictatorial power of the conservative Speaker, Joseph Cannon. Taft waffled, first supporting them and then abandoning them to preserve the tariff reductions he was seeking. When progressives later broke Cannon's power without Taft's help, they scorned the president. And Taft's compromise was wasted. Senate protectionists peppered the tariff bill with so many amendments that rates jumped nearly to their old levels.

Late in 1909, the rift between Taft and the progressives reached the breaking point in a dispute over conservation. Taft had appointed Richard Ballinger secretary of the interior over the objections of Roosevelt's old friend and mentor Chief Forester Pinchot. When Ballinger opened a million acres of public lands for sale, Pinchot charged that shady dealings had led Ballinger to transfer Alaskan public coal lands to a syndicate that included J. P. Morgan. Early in 1910, Taft fired Pinchot for insubordination. Angry progressives saw the Ballinger-Pinchot controversy as another betrayal by Taft. They began to look longingly across the Atlantic, where TR was stalking big game in Africa.

Despite his failures, Taft was no conservative pawn. He ended up protecting more land than Roosevelt, and he pushed Congress to enact a progressive program regulating safety standards for mines and railroads, creating a federal children's bureau, and setting an eight-hour workday for federal employees. Taft's support of a graduated income tax—sometimes staunch, sometimes mild—was finally decisive. Early in 1913 it became the Sixteenth Amendment. Historians view it as one of the most important reforms of the century, for it eventually generated the revenue for many new social programs.

Taft's Accomplishments

Yet no matter what Taft did, he managed to alienate conservatives and progressives alike. That spelled trouble for the Republicans as the presidential election of 1912 approached.

Roosevelt Returns

In June 1910 Roosevelt had come home laden with hunting trophies and exuberant as ever. He found Taft unhappy and progressive Republicans threatening to defect. Party loyalty kept Roosevelt quiet through most of 1911, but in October Taft pricked him personally on the sensitive matter of busting trusts. Like TR, Taft accepted trusts as natural, but he failed to make Roosevelt's distinction between "good" and "bad" ones. He demanded, more impartially, that all trusts be prevented from restraining trade. In four years as president, Taft had brought nearly twice the antitrust suits Roosevelt had in seven years.

In October 1911 the Justice Department charged U.S. Steel with having violated the Sherman Antitrust Act by acquiring the Tennessee Coal and Iron Company. Roosevelt regarded the action as a personal rebuke, because he himself had allowed U.S. Steel to proceed with the acquisition. Taft "was playing small, mean, and foolish politics," complained TR.

New Nationalism

Roosevelt decided to play big, high-minded, and presidential. Already, in a speech at Osawatomie, Kansas, in 1910, he had outlined a program of sweeping reform. His "New Nationalism" stressed the interests of the nation as a whole and the value of government as an agent of reform. It accepted consolidation in the economy—whether big business or big labor—but insisted on protecting the interests of individuals through big government. The New Nationalism promised government planning and efficiency under a powerful executive, "a steward of the public welfare." It promoted taxes on incomes and inheritances and greater regulation of industry. And it embraced social justice, specifically workers' compensation for accidents, minimum wages and maximum hours, child labor laws, and "equal suffrage"—a nod to women and loyal black Republicans. Roosevelt, a cautious reformer as president, grew daring as a campaigner who set his sights again on the White House.

The Election of 1912

"My hat is in the ring!" Roosevelt announced in February 1912. The enormously popular Roosevelt won most of the primaries, but by the time Republicans met in Chicago in June 1912, Taft had used presidential patronage and promises to secure his renomination. A frustrated Roosevelt bolted and took progressive Republicans with him. Two months later, amid choruses of "Onward Christian Soldiers," delegates to the newly formed Progressive party nominated Roosevelt for the presidency. "I'm feeling like a bull moose!" he bellowed. Progressives suddenly had a symbol for their breakaway party.

Progressive, or "Bull Moose," Party

Woodrow Wilson's New Freedom

The Democrats chose as their candidate Woodrow Wilson, the progressive governor of New Jersey. Wilson wisely concentrated his fire on Roosevelt. He countered the New Nationalism with his "New Freedom." It rejected the economic consolidation that Roosevelt embraced. Bigness itself was a sin, no matter how big corporations acted, because it crowded out competition, thereby promoting inefficiency and reducing economic opportunity. Only by strictly limiting the size of business enterprises could the free market be preserved and Americans be released from the control of the wealthy and powerful. And only by keeping government small could individual liberty be protected. "Liberty," Wilson cautioned, "has never come from government," only from the "limitation of governmental power."

Increasingly voters found the Republican Taft beside the point. In an age of reform, even the Socialists looked good. Better led, financed, and organized than ever, the Socialist party had enlarged its membership to nearly 135,000 by 1912. Socialist mayors ran 32 cities. The party also had an appealing candidate in Eugene V. Debs, a home-grown Indiana radical. He had won 400,000 votes for president in 1904. Now, in 1912, he summoned voters to make "the working class the ruling class."

On Election Day voters gave progressive reform a resounding endorsement. Wilson won 6.3 million votes, Roosevelt 4.1 million, Taft just 3.6 million. Debs received almost a million votes. Together the two progressive

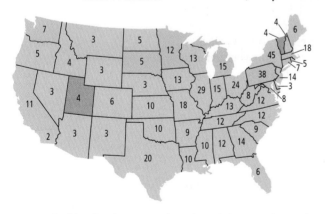

Candidate (Party)	Electoral Vote (%)	Popular Vote (%)
Woodrow Wilson (Democratic)	435 (82)	6,293,152 (42)
Theodore Roosevelt (Progressive/Bull Moose)	88 (17)	4,119,207 (28)
William H. Taft (Republican)	8 (1)	3,484,980 (24)
Eugene V. Debs (Socialist)	—	900,672 (6)

Election of 1912

candidates amassed a three to one margin. The Republican split, moreover, had broken the party's hold on national politics. For the first time since 1896, a Democrat would sit in the White House with his party in control of Congress.

Woodrow Wilson and the Politics of Morality

Woodrow Wilson was not shy about his good fortune. Soon after the election he confessed to William McCombs, chairman of the Democratic National Committee: "God ordained that I should be the next President of the United States." To the White House Wilson brought a passion for reform and the conviction that he was meant to accomplish great things. Under him, progressivism peaked.

Early Career

From the moment of his birth in 1856, Thomas Woodrow Wilson could not escape a sense of destiny. In the family's Presbyterian faith, in the sermons of his minister father, in dinnertime talk ran the unbending belief in a world predetermined by God and ruled by saved souls, the "elect." Wilson ached to be one of them.

To prepare to lead, young Tommy Wilson studied the fiery debates of the British Parliament and wandered the woods reciting them from memory. Like most southerners, he grew up loving the Democratic party and small government, hating the tariff, and accepting racial segregation. (Under his presidency, segregation would return to Washington for the first time since Reconstruction.)

An early career in law bored him, so he turned to political science and became a professor. His studies persuaded him that a modern president must act as a "prime minister," directing and uniting his party, shaping legislation and public opinion, exerting continuous leadership. In 1910, after a stormy tenure as head of Princeton University, Wilson was helped by Democratic party bosses to win the governorship of New Jersey. In 1912 they helped him again, this time to the presidency of the country.

The Reforms of the New Freedom

As governor, Wilson had led New Jersey on the path of progressive reform. As president, he was a model of executive leadership. More than Theodore Roosevelt, he shaped policy and legislation. He went to Congress to let members know he intended to work personally with them. He kept party discipline tight and mobilized public opinion when Congress refused to act.

Lowering the high tariff was Wilson's first order of business. Progressives had long attacked the tariff as another example of the power of trusts. By protecting American manufacturers, Wilson argued, such barriers weakened the competition he cherished. When the Senate threatened to raise rates, the new president appealed directly to the public. "Industrious" and "insidious" lobbyists were blocking reform, he cried to reporters. A "brick couldn't be thrown without hitting one of them."

The Underwood-Simmons Tariff of 1913 marked the first downward revision of the tariff in 19 years and the biggest since before the Civil War. To compensate for lost revenue, Congress enacted a graduated income tax under the newly adopted Sixteenth Amendment. It applied solely to corporations and the tiny fraction of Americans who earned more than $4,000 a year. It nonetheless began a momentous shift in government revenue from its nineteenth-century base—public lands, alcohol taxes, and customs duties—to its twentieth-century base—personal and corporate incomes.

Underwood-Simmons Tariff

Wilson turned next to the perennial problems of money and banking. Early in 1913 a congressional committee under Arsene Pujo revealed that a few powerful banks controlled the nation's credit system. They could choke Wilson's free market by raising interest rates or tightening the supply of money. As a banking reform bill moved through Congress in 1913, Wall Street conservatives lobbied for a privately controlled,

Woodrow Wilson came to the White House with promises to reform government. In this 1913 cartoon titled "A New Captain in the District," the newly elected president strides through corrupt Washington, ready to police such abuses as easy land grants and pork barreling, the much-criticized congressional practice of voting for projects that benefit home districts and constituents.

centralized banking system that could issue currency and set interest rates. Rural Democrats favored a decentralized system of regional banks run by local bankers. Populists and progressives—including William Jennings Bryan and Robert La Follette—wanted government control.

Federal Reserve Act

Wilson split their differences in the Federal Reserve Act of 1913. The new Federal Reserve System contained 12 regional banks scattered across the country. But it also created a central Federal Reserve Board in Washington, appointed by the president, to supervise the system. The board could regulate credit and the money supply by setting the interest rate it charged member banks, by buying or selling government bonds, and by issuing paper currency called Federal Reserve notes. Thus the Federal Reserve System sought to stabilize the existing order by increasing federal control over credit and the money supply.

Federal Trade Commission

When Wilson finally took on the trusts, he moved closer to the New Nationalism of Theodore Roosevelt. The Federal Trade Commission Act of 1914 created a bipartisan executive agency to oversee business activity. The end—to enforce orderly competition—was distinctly Wilsonian, but the means—an executive commission to regulate commerce—were pure Roosevelt.

Clayton Antitrust Act

Roosevelt would have stopped there, but Wilson made good on his campaign pledge to attack trusts. The Clayton Antitrust Act (1914) barred some of the worst corporate practices—price discrimination, holding companies, and interlocking directorates (directors of one corporate board sitting on others). Yet despite Wilson's bias against size, the advantages of large-scale production and distribution were inescapable. In practice his administration chose to regulate rather than break up bigness. Under Wilson the Justice Department filed fewer antitrust suits than under the Taft administration and negotiated more "gentlemen's agreements" (voluntary agreements by companies to change practices) than under Roosevelt.

Labor and Social Reform

For all of Wilson's impressive accomplishments, voters turned lukewarm toward the New Freedom. In the elections of 1914 Republicans cut Democratic majorities in the House and won important industrial and farm states. To strengthen his hand in the presidential election of 1916, Wilson began edging toward the social reforms of the New Nationalism he had once criticized as paternalistic and unconstitutional. Early in 1916 he signaled the change when he nominated his close adviser Louis D. Brandeis to the Supreme Court. The progressive Brandeis had fought for the social reforms lacking on Wilson's agenda. His appointment also broke the tradition of anti-Semitism that had previously kept Jews off the Court.

In a host of other ways, Wilson revealed his willingness to intervene more actively in the economy. He helped pass laws improving the working conditions of merchant seamen and setting an eight-hour day for workers on interstate railroads. He endorsed the Keating-Owen Child Labor Act (see page 639) and threw his support to legislation providing farmers with low-interest loans. And just before the election Wilson intervened to avert a nationwide strike of rail workers.

Woodrow Wilson's administration capped a decade and a half of heady reform. But the United States was hardly first among reformers. The Machine Age triggered a wave of progressive reform across the industrialized world. Movements for social justice and social welfare sprang up first in Great Britain, where the industrial revolution began. The Factory Act of 1833 outlawed child labor in textile mills for those under the age of nine. The Mines Act of 1842 made it illegal to employ all women as well as children younger than ten in work underground. In comparison, the United States failed even to enact a law prohibiting child labor until 1916. In 1884 Toynbee Hall, the world's first social settlement house, opened in London's East End to minister to the needs of the poor. It became the model for Jane Addams' Hull House in Chicago.

As for political reform the world lagged behind the United States, on the issue of woman suffrage. Except in Scandinavia, most European women did not receive the vote until after World War I. Finland enacted women's suffrage in 1906, followed by Norway in 1914. And despite the democratic revolutions that swept across Latin America in the nineteenth century, national women's suffrage was opposed by the Catholic Church and did not come to Ecuador until 1929, Brazil until 1932, and El Salvador until 1939. Asia was slower still, often because colonial rulers denied or limited suffrage or because patriarchal Asian societies looked on women as subordinate to men. Only in 1950, for example, after India achieved independence did women receive the right to vote. In Japan, although Japanese suffragists founded the *Fusen Kakutoku Domei* (Women's Suffrage League) in 1924, Japanese militarists crushed the fledgling Japanese democracy in the 1930s, as well as any hope of women's suffrage.

Perhaps inevitably, progressive reform was a patchwork affair, uneven and incomplete. Reformers sometimes betrayed their high ideals by denying equality to African Americans, Asians, and other minorities. They preferred to Americanize foreigners rather than accept the contributions of their cultures. Too often government commissions that were designed to be "watchdog" agencies found themselves captured by the interests they were supposed to oversee. Well-meaning but cumbersome regulation crippled industries like the railroads for decades. Although the direct primary, the popular election of senators, and other reforms weakened the power of political machines, boss rule survived.

For all its claims of sweeping change, progressivism left the system of market capitalism intact. Neither the New Nationalism of Theodore Roosevelt, with its emphasis on planning and regulation, nor Woodrow Wilson's New Freedom, which promoted competition through limits on corporate size, aimed to do more than improve the system. But the Gilded Age philosophy of laissez faire—of giving private enterprise a free hand—had clearly been rejected. Both state and federal governments established their right to regulate the actions of private corporations for the public good.

The reforms thus achieved, including the eight-hour workday, woman suffrage, direct election of senators, graduated income taxes, and public ownership of utilities, began to address the problems of an urban industrial society. Under progressive leadership, the modern state—active and interventionist—was born.

Significant Events

1890	General Federation of Women's Clubs organized
1892	Sierra Club founded
1893	Illinois legislature enacts eight-hour workday law for women; Anti-Saloon League created
1895	*United States v. E. C. Knight*
1899	National Consumers League founded
1900	Robert La Follette elected governor of Wisconsin
1901	Leon Czolgosz assassinates President McKinley; Theodore Roosevelt becomes president
1902	Northern Securities Company dissolved under Sherman Antitrust Act; anthracite coal miners strike in Pennsylvania
1903	Elkins Act ends railroad rebates; Wisconsin first state to enact direct primary; W. E. B. Du Bois publishes *The Souls of Black Folk*
1904	Lincoln Steffens's *The Shame of the Cities* published; Theodore Roosevelt elected president
1906	Hepburn Act strengthens Interstate Commerce Commission; Upton Sinclair's *The Jungle* published; Meat Inspection and Pure Food and Drug acts passed
1908	*Muller v. Oregon* upholds the right of states to regulate working hours of women; William Howard Taft elected president
1909	NAACP founded
1911	Triangle Shirtwaist fire
1912	Progressive ("Bull Moose") party nominates Theodore Roosevelt for presidency; Woodrow Wilson elected president
1913	Sixteenth and Seventeenth amendments passed, allow for federal income taxes and direct election of senators
1914	Clayton Antitrust Act passed; Federal Trade Commission created
1916	Margaret Sanger organizes New York Birth Control League; Woodrow Wilson reelected
1920	Nineteenth Amendment grants women the right to vote

Chapter Summary

Progressivism was a broad-based reform movement, the first truly national reform movement in American history, that attempted to address problems arising from industrialization, urbanization, and immigration.

- Progressive reform sprang from many impulses:

  —Desires to curb the advancing power of big business and to end political corruption.

  —Efforts to bring order and efficiency to economic and political life.

  —Attempts by new interest groups to make business and government more responsive to the needs of ordinary citizens.

  —Moralistic urges to rid society of industries such as the liquor trade that profited from human misery, to bridge the gap between immigrants and native-born Americans, and to soften the consequences of industrialization through social justice and social welfare.

- Led by members of the urban middle class, progressives were moderate modernizers, supporting traditional American values as democracy, Judeo-Christian ethics, and the spirit of volunteerism and public service while employing the new techniques of management and planning, coordinated systems, and bureaucracies of experts.

- Progressive women extended their traditional sphere of home and family to become "social housekeepers" and crusaders for women's rights, especially the right to vote.

- Increasingly, progressivism animated politics, first at the local and state levels, then in the presidencies of Theodore Roosevelt and Woodrow Wilson.

- In the end, the weaknesses of progressivism—the fuzziness of its conception of the public interest, the exclusion of African Americans and other minorities, the ease with which its regulatory mechanisms were "captured" by those being regulated—were matched by its accomplishments in establishing the modern, activist state.

Additional Reading

The long interpretive debate over progressivism is best covered in Arthur Link and Richard L. McCormick, *Progressivism* (1985). Benchmarks in that debate include George Mowry, *The California Progressives* (1951), and Richard Hofstadter, *The Age of Reform: From Bryan to FDR* (1955), both of which see progressives as a small elite seeking to recapture its fading status and influence. Gabriel Kolko, *The Triumph of Conservatism: A Reinterpretation of American History 1900–1916* (1963), makes the controversial case of the New Left that business "captured" reform to control competition and stave off stricter federal regulation. Richard McCormick stresses the transformation of political culture accompanying the decline of political parties and the rise of interest groups in *From Realignment to Reform: Political Change in New York State, 1893–1910* (1981). Michael McGerr's *A Fierce Discontent: The Rise and Fall of the Progressive Movement* (2003), sees progressivism as a daring middle-class movement to transform society in four classically progressive ways: "to change other people; to end class conflict; to control big business; and to segregate society." David Traxel examines the reforming spirit of the Progressive Era and the First World War he sees it spawning in *Crusader Nation: The United States in Peace and the Great War, 1898–1920* (2006).

The social history of progressivism is best covered in Steven J. Diner's *A Very Different Age: Americans of the Progressive Era* (1998). Eric Rauchway's *Murdering McKinley: The Making of Theodore Roosevelt's America* (2003) presents a revisionist account of American politics and society ranging from criminal psychology to nativism, tariff and currency reform, and ideological conflict. James Chace provides a deft narrative in *1912: Wilson, Roosevelt, Taft, and Debs and the Election that Changed the Country* (2004).

John M. Blum, *The Republican Roosevelt* (1954), remains the most incisive rendering of TR, and Lewis L. Gould, *The Presidency of Theodore Roosevelt* (1991), is the best single-volume study of the White House years. Unsurpassed for its detail and depth is Arthur Link, *Woodrow Wilson*, 5 vols. (1947–1965). Robert Crunden, *Ministers of Reform: The Progressives' Achievements in American Civilization, 1889–1920* (1982), emphasizes the cultural origins and impact of progressivism, and Ellen Chesler, *Woman of Valor: Margaret Sanger and the Birth Control Movement in America* (1992), looks through a feminist lens at the life and times of social reformer Margaret Sanger. In *Triangle: The Fire That Changed America* (2004), David Von Drehle offers the fullest account yet of the fire at the Triangle Shirtwaist Company and the ways in which it sparked reform.

For a fuller list of readings, see the Bibliography at www.mhhe.com/davidsonnation6.

CHAPTER 23

The United States & The Collapse of the Old World Order

1901~1920

"A Path Between the Seas"

War! War! WAR!" The news had flashed across the country in the spring of 1898. As tens of thousands of eager young men signed up to fight the Spanish in Cuba, the USS *Oregon* left San Francisco Bay on a roundabout route toward its battle station in the Caribbean. It first headed south through the Pacific, passing Central America and leaving it thousands of miles behind. Then, in the narrow Strait of Magellan at South America's tip, the ship encountered a gale so ferocious that the shore could not be seen. All communication ceased, and Americans at home feared the worst. But the *Oregon* passed into the Atlantic and steamed north until finally, after 68 days and 13,000 miles at sea, it helped win the Battle of Santiago Bay.

The daring voyage electrified the nation but worried its leaders. Since the defeat of Mexico in 1848, the United States had stretched from the Atlantic to the Pacific without enough navy to go around. As an emerging power, the country needed a "path between the seas"—a canal across the narrow isthmus of Colombia's Panamanian province in Central America—to defend itself and to promote its growing trade.

"I took the isthmus," Theodore Roosevelt later told a cheering crowd. In a way he did. As president, in 1903 he negotiated an agreement with Colombia to lease the needed strip of land. Holding out for more money and greater control over the canal, the Colombian senate refused to ratify the agreement.

Privately, TR talked of seizing Panama. But when he learned of a budding independence movement in Panama, he let it be known that he would welcome a revolt. On schedule and without bloodshed, the Panamanians rebelled late in 1903. The next day a U.S. cruiser dropped anchor offshore to prevent Colombia from landing troops. The United States quickly recognized the new Republic of Panama and signed a treaty for a renewable lease on a canal zone 10 miles wide. Panama received $10 million plus an annual rent of $250,000 (the same terms offered to Colombia). One of the few critics called it "a rough-riding assault upon another republic."

TR never blinked. Arriving in Panama in 1906, he spent three days traveling the canal site in the pouring rain, his huge panama hat and white suit sagging about his body as he splashed through the labor camps, asked workers for

The horror of battle is graphically captured in this detail from a painting by Georges Leroux titled L'Enfer. *The figures in the center, with helmets and gas masks, crouch in what looks like a muddy shell hole as they try to escape artillery fire and poison gas. "My impression," according to one report of a battle, "was that if the men at the heads of all the warring governments had to spend a few hours in the hell on earth that was going on there, the war would be over in short order."*

their complaints, and took the helm of a giant steam shovel. He did not apologize for his nation's conduct, although in 1921, after oil had been discovered in the Canal Zone, Congress voted $25 million to Colombia.

The Panama Canal embodied Roosevelt's muscular foreign policy of respect through strength. He modernized the army and tripled its size, created a general staff for planning and mobilization, and established the Army War College. As a pivot point between the two hemispheres, his canal allowed the United States to flex its strength across the globe.

These expanding horizons came about largely as an outgrowth of American commercial and industrial expansion, just as the imperialist empires of England, France, Germany, Russia, and Japan reflected the spread of their own industrial and commercial might. The Americans, steeped in democratic ideals, frequently seemed uncomfortable with the naked ambitions of European empire-builders. Roosevelt's embrace of the canal, however, showed how far some progressives had come in being willing to shape the world.

Expansionist diplomats at home and abroad assured each other that global order could be maintained by balancing power through a set of carefully crafted alliances. But that system and the spheres of influence it spawned did not hold. In 1914, the year the Panama Canal opened, this old world order collapsed in a terrible war.

Progressive Diplomacy

Foundations of Progressive Diplomacy

As the Panama Canal was being built, progressive diplomacy was taking shape. Like progressive politics, it stressed moralism and order as it stretched presidential power to new limits in an effort to mold and remake the international environment. It rested on faith in the superiority of Anglo-American stock and institutions. "Of all our race, [God] has marked the American people as His chosen nation to finally lead in the redemption of the world," said one senator in 1900. In this global vision of Manifest

Panama Canal—Old and New Transoceanic Routes *Tropical forests cover three-fourths of Panama, including the Canal Zone. Vegetation is denser at high elevations but tightly packed even below 1,000 feet. The terrain is rugged, but the distance saved by the canal (nearly 8,000 miles) convinced Roosevelt and other American leaders that the ordeal of construction and the loss of lives was worthwhile in the long run.*

Destiny, few progressives questioned the need to uplift the "darker peoples" of the tropical zones.

Economic expansion underlay the commitment to a "civilizing" mission. The depression of 1893 had encouraged American manufacturers and farmers to look overseas for markets, and that expansion continued after 1900. By 1918, at the end of World War I, the United States had become the largest creditor in the world. Every administration committed itself to opening doors of trade and keeping them open.

Big Stick in the Caribbean

Theodore Roosevelt liked to invoke the old African proverb "Walk softly and carry a big stick." But in the Caribbean he moved both loudly and mightily. The Panama Canal gave the United States a commanding position in the Western Hemisphere. Its importance required the country to "police the surrounding premises," explained Secretary of State Elihu Root. Before granting Cuba independence in 1902, the United States reorganized its finances and attached the Platt Amendment to the Cuban constitution. The amendment gave American authorities the right to intervene in Cuba if the independence or internal order of the country were threatened. Claiming that power, U.S. troops occupied the island twice between 1906 and 1923.

Platt Amendment

In looking to enforce a favorable environment for trade in the Caribbean, Roosevelt also worried about European intentions. The Monroe Doctrine of 1823 had declared against further European colonization of the Western Hemisphere, but in the early twentieth century the rising debts of Latin Americans to Europeans invited intrusion. "If we intend to say hands off to the power of Europe, then sooner or later we must keep order ourselves," Roosevelt warned. In his balance-of-power system, it was the obligation of great powers to avoid the spheres of others while keeping order in their own. Across the globe, great powers would thus check each other, much as big government held big business in check at home.

Going well beyond Monroe's concept of resisting foreign intrusions into the Western Hemisphere, Roosevelt tightened his grip on the region. In 1904, when the Dominican Republic defaulted on its debts, he added the "Roosevelt Corollary" to the Monroe Doctrine by claiming the right to intervene directly if Latin Americans failed to keep their own financial households in order. Invoking its sweeping (and self-proclaimed) power, the United States assumed responsibility for several Caribbean states, including the Dominican Republic, Cuba, and Panama.

Roosevelt Corollary to the Monroe Doctrine

A "Diplomatist of the Highest Rank"

In the Far East Roosevelt exercised ingenuity rather than force, because he realized that few Americans would support armed intervention half a world away. Like McKinley before him, TR committed himself only to maintaining an "open door" of equal access to trade in China and to protecting the Philippines, which he saw as "our heel of Achilles."

The key to success lay in offsetting Russian and Japanese ambitions in the region. When Japan attacked Russian holdings in the Chinese province of Manchuria in 1904, Roosevelt offered to mediate. He worried that if unchecked, Japan might threaten American interests in China and the Philippines. At the U.S. Naval Base near Portsmouth, Maine, Roosevelt guided the Russians and the Japanese to the Treaty of Portsmouth in 1905. It recognized the Japanese victory (the first by an Asian power over a European country) and ceded to Japan Port Arthur, the southern half of Sakhalin Island, and, in effect, control of Korea. Japan promised to leave Manchuria as part of China and keep trade open to all foreign nations. The balance of power in Asia and the open door in China thus had been preserved. For his contributions, Roosevelt received the Nobel Peace Prize in 1906.

Treaty of Portsmouth

Japanese nationalists resented the peace treaty for curbing Japan's ambitions in China. Their anger surfaced in a protest lodged, of all places, against the San Francisco

Gentlemen's Agreement

Newsrunners in Japan bringing latest word on the Russo-Japanese war

school board. In 1906, rising Japanese immigration led San Francisco school authorities to place the city's 93 Asian students in a separate school. In Japan citizens talked of war over the insult. Roosevelt, furious at the "infernal fools in California," summoned the mayor of San Francisco and seven school board members to the White House. In exchange for an end to the segregation order Roosevelt offered to arrange a mutual restriction of immigration between Japan and the United States. In 1907 all sides accepted his "gentlemen's agreement."

The San Francisco school crisis sparked wild rumors that Japan was bent on taking Hawaii, or the Philippines, or the Panama Canal. In case Japan or any other nation thought of upsetting the Pacific balance, Roosevelt sent 16 gleaming white battleships on a world tour. "By George, isn't it magnificent!" he crowed as the "Great White Fleet" steamed out of Hampton Roads, Virginia, in 1907 (see pages 618–619). The fleet made its most conspicuous stop in Japan, where a group of Japanese children stood on the docks of Yokohama and sang "The Star-Spangled Banner" in English. The show of force heralded a new age of American naval might but had an unintended consequence that haunted Americans for decades: it spurred Japanese admirals to expand their own navy.

Watching Roosevelt in his second term, an amazed London *Morning Post* honored him as a "diplomatist of the highest rank." Abroad as at home, his brand of progressivism was grounded in an enthusiastic nationalism that mixed force with finesse to achieve balance and order. Yet despite TR's efforts, imperial rivalries, an unchecked arms race, and unrest in Europe threatened to plunge the world into chaos.

Dollar Diplomacy

Instead of force or finesse, Roosevelt's successor in the White House turned to economic means to advance U.S. interests abroad. William Howard Taft stressed private investment to promote economic stability, keep peace, and tie debt-ridden nations to the United States. "Dollar diplomacy" simply amounted to "substituting dollars for bullets," Taft explained. He and Philander Knox, his prickly secretary of state, treated the restless nations of Latin America like ailing corporations, injecting capital and reorganizing management. By the time Taft left office in 1913, half of all American investments abroad were in Latin America.

Failure dogged Taft overseas as it did at home. In the Caribbean his dollar diplomacy was linked so closely with unpopular regimes, corporations, and banks that Woodrow Wilson scrapped it as soon as he entered the White House. Taft's efforts to strengthen China with investments and trade only intensified rivalry with Japan and made China more suspicious of all foreigners, including Americans. In 1911 the southern Chinese provinces rebelled against foreign intrusion and overthrew the monarchy. Only persistent pressure from the White House kept dollar diplomacy in Asia alive at all.

Great White Fleet

Woodrow Wilson and Moral Diplomacy

The Lightfoot Club had been meeting in the Reverend Wilson's hayloft for months when the question of whether the pen was mightier than the sword came up. Young Tommy Wilson, who had organized the debating society, jumped at the chance to argue that written words were more powerful than armies. But when the boys drew lots, Tommy ended up on the other side. "I can't argue that side," he protested. "I can't argue for something I don't believe in." Thomas Woodrow Wilson eventually dropped his first name, but he never gave up his boyhood conviction that morality, at least as he defined it, should guide all conduct. To the diplomacy of order, force, and finance, Wilson added a missionary's commitment to spreading what he saw as the American system of beliefs—justice, democracy, and the Judeo-Christian values of harmony and cooperation.

Missionary Diplomacy

Although Wilson's missionary diplomacy was deeply idealistic, it had a practical side. In the twentieth century foreign markets would serve as America's new frontier. American industries "will burst their jackets if they cannot find free outlets in the markets of the world," Wilson cautioned in 1912. His special genius lay in reconciling this commercial self-interest with a global idealism. In his eyes, exporting American democracy and capitalism would promote peace, prosperity, and human advancement throughout the world.

Solitary and self-assured, Wilson conducted foreign policy on his own. Bypassing the State Department, he sent personal emissaries to foreign leaders and often typed his own dispatches. Sometimes Secretary of State William Jennings Bryan had no idea of what was happening. In rare moments of doubt, Wilson turned to his trusted friend, Edward M. House. The honorary "Colonel" House had yoked himself to Wilson in the early days of his political career and wielded power behind the scenes.

American Interventions in the Caribbean, 1898–1930   *In the first three decades of the twentieth century, U.S. diplomacy transformed the Caribbean into an American lake as armed and unarmed intervention became part of the country's diplomatic arsenal.*

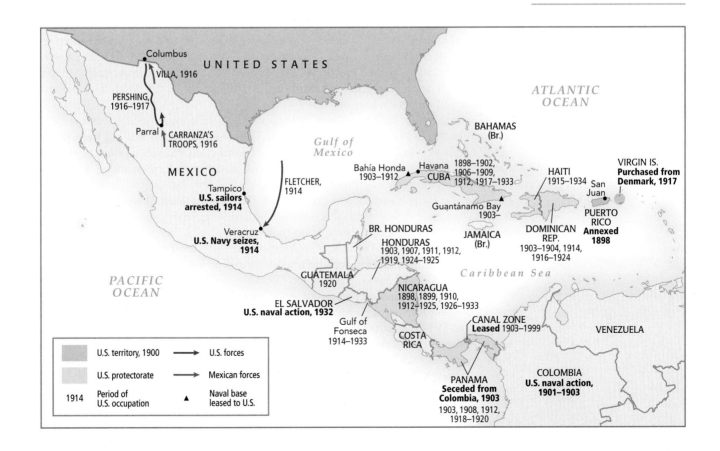

In Asia and the Pacific Wilson moved to put "moral and public considerations" ahead of the "material interests of individuals." He pulled American bankers out of a six-nation railroad project in China backed by President Taft. The scheme encouraged foreign intervention and undermined Chinese sovereignty, said Wilson. The United States became the first major power to recognize the new Republic of China in 1911 when nationalists overthrew the last Manchu emperor. And in 1915 Wilson strongly opposed Japan's "Twenty-one Demands" for control of China. At the end of Wilson's first administration, the Philippines gained limited self-government, the first step toward independence finally granted in 1946.

Twenty-One Demands

In the Caribbean and Latin America, Wilson discovered that interests closer to home could not be pursued through high-minded words alone. In August 1914 he convinced Nicaragua, already occupied by American troops, to yield control of a naval base and grant the United States an alternate canal route. Upheavals in Haiti and the Dominican Republic brought in the U.S. Marines. By the end of his administration American troops were still stationed there and also in Cuba. All four nations were economically dependent on the United States and were virtual protectorates. Missionary diplomacy, it turned out, could spread its gospel with steel as well as cash.

Intervention in Mexico

Mexican Revolution

A lingering crisis in Mexico turned Wilson's "moral diplomacy" into a mockery. A common border, 400 years of shared history, and millions of dollars in investments made what happened in Mexico of urgent importance to the United States. In 1910 a revolution overthrowing the aged dictator Porfirio Díaz plunged the country into turmoil. Just as Wilson was entering the White House in 1913, the ruthless general Victoriano Huerta emerged as head of the government. Wealthy landowners and foreign investors endorsed Huerta, a conservative likely to protect their holdings. Soon a bloody civil war was raging between Huerta and his rivals.

Most European nations recognized the Huerta regime immediately, but Wilson refused to accept the "government of butchers." (Huerta had murdered the popular leader Francisco Madera with the approval of the Taft administration.) When Huerta proclaimed himself dictator, Wilson banned arms shipments to Mexico. He threw his support to rebel leader Venustiano Carranza, on the condition that Carranza participate in American-sponsored elections. No Mexican was ready to tolerate such foreign interference. Carranza and his "constitutionalists" rejected the offer. With few options, Wilson armed the rebels anyway.

Wilson's distaste for Huerta was so great that he used a minor incident as a pretext for an invasion. In April 1914 the crew of the USS *Dolphin* landed without permission in the Mexican port city of Tampico. Local police arrested the sailors, only to release them with an apology. Unappeased, their squadron commander demanded a 21-gun salute to the American flag. Agreed, replied the Mexicans, but only if American guns returned the salute to Mexico. Learning of a German shipload of weapons about to land at Veracruz, Wilson broke the impasse by ordering American troops to take the city. Instead of the bloodless occupation they expected, U.S. marines encountered stiff resistance as they stormed ashore; 126 Mexicans and 19 Americans were killed before the city fell. The intervention accomplished little except the unlikely feat of uniting the rival Mexican factions against the United States.

Only the combined diplomacy of Argentina, Brazil, and Chile (the "ABC powers") staved off war between Mexico and the United States. When a bankrupt Huerta resigned in 1914, Carranza formed a new constitutionalist government but refused to follow Wilson's guidelines. Wilson turned to Francisco "Pancho" Villa, a wily, peasant-born general who had broken from Carranza. Together with Emiliano Zapata, another peasant leader, Villa kept a rebellion flickering.

Pancho Villa

A year later, Wilson finally recognized the Carranza regime, which only turned Villa against the United States. In January 1916 Villa abducted 18 Americans from a train in Mexico and slaughtered them. In March, he galloped into Columbus, New

General John J. "Black Jack" Pershing led U.S. forces into Mexico to catch rebel leader Pancho Villa "dead or alive." Villa (pictured here on horseback leading a band of his rebels) eluded the Americans for several months before they abandoned the expedition. Audacious and ruthless, he was worshiped by Mexican peasants, who extolled his exploits in folktales and ballads after his assassination in 1923 by Mexican political rivals.

Mexico, killed 19 people, and left the town in flames. Wilson ordered 6,000 troops into Mexico to capture Villa "dead or alive." A reluctant Carranza agreed to yet another American invasion.

For nearly two years, General John "Black Jack" Pershing (nicknamed for the all-black unit he commanded in the Spanish-American War) chased Villa on horseback, by automobile, and in airplanes. There were bloody skirmishes with government troops but not a single one with Villa and his rebels. As the chase grew wilder and wilder, Carranza withdrew his consent for U.S. troops on Mexican soil. Early in 1917 Wilson pulled Pershing home. The "punitive expedition," as the president called it, poisoned Mexican-American relations for the next 30 years.

The Road to War

In early 1917, around the time Wilson recalled Pershing, the British liner *Laconia* was making a voyage across the Atlantic. As the ship steamed through the inky night, passengers below decks talked almost casually of the war raging in Europe since 1914. "What do you think are our chances of being torpedoed?" asked Floyd Gibbons, an American reporter who was aboard. Since Germany had stepped up its submarine attacks, the question was unavoidable. "I should put our chances at 250 to 1 that we don't meet a sub," replied a British diplomat.

"At that minute," recalled Gibbons, "the torpedo hit us." Whistle blasts echoed through the corridors and the passengers were forced to abandon ship. They watched in horror from lifeboats as a second torpedo struck its target, and the *Laconia* slid silently beneath icy waters. After a miserable night bobbing in the waves, Gibbons was rescued. But by 1917 other neutral Americans had already lost their lives at sea. And in April, despite Woodrow Wilson's best efforts at peace, the United States found itself dragged into war.

The Guns of August

For a century, profound strains had been pushing Europe toward war. Its population tripled, its middle and working classes swelled, discontent with industrial society grew. The United States had experienced many of the same strains, of course, yet in Europe these pressures played out on a field that was at once more stratified socially and more divided ethnically and culturally. As European nations competed for empire, nationalism

Causes of World War I

Fervent nationalism heightened the imperial rivalries that pulled European nations into World War I. Flags became important patriotic symbols, masses of morale-boosting color deployed above parades of marching troops and cheering citizens. The American artist Childe Hassam demonstrated that Americans shared this patriotic penchant. Here, Allied flags are featured.

helped paper over these internal divisions by directing ambitions and rivalries toward other nations. By 1914 empires jostled uneasily against one another across the globe.

Europe responded to the increased competition with an arms race. Great Britain became convinced that its mastery of the seas depended on maintaining a navy equal in power to the combined navies of its closest two rivals. France and Germany both doubled the size of their standing armies between 1870 and 1914. Led by Kaiser Wilhelm II, Germany aligned itself with Turkey and Austria-Hungary. The established imperial powers of England and France looked to contain Germany by supporting its foe, Russia. Soon Europe bristled with weapons, troops, and armor-plated navies. These war machines were linked to one another through a web of diplomatic alliances—all of them committed to war should someone or some nation set chaos in motion.

That moment came in 1914, in the Slavic province of Bosnia in southwestern Austria-Hungary. Since the 1870s the Ottoman, or Turkish, empire had been slowly disintegrating, allowing a host of smaller, ethnically based states to emerge. Serbia was one of them, and many Serbs dreamed of uniting other Slavic peoples in a "Pan-Slavic" nation. Their ambitions had been blocked in 1908, when Austria-Hungary annexed neighboring Bosnia. Tensions in the region were high when the Archduke Franz Ferdinand, heir to the Austro-Hungarian throne, visited Sarajevo, Bosnia's capital. On June 28, 1914, the Archduke and his wife were gunned down by a Serbian nationalist as they drove through the streets of Sarajevo.

Austria-Hungary mobilized to punish Serbia. In response, rival Russia called up its 6-million-soldier army to help the Serbs. Germany joined with Austria-Hungary, France with Russia. On July 28, after a month of insincere demands for apologies, Austria-Hungary declared war on Serbia. On August 1, Germany issued a similar declaration against Russia, and, two days later, against France. Following a battle plan drawn up well in advance, German generals pounded neutral Belgium with siege cannons the size of freight cars. Within days, five German columns were slicing west through the Belgian countryside, determined to overrun France before Russia could position its slow-moving army on the eastern front.

The guns of August heralded the first global war. Like so many dominoes, the industrialized nations fell into line: Britain, Japan, Romania, and later Italy to the side of "Allies" France and Russia; Bulgaria and Turkey to the "Central Powers" of Germany and Austria-Hungary. Armies fought from the deserts of North Africa to the plains of Flanders in Belgium. Fleets battled off the coasts of Chile and Sumatra. Soldiers came from as far away as Australia and India. Nearly 8 million never returned.

Neutral but Not Impartial

The outbreak of war shocked most Americans. Few knew Serbia as anything but a tiny splotch on the map of Europe. Fewer still were prepared to go to war in its defense.

Assassination of Archduke Franz Ferdinand

The Course of War in Europe, 1914–1917 *When World War I erupted between the Central and Allied Powers in 1914, few countries in Europe remained neutral. The armies of the Central Powers penetrated as far west as France and as far east as Russia, but by 1917, the European war had settled into a hideous standoff along the deadly line of trenches on the western front that stretched from the North Sea to the border of Switzerland.*

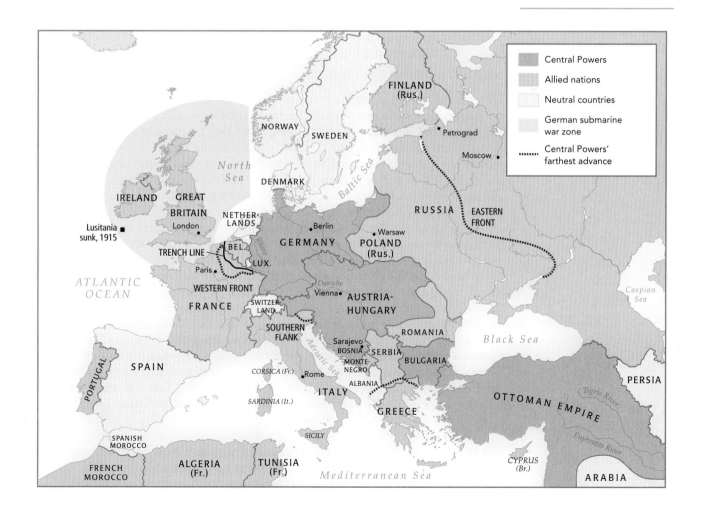

President Wilson issued an immediate declaration of neutrality and approved a plan for evacuating Americans stranded in Belgium.

Wilson's Neutral Ideals   Wilson came to see the calamity as an opportunity. America could lead warring nations to a new world order. Selfish nationalism would give way to cooperative internationalism, power politics to collective security and Christian charity. Progressive faith in reason would triumph over irrational violence. Only if the United States stood above the fray could it lead the way to a higher peace. Americans must remain "impartial in thought as well as action," Wilson insisted in 1914.

True impartiality was impossible. Americans of German and Austrian descent naturally sympathized with the Central Powers, as did Irish Americans, on the grounds of England's centuries-old domination of Ireland. The bonds of language, culture, and history tied most Americans to Great Britain. And gratitude for French aid during the American Revolution still lived. When the first American division marched through Paris over a century later, its commander stopped to salute Lafayette's tomb with the cry, "Nous voilà, Lafayette!"—Lafayette, we are here!

American economic ties to Britain and France also created a financial investment in Allied victory. The American economy boomed with the flood of war orders. The commanding British navy ensured that the Atlantic trade went mostly to the Allies. Between 1914 and 1916 trade with the Allies rocketed from $800 million to $3 billion. The Allies eventually borrowed more than $2 billion from American banks to finance their purchases. In contrast, a British naval blockade reduced American **contraband** commerce with the Central Powers to a trickle.

Few Americans cared. Although some progressives admired German social reforms, Americans generally saw Germany as an iron military power bent on conquest. Americans read British propaganda about spike-helmeted "Huns" raping Belgian women, bayoneting their children, pillaging their towns. Some of the stories were true, some embellished, some utterly false, but all worked against Germany in the United States.

The Diplomacy of Neutrality

Though Wilson insisted that all warring powers respect the right of neutrals to trade with any nation, he hesitated to retaliate against Great Britain's blockade of Germany. He recognized that the key to strangling Germany, a land power, was Britain's all-powerful navy and its iron blockade. Breaking it would cripple the Allied war effort. Meanwhile, Great Britain enforced its blockade with caution where the Americans were concerned. When Britain forbade the sale of cotton to the Central Powers in 1915, the British government bought American surpluses. It also agreed to compensate American firms for their losses when the war was over. By the end of 1915 the United States had all but accepted the British blockade of Germany, while American supplies continued to flow to England. True neutrality was dead. America became the quartermaster of the Allies.

Submarine Warfare   Early in 1915, Germany turned to a dreadful new weapon to even the odds at sea. It mounted a counterblockade of Great Britain with two dozen submarines, or *Unterseebootes,* called U-boats. Before submarines, sea raiders usually gave crews and passengers the chance to escape. But if thin-skinned U-boats surfaced to obey these conventions, they risked being rammed or blown from the water. So submarines attacked without warning and spared no lives. Invoking international law and national honor, President Wilson threatened to hold Germany to "strict accountability" for any American losses. Germany promised not to sink any American ships, but soon a new issue grabbed the headlines: the safety of American passengers on belligerent vessels.

Lusitania   On the morning of May 7, 1915, the British passenger liner *Lusitania* appeared out of a fog bank off the coast of Ireland on its way from New York to England. The commander of the German U-20 could hardly believe his eyes: the giant ship filled the viewfinder of his periscope. He fired a single torpedo. A tremendous roar followed as one of the *Lusitania*'s main boilers exploded. The ship stopped dead in the water and listed so badly that lifeboats could barely be launched before the vessel sank. Nearly 1,200 men, women, and children perished, including 128 Americans.

Wilson, horrified at this "murder on the high seas," nevertheless urged restraint. "There is such a thing as a nation being so right that it does not need to convince others by force," he said a few days later. He sent notes of protest but did little more. Secretary of State Bryan, an advocate of what he called "real neutrality," wanted equal protests lodged against both German submarines and British blockaders. He suspected that the *Lusitania* carried munitions as well as passengers and was thus a legitimate target. (Much later, evidence proved him right.) Relying on passengers for protection against attack, Bryan argued, was "like putting women and children in front of an army." Rather than endorse Wilson's policy, Bryan resigned.

Battling on two fronts in Europe, Germany wanted to keep the United States out of the war. But in February 1916 a desperate Germany declared submarine warfare on all *armed* vessels, belligerent or neutral. A month later a U-boat commander mistook the French steamer *Sussex* for a mine layer and torpedoed the unarmed vessel as it ferried passengers and freight across the English Channel. Several Americans were injured.

In mid-April, Wilson issued an ultimatum. If Germany refused to stop sinking nonmilitary vessels, the United States would break off diplomatic relations. War would surely follow. Without enough U-boats to control the seas, Germany agreed to Wilson's terms, all but abandoning its counterblockade. This *Sussex* pledge gave Wilson a great

Sussex Pledge

diplomatic victory but carried a grave risk. If German submarines resumed unrestricted attacks, the United States would have to go to war. "Any little German [U-boat] commander can put us into the war at any time," Wilson admitted to his cabinet.

Peace, Preparedness, and the Election of 1916

While hundreds of young Yanks slipped across the border to enlist in the Canadian army, most Americans agreed neutrality was the wisest course. Before the war a peace movement had taken seed in the United States, nourished in 1910 by a gift of $10 million from Andrew Carnegie. In 1914 social reformers Jane Addams, Charlotte Perkins Gilman, and Lillian Wald founded the Women's International League for Peace and Freedom and the American Union Against Militarism. Calling on Wilson to convene a peace conference, they lobbied for open diplomacy, disarmament, an end to colonial empires, and an international organization to settle disputes. In time these aims would become the core of Wilson's peace plan.

Pacifists might condemn the war, but Republicans and corporate leaders argued that the nation was woefully unprepared to keep peace. The army numbered only 80,000 men in 1914, the navy just 37 battleships and a handful of new "dreadnoughts," or supercruisers. Advocates of "preparedness" called for a navy larger than Great Britain's, an army of millions of reservists, and universal military training.

By the end of 1915, frustration with German submarines led Wilson to join the preparedness cause. He toured the country promoting preparedness and promised a "navy second to none." In Washington, he pressed Congress to double the army, increase the National Guard, and begin construction of the largest navy in the world. To foot the bill progressives pushed through new graduated taxes on higher incomes and on estates as well as additional levies on corporate profits.

Whoever paid for it, most Americans in 1916 were thinking of preparedness for peace, not war. The Democrats discovered the political power of peace early in the presidential campaign. As their convention opened in St. Louis in June, the keynote

J. H. Cassel's 1915 cartoon "Without Warning!" captures the horror of the submarine attack on the Lusitania. *A bloody saber in the hand of a spikehelmeted German knifes through the ship from beneath the waves. Flag-waving Americans fall helplessly into the sea and drown.*

"He Kept Us Out of War"

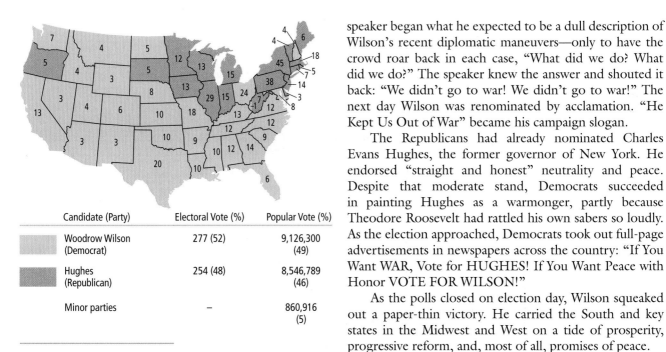

Candidate (Party)	Electoral Vote (%)	Popular Vote (%)
Woodrow Wilson (Democrat)	277 (52)	9,126,300 (49)
Hughes (Republican)	254 (48)	8,546,789 (46)
Minor parties	–	860,916 (5)

Election of 1916

speaker began what he expected to be a dull description of Wilson's recent diplomatic maneuvers—only to have the crowd roar back in each case, "What did we do? What did we do?" The speaker knew the answer and shouted it back: "We didn't go to war! We didn't go to war!" The next day Wilson was renominated by acclamation. "He Kept Us Out of War" became his campaign slogan.

The Republicans had already nominated Charles Evans Hughes, the former governor of New York. He endorsed "straight and honest" neutrality and peace. Despite that moderate stand, Democrats succeeded in painting Hughes as a warmonger, partly because Theodore Roosevelt had rattled his own sabers so loudly. As the election approached, Democrats took out full-page advertisements in newspapers across the country: "If You Want WAR, Vote for HUGHES! If You Want Peace with Honor VOTE FOR WILSON!"

As the polls closed on election day, Wilson squeaked out a paper-thin victory. He carried the South and key states in the Midwest and West on a tide of prosperity, progressive reform, and, most of all, promises of peace.

Wilson's Final Peace Offensive

Twice since 1915 Wilson had sent his trusted adviser Edward House to Europe to negotiate a peace among the warring powers, and twice House had failed. With the election over, Wilson opened his final peace offensive. But when he asked the belligerents to state their terms for a cease-fire, neither side responded. Frustrated, fearful, and genuinely agonized, Wilson called for "peace without victory": no victor, no vanquished, no embittering division of the spoils of war, only "a peace among equals," he said in January 1917.

As Wilson spoke, a fleet of U-boats was cruising toward the British Isles. Weeks earlier German military leaders had persuaded the Kaiser to take one last desperate gamble to starve the Allies into submission. On January 31, 1917, the German ambassador in Washington announced that unrestricted submarine warfare would resume the next day.

Wilson's dream of keeping the country from war collapsed. He asked Congress for authority to arm merchant ships and early in February severed relations with Germany. Then British authorities handed him a bombshell—an intercepted telegram from the German foreign secretary, Arthur Zimmermann, to the Kaiser's ambassador in Mexico. In the event of war with the United States, the ambassador was instructed to offer Mexico guns, money, and its "lost territory in Texas, New Mexico, and Arizona" to attack the United States. Already frustrated by Pancho Villa's raids across the U.S.-Mexican border, Wilson angrily released the Zimmermann telegram to the press. Soon after, he ordered gun crews aboard merchant ships and directed them to shoot U-boats on sight.

The momentum of events now propelled a reluctant United States toward war. On March 12, U-boats torpedoed the American merchant vessel *Algonquin*. On March 15, a revolution in Russia toppled Czar Nicholas II. A key ally was crumbling from within. By the end of the month U-boats had sunk nearly 600,000 tons of Allied and neutral shipping. For the first time reports came to Washington of cracking morale in the Allied ranks.

On April 2, 1917, accompanied by armed cavalry, Wilson rode down Pennsylvania Avenue and trudged up the steps of the Capitol. He delivered to Congress a stirring war message, full of idealistic purpose. "We shall fight for the things we have always carried nearest our hearts—for democracy, for the right of those who submit to authority to have a voice in their own governments, for the rights and liberties of small nations."

Pacifists held up the war resolution until it finally passed on April 6, Good Friday. Six senators and 50 House members opposed it, including the first woman in Congress,

Zimmermann Telegram

Jeannette Rankin

Jeannette Rankin of Montana. Cultural, economic, and historical ties to the Allies, along with the German campaign of submarine warfare, had tipped the country toward war. Wilson had not wanted it, but now the battlefield seemed the only path to a higher peace.

War and Society

In 1915 the German zeppelin LZ-38, hovering at 8,000 feet, dropped a load of bombs that killed seven Londoners. For the first time in history, civilians died in an air attack. Few aerial bombardments occurred during World War I, but they signaled the growing importance of the home front in modern combat. Governments not only fielded armies but also mobilized industry, controlled labor, even rationed food. In the United States, traditions of cooperation and volunteerism helped government to organize the home front and the battle front, often in ways that were peculiarly progressive.

The Slaughter of Stalemate

While the United States debated entry into the Great War, the Allies were coming perilously close to losing it. Following the German assault in 1914, the war had settled into a grisly stalemate. A continuous, immovable front stretched from Flanders in the north to the border of Switzerland in the south. Troops dug ditches, six to eight feet deep and four to five feet wide, to escape bullets, grenades, and artillery. Twenty-five thousand miles of these "trenches"—enough to circle the globe—cut a muddy scar across Europe. Men lived in them for years, prey to disease, lice, and a plague of rats.

Trench Warfare

War in the machine age gave the advantage to the defense. When soldiers bravely charged "over the top" of the trenches, they were shredded by machine guns that fired 600 rounds a minute. Poison gas choked them in their tracks. Giant howitzers lobbed shells on them from positions too distant to see. In the Battle of the Somme River in 1916 a million men were killed in just four months of fighting, all to enable the British army to advance barely seven miles. Only late in the war did new armored "landships"—code-named "tanks"—return the advantage to the offense by surmounting the trench barriers with their caterpillar treads.

Trench warfare, wrote one general, was "marked by uniform formations, the regulation of space and time by higher commands down to the smallest details . . . fixed distances between units and individuals." The reality was something else again.

Felix Sanchez, a Mexican–American recruit from New Mexico.

By then Vladimir Lenin was speeding home to Russia aboard a special train provided by the Germans. Lenin had been exiled to Switzerland during the early stages of the Russian Revolution but returned to lead his Bolshevik ("majority" in Russian) party to power in November 1917. Soon the Bolshevik-controlled government negotiated a separate peace with Germany, which promptly transferred a million of its soldiers to the western front for the coming spring offensive.

"You're in the Army Now"

The Allies' plight forced the U.S. Army into a crash program to send a million soldiers to Europe by the spring of 1918. The United States had barely 180,000 men in uniform. Volunteers rushed to recruitment offices, especially in ethnic communities, where Mexican Americans enlisted in numbers proportionately higher than any other group. But they were not enough.

To raise the necessary force, Congress passed the Selective Service Act in May 1917. Men between the ages of 20 and 30 would be conscripted into the armed forces. Feelings over forced military service ran high. "There is precious little difference between a conscript [draftee] and a convict," protested the House Speaker in 1917. Progressives were more inclined to see military service as an opportunity to unite America and promote democracy: "Universal [military] training will jumble the boys of America all together, . . . smashing all the petty class distinctions that now divide, and prompting a brand of real democracy."

At ten in the morning on July 20, 1917, Secretary of War Newton Baker tied a blindfold over his eyes, reached into a huge glass bowl, and drew the first number in the new draft lottery. Some 24 million men were already registered. Almost 3 million were drafted; another 2 million volunteered. Most were white and young, between the ages of 21 and 31. Some 20,000 women served as clerks, telephone operators, and nurses. In a nation of immigrants, nearly one draftee in five was born in another country. Training often aimed at educating and Americanizing ethnic recruits. In special "development battalions" drill sergeants barked out orders while volunteers from the YMCA taught American history and English.

With hostility remaining high between Mexico and the United States after President Wilson sent U.S. troops into Mexico, many Mexican laborers returned to Mexico rather than be drafted into a foreign army whose goals they did not share. On the other hand, Mexican Americans, especially those whose families had long lived in the United States, enlisted in the U.S. Army.

Like Mexican Americans, African Americans volunteered in disproportionately high numbers. They quickly filled the four all-black army and eight National Guard units already in existence. They were also granted fewer exemptions from the draft than white Americans were. Only 10 percent of the population, blacks made up 13 percent of all draftees. Abroad, where 200,000 black troops served in France, just one in five (compared with two of every three whites) was permitted in combat. Southern Democrats in Congress had opposed training African Americans to arms, fearful of the prospect of putting "arrogant, strutting representatives of black soldiery in every community." But four regiments of the all-black 93rd Division, brigaded with the French army, were among the first Americans in the trenches and the most decorated units in the U.S. Army.

Houston Riot   Racial violence sometimes flared among the troops, notably in Houston in the summer of 1917. Harassed by white soldiers and by the city's Jim Crow laws, seasoned black regulars rioted and killed 17 white civilians. Their whole battalion was disarmed and sent under arrest to New Mexico. Thirteen troopers were condemned to death and hanged within days, too quickly for appeals even to be filed.

Bias also surfaced as progressive reformers enlisted the social sciences in army testing. Most recruits had fewer than seven years of education, yet they had to be classified and assigned quickly to units. Psychologists saw the chance to use new intelligence tests to help the army and prove their own theories about the value of "IQ" (intelligence quotient) in measuring the mind. In fact, these new "scientific" IQ tests often measured little more than class and cultural origins. Questions such as "Who wrote 'The Raven'?" exposed background rather than intelligence. More than half the Russian, Italian, and Polish draftees and almost 80 percent of blacks showed up as "inferior." The army stopped the testing program in January 1919, but schools across the country adopted it after the war, reinforcing many ethnic and racial prejudices.

On the home front, moral crusaders waged a war against sin, often pursuing old reforms with the help of mushrooming patriotism. Temperance leaders pressured the War Department to prohibit the sale of liquor to anyone in uniform in the vicinity of training camps. Alcohol would only impair a soldier's ability to fight. The army also declared war on venereal disease. "A Soldier who gets a dose is a Traitor!" warned one poster. The drive against sexual misconduct constituted the first serious sex education many young Americans had ever received.

Mobilizing the Economy

To equip, feed, and transport an army of nearly 5 million demanded a national effort. The production of even a single ammunition shell brought components from every section of the country (plus vital nitrates from Chile) to assembly plants in New Jersey, Virginia, and Pennsylvania and from there to military installations or Atlantic ports.

At the Treasury Department, Secretary William Gibbs McAdoo fretted over how to finance the war, which cost, finally, $32 billion. New taxes paid about a third of all war costs. The rest came from the sale of "Liberty" and "Victory" bonds and war savings certificates. At huge bond drives, movie stars Douglas Fairbanks, Mary Pickford, and other celebrities, exhorted Americans to buy bonds. Boy Scouts sold them under the slogan "Every Scout to Save a Soldier." More than money was at stake. The fund-raising campaign was also designed to raise patriotism. "Every person who refuses to subscribe," Treasury Secretary McAdoo warned a California audience, "is a friend of Germany." The **national debt,** which had stood at $2 billion in 1917, soared to $20 billion only three years later.

War Costs

With sweeping grants of authority provided by Congress, President Wilson constructed a massive bureaucracy to manage the home front. What emerged was a more **managed economy,** ironically similar to the New Nationalism envisioned by Theodore Roosevelt. Nearly 5000 new executive agencies employed business leaders from mammoth machinery makers John Deere and Evinrude to other corporate giants, the readiest source of expert managers. For a nominal "dollar a year," these executives served their country and built a partnership between big business and government. Industrial and **trade associations** as well as professional associations of engineers and scientists tied industry and science to a web of federal agencies. Antitrust suits, recalled one official, were simply put "to sleep until the war was over."

Under the leadership of Wall Street wizard Bernard Baruch, a War Industries Board (WIB) coordinated production through networks of industrial and trade associations. Though it had the authority to order firms to comply, the WIB relied instead on persuasion through publicity and "cost-plus" contracts that covered all costs, plus a guaranteed profit. When businesses balked—as when Henry Ford refused to accept government curbs on the manufacture of civilian automobiles—Baruch could twist arms. In this case, he threatened to have the army run Ford's factories. Ford quickly reversed himself. Overall, corporate profits tripled and production soared during the war years.

War Industries Board

The Food Administration encouraged farmers to grow more and citizens to eat less wastefully. Herbert Hoover, who had saved starving refugees as chairman of the Commission for Relief in Belgium in 1914, was appointed administrator. Like the WIB, the Food Administration mobilized what Hoover called "the spirit of self-sacrifice." Huge publicity campaigns promoted "wheatless" and "meatless" days each week and encouraged families to plant "victory" gardens. Stirred by high commodity prices, farmers brought more marginal lands into cultivation, and their real income jumped 25 percent.

A Fuel Administration met the army's energy needs by increasing production and limiting domestic consumption. Transportation snarls required more drastic action. In

December 1917 the U.S. Railroad Administration took over rail lines for the duration of the war. Government coordination, together with a new system of permits, got freight moving and kept workers happy. Federally imposed "daylight savings time" stretched the workday and saved fuel as well. Rail workers saw their wages grow overall by $300 million. Railroad unions won recognition, an eight-hour day, and a grievance procedure. For the first time in decades labor unrest subsided, and the trains ran on schedule.

Bureaucratic State

The modern **bureaucratic state** received a powerful boost during the 18 months of American participation in the war. Accelerating trends that were already under way, hundreds of federal agencies centralized authority as they cooperated with business and labor to mount an unprecedented war effort. The number of federal employees more than doubled between 1916 and 1918, to over 850,000. The wartime bureaucracy was quickly dismantled at the end of the war, but it set an important precedent for the growth of government.

War Work

The war benefited working men and women, though not as much as it benefited their employers. Government contracts guaranteed high wages, an eight-hour day, and equal pay for comparable work. To encourage people to stay on the job, federal contracting agencies set up special classes to teach employers the new science of personnel management in order to supervise workers more efficiently and humanely. American industry moved one step closer to the **welfare capitalism** of the 1920s, with its promises of profit sharing, company unions, and personnel departments to forestall worker discontent.

National War Labor Board

Personnel management was not always enough to guarantee industrial peace. In 1917 American workers called over 4,000 strikes, the largest annual outbreak in American history. To keep factories running smoothly, President Wilson created the National War Labor Board (NWLB) early in 1918. The NWLB arbitrated more than 1,000 labor disputes, helped to increase wages, established overtime pay, and supported the principle of equal pay for women. In return for pledges not to strike, the board guaranteed the rights of unions to organize and bargain collectively. Membership in the American Federation of Labor jumped from 2.7 million in 1914 to nearly 4 million by 1919.

Women in the Workforce

As doughboys went abroad, the war brought nearly a million more women into the labor force. (Infantrymen were called "doughboys" for the "dough" of clay that soldiers used to clean their white belts in the 1850s.) Most were young and single. Sometimes they took over jobs once held by men as railroad engineers, drill press operators, and electric lift truck drivers. Here, too, government tried to mediate between labor and management. In 1917 the Labor Department opened the Women in Industry Service (WIS) to recommend guidelines for using female labor. Among the most important were an eight-hour day, rest periods and breaks for meals, and equal pay for equal work. Most women never worked under such conditions, but for the first time, the federal government tried to upgrade their working conditions.

The prewar trend toward higher-paying jobs for women intensified. Most still earned less

The constraints of war brought more women than ever into the job market. These women work on a production line manufacturing bullets. The novelty of the situation seems evident from the fashionable high-heeled high-button shoes that they wear—ill suited to the conditions in an armaments plant.

than the men they replaced as they moved into clerical and light industrial work. And some of the most spectacular gains in defense and government work evaporated after the war as male veterans returned. Tens of thousands of army nurses, defense workers, and war administrators lost their jobs. Agencies such as the Women's Service Section of the Railroad Administration, which fought sexual harassment and discrimination, simply went out of business.

Women in war work nonetheless helped to energize a number of women's causes and organizations. Radical suffragist Alice Paul and others who had protested against the war now argued for women's rights, including the right to vote, on the basis of it. As women worked side by side with men in wartime factories and offices, in nursing stations at home or at the front, they could argue more convincingly for both economic and political equality. One step in that direction came after the war with the ratification of the Nineteenth Amendment in 1919 granting women the right to vote (see page 641).

Great Migrations

War work sparked massive migrations of laborers. As the fighting abroad choked off immigration and the draft depleted the workforce, factory owners and large-scale farmers scoured the country and beyond for willing workers. Congress waived immigration requirements in 1917 for agricultural workers from Mexico and in 1918 for workers on railroads, in mines, and on government construction projects.

Latino Migrations

Industrial cities soon swelled with newcomers, many of them Mexican and Mexican American. Between 1917 and 1920, some 50,000 Mexicans legally crossed the border into Texas, California, New Mexico, and Arizona. At least another 100,000 entered illegally. Some Mexican Americans left the segregated barrios and farmlands of the West, pushed out by this cheaper labor from Mexico, and migrated to Chicago, Omaha, and other midwestern cities. Mexican *colonias*, or communities, sprang up across the industrial heartland. But most Mexicans and Mexican Americans continued to work on the farms and ranches of the Southwest, where they were freed from military service by the deferment granted to all agricultural labor.

African Americans

Northern labor agents fanned out across the rural South to recruit young African Americans, while black newspapers like the Chicago *Defender* summoned them north to the "Land of Hope." Over the war years more than 400,000 moved to the booming industrial centers of the North. Largely unskilled and semiskilled, they worked in the steel mills of Pennsylvania, the war plants of Massachusetts, the brickyards of New Jersey. Southern towns were decimated by the drain. Finally, under pressure from southern politicians, the U.S. Employment Service suspended its program to assist blacks moving north.

These migrations—of African Americans into the army as well as into the city—aggravated racial tensions. Lynching parties murdered 38 black southerners in 1917 and 58 in 1918. In 1919, after the war ended, more than 70 African Americans were hanged, some still in uniform. Housing shortages and job competition helped spark race riots across the North.

In almost every city black citizens, stirred by war rhetoric of freedom and democracy, showed new militancy by fighting back. In mid-1917 some 40 black and 9 white Americans died when East St. Louis erupted in racial violence. During the "red summer" of 1919, blood flowed in the streets of Washington, D.C., Omaha, Nebraska, New York City, and Chicago, where thousands of African Americans were burned out of their homes and hundreds injured. "The Washington riot gave me the *thrill that comes once in a life time,*" wrote a young black woman in 1919. "At last our men had stood like men, struck back, were no longer dumb driven cattle."

Propaganda and Civil Liberties

"Once lead this people into war," President Wilson warned before American entry into World War I, "and they'll forget there ever was such a thing as tolerance." Americans

Committee on Public
Information

succumbed to war hysteria, but they had help. Wilson knew how reluctant Americans had been to enter the war, and he created the Committee on Public Information (CPI) to boost American commitment to the war.

Under George Creel, a California journalist, the CPI launched "a fight for the *minds* of men, for the conquest of their convictions." A zealous publicity campaign produced 75 million pamphlets, patriotic "war expositions" attended by 10 million people in two dozen cities, and colorful war posters, including James Flagg's famous "I Want *You* for the U.S. Army." Seventy-five thousand fast-talking "Four-Minute Men" invaded movie theaters, lodge halls, schools, and churches to keep patriotism at "white heat" with four minutes of war tirades. The CPI organized "Loyalty Leagues" in ethnic communities and sponsored parades and rallies, among them a much-publicized immigrant "pilgrimage" to the birthplace of George Washington.

100 Percent Americanism

The division between patriotism and intolerance proved impossible to maintain. As war fever rose, voluntary patriotism blossomed into an orgy of "100 percent Americanism" that distrusted all aliens, radicals, pacifists, and dissenters. German Americans became special targets. In Iowa the governor made it a crime to speak German in public. Hamburgers were renamed "Salisbury steak"; German measles, "liberty measles." When a mob outside St. Louis lynched a naturalized German American who had tried to enlist in the navy, a jury found the leaders not guilty.

Espionage and
Sedition Acts

Congress gave concern about espionage and **sedition** more legal bite by passing the Espionage and Sedition acts of 1917 and 1918. Both set out harsh penalties for any actions that hindered the war effort or that could be viewed as even remotely unpatriotic. Following their passage, 1500 citizens were arrested for offenses that included denouncing the draft, criticizing the Red Cross, and complaining about wartime taxes.

Radical groups received especially severe treatment. The Industrial Workers of the World (IWW), a militant labor union centered in western states, saw the war as a battle among capitalists and threatened to strike mining and lumber companies in protest. Federal agents raided the Chicago headquarters of the IWW—familiarly known as the "Wobblies"—and arrested 113 of its leaders in September 1917. The

The Final German Offensive and Allied Counterattack, 1918 *On the morning of March 21, 1918, the Germans launched a spring offensive designed to cripple the Allies. Sixty-three German divisions sliced through Allied lines for the first time since 1914 and plunged to within 50 miles of Paris. The tide turned in July, when the Germans were stopped at the Marne. The Allied counterattack, with notable American successes at Château-Thierry, Belleau Wood, Saint-Mihiel, and Meuse-Argonne, broke the German war effort.*

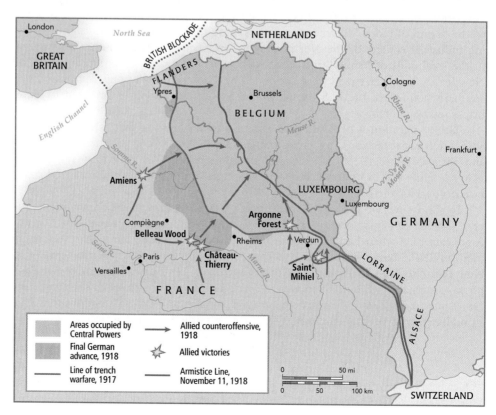

crusade destroyed the union. Similarly, the Socialist party opposed the "capitalist" war. In response, the postmaster general banned a dozen Socialist publications from the mail, though the party was a legal organization that had elected mayors, municipal officials, and members of Congress. In June 1918 government agents arrested Eugene V. Debs, the Socialist candidate in the presidential election of 1912, for attacking the draft. A jury found him guilty of sedition and sentenced him to 10 years in jail. Running for the presidency from his jail cell in 1920, Debs received nearly 1 million votes.

The Supreme Court endorsed such actions. In *Schenck v. United States* (1919), the Court unanimously affirmed the use of the Espionage Act to convict a Socialist party officer who had mailed pamphlets urging resistance to the draft. Free speech had limits, wrote Justice Oliver Wendell Holmes, and the pamphlets created "a clear and present danger" to a nation at war.

Schenck v. United States

Over There

The first American doughboys landed in France in June 1917, but General John Pershing held back his raw troops for nearly six months, until they could receive more training. He also separated them in a distinct American Expeditionary Force to preserve their identity and avoid Allied disagreements over strategy.

In the spring of 1918, as the Germans pushed within 50 miles of Paris, Pershing rushed 70,000 American troops to the front. American units helped block the Germans both at the town of Château-Thierry and a month later, in June, at Belleau Wood. At Belleau, it cost half their force to drive the enemy from the woods. Two more German attacks, one at Amiens, the other just east of the Marne River, ended in costly German retreats. On September 12, 1918, half a million American soldiers and a smaller number of French troops overran the German stronghold at Saint-Mihiel in four days.

With their army in retreat and civilian morale low, Germany's leaders sought an **armistice.** They hoped to negotiate terms along the lines laid out by Woodrow Wilson in a speech to Congress in January 1918. Wilson's bright vision of peace encompassed his "Fourteen Points." The key provisions called for open diplomacy, free seas and free trade, disarmament, democratic self-rule, and an "association of nations" to guarantee collective security. It was nothing less than a new world order to end selfish nationalism, imperialism, and war.

Wilson's Fourteen Points

Allied leaders were not impressed. "President Wilson and his Fourteen Points bore me," French premier Georges Clemenceau said. "Even God Almighty has only ten!" But Wilson's idealistic platform was also designed to save the Allies deeper embarrassment. Almost as soon as it came to power in 1917, the new Bolshevik government in Moscow began publishing secret treaties from the czar's archives. They revealed that the Allies had gone to war for territory and colonies, not the high principles they claimed. Wilson's Fourteen Points now gave their cause a nobler purpose.

Wilson's ideals also stirred German liberals. On October 6, 1918, the liberals gave him the chance when a telegram arrived from Berlin requesting an immediate truce on the basis of the Fourteen Points. Within a month Turkey and Austria surrendered. Early in November the Kaiser was overthrown and fled to neutral Holland. On November 11, 1918, just before dawn, German officers filed into Allied headquarters in a converted railroad car near Compiègne, France, and signed the armistice.

Of the 2 million Americans who served in France, some 116,500 died. Over 200,000 were wounded. By comparison, the war claimed 1.8 million Germans, 1.7 million Russians, 1.4 million French, 1.2 million Austro-Hungarians, and nearly a million Britons. The American contribution had nonetheless been crucial, providing vital convoys at sea and fresh, confident troops on land. The United States emerged from the war stronger than ever. Europe, on the other hand, looked forward—as one newspaper put it—to "Disaster . . . Exhaustion . . . Revolution."

When Secretary of War Newton Baker drew the first number in a new draft lottery on July 20, 1917, the United States had barely 180,000 men in the service. By the time World War I ended in November 1918, nearly 2 million men had donned uniforms and gone off to fight in Europe. For the first time the New World was invading the Old, and for most of those who went, it was their first trip from home.

The "doughboys" marched out of their training camps and up the gangplanks of the "Atlantic Ferry"—the ships that conveyed them to Europe. Some soldiers were fortunate enough to ship out on refitted luxury liners, but most made the voyage below decks in converted freighters, "the blackest, foulest, most congested hole that I ever set foot into," reported one private. A few died from anthrax in the horsehair of their

After months of training stateside, the American Expeditionary Force sailed to Europe on the troop ships of the "Atlantic Ferry." Most soldiers departed from Hoboken, New Jersey, and almost half made the journey aboard British vessels.

The Influenza Pandemic of 1918–1919

In the months before the armistice, a scourge more lethal than war began to engulf the globe. It started innocently enough. At Fort Riley, Kansas, on the morning of March 11, 1918, company cook Albert Mitchell reported to the infirmary on sick call. His head and muscles ached, his throat was sore, and he had a low-grade fever.

It was the flu, dangerous for infants and the old but ordinarily no threat to a robust young man like Mitchell. By noon, 107 soldiers had reported symptoms. Within a week, the number had jumped to over 500. Cases of the flu were being reported in virtually every state in the Union, even on the isolated island of Alcatraz in San Francisco Bay. And robust young adults Mitchell's age were dying from it.

The first wave of flu produced few deaths in the United States. But as the virus mutated over the next year, its victims experienced more distressing symptoms: vomiting, dizziness, labored breathing, incessant sweating. Eventually victims drowned in their own bodily fluids from the pneumonia that accompanied the infection.

Soldiers and others living in close quarters were especially vulnerable, and for reasons that are still uncertain, so were young adults 20 to 34 years old, precisely the ages of most in the services. For every 50 people infected, 1 died. In the United States alone, the death toll rose to at least 600,000, more than the American battle deaths in World War I, World War II, the Korean War, and the war in Vietnam combined.

Global Spread of the Pandemic

Ironically, the United States was the country least affected by this worldwide epidemic, called a **pandemic.** American soldiers seem to have carried the disease to Europe, where it jumped from one country to another in the spring and summer of 1918. French troops and civilians soon were suffering from it, then British and Germans. General Eric von Ludendorf counted the flu as one of the causes of the failure of the final German offensive in July 1918, which almost won the war for Germany.

With steamships and railroads carrying people all over the globe, virtually no place was safe. By the summer of 1918, the virus had leapt from North America and Europe new shaving brushes. It was a poignant taste of things to come. Disease killed more Americans than enemy fire.

The first American troops arrived during the summer of 1917 and were promptly squeezed into "40-and-8's"—French freight cars designed to hold 40 men and 8 horses—and carried inland to training areas.

With the United States at war for such a short time, most American soldiers spent more time in training and on leave than in the trenches. To keep the men from becoming restless, company commanders marched their troops against imaginary enemies in never-ending exercises. Soldiers complained about "cooties" (lice) and food (so bad that many reported a 10 percent weight loss within weeks of arriving). Used to freewheeling individualism and equality, they positively hated military discipline.

Enlisted men groused about army life, but the Old World awed them. Paris was titillating, with women who danced the "Can-Can" and cried "oo-la-la." The antiquity of Europe struck the doughboys even more: "The church here is very, very old. . . . Saint Louis the Crusader, King of France, attended a service there on three occasions and Jeanne d'Arc was there several times." The Europeans seemed both old and old-fashioned. Elderly women in black shawls of mourning often were the only ones left in shattered villages. "They still harvest with cradles and sickles," noted one soldier. Everything endorsed the American myth of the Old World as hidebound and worn and the New as modern and vital.

Disillusion and discontent overcame British and French troops after years in the trenches, but most doughboys never fought long enough to lose their sense of wonder and delight. They returned with a war veteran's sense of dislocation and a new appreciation of the world outside the United States. A year after the war ended a veteran wrote: "I know how we all cried to get back to the States. But now that we are here, I must admit for myself at least that I am lost and somehow strangely lonesome. These our own United States are truly artificial and bare. There is no romance or color here, nothing to suffer for and laugh at."

*In October 1918 artist D. C. Boonzaier drew this grim cartoon of the Spanish flu—*Spaanse Griep*—when it came to South Africa. In his diary Boonzaier spoke of "the presence of some universal calamity, from which there was no escape. Death stalked by your side incessantly, you looked into its face wherever you turned."*

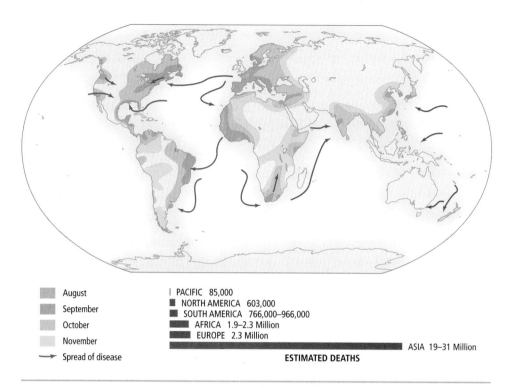

August

September

October

November

→ Spread of disease

| PACIFIC 85,000
■ NORTH AMERICA 603,000
■ SOUTH AMERICA 766,000–966,000
■ AFRICA 1.9–2.3 Million
■ EUROPE 2.3 Million

ASIA 19–31 Million

ESTIMATED DEATHS

Spread of Influenza Pandemic: Second Stage, Autumn 1918   *After the milder outbreak in the spring of 1918, a more deadly form of influenza spread outward from the coast of France at the beginning of August. The worldwide transportation system quickly dispersed the disease, sending it first to the western coast of Africa (beginning at Freetown, Liberia) and the eastern coast of North America (at Boston). The disease reached virtually all continents, although Australia's strict quarantine delayed entrance of the flu there until 1919. By far, the continent hardest hit was Asia, where anywhere from 12 to 20 million died in India alone. American fatalities, though serious, totaled only about 550,000.*

to Asia and Japan; by fall, to Africa and South America. As far north as the Russian city of Archangel, officials were reporting 30 influenza deaths a day by October 1918. In densely packed India, one account claimed that at least 12 million perished from influenza.

Sixteen months after Albert Mitchell had first reported to sick call, the flu vanished as quickly as it had appeared. Conservative estimates placed the number of dead worldwide at 50 million, making the influenza pandemic of 1918–1919 the most lethal outbreak of disease on an annual basis in human history.

The Lost Peace

As the USS *George Washington* approached the coast of France in mid-December 1918 the mist suddenly lifted in an omen of good hope. Woodrow Wilson had come to represent the United States at the Paris peace conference at Versailles, once the glittering palace of Louis XIV. A world of problems awaited him and the other Allied leaders. Europe had been shelled into ruin and scarred with the debris of war. Fifty million people lay dead or maimed from the fighting. Throughout the Balkans and the old Turkish empire, ethnic rivalries, social chaos, and revolution loomed.

With the old world order in shambles, Wilson felt the need for vigorous action. Thus the president handpicked the peace commission of experts that accompanied him. It included economists, historians, geographers, and political scientists—but not a single member of the Republican-controlled Senate. What promised to make

As Practical as the Ten Commandments?

Placing a Document in Context

Woodrow Wilson's famous Fourteen Points for establishing a new world order struck some observers, including this cartoonist, as being as idealistic as the Ten Commandments. Didn't Wilson understand that a bold proclamation in favor of democracy and self-determination would be ignored by imperialists who prided themselves on being Great Powers? But for historians, the *context* of Wilson's Fourteen Points speech is as important as its content, and it reveals purposes far more practical.

To begin with, when was the speech delivered? Wilson laid his principles before Congress on January 8, 1918, just when the new Bolshevik government in Russia was negotiating an armistice with Germany. That agreement was based on the "Petrograd Formula" of peace "without annexations or indemnities" but guaranteeing "the self-determination of peoples." With Russia about to leave the fight and peace nowhere in sight, morale among the Allies was at low ebb.

Thus, for Wilson, the Fourteen Points speech, with its call for a peace based on national self-determination and a League of Nations, had quite practical political ends. The president hoped to keep Russia in the war and steal the revolutionary thunder of the Petrograd Formula. He aimed to bolster German liberals who wanted an end to war. And he meant to boost sagging morale among the Allies with the promise of peace. Although the Fourteen Points, like the Ten Commandments, set a lofty standard of ideals, Wilson (like God) had practical results in mind as well.

GOD: Woodrow Wilson, where are your 14 points?
WILSON: Don't get excited, Lord, we didn't keep your Ten Commandments either!

peace negotiations easier, however, created a crippling liability in Washington, where Republicans cast a hostile eye on the mirrored halls of Versailles.

The Treaty of Versailles

Everywhere he went, cheers greeted the president. In Paris 2 million people showered him with flowers. In Italy they hailed him as the "peacemaker from America." And Wilson believed them, unaware of how determined the victors were to punish the vanquished Germans. David Lloyd George of England, Georges Clemenceau of France, Vittorio Orlando of Italy, and Wilson made up the Big Four at the conference that included some 27 nations. War had united them; now peacemaking threatened to divide them.

Wilson's sweeping call for reform had taken Allied leaders by surprise. Hungry for new colonies, eager to see Germany crushed and disarmed, they had already drawn up secret treaties dividing the territories of the Central Powers. Germany had offered to surrender on the basis of Wilson's Fourteen Points, but the Allies refused to accept them. When Wilson threatened to negotiate peace on his own, Allied leaders finally agreed—but only for the moment.

Noticeably absent when the peace conference convened in January 1919 were the Russians. None of the Western democracies had recognized the Bolshevik regime in Moscow out of fear that the communist revolution might spread. Instead, France and Britain were helping to finance a civil war to overthrow the Bolsheviks. Even Wilson had been persuaded to send a small number of American troops to join the Allied occupation of Murmansk in northern Russia and Vladivostok on the Sea of Japan. The Soviets would neither forget nor forgive this invasion of their soil.

Grueling peace negotiations forced Wilson to yield several of his Fourteen Points. Britain, with its powerful navy, refused even to discuss the issues of free trade and freedom of the seas. Wilson's "open diplomacy" was conducted behind closed doors by the Big Four. The only mention of disarmament involved Germany, which was permanently barred from rearming. Wilson's call for "peace without victory" gave way to a "guilt clause" that saddled Germany with responsibility for the war. Worse still, the victors imposed on the vanquished an impoverishing debt of $33 billion in reparations.

Wilson did achieve some successes. His pleas for national self-determination led to the creation of a dozen new states in Europe, including Yugoslavia, Hungary, and Austria. (Newly created Poland and Czechoslovakia, however, contained millions of ethnic Germans.) Former colonies gained new status as "mandates" of the victors, who were obligated to prepare them for independence. The old German and Turkish empires in the Middle East and Africa became the responsibility of France and England, while Japan took over virtually all German possessions in the Pacific north of the equator.

League of Nations   Wilson never lost sight of his main goal—a League of Nations. He had given up so much ground precisely because he believed this new world organization would correct any mistakes in the peace settlement. As constituted, the League comprised a general Body of Delegates, a select Executive Council, and a Court of International Justice. Members promised to submit all war-provoking disagreements to arbitration and to isolate aggressors by cutting off commercial and military trade. Article X (Wilson called it "the heart of the covenant") bound members to respect one another's independence and territory and to join together against attack. "It is definitely a guarantee of peace," the president told the delegates in February 1919.

The Battle for the Treaty

Wilson left immediately for home to address growing opposition in Congress. In the off-year elections of 1918, voters unhappy with wartime controls, new taxes, and attacks on civil liberties had given both houses to the Republicans. A slim Republican majority in the Senate put Wilson's archrival, Henry Cabot Lodge of Massachusetts, in the chairman's seat of the all-important Foreign Relations Committee. "I never expected to hate anyone in politics with the hatred I feel toward Wilson," Lodge confessed.

While most of the country favored the League, Lodge was against it. For decades he had fought to preserve American freedom of action in foreign affairs. Now he worried that the League would force Americans to subject themselves to "the will of other nations." And he certainly did not want Democrats to win votes by taking credit for the treaty. Securing the signatures of enough senators to block any treaty, Lodge rose in the Senate just before midnight on March 3, 1919, to read a "round robin" resolution against the League. "Woodrow Wilson's League of Nations died in the Senate tonight," concluded the New York *Sun*.

Wilson formally presented the treaty in July. "Dare we reject it and break the heart of the world?" he asked the senators. Fourteen Republicans and two Democrats were happy to do just that. Wilson's only hope of winning the necessary two-thirds majority for passage of the treaty lay in compromise, but temperamentally he could not abide it. Worn out by the concessions already wrung from him in Paris, afflicted increasingly by numbing headaches and a twitch in his left eye, he resisted any more changes. Despite

Europe After World War I

- Demilitarized zones
- 1926 boundaries
- Territory lost by Austro-Hungarian empire
- Territory lost by Russia
- Territory lost by Germany
- Territory lost by Bulgaria

- Ottoman empire, 1914
- British protectorate, 1914
- League of Nations mandates, 1920
- International boundaries, 1923

Europe & Mid-East After WWI

Wilson's Stroke

his doctor's warnings, Wilson took his case to the people in a month-long stump across the nation in hopes of rallying public opinion and bending the Senate to his will.

In Pueblo, Colorado, a crowd of 10,000 heard perhaps the greatest oration of Wilson's career. He spoke that evening, utterly exhausted, and collapsed in a spasm of pain. On October 2, four days after being rushed to the White House, the president fell to the bathroom floor, knocked unconscious by a stroke.

For six weeks Wilson could do no work at all and for months after worked little more than an hour a day. His second wife, Edith Bolling Wilson, handled the routine business of government along with the president's secretary and his doctor. The country knew nothing of the seriousness of his condition. Wilson recovered slowly but never fully. More and more the battle for the treaty consumed his fading energies.

On November 19 Lodge finally reported the treaty out of committee with 14 amendments to match Wilson's Fourteen Points. The most important asserted that the United States assumed no obligation under Article X to come to the aid of League members unless Congress consented. Wilson believed Lodge had delivered a "knife thrust at the heart of the treaty" and refused to accept any changes. Whatever ill will Lodge bore Wilson, his objections did not destroy the treaty but only weakened it by protecting the congressional prerogative to declare war.

Under orders from the president, Democrats joined Republicans to defeat the treaty with Lodge's reservations. An attempt to pass the unamended treaty failed. Although four-fifths of the senators favored it in some form, Wilson and Lodge refused to compromise. The Treaty of Versailles was dead, and loyal Democrats had been forced to deliver the killing blow. Not until July 1921 did Congress enact a joint resolution ending the war. The United States, which had fought separately from the Allies, made a separate peace as well.

Red Scare

Peace abroad did not bring peace at home. On May Day 1919, six months after the war ended, mobs in a dozen cities broke up Socialist parades, injured hundreds, and killed three people. On the floor of the Senate Kenneth McKellar of Tennessee advocated sending citizens with radical beliefs to a penal colony on Guam.

Radicals and Labor Unrest

The spontaneous violence and extremism occurred because Americans believed they were under attack. Millions of soldiers had returned home, now unemployed

In September 1919 some 350,000 steelworkers struck for higher wages, recognition of their union, and a reduction in their 70-hour workweeks. Mill owners countered by hiring black strikebreakers and armed guards and by launching a potent publicity campaign that depicted the strike as a plot of "Red agitators." Here, armed police ride down strikers in Philadelphia.

and looking for jobs. With prices rising and war regulations lifted, laborers were demanding higher wages and striking when they failed to get them. In Boston even the police walked off their jobs. When a strike by conservative trade unionists paralyzed Seattle for five days in January, Mayor Ole Hanson draped his car in an American flag and led troops through the streets in a show of force. Hanson blamed radicals, while Congress ascribed the national ills to Bolshevik agents inspired by the revolution in Russia.

The menace of radical subversion appeared greater than it was. With Socialist Eugene Debs in prison, his dwindling party numbered only about 30,000. Radicals at first hoped that the success of the Russian Revolution would help reverse their fortunes in the United States. But most Americans found the prospect of "Bolshevik" agitators threatening, especially after March 1919, when the new Russian government formed the Comintern to spread revolution abroad. Furthermore, the Left itself splintered. In 1919 dissidents deserted the Socialists to form the more radical Communist Labor party. About the same time, a group of mostly Slavic radicals created a separate Communist party. Both organizations together counted no more than 40,000 members.

Terrorism now stoked the flames of fear. On April 28 Mayor Hanson received a small brown parcel at his office, evidently another present from an admirer of his tough patriotism. It was a homemade bomb. Within days, 20 such packages were discovered, including ones sent to John D. Rockefeller, Supreme Court Justice Oliver Wendell Holmes, and Postmaster General Albert Burleson. On June 2 bombs exploded simultaneously in eight different cities. One of them demolished the front porch of A. Mitchell Palmer, the attorney general of the United States. The bomb thrower was blown to bits, but enough remained to identify him as an Italian anarchist from Philadelphia. Already edgy over Bolshevism and labor militancy, many Americans assumed that an organized conspiracy was being mounted to overthrow the government.

Palmer, a Quaker and a staunch progressive, hardened in the wake of the bombings. In November 1919 and again in January 1920, he launched raids in cities across the United States. In a single night in January, government agents invaded private homes, meeting halls, and pool parlors in 33 cities. They took 4,000 people into custody without warrants, sometimes beating those who resisted. Many were Russians, some were communists, but most were victims of suspicion run amok. In Detroit, 300 innocent people were arrested and confined for a week, one day without food. Prisoners were marched through streets in chains, crammed into dilapidated jails, and held incommunicado without hearings. Over 200 aliens, most of whom had no criminal records, were deported to the Soviet Union. Arrests continued at the rate of 200 a week through March.

Palmer Raids

Such abuses of civil liberties finally provoked a backlash. After the New York legislature expelled five duly elected Socialists in 1919, responsible politicians—from former presidential candidate Charles Evans Hughes to Ohio senator Warren Harding—began to denounce the action. Assistant Secretary of Labor Louis Post refused to issue more deportation orders, and the "deportation delirium" ended early in 1920.

Palmer finally overreached himself by predicting a revolutionary uprising for May 1, 1920. Buildings were put under guard and state militia called to readiness. Nothing happened. Four months later, when a wagonload of bombs exploded on Wall Street, Palmer blamed a Bolshevik conspiracy. Despite 35 deaths and more than 200 injuries, Americans saw it as the work of a few fanatic anarchists (which it probably was) and went about business as usual.

In early August 1914 the Panama Canal opened without fanfare, but no one could miss its significance: the new American empire now spanned the globe, stretching from the Caribbean to the Pacific and linked by a path between the seas. There were plans for a tremendous celebration in which the battleship *Oregon*, whose 1898 "race around the Horn" had inspired the idea of an American-owned canal, would lead a flotilla of ships through the locks. But the plans had to be scrapped, for in that fateful month of August, the old world order collapsed into a world war.

World War I was rightly named "the Great War" by Europeans, because it transformed the continent and left a bitter legacy that shaped the emerging world of the twentieth century. In Europe, France and Great Britain triumphed, only to find their economies enfeebled, their people dispirited and fearful, their empires near collapse. Two other empires—of vanquished Austria-Hungary and Turkey—were dismembered. Revolution toppled the once mighty czars of Russia, bringing an end to the Russian empire and the beginning of the Soviet Union under the direction of Joseph Stalin. Germany suffered defeat, humiliation, and a crushing burden of debt, which together paved the way for Adolf Hitler and the Nazis.

Elsewhere, a victorious Japan left the Paris peace table shamed by what it regarded as paltry spoils of war and determined to rise to global greatness. Japan's flickering democracy soon crumbled as a cult of militarism and emperor worship took hold. In the Middle East, in Africa, and on the Indian subcontinent, the unfulfilled promises of a world made "safe for democracy" sparked a growing number of nationalist and anticolonialist movements. The twentieth century, a century of global change and violence, was indeed forged in the crucible of the Great War.

Significant Events

1901	Hay-Paunceforte Treaty authorizes United States to build a canal across the Central American isthmus
1904	Roosevelt Corollary to Monroe Doctrine
1905	Treaty of Portsmouth ends Russo-Japanese War
1907	"Gentlemen's agreement" with Japan; "Great White Fleet" embarks on world tour
1911	Mexican Revolution erupts
1914	Archduke Franz Ferdinand assassinated; World War I begins; Panama Canal opens
1915	Germany proclaims war zone around British Isles; *Lusitania* torpedoed; Wilson endorses preparedness
1916	General John Pershing invades Mexico in pursuit of Pancho Villa; Wilson reelected president
1917	Germany resumes unrestricted submarine warfare; Russian Revolution breaks out; United States enters World War I
1918	Wilson's Fourteen Points for peace; influenza epidemic; armistice declared
1919	Paris Peace Conference; *Schenck v. United States* affirms Espionage Act; Senate rejects Treaty of Versailles
1920	Palmer raids; Red scare

Chapter Summary

World War I marked the beginning of the end of the old world order of colonial imperialism, military alliances, and balances of power; it also marked a failed effort to establish a new world order based on the progressive ideals of international cooperation and collective security.

- Progressive diplomacy—whether through Theodore Roosevelt's big stick diplomacy, William Taft's dollar diplomacy, or Woodrow Wilson's missionary diplomacy—stressed moralism and order, championed "uplifting" nonwhites, and stretched presidential authority to its limits.

- With the outbreak of World War I in 1914, Woodrow Wilson saw an opportunity for the United States to lead the world to a higher peace of international cooperation and collective security by remaining neutral and brokering the peace settlement.

- However, American sympathy for the Allies, heavy American investments in the Allies, and the German campaign of unrestricted submarine warfare finally drew the country into the war in 1917.

- Progressive faith in government, planning, efficiency, and publicity produced a greatly expanded bureaucratic state that managed the war effort on the home front.

  - The darker side of progressivism also flourished as the war transformed progressive impulses for assimilation and social control into campaigns for superpatriotism and conformity that helped to produce a postwar Red scare in 1919 and 1920.
  - Meanwhile, changes already under way, including more women in the labor force and migrations of African Americans and Mexican Americans from rural to urban America, vastly accelerated with the expansion of opportunities for war work.

- When the war ended, Wilson's hopes for "peace without victory" and a new world order, embodied in his Fourteen Points, were dashed when his European allies imposed a harsh settlement on Germany and the U.S. Senate failed to ratify the Treaty of Versailles.

Additional Reading

The diverse vectors of progressive diplomacy, as practiced by Theodore Roosevelt and Woodrow Wilson, are the subject of Howard K. Beale, *Theodore Roosevelt and the Rise of America to World Power* (1956), and Arthur Link, *Woodrow Wilson: Revolution, War, and Peace* (1968). Ernest R. May examines American prewar diplomacy and the policies of the Great Powers, especially Germany's U-boat campaign, in *The World War and American Isolation, 1914–1917* (1957).

The debate over American entry into World War I has a long history. Early revisionist accounts emphasizing a financial conspiracy to bring the nation to war include Charles Beard, *The Open Door to War* (1934), and Charles C. Tansill, *America Goes to War* (1938). A good account from the school of realism, critical of Wilson's moral motives, is George Kennan, *American Diplomacy, 1900–1950* (rev. ed, 1971). David M. Kennedy, *Over Here: The First World War and American Society* (1980), is the definitive account of mobilization and the home front, but see also Maurine W. Greenwald, *Women, War, and Work* (1980), Susan Zeiger, *In Uncle Sam's Service: Women Workers with the American Expeditionary Force, 1917–1919* (1999), and Kathleen Kennedy, *Disloyal Mothers and Scurrilous Citizens: Women and Subversion During World War I* (1999), on the status and role of women during the war. Joe William Trotter, *The Great Migration in Historical Perspective* (1991), is a fine collec-

tion of essays that stresses gender and class in the wartime experience of African Americans. Mark Ellis, *Race, War, and Surveillance: African Americans and the United States Government during World War I* (2001), and Mark Robert Schneider, *"We Return Fighting": The Civil Rights Movement in the Jazz Age* (2001), look at the effects of the war on African American civil rights. Frank Freidel re-creates the horrors of trench warfare in *Over There: The Story of America's First Great Overseas Crusade* (1964), while Jennifer D. Keene, *Doughboys, the Great War, and the Remaking of America* (2001), looks at the impact of the war on soldiers and on the country. For African Americans on the battle front, see Arthur E. Barbeau and Henri Florette, *The Unknown Soldiers: Black American Troops in World War I* (1974). Robert Ferrell, *Woodrow Wilson and World War I* (1985), analyzes Wilson's wartime diplomacy, the peace negotiations, and the fate of the Treaty of Versailles. The most informed account of the influenza pandemic can be found in Alfred W. Crosby, *America's Forgotten Pandemic: The Influenza of 1918* (1989). For a colorful, thorough, and thoughtful account of the Paris Peace Conference, see Margaret Macmillan and Richard Holbrooke, *Paris, 1919: Six Months That Changed the World* (2001).

For a fuller list of readings, see the Bibliography at www.mhhe.com/davidsonnation6.

CHAPTER 24
The New Era
1920~1929

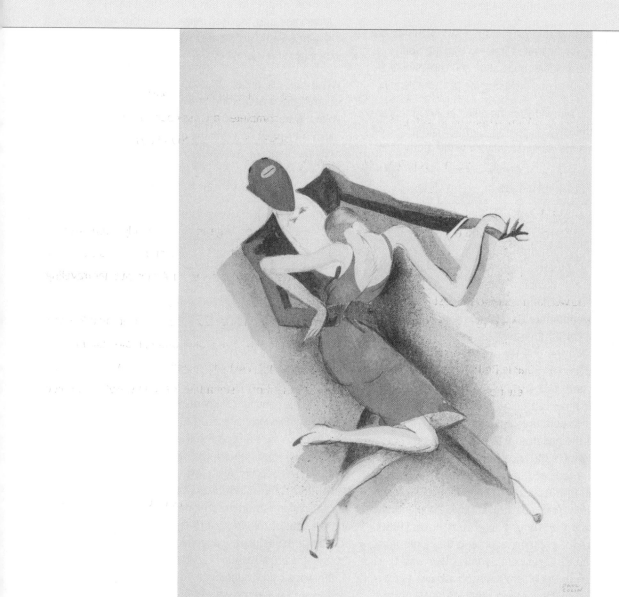

Yesterday Meets Today in the New Era

Just before Christmas 1918 the "Gospel Car" pulled into Los Angeles. Bold letters on the side announced: "JESUS IS COMING—GET READY." Aimee Semple McPherson, the ravishing redheaded driver, had completed a cross-country drive to seek her destiny in the West. With only "ten dollars and a tambourine" to her name, Sister Aimee at first found destiny elusive. After three years of wandering the state, she landed in San Diego. With the highest rates of illness and suicide in California, it was the perfect place for Sister Aimee to preach the healing message of her "Foursquare Gospel." Her revival attracted 30,000 people, who witnessed her first proclaimed miracle: a paralytic walked.

After the miracle in San Diego, her fame spread. She returned triumphantly to Los Angeles, where nearly three-quarters of a million people, many from the nation's heartland, had migrated in search of opportunity, sun, and perhaps salvation. In heading west, most had lost touch with the traditional Protestant denominations at home. Sister Aimee put her traveling gospel tent away. She would minister to the lost flock at her doorstep.

To the blare of trumpets on New Year's Day, 1923, she unveiled the $1.5 million Angelus Temple, graced by a 75-foot, rotating electrified cross. It was visible at night from 50 miles away. Inside was a 5,000-seat auditorium, radio station KFSG (Kall Four Square Gospel), a "Cradle Roll Chapel" for babies, and a "Miracle Room" filled with crutches and canes discarded by the cured faithful. Services were not simply a matter of hymn, prayer, and sermon. Sister added pageants, Holy Land slide shows, circuses, and healing sessions.

Aimee Semple McPherson succeeded because she was able to blend old and new. Where country preachers menaced their congregations with visions of eternal damnation, Sister Aimee, wrote a reporter, offered "flowers, music, golden trumpets, red robes, angels, incense, nonsense, and sex appeal." Her approach revealed a nose for publicity and a sophisticated understanding of the booming media industries of the 1920s. Here was one brand of evangelism suited to what contemporaries were calling the "New Era" of prosperity and consumption.

Modernizing the gospel was just one symptom of the New Era. Writing in 1931, journalist Frederick Lewis Allen found the changes of the preceding decade so breathtaking that he could not believe that 1919 was *Only Yesterday*, as he titled his book.

The "Dancing Pair with Woman in Orange" comes from Le Tumulte Noir *("The Black Craze"), a collection of lithographs by French artist Paul Colin (1892–1985) published in 1929. The vibrant images were inspired by the African American performer Josephine Baker, whose* La Revue Négre *burst onto the Paris club scene in 1925 at the height of the Jazz Age. The French embraced jazz with an exuberance and a tolerance captured in this Art Deco rendering of a biracial couple locked in the most popular dance of the era, the Charleston.*

To give a sense of the transformation, Allen followed an average American couple, the fictitious "Mr. and Mrs. Smith," through the 1920s. The same revolution in industry and technology that allowed the sweet-voiced Aimee McPherson to save souls by the thousands had also transformed the Smiths' home with the sounds of radio, the miracles of canned foods, and the savings in time and energy generated by a host of new electrical gadgets. Perhaps the most visible changes involved the revolution in women's fashions and behavior. By the end of the decade, Mrs. Smith's corset vanished, and her hemline jumped from her ankle to her knee. Mimicking stylish young flappers, she bobbed, or cut, her long hair to the popular, near-boyish length and flattened her breasts for greater freedom of movement.

With Prohibition in full force, Mrs. Smith and other women of her day walked into illegal speakeasy saloons as readily as men. In the trendy hotels she and her husband danced to jazz. Modern couples like the Smiths sprinkled their conversations with references to "repressed sexual drives" and the best methods of contraception. But the most striking change about these "average" Americans was that they lived in the city. The census of 1920 showed that for the first time just over half the population were urbanites. Here, in urban America, the New Era worked its changes and sent them rippling outward.

Yet the city-dwelling Smiths of Frederick Allen's imagination were hardly average. Nearly as many Americans still lived on isolated farms, in villages, and in small towns as in cities. In fact, many "city" dwellers lived there, too. By defining cities as incorporated municipalities with 2,500 people or more, the Census Bureau had created hundreds of statistical illusions. New York with its millions of inhabitants ranked in the census tables alongside tiny Hyden, located on the Cumberland plateau of eastern Kentucky.

Most citizens, the Smiths aside, dwelled in an earlier America and clung to its traditions. The technology of the New Era had yet to penetrate many urban American homes, let alone the hinterlands. As late as 1927, two-thirds of American households still had no washing machines or vacuum cleaners and half had no telephones. Nearly all American farms lacked electricity. In Hyden, Main Street was still unpaved. By 1930 there were still only 10 automobiles in the county. God-fearing

Aimee Semple McPherson (center left), billed as the "world's most pulchritudinous evangelist," conducts a revival. Congregants raise their arms in religious ecstasy, while those overcome with the healing power of the Lord fall to the ground. "I am not the healer," Sister Aimee modestly confessed. "Jesus is the healer. I am only the little office girl who opens the door and says, 'Come in.'"

Baptists worshiped together as their parents had before them and still repaired to the Middle Fork of the Kentucky River for an open-air baptism when they declared their new birth in Christ. They would have nothing to do with flapper girls or the showy miracles of Aimee McPherson.

As much as some Americans resisted the transforming forces of modern life, the New Era could not be walled out. Industrial breakthroughs led to a host of new consumer goods, while large corporations developed more "modern" bureaucracies to make production more efficient and profitable. Whether Americans embraced the New Era or condemned it, change came nonetheless, in the form of a mass-produced consumer economy, a culture shaped by mass media, and a more materialistic society. A new ethic of getting and spending took hold, driving the economy to dizzying heights. Most Americans believed the New Era of prosperity would last forever and ripple outward across the globe. Little did they realize that their roaring economy was honeycombed with weaknesses, and in 1929, to their astonishment, it came crashing down.

The Roaring Economy

In the 1920s, the United States was in the midst of a revolution in production. Not only did the amount of goods manufactured increase sharply—by 64 percent over the decade—but workers became more efficient in manufacturing them. Output per worker—productivity—increased by 40 percent. The sale of electricity doubled; the consumption of fuel oil more than doubled. Between 1922 and 1927 the economy grew by 7 percent a year—the largest peacetime rate ever. If anything roared in the "Roaring Twenties," it was the economy.

Technology and Consumer Spending

Technology was partly responsible. Steam turbines and shovels, electric motors, belt and bucket conveyors, and countless other new machines became common at work sites. Machines replaced 200,000 workers each year, and a new phrase—"technological unemployment"—entered the vocabulary. Even so, rising demand, especially for new consumer goods, kept the labor force growing at a faster rate than the population. And pay improved. Between 1919 and 1927, average income climbed nearly $150 for each industrial worker.

As the industrial economy matured, more consumer goods appeared on store shelves—cigarette lighters, wristwatches, radios, panchromatic film. As production of consumer goods grew, improvements in productivity helped keep prices down. The cost of a tire and an inner tube, for example, dropped by half between 1914 and 1929. Meanwhile, real wages (wages valued in purchasing power) jumped by 20 percent. Americans enjoyed the highest standard of living any people had ever known.

Yet for all the prosperity, a dangerous imbalance was developing in the economy. Most Americans saved little in the mistaken belief that prosperity was here to stay. Falling prices made many items seem like good buys, and the rapid expansion of credit allowed consumers to put off paying for what they purchased. As a result, personal debt was rising two and a half times faster than personal income, an unhealthy sign of consumers scrambling to spend.

The Booming Construction Industry

Along with technology and consumer spending, new "boom industries" promoted economic growth. In a rebound after the war years, construction soared. Even cities the size of Beaumont, Texas; Memphis, Tennessee; and Syracuse, New York, were erecting buildings of 20 stories or more. New York got a new skyline of tall towers, topped in 1931 when the Empire State Building rose to the world-record height of 86 stories.

Residential construction doubled as people moved from cities to suburbs. Suburban Grosse Point, near Detroit, grew by 700 percent, and Beverly Hills, on the outskirts of Los Angeles, by 2,500 percent. Road construction made suburban life possible and pumped millions of dollars into the economy. In 1919 Oregon, New Mexico, and Colorado hit on a novel idea for financing roads—a tax on gasoline. Within a decade every state had one.

Construction stimulated other businesses: steel, concrete, lumber, home mortgages, and insurance. It even helped change the nation's eating habits. The limited storage space of small "kitchenettes" in new apartments boosted supermarket chains and the canning industry. As shipments of fresh fruits and vegetables sped across new roads, interest in nutrition grew. Vitamins, publicized with new zeal, appeared on breakfast tables.

The Automobile

No industry boomed more than automobile manufacturing. Although cars had first appeared on streets at the turn of the century, for many years they remained little more than expensive toys. By 1920 there were 10 million in America, a sizable number. But by 1929 the total had jumped to 26 million, 1 for every 5 people (compared to 1 for every 43 in Britain and 1 for every 7,000 in Russia). Automakers bought one-seventh of the nation's steel and more rubber, plate glass, nickel, and lead than any other industry. By the end of the decade, one American in four somehow earned a living from automobiles.

Henry Ford at the turn of the century.

Henry Ford

Henry Ford helped to make the boom possible by pushing standardization and mass production to such ruthless extremes that the automobile became affordable. Trading on his fame as a race-car manufacturer, he founded the Ford Motor Company in 1903 with the dream of building a "motor car for the multitude." The way to succeed was to drive down costs by making all the cars alike, "just like one pin is like another pin." In 1908 Ford perfected the Model T. It had a 20-horsepower engine and a body of steel. It was high enough to ride the worst roads, and it came in only one color: black.

Priced at $845, the Model T was cheap by industry standards but still too costly and too time-consuming to build. Two Ford engineers suggested copying a practice of Chicago meatpacking houses, where beef carcasses were carried on moving chains past meat dressers. In 1914 Ford introduced the moving assembly line. A conveyor belt, positioned waist high to eliminate bending or walking, propelled the chassis at six feet per minute as stationary workers put the cars together. The process cut assembly time in half. In 1925 new Model Ts were rolling off the line every 10 seconds. At $290, almost anybody could buy one. By 1927 Ford had sold 15 million of his "tin lizzies."

Doctrine of High Wages

Ford was also a social prophet. Breaking with other manufacturers, he preached a "doctrine of high wages." According to it, workers with extra money in their pockets would buy enough to sustain a booming prosperity. In 1915 Ford's plants in Dearborn established the "Five-Dollar Day," twice the wage rate in Detroit. He reduced working hours from 48 to 40 a week and cut the workweek to five days. By 1926 he also employed 10,000 African Americans, many of whom had advanced far enough to hire and fire their white subordinates.

Yet Ford workers were not happy. Ford admitted that the repetitive operations on his assembly line made it scarcely possible "that any man would care to continue long at the same job." The Five-Dollar Day was designed, in part, to reduce the turnover rate of 300 percent a year at Ford plants. And Ford recouped his profits by speeding up the assembly line and enforcing ruthless efficiencies. Ford workers could not talk, whistle, smoke, or sit on the job. A Sociological Department spied on workers in their homes, and the Education Department taught plant procedures but also Americanization classes where immigrant workers learned English, proper dress, and even etiquette.

General Motors copied Ford's production techniques but not his business strategies. While Ford tried to sell everyone the same car, GM created "a car for every purse and purpose." There were Cadillacs for the wealthy, Chevrolets for the modest. GM cars were painted in a rainbow of colors, and every year the style changed. In a standardized society, such details made automobiles symbols of distinction as well as prestige.

By making automobiles available to nearly everyone, the industry changed the face of America. The spreading web of paved roads fueled urban sprawl, real estate booms in California and Florida, and a new roadside culture of restaurants, service stations, and motels. Thousands of "auto camps" opened to provide tourists with tents and crude toilets. Automobile travel broke down the isolation and provincialism of Americans and helped to standardize dialects and manners.

A Car Culture

Across the country the automobile gave the young unprecedented freedom from parental authority. After hearing 30 cases of "sex crimes" (19 had occurred in cars), an exasperated juvenile court judge declared that the automobile was "a house of prostitution on wheels." It was, of course, much more. The automobile was to the 1920s what the railroad had been to the nineteenth century: the catalyst for economic growth, a transportation revolution, and a cultural symbol.

The Business of America

In business, said Henry Ford, the "fundamentals are all summed up in the single word, 'service.'" President Calvin Coolidge echoed the theme of service to society in 1925: "The business of America is business. The man who builds a factory builds a temple. The man who works there worships there." A generation earlier, progressives had criticized business for its social irresponsibility. But the wartime contributions of business managers and the return of prosperity in 1922 gained them a renewed respect.

Encouraged by federal permissiveness, a wave of mergers swept the country. Between 1919 and 1930, some 8,000 firms disappeared as large gobbled small. Oligopolies (where a few firms dominated whole industries) flourished in steel, meatpacking, cigarettes, and other businesses. National chains began to replace local "mom and pop" stores. By 1929, one bag of groceries in ten came from the 15,000 red-and-gold supermarkets of the Great Atlantic and Pacific Tea Company, commonly known as A&P.

Corporate Consolidation

This expansion and consolidation meant that the capital of the nation was being controlled not by individuals but by corporations. The model of modern business was the large, bureaucratic corporation, in which those who actually managed the company had little to do with those who owned it—the shareholders. Stocks and bonds were becoming so widely dispersed that few individuals held more than 1 or 2 percent of any company.

Managerial Elite

A salaried bureaucracy of executives and plant managers formed a new elite, which no longer set their sights on becoming swashbuckling entrepreneurs like the Carnegies and Rockefellers of old. The new managers looked to work their way up a corporate ladder. They were less interested in risk than in productivity and stability. Managers subdivided operations and put experts in charge. Corporate leaders learned the techniques of **scientific management** taught at Harvard and other new schools of business through journals, professional societies, and consulting firms. They channeled earnings back into their companies to expand factories, carry on research, and grow in size and wealth. By the end of the decade, more than a thousand firms had research laboratories and half the total industrial income was concentrated in 100 corporations.

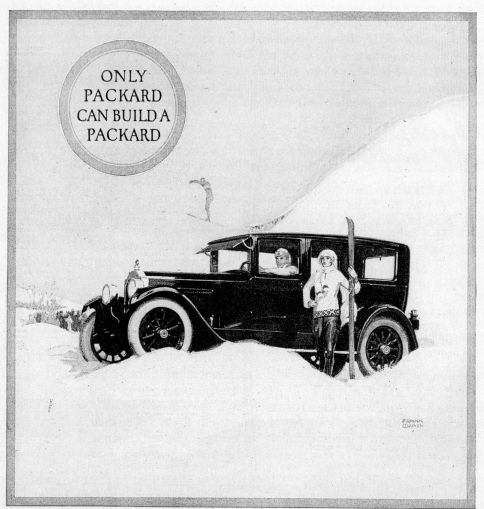

ONLY
PACKARD
CAN BUILD A
PACKARD

A MAN IS KNOWN BY THE CAR HE KEEPS

In the old days men were rated by the homes in which they lived

and few but their friends saw them.

Today, men are rated by the cars they drive

and everybody sees them—

for the car is mobile and the home is not.

To own a Packard is an evidence of discriminating taste.

Woman, with her observing eye, has known this for twenty-five years.

And woman, proverbial for her greater thrift, will insist upon the family motor car being a Packard once she learns that the Packard Six costs less to own, operate and maintain than the ordinary car the family has been buying every year or two.

Packard Six and Packard Eight both furnished in ten body types, open and enclosed. Packard's extremely liberal monthly payment plan makes possible the immediate enjoyment of a Packard, purchasing out of income instead of capital.

A S K　T H E　M A N　W H O　O W N S　O N E

In the 1920s, automobile advertising shifted gears by broadening its audience and making the automobile a symbol of social success. Earlier advertisements had stressed the technical advantages of automobiles and were aimed strictly at men. Here an automobile advertisement from 1925 emphasizes the subliminal rewards of owning a luxury car. Prestige, power, wealth, and romantic love belong to a man who owns a Packard automobile. And women are not ignored. The advertisement points out to women that owning a Packard is not only "evidence of discriminating taste" but also a sign of cost-consciousness for family-minded women.

Welfare Capitalism

The new "scientific management" also stressed smooth relations between managers and employees. The rash of postwar strikes had left business leaders as suspicious as ever of labor unions and determined to find ways to limit their influence.

Some tactics were more strong-armed than scientific. In 1921 the National Association of Manufacturers, the Chamber of Commerce, and other employer groups launched the "American Plan," aimed at opening "closed shops," factories where only union members could work. Employers made workers sign agreements disavowing union membership. Labor organizers called them "yellow dog contracts." Companies infiltrated unions with spies, locked union members out of factories if they protested, and boycotted firms that hired union labor.

The gentler side of the American Plan involved a social innovation called "welfare capitalism." Companies such as General Electric and Bethlehem Steel pledged to care for their employees and give them incentives for working hard. They built clean, safe factories, installed cafeterias, hired trained dietitians, formed baseball teams and glee clubs. Several hundred firms encouraged perhaps a million workers to buy company stock. Millions more enrolled in company unions. Called "Kiss-Me Clubs" for their lack of power, they offered what few independent unions could match: health and safety insurance; a grievance procedure; and representation for African Americans, women, and immigrants.

Welfare capitalism embraced barely 5 percent of the workforce and often gave benefits only to skilled laborers, the hardest to replace. In the 1920s almost one working-class family in six was labeled as "chronically destitute." With little to restrain the antiunion policies of companies, union membership sank from its postwar peak of almost 5 million in 1921 to less than 3.5 million by 1929. Still, by the end of the decade the grievances of workers sometimes boiled over into massive strikes. In 1927, the most famous strike of the decade idled 2,500 mill hands in Gastonia, North Carolina, where workers labored for 10- to 12-hour shifts in 90-degree heat and endured regular "stretch-outs," the textile equivalent of assembly-line speedups. Even strikebreakers walked out. Eventually, however, authorities broke the strike, presaging a national trend. A year later there were a record-low 629 strikes.

The American Plan

Gastonia Strike

The Consumer Culture

During the late nineteenth century the economy had boomed, too, but much of its growth had gone into producer goods: huge steel factories and rail, telephone, and electric networks. By World War I, these industrial networks had penetrated enough of the country to create mass markets for consumer goods such as refrigerators, bicycles, and other products for ordinary Americans. As an increasing percentage of the nation's industries turned out consumer goods, prosperity hinged more and more on consumption. If consumers purchased more goods, production would increase at the same time that costs would decrease. Lower production costs would allow for lower prices, which would lift sales, production, and employment still higher.

Everything in this cycle of prosperity depended on consumption. In the consumer economy, wives ceased to be homemakers and became purchasers of processed food and manufactured goods. Husbands were not merely workers but, equally important, consumers of mortgages and other forms of credit. Even vacationers became consumers—in this case, consumers of leisure time as more employees enjoyed two-week (unpaid) vacations. Consumption was the key to prosperity, and increased consumption rested on two innovations: advertising to help people buy, and credit to help them pay.

Around the turn of the century, advertisers began a critical shift from emphasizing *products* to stressing a consumer's *desires:* health, popularity, social status. During World War I the Committee on Public Information, the federal propaganda agency, demonstrated the power of emotional appeals as an instrument of mass persuasion. Like the war propaganda, advertising copy aimed at emotions and cynically regarded

Role of Advertising

This pen-and-ink drawing depicts a cavernous street in New York City awash in advertising. Its title, Picturesque America, *is a play on the growing use of signs to sell products. Already by 1909, when the graphic artist Harry Grant Dart drew the piece, advertising and the consumer culture were overtaking the country; in this case transforming buildings into billboards for hawking everything from foreign language courses to cigars, furs, and automobiles. "Electric signs," promises one electrified sign, "make night beautiful." The artist did not agree.*

the "average normal American," in the words of one executive, as having the "literate capacity of a 12- or 14-year-old." Behavioral psychologists like John B. Watson, who left Johns Hopkins University for an advertising agency in the 1920s, helped advertisers develop more sophisticated techniques for attracting customers.

Earlier in the century Albert Lasker, the owner of Chicago's largest advertising firm, Lord and Thomas, had created modern advertising in America. His eye-catching ads were hard-hitting, positive, and often preposterous. To expand the sales of Lucky Strike cigarettes, Lord and Thomas advertisements claimed smoking made people slimmer and more courageous. "Luckies" became one of the most popular brands in America. Bogus doctors and dentists endorsed all kinds of products, including toothpaste containing potassium chloride—eight grams of which was lethal. "Halitosis" was plucked from the pages of an obscure medical dictionary and used to sell Listerine mouthwash.

Installment Buying as Credit

Advertisers encouraged Americans to borrow against tomorrow to purchase what advertising convinced them they wanted today. Installment buying had once been confined to sewing machines and pianos. In the 1920s it grew into the tenth biggest business in the United States. In 1919 Alfred Sloan created millions of new customers by establishing the General Motors Acceptance Corporation, the nation's first consumer credit organization. By 1929 Americans were buying most of their cars, radios, and furniture on the installment plan. Consumer debt jumped to $7 billion, almost twice the federal budget.

A Mass Society

In the evening after a day's work in the fields—perhaps in front of an adobe house built by one of the western sugar-beet companies—Mexican American workers might gather to chat or sing a *corrido* or two. The *corrido,* or ballad, was an old

Mexican folk tradition whose subjects matched the concerns of the day. One corrido during the 1920s told of a field laborer distressed that his family had rejected old Mexican customs in favor of new American fashions. His wife, he sang, now had "a bob-tailed dress of silk" and, wearing makeup, went about "painted like a *piñata*." As for his children:

> My kids speak perfect English
> And have no use for our Spanish
> They call me "fader" and don't work
> And are crazy about the Charleston.

It was enough to make him long for Mexico.

For Americans from all backgrounds, the New Era was witness to "a vast dissolution of ancient habits," commented columnist Walter Lippmann. Mass marketing and mass distribution led not simply to a higher standard of living but also to a life less regional and diverse. In the place of moral standards set by local communities and churches came "modern" fashions and attitudes, spread by the new mass media of movies, radio, and magazines. In the place of "ancient habits" came the forces of mass society: independent women, freer love, standardized culture, urban energy and impersonality, and deep alienation.

A "New Woman"

In the tumultuous 1890s, a "New Woman" appeared, one who was more assertive, athletic, and independent than her Victorian peers. By the 1920s, more modern versions of this New Woman were being charged with nothing less than leading what Frederick Lewis Allen called the "revolution in manners and morals." The most flamboyant of them wore close-fitting felt hats and makeup, long-waisted dresses and few undergarments, strings of beads, and unbuckled galoshes (which earned them the nickname "flappers"). Cocktail in hand, cigarette in mouth, footloose and economically free, the New Woman became a symbol of liberation and sexuality to some. To others she represented the decline of civilization.

"Street selling was torture for me," Margaret Sanger *recalled of her efforts to promote the* Birth Control Review. *Hecklers often taunted Sanger and her colleagues. "Have you never heard God's word to 'be fruitful and multiply and replenish the earth'?" one asked. The reply came back, "They've done that already."*

Margaret Sanger

World War I served as a social catalyst, while the decade before it had stimulated changes for women workers. Single and married women poured into the workforce after the turn of the century. From a fifth of the labor force in 1900, women jumped to a quarter by 1930, with the greatest gains coming before the war. But most female workers remained in poor-paying jobs, and few found new freedom after quitting time. The war nonetheless prompted a change in attitudes. Before it, women were arrested for smoking cigarettes openly, using profanity, and driving automobiles without men beside them. With women bagging explosives, running locomotives, and drilling with rifles during the war, the old taboos often seemed silly.

Disseminating birth control information by mail had also been a crime before the war. By the armistice there was a birth control clinic in Brooklyn, a National Birth Control League, and later an American Birth Control League led by Margaret Sanger. Sanger's crusade had begun as an attempt to save poor women from the burdens of unwanted pregnancies (see page 639). In the 1920s her message found a receptive middle-class audience. Surveys showed that by the 1930s nearly 90 percent of college-educated couples practiced contraception.

Being able to a degree to control the matter of pregnancy, women felt less guilt about enjoying sex and less fear over the consequences. In 1909 Sigmund Freud had come to America to lecture on his theories of coping with the unconscious and overcoming harmful repressions. Some of Freud's ideas, specifically his emphasis on childhood sexuality, shocked Americans, while most of his complex theories sailed blissfully over their heads. As popularized in the 1920s, however, Freudian psychology stamped sexuality as a key to health.

Early in September 1921 eight young women stood nervously on the boardwalk at Atlantic City, New Jersey. For a week the seaside resort had presented a succession of swimming exhibitions, dance contests, automobile races, and a giant parade featuring clowns, bands, and a float carrying King Neptune escorted by mermaids, all in preparation for the week's central event—a national beauty contest to select the first "Miss America."

The American beauty contest drew on an old heritage. In colonial times the traditional May Day celebration crowned a Queen of the May as a symbol of fertility. Though physical beauty mattered in the selection, qualities such as civic leadership and popularity also counted.

In 1854 showman P. T. Barnum conceived of a competition among women to judge their beauty. Because Victorian codes prohibited such displays, Barnum attracted only contestants of "questionable reputation." To lure middle-class women, he announced that "daguerreotypes," or photographs, could be submitted. Participants did not even have to send their names. The idea spread. When the promoters of the St. Louis Exposition advertised a beauty contest in 1905, 40,000 women applied.

Promoters had conceived of the Miss America pageant as a way of extending the summer season past September 1. The contest measured physical beauty alone, with the high point being a bathing suit competition. (Only later did the pageant add a talent show.) After the turn of the century, bathing suits had grown alarmingly scant, exposing arms and discarding billowy bloomers in favor of revealing tights.

Aware of such perils, pageant officials depicted entrants as wholesome, conventional, and unsophisticated. The contestants were not permitted to wear short bobbed hair or makeup—both symbols of the racy modern woman.

As the contestants waited anxiously, officials announced the winner—Margaret Gorman of Washington, D.C. She radiated wholesomeness and athletic vigor. "She represents the type of womanhood America needs," observed Samuel Gompers of the American Federation of Labor, "—strong, red-blooded, able to shoulder the responsibilities of homemaking and motherhood."

The Miss America pageant was an immediate success. Newspapers across the country reported the results. In 1922 representatives of 58 cities competed, and a crowd of 200,000 watched the opening parade.

Miss America and other beauty contests evolved as commercialism and advertising took hold and Victorianism declined in the early twentieth century. But the lengths to which pageant organizers went to gain respect demonstrated the strength of the older social ideals.

Margaret Gorman of Washington, D.C., crowned in 1921 as the first Miss America.

The Miss America pageant in particular came to symbolize the middle-class ideal of womanhood. Physical beauty remained the chief component, marriage and motherhood the chief ends. The message was graphic: men competed in sports gear, business attire, and professional garb; women, in bathing suits.

Such changes in the social climate were real enough, but the life of a flapper girl hardly mirrored the lives and work routines of most American women. Over the decade, the female labor force grew by only 1 percent. As late as 1930 nearly 60 percent of all working women were African American or foreign-born and generally held low-paying jobs in domestic service or the garment industry.

The New Era did spawn new careers for women. The consumer culture capitalized on a preoccupation with appearance and led to the opening of some 40,000 beauty parlors staffed by hairdressers, manicurists, and cosmeticians. "Women's fields" carved out by progressive reformers expanded opportunities in education, libraries, and social welfare. Women earned a higher percentage of doctoral degrees (from 1 percent in 1910 to 15.4 percent in 1930) and held more college teaching posts than ever (32 percent). But in most areas, professional men resisted the "feminization" of the workforce.

The number of female doctors dropped by half as medical schools imposed restrictive quotas and hospitals rejected female interns.

In 1924 two women—Nellie Ross in Wyoming and Miriam ("Ma") Ferguson in Texas—were elected governors, the first female chief executives. But for the most part, women continued to be marginalized in party politics while remaining widely involved in educational and welfare programs. Operating outside male-dominated political parties, women activists did succeed in winning passage of the Sheppard-Towner Federal Maternity and Infancy Act in 1921 to fight infant mortality with rural prenatal and baby-care centers. It was the first federal welfare statute. Yet by the end of the decade the Sheppard-Towner Act had lapsed.

In the wake of their greatest success, the hard-won vote for women, feminists splintered. The National Woman Suffrage Association disbanded in 1920. In its place the new League of Women Voters encouraged informed voting with nonpartisan publicity. For the more militant Alice Paul and her allies, that was not enough. Their National Woman's party pressed for a constitutional Equal Rights Amendment (ERA). Social workers and others familiar with the conditions under which women labored opposed it. Death and injury rates for women were nearly double those for men. To them the ERA meant losing the protection as well as the benefits women derived from mothers' pensions and maternity insurance. Joined by most men and a majority of Congress, they fought the amendment to a standstill.

Equal Rights Amendment

Mass Media

In balmy California, where movies could be made year-round, Hollywood helped give the New Woman notoriety as a temptress and trendsetter. When sexy Theda Bara (a stage name and an anagram of Arab Death) appeared in *The Blue Flame* in 1920, crowds mobbed theaters. And just as Hollywood dictated standards of physical attraction, it became the judge of taste and fashion in countless other ways because motion pictures were a virtually universal medium. There was no need for literacy or fluency, no need even for sound, given the power of the pictures parading across the screen.

Motion Pictures

Motion pictures, invented in 1889, had first been shown in tiny neighborhood theaters called "nickelodeons." For a nickel, patrons watched a silent screen flicker with moving images as an accompanist played music on a tinny piano. The audience was anything but silent. The theater reverberated with the cracking of Indian nuts, the day's equivalent of popcorn, while young cowboys shot off their Kilgore repeating cap pistols during dramatic scenes. Often children read the subtitles aloud to their immigrant parents, translating into Italian, Yiddish, or German.

After the first feature-length film, *The Great Train Robbery* (1903), productions became rich in spectacle, attracted middle-class audiences, and turned into America's favorite form of entertainment. By 1926 more than 20,000 movie houses offered customers lavish theaters with overstuffed seats, live music, and a celluloid dream world— all for 50 cents or less. At the end of the decade, they were drawing over 100 million people a week, roughly the equivalent of the national population.

In the spring of 1920 Frank Conrad of the Westinghouse Company in East Pittsburgh rigged up a research station in his barn and started transmitting phonograph music and baseball scores to local wireless operators. An ingenious Pittsburgh newspaper began advertising radio equipment to "be used by those who listen to Dr. Conrad's programs." Six months later Westinghouse officials opened the first licensed broadcasting station in history, KDKA, to stimulate sales of their supplies. By 1922 the number of licensed stations had jumped to 430. By 1930 nearly one home in three had a radio ("furniture that talks," comedian Fred Allen called it).

The vibrant energy of the New Woman is reflected in the geometric designs of this fashionable evening wrap (1928), whose jagged lines also suggest the era's newest vaulting skyscrapers.

At first radio was seen as a civilizing force. "The air is your theater, your college, your newspaper, your library," exalted one ad in 1924. But with the growing number of sets came commercial broadcasting, catering to more common tastes. By 1931 advertisers were paying $10,000 an hour for a national hookup, and the most popular show on radio was *Amos 'n' Andy,* a comedy about African Americans created by two white vaudevillians in 1926. It borrowed its style from black comedians Aubrey Lyles and Flournoy Miller, who occasionally wrote dialogue for the show. A slice of black culture, often stereotyped, nonetheless entered mainstream American life.

At night families gathered around the radio instead of the hearth, listening to a concert, perhaps, rather than going out to hear music. Ticket sales at vaudeville theaters collapsed. The aged, the sick, and the isolated, moreover, could be "at home but never alone," as one radio ad declared. Linked by nothing but airwaves, Americans were finding themselves part of a vast new community of listeners.

Newspaper Chains

Print journalism also broadened its audience during the 1920s. In 1923 Yale classmates Henry R. Luce and Briton Hadden rewrote news stories in a snappy style, mixed them with photographs, and created the country's first national weekly, *Time* magazine. By 1927, 55 giant newspaper chains distributed 230 newspapers with a combined circulation of 13 million. Though they controlled less than 10 percent of all papers, the chains pioneered modern mass news techniques. Editors relied on central offices and syndicates to prepare editorials, sports, gossip, and Sunday features for a national readership.

The Culture of Celebrity

In a world in which Americans were rapidly being reduced to anonymous parts of mass, industrialized society, media offered them a chance to identify with the achievements of individuals by creating a world of celebrities and heroes. Sports figures, business executives, and movie stars found their exploits splashed across the front pages of newspapers and magazines and followed on radio by millions hungry for excitement and eager to project their own dreams onto others.

Charles Lindbergh

No hero attracted more attention than a shy, reed-thin young man named Charles Lindbergh. Early on the morning of May 20, 1927, "Lucky Lindy" streaked into the skies above Long Island aboard a silver-winged monoplane called the *Spirit of St. Louis* and headed east. Thirty-three hours and thirty minutes later he landed just outside Paris, the first flier to cross the Atlantic alone. Eight others had died trying. An ecstatic mob swamped him and nearly tore his plane to pieces in search of souvenirs.

Lindbergh, dubbed by reporters the "Lone Eagle," returned with his plane aboard the warship USS *Memphis.* In New York City alone, he was greeted by nearly 4 million cheering fans. Lindbergh had "fired the imagination of mankind," observed one newspaper. Never had one person mastered a machine so completely or conquered nature so courageously. To Americans ambivalent about mass society and worried about being overwhelmed by technology and bureaucracy, Lindbergh's accomplishment was a sign. Perhaps they could control the New Era without losing their cherished individualism.

"Ain't We Got Fun?"

Spectator Sports

"Ev'ry morning, ev'ry evening, ain't we got fun?" ran the 1921 hit song. As the average hours on the job each week decreased from 47.2 in 1920 to 42 by 1930, spending on amusement and recreation tripled. Spectator sports came of age. In 1921, some 60,000 fans paid $1.8 million to see Jack Dempsey, the "Manassas Mauler," knock out French champion Georges Carpentier. Millions more listened as radio took them ringside for the first time in sports history. Universities

The Roxy, the largest theater in the world when it opened in 1926, in all its palatial glory. Such lavish movie houses sought to attract more prosperous middle-class audiences with splendor reminiscent of European cathedrals. On opening night, pealing chimes heralded the entrance of a man dressed as a monk who pointed to the balcony and declaimed, "Let there be light!" Blazing spotlights then set the orchestra aglow. "Does God live here?" asked a little girl in a New Yorker *cartoon.*

constructed huge stadiums for football—a 60,000-seater at Berkeley, a 64,000-seater at Ohio State. By the end of the decade college football games were outdrawing major league baseball.

Baseball remained the national pastime but became a bigger business. An ugly World Series scandal in 1919 led owners to appoint Judge Kenesaw Mountain Landis as "czar" of the sport to avoid the possibility of more stringent government regulation. His iron-fisted rule reformed the game. In 1920 the son of immigrants revolutionized it. George Herman "Babe" Ruth hit 54 home runs and made the New York Yankees the first club to attract a million fans in one season. A heroic producer in an era of consumption, Ruth was also baseball's bad boy. He smoked, drank, cursed, and chased every skirt in sight. Under the guidance of the first modern sports agent, Christy Walsh, Ruth became the highest-paid player in the game and made a fortune endorsing everything from clothing to candy bars.

At parties old diversions—charades, card tricks, recitations—faded in popularity as dancing took over. The ungainly camel walk, the sultry tango, and in 1924 the frantic Charleston were the urban standards. As a cultural counterweight to what some regarded as such unseemingly displays, country barns featured a revival of square dancing with music provided by Detroit's WBZ, courtesy of Henry Ford. But the new energy could not be contained. From the turn-of-the-century brothels and gaming houses of New Orleans, Memphis, and St. Louis came a rhythmic, compelling music that swept into nightclubs and over the airwaves: jazz.

Jazz was a remarkably complex blend of several older African American musical traditions, combining the soulfulness of the blues with the brighter syncopated rhythms of ragtime music. The distinctive style of jazz bands came from a marvelous improvising as the musicians embellished melodies and played off one another. The style spread when the "Original Dixieland Jazz Band" (hardly original but possessed of the advantage of being white) recorded a few numbers for the phonograph. The music became a sensation in New York in 1917 and spread across the country. Black New Orleans stalwarts like Joe "King" Oliver's Creole Jazz Band began touring. In 1924 Paul Whiteman inaugurated respectable "white" jazz in a concert at Carnegie

Jazz

Hall. When self-appointed guardians of good taste denounced such music as "intellectual and spiritual debauchery," Whiteman disagreed: "Jazz is the folk music of the machine age."

The Art of Alienation

Before World War I a generation of young writers had begun to rebel against Victorian purity. The savagery of the war drove many of them even farther from any faith in reason or progress. Instead they embraced a "nihilism" that denied all meaning in life. When the war ended, they turned their resentment against American life, especially its small towns and big businesses, its conformity, technology, and materialism. Some led unconventional lives in New York City's Greenwich Village. Others, called **expatriates,** left the country altogether for the artistic freedom of London and Paris. Their alienation helped produce a literary outpouring unmatched in American history.

Expatriates

On the eve of World War I the poet Ezra Pound had predicted an "American Risorgimento" that would "make the Italian Renaissance look like a tempest in a teapot." From Europe the expatriate Pound began to make it happen. Abandoning rhyme and meter in his poetry, he decried the "botched civilization" that had produced the war. Another voluntary exile, T. S. Eliot, bemoaned the emptiness of modern life in his epic poem *The Waste Land* (1922). Ernest Hemingway captured the disillusionment of the age in *The Sun Also Rises* (1926) and *A Farewell to Arms* (1929), novels where resolution came as it had in war—by death.

At home Minnesota-born Sinclair Lewis, the first American to win a Nobel Prize in literature, sketched a scathing vision of midwestern small-town life in *Main Street* (1920). The book described "savorless people . . . saying mechanical things about the excellence of Ford automobiles, and viewing themselves as the greatest race in the world." His next novel, *Babbitt* (1922), dissected small-town businessman George Follansbee Babbitt, a peppy realtor from the fictional city of Zenith. Faintly absurd and supremely dull, Babbitt was the epitome of the average.

The novels of another Minnesotan, F. Scott Fitzgerald, glorified youth and romantic individualism but found redemption nowhere. Fitzgerald's heroes, like Amory Blaine in *This Side of Paradise* (1920), spoke for a generation "grown up to find all Gods dead, all wars fought, all faiths in man shaken." Like most writers of the decade, Fitzgerald saw life largely as a personal affair—opulent, self-absorbing, and ultimately tragic.

A "New Negro"

As World War I seared white intellectuals, so too did it galvanize black Americans. Wartime labor shortages had spurred a migration of over a million African Americans out of the rural South into northern industrial cities. But postwar unemployment and racial violence quickly dashed black hopes for equality. Common folk in these urban enclaves found an outlet for their alienation in a charismatic black nationalist from Jamaica named Marcus Garvey.

Marcus Garvey

Garvey brought his organization, the Universal Negro Improvement Association (UNIA), to America in 1916 in hopes of restoring black pride by returning African Americans to Africa and Africa to Africans. Whereas Booker T. Washington had counseled accommodation of segregated America and W. E. B. Du Bois and the NAACP had pursued racial integration, Garvey urged separation of the races. Yet he stood not entirely apart from these other activists. Garvey relied, like Washington, on a message of self-help and demanded, like Du Bois, an end to colonialism. "Up you mighty race," Garvey told his followers, "you can accomplish what you will." When Garvey spoke at the first national UNIA convention in 1920, over 25,000 supporters jammed Madison Square Garden in New York to listen. Even his harshest critics admitted there were at least half a million members in more than 30 branches of his organization. It was the

Blues, painted in 1929 by African American artist Archibald Motley Jr., evokes the improvised rhythms of the Jazz Age. New Orleans–born Motley was one of a group of black genre painters in the 1920s who became part of the Harlem Renaissance.

first mass movement of African Americans in history. But in 1925 Garvey was convicted of mail fraud and sentenced to prison for having oversold stock in his Black Star Line, the steamship company founded to return African Americans to Africa. His dream shattered, but not the image of a proud black man standing up against racial bigotry and intolerance. The memory of Garvey and his movement nurtured budding black nationalism for decades to come.

As Garvey rose to prominence a renaissance of black literature, painting, and sculpture was brewing in Harlem at the northern end of Manhattan. Since the completion of Manhattan's subway system in 1904, Harlem had grown black after eagerly expected white renters failed to appear. By the end of World War I, Harlem had become the cultural capital of black America.

The first inklings of a renaissance in Harlem came in 1922 when Claude McKay, another Jamaican immigrant, published a book of poems entitled *White Shadows*. In his most famous, "If We Must Die," McKay mixed defiance and dignity: "Like men we'll face the murderous, cowardly pack / Pressed to the wall, dying but fighting back!" Often supported by white patrons, or "angels," the young black writers and artists of Harlem found their subjects in the street life of cities, the folkways of the rural South, and the primitivism of preindustrial cultures. They wrote without embarrassment of prostitution and pimping, celebrated sex and alcohol, and reveled in the joys of life and

Harlem Renaissance

love on the streets of Harlem. Middle-class reformers such as Du Bois often shuddered at such frank depictions, bent as they were on demonstrating the moral equivalency of the races. Descriptions of "brown lips full and pouted for sweet kissing" and "brown breasts throbbing with love" seemed only to reinforce the stereotypes of unbridled black sexuality and made Du Bois, for one, feel "like taking a bath." Renaissance writers did not care. For them, vitality and instinct were among the hallmarks of the New Negro. So, too, were these hallmarks for painters such as Aaron Douglas. His vibrant murals and illustrations fused geometric designs with African myth and everyday African American life and religion. Poet Langston Hughes reminded his readers of the ancient heritage of African Americans in "The Negro Speaks of Rivers," while Zora Neale Hurston collected folktales, songs, and prayers of black southerners.

Though generally not a racial protest, the Harlem Renaissance drew on the new assertiveness of African Americans as well as on the alienation of white intellectuals. In 1925 Alain Locke, a black professor from Howard University, collected a sampling of their works in *The New Negro*. The New Negro, Locke wrote, was "not a cultural foundling without his own inheritance" but "a conscious contributor . . . collaborator and participant in American civilization." The title of the book reflected not only a distinctively black artistic movement but also a new racial consciousness: militant, uncompromising, and self-consciously proud.

Defenders of the Faith

As mass society pushed the country into a future of machines, organization, middle-class living, and cosmopolitan diversity, not everyone approved. Dr. and Mrs. Wilbur Crafts, the authors of *Intoxicating Drinks and Drugs in All Lands and Times*, set forth

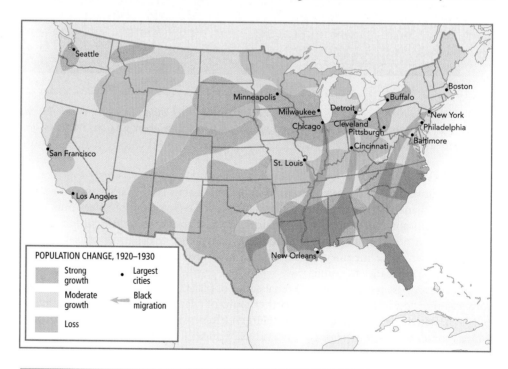

Areas of Population Growth   *In the 1920s the population of urban America grew by some 15 million people, at the time the greatest 10-year jump in American history. Spurred first by the industrial demands of World War I and then by declining farm income, cities grew largely by depopulating rural areas. The biggest gains were in the South and West, where farmers followed opportunity to cities in climates similar to their own. In the most dramatic manifestation of the overall trend, more than a million African Americans migrated from the rural South to the urban North in hopes of escaping poverty and discrimination.*

a litany of sins that tempted young people in this "age of cities." "Foul pictures, corrupt literature, leprous shows, gambling slot machines, saloons, and Sabbath breaking. . . . *We are trying to raise saints in hell.*"

The changing values of the New Era seemed especially threatening to traditionalists like the Crafts. Their deeply held beliefs reflected the rural roots of so many Americans: an ethic that valued neighborliness, small communities, and a sameness of race, religion, and ethnicity. Improvements in mass media—radio, movies, magazines—made it impossible for isolated communities to avoid national trends, even when they disapproved of them. Opponents of the new ways could be found among countryfolk and rural migrants to cities as well as an embattled Protestant elite. All were determined to defend the older faiths against the modern age.

Nativism and Immigration Restriction

In 1921, two Italian immigrants, who freely admitted to being radical anarchists, presented a dramatic challenge to those older faiths. Nicola Sacco and Bartolomeo Vanzetti were sentenced to death—on the face of it, for a shoe company robbery and murder in South Braintree, Massachusetts, committed a year earlier. But the evidence against them was controversial, and critics charged that Sacco and Vanzetti were convicted primarily because they were foreign-born radicals. During the trial, the presiding judge had scorned them in private as "anarchist bastards" and later refused all motions for a retrial, in spite of a confession to the robbery by a member of a well-known gang. For protesters around the world, Sacco and Vanzetti's execution in 1927 was a symbol of American bigotry and prejudice.

By then, nativism—a rabid hostility to foreigners—had produced the most restrictive immigration laws in American history. In the aftermath of World War I immigration was running close to 1 million a year, almost as high as prewar levels. Most immigrants came from eastern and southern Europe and from Mexico; most were Catholics and Jews. Alarmed white native-born Protestants warned that if the flood continued, Americans might become "a hybrid race of people as worthless and futile as the good-for-nothing mongrels of Central America and Southeastern Europe." Appreciating the wage benefits of a shrunken labor pool, the American Federation of Labor supported restriction.

In the Southwest, Mexicans and Mexican Americans became a target of concern. The Spanish had inhabited the region for nearly 400 years, producing a rich blend of European and Indian cultures. By 1900 about 300,000 Mexican Americans lived in the United States. In the following decade Mexicans fleeing poverty and a revolution in 1910 almost doubled the Latino population of Texas and New Mexico. In California it quadrupled. During World War I, labor shortages led authorities to relax immigration laws, and in the 1920s American farmers opened a campaign to attract Mexican farm workers.

Thousands of single young men, known as *solos,* also crossed the border to catch trains for northern industrial cities. By the end of the 1920s, thriving communities of Mexicans could be found in the "barrios"—Mexican neighborhoods—of Kansas City, Detroit, and elsewhere. Spanish-speaking newcomers settled into an immigrant life of family and festivals, churchgoing, hard work, and slow adaptation. As with other immigrants, some returned home, but some brought their families. The census of 1930 listed nearly 1.5 million Mexicans living in the United States, not including an untold number who had entered the country illegally.

Mexicans were just one target of the first National Origins Act, passed in 1921. It capped all immigration at 350,000 and parceled out entry by admitting up to 3 percent of each nationality living in the United States as of 1910. That system of quotas privileged "races" commonly believed to be superior—"Nordics" (from northern and western Europe)—over those considered inferior—"Alpines" and "Mediterraneans" (from southern and eastern Europe). Asian immigration was virtually banned. In 1924 a second National Origins Act cut the quota to 150,000, reduced the percentage to 2, and

Sacco and Vanzetti

Mexican Americans

National Origins Acts

pushed the base year back to 1890, before the bulk of southern and eastern Europeans had arrived. To control the flow of illegal aliens, Congress also created the Border Patrol. Its 450 agents, stationed along the boundaries with Canada and Mexico, were scarcely enough to make anything other than a symbolic statement of restrictionist sentiment.

The National Origins Act fixed the pattern of immigration for the next four decades. Immigration from southern and eastern Europe was reduced to a trickle. The free movement of Europeans to America, a migration of classes and nationalities that had been unimpeded for 300 years, came to an end.

The "Noble Experiment"

For nearly a hundred years reformers had tried—with sporadic success—to reduce the consumption of alcohol. Their most ambitious campaign climaxed in January 1920 when the Eighteenth Amendment, sanctioning the prohibition of liquor, went into effect. Prohibition was not total: private citizens could still drink. They simply could not make, sell, transport, or import any "intoxicating beverage" containing 0.5 percent alcohol or more. The aim was to take the profit out of the liquor trade and reduce alcohol consumption without trampling too heavily on the rights of individuals. By some estimates, the consumption of liquor was cut in half.

From the start, however, enforcement was underfunded and understaffed. In large cities "speakeasies"—taverns operating under cover—were plentiful. Rural stills continued to turn out "moonshine." Even so, the consequences of so vast a social experiment were significant and often unexpected. Prohibition reversed the prewar trend toward beer and wine, because hard liquor brought greater profits to bootleggers. Prohibition also advanced women's rights. Whereas saloons had discriminated against "ladies," either barring them or having them enter by a separate door, speakeasies welcomed them. Prohibition helped to line the pockets and boost the fame of gangsters, including "Scarface" Al Capone. Like Capone, thousands of poor immigrants looked to illegal **bootlegging** to move them out of the slums. As rival gangs fought over territory, cities erupted in violence. To save lives and profits, gangsters organized crime as if they

Eighteenth Amendment

Consequences of Prohibition

Prohibition spawned a new industry—"bootlegging," or the illegal manufacture and sale of alcohol. The term derived from the practice of hiding an object, say a bottle of alcohol, in the leg of a high boot. This pen-and-ink illustration by Winsor McCay depicts the bootlegger, as its title, A Giant of Evil, *indicates, as raining down bottles of whiskey.*

were nineteenth-century business moguls, dividing their operations and territory and imposing a hierarchical structure of management.

For all its unhappy consequences, Prohibition enjoyed wide backing. The best science of the day taught that alcohol was bad for health; the best social science, that it corroded family life and weakened society. Corporate executives and labor leaders supported Prohibition to promote an efficient and healthy workforce. So did many Catholics, who saw the road to pain and perdition lined with liquor bottles. And the liquor industry hurt itself with a terrible record of corrupting legislatures and, worse still, corrupting minors, who were one target of its aggressive campaign to recruit new drinkers in the competitive saloon business.

Yet Prohibition can also be understood as cultural and class legislation. Support had always run deepest in Protestant churches, especially among the evangelical Baptists and Methodists. And there had always been a strong antiurban and anti-immigrant bias among reformers. As it turned out, the steepest decline in drinking occurred among working-class ethnics. Only the well-to-do had enough money to drink regularly without risking death or blindness, the common effects of cheap, tainted liquor. Traditionalists might celebrate the triumph of the "noble experiment," but modern urbanites either ignored or resented it.

Fundamentalism versus Darwinism

Although Aimee Semple McPherson embraced the fashions of the New Era, many Protestants, especially in rural areas, felt threatened by the secular aspects of modern life. Beginning in the late nineteenth century, scientists and intellectuals spoke openly about the relativity of moral values, questioned the possibility of miracles, and analyzed the Bible as if it were simply a historical document. Darwinism, pragmatism, and other philosophical and scientific theories left traditional religious teachings open to skepticism or even scorn. Pastors noted that despite an increase of nearly 13 million in church membership, church attendance was slipping.

Among Protestants, conservatives of various sects worried that their liberal brethren had wandered too far from their faith. As early as the 1870s, liberal Protestants had sought to make Christianity more relevant to contemporary life. Their movement became known as "Modernism," defined by one leader as "the use of scientific, historical and social methods in understanding and applying evangelical Christianity to the needs of living persons."

Conservatives disagreed with this updating of orthodoxy, nowhere more publicly than in a series of pamphlets called *The Fundamentals* published between 1910 and 1915 and subsidized by two wealthy oilmen from Los Angeles, Lyman and Milton Stewart. The 3 million copies distributed nationwide called for a return to what they considered to be the fundamentals of belief, among them the virgin birth and resurrection of Jesus, a literal reading of the Creation account in Genesis, and the divinely inspired authorship of the Bible. Whereas liberal theologians saw the Bible as the product of human beings observing and interpreting godly action within their historical and cultural context, conservatives insisted the Bible was the timeless, revealed word of God. After 1920 a wide variety of conservative Protestants began calling themselves "Fundamentalists."

The Fundamentals

The Fundamentalist movement grew dramatically in the first two decades of the twentieth century, fed by fears of Protestant Modernism but also of the Catholic and Jewish immigrants flooding into the country and by colorful evangelists such as former baseball player Billy Sunday. Fundamentalists maintained effective ministries nationwide but especially among Southern Baptists. Nothing disturbed them more than Darwinian theories of evolution that called into question the divine origins of humankind. In 1925 what began as an in-house fight among Protestants became a national brawl when the Tennessee legislature made it illegal to teach that "man has descended from a lower order of animals." Oklahoma, Florida, Mississippi, and Arkansas passed similar statutes.

Encouraged by the newly formed American Civil Liberties Union, a number of skeptics in the town of Dayton, Tennessee, decided to test the law. In the spring of

Scopes Trial

The "Monkey Trial" as Media Event

In 1994 the sensational murder trial of ex-football star O. J. Simpson struck many as the media event of the century, but it was hardly the first trial to create a national news frenzy. In 1925, the Scopes Trial captivated Americans. In the way it drew attention, the court case revealed much more than a battle over evolution.

No trial had been covered so thoroughly before because none had unfolded under the glare of modern media. Over 150 reporters sent more than two million words across telephone and telegraph lines strung to the courthouse expressly to provide coverage. Photographers and movie cameramen recorded the event, while a monkey named Joe Mendl greeted them wearing a fedora, a bow tie, and white spats. A new variety of news reporter—radio broadcasters—brought the trial into the homes of millions of Americans. Songs, including "You Can't Make a Monkey Out of Me," appeared in record stores and across the airwaves. The Scopes Trial, in short, signaled a new age of media-driven ballyhoo and advertising, as noteworthy a development as the controversy over evolution.

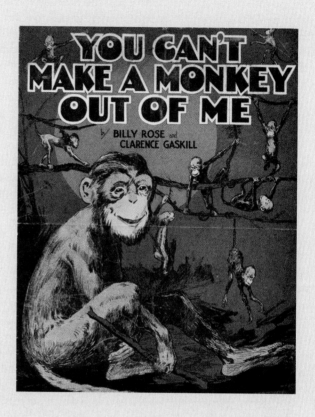

1925 a bespectacled biology teacher named John T. Scopes was arrested for teaching evolution. Behind the scenes, Scopes's sponsors were as much preoccupied with boosting their town's commercial fortunes as with the defense of academic freedom.

When the Scopes trial opened in July, it took on the flavor of a championship boxing match. Millions listened over the radio to the first trial ever broadcast. Inside the courtroom Clarence Darrow, the renowned defense lawyer from Chicago and a professed agnostic, acted as co-counsel for Scopes. Serving as a coprosecutor was William Jennings Bryan, the three-time presidential candidate who had recently joined the antievolution crusade. It was urban Darrow against rural Bryan in what Bryan described as a "duel to the death" between Christianity and evolution.

As Bryan saw it, nonbelievers as well as believers had a stake in the trial's outcome, at least if they lived in small-town America. The industrial revolution, he argued, had brought unprecedented organization to society and had concentrated power in big business and big government. The result was the erosion of community control and personal autonomy. Thus, for Bryan, the teaching of evolution became another battlefield in the struggle between localities and centralized authority, whether in business or government or even science, that was far removed from ordinary citizens.

The presiding judge ruled that scientists could not be used to defend evolution. He considered their testimony "hearsay" because they had not been present at the Creation. The defense virtually collapsed until Darrow called Bryan to the stand as an "expert on the Bible." Under withering examination Bryan admitted, to the horror of his followers, that the Earth might not have been made "in six days of 24-hours." Even so, the Dayton jury took only eight minutes to find Scopes guilty of violating the law and fine him $100.

By then the excesses of the Scopes trial had transformed it into more of a national joke than a confrontation between darkness and light. Yet the debate over evolution raised a larger issue that continues to reverberate. As scientific, religious, and cultural standards clash, how much should religious beliefs influence public education?

In the wake of the Scopes trial, the question was resolved in favor of secular over religious instruction, at least in public schools. Before the trial, public education had always contained explicitly religious—indeed, Protestant—components. Now it became increasingly nonreligious. As for the Fundamentalists, they sought shelter. In the public mind, all Fundamentalism had collapsed into the single image of the Bible-thumping southern redneck clinging to outmoded beliefs. The faith of these true believers never wavered, however. They spent the next two decades spreading their word over the radio and through Bible study and other parachurch groups, biding their time and growing in numbers.

KKK

On Thanksgiving Day 1915, just outside Atlanta, 16 men trudged up a rocky trail to the crest of Stone Mountain. There, as night fell, they set ablaze a large wooden cross and swore allegiance to the Invisible Empire, Knights of the Ku Klux Klan. The KKK was reborn.

As the Ku Klux Klan grew in influence after World War I, race riots erupted in over 25 cities beginning in 1919, including Chicago; Longview, Texas; Knoxville, Tennessee; and Omaha, Nebraska. More than 70 African Americans were lynched in the first year after the end of the war, and 11 were burned alive. Many blacks fought back, their experience in World War I having made them determined to resist repression. In June 1921, rioting in Tulsa left 21 African Americans as well as 11 whites dead. As the billowing smoke in this photograph indicates, white mobs burned down entire neighborhoods belonging to the black community. The National Guard was called out to reestablish order.

New Klan

The modern Klan, a throwback to the hooded order of Reconstruction days (see page 491), reflected the insecurities of the New Era. Klansmen worried about the changes and conflicts in American society, which they attributed to the rising tide of new immigrants, "uppity women," and African Americans who refused to "recognize their place." Whereas any white man could join the old Klan, the new one admitted only "native born, white, gentile [Protestant] Americans." And the reborn Klan was not confined to the rural South, like the hooded nightriders of Reconstruction. In Texas, Klansmen fed off hatred of Mexicans; in California, of Japanese; in New York, of Jews and other immigrants. By the 1920s the capital of the Klan was Indianapolis, Indiana. More than half of its leadership and over a third of its members came from cities of more than 100,000 people.

Thenew Klan drew on the culture of small-town America and responded to some of its anxieties about lost personal independence and waning community control. The Klan, organized in local units called "klaverns," gave to local charities and was avowedly patriotic. It boasted the kind of outfits and rituals familiar in any of the fraternal lodges that blanketed towns and villages across the country. Klan members wore white hooded sheets and satin robes, sang songs called "klodes," and even used a secret hand "klasp."

Women of the KKK

The "Women of the Ku Klux Klan" had chapters in 36 states, including Indiana, where almost a third of all native-born white women joined. Klanswomen were often God-fearing members of their communities who shunned the "revolution in manners and morals" and saw the Klan as the keeper of traditional values. A typical gathering brought the whole family to a barbecue with fireworks and hymn singing, the evening capped by the burning of a giant cross.

Members came mostly from the middle and working classes: small businesspeople, clerical workers, independent professionals, farmers, and laborers with few skills. Some lived on the edge of poverty. The Klan offered them status, security, and the promise of restoring an older America. It touted white supremacy, chastity, fidelity, and parental authority and fought for laissez-faire capitalism and fundamental Protestantism. When boycotts and whispering campaigns failed to cleanse communities of Jews, Mexicans, Japanese, or others who offended their social code, the Klan resorted to floggings, kidnappings, acid mutilations, and murder.

Using modern methods of promotion, the Klan enrolled perhaps 3 million dues-paying members by the early 1920s. Moving into politics, Klan candidates won control of legislatures in Indiana, Texas, Oklahoma, and Oregon. The organization was instrumental in electing six governors, three senators, and thousands of local officials. In the end, however, the Klan was undone by sex scandals and financial corruption. In November 1925 David Stephenson, grand dragon of the Indiana Klan and the most powerful leader in the Midwest, was sentenced to life imprisonment for rape and second-degree murder.

Republicans Ascendant

"The change is amazing," wrote a Washington reporter shortly after the inauguration of Warren G. Harding on March 4, 1921. Sentries disappeared from the gates of the White House, tourists again walked the halls, and reporters freely questioned the president. The reign of "normalcy," as Harding called it, had begun. "By 'normalcy,'" he explained, ". . . I mean normal procedure, the natural way, without excess."

The Politics of "Normalcy"

"Normalcy"—Harding's misreading of the word *normality*—turned out to be anything but normal. After eight years of Democratic rule, Republicans controlled the White House from 1921 to 1933 and both houses of Congress from 1918 to 1930. Fifteen years of bold reform gave way to eight years of cautious pro-business governing. A strengthened executive fell into weak hands. The cabinet and the Congress set the course of the nation.

Harding and his successor, Calvin Coolidge, were content with delegating power. Harding appointed to the cabinet some men of quality, what he called the "best minds": jurist Charles Evans Hughes as secretary of state, farm leader Henry C. Wallace as secretary of agriculture, and Herbert Hoover, savior of Belgian war refugees and former head of the Food Administration, as secretary of commerce. He also made, as one critic put it, some "unspeakably bad appointments": his old crony Harry Daugherty as attorney general and New Mexico senator Albert Fall as interior secretary. Daugherty sold influence for cash and resigned in 1923. Only a divided jury saved him from jail. In 1929 Albert Fall became the first cabinet member to be convicted of a felony. In 1922 he had accepted bribes of more than $400,000 for secretly leasing naval oil reserves at Elk Hills, California, and Teapot Dome, Wyoming, to private oil companies.

Harding died suddenly in August 1923, before most of the scandals came to light. Though he would be remembered as lackluster, his tolerance and moderation had a calming influence on the strife-ridden nation. Slowly he had even begun to lead. In 1921 he created a new Bureau of the Budget, which brought modern accounting techniques to the management of federal revenues. Toward the end of his administration he cleared an early scandal from the Veterans' Bureau and set an agenda for Congress that included expanding the merchant marine.

To his credit Calvin Coolidge handled Harding's unfavorable legacy with skill and dispatch. He created a special investigatory commission, prosecuted the wrongdoers, and restored public confidence. Decisiveness, when he chose to exercise it, was one of Coolidge's hallmarks. He believed in small-town democracy and minimalist government. "One of the most important accomplishments of my administration has been minding my own business," he boasted. Above all Coolidge worshiped wealth. "Civilization and profits," he once said, "go hand in hand."

Coolidge had been in office barely a year when voters returned him to the White House by a margin of nearly two to one in the election in 1924. It was another sign that Americans had wearied of reform and delighted in surging prosperity. Whether the business-dominated policies served the economy or the nation well in the long term is open to question.

The Policies of Mellon and Hoover

Coolidge retained most of Harding's cabinet, including his powerful treasury secretary, Andrew Mellon. The former president of aluminum giant Alcoa, Mellon believed that prosperity "trickled down" from rich to poor through investment, which would raise production, employment, and wages. For more than a decade Mellon devoted himself to encouraging investment by reducing taxes on high incomes and corporations. By the time he was through, Congress had nearly halved taxes.

Unlike Mellon, Commerce Secretary Herbert Hoover (another Harding holdover) was not a traditional Republican. Hoover promoted a progressive brand of capitalism called "associationalism." It involved cooperation between business and government through trade associations, groups of private companies organized industry by industry. Approximately 2,000 trade associations had come into being by 1929, many of them nurtured in the heyday of business-government cooperation during World War I. The role of government, as Hoover saw it, was to promote cooperation among businesses, to advise them on how best to act in the public interest, and to ensure that everyone obeyed the rules. Through associationalism, Hoover married the individualism of the past with what progressives had seen as the efficiency, organization, and cooperation of the future. As such, he represented the best of the New Era.

Both Hoover and Mellon ended up placing government in service of business. Mellon's tax policies helped concentrate wealth in the hands of fewer individuals and corporations, while Hoover's associationalism, for all its faith in the ability of businesses to act for public good, helped them consolidate their power at the expense of the public.

Warren G. Harding

Calvin Coolidge

Associationalism

Andrew Mellon, secretary of the treasury and the millionaire head of an aluminum monopoly, is flanked by Grace and Calvin Coolidge on the lawn of the White House. A disciple of business, President Coolidge believed that what was of "real importance to wage-earners was not how they might conduct a quarrel with their employers but how the business of the country might be so organized as to insure steady employment at a fair rate of pay. If that were done there would be no occasion for a quarrel, and if it were not done a quarrel would do no good."

By the end of the decade, 200 giant corporations controlled almost half the corporate wealth and nearly a fifth of national wealth. In keeping with this government-sponsored trend, the Anti-Trust Division of the Justice Department offered few objections and brought few antitrust suits, while the Supreme Court affirmed the constitutionality of trade associations. And for all the talk of limiting government, its role in the economy grew. So did its size, by more than 40,000 employees between 1921 and 1930. Building on their wartime partnership, government and business dropped all pretense of a laissez-faire economy. "Never before, here or elsewhere, has a government been so completely fused with business," noted the *Wall Street Journal.*

Distress Signals at Home and Abroad

Some economic groups remained outside the magic circle of Republican prosperity. Ironically, they included those people who made up the biggest business in America: farmers.

In 1920 farming still had an investment value greater than manufacturing, all utilities, and all railroads combined. A third of the population relied on farming for a living. Yet the farmers' portion of the national income shrank by almost half during the 1920s. The government withdrew wartime price supports for wheat and ended its practice of feeding refugees with American surpluses. As European farms began producing again, the demand for American exports dropped. New dietary habits meant that average Americans of 1920 ate 75 fewer pounds of food annually than they had 10 years earlier. New synthetic fibers drove down demand for natural wool and cotton fibers.

In 1921 a group of southern and western senators organized the "farm bloc" in Congress to coordinate relief for farmers. Over the next two years they succeeded in bringing stockyards, packers, and grain exchanges under federal supervision. Other legislation exempted farm cooperatives from antitrust actions and created a dozen banks for low-interest farm loans. But regulation and credit were not enough, and over the decade the purchasing power of farmers continued to slide.

For the five years that Coolidge ran a "businessman's government," workers reaped few gains in wages, purchasing power, and bargaining rights. Although welfare capitalism promised workers profit-sharing and other benefits, only a handful of companies put it into practice. Those that did often used it to weaken independent unions. As dangerous imbalances in the economy developed, Coolidge ignored them.

One sign of distress no one could ignore: the great Mississippi flood of 1927. After years of deforestation and months of heavy rain, the Mississippi River burst through its

The Great Flood of 1927

levees, rampaging across an area roughly the size of New England from southern Missouri to Louisiana. Floodwaters reached 100 feet in some places and did not recede for three months. A network of private agencies was quickly knit together and placed under the control of Commerce secretary Herbert Hoover. An army of local citizens, many of them black and some conscripted at gunpoint, erected a series of refugee camps to cope with the 700,000 people displaced by the flood, but relief efforts were hardly equal to the task. Nearly 250 people died, and 130,000 homes were destroyed. Property damage ran to $350 million ($5 billion in today's dollars). Before the end of 1928, half the African American population of the Mississippi Delta's black belt had fled the region. For the rest of the decade commerce throughout the central United States suffered. Still, federal legislation had been passed—for the first time—giving the government responsibility for controlling such disasters along the Mississippi.

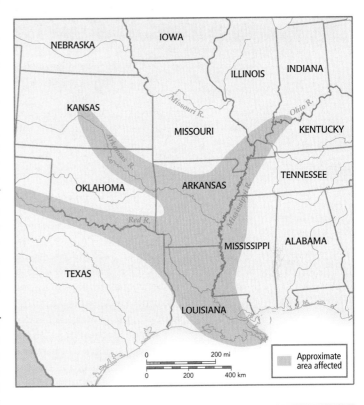

The Great Flood of 1927

If most Americans paid little attention to many of the distress signals at home, they ignored economic unrest abroad. At the end of World War I, Europe's victors had forced Germany to take on $33 billion in war costs or reparations, partly to repay their own war debts to the United States. When Germany defaulted in 1923, French forces occupied the Ruhr valley, the center of German industry. Germany struck back by printing more money to cope with the crushing burden of debt. Runaway inflation soon wiped out the savings of the German middle class, shook confidence in the new democratic Weimar Republic, and eventually threatened the economic structure of all Europe.

The Dawes Plan

In 1924 American business leader Charles G. Dawes persuaded the victorious Europeans to scale down reparations. In return the United States promised to help stabilize the German economy. Encouraged by the State Department, American bankers made large loans to Germany, with which the Germans paid their reparations. The European victors then used those funds to repay *their* war debts to the United States. It amounted to taking money out of one American vault and depositing it in another. In 1926 the United States also reduced European war debts. Canceling them altogether would have made more sense, but few Americans were that forgiving.

Two grand, if finally futile, gestures reflected the twin desires for peace and economy. In 1921, in a conference held in Washington, the sea powers of the world agreed to freeze battleship construction for 10 years and to set ratios on the tonnage of each navy. The Five-Power Agreement was the first disarmament treaty in modern history. A more extravagant gesture came in 1928, when the major nations of the world (except the Soviet Union) signed the Kellogg-Briand Pact outlawing war. "Peace is proclaimed," announced Secretary of State Frank Kellogg as he signed the document with a foot-long pen of gold.

Kellog-Briand Pact

But what seemed so bold on paper proved timid in practice. The French and Japanese resented the lower limits set on their battleships under the Five-Power Agreement and touched off a new arms race by building smaller warships such as submarines, cruisers, and destroyers. And with no means of enforcement, the Kellogg-Briand Pact remained a hollow proclamation.

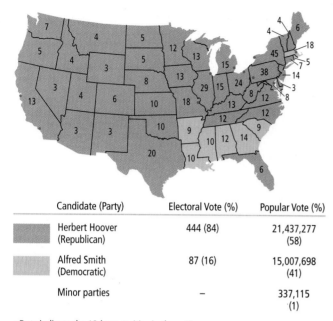

Candidate (Party)	Electoral Vote (%)	Popular Vote (%)
Herbert Hoover (Republican)	444 (84)	21,437,277 (58)
Alfred Smith (Democratic)	87 (16)	15,007,698 (41)
Minor parties	–	337,115 (1)

* Dots indicate the 12 largest cities in the nation.

Election of 1928

The Election of 1928

On August 2, 1927, in a small classroom in Rapid City, South Dakota, Calvin Coolidge handed a terse, typewritten message to reporters: "I do not choose to run for President in nineteen twenty-eight." Republicans honored the request and nominated Herbert Hoover. Hoover was not a politician but an administrator who had never once campaigned for public office. It did not matter. Republican prosperity made it difficult for any Democrat to win. Hoover, perhaps the most admired public official in America, made it impossible.

The Democratic party continued to fracture between its rural supporters in the South and West and ethnic laborers in the urban Northeast. The two factions had clashed during the 1924 convention, scuttling the presidential candidacy of New York governor Al Smith. By 1928 the shift in population toward cities had given an edge to the party's urban wing. Al Smith won the nomination on the first ballot, even though his handicaps were evident. When the New York City–bred Smith spoke "poysonally" on the "rha-dio," his accent made voters across America wince. Though he pledged to enforce Prohibition, he campaigned against it and even took an occasional drink (which produced the false rumor that he was a hopeless alcoholic). Most damaging of all, Smith was Catholic at a time when anti-Catholicism remained strong in many areas of the country.

In the election of 1928, nearly 60 percent of the eligible voters turned out to give all but eight states to Hoover. The solidly Democratic South cracked for the first time. Still, the stirrings of a major political realignment lay buried in the returns. The 12 largest cities in the country had gone to the Republicans in 1924; in 1928 the Democrats won them. Western farmers, ignored by Republicans for a decade, also voted for Smith. The Democrats were becoming the party of the cities, of immigrants, and of the long-ignored. Around this core, they would build the most powerful vote-getting coalition of the twentieth century.

As important, a new kind of electorate was emerging. No longer were voters part of a vast partisan army whose loyalties were tied to the party year in and year out by barbecues, rallies, and torchlight parades. The reforms of the progressive era had restricted the power of political machines and the discipline they could exert over voters. The culture of consumption that had shaped American life in the 1920s also shaped politics. Increasingly, parties courted voters with newspaper advertisements and radio "spots." In 1929 the Democrats created the first public relations department in American politics. Paradoxically, the twentieth century would witness a deterioration of party loyalty as the growing reliance on the media to communicate with "consumer/voters" weakened traditional party networks.

The Great Bull Market

Strolling across the felt-padded floor of the New York Stock Exchange, Superintendent William Crawford greeted the New Year with swaggering confidence. Nineteen twenty-eight had broken all stock-buying records. The "bulls," or buyers of stock, had routed the bears, those who sell. It was the greatest bull market in history as eager purchasers drove prices to new highs. At the end of the last business day, Crawford surveyed the floor and declared flatly, "The millennium's arrived."

Veteran financial analyst Alexander Noyes had his doubts. Speculation—buying and selling on the expectation that rising prices will yield quick gains—had taken over the stock market. "Something has to give," said Noyes in September 1929. Less than a month later, the Great Bull Market fell in a heap.

The Rampaging Bull

No one knows exactly what caused the wave of speculation that boosted the stock market to dizzying heights. Driven alternately by greed and fear, the market succumbed to greed in a decade that considered it a virtue. A new breed of aggressive outsiders helped spread the speculative fever. William Durant of General Motors, the Fisher brothers from Detroit, and others like them bought millions of shares, crowded out more conservative investors from the East, and helped send prices soaring.

New Breed

Money and credit to fuel the market became plentiful. From 1922 to 1929, some $900 million worth of gold flowed into the country. The money supply expanded by $6 billion. Over the decade corporate profits grew by 80 percent. At interest rates as high as 25 percent, more could be made from lending money to brokers (who then made "brokers' loans" to clients for stock purchase) than from constructing new factories. By 1929 brokers' loans had almost tripled from two years earlier.

New Money

"Margin requirements," the cash actually put down to purchase stock, hovered around 50 percent for most of the decade. Thus buyers had to come up with only half the price of a share. The rest came from credit furnished by brokers' loans. As trading reached record heights in August 1929, the Federal Reserve Board tried to dampen speculation by raising the interest rates. Higher interest rates made borrowing more expensive and, authorities hoped, would rein in the galloping bull market. They were wrong. It was already too late.

The Great Crash

At the opening bell on Thursday, October 24, 1929, a torrent of sell orders flooded the Exchange, triggered by nervous speculators who had been selling for the past week. Prices plunged as panic set in. By the end of "Black Thursday" nearly 13 million shares had been traded—a record. Losses stood at $3 billion, another record.

Prices rallied for the rest of the week, buoyed by a bankers' buying pool organized at the House of Morgan. The following Tuesday, October 29, 1929, the bubble burst. Stockholders lost $10 billion in a single day. And the downward slide continued for almost four years. At their peak in 1929 stocks had been worth $87 billion. In 1933 they bottomed out at $18 billion.

The Great Crash did not cause the Great Depression, but it did damage the economy and break the unbounded optimism on which the New Era rested. Although only about 500,000 people were actually trading stocks by the end of the decade, their investments had helped to sustain prosperity. Thousands of middle-class investors lost their savings and their futures. Commercial banks—some loaded with corporate stocks, others financing brokers' loans—reeled in the wake of the crash.

Role of the Crash

ON THE FLOOR — N.Y. STOCK EXCHANGE   REGINALD MARSH

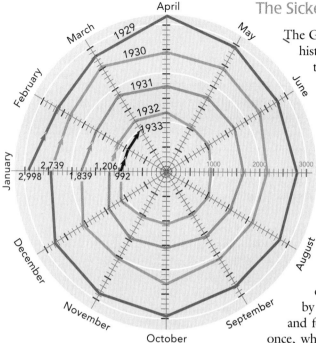

(in millions of dollars)

Declining World Trade, 1929–1933 *As the Great Depression deepened, world trade spiraled downward. Here the imports of 75 countries are tracked from 1929 to 1933. (The amounts are measured in millions of U.S. gold dollars.) The greatest annual decline occurred between 1930 and 1931 as production plummeted and nation after nation began to erect high tariff barriers to protect their domestic markets from cheaper imports. Over the four-year period, world import trade fell by almost two-thirds, only underscoring the growing interdependence of the global economy.*

Overexpansion and Relative Decline In Purchasing Power

The Sickening Slide in Global Perspective

The Great Crash signaled the start of the greatest depression in the history of the modern world. In the United States, the gains of the 1920s were wiped out in a few years. In the first three years after the crash, national income fell by half, factory wages by almost half. By some estimates 85,000 businesses failed.

Although the Great Depression was less prolonged in other countries, the shock waves from the United States rippled across the globe, helping to topple already fragile economies in Europe. American loans, investments, and purchases had propped up Europe since the end of World War I. When American resources dried up, European governments defaulted on war debts. More European banks failed; more businesses collapsed; unemployment surged to at least 30 million worldwide by 1932.

Europeans scrambled to protect themselves. Led by Great Britain in 1931, 41 nations abandoned the gold standard. Foreign governments hoped to devalue their currencies by expanding their supplies of money. Exports would be cheaper and foreign trade would increase. But several countries did so at once, while each country raised tariffs to protect itself from foreign competition. Devaluation failed, and the resulting trade barriers only deepened the crisis. Between 1929 and 1933 world exports declined by two-thirds, from a high of nearly $3 billion to less than $1 billion. (See the chart at left.)

In Latin America and other regions where countries depended on exporting raw materials, the slide varied. Shrinking sales of metallic minerals, timber, and hides crippled Chile, Bolivia, Peru, and Malaya, while exports of fuel oils still needed to warm homes and run factories shielded Venezuela. Only the Soviet Union escaped catastrophe, with its limited exports and a command economy that had launched a breakneck campaign of industrialization. Even in the Soviet Union, however, bumper crops of Russian wheat forced onto the world market at deflated prices led millions of peasants to starve to death in 1932–1933. Virtually everywhere else economies cracked under the weight of slackening demand and contracting world trade.

In the United States declining sales abroad sent crop prices to new lows. Farm income dropped by more than half. The epidemic of rural bank failures spread to the cities. Nervous depositors rushed to withdraw their cash. Even healthy banks could not bear the strain. In August 1930 every bank in Toledo but one closed its doors. Between 1929 and 1933 collapsing banks took more than $20 billion in assets with them. The economy was spiraling downward, and no one could stop it.

The Causes of the Great Depression

What, then, caused the Great Depression in the United States? In the months before the crash, with national attention riveted on the booming stock market, hardly anyone paid attention to existing defects in the American economy. But by 1928 the booming construction and automobile industries began to lose vitality as demand sagged. In fact, increases in consumer spending for all goods and services slowed to a lethargic 1.5 percent for 1928–1929. Warehouses began to fill as business inventories climbed, from $500 million in 1928 to $1.8 billion in 1929.

In one sense, businesses had done all too well. Corporations had boosted their profits by some 80 percent during the 1920s. They had done so by keeping the cost of labor and raw materials low as well as by increasing productivity. But the profits that business reaped were used to expand factories rather than to pay workers higher wages. Without strong labor unions or government support, real wages increased (largely because of falling prices) but never kept pace with productivity, which led to a paradox. As consumers, workers did not have enough money to buy the products they were making ever more efficiently and at lower cost.

People made up the difference between earnings and purchases by borrowing. Consumers bought "on time," paying for merchandise a little each month. During the decade, consumer debt rose by 250 percent. Few could afford to keep spending at that rate. Nor could the distribution of wealth sustain prosperity. By 1929, 1 percent of the population owned 36 percent of all personal wealth. The wealthy had more money than they could possibly spend and saved too much. The working and middle classes had not nearly enough to keep the economy growing, spend though they might.

Consumer Debt and Uneven Distribution of Wealth

Another problem lay with the banking system. Mismanagement, greed, and the emergence of a new type of executive—half banker, half broker—led banks to divert more funds into speculative investments. The uniquely decentralized American banking system left no way to set things right if a bank failed. At the end of the decade, half of the 25,000 banks in America lay outside the Federal Reserve System. Its controls even over member banks were weak, and during the decade, 6,000 banks failed.

Banking System

A shaky corporate structure only made matters worse. No government agency at all monitored the stock exchanges, while big business operated largely unchecked. Insider stock trading, shady stock deals, and outright stock fraud ran rampant. Meanwhile, public policy encouraged corporate consolidation and control because the government filed few antitrust suits. High profits and the Mellon tax program helped make many corporations wealthy enough to avoid borrowing. Thus changes in interest rates—over which the Federal Reserve exercised some control—had little influence on such corporations. Free from government regulation, fluctuating prices, and the need for loans, big businesses ruled the economy. And they ruled badly.

Corporate Structure and Public Policy

Unemployment began to increase as early as 1927, a sign of growing softness in the economy. By the fall of 1929 some 2 million people were out of work. Many of them were in textiles, coal mining, lumbering, and railroads. All were "sick" industries during the decade because they suffered from overexpansion, reduced demand, and weak management. Farmers were in trouble too. As European agriculture revived after World War I, farm prices tumbled. American farmers earned 16 percent of the national income in 1919 but only 9 percent in 1929. As more farmers went bust, so did many of the rural banks that had lent them money.

"Sick" Industries

Finally, plain economic ignorance contributed to the calamity. High tariffs protected American industries but discouraged European business from selling to the world's most profitable market. Because Europeans weren't profiting, they lacked the money for American goods being shipped to Europe. Only American loans and investments supported demand abroad. When the American economy collapsed, those vanished and with them went American foreign trade. Furthermore, the Federal Reserve had been stimulating the economy both by expanding the money supply and by lowering interest rates. Those moves only fed the speculative fever by furnishing investors with more money at lower costs. A decision finally to raise interest rates in 1929 to stem speculation ended up speeding the slide.

Economic Ignorance

"Everyone ought to be rich," proclaimed one enthusiastic investment adviser in *The Ladies Home Journal*—at a time when the economy was still bubbling and the stock market was setting new highs. Americans like him had nothing but faith in their New Era: in its capacity to produce abundance and spread wealth, in its promise of technological freedom from toil and want, in its ability to blend the vast differences among Americans into a mass culture in which individuals would nonetheless retain their identities. They put their money, some quite literally, on this modernism. Others objected to the price being paid in lost community and independence. They wanted to resurrect a world less organized, less bureaucratized, less complex and varied—a world less modern. In the 1920s, the tensions between these contrasting ideals sparked the first culture wars of the twentieth century.

The mix of exuberance, hedonism, and anxiety was mirrored in other nations. As the postwar recession lifted, many of the world's political systems seemed to sustain Woodrow Wilson's dream of a world made safe for democracy. Hapsburg Germany transformed itself into the Weimar Republic, whose constitution provided universal suffrage and a bill of rights. The new nations carved out of the old Russian and Austro-Hungarian empires attempted to create similarly democratic governments, while in Turkey, Kemal Ataturk abolished the sultanate and established the Turkish Republic. In India, the Congress party formed by Mohandas K. Gandhi united socialists and powerful industrial capitalists and pushed the British to grant them greater political representation. Even where the political mix was more volatile, as in China and Indochina (Vietnam), nationalism mixed with communism as a means of liberating colonial peoples from imperialist rule.

The Great Crash and the Great Depression rocked these fragile beginnings. Fledgling democracies in Japan and Germany gave way to authoritarian states, while dire economic straits strengthened the hands of dictators in Italy and the Soviet Union. Japan, too, departed from its peaceful path of trade and foreign investment toward aggressive militarism and expansion. No one—not the brokers of Wall Street, not the captains of industry, not the diplomats at the League of Nations—could predict the future in such an unstable world.

Significant Events

Year	Event
1914	Henry Ford introduces moving assembly line
1915	Modern Ku Klux Klan founded
1916	Marcus Garvey brings Universal Negro Improvement Association to America
1919	Eighteenth Amendment outlawing alcohol use ratified
1920	First commercial radio broadcast; Nineteenth Amendment grants women right to vote; Warren Harding elected president
1921	Congress enacts quotas on immigration
1921–1922	Washington Naval Disarmament Conference
1922	Sinclair Lewis's *Babbitt* and T. S. Eliot's *The Waste Land* published
1923	Harding dies; Calvin Coolidge becomes president
1924	Dawes plan to stabilize German inflation; Coolidge elected president
1925	John T. Scopes convicted of teaching evolution in Tennessee; Alain Locke's *The New Negro* published
1927	Charles Lindbergh's solo flight across the Atlantic; Sacco and Vanzetti executed; the Mississippi flood
1928	Herbert Hoover elected president
1929	Stock market crashes

Chapter Summary

The New Era of the 1920s brought a booming economy and modern times to America, vastly accelerating the forces of change—bureaucracy, productivity, technology, advertising and consumerism, mass media, peer culture, and suburbanization. Urban-rural tensions peaked with shifts in population that gave cities new power. But as the decade wore on, weaknesses in the economy and a new ethos of getting and spending, too much of it on credit, proved to be the New Era's undoing.

• Technology, advertising and consumer spending, and such boom industries as automobile manufacturing and construction fueled the largest peacetime economic growth in American history.

• Key features of modern life—mass society, mass culture, and mass consumption—took hold, fed by mass media in the form of radio, movies, and mass-circulation newspapers and magazines.

• Modern life unsettled old ways and eroded social conventions that had limited life especially for women and children, leading to the emergence of a New Woman and a youth culture.

• Great migrations of African Americans from the rural South to the urban North and of Latinos from Mexico to the United States reshaped the social landscape.

• Traditional culture, centered in rural America, hardened and defended itself against change through immigration restriction, Prohibition, Fundamentalism, and a reborn Ku Klux Klan.

• A galloping bull market in stocks reflected the commitment of government to big business and economic growth.

• When the stock market crashed in 1929, weaknesses in the economy—overexpansion, declining purchasing power, uneven distribution of wealth, weak banking and corporate structures, "sick" industries, and economic ignorance—finally brought the economy down, and with it the New Era came to a close.

Additional Reading

For years, Frederick Lewis Allen, *Only Yesterday: An Informal History of the 1920s* (1931), shaped the stereotyped view of the decade as a frivolous interlude between World War I and the Great Depression. William Leuchtenburg, *The Perils of Prosperity, 1914–1932* (1958), began an important reconsideration by stressing the serious conflict between urban and rural America and the emergence of modern mass society. Lynn Dumenil updates Leuchtenburg in her excellent *The Modern Temper: American Culture and Society in the 1920s* (1995). Ann Douglas, *Terrible Honesty: Mongrel Manhattan in the 1920s* (1995), puts Manhattan at the core of the cultural transformation in the 1920s, especially its success at bringing African American folk and popular art into the mainstream. On immigration restriction beginning in 1882 and ending with debates sparked by 9/11, see Roger Daniels, *Guarding the Golden Door: American Immigration Policy and Immigrants Since 1882* (2004). On the Scopes trial, see Edward J. Larson, *Summer for the Gods: The Scopes Trial and America's Continuing Debate over Science and Religion* (1997).

Roland Marchand, *Advertising the American Dream: Making Way for Modernity, 1920–1940* (1985), analyzes the role of advertising in shaping mass consumption, values, and culture, and Ellis Hawley, *The Great War and the Search for a Modern Order* (1979), emphasizes economic institutions. For women in the 1920s, see: Kathleen M. Blee, *Women of the Klan: Racism and Gender in the 1920s* (1991); Virginia Scharff, *Taking the Wheel: Women and the Coming of the Motor Age* (1991); and Jacqueline Jones, *Labor of Love, Labor of Sorrow: Black Women, Work, and Family, from Slavery to the Present* (1985). In a penetrating and gendered discussion of Garveyism and of the Harlem Renaissance, Martin Summers profiles evolving notions of what it meant to be a black man in the early years of the twentieth century in *Manliness and Its Discontents: The Black Middle Class & the Transformation of Masculinity, 1900–1930* (2004).

The most thorough and readable examination of the stock market and its relation to the economy and public policy in the 1920s is still Robert Sobel, *The Great Bull Market: Wall Street in the 1920s* (1968). For a colorful survey, particularly of the two years before the crash, see Maury Klein, *Rainbow's End: The Crash of 1929* (2001). The best books on the disintegration of the American economy remain Lester Chandler, *America's Greatest Depression, 1929–1941* (1970), and, from a global standpoint, Charles Kindleberger, *The World in Depression, 1929–1939* (1973). For an analysis of the Great Depression from the perspective of Keynesian economics that stresses declining purchasing power and investment, see John Kenneth Galbraith, *The Great Crash* (rev. ed., 1988). For the argument of monetarists, who see the roots of the depression in the shrinking money supply, see Milton Friedman and Anna Jacobson Schwartz, *Monetary History of the United States* (1963), and Peter Temin, *Did Monetary Forces Cause the Great Depression?* (1976). John M. Barry, *Rising Tide: The Great Mississippi Flood of 1927 and How It Changed America* (1997), is especially good in describing the fate of African Americans and the failure of government and private aid organizations.

For a fuller list of readings, see the Bibliography at www.mhhe.com/davidsonnation6.

CHAPTER 25

The Great Depression &
the New Deal

1929~1939

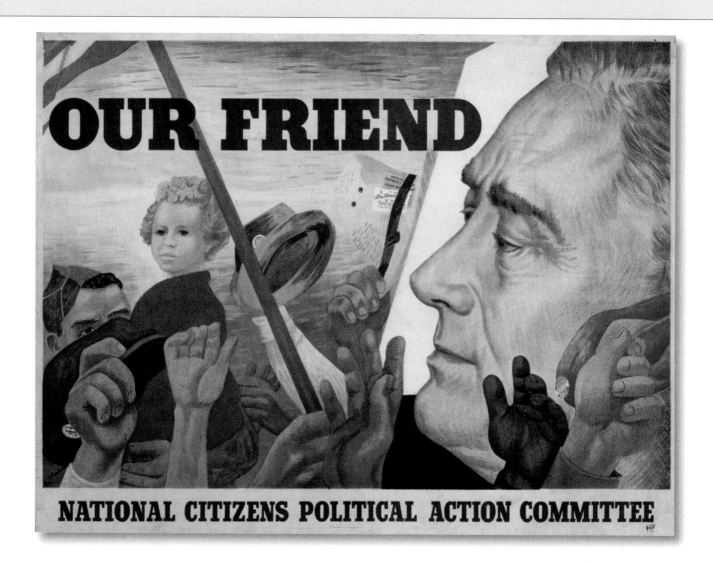

In 1944, painter and political activist Ben Shahn made this poster for the Political Action Committee of the Congress of Industrial Organizations (CIO), a federation of labor unions, as part of a voter registration drive to help re-elect Franklin Roosevelt for a record 4th term as president.

Hard Times

Subsistence Incomes

Hard times lasted for a decade. Even before the Great Crash many Americans were having trouble making a living. Economists calculated that for the barest necessities a family of four in the golden year of 1929 required $2,000 a year—more money than 60 percent of American families earned.

As soup kitchens opened and breadlines formed in cities across the nation, survival often became the goal. Millions stayed alive by foraging like animals, and city hospitals began receiving new patients ill from starvation. Pellagra and other diseases associated with malnutrition increased. Despite official claims that "no one has starved," the New York City Welfare Council reported 29 victims of starvation and 110 dead of malnutrition in 1932. Most were children.

Unable to pay mortgages or rent, many families lived off the generosity of forgiving landlords. Some traded down to smaller quarters or simply lost their homes. By 1932 between 1 million and 2 million Americans were homeless wanderers, among them an estimated 25,000 nomadic families. For the first time, emigration out of the United States exceeded immigration into it because Americans could find no work in their own country.

Marriage and Family

Marriages and births, symbols of faith in the future, decreased. For the first time in three centuries the curve of population growth began to level, as many young couples postponed having children. Experts worried about an impending "baby crop shortage." Strong families hung together and grew closer; weak ones languished or fell apart. Although divorce declined, desertion—the "poor man's divorce"—mushroomed. Under the strain, rates of mental illness and suicide rose as well.

Fathers and Mothers

Many fathers, whose lives had been defined by work, suddenly had nothing to do. They grew listless and depressed. Most mothers stayed home and found their traditional roles as nurturer and household manager less disrupted than the roles of their husbands as breadwinners. Between 1929 and 1933 living costs dropped 25 percent, but family incomes tumbled by 40 percent. Homemakers watched household budgets with a closer eye than ever. They canned more food and substituted less expensive fish for meat. When they earned extra money, they often did so within the confines of the "woman's sphere" by taking in boarders, laundry, and sewing; opening beauty parlors in their kitchens; and selling baked goods.

Monopoly, patented in 1935 by Charles Darrow, became the best-selling board game in the world.

Family life took on new importance, and the home emerged as the center of recreation. Surveys showed that while Americans dreamed of the outdoors—swimming, boating, or playing tennis—they spent most of their free time at home. Board games such as Monopoly and card games like contract bridge enjoyed great popularity. Between 1934 and 1937, phonograph record sales jumped a hundredfold; reading became the number one form of entertainment.

For those women who worked outside the home, prejudice still relegated them to so-called women's work. Over half the female labor force continued to work in domestic service or the garment trades, while others found traditional employment as schoolteachers, social workers, and secretaries. Only slowly did the female proportion of the workforce reach pre-Depression levels, until it rose finally to 25 percent by 1940, largely because women were willing to take almost any job.

Psychological Impact

Whether in the renewed importance of homemaking and family life or the re-emergence of home industries, the Great Depression sent ordinary Americans scurrying for the reassuring shelter of past practices and left many of them badly shaken. Shame, self-doubt, and pessimism became epidemic as people blamed themselves for their circumstances and turned their anger inward. "Shame? You tellin' me?" recalled one man. "I would go stand on the relief line [and] bend my head low so nobody would recognize me." The lasting legacy of humiliation and fear—that you had caused your own downfall; that the bottom would drop out again; that life would be leveled once more; that the next depression might not end—was what one writer called an "invisible scar."

The Golden Age of Radio and Film

Programming

By the end of the decade almost 9 out 10 families owned radios. People depended on radios for nearly everything—news, sports, and weather; music and entertainment; advice on how to bake a cake or find God. Some programming helped change national habits. When *The Sporting News* conducted a baseball poll in 1932, editors were surprised to discover that a "new crop of fans has been created by radio . . . the women." Many women were at home during the day when most games were played, and broadcasters went out of their way to educate these new listeners.

Radio entered a golden age of commercialism. Advertisers hawked their products on variety programs like *Major Bowes' Amateur Hour* and comedy shows with George Burns and Gracie Allen. Daytime melodramas (called "soap operas" because they were sponsored by soap companies) aimed at women with stories of the personal struggles of ordinary folk.

Radio continued to bind the country together. A teenager in Splendora, Texas, could listen to the same wisecracks from Jack Benny, the same music from Guy Lombardo, as kids in New York and Los Angeles. In 1938 Orson Welles broadcast H. G. Wells's classic science fiction tale *The War of the Worlds*. Americans everywhere listened to breathless reports of an "invasion from Mars," and many believed it. In Newark, New Jersey, cars jammed roads as families rushed to evacuate the city.

Art Deco radio, 1930. Art Deco, popularized in the 1920s, relied on the geometrical patterns of machines arranged in decorative designs.

In Hollywood an efficient but autocratic studio system churned out a record number of feature films. Eight motion picture companies produced more than two-thirds of them. Color, first introduced to feature films in *Becky Sharp* (1935), soon complemented sound, which had debuted in the 1927 version of *The Jazz Singer*. Neither alone could keep movie theaters full. As attendance dropped early in the Depression, big studios such as Metro-Goldwyn-Mayer and Universal lured audiences back with films that often shocked and titillated. In the face of growing criticism the industry began regulating its movie content. In 1933 the Catholic Church created the Legion of Decency to monitor features. To avoid censorship and boycotts, studios stiffened their own regulations. Producers could not depict homosexuality, abortion, drug use, or sex. (Even the word *sex* was banned, as was all profanity.) If couples were shown in bed, they had to be clothed and one foot of each partner had to touch the floor. Middle-class morality reigned on the screen, and most Depression movies, like most of popular culture, preserved traditional values.

Still, the "mass" aspects of media could cut more than one way politically. While Hollywood produced films that affirmed popular faith in democratic government, a capitalist economy, and the success ethic, **totalitarian** Nazi Germany broadcast the fiery mass rallies of Adolf Hitler, which seemed bent on encouraging racist fears and inflaming public hysteria. German director Leni Riefenstahl used her cinematic gifts to combine myth, symbol, and documentary into an evocation of Hitler as the Führer, a national leader with the strength of a pagan god and the charity of a Christian savior.

"Dirty Thirties": An Ecological Disaster

Dust Bowl

Each year between 1932 and 1939 an average of nearly 50 dust storms, or "black blizzards," turned 1,500 square miles between the Oklahoma panhandle and western Kansas into a gigantic "Dust Bowl." The baleful effects were felt as far north as the Dakotas and as far south as Texas. It was one of the worst ecological disasters in modern history.

Nature played its part, scorching the earth and whipping the winds. But the "dirty 30s" were mostly human-made. The semiarid lands west of the 98th meridian were not suitable for agriculture or livestock. Sixty years of intensive farming and grazing had stripped the prairie of its natural vegetation and rendered it defenseless against the elements. When the dry winds came, one-third of the Great Plains just blew away.

The dust storms lasted anywhere from hours to days. Walking into one was like walking into "a wall of dirt." "This is the ultimate darkness," despaired a Kansan in

"Black blizzards" dwarfed all fabricated structures. The drought that gave rise to the huge dust storms lasted from 1932 until 1939, and few who lived through a black blizzard ever forgot it. "Noon was like night," reported a conductor on the Santa Fe railroad. "There was no sun, and, at times, it was impossible to see a yard. The engineer could not see the signal lights." In a single day in 1934, 12 million tons of western dirt fell on Chicago.

the midst of one storm. "So must come the end of the world." Winds carried the dust aloft so high that yellow grit from Nebraska collected on the windowsills of the White House. Ships 300 miles off the East Coast found bits of Montana and Wyoming on their decks. Even the fish died—from lack of oxygen in dust-coated rivers.

Some 3.5 million plains people abandoned their farms. Landowners or corporations forced off about half of them as large-scale commercial farming slowly spread into the heartland of America. Commercial farms were more common in California, where 10 percent of the farms grew more than 50 percent of the crops. As in industrial America, the strategy in agricultural America was to consolidate and mechanize. As farms grew in size, so did the number of tenants. In most Dust Bowl counties people owned less than half the land they farmed. American agriculture was turning from a way of life into an industry. And, as the economy contracted, owners cut costs by cutting workers on farms as well as in factories.

Relief offices around the country reported a change in migrant families. Rather than black or brown, more and more were white and native-born, typically a young married couple with one child. Most did not travel far, perhaps to the next county. Long-distance migrants from Oklahoma, Arizona, and Texas usually set their sights on California. Handbills and advertisements promised jobs picking fruit and harvesting vegetables. If they were like the Joad family in John Steinbeck's classic novel *The Grapes of Wrath* (1939), they drove west along Route 66 through Arizona and New Mexico, their belongings piled high atop rickety jalopies, heading for the West Coast.

More than 350,000 Oklahomans migrated to California—so many that "Okie" came to mean any Dust Bowler, even though most of Oklahoma lay outside the Dust Bowl. The poor were only a small minority of new arrivals, but enough came to make Californians edgy. By the middle of the decade Los Angeles police had formed "bum blockades" to keep migrants out. "Negroes and Okies upstairs," read one sign in a San Joaquin Valley theater. Native-born whites had never encountered such discrimination before.

Only one in two or three migrants found work, and the labor surplus allowed growers to set their own terms. A migrant family earned about $450 a year, less than a third the subsistence level. Families that did not work formed wretched enclaves called "little Oklahomas." The worst were located in the fertile Imperial Valley. There, at the end of the decade, relief officials discovered a family of 10 living in a 1921 Ford. When told to go, the mother responded vacantly, "I wonder where?"

Effect of Commercial Farming

Okies

Mexican Americans and Repatriation

Cesar Chavez

The Chavez family lost their farm in the North Gila River valley of Arizona in 1934. They had owned a small homestead near Yuma for two generations, but the Depression pushed them out. Cesar, barely six years old at the time, remembered only images of the departure: a "giant tractor" leveling the corral; a beat-up Chevy hauling the family west; his father promising to buy another farm someday.

The elder Chavez could never keep his promise. Instead he and his family lived on the road, "following the crops" in California. In eight years Cesar went to 37 schools. The family was forced to sell their labor to unscrupulous *enganchistas,* or contractors, for less than $10 a week. The father joined strikers in the Imperial Valley in the mid-1930s, but they were easily crushed. "Some people put this out of their minds and forget it," said Cesar Chavez years later. "I don't." Thirty years later he founded the United Farm Workers of America, the first union of migratory workers in the country.

Repatriation

A deep ambivalence had always characterized American attitudes toward Mexicans, but the Great Depression turned most Anglo communities against them. Cities such as Los Angeles, fearing the burden of relief, found it cheaper to ship Mexicans home. Beginning in 1931 the federal government launched a series of deportations, or **repatriations,** of Mexicans back to Mexico. These deportations often included the Mexicans' American-born children, who by law were citizens of the United States. During the decade the Latino population of the Southwest dropped by 500,000. In Chicago, the Mexican community shrank almost by half. Staying in the United States often turned out to be as difficult as leaving. The average income of Mexican American families in the Rio Grande valley of Texas was $506 a year. The sum represented the combined income of parents and children. Following the harvest made schooling particularly difficult: fewer than 2 Mexican American children in 10 completed five years of school.

LULAC and Ethnic Identity

For Americans of Mexican descent, the Great Depression only deepened anxiety over identity. Were they Mexicans, as many Anglos regarded them, or were they Americans, as they regarded themselves? In the 1920s, such questions had produced several organizations founded to assert the American identity of native-born and naturalized Mexican Americans and to pursue their civil rights. In 1929, on the eve of the Depression, many of these organizations were consolidated into the League of United Latin American Citizens (LULAC). By the early 1940s, "Flying Squadrons" of LULAC organizers had founded some 80 chapters nationwide, making it the largest Mexican American civil rights association in the country.

LULAC permitted only those Latinos who were American citizens to join, thus excluding hundreds of thousands of ethnic Mexicans who nonetheless regarded the United States as their home. It pointedly conducted meetings in English, relied heavily on the assimilated middle class for leadership, and stressed desegregation of public schools, voter registration, and an end to discrimination in public facilities and on juries.

Perhaps LULAC's clearest statement of intent in the 1930s came in its support for immigration restriction from Mexico as a means of both establishing the "Americanness" of its members and creating more jobs for Mexican Americans already here. Still, LULAC counted small farmers, ranchers, and wage laborers among its rank and file, many of whom identified strongly with Mexico. And, despite LULAC's efforts to distance itself from Mexican immigrants, women members nonetheless raised funds for milk, eyeglasses, Christmas toys, and clothes for the new arrivals.

African Americans in the Depression

Hard times were nothing new to African Americans. "The Negro was born in depression," opined one black man. "It only became official when it hit the white man." Still, when the Depression struck, black unemployment surged. By 1932 it reached 50 percent, twice the national level. By 1933 several cities reported between 25 and 40 percent of their black residents with no support except relief payments. Even skilled

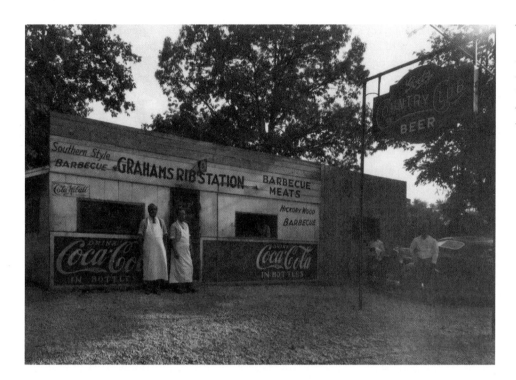

Graham's Rib Station, a black-owned restaurant in Springfield, Missouri, found it increasingly difficult to make a living during the Great Depression.

black workers who retained their jobs saw their wages cut in half, according to one study of Harlem in 1935.

Migration out of the rural South, up by 800,000 during the 1920s, dropped by 50 percent in the 1930s. As late as 1940 three of four African Americans still lived in rural areas, yet conditions there were just as bad as in cities. In 1934 one study estimated the average income for black cotton farmers at under $200 a year.

Like many African Americans, George Baker refused to be victimized by the Depression. Baker had moved from Georgia to Harlem in 1915. He changed his name to M. J. Divine and founded a religious cult that promised followers an afterlife of full equality. In the 1930s "Father Divine" preached economic cooperation and opened shelters, or "heavens," for regenerate "angels," black and white. In Detroit, Elijah Poole changed his name to Elijah Muhammad and in 1931 established the Black Muslims, a blend of Islamic faith and black nationalism. He exhorted African Americans to celebrate their African heritage, to live a life of self-discipline and self-help, and to strive for a separate all-black nation.

Father Divine and Elijah Muhammad

The Depression inflamed racial prejudice. "Dust has been blown from the shotgun, the whip, and the noose," reported *The New Republic* in 1931. Lynchings tripled between 1932 and 1933. In 1932 the Supreme Court ordered a retrial in the most celebrated racial case of the decade. A year earlier nine black teenagers had been accused of raping two white women on a train bound for Scottsboro, Alabama. Within weeks all-white juries had sentenced eight of them to death. The convictions rested on the testimony of the women, one of whom later admitted that the boys had been framed. Appeals kept the case alive for almost a decade. In the end charges against four of the "Scottsboro boys" were dropped. The other five received substantial prison sentences.

Scottsboro Boys

The Tragedy of Herbert Hoover

The presidency of Herbert Hoover began with great promise but soon turned into a tragedy both personal and professional. "I have no fears for the future of our country," he had announced at his inauguration in March 1929. "It is bright with hope." Within seven months a "depression" had struck. (Hoover himself invented the label to downplay the emergency.) For all his efforts, he failed to end it. Worse, people blamed him for it. "People were starving because of Herbert Hoover," fumed an angry mother in 1932. "Men were killing themselves because of Herbert Hoover, and their fatherless children were being packed away to orphanages . . . because of Herbert Hoover." The claim was as unfair as it was widely believed. For all of Hoover's promise and innovative intelligence, his was to be a transitional presidency, important as a break from do-nothing presidents of past depressions and as a herald of new, more active presidents to come.

The Failure of Relief

Private Charity

By the winter of 1931–1932 the picture was bleak; relief organizations with too little money and too few resources to make much headway against the Depression. Once-mighty private charity had dwindled to 6 percent of all relief funds.

Ethnic charities tried to stave off disaster for their own. Mexican Americans and Puerto Ricans turned to *mutualistas,* traditional societies that provided members with social support, life insurance, and sickness benefits. In San Francisco, the Chinese Six Companies offered food and clothing to needy Chinese Americans. But as the head of the Federation of Jewish Charities warned, private efforts were failing. The government would be "compelled, by the cruel events ahead of us, to step into the situation and bring relief on a large scale."

City Services

City treasuries, already pressed because nearly 30 percent of city taxpayers had fallen behind in paying their taxes, were quickly depleted. In Philadelphia relief payments to a family of four totaled $5.50 a week, the highest in the country. Some cities gave nothing to unmarried people or childless couples, no matter how impoverished they were. By the end of 1931, Detroit, Boston, and scores of other cities were bankrupt.

Cities clamored for help from state capitals, but after a decade of extravagant spending and sloppy bookkeeping, many states were already running in the red. As businesses and property values collapsed, tax bases shrank and with them state revenues. Michigan, one of the few states to provide any relief, reduced funds by more than half

TERA

between 1931 and 1932. Until New York established its Temporary Emergency Relief Administration (TERA) in 1931, no state had any agency at all to handle the problem of unemployment.

Louis Ribak's Home Relief Station *grimly portrays the failing relief efforts of private charities and the humiliation of applying for relief. A crowd of broken men and women sits anxiously as a burly administrator interrogates a frail relief applicant. To go on relief, said one man, was to endure a "crucifixion."*

The Hoover Depression Program

Beginning in 1930, Herbert Hoover assumed leadership in combatting the depression with more vigor and compassion than had any other president. It was a mark of his character. Orphaned at nine, he became one of Stanford University's first graduates and, before the age of 40, the millionaire head of one of the most successful mine engineering firms in the world. As a Quaker, he turned his energies to doing good, saving starving Belgian refugees in 1915 after war broke out in Europe. He worked 14 hours a day, paid his own salary, and convinced private organizations and businesses to donate food, clothing, and other necessities. In his honor, Finns coined a new word: to "hoover" meant to help.

As secretary of commerce under Harding and Coolidge, Hoover perfected his associational philosophy (see page 713). It rested on the notion that government should foster private solutions to public problems by promoting voluntary cooperation among businesses and between businesses and government. Even so, when the Depression struck, he and his government acted. Past presidents had feared that any intervention at all by government would upset the natural workings of the economy and that their sole responsibility was to keep the budget balanced. But Hoover understood the vicious cycle in which rising unemployment drove down consumer demand, and he appreciated the need for stimulating investment. He set in motion an unprecedented program of government activism.

Despite the president's best efforts, his programs failed. As a good associationalist, Hoover rallied business leaders, who pledged to maintain employment, wages, and prices—only to see those leaders back down as the economy sputtered. He pushed a tax cut through Congress in 1930 in order to increase the purchasing power of consumers. But when the cuts produced an unbalanced federal budget, Hoover reversed course. At bottom he firmly believed that capitalism would generate its own recovery and that a balanced federal budget was required in order to restore the confidence of business. Too much government action, he worried, might destroy the very economic system he was seeking to save. So he agreed to tax increases in 1932, further undermining investment and consumption.

Equally disastrous, the president endorsed the Smoot-Hawley Tariff (1930) to protect the United States from cheap foreign goods. That bill resulted in little but retaliatory tariffs from abroad, which choked world trade and reduced American sales overseas. Even the $1 billion that Hoover spent on **public works**—more than the total spent by all his predecessors combined—did not approach the $10 billion needed to employ only half the jobless. Spending such huge sums seemed unthinkable, for the entire federal budget at the time was only $3.2 billion.

Under pressure from Congress, Hoover took his boldest action to save the banks. Between 1930 and 1932 some 5,100 banks went under as worried depositors took their money and ran. Hoover agreed to permit the creation of the Reconstruction Finance Corporation (RFC) in 1932, an agency that could lend money to banks and their chief corporate debtors—insurance companies and railroads. Within three months bank failures dropped from 70 a week to 1 every two weeks. The Glass-Steagall Banking Act (1932) made it easier for banks to loan money by adding $2 billion of new currency to the money supply, backed by Federal Reserve government bonds.

Yet, in spite of this success, Hoover drew criticism for rescuing banks and not people. From the start he refused to give federal aid to the unemployed. He feared that a "dole," or giveaway program (of the kind being used in Britain), would damage the freedom and initiative of recipients, perhaps even produce a permanent underclass. The bureaucracy needed to police recipients would inevitably meddle in the private lives of citizens and bring a "train of corruption and waste." Hoover assumed that neighborliness and cooperation would be enough.

As unemployment continued to worsen, Hoover slowly softened his stand on federal relief. In 1932 he allowed Congress to pass the Emergency Relief and Construction Act.

Herbert Hoover

Reconstruction Finance Corporation

Unemployment Relief

It authorized the RFC to lend up to $1.5 billion for "reproductive" public works that paid for themselves—like toll bridges and slum clearance. Another $300 million went to states as loans for the direct relief of the unemployed. Yet in this Depression $300 million was a pittance. When the governor of Pennsylvania requested loans to furnish the destitute with 13 cents a day for a year, the RFC sent only enough for 3 cents a day.

Stirrings of Discontent

Despite unprecedented action, Hoover could not stem rising discontent. "The word revolution is heard at every hand," one writer warned in 1932. Some wondered if capitalism itself had gone bankrupt.

In 1932, anger erupted into action. Wisconsin diary farmers overturned tens of thousands of milk cans in a fruitless effort to increase prices. A 48-mile long "Coal Caravan" of striking miners drove through southern Illinois in protest. In Dearborn, Michigan, 3,000 marchers stormed Henry Ford's plant, only to have Ford police turn power water hoses and guns on them. Before it was over, four lay dead, and more than 20 were wounded.

Communist Party

For all the stirrings of discontent, revolution was never a danger. In 1932 the Communist party of the United States had 20,000 members—up from 6,500 only

In the early years of the Depression, demonstrations by the unemployed, some organized by Communists and other radicals, broke out all over the country. On March 6, 1930, a Communist-led protest at Union Square in New York turned into an ugly riot. In 1935 Communist parties, under orders from Moscow, allied with democratic and socialist groups against fascism, proclaiming in the United States that "Communism is twentieth-century Americanism."

three years earlier but hardly large enough to constitute a political force. Deeply suspicious of Marxist doctrine, most Americans were unsympathetic to their cries for collectivism and an end to capitalism. Fewer than 1,000 African Americans joined the party in the early 1930s, despite its strong support of civil rights. At first hostile to established politics, the Communists adopted a more cooperative strategy to contain Adolf Hitler when his Nazi party won control of Germany in 1933. The Soviet Union ordered Communist parties in Europe and the United States to join with liberal politicians in a "popular front" against Nazism. Thereafter party membership peaked in the mid-1930s at about 80,000.

The Bonus Army

Hoover sympathized with the discontented, but as the "Bonus Army" learned in the summer of 1932, his compassion had limits. The army, a scruffy collection of World War I veterans, was hungry and looking to cash in the bonus certificates they had received from Congress in 1924 as a reward for wartime service. By the time they reached Washington, D.C., in June 1932, their numbers had swelled to nearly 20,000, the largest protest in the city's history. The House voted to pay them immediately. When the Senate blocked the bonus bill, most veterans left.

About 2,000 stayed to dramatize their plight, camping with their families and parading peaceably. Despite the efforts of the Washington police to evict them, the protesters refused to leave. By the end of July, the president had had enough. He called in the U.S. Army under the command of Chief of Staff General Douglas MacArthur. MacArthur arrived with four troops of saber-brandishing cavalry, six tanks, and a column of infantry with bayonets ready for action. By the time the smoke cleared the next morning, the Bonus marchers had vanished except for 300 wounded veterans.

Though he had intended that the army only assist the police, Hoover accepted responsibility for the action. The sight of unarmed and unemployed veterans under attack by American troops soured most Americans. In Albany, New York, Governor Franklin D. Roosevelt exploded at the president's failure: "There is nothing inside the man but jelly."

The Election of 1932

At their convention in Chicago, Republicans still stuck with Hoover and endorsed his entire Depression program. Democrats countered with Franklin D. Roosevelt, the charismatic New York governor. As a sign of things to come, Roosevelt broke all precedent by flying to Chicago and addressing the delegates in person: "I pledge you, I pledge myself to a new deal for the American people."

Without a national following, Roosevelt zigged and zagged in an effort to appeal to the broadest possible bloc of voters. One minute he attacked Hoover as a "profligate spender" and vowed to balance the budget; the next he called for costly public works and aid to the unemployed. He promised to help business, then spoke vaguely of remembering the "forgotten man" and "distributing wealth and products more equitably." For his part, Hoover denounced Roosevelt's New Deal as a "dangerous departure" from time-honored traditions, one that would destroy American values and institutions and "build a bureaucracy such as we have never seen in our history." None of it mattered. The deepening Depression ensured that virtually any Democratic candidate would defeat Hoover.

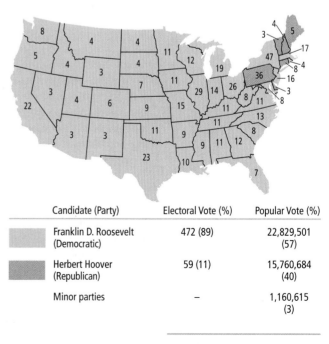

Candidate (Party)	Electoral Vote (%)	Popular Vote (%)
Franklin D. Roosevelt (Democratic)	472 (89)	22,829,501 (57)
Herbert Hoover (Republican)	59 (11)	15,760,684 (40)
Minor parties	–	1,160,615 (3)

Election of 1932

On Election Day, Roosevelt captured a decisive 57 percent of the popular vote and carried with him large Democratic majorities in the Congress. Just as telling as the margin of victory were its sources. Industrial workers in the North, poor farmers in the South and West, immigrants and big-city dwellers everywhere were being galvanized into a broad new coalition. These people had experienced firsthand the savage effects of the boom-and-bust business cycle and wanted change. But they were not radicals and found no appeal in the presidential campaigns of Socialist Norman Thomas or Communist William Z. Foster, both of whom had called for worker ownership of businesses. Instead Depression-era voters turned to Roosevelt and the Democrats, who recognized that in a modern industrial state it was not enough to rally around business and hope that capitalism would right itself. Over 30 years of nearly unbroken Republican rule had come to an end.

The Early New Deal (1933–1935)

On March 4, 1933, as the clocks struck noon, Eleanor Roosevelt wondered if it were possible to "do anything to save America now." One-fourth of the workforce was unemployed. Thirty million families had no means of support. There wasn't enough money in the Treasury to meet the federal payroll.

Eleanor looked at her husband, who had just been sworn in as thirty-second president of the United States. Franklin faced the crowd of over 100,000 as millions more huddled around their radios: "Let me assert my firm belief that the only thing we have to fear is fear itself." Heeding the nation's call for "action, and action now," he promised to exercise "broad Executive power to wage a war against the emergency." The crowd cheered. Eleanor was terrified: "One has the feeling of going it blindly because we're in a tremendous stream, and none of us know where we're going to land."

Recovery, Relief, Reform

The early New Deal unfolded in the spring of 1933 with a chaotic, three-month burst of legislation known as "the Hundred Days." It stressed recovery through planning and cooperation with business. It also furnished relief for the unemployed and began a reform of the economic system. Above all, the early New Deal revived national confidence. With Roosevelt in the White House, most Americans believed that they were in good hands, wherever they landed.

The Democratic Roosevelts

From the moment they entered it in 1933, Franklin and Eleanor—the Democratic Roosevelts—transformed the White House. No more footmen bowing and buglers playing, as they had when Hoover arrived in the dining room to partake of his customary seven-course meal. Instead visitors got fare fit for a boardinghouse. Roosevelt's lunches of hash and a poached egg cost 19 cents. With millions of Americans tightening their belts, the president joined them with a symbolic gesture that made his point of ending business as usual.

Franklin Roosevelt

Such belt-tightening was new to Franklin Roosevelt. Born in 1882 of an old Dutch New York family, he grew up rich and pampered. He idolized his Republican cousin Theodore Roosevelt and mimicked his career, except as a Democrat. Like Theodore, Franklin had graduated from Harvard University (in 1904), won a seat in the New York State legislature (in 1910), secured an appointment as assistant secretary of the navy (in 1913), and ran for the vice presidency (in 1920). Then a disaster all his own struck. On vacation in the summer of 1921, Roosevelt fell ill with poliomyelitis. The disease paralyzed him from the waist down. For the rest of his life, he walked only with the aid of crutches and heavy steel braces. To foster the illusion that he could walk, Roosevelt developed a technique for shifting his weight from one leg to the other as he leaned forward and supported himself on guard rails (as pictured in the photo) or on the sturdy shoulder of an aide.

Roosevelt seems to have emerged from the ordeal with greater patience, deeper conviction, and more empathy for the unfortunates of the world. He won the governorship of New York in 1928. When the Depression struck, he created the first state relief agency in 1931, the Temporary Emergency Relief Administration. Aid to the jobless "must be extended by Government, not as a matter of charity, but as a matter of social duty," he explained. He considered himself a progressive but moved well beyond the cautious use of federal power advocated by most progressives. A conventional budget balancer, he could abandon convention and be bold with sometimes costly social programs. He cared little about economic principles. What he wanted were results. "Take a method and try it," he instructed his staff. "If it fails, try another. But above all try something." Experimentation became a hallmark of the New Deal.

Having followed a political path to the presidency, Roosevelt understood the value of public relations. As president, he held an unequaled number of press conferences (998) and hired the first press secretary. His famous "fireside chats" on radio brought him into American homes. When Roosevelt's reassuring voice came over the airwaves ("My friends, I want to tell you what has been done in the last few days, why it was done, and what the next steps are going to be"), people felt as if he had each of them in mind.

Eleanor Roosevelt redefined what it meant to be First Lady. Never had a president's wife been so visible, so much of a crusader, so cool under fire. She was the first First Lady to hold weekly press conferences. Her column, "My Day," appeared in 135 newspapers, and her twice-weekly broadcasts made her a radio personality rivaling her husband. She became his eyes, ears, and legs, traveling 40,000 miles a year. Secret Service men code-named her "Rover."

Eleanor believed that she was only a spur to her husband. But she was an activist in her own right, as a teacher and social reformer before Franklin became president and afterward as a tireless advocate of the underdog. In the White House, she pressed him to hire more women and minorities. She supported antilynching and anti–poll tax measures when he would not and experimental towns for the homeless. By 1939 more Americans approved of her than of her husband.

Before the election Roosevelt had gathered a group of lawyers and university professors called the "Brains Trust" to advise him on economic policy. Out of their recommendations came the early, or "first," New Deal of government planning, intervention, and experimentation. Brain Trusters disagreed over the means of achieving their goals but shared the broad aims of economic recovery, relief for the unemployed, and sweeping reform to soften the impact of the industrial order and to guard against another depression.

Franklin Roosevelt contracted polio in 1921 and remained paralyzed from the waist down for the rest of his life. Out of respect for his politically motivated wishes, photographers rarely showed him wearing heavy leg braces or sitting in a wheelchair. This photograph, snapped outside his New York City brownstone in September 1933 during his first year as president, is one of the few in which Roosevelt's braces are visible (just below the cuffs of his trousers). Note the wooden ramp constructed especially to help hold him up.

Saving the Banks

Roosevelt launched the New Deal with a record-breaking barrage of legislation in his first hundred days in office. Congress helped to shape the laws, but with an urgency and speed that left even the president feeling "a bit shell-shocked." Government began to dominate economic life so much that conservatives feared the end of capitalism had come, not from the Depression but from the White House. They need not have worried. Roosevelt meant to save capitalism by regulating and reforming it. The banks came first. Without a sound credit structure, there could be no borrowing; without borrowing, no investment; without investment, no recovery.

By the eve of the inauguration, governors in 38 states had temporarily closed their banks to stem the withdrawals of nervous depositors and to stop the failure of so many banks. On March 5, the day after his inauguration, Roosevelt ordered every bank in the country closed for four days (later extended to eight). He called it a "bank holiday." Instead of panicking, Americans acted as if it were a holiday, using homemade currencies called "scrip" and bartering their services. On March 9, the president introduced emergency banking legislation. The House passed the measure, sight unseen, and the Senate endorsed it later in the day. Roosevelt signed it that night.

Emergency Banking Act

According to the Emergency Banking Act, sound banks would reopen immediately with government support. Troubled banks would be handed over to federal "conservators," who would guide them to solvency. On Sunday, March 12, Roosevelt explained what was happening in the first of his fireside chats. When banks reopened the next day, deposits exceeded withdrawals, even though legislation to insure those deposits had yet to be enacted.

To restore confidence in government, Roosevelt pushed through the Economy Act in March 1933, slashing $400 million in veterans' payments and $100 million in salaries from the federal budget. To guard against future stock crashes, financial reforms gave government greater authority to manage the currency and regulate stock transactions. In April 1933, Roosevelt dropped the gold standard and began experimenting with the value of the dollar to boost prices. Later that spring the Glass-Steagall Banking Act restricted speculation by banks and, more important, created federal insurance for bank deposits of up to $2,500. Under the Federal Deposit Insurance Corporation, fewer banks failed for the rest of the decade than in the best year of the 1920s. The Securities Exchange Act (1934) established a new federal agency, the Securities and Exchange Commission, to oversee the stock market.

Federal Deposit Insurance

Relief for the Unemployed

Saving the banks and financial markets meant little if human suffering could not be relieved. Mortgage relief for the millions who had lost their homes came eventually in 1934 in the Home Owners' Loan Act. But to meet the need to alleviate starvation, Congress created the Federal Emergency Relief Administration (FERA) in May 1933. Sitting amid unpacked boxes, gulping coffee and chain-smoking, former social worker Harry Hopkins spent $5 million of a $500 million appropriation in his first two hours on the job. In its two-year existence, FERA furnished more than $1 billion in grants to states, local areas, and private charities.

Work Relief

Hopkins persuaded the president to expand relief with an innovative shift from government giveaways to a work program to see workers through the winter of 1933–1934. Paying someone "to do something socially useful preserves a man's morale," Hopkins argued. The Civil Works Administration (CWA) employed 4 million Americans on projects such as repairing schools, laying sewer pipes, and building roads. Alarmed at the high cost of the program, Roosevelt disbanded the CWA in the spring of 1934. It nonetheless furnished a new weapon against unemployment and an important precedent for future relief programs.

Another work relief program established during Roosevelt's first hundred days proved even more creative. The Civilian Conservation Corps (CCC) was Roosevelt's pet project. It combined his concern for conservation with compassion for youth. The CCC took unmarried 18- to 25-year-olds from relief rolls and sent them into the woods and fields to plant trees, build parks, and fight soil erosion. During its 10 years, the CCC provided 2.5 million young men with jobs (which prompted critics who felt women were being neglected to chant, "Where's the she, she, she?").

Tennessee Valley Authority

New Dealers intended relief programs to last only through the crisis. The Tennessee Valley Authority (TVA)—a massive public works project created in 1933—helped to relieve unemployment but also made a continuing contribution to regional planning. For a decade, planners had dreamed of transforming the flood-ridden basin of the Tennessee River, one of the poorest areas of the country, with a program of regional development and social engineering. The TVA constructed a series of dams along the seven-state basin to control flooding, improve navigation, and generate cheap electric

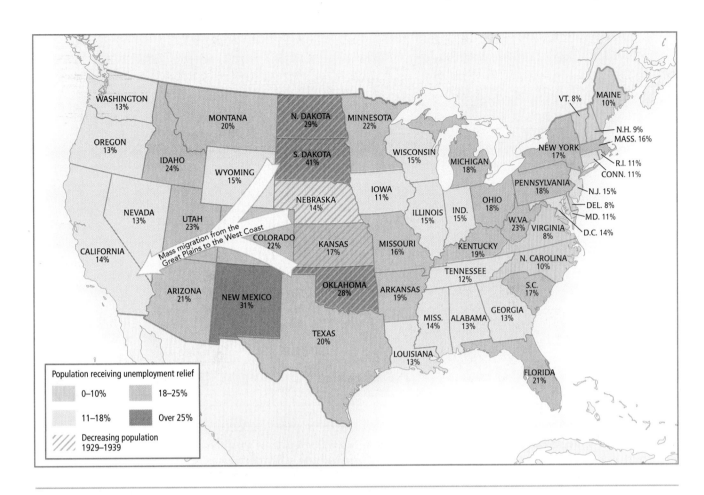

Unemployment Relief, 1934 *The percentage of people receiving unemployment relief differed markedly throughout the nation. The farm belt of the plains was hit especially hard, with 41 percent of South Dakota's citizens receiving federal benefits. In the East, the percentage dropped as low as 8 percent in some states.*

power. In cooperation with state and local officials, it also launched social programs to stamp out malaria, provide library bookmobiles, and create recreational lakes.

Like many New Deal programs, the TVA left a mixed legacy. It saved three million acres from erosion, multiplied the average income in the valley tenfold, and repaid its original investment in federal taxes. Its cheap electricity helped bring down the rates of private utility companies and increase usage. But the experiment in regional planning also pushed thousands of families from their land, failed to end poverty, and created an agency that became one of the worst polluters in the country.

Planning for Industrial Recovery

Planning, not just for regions but for the whole economy, seemed to many New Dealers the key to recovery. Some held that if businesses were allowed to plan and cooperate, the ruthless competition that was driving down the economy might be controlled and the riddle of industrial recovery solved. Business leaders had been urging such a course since 1931. In June 1933, under the National Industrial Recovery Act (NIRA), Roosevelt put planning to work for industry.

The legislation created two new agencies. The Public Works Administration (PWA) was designed to boost consumer purchasing power and industrial activity with a $3.3 billion public works program. The workers it hired would spend their paychecks and stimulate production, while its orders for factory and other goods would send waves of capital rippling through the economy. Harold Ickes, the prickly interior secretary who headed PWA, built the Triborough Bridge and Lincoln Tunnel in New York, the port city of

Public Works
Administration

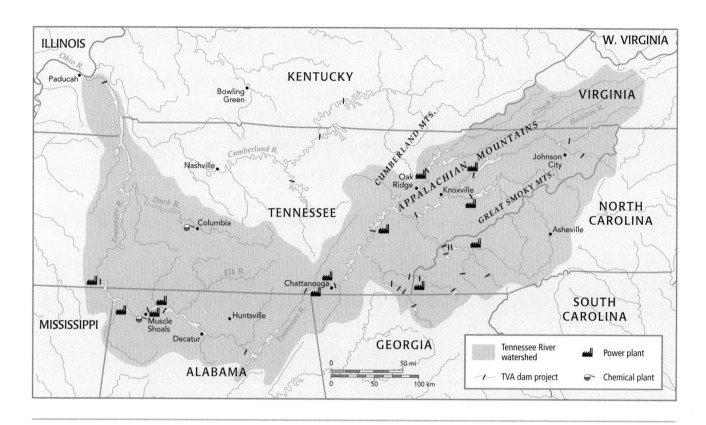

The Tennessee Valley Authority   *The Tennessee River basin encompassed parts of seven states. Rivers honeycombed the area, which received some of the heaviest rainfall in the nation. A longtime dream of Senator George Norris, the Tennessee Valley Authority, created in 1933, constructed some 20 dams and improved 5 others over the next 20 years to control chronic flooding and erosion and to produce cheap hydroelectric power and fertilizers.*

Brownsville, Texas, and two aircraft carriers. But he was so fearful of waste and corruption that he never spent funds quickly enough to jump-start the economy.

National Recovery
Administration

A second federal agency, the National Recovery Administration (NRA), aimed directly at controlling competition. Under NRA chief Hugh Johnson, representatives from government and business (and also from labor and consumer groups) drew up "codes of fair practices." Industry by industry, the codes established minimum prices and wages and maximum hours. They also required business to accept key demands of labor, including union rights to organize and bargain with management (thus ensuring that if prices jumped, so too might wages). Each code promised improvements in working conditions and outlawed such practices as child labor and sweatshops.

No business was forced to comply, for fear that government coercion might be ruled unconstitutional. The NRA relied instead on voluntary participation. A publicity campaign of parades, posters, and massive public pledges exhorted businesses to join the NRA and consumers to buy only NRA-sanctioned products. More than two million employers eventually signed up. In store windows and on merchandise, shiny decals with blue-eagle crests alerted customers that "We Do Our Part."

For all the hoopla, the NRA failed to bring recovery. Big businesses shaped the codes to their advantage. Often they limited production and raised prices, sometimes beyond what they normally might have been. Not all businesses joined, and those that did often found the codes too complicated or costly to follow. The relatively few NRA inspectors had trouble keeping up with all the complaints. Even NRA support for labor faltered, because the agency had no way to enforce the rules granting unions the right to bargain. Business survived under the NRA but did not grow. And without increased production and sales, there was no incentive for expansion, employment, and investment. Under such conditions hard times could last indefinitely.

On May 27, 1935, the Supreme Court struck down the floundering NRA in *Schecter Poultry Corp. v. United States.* The justices unanimously ruled that when the NRA regulated the Schecter brothers' poultry business within the state of New York, it exceeded the power granted the federal government to regulate interstate commerce among the states. Privately Roosevelt was relieved to be rid of the NRA. But he and other New Dealers were plainly shaken by the Court's reasoning. They were relying on federal power to regulate interstate commerce as a means of fighting the Depression. Their distress only grew when Justice Benjamin Cardozo added a chilling afterthought: the NRA's code-making represented "an unconstitutional delegation of legislative power" to the executive branch. Without the ability to make rules and regulations, *all* the executive agencies of the New Deal might flounder.

Schecter Decision

Planning for Agriculture

Like planning for industry, New Deal planning for agriculture relied on private interests—the farmers—to act as the principal planners. Under the Agricultural Adjustment Act of 1933, producers of basic commodities agreed to limit their own production. The government, in turn, paid farmers for not producing, while a tax on millers, cotton ginners, and other processors financed the payments. In theory, production quotas would reduce surpluses, and demand for farm commodities would rise, as would prices. Agriculture would recover.

Agricultural Adjustment Administration

In practice, the Agricultural Adjustment Administration (AAA) did help increase prices. Unlike the code-ridden NRA, the AAA wisely confined coverage to seven major commodities. As a way to push prices even higher, the new Commodity Credit Corporation gave loans to farmers to store their crops rather than to sell them—a revival of the Populists' old subtreasury plan (see page 604). Farm income rose from $5.5 billion in 1932 to $8.7 billion in 1935.

Not all the gains in farm income were due to government actions or were free of problems. The dust storms, droughts, and floods of the mid-1930s helped reduce harvests and push up prices. The AAA, moreover, failed to distribute its benefits equally. Large landowners were in a position to decide which of their fields would be left fallow. In the South this decision frequently meant that big farmers would cut the acreage of tenants and sharecroppers or force them out. Even when big farmers reduced the acreage that they themselves plowed, they could increase yields, because they had the money and equipment to cultivate more intensively.

In 1936 the Supreme Court voided the AAA. In *Butler v. U.S.,* the six-justice majority concluded that the government had no right to regulate agriculture, either by limiting production or by taxing processors. Congress hastily passed a replacement bill, the Soil Conservation and Domestic Allotment Act (1936), which addressed the Court's complaints. Farmers were now subsidized for practicing "conservation"—taking soil-depleting crops off the land—and paid from general revenues instead of a special tax. A second Agricultural Adjustment Act in 1938 returned production quotas.

Other agencies tried to help impoverished farmers. The Farm Credit Administration refinanced about a fifth of all farm mortgages. In 1935 the Resettlement Administration gave marginal farmers a fresh start by moving them to better land. Beginning in 1937 the Farm Security Administration furnished low-interest loans to help tenants buy family farms. In neither case did the rural poor have enough political leverage

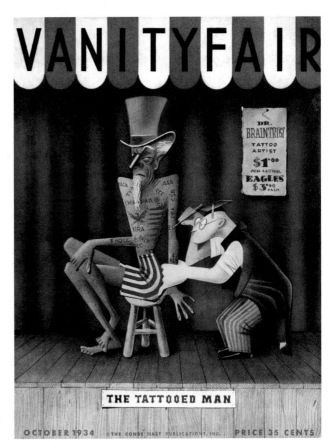

Despite the popularity of the New Deal, there were critics. New federal agencies, designated by their initials, became easy targets of satirists. In this 1934 cartoon, a wincing Uncle Sam receives an unwelcome set of tattoos, each signifying a New Deal agency.

to obtain sufficient funds from Congress. Fewer than 5,000 families (of a projected 500,000) were resettled, and less than 2 percent of tenant farmers received loans.

Here, as elsewhere, the net effect was mixed. New Deal programs did help to stabilize the farm economy and provided an important precedent for future aid to farmers. At the same time, the favoritism shown large farmers promoted large-scale agribusiness or corporate-run farming.

After years of Hoover paralysis, Roosevelt's first hundred days finally broke national despair. The economic depression proved more resistant. Though Roosevelt regarded recovery as his primary goal, the New Deal never achieved it. Conditions improved, but the economy only limped along. Perhaps no one could have solved the riddle of recovery, but Roosevelt tried, and in 1935 he began to address a second riddle: how to reform the system so that the Great Depression did not return.

Recovery in Global Perspective

The Great Depression spread across the globe like a plague (see page 718). In Europe and Asia, the economies of most industrial nations collapsed. But several countries did recover, and more quickly than the United States. By applying some of the same techniques of government planning but spending much more aggressively than did the United States, they were able to solve the riddle of recovery.

In Germany, where the Depression helped to install Adolf Hitler and his Nazi dictatorship in 1933, a bold program of public works—including a system of highways, or *Autobahns,* as well as housing, navigation, and railroad projects—far outspent the New Deal on a per capita basis. The Germans also stimulated economic growth through rearmament, subsidies to farmers and exporters, tax rebates to businesses, and

Cartels   government-sponsored **cartels** that regulated industrial output and prices. By 1936, the German economy had largely recovered and was approaching full employment.

Other industrial powerhouses had different experiences. Often recovery depended on how fast and how much they spent. In Britain, where unemployment was high during the 1920s and the economy listless, a similar program of government subsidies to industry and agriculture and government-sponsored cartels and public works (in this case, to clear slums and to construct low-income housing) helped to jump-start the economy. Unlike Germany, Britain already had unemployment insurance and relief services available, but it greatly expanded them in 1934. By 1937 limited British recovery, aided by booms in private residential construction and consumer goods, was under way. Although the Depression struck France later than either Britain or Germany, by 1935 conditions there were as bad as anywhere. Despite a wave of protests and strikes and a burst of reforms in 1936, no French government had the will, imagination, or staying power to do much. Industrial production remained below 1929 levels throughout the 1930s. Japan, on the other hand, dampened the effects of the Depression by arming itself to the teeth in preparation for expanding into Asia. The Japanese economy actually *grew* each year between 1929 and 1938 at an annual rate of 5 percent, the highest in the world.

A Second New Deal (1935–1936)

"Boys—this is our hour," concluded Harry Hopkins in the spring of 1935. A year earlier voters had broken precedent by returning the party in power to office, giving the Democrats their largest majorities in decades. With the presidential election of 1936 only a year away, Hopkins figured that time was short: "We've got to get everything we want—a works program, social security, wages and hours, everything—now or never."

Hopkins calculated correctly. Swept along by a torrent of protest, Roosevelt and the Congress produced a "second hundred days" of lawmaking and a "Second New Deal." The emphasis shifted from planning and cooperation with business to greater regulation of business, broader relief, and bolder reform to protect Americans against another perilous plummet. A limited welfare state emerged, in which government was finally committed—at least symbolically—to guaranteeing the well-being of needy Americans.

Voices of Protest

Conditions were improving but not quickly enough, and across the country, voices of protest gathered strength. From the right came the charges of some wealthy business executives and conservatives that Roosevelt was an enemy of private property and a dictator in the making. In August 1934 they founded the American Liberty League. Despite spending $1 million in anti–New Deal advertising, the league won little support and only helped to convince the president that cooperation with business was failing. | *Liberty League*

In California discontented voters took over the Democratic party and nominated novelist Upton Sinclair, a Socialist, for governor. Running under the slogan "End Poverty in California," Sinclair proposed to confiscate idle factories and land and permit the unemployed to produce for their own use. Republicans mounted a no-holds-barred counterattack, including fake newsreels depicting Sinclair as a Bolshevik, atheist, and advocate of free love. Sinclair lost the election but won nearly one million votes. | *"End Poverty in California"*

Huey P. Long, the flamboyant senator from Louisiana, had ridden to power on a wave of rural discontent against banks, corporations, and machine politics as usual. | *Huey Long*
As governor of Louisiana, he pushed through reforms regulating utilities, building roads and schools, even distributing free schoolbooks. By turns comical and ruthless, Long used his power to feather his own financial nest, and his private police force was not above kidnapping political opponents. Detractors called him "dictator"; most Louisianans affectionately called him the "Kingfish" after a conniving character in the popular *Amos 'n' Andy* radio show.

Louisiana governor and one-time U.S. senator Huey Long promised to make "every man a king," but critics predicted that only Long would wear the crown. Power-hungry and charismatic, the Kingfish made no secret of his presidential aspirations.

Breaking with Roosevelt in 1933, Long pledged to bring about recovery by making "every man a king." His "Share Our Wealth" proposal was a drastic but simple plan: the government would limit the size of all fortunes and confiscate the rest. Every family would then be guaranteed an annual income of $2,500 and an estate of $5,000, enough to buy a house, an automobile, and a radio. (Long had already built a national following over the airwaves.)

Despite his wild underestimates of the cost of subsidies for the have-nots, Long's Share Our Wealth organization boasted 27,000 clubs by 1935. Democratic National Committee members shuddered at polls showing that Long might capture up to 4 million votes in 1936, enough to put a Republican in the White House. But late in 1935, in the corridors of the Louisiana capitol, Long was shot to death by a disgruntled constituent whose family had been wronged by the Long political machine.

Father Charles Coughlin was Long's urban counterpart. Whereas Long explained the Depression as the result of bloated fortunes, Coughlin blamed the banks. In weekly broadcasts from the Shrine of the Little Flower in suburban Detroit, the Radio Priest told his working-class, largely Catholic audience that international bankers (many of them Jewish, Coughlin also charged) had toppled the world economy by manipulating gold-backed currencies. | *Charles Coughlin*

Across the urban North, 30 to 40 million Americans—the largest audience in the world—sat by their radios to listen. Like Long, Coughlin promised to cure the Depression with simple strokes: nationalizing banks; inflating the currency with silver; spreading work. When Roosevelt refused to adopt Coughlin's schemes, the priest broke with the president. In 1934 Coughlin organized the National Union for Social Justice to pressure both parties. As the election of 1936 approached, the union loomed ominously as a third-party threat.

Francis Townsend

A less ominous challenge came from Dr. Francis Townsend, a recently retired California physician. Moved by the plight of elderly Americans without pensions or medical insurance, Townsend set up Old Age Revolving Pensions, Limited, in 1934. He proposed to have the government pay $200 a month to Americans aged 60 years or older who quit their jobs and spent the money within 30 days. For funding, the government would levy a 2 percent tax on commercial transactions. Thus Townsendites expected to spend more than half the national income to compensate less than one-tenth of the population. By 1936 Townsend clubs counted 3.5 million members, most of them small businesspeople and farmers at or beyond retirement age.

For all their differences, Sinclair, Long, Coughlin, and Townsend struck similar chords. Each proposed simplistic solutions for serious problems: an uneven distribution of goods and wealth, inadequacies in the money supply, the plight of the elderly. Each attacked the growing control of corporations, banks, and government over individuals and communities. And they created mass political movements based on social as well as economic dissatisfaction. When Sinclair supporters pledged to produce for their own use and Long's followers swore to "share our wealth," when Coughlinites damned the "monied interests" and Townsendites thumped their Bibles at foul-ups in Washington, they were all also trying to protect their freedom and their communities from what they saw as the ills and intrusions of big business and big government.

The Second Hundred Days

The 100 days from April through mid-July of 1935, the "second hundred days," produced a legislative barrage that moved the New Deal toward Roosevelt's ultimate destination—"a little to the left of center," where government would permanently seek to soften the impact of industrial excesses, protect the needy, and compensate for the boom-and-bust business cycle.

Works Progress Administration

To help the many Americans who were still jobless, Roosevelt proposed the Emergency Relief Appropriation Act of 1935, with a record of $4.8 billion for relief and employment. Some of the money went to the new National Youth Administration for more than 4.5 million jobs for young people. The lion's share went to the new Works

Unemployment, 1925–1945
Unemployment mushroomed in the wake of the stock market crash of 1929. It did not drop to 1929 levels until American entry into the Second World War in 1941. The yellow bands indicate periods of declining unemployment. Note that unemployment begins to rise in 1945 as the military services begin to stand down, wartime industries begin the slow shift to peacetime production, and returning veterans begin to flood the labor force.

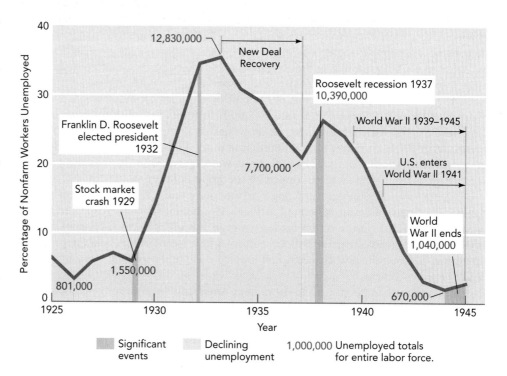

Progress Administration (WPA), where Harry Hopkins mounted the largest work-relief program in history. Because his agency was not permitted to compete with private industry and stressed spending its money on wages, Hopkins showed remarkable ingenuity. WPA workers taught art classes in a Cincinnati mental hospital, drafted a Braille map for the blind in Massachusetts, and pulled a library by packhorse through the hills of Kentucky. Before its end in 1943, the WPA employed at least 8.5 million people, built or improved over 100,000 schools, post offices, and other public buildings, and spent 30 percent of its money on wages.

The ambitious Social Security Act, passed in 1935, sought to help those who could not help themselves—the aged poor, the infirm, dependent children. But Social Security went further, extending the umbrella of protection in the form of pensions for retirees and insurance for those suddenly laid off from their jobs. Equally important, the financial assistance Social Security provided would also act as an economic stabilizer to sustain consumer purchasing power in good times and bad. A payroll tax on both employers and employees underwrote pensions given to retirees over age 65, while an employer-financed system of insurance made possible government payments to unemployed workers.

Social Security

Social Security marked a historic reversal in American political values. A new social contract between the government and the people replaced the gospel of self-help and the older policies of laissez faire. Government acknowledged a broad responsibility to protect the social rights of citizens. The welfare state, foreshadowed in the aid given veterans and their families after the Civil War, was institutionalized, though its coverage was limited. To win the votes of southern congressmen hostile to African Americans, the legislation excluded farm workers and domestic servants, doubtless among the neediest Americans but often black and disproportionately southern.

Congress had whittled down Roosevelt's plan for Social Security, but its labor legislation pushed well beyond the president's paternalistic goals. Roosevelt would have been happy providing moderate aid for workers in the form of pension plans, unemployment insurance, and, later, federal minimum wage standards. But New York senator Robert Wagner, the son of a janitor, wanted to give workers the power to fight their own battles. In 1933 Wagner had included union recognition in the NRA. When the Supreme Court killed the agency in 1935, Wagner introduced what became the National Labor Relations Act. (So important had labor support become to Roosevelt that he gave the bill his belated blessing.) The "Wagner Act" created a National Labor Relations Board (NLRB) to supervise the election of unions and ensure union rights to bargain. Most vital, the NLRB had the power to enforce these policies. By 1941, union membership had doubled.

National Labor Relations Act

Roosevelt responded to the growing hostility of business by turning against the wealthy and powerful in 1935. The popularity of Long's tirades against the rich and Coughlin's against banks sharpened Roosevelt's points of attack. The Revenue Act of 1935 (called the "Wealth Tax Act") threatened to "soak the rich," although Congress's final version of the law levied only moderate taxes on the relatively small number of high incomes and inheritances. To control the powerful banking industry, the Banking Act of 1935 centralized the money market in the Federal Reserve Board. By controlling interest rates and the money supply, government increased its ability to compensate for swings in the economy. Finally, the Public Utilities Holding Company Act (1935) limited the size of widely unpopular utility empires. Long the target of progressive reformers, the giant holding companies produced high profits for speculators and higher prices for consumers. Although Congress diluted the act, as it had the wealth tax, New Dealers could still claim a political victory.

The Election of 1936

In June 1936 Roosevelt traveled to Philadelphia to accept the Democratic nomination for a second term as president. "This generation of Americans has a rendezvous with destiny," he told a crowd of 100,000. Whatever destiny had in store for his generation,

Roosevelt knew that the coming election would turn on a single issue: "It's myself, and people must be either for me or against me."

Roosevelt ignored his Republican opponent, Governor Alfred Landon of Kansas. Despite a bulging war chest of $14 million, Landon lacked luster as well as issues, because he favored so much of the New Deal. For his part Roosevelt turned the election into a contest between haves and have-nots. The forces of "organized money are unanimous in their hate for me," he told a roaring crowd at New York's Madison Square Garden, "and I welcome their hatred." The election returns shocked even experienced observers. Roosevelt won the largest electoral victory ever—523 to 8—and a whopping 60.8 percent of the popular vote. The margin of victory came from those at the bottom of the economic ladder, grateful for help furnished by the New Deal.

Roosevelt Coalition

A dramatic political realignment was now clearly in place, one as important as the Republican rise to power in 1896. No longer did the Democratic Party depend for its strength primarily on the regional support of the "Solid South." Class replaced region as the dominant element in American politics. For the next 30 years, the Democrats would reign as the new majority party. The "Roosevelt coalition" rested on three pillars: traditional Democratic support in the South; citizens in the industrial cities, particularly ethnics and African Americans; and labor, both organized and unorganized. The minority Republicans became the party of big business and small towns.

The American People under the New Deal

Before 1939, farmers in the hill country of Texas spent their evenings in the light of 25-watt kerosene lamps. Their wives washed eight loads of laundry a week, all by hand. Every day the women hauled home 200 gallons of water—about 1,500 pounds—from nearby wells. Farms had no milking machines, no washers, no water heaters, no refrigerators, and no radios. "Living—just living—was a problem," recalled one woman.

Rural Electrification Administration

The reason for this limited life was simple: the hill country had no electricity. Thus no agency of the Roosevelt administration changed the way people lived more dramatically than did the Rural Electrification Administration (REA), created in 1935. At the time, less than 10 percent of American farms had electricity. Six years later, 40 percent did, and by 1950, 90 percent did. The New Deal did not always make such a dramatic impact, and its overall record was mixed. But time and again it changed the lives of ordinary people as government never had before.

The New Deal and Western Water

In September 1936, President Roosevelt pushed a button in Washington, D.C., and sent electricity pulsing westward from the towering Boulder Dam on the Colorado River to cities as far away as Los Angeles. Its generators and turbines were the largest ever installed and could produce four times the electricity of Niagara Falls. The diverted waters irrigated 2.5 million acres, while the dam's floodgates protected millions in southern California, Nevada, and Arizona from the ravages of the Colorado River, the wildest in the West. In its water management programs, the New Deal further extended federal power, literally, across the country.

Stringing TVA electric power lines

The Hoover Dam (begun under the Hoover administration) was one of several multipurpose dams completed under the New Deal in the arid West. The aim was simple: to control whole river systems for regional use. The task, of course, was more complicated, involving strings of dams, channels, and other projects costing billions. The Buchanan Dam on the lower Colorado River, the Bonneville and Grand Coulee dams on the Columbia, and many smaller versions curbed floods, generated cheap electric power, and developed river basins from Texas to Washington State. Beginning in 1938, the All-American Canal diverted the Colorado River to the Imperial Valley in California, 80 miles away, with a 130-mile extension to the Coachella Valley.

Such projects made the Bureau of Reclamation a powerful force in Washington and the West. It oversaw most water development and so provided not only employment for tens of thousands of westerners but also some of the cheapest electricity in the United States. Inexpensive power also helped to attract industry and to free regions, particularly the Pacific Northwest, from their dependence on extractive industries such as logging and mining. It was no wonder, then, that Franklin Roosevelt carried the West in every one of his four presidential elections.

The environmental price for such rewards soon became evident, as it did with the New Deal's experiment in eastern water use, the Tennessee Valley Authority. The once-mighty Columbia River, its surging waters checked by dams, flowed tamely from human-made lake to human-made lake, but without the salmon whose spawning runs were also checked. Blocked by the All-American Canal of its path to the sea, the Colorado River slowly turned salty. By 1950 its water was unfit for drinking or irrigation.

Bureau of Reclamation

The Limited Reach of the New Deal

In the spring of 1939, the Daughters of the American Revolution (DAR) refused to permit the black contralto Marian Anderson to sing at Constitution Hall. Eleanor Roosevelt quit the DAR in protest, and Secretary of the Interior Harold Ickes began looking for another site. On a nippy Easter Sunday, in the shadow of the Lincoln Memorial, Anderson finally stepped to the microphone and sang to a crowd of 7,500. Lincoln himself would not have missed the irony.

In 1932 most African Americans cast their ballots as they had since Reconstruction—for Republicans, the party of Abraham Lincoln and emancipation. But disenchantment with decades of broken Republican promises was spreading, and by 1934 African Americans were voting for Democrats. "Let Jesus lead you and Roosevelt feed you," a black preacher told his congregation on the eve of the 1936 election. When the returns were counted, three of four black voters had cast their ballots for Roosevelt.

African Americans

The New Deal accounted for this voting revolution. Sympathetic but never a champion, Roosevelt regarded African Americans as one of many groups whose interests he brokered. Even that attitude was an improvement. Federal offices had been segregated since Woodrow Wilson's day, and in the 1920s black leaders called Hoover "the man in the lily-White House." Under Roosevelt, racial integration slowly returned to government, whose doors opened a bit wider to African Americans. Supporters of civil rights, such as Eleanor Roosevelt and Secretary of the Interior Ickes, brought economist Robert C. Weaver and other black advisers into the administration. Mary McLeod Bethune, a sharecropper's daughter and founder of Bethune-Cookman College, ran a division of the National Youth Administration. Important as both symbols and activists, African American administrators created a "Black Cabinet" to help design federal policy.

Outside government the Urban League continued to lobby for economic advancement, and the National Association for the Advancement of Colored People pressed to make lynching a federal crime. (Though publicly against lynching and privately in favor of an antilynching bill, Roosevelt refused to make it "must" legislation for fear of losing the powerful white southern members of Congress whom he needed "to save America.") In New York's Harlem, the Reverend John H. Johnson organized the Citizens' League for Fair Play in 1933 to persuade white merchants to hire black clerks. After picketers blocked storefronts, hundreds of African Americans got jobs with Harlem

California's multiethnic workforce is captured in this detail from one of the murals that adorned Coit Tower, built in 1933 on San Francisco's Telegraph Hill. Like other American muralists, John Langley Howard drew on the work of Mexican artists such as Diego Rivera and David Alfaro Siqueiros to paint murals and frescos with political themes. Here Howard shows resolute workers rallying on May Day, an international labor holiday commemorating, among other things, the Haymarket Square Riot of 1886.

retailers and utility companies. Racial tension over employment and housing continued to run high, and in 1935 Harlem exploded in the only race riot of the decade.

Racial discrimination persisted under the New Deal. Black newspapers reported hundreds of cases in which businesses, under the guise of following NRA codes, replaced black workers with white ones or paid black workers lower wages than whites. Disgusted editors renamed the agency "Negroes Ruined Again." New Deal showplaces like the TVA's model town of Norris, Tennessee, and the subsistence homestead village of Arthurdale, West Virginia, were closed to African Americans.

African Americans reaped a few benefits from the New Deal. The WPA hired black workers for almost 20 percent of its jobs, even though African Americans made up less than 10 percent of the population. When it was discovered that the WPA was paying black workers less than whites, Roosevelt issued an executive order to halt the practice. Public Works Administrator Ickes established the first quota system for hiring black Americans. By 1941 the number of African Americans working for the government exceeded their percentage of the population.

Mexican Americans

Civil rights never became a goal of the New Deal, but for the nearly one million Mexican Americans in the United States, Latino culture sometimes frustrated even meager federal efforts to help. Mexican folk traditions of self-help inhibited some from seeking aid; others remained unfamiliar with claim procedures. Still others failed to meet residency requirements, and some feared that applying for aid might lead to deportation, even when they were legal residents. Low voter turnout hampered the political influence of Latinos, and discrimination limited economic advancement. More important, from the Rio Grande Valley in Texas to the Imperial Valley in California, the majority of Mexicans and Mexican Americans served as farm workers, picking and planting for others. As such, they lay beyond most New Deal programs.

On Capitol Hill, Dennis Chavez of New Mexico, the only Mexican American in the Senate, channeled what funds he could into Spanish-speaking communities of the Southwest, but the results of his and other federal efforts were often limited. The CCC and the WPA furnished some jobs for Mexican Americans in the Southwest and California, though fewer of them and for less pay than Anglos received. In southern Colorado, New Deal relief measures alleviated unemployment among Latinos, but the policy of emptying relief rolls just before the beet harvest to avoid competing with the wages offered by local growers only drove wages down. Crafts programs meant to generate income and preserve village life ended up preserving a marginalized, under-paid workforce as well. Federal training programs for midwives helped to bring down high rates of infant mortality but also raised the cost to patients and threatened village control of custom and culture. Like African Americans, most Mexican Americans remained mired in poverty.

Tribal Rights

The New Deal renewed federal interest in the 320,000 Indians living on reservations in Oklahoma, New Mexico, and other western states. Among the most disadvantaged Americans, Indian families rarely earned more than $100 a year. Their infant mortality was the highest in the country; their life expectancy the shortest; their education level—usually no more than five years—the lowest. Their rate of unemployment was three times the national average.

Part of the reason for new attention from Washington was John Collier. In the 1930s, Indians had no stronger friend. For years he had fought to restore tribal lands and culture, first as a social worker among the Pueblos and later as executive secretary of the American Indian Defense Association. Appointed as the new commissioner of the Bureau of Indian Affairs in 1933, Collier hired over 4,000 Indians. By the end of the decade they made up a fourth of all BIA employees. He cleaned out corruption and incompetence from the bureau, placed 77,000 young Indians in the CCC, and built Indian day schools with funds from the Public Works Administration.

The centerpiece of Collier's new program was the Indian Reorganization Act of 1934. It reversed the decades-old policy of assimilation and promoted tribal life. The 200 tribes on reservations, explained Collier, would be "surrounded by the protective guardianship of the federal government and clothed with the authority of the federal government." A special Court of Indian Affairs removed Indians from state jurisdiction.

John Collier's Indian Reorganization Act

In 1937 artist Amy Jones painted life on an Iroquois Indian reservation in the Adirondack Mountains. Indian rates for tuberculosis were high, and a doctor and nurse examine an Indian child for the disease (left side of the painting). On the right, Iroquois women and children weave baskets from wooden splints while Indian workers split logs to be made into splints for baskets. These themes of public health, manual labor, and Indian crafts formed powerful points of emphasis in the New Deal.

Tribal governments ruled reservations. Elders were urged to celebrate festivals, artists to work in native styles, children to learn the old languages. Perhaps most important, tribes regained control over Indian land. Since the Dawes Act of 1887, land had been allotted to individual Indians, who were often forced by poverty to sell to whites. By the end of the 1930s, Indian landholding had increased.

Indians split over Collier's policies. The Pueblos, with a strong communal spirit and already functioning communal societies, favored them. The tribes of Oklahoma and the Great Plains tended to oppose them. Individualism, the profit motive, and an unwillingness to share property with other tribe members fed their resistance. So did age-old suspicion of all government programs. And some Indians genuinely desired assimilation. The Navajos, under the leadership of J. C. Morgan, rejected the Indian Reorganization Act in 1935. Morgan saw tribal government as a step backward.

A New Deal for Women

As the tides of change washed across the country, a new deal for women was unfolding in Washington. The New Deal's welfare agencies offered unprecedented opportunity for social workers, teachers, and other women who had spent their lives helping the downtrodden. They were already experts on social welfare. Several were also friends with professional ties, and together they formed a network of activists in the New Deal promoting women's interests and social reform. Led by Eleanor Roosevelt and labor secretary Frances Perkins, women served on the consumers' advisory board of the NRA, helped to administer the relief program, and won appointments to the Social Security Board.

In growing numbers women became part of the Democratic party machinery. At the 1936 Democratic National Convention 219 women served as delegates while more than 300 stood by as alternates. Social worker Mary W. "Molly" Dewson led the new Women's Division of the Democratic National Committee. It played a critical role in the election. Thousands of women mounted a "mouth-to-mouth" campaign, literally traveling from door to door to drum up support for Roosevelt and other Democrats. When the ballots were finally tallied, women formed an important part of the new Roosevelt coalition.

Federal appointments and party politics broke new ground for women, but in general the New Deal abided by existing social standards. Gender equality, like racial equality, was never high on its agenda. One quarter of all NRA codes permitted women to be paid less than men. WPA wages averaged $2 a day more for men. The New Deal gave relatively few jobs to women, and when it did, the jobs were often in gender-segregated trades such as sewing. The percentage of women hired by the government fell below even that of the private sector.

During the wave of agricultural strikes in California in 1933, Mexican laborers who had been evicted from their homes settled in camps such as this one in Corcoran. The camp held well over 3,000 people, each family provided an old tent or burlap bags to live in. Makeshift streets were named in honor of Mexican towns and heroes. By chance the field had been occupied previously by a Mexican circus, the Circo Azteca, which provided nightly entertainment.

Reflecting old conceptions of reform, New Dealers placed greater emphasis on aiding and protecting women than on employing them. The FERA built 17 camps for homeless women in 11 states. Social Security furnished subsidies to mothers with dependent children, and the WPA established emergency nursery schools (which became the government's first foray into early childhood education). But evenhanded protection for women was lacking. Those domestic servants left out of Social Security, for example, were mostly women.

The Rise of Organized Labor

Although women and minorities discovered that the New Deal had limits to the changes it promoted, a powerful union movement arose in the 1930s by taking full advantage of the new climate. Workers themselves took the lead and ended up pushing Roosevelt further than he wished to go in his support for labor.

At the outset of the Great Depression, most workers were demoralized and languishing. Barely 6 percent belonged to a union. Though the New Deal left farm workers officially outside its coverage, its promise of support encouraged these workers, traditionally among the most unorganized laborers, to act on their own. In California, where large agribusinesses employed migrant laborers to pick vegetables, fruit, and cotton, some 37 strikes involving over 50,000 workers swept the state after Roosevelt took office.

The most famous strike broke out in the cotton fields of the San Joaquin Valley under the auspices of the Cannery and Agricultural Workers Industrial Union (CAWIU). Most of the strikers were Mexican, supported more by a complex network of families, friends, and coworkers than by the weak CAWIU. Before the strike was over, local farmers killed three people, and local officials threatened to cut off all relief aid to strikers and to send them back to Mexico. The government finally stepped in to arbitrate a wage settlement. It ended the strike but at a fraction of the pay the workers had sought.

CAWIU Farm Strike

Such government support was not enough to embolden the cautious American Federation of Labor, the nation's premier union. Historically bound to skilled labor and organized on the basis of craft, it ignored the unskilled workers who by the 1930s made up most of the industrial labor force. And it almost never organized women or black workers. Thus the AFL avoided major industries such as rubber, automobiles, and steel. Because the NRA's regulations gave unions the right to organize and bargain, the AFL increased its membership, but its president, William Green, sought cooperation with management and made no changes in its policies toward the unskilled.

The thundering, barrel-chested John L. Lewis fought to unionize unskilled laborers. Tough, charismatic, practical, and dedicated to organizing all workers, Lewis

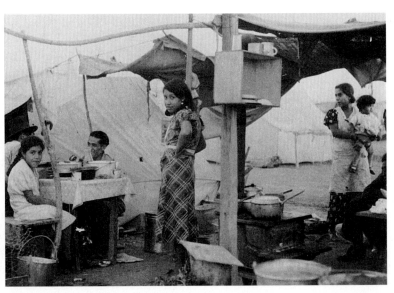

headed the United Mine Workers (UMW), an affiliate of the AFL. He had supported Herbert Hoover in the 1932 presidential election, but when Roosevelt won, Lewis promptly paid a call on the new president to shore up his ties to the White House. He received little more than consolation from Roosevelt for his shrinking union. Yet the shrewd Lewis returned to the coalfields with a message he had never been given: "The president wants you to join a union." Within a year the UMW had 400,000 members. Raising his sights, Lewis called for the creation of a Steel Workers' Organizing Committee and for the admission of the United Auto Workers into the AFL.

At the annual AFL convention in Atlantic City in 1935, Lewis demanded a commitment to the "industrial organization of mass production workers." The delegates, mostly from craft unions, voted down the proposal. Near the end of the convention, as he passed "Big Bill" Hutcheson of the carpenters union, angry words passed between the two. Lewis spun and with a single punch sent Hutcheson sprawling in a bloody heap.

Congress of Industrial Organizations

The blow signaled the determination of industrial unions to break the AFL's domination of organized labor. A few weeks later, Lewis and the heads of seven other AFL unions announced the formation of the Committee for Industrial Organization (CIO). The AFL suspended the rogue unions in 1936. The CIO, later rechristened the Congress of Industrial Organizations, turned to the unskilled and embarked on a series of organizing drives in large-scale, mass-production industries.

Campaigns of the CIO

CIO representatives concentrated on the mighty steel industry, which had clung to the open, or nonunion, shop since 1919. In other industries, militant members of the rank

Men looking through the broken windows of an automobile plant during the wave of sit-down strikes in 1937. The windows were smashed not by the men in this photograph but by women of the newly established "Emergency Brigade" when they heard that the men inside were being gassed. Women played a vital role in supporting the strikes, collecting and distributing food to strikers and their families, setting up a first-aid station, and furnishing day care. Women of the Emergency Brigade wore red tams, armbands with the initials "EB" ("Emergency Brigade"), and political buttons.

"Look in Her Eyes"

Selection and Photographic Evidence

A picture may be worth a thousand words, but to historians it is only the first word. Dorothea Lange took these photographs of destitute pea-picker Florence Thompson and her children at a migrant camp in March 1936. The haunting picture called "Migrant Mother" (below left) has become perhaps the most widely circulated image of the era. "Look in her eyes," ran the caption when the photo was first run. "This woman is watching something happen to America and to herself and her children who are part of America."

Yet even before the days when digital photographs could be easily altered, the taking of photographs—like the writing of text—involved the act of selection. Lange's aim was to capture the suffering of the needy in the worst economic disaster the nation had ever experienced. It was part of a government effort to document the human costs of the Great Depression, along with another aim: to justify the expenditure of federal relief funds.

Lange took at least six photos of the mother and her children. As the alternative on the right demonstrates, some moments were more haunting than others. Note, for example, how the little girl beside her mother smiles into Lange's camera while the older child at the left looks down, seemingly bored with her lot. The moving image of tragedy in the celebrated photo reveals nothing of the possibility of triumph in the little girl's smile moments earlier. To compare Lange's other photos, go to www.loc.gov/rr/print/list/128_migm.html. Does the act of selection necessarily invalidate Lange's message?

and file did not wait. Emboldened by the recent passage of the Wagner Act, a group of rubber workers in Akron, Ohio, simply sat down on the job in early 1936. Because the strikers occupied the plants, managers could not replace them with strikebreakers. Nor could the rubber companies call in the military or police without risk to their property. The leaders of the United Rubber Workers Union opposed the "sit-downs," but when the Goodyear Tire and Rubber Company laid off 70 workers, 1,400 rubber workers struck on their own. An 11-mile picket line sprang up outside. Eventually Goodyear settled by recognizing the union and accepting its demands on wages and hours.

Sit-Down Strikes

The biggest strikes erupted in the automobile industry. A series of spontaneous strikes at General Motors plants in Atlanta, Kansas City, and Cleveland spread to Fisher Body No. 2 in Flint, Michigan, late in December 1936. Singing the unionists' anthem, "Solidarity Forever," workers took over the plant while wives, friends, and fellow union members handed food and clothing through the windows. Local police tried to break up supply lines but were driven off by a hail of nuts, bolts, coffee mugs, and bottles.

In the wake of this "Battle of Running Bulls" (a reference to the retreating police), Governor Frank Murphy finally called out the National Guard, not to arrest but

Could a citizen be properly cultured or "finished" if he lived in "an artless town?" That was the question asked by the postmaster of Pleasant Hill, Missouri, in 1939. Such weighty matters as citizenship and art might have seemed beyond an ordinary postmaster, but he did not think so. Neither did the New Dealers in Washington. They had just made his post office the recipient of a new painting, titled *Back Home: April 1865*. His town, like so many others across America, had been "wholly without objects of art." Now it had one that showed common people at an epic moment in American history, the end of the Civil War. Townsfolk saw it every day, and every day it made them a bit more comfortable with art, more appreciative of the heritage of democracy, more se-cure in the knowledge that the Republic had endured other crises.

The Fine Arts Section (FAS) of the Treasury Department sponsored the

Back Home: April 1865, *presented to the Pleasant Hill, Missouri, post office in 1939, was commissioned by the Fine Arts Section of the Treasury Department as part of its program to democratize American art by adorning public buildings with it.*

to protect strikers. General Motors surrendered in February 1937. Less than a month later U.S. Steel capitulated to the Steel Workers Organizing Committee without a strike. By the end of the year every automobile manufacturer except Henry Ford had negotiated with the UAW. Not until 1941 with the pressure of an impending war did Ford finally recognize the union.

Union Gains

Bloody violence accompanied some drives. On Memorial Day 1937, 10 strikers lost their lives when Chicago police fired on them as they marched peacefully toward the Republic Steel plant. Sit-down strikes often alienated an otherwise sympathetic middle class. (In 1939 the Supreme Court outlawed the tactic.) Yet a momentous transfer of power had nonetheless taken place. By 1940 nearly one worker in three belonged to a union. The unskilled had a powerful voice in the CIO. Membership in the craft unions of the AFL still outnumbered CIO membership by more than a million but women's membership in unions tripled between 1930 and 1940, and African Americans also made gains. Independent unions had become a permanent part of industrial America.

Government played an important but secondary role in the industrial union movement. Roosevelt courted workers, both organized and unorganized, but stood aside in the toughest labor battles. When the CIO tried to unionize the steel industry, the president declared "a plague o' both your houses." Yet doing nothing in favor of strikers was a vast improvement over the active hostility shown by earlier presidents. The Wagner Act afforded laborers an opportunity to organize and protection if they chose to request it. Leaders such as John L. Lewis, Walter Reuther of the United Auto Workers, and Philip Murray of the Steel Workers' Organizing Committee galvanized workers, who won their own victories.

"Art for the Millions"

No agency of the New Deal touched more Americans than Federal One, the bureaucratic umbrella of the WPA's arts program. For the first time, thousands of unemployed artwork for Pleasant Hill. It was only one of the New Deal programs for artists. The largest and most famous, the Works Progress Administration's Federal Art Project (1935–1943), produced 18,000 easel paintings, 17,000 sculptures, and 2,500 murals. It employed thousands of needy artists and placed their work in state and municipal institutions.

The Treasury Department had a similar mission but focused on federal buildings. During its nine-year existence, the FAS hired 850 artists and authorized nearly 1,400 works. Most were for the 1,100 new post offices built during the New Deal.

Post offices were an ideal medium for democratizing art because they were often at the center of town and almost everyone used them. The rectangular brick buildings reflected the solidity, permanence, and service for which government stood.

Unlike the muralist Diego Rivera, whose controversial work had glorified the Mexican Revolution, post office muralists were encouraged to avoid controversy. Artists were rarely permitted to deal with inflammatory subjects such as war, radicalism, or poverty.

In a decade of fear and insecurity, the murals stressed the continuity of past and present. Grand themes were distilled to simple, timeless symbols embodied in everyday experiences: a family enjoying a Sunday picnic, friends picking fruit, skaters gliding across a frozen pond. Family, work, community— these lasting values bound Americans together in good times and saw them through bad.

Regionalism often influenced subject matter. Colonial and urban scenes predominated in New England and the mid-Atlantic states; agriculture and country life in the South; the frontier and Indian and Spanish culture in the West.

The caliber of the murals varied greatly, but in the end they achieved their aim. They reached millions of common folk by combining the ordinary and the aesthetic.

writers, musicians, painters, actors, and photographers went on the federal payroll, and millions of ordinary Americans saw their work. Public projects—from massive murals to tiny guidebooks—would make, as one New Dealer put it, "art for the millions."

A Federal Writers Project (FWP) produced about a thousand publications. Its 81 state, territorial, and city guides were so popular that commercial publishers happily printed them. A Depression-bred interest in American history prompted the FWP to collect folklore, study ethnic groups, and record the reminiscences of former slaves. Meanwhile, the Federal Music Project (FMP) employed some 15,000 out-of-work musicians. For a token charge, Americans could hear the music of Bach and Beethoven or the commissioned compositions of American composers such as Aaron Copland. In the Federal Art Project (FAP), watercolorists and drafters painstakingly prepared the Index of American Design, which offered elaborate illustrations of American material culture, from skillets to cigar-store Indians. At night, artists taught sculpture, painting, clay modeling, and carving in country churches, settlement houses, and schools.

The most notable contribution of the FAP came in the form of murals. Under the influence of Mexican muralists Diego Rivera and José Clemente Orozco, American artists adorned the walls of thousands of airports, post offices, and other government buildings with murals glorifying local life and work. The rare treatment of class conflict later opened the FAP to charges of communist infiltration, but most of the murals stressed the enduring qualities of American life—family, work, community.

Rivera and Orozco

The Federal Theater Project (FTP) reached the greatest number of people—some 30 million—and aroused the most controversy. As its head, Hallie Flanagan made government-supported theater vital, daring, and relevant. Living Newspapers dramatized headlines of the day in play-like form. Under the direction of Orson Welles and John Houseman, an all-black company (one of 16 "Negro Units") set Shakespeare's *Macbeth* in Haiti with voodoo priestesses and African drummers. Occasionally frank depictions of class conflict riled congressional conservatives, and beginning in 1938,

Documentary Realism
the House Un-American Activities Committee investigated the FTP as "a branch of the Communistic organization." A year later Congress slashed its budget and brought government-sponsored theater to an end.

The documentary impulse to record life permeated the arts in the 1930s. Novels such as Erskine Caldwell's *Tobacco Road,* feature films such as John Ford's *The Grapes of Wrath,* and such federally funded documentaries as Pare Lorentz's *The River* stirred the social conscience of the country. New Dealers had practical motives for promoting such documentary realism. They wanted to blunt criticism of New Deal relief measures by showing the depth and dimensions of want. In 1937 Rexford Tugwell established an Information Division in his Resettlement Administration. He put Roy Stryker, his former Columbia University teaching assistant, in charge of its Historical Section. Stryker hired talented photographers to produce an unvarnished record of the Great Depression. Their raw and haunting photographs turned history into both propaganda and art.

The End of the New Deal (1937–1940)

"I see one-third of a nation ill-housed, ill-clad, ill-nourished," the president la-mented in his second inaugural address on January 20, 1937 (the first January inauguration under a new constitutional amendment). Industrial output had doubled since 1932; farm income had almost quadrupled. But full recovery remained elusive. Over 7 million Americans were still out of work. At the height of his popularity, with bulging majorities in Congress, Roosevelt planned to expand the New Deal. Within a year, however, the New Deal was largely over—drowned in a sea of economic and political troubles, some of them Roosevelt's own doing.

Packing the Courts

As Roosevelt's second term began, only the Supreme Court clouded the political horizon. In its first 76 years the Court had invalidated only two acts of Congress. Between 1920 and 1933 it struck down portions of 22 laws. This new judicial activism, spearheaded by a conservative majority, rested on a narrow view of the constitutional powers of Congress and the president. As the New Deal broadened those powers, the Supreme Court let loose a torrent of anti-New Deal decisions.

In 1935 the Court wiped out the NRA on the grounds that manufacturing was not involved in interstate commerce and thus lay beyond federal regulation. In 1936 it canceled the AAA, reducing federal authority that had been formerly justified under the taxing power and the general welfare clause of the Constitution. In *Moorehead v. Tipaldo* (1936) the Court ruled that a New York minimum-wage law was invalid because it interfered with the right of workers to negotiate a contract. A frustrated Roosevelt complained that the Court had thereby created a "'no-man's land,' where no government—State or Federal" could act.

Roosevelt's Plan
Roosevelt was the first president since James Monroe to serve four years without having the opportunity to make a Supreme Court appointment. Among federal judges, Republicans outnumbered Democrats by more than two to one in 1933. Roosevelt intended to redress the balance by adding new judges to the federal bench, including the Supreme Court. Too many judges were "aged or infirm," Roosevelt declared early in February 1937. In the interest of efficiency he proposed to "vitalize" the judiciary with new members. When a 70-year-old judge who had served at least 10 years failed to retire, the president would add another, up to six to the Supreme Court and 44 to the lower federal courts.

Roosevelt badly miscalculated. He unveiled his plan without warning, expecting widespread support. He regarded courts as political, not sacred, institutions and had ample precedent for altering even the Supreme Court. (As recently as 1869 Congress had increased its size to nine.) But most Americans clung to the courts as symbols of stability. Few accepted Roosevelt's efficiency argument, and no one on Capitol Hill, with its share of 70-year-olds, believed that seven decades of life made a person incompetent. Worse still, the proposal ignited conservative-liberal antagonisms within the Democratic party.

In the midst of the controversy, the Court suddenly began to reverse direction. In April 1937, *N.L.R.B. v. Jones and Laughlin Steel Corporation* upheld the Wagner Act by one vote. A month later the justices sustained the Social Security Act as a legitimate exercise of the commerce power. And when Justice Willis Van Devanter, the oldest and most conservative justice, retired later that year, Roosevelt at last made an appointment to the Supreme Court.

With Democrats deserting him, the president abandoned his proposal in favor of a substitute measure that modestly reformed the lower federal courts. Roosevelt claimed victory nonetheless. After all, the Court had finally shifted course (and eventually he appointed nine Supreme Court justices). But victory came at a high price. The momentum of the 1936 election was squandered, the unity of the Democratic party was destroyed, and opponents learned that Roosevelt could be beaten. Perhaps most important, a conservative coalition of Republicans and rural Democrats had joined forces in the first of several anti–New Deal causes.

The Court Reverses Direction

The New Deal at Bay

As early as 1936 Secretary of the Treasury Henry Morgenthau began to plead for fiscal restraint. With productivity rising and unemployment falling, Morgenthau felt that it was time to reduce spending, balance the budget, and let business lead the recovery. "Strip off the bandages, throw away the crutches," he said, and let the economy "stand on its own feet."

Morgenthau was preaching to the converted. Although the president had been willing to run budget deficits in a time of crisis, he was never comfortable with them. To be sure, the British economist John Maynard Keynes had actually recommended the kind of deficit spending that Roosevelt was using. Keynes's startling theory called on government not to balance the budget but to spend its way out of depression. When prosperity returned, Keynes argued, government could pay off its debts through taxes. This deliberate policy of "countercyclical" action (spending in bad times, taxing in good) was designed to compensate for swings in the economy.

John Maynard Keynes

Roosevelt ordered cuts in federal spending early in 1937. He slashed relief rolls by half and virtually halted spending on public works. Within six months, the economy collapsed. Industrial activity plummeted to 1935 levels and unemployment stood at 10.5 million. As the "Roosevelt recession" deepened, spenders convinced the president to propose a $3.75 billion omnibus measure in April 1938. Facing an election, Congress happily reversed relief cuts, quadrupled farm subsidies, and embarked on a new shipbuilding program. The economy revived but never recovered. Keynesian economics was vindicated, though decades would pass before it became widely accepted.

With Roosevelt vulnerable, conservatives in Congress struck. They cut back on public housing programs and minimum wage guarantees in the South. The president, wrote Harold Ickes in August 1938, "is punch drunk from the punishment." Vainly Roosevelt fought back. In the off-year elections of 1938, he tried to purge Democrats who had deserted him but to no avail. The five senators he targeted for defeat all won. Republicans posted gains in the House and Senate and won 13 governorships. Democrats still held majorities in both houses but conservatives had the votes to block new programs. With the economy limping toward recovery, the New Deal passed into history, and the nation turned to a new crisis—a looming war abroad.

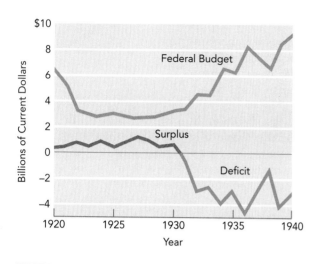

Federal Budget and Surplus/Deficit, 1920–1940 *During the 1920s the federal government ran a modest surplus as spending dropped back sharply after World War I. Deficits grew steadily as Franklin Roosevelt's New Deal spent boldly and as revenues from taxes and tariffs continued to sink. In 1937 federal spending cuts to balance the budget reduced the deficit but brought on a recession that was quickly followed by renewed federal spending and increasing deficits.*

The Legacy of the New Deal

The New Deal lasted only five years, from 1933 to 1938. In many ways it was quite conservative. It left capitalism intact, even strengthened, and it overturned few cultural conventions. Though it pledged itself to the "forgotten" Americans, it failed the neediest among them—sharecroppers, tenant farmers, migrant workers. Even its reforms followed the old progressive formula of softening industrial capitalism by strengthening the state. And it never spent enough to end the Depression.

Yet for all its conservatism and continuities, the New Deal left a legacy of change. Under it, government assumed a broader role in the economy than progressives had ever undertaken. To the progressive goal of regulation was now added the more complicated task of maintaining economic stability—compensating for swings in the business cycle. In its securities and banking regulations, unemployment insurance, and requirements for wages and hours the New Deal created stabilizers to avoid future breakdowns. Bolstering the Federal Reserve system and enhancing control over credit strengthened the means by which government could shape the economy.

Franklin Roosevelt modernized the presidency. He turned the White House into the heart of government, the place where decisions were made. Americans looked to the president to set the public agenda, spread new ideas, initiate legislation, and assume responsibility for the nation. The power of Congress diminished but the scope of government grew. In 1932 there were 605,000 federal employees; by 1939 there were nearly a million (and by 1945, after World War II, some 3.5 million). The many programs of the New Deal—home loans, farm subsidies, bank deposit insurance, relief payments and jobs, pension programs, unemployment insurance, aid to mothers with dependent children, rural electrification, western water management—touched the lives of ordinary Americans, made them more secure, and formed the outlines of the new welfare state.

The welfare state had limits. Most of its relief measures were designed to last no longer than the crisis. Millions fell through even its more nearly permanent safety nets. Yet the commitment to furnishing minimum standards of life, not the failure to do so, marked a change so dramatic that the poor and working class threw their support to Roosevelt. He was, after all, the first president to try.

Under the New Deal, the Democratic party became a mighty force in politics. In a quiet revolution, African Americans came into the party's fold, as did workers and farmers. Political attention shifted to bread-and-butter issues. In 1932 people had argued about Prohibition and European war debts. By 1935 they were debating Social Security, labor relations, tax reform, public housing, and the TVA. With remarkable speed, the New Deal had become a vital part of American life.

The Depression shook both the political and material pillars of democratic culture—even more turbulently around the world than at home. By 1939, on the eve of World War II, the Soviet Union, Germany, and Italy were firmly under the control of dictators bent on expanding both their powers and their nations' territory. The number of European democracies had shrunk from 27 to 10. Latin America was ruled by a variety of dictators and military juntas, little different from the new despots of Europe. China suffered not only from invasion by Japan's militarists but also from the corrupt and ineffectual one-party dictatorship of Chiang Kai-shek.

Almost alone, the New Deal attempted to combat the Depression through the methods of parliamentary democracy. Blending public and private controls, Roosevelt's

What the New Deal Did . . .

	RELIEF	RECOVERY	REFORM
FOR THE FARMER:	Rural Electrification Administration (1936) Farm Security Administration (1937)	Agriculture Adjustment Act (1933)	
FOR THE WORKER:		National Industrial Recovery Act (1933)	National Labor Relations Act (1935) Fair Labor Standards Act (1938)
FOR THE MIDDLE CLASS:	Home Owner's Loan Act (1934)		Revenue ("Wealth Tax") Act (1935) Public Utilities Holding Company Act (1935)
FOR THE NEEDY:	Federal Emergency Relief Act (1933) Civilian Conservation Corp (1933) Civil Works Administration (1933) National Public Housing Act (1937) Emergency Relief Appropriation Act (1935)		
FOR PROTECTION AGAINST FUTURE DEPRESSIONS:			Federal Deposit Insurance Corporation (1933) Securities Exchange Act (1934) Social Security Act (1935)

program humanized industrial society and attempted to generate prosperity without sacrificing capitalism or democracy. And through it all, government—embodied in the leadership of FDR—had taken the lead. New Dealers from the president on down recognized that the federal government could not do everything. But "it bought us time to think," commented Eleanor Roosevelt, in a speech to the National Youth Congress in 1939.

As Eleanor spoke those words, a measure of doubt crept into her voice. "Is it going to be worthwhile?" With the threat of war on the horizon, only future generations would know for certain.

Significant Events

1928   Herbert Hoover elected president

1929   "Great Crash" of stock market ushers in Great Depression

1931   Repatriation of Mexicans; Scottsboro boys arrested in Alabama on charges of rape; New York establishes first state welfare agency, Temporary Emergency Relief Administration

1932   Bonus Army marches on Washington, D.C.; Franklin Roosevelt elected president

1933	Roosevelt inaugurated; black blizzards begin to form Dust Bowl; Hundred Days legislation enacted
1934	Huey Long organizes Share Our Wealth Society to redistribute wealth; Father Charles Coughlin creates National Union for Social Justice
1935	Second Hundred Days legislation enacted; *Schecter Poultry Corporation v. United States* invalidates National Recovery Administration
1936	Congress of Industrial Organization formed to unionize unskilled industrial workers; Roosevelt reelected; United Auto Workers begin sit-down strikes
1937	Roosevelt announces his court-packing plan; war between Japan and China breaks out
1938	Fair Labor Standards Act sets minimum wages and maximum work hours; Orson Welles's radio broadcast of *The War of the Worlds*
1939	Marian Anderson gives concert at Lincoln Memorial; war in Europe breaks out

Chapter Summary

The Great Depression of the 1930s was the longest in the history of the nation; it forced virtually all Americans to live leaner lives and it spawned Franklin Roosevelt's New Deal.

- The Great Depression acted as a great leveler that reduced differences in income and status and left many Americans with an "invisible scar" of shame, self-doubt, and lost confidence.

  —Unemployment and suffering were especially acute among agricultural migrants, African Americans, Latinos, and American Indians.
  —Rates of marriage and birth declined, and many women found themselves working additional hours inside and outside the home to supplement family incomes.
  —Popular culture rallied to reinforce basic tenets of American life: middle-class morality, family, capitalism, and democracy.

- President Herbert Hoover represented a transition from the old, do-nothing policies of the past to the interventionist policies of the future. In the end, his program of voluntary cooperation and limited government activism failed, and in 1932 he lost the presidency to Franklin Roosevelt.

- Roosevelt's New Deal attacked the Great Depression along three broad fronts: recovery for the economy, relief for the needy, and reforms to ward off future depressions.

- The New Deal failed to achieve full recovery but did result in lasting changes:

  —The creation of economic stabilizers such as federal insurance for bank deposits, unemployment assistance, and greater control over money and banking that were designed to compensate for swings in the economy.
  —The establishment of a limited welfare state to provide minimum standards of well-being for all Americans.
  —The revitalization of the Democratic Party and the formation of a powerful new political coalition of labor, urban ethnics, women, African Americans, and the South.
  —The modernization of the presidency.

Additional Reading

The best overall examination of the period encompassing the Great Depression and the Second World War is David M. Kennedy's *Freedom from Fear: The American People in Depression and War, 1929–1945* (1999). For a comparative look at responses to the Great Depression, see John A. Garraty, *The Great Depression* (1987). Robert Sobel, *The Great Bull Market:* *Wall Street in the 1920s* (1968), is a brief, evenhanded study of the stock market and Republican fiscal policies in the 1920s. Caroline Bird, *The Invisible Scar* (1966), remains the most sensitive treatment of the human impact of the Great Depression, but it should not be read without Studs Terkel, *Hard Times: An Oral History of the Great Depression* (1970), and Robert

McElvaine, *The Great Depression: America, 1929–1941* (1984), which are especially good on Depression culture and values. Joan Hoff Wilson, *Herbert Hoover: Forgotten Progressive* (1975), traces Hoover's progressive impulses before and during his presidency.

Frank Freidel, *Franklin D. Roosevelt: A Rendezvous with Destiny* (1990), is the best single-volume biography of Roosevelt, and William Leuchtenburg, *Franklin D. Roosevelt and the New Deal, 1932–1940* (1963), is the best single-volume study of the New Deal. Both fall within the liberal tradition of New Deal scholarship and are admiringly critical of Roosevelt's use of power. They emphasize the limits of political feasibility faced by New Dealers. Jean Edward Smith's *FDR* (2007) offers a positive, if critical, reinterpretation of FDR with greater emphasis on his personal life than found in earlier biographies. For sharp criticism of New Left historians, see Paul Conkin, *The New Deal* (1967). For the bureaucratic constraints faced by the New Deal and the absence of "state capacity," see Theda Skocpol and Kenneth Finegold, "State Capacity and Economic Intervention in the Early New Deal," *Political Science Quarterly* (1982), 255–278. Stephen Lawson's *A Commonwealth of Hope: The New Deal Response to Crisis* (2006) argues that the New Deal was less a makeshift reaction to the Great Depression and more a part of a longer tradition of planning and reform.

Eleanor Roosevelt is analyzed in rich detail and from a frankly feminist viewpoint in Blanche Wiesen Cook, *Eleanor Roosevelt, Volume One, 1884–1993* (1992), and *Eleanor Roosevelt: Volume Two, 1933–1938* (1999). Susan Ware, *Beyond Suffrage: Women and the New Deal* (1981), locates a women's political network within the New Deal, and Harvard Sitkoff, *A New Deal for Blacks* (1978), studies a similar network of blacks and whites and surveys the mixed record of the New Deal for African Americans. The culture and politics of working men and women during the Great Depression are the subject of Lisabeth Cohen, *Making a New Deal: Industrial Workers in Chicago, 1919–1939* (1990), which depicts the erosion of ethnic communities and the acceptance among workers of federal activism and welfare capitalism during the Great Depression. Steve Fraser and Gary Gerstle, eds., *The Rise and Fall of the New Deal Order, 1930–1980* (1989), is an excellent collection of interpretive essays examining the origins, impact, and legacy of the New Deal. For a probing analysis of New Deal liberalism and its retreat from reform, see Alan Brinkley, *The End of Reform: New Deal Liberalism in Recession and War* (1995).

For a fuller list of readings, see the Bibliography at www.mhhe.com/davidsonnation6.

CHAPTER 26
America's Rise to Globalism
1927~1945

"Oh Boy"

John Garcia, a native Hawaiian, worked as a pipe fitter's apprentice at the Pearl Harbor Navy Yard in Honolulu. On Sunday, December 7, 1941, Garcia planned to enjoy a lazy day off. By the time his grandmother rushed in to wake him that morning at eight, he had already missed the worst of it. "The Japanese were bombing Pearl Harbor," he recalled her yelling at him. John listened in disbelief. "I said, 'They're just practicing.'" "No," his grandmother replied. It was real. He catapulted his huge frame from the bed, ran to the front porch, and caught sight of the antiaircraft fire in the sky. "Oh boy" were his only words.

Hopping on his motorcycle, Garcia sped the four miles to the harbor in 10 minutes. "It was a mess," he remembered. The USS *Shaw* was in flames. The battleship *Pennsylvania,* a bomb nesting one deck above the powder and ammunition, was about to blow. When ordered to put out its fires, he refused. "There ain't no way I'm gonna go down there," he told the navy officer. Instead, he spent the rest of the day pulling bodies from the water. There were so many, he lost count. Surveying the wreckage the following morning, he noted that the battleship *Arizona* "was a total washout." So was the *West Virginia*. The *Oklahoma* had "turned turtle, totally upside down." It took two weeks to get all the fires out.

The world had been at war since 1937, but Americans had largely been spared. The surprise attack at Pearl Harbor suddenly transformed the Pacific into an avenue of potential assault. Dennis Keegan, a young college student at the University of San Francisco, could not believe the radio reports on Pearl Harbor. "These places were so far away from us," he remembered. "It just didn't seem possible that we were at war."

All along the West Coast panic spread. That night Keegan drove into downtown San Francisco. Market Street was "bedlam." "The United Artists Theater had a huge marquee with those dancing lights, going on and off," he recalled. "People were throwing everything they could to put those lights out, screaming Blackout! Blackout!" The next day a false army report of 30 Japanese planes flying toward the coast triggered air-raid sirens throughout the city. Los Angeles turned trigger

News of U.S. battleships in flames, from the Japanese surprise attack at Pearl Harbor, sent the nation into global war. The West Virginia, *shown here, settled to the bottom of the harbor with guns firing, but was later repaired and sent into service the Pacific.*

happy. A young police officer named Tom Bradley (who later served as mayor of the city) heard "sirens going off, aircraft guns firing." "Here we are in the middle of the night," he said; "there was no enemy in sight, but somebody thought they saw the enemy." In January 1942 worried officials moved the Rose Bowl from Pasadena, California, to Durham, North Carolina. Though overheated, their fears were not entirely imaginary. Japanese submarines shelled an oil facility near Santa Barbara and Fort Stevens in Oregon. Balloons carrying incendiary devices caused several deaths in Oregon.

Although the Japanese would never invade the mainland, in a world with long-range bombers and submarines no place seemed safe. The global scale of this war was unprecedented. Arrayed against the Axis powers of Germany, Italy, and Japan were the Allies—Great Britain, the Soviet Union, the United States, China, and the Free French. Their armies fought from the Arctic to the southwestern Pacific, in the great cities of Europe and Asia and the small villages of North Africa and Indochina, in malarial jungles and scorching deserts, on six continents and across four oceans. Perhaps as many as 100 million people took up arms; some 40 to 50 million lost their lives.

Tragedy on such a scale taught a generation of Americans that they could no longer isolate themselves from any part of the world, no matter how remote. Manchuria, Ethiopia, and Poland had once seemed far away to many Americans, yet the road to war had led from those distant places to the United States. Retreat into isolation had not cured the worldwide depression or preserved the peace. To avoid other such disasters, the United States eventually assumed a far wider role in managing the world's geopolitical and economic systems.

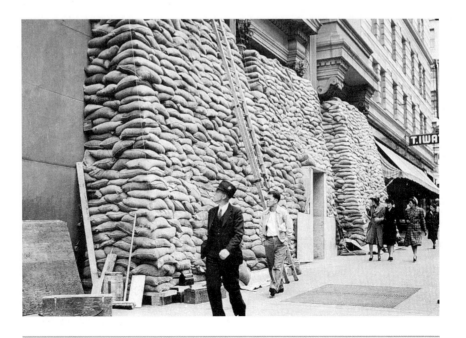

The Japanese attack on Pearl Harbor created a panic along the West Coast of the United States. Hasty defenses such as these sandbags stacked in front of the telephone company in San Francisco were piled high to ward off an attack that never came.

The United States in a Troubled World

The outbreak of World War II had its roots in World War I. So vast was the devastation of the Great War that the victors suffered almost as much as the vanquished. Many of the victorious as well as the defeated nations were deeply dissatisfied with the peace terms adopted at Versailles. Over the next two decades Germany, the Soviet Union, Italy, Poland, and Japan all sought to achieve unilaterally what Allied leaders had denied them at Versailles. In central and eastern Europe rivalry among fascists, communists, and other political factions led to frequent violence and instability. Reparations imposed at Versailles shackled Germany's economy. As Germany struggled to recover, so did all of Europe. Although the United States possessed the resources to ease international tensions, it declined to lead in world affairs. It even rejected membership in the League of Nations.

Pacific Interests

A preference for isolation did not mean the United States could simply ignore events abroad. In assuming colonial control over the Philippines, Americans acquired a major interest in the western Pacific that created a potentially dangerous rivalry with Japan. The United States had also committed itself to an open-door policy (see pages 624–625) to prevent China from being divided up by foreign powers. That temptation seemed especially great during the 1920s, because China was wracked by civil war. In 1927 the Nationalist party, led by Chiang Kai-shek, consolidated power by attacking their former Communist party allies.

The Japanese had long dominated Korea, and during the 1920s they expanded their influence on the Chinese mainland. In 1931 Japanese agents staged an explosion on a rail line in Manchuria (meant to appear as if carried out by Chinese nationalists) that provided Japan with an excuse to occupy the whole province. A year later Japan converted Manchuria into a puppet state called Manchukuo.

Here was a direct threat to the Versailles system and the open door. But neither the major powers in Europe nor the United States was willing to risk a war with Japan over China. President Hoover would allow Secretary of State Henry Stimson only to protest that the United States would refuse to recognize Japan's takeover of Manchuria. The policy of "nonrecognition" became known as the Stimson Doctrine, even though Stimson himself doubted its worth. He was right to be skeptical. Three weeks later Japan's imperial navy shelled the Chinese port city of Shanghai. When the League of Nations condemned Japan in 1933, the Japanese withdrew from the League. The seeds of war in Asia had been sown.

Stimson Doctrine

Becoming a Good Neighbor

Trouble abroad encouraged the United States to improve relations with nations closer to home. By the late 1920s the United States had intervened in Latin America so often that the Roosevelt Corollary (see page 663) had become an embarrassment. Slowly, Washington began to abandon some of its highhanded policies. In 1927, when Mexico confiscated American-owned properties, President Coolidge sent an ambassador, instead of the marines, to settle the dispute. In 1933, when critics compared the American position in Nicaragua to Japan's in Manchuria, Secretary Stimson ordered U.S. troops to withdraw. In those gestures and in President Hoover's efforts to cultivate goodwill south of the border lay the roots of a "Good Neighbor" policy.

Good Neighbor Policy

Franklin Roosevelt pushed the good neighbor idea. To Roosevelt that meant correcting the political inequities between the United States and Latin America. At the seventh Pan-American Conference in 1933, his administration accepted a resolution denying any country "the right to intervene in the internal or external affairs of another." The following year he negotiated a treaty with Cuba that renounced the American right to intervene under the Platt Amendment (see page 663). Henceforth the United States would replace direct military presence with indirect (but still substantial) economic influence.

The Good Neighbor policy made Franklin Roosevelt unusually popular in Latin America, as this sheet music suggests. Roosevelt was the first American president to visit South America, and his diplomacy paid dividends when a largely united Western Hemisphere faced the world crisis.

As the threat of war increased during the 1930s, the United States found a new Latin willingness to cooperate in matters of common defense. In the first visit of an American president to the capital of Argentina, Roosevelt opened the Pan-American Conference in 1936. In a speech he declared that outside aggressors "will find a Hemisphere wholly prepared to consult together for our mutual safety and our mutual good." By the end of 1940 the administration had worked out defense agreements with every Latin American country but Argentina. The United States faced the threat of war with the American hemisphere largely secured.

The Diplomacy of Isolationism

During the 1920s Benito Mussolini had appealed to Italian nationalism and fear of communism to gain power in Italy. Spinning dreams of a new Roman empire, Mussolini em-

The Rise of Fascism

bodied the rising force of fascism. Mussolini's *Fasci di Combattimento,* or fascists, used terrorism and murder to create an "all-embracing" single-party state, outside which "no human or spiritual values can exist, let alone be desirable." Italian fascists rejected the liberal belief in political parties in favor of a glorified nation-state dominated by the middle class, small businesspeople, and small farmers. Then, on March 5, 1933, one day after the inauguration of Franklin Roosevelt, the German legislature gave Adolf Hitler control of Germany. Riding a wave of anticommunism and anti-Semitism, Hitler's Nazi party promised to unite all Germans in a Greater Third Reich that would last a thousand years. Just over a week earlier, Yosuke Matsuoka had led the Japanese out of the League of Nations. Governed by militarists, Japan began to carve out its own empire, which it called the Greater East Asia Co-Prosperity Sphere. The rise of fascism and militarism in Europe and Asia brought the world to war.

As much as Roosevelt wanted the United States to play a leading role in world affairs, the nation proved unwilling to follow. "It's a terrible thing to look over your shoulder when you are trying to lead—and to find no one there," he commented during the mid-1930s. Programs to pull the economy out of the Great Depression gained broad support; efforts to resolve crises abroad provoked controversy.

The reluctance to become involved in foreign affairs received additional support in 1935 after Senator Gerald P. Nye of North Dakota held hearings on the role of bankers and munitions makers in World War I. These **merchants of death,** Nye's committee revealed,

Nye Committee

had made enormous profits during World War I. The Nye Committee report implied, but could not prove, that business interests had even steered the United States into war. "When Americans went into the fray," declared Senator Nye, "they little thought that they were there and fighting to save the skins of American bankers who had bet too boldly on the outcome of the war and had two billions of dollars of loans to the Allies in jeopardy."

Such charges provoked debate over how the United States should respond to the growing threats to peace. Internationalists such as the League of Women Voters and

Internationalists Versus Isolationists

former secretary of state Henry Stimson favored a policy of collective security—working actively with other nations. "The only certain way to keep out of a great war is to prevent war," Stimson declared. "The only hope of preventing war . . . is by the earnest, intelligent, and unselfish cooperation of the nations of the world towards that end."

On the other side stood the **isolationists,** united by their firm opposition to war and the conviction that the United States should avoid alliances with other nations. Yet many strange bedfellows made up the isolationist movement. It included liberal reformers such as George W. Norris and conservatives such as Robert A. Taft of Ohio, a concentration of midwesterners as well as major leaders from both coasts, and a number of Democrats as well as leading Republicans. Pacifists added yet another element to the debate. Powerful groups like the Women's International League for Peace and Freedom insisted that disarmament was the only road to peace.

Neutrality Legislation

Roused by the Nye Committee hearings, Congress debated the Neutrality Act of 1935, which prohibited the sale of arms to all belligerents in time of war. Internationalists protested: the embargo should apply only to aggressor nations. Otherwise, aggressors could strike when they were ready and their victims would be ill prepared. A troubled Roosevelt argued that, without the power to apply the embargo selectively, the Neutrality Act might "drag us into war rather than keeping us out."

The limitations of the Neutrality Act became immediately apparent. In October 1935 Benito Mussolini ordered Italian forces into the North African country of Ethiopia. Against tanks and planes, the troops of Emperor Haile Selassie fought with spears and flintlock rifles. Roosevelt immediately invoked the act in hopes of depriving Italy of war goods. Unfortunately for Roosevelt, Italy needed not arms but oil, steel, and copper— materials not included under the Neutrality Act. When Secretary of State Cordell Hull called for a "moral embargo" on such goods, hard-pressed American businesses shipped them anyway. With no effective opposition from the League of Nations or the United States, Mussolini quickly completed his conquest. In a second Neutrality Act Congress added a ban on loans or credits to belligerents.

Neutrality legislation also benefited Nazi dictator Adolf Hitler. In March 1936 German troops thrust into the demilitarized area west of the Rhine River. This flagrant act violated the Treaty of Versailles. As Hitler shrewdly calculated, Britain and France did nothing, while the League of Nations sputtered out a worthless condemnation. Roosevelt remained aloof. The Soviet Union's lonely call for collective action fell on deaf ears.

Then came a rebellion against Spain's fledgling democracy. In July 1936 Generalissimo Francisco Franco, made bold by Hitler's success, revolted against the newly elected Popular Front government. The civil war that followed became a staging ground for World War II. Hitler and Mussolini sent supplies, weapons, and troops to Franco's Fascists, while the Soviet Union and Mexico aided the left-leaning government. The war divided opinion in Europe and America. Catholics supported the anti-communist

Spanish Civil War

A flag company of Hitler Youth parades past its Führer, *Adolf Hitler (centered in the balcony doorway). Hitler's shrewd use of patriotic and party symbols, mass rallies, and marches exploited the possibilities for mass politics and propaganda.*

Franco forces. Leftists embraced the Loyalists, who backed the democratic government. In the face of domestic political divisions Roosevelt refused to become involved in the conflict. By 1939 the Spanish republic had fallen to Franco.

Cash-and-Carry

For its part, Congress searched for a way to allow American trade to continue (and thus to promote economic recovery at home) without drawing the nation into war itself. Under new "cash-and-carry" provisions in the Neutrality Act of 1937, belligerents could buy supplies other than munitions. But they would have to pay beforehand and carry the supplies on their own ships. If war spread, these terms favored the British, whose navy would ensure that supplies reached England.

Aggression in China

But the policy of cash-and-carry hurt China. In 1937 Japanese forces pushed into its southern regions. In order to give China continued access to American goods, Roosevelt refused to invoke the Neutrality Act, which would have cut off trade with both nations. But Japan had by far a greater volume of trade with the United States. Because the president lacked the freedom to impose a selective embargo, Japan could use American resources to support the invasion.

Inching toward War

With Italy, Germany, and Japan turning into armed camps, war seemed inevitable in both Europe and Asia. The three militant nations signed the Anti-Comintern Pact in 1937. On the face of it, the pact was merely a pledge of mutual support against the Soviet Union. But the Rome-Berlin-Tokyo axis freed those nations for further expansion. Roosevelt groped for a way to contain the Axis powers—these "bandit nations." In his first foreign policy speech in 14 months, he called for an international "quarantine" of aggressor nations. Most newspaper editorials applauded his remarks, yet the American public remained skeptical, and Roosevelt quickly retreated. When Japanese planes sank the American gunboat *Panay* on China's Yangtze River in December, only two months later, he meekly accepted an apology for the unprovoked attack.

Quarantine Speech

Appeasement

In Europe the Nazi menace continued to grow as German troops marched into Austria in 1938, in yet another violation of the Treaty of Versailles. Hitler then insisted that the 3.5 million ethnic Germans in the Sudetenland of Czechoslovakia be brought into the Reich. With Germany threatening to invade Czechoslovakia, the leaders of France and Britain flew to Munich in September 1938, where they struck a deal to appease Hitler. Czechoslovakia would give up the Sudetenland in return for German pledges to seek no more territory in Europe. When British prime minister Neville Chamberlain returned to England, he told cheering crowds that the Munich Pact would bring "peace in our time." Six months later, in open contempt for the European democracies, Hitler took over the remainder of Czechoslovakia. **"Appeasement"** became synonymous with betrayal, weakness, and surrender.

"I believe it is peace in our time," announced Prime Minister Neville Chamberlain, who flourished the agreement he and Hitler signed at Munich, promising to resolve differences peacefully. Hitler overran Czechoslovakia six months later.

Hitler's Invasion

By 1939 Hitler made little secret that he intended to recapture territory lost to Poland after World War I. Russia was the key to his success. If Soviet leader Joseph Stalin joined the Western powers, Hitler might be blocked. But Stalin suspected that the West hoped to turn Hitler against the Soviet Union. On August 24, 1939, the foreign ministers of Russia and Germany signed a nonaggression pact, shocking the rest of the world. The secret protocols of the agreement freed Hitler to invade Poland without having to fight a war with enemies attacking on two fronts. Stalin could extend his western borders by bringing eastern Poland, the Baltic states (Latvia, Estonia, and Lithuania), and parts of Romania and Finland into the Soviet sphere.

On the hot Saturday of September 1, 1939, German tanks and troops surged into Poland. "It's come at last," Roosevelt sighed. "God help us all." Within days France and England declared war on Germany. Stalin quickly moved into eastern Poland, where German and Russian armor took just three weeks to crush the Polish cavalry. As Hitler consolidated his hold on eastern Europe, Stalin invaded Finland.

Germany Begins
World War II

Once spring arrived in 1940, Hitler moved to protect his sea lanes by capturing Denmark and Norway. The French retreated behind their Maginot Line, a steel and concrete fortification at the German border. Undeterred, German panzer divisions supported by air power knifed through Belgium and Holland in a blitzkrieg—a "lightning war." The Low Countries fell in 23 days, giving the Germans a route into France. By May a third of a million British and French troops had been driven back onto the Atlantic beaches of Dunkirk. Only a strenuous rescue effort, staged by the Royal Navy and a flotilla of English pleasure craft, saved them. The way was clear for the Germans to march to Paris.

On June 22, less than six weeks after the German invasion, France capitulated. Hitler insisted that the surrender come in the very railway car in which Germany had submitted in 1918. William Shirer, an American war correspondent standing 50 yards away, watched the dictator through binoculars: "He swiftly snaps his hands on his hips, arches his shoulders, plants his feet wide apart. It is a magnificent gesture of defiance, of burning contempt for this place and all that it has stood for in the twenty-two years since it witnessed the humbling of the German Empire."

Retreat from Isolationism

Now, only Britain stood between Hitler and the United States. If the Nazis defeated the British fleet, the Atlantic Ocean could easily become a gateway to the Americas. Isolationism suddenly seemed dangerous. By the spring of 1940 Roosevelt had abandoned impartiality in favor of outright aid to the Allies. In May he requested funds to motorize the army (it had only 350 tanks) and build 50,000 airplanes a year (fewer than 3,000 existed, most outmoded). Over isolationist protests he soon persuaded Congress to adopt a bill for the first peacetime draft in history.

That summer thousands of German fighter planes and heavy bombers struck targets in England. In the Battle of Britain Hitler and his air chief, Hermann Goering, sought to soften up England for a German invasion from occupied France. Radio reporters relayed graphic descriptions of London in flames and Royal Air Force pilots putting up a heroic defense. Such tales convinced a majority of Americans that the United States should help Britain win the war, though few favored military involvement.

Battle of Britain

In the 1940 election campaign both Roosevelt and his Republican opponent, Wendell Willkie, favored an internationalist course short of war. In defeating Willkie, Roosevelt promised voters that "your boys are not going to be sent into any foreign wars." He portrayed the United States, instead, as "the great arsenal of democracy." Because the British no longer could pay for arms under the provisions of cash-and-carry, Roosevelt proposed a scheme to "lease, lend, or otherwise dispose of" arms and supplies to countries whose defense was vital to the United States. That meant sending supplies to England on the dubious premise that they would be returned when the war ended. Roosevelt likened "lend-lease" to lending a garden hose to a neighbor whose house was on fire. Isolationist senator Robert Taft thought a comparison to "chewing gum" more apt. After a neighbor used it, "you don't want it back." In March 1941 Congress rejected isolationism, passing the Lend-Lease Act by a large majority.

Lend-Lease Aid

By the summer of 1941 the United States and Germany were on the verge of war. American destroyers had begun to escort British ships as far as Iceland (though Roosevelt insisted it was a "patrol," not a convoy). The United States extended its defensive sphere to include Greenland and Iceland. Then Hitler, as audacious as ever, broke his alliance with the Soviet Union by launching a surprise invasion in June 1941. The Allies expected a swift Russian collapse. Soviet armies had fought poorly in the Finnish War, and Stalin in a series of purges three years earlier had executed much of his officer corps.

During World War II, President Franklin Roosevelt and British Prime Minister Winston Churchill developed the closest relationship ever between an American president and the head of another government. These distant cousins shared a sense of the continuities of Anglo-American culture and of the global strategy for pursuing the war to a successful end.

But when the Russians threw up a heroic resistance, Roosevelt extended lend-lease to the Soviet Union.

In August 1941 Roosevelt took a secret voyage to Argentia Bay off the coast of Newfoundland. There he met Britain's new war prime minister, Winston Churchill. Almost every day since England and Germany had gone to war, the two leaders had exchanged phone calls, letters, or cables. The Argentia meetings cemented this friendship—one key to Allied victory. Roosevelt and Churchill also drew up the Atlantic Charter, a statement of principles that the two nations held in common. The charter condemned "Nazi tyranny" and embraced the "Four Freedoms"—freedom of speech and expression, freedom of worship, freedom from want, and freedom from fear. In effect, the Atlantic Charter was an unofficial statement of war aims. It put humanitarian values ahead of narrow interests.

Atlantic Charter

By the time of the Argentia meetings, American destroyers in the North Atlantic were stalking German U-boats and reporting their whereabouts to British commanders. Given the harsh weather and aggressive American policy, incidents were inevitable. In October a U-boat sank the destroyer *Reuben James* with the loss of more than 100 American sailors. That attack increased public support for the Allied cause. Yet as late as September 1941 eight of ten Americans opposed entering the hostilities. Few in the United States suspected that an attack by Japan, not Germany, would bring a unified America into the war.

Disaster in the Pacific

Worried most by the prospect of a German victory in Europe, Roosevelt avoided a showdown with Japan. The navy, the president told his cabinet, had "not got enough ships to go round, and every little episode in the Pacific means fewer ships in the Atlantic." But precisely because American and European attention lay elsewhere, Japan was emboldened to expand militarily into Southeast Asia.

Japanese Expansion

Japanese leaders viewed their sphere of influence—what they called the Greater East Asia Co-Prosperity Sphere—as an Asian version of the Monroe Doctrine. Japan, the preeminent power in the region, would replace the Europeans as a promoter of economic development. To American leaders, however, Japan's actions threatened the policy of

Did FDR Invite War?

Filtering Out the Noise in a Pivotal Historical Moment

Historians constantly attempt to view events from the perspective of the participants in a situation. What were Roosevelt and his intelligence agencies thinking in the days before Pearl Harbor? Researchers have long known that American intelligence at the time had cracked some of Japan's secret code traffic. Among the files of intercepted cables lay information that suggested that Pearl Harbor was at risk. Why, then, did the nation's leaders fail to take the necessary steps to protect against a Japanese attack? Some historians have charged, as did many of Roosevelt's critics, that the president purposely left the fleet at Pearl Harbor unprotected. In that way he invited an attack in order to push the country into war.

Most historians studying the available intelligence have suggested, however, that the problem was too much, not too little, information. Intelligence experts refer to this condition as "noise." With noise, more important signals are hidden in a mass of unimportant ones. The needle is lost in the haystack. Messages captured from the Japanese suggested many potential targets for Japanese attack: the Soviet Union, Dutch and British possessions, as well as the Philippines and Guam. With so many possible targets to consider, spread across the vast Pacific and

New code breaking machines provided vital information from intercepted enemy cables.

Southeast Asia, analysts on the ground assumed that the naval fleet at Pearl Harbor was sufficient to deter any attack there. And, in fact, the Japanese did eventually attack the Dutch and the British possessions as well as the Philippines and Guam— although not until after the attack on Hawaii. By putting aside hindsight—the luxury of knowing what actually happened— historians get a better sense of how the intelligence noise in the months before Pearl Harbor disguised the real threat.

keeping an open door to China and preserving that country's independence. By the summer of 1941 Japanese forces controlled the Chinese coast and all major cities. When its army marched into French Indochina (present-day Vietnam) in July, Japan stood ready to conquer the entire Southeast Asian peninsula and the oil-rich Dutch East Indies.

Roosevelt was forced to act. He embargoed trade, froze Japanese assets in American banks, and barred shipments of vital scrap iron and petroleum. Japanese leaders indicated a willingness to negotiate with the United States, but diplomats from both sides were only going through the motions. The two nations' goals were totally at odds. Japan demanded that its conquests be recognized; the United States insisted that Japan withdraw from China and renounce the alliance it had made with Germany and Italy in 1940. As negotiations sputtered on, the Japanese secretly prepared for an attack on American positions in Guam, the Philippines, and Hawaii.

In late November American intelligence located, and then lost, a Japanese armada in Hitokappu Bay in Japan. Observing strict radio silence, the six carriers and their escorts steamed across the North Pacific toward the American base at Pearl Harbor in Hawaii. On Sunday morning, December 7, 1941, the first wave of Japanese planes roared down on the Pacific Fleet lying at anchor. For more than an hour the Japanese pounded the harbor and nearby airfields. Altogether 19 ships—the heart of the Pacific Fleet—were sunk or battered. Practically all of the 200 American aircraft were damaged or destroyed. Only the aircraft carriers, by chance on maneuvers, escaped the worst naval defeat in American history.

Pearl Harbor

In Washington, Secretary of War Henry Stimson could not believe the news. "My God! This can't be true, this must mean the Philippines." Later that day the Japanese did attack the Philippines, along with Guam, Midway, and British forces in Hong Kong and on the Malay peninsula. On December 8, Franklin Roosevelt told a stunned nation that "yesterday, December 7, 1941," was "a date which will live in infamy." America, the "reluctant belligerent," was in the war at last. Three days later Hitler declared war on the "half Judaized and the other half Negrified" people of the United States. Italy quickly followed suit.

A Global War

Prime Minister Churchill greeted the news of Pearl Harbor with shock but, even more, relief. Great Britain would no longer stand alone in the North Atlantic and the Pacific wars. "We have won the war," he thought, and that night he slept "the sleep of the saved and thankful."

Japan's shocking triumph over U.S. forces united Americans in a way Roosevelt never could. And, as Churchill recognized, only with the Americans fully committed to war could the Allies make full use of the enormous material and human resources of the United States. Still, the Allies needed to secure an alliance between the Anglo-American democracies and the Soviet Communist dictatorship. And they needed to find a strategy to win both the war and the peace to follow.

Strategies for War

Within two weeks, Churchill was in Washington, meeting with Roosevelt to coordinate production schedules for ships, planes, and armaments. The numbers they announced were so large that some critics openly laughed—at first. A year later combined British, Canadian, and American production boards not only met but exceeded the schedules.

Defeat Germany First

Roosevelt and Churchill also planned grand strategy. Outraged by the attack on Pearl Harbor, many Americans thought Japan should be the war's primary target. But the two leaders agreed that Germany posed the greater threat. The Pacific war, they decided, would be fought as a holding action while the Allies concentrated on Europe. In a global war, in which arms and resources had to be allocated carefully, the Allies faced a daunting future indeed.

Gloomy Prospects

By summer's end in 1942 the Allies faced defeat. The Nazis were massed outside the Soviet Union's three major cities—Leningrad, Moscow, and Stalingrad. In North Africa General Erwin Rommel, the famed "Desert Fox," swept into Egypt with his Afrika Korps and stood within striking distance of the Suez Canal—a crucial link to the resources of the British empire. German U-boats in the North Atlantic threatened to break the ocean link between the United States and Britain. U-boat sailors called the first six months of 1942 "the American hunting season" as they sank 400 Allied ships in U.S. territorial waters. So deadly were these "Wolfpacks" that merchant sailors developed a grim humor about sleeping. Those on freighters carrying iron ore slept above decks because the heavily laden ships could sink in less than a minute. On flammable oil tankers, however, sailors closed their doors, undressed, and slept soundly. If a torpedo hit, no one would survive.

U-Boat War

Fall of the Philippines

In the Far East the Allies fared no better. Japanese forces had invaded the Philippines, British Malaya, and the Dutch East Indies. The supposedly impregnable British bastion of Singapore fell in just one week, and at the Battle of Java Sea, the Japanese navy destroyed almost the entire remaining Allied naval force in the western Pacific. In April 1942 General Douglas MacArthur, commander of American forces in the Philippines,

Axis and controlled
areas, Nov. 1942

Allies and controlled
areas, Nov. 1942

Allied supply routes
to Soviet Union

U-boat sinkings:
- Sept. 1939–Dec. 1941
- Dec. 1941–Sept. 1943
- Sept. 1943–May 1945

The U-Boat War *In the world's first truly global war, the need to coordinate and supply troops and matériel became paramount. But as German U-boats took a heavy toll on Allied shipping, it became difficult to deliver American supplies to Europe. Avoiding the North Atlantic route forced an arduous 12,000-mile journey around Africa to the Persian Gulf and then across Iran by land. The elimination of German submarines greatly eased the shipping problem and, as much as any single battle, ensured victory.*

fled to Australia. In what appeared to be an empty pledge, he vowed, "I shall return." Left behind with scant arms and food, American and Philippine troops on Bataan and Corregidor put up a heroic but doomed struggle. By summer no significant Allied forces stood between the Japanese and India or Australia.

The chain of spectacular victories disguised fatal weaknesses within the Axis alliance. Japan and Germany were fighting separate wars, each on two fronts. They never coordinated strategies. Vast armies in China and Russia drained them of both personnel and supplies. Brutal occupation policies made enemies of conquered populations. Axis armies had to use valuable forces to maintain control and move supplies. The Nazis were especially harsh. They launched a major campaign to exterminate Europe's Jews, Slavs, and Gypsies. Resistance movements grew as the victims of Axis aggression fought back. At the war's height 50 countries joined the Allies, who referred to themselves as the United Nations.

A Grand Alliance

Defeat at first obscured the Allies' strengths. Chief among these were the human resources of the Soviet Union and the industrial capacity of the United States. During World War II Americans would develop a global economy. Safe from the fighting, American farms and factories could produce enough food and munitions to supply two separate wars at once. By the end of the war American factories had turned out 300,000 airplanes, 87,000 ships, 400,000 artillery pieces, 102,000 tanks and self-propelled guns, and 47 million tons of ammunition.

The Allies benefited too from exceptional leadership. The "Big Three"—Joseph Stalin, Winston Churchill, and Franklin Roosevelt—all had shortcomings but were able to maintain a unity of purpose that eluded Axis leaders. All three understood the global nature of the war. To a remarkable degree they managed to set aside their differences in pursuit of a common goal—the defeat of Nazi Germany. The staunch anti-Communist Churchill pledged Britain's resources to assist the defense of the world's largest Communist state. The anti-imperialist Roosevelt poured American resources into the war effort of two of Europe's major imperial powers, Britain and France.

The Big Three

To be sure, each nation had its own needs. Russian forces faced 3.5 million Axis troops along a 1,600-mile front in eastern Europe. To ease the pressure on those troops, Stalin repeatedly called on the Allies to open a second front in western Europe. So urgent were his demands that one Allied diplomat remarked that Stalin's foreign minister knew only four words in English: *yes, no,* and *second front*. But Churchill and

World War II in Europe and North Africa   *Coordination of Allied strategy was crucial to victory. Until 1944 Soviet forces engaged the bulk of the Axis armies across a massive front. The battle of Stalingrad prevented Hitler from reinforcing Rommel against the British in North Africa. After winning North Africa, the Allies turned north to knock Italy out of the war. The final key to defeating the Nazis was the invasion of western Europe at Normandy. D-Day would not have been possible had the Allies been unable to use England as a base to gather their forces. Stalin supported D-Day with a spring offensive in eastern Europe.*

Roosevelt felt compelled to turn Stalin down. In August 1942 the western Allies lacked the massive, well-trained force needed for a successful invasion of Europe. Churchill himself flew to Moscow to give Stalin the bad news: no second front in Europe until 1943. Postponed again until mid-1944, the second front became a source of festering Russian discontent.

Operation Torch

Yet, after his initial anger over the postponement, Stalin accepted Churchill's rationale for a substitute action. British and American forces would invade North Africa by the end of 1942. Code-named Operation Torch, the North African campaign could be mounted quickly. Equally important, it could bring British and American troops into direct combat with the Germans and stood an excellent chance of succeeding. Here was an example of how personal contact among the Big Three ensured Allied cooperation. The alliance sometimes bent but never broke.

The Naval War in the Pacific

Despite the decision to concentrate on defeating Germany first, the Allies' earliest successes came in the Pacific. At the Battle of Coral Sea in May 1942 planes from the aircraft carriers *Yorktown* and *Lexington* stopped a large Japanese invading force headed for Port Moresby in New Guinea (see map, page 786). For the first time in history two fleets fought without seeing each other. The age of naval aviation had arrived. The Japanese fleet actually inflicted greater damage but decided to turn back to nurse its wounds. Had they captured Port Moresby, the Japanese could have severed Allied shipping routes to Australia.

Midway

To extend Japan's defenses, Admiral Isoruku Yamamoto ordered the capture of Midway, a small island guarding the approach west of Hawaii. The Americans, in possession of decoded messages, knew the Japanese were coming. On June 3, as the Japanese main fleet bore down on Midway, American aircraft sank four enemy carriers, a cruiser, and three destroyers. The Japanese sank only one American aircraft carrier, the *Yorktown*. More important, the Japanese lost many of their best carrier pilots, who were more difficult to replace than planes. The Battle of Midway broke Japanese naval supremacy in the Pacific. In August 1942 American forces launched their first offensive—on the Solomon Islands, east of New Guinea. With the landing of American marines on the key island of Guadalcanal, the Allies started on the bloody road to Japan and victory.

Turning Points in Europe

By the fall of 1942 the Allies had their first successes in the European war. At El Alamein, 75 miles from the Suez Canal, British forces under General Bernard Montgomery broke through Rommel's lines. Weeks later, the Allies launched Operation Torch, the invasion of North Africa. Under the command of General Dwight D. Eisenhower, Allied forces swept eastward through Morocco and Algeria. They were halted in February 1943 at the Kasserine Pass in Tunisia, but General George S. Patton regrouped them and masterminded an impressive string of victories. By May 1943 Rommel had fled from North Africa, leaving behind 300,000 German troops.

Stalingrad

Success in North Africa provided a stirring complement to the Russian stand at Stalingrad. From August 1942 until February 1943 Axis and Soviet armies threw into battle more than a million troops. In one of the bloodiest engagements in history, each side suffered more casualties than the Americans did during the entire war. When it was over, the Germans had lost an army and their momentum. Stalin's forces went on the offensive, moving south and west through the Ukraine toward Poland and Romania. By the fall of 1942 the Allies had also gained the edge in the war for the Atlantic. Supplies moved easily after antisubmarine forces sank 785 out of the nearly 1,200 U-boats the Germans built.

Those Who Fought

Mobilizing for war brought together Americans from all regions, social classes, and ethnic backgrounds. "The first time I ever heard a New England accent," recalled a midwesterner, "was at Fort Benning. The southerner was an exotic creature to me." More than any other social institution the army acted as a melting pot. It also offered educational opportunities and job skills or suggested the need for them. "I could be a technical sergeant only I haven't had enough school," reported one Navajo soldier in a letter home to New Mexico. "Make my little brother go to school even if you have to lasso him."

In waging the world's first global war, the U.S. armed forces swept millions of Americans into new worlds and new experiences. When Pearl Harbor came, the army had 1.6 million men in uniform. By 1945 it had more than 7 million; the navy,

Many young GIs at first looked forward to going into battle. "I was going to gain my manhood," recalled one soldier. But combat soon hardened such troops. Donald Dickson's portrait of one such war-weary GI is titled Too Many, Too Close, Too Long.

3.9 million; the army air corps, 2.3 million; and the marines, 600,000. Nineteen-year-olds who had never left home found themselves swept off to Europe or to the South Pacific. At basic training new recruits were subjected to forms of regimentation—the army haircut, foul-mouthed drill sergeants, and barracks life—they had seldom experienced in other areas of America's democratic culture.

In this war, as in most wars, the infantry bore the brunt of the fighting and dying. They suffered 90 percent of the battlefield casualties. In all, almost 400,000 Americans died and more than 600,000 were wounded. But service in the military did not mean constant combat. Most battles were reasonably short, followed by long periods of waiting and preparation. The army used almost 2 million soldiers just to move supplies. Yet even during the lull in battle, the soldiers' biggest enemy, disease, stalked them: malaria, dysentery, typhus, and even plague. In the Pacific theater, the thermometer sometimes rose to over 110 degrees Fahrenheit.

Wherever they fought, American soldiers usually lived in foxholes dug by hand with small shovels. Whenever possible they turned a hole in the ground into a home. "The American soldier is a born housewife," observed war correspondent Ernie Pyle. Between battles, movies were about the only entertainment many troops had. Each film was a tenuous link to a more comfortable world at home, a place American soldiers yearned for with special intensity. It was not a country or an idea for which they fought so much as a set of memories—a house, a car, Mom and Pop.

Minorities at War

African Americans

Minorities enlisted in unusually large numbers because the services offered training and opportunities unavailable in civilian life. Still, prejudice against African Americans and other minorities remained high. The army was strictly segregated and generally assigned black soldiers to noncombatant roles. The navy accepted them only as cooks and servants. At first the air corps and marines would not take them at all. The American Red Cross even kept "black" and "white" blood plasma separated, as if there were a difference. (Ironically, a black physician, Charles Drew, had invented the process allowing plasma to be stored.)

Despite the persistence of prejudice, more than a million black men and women served. As the war progressed, leaders of the black community pressured the military to ease segregation and allow black soldiers a more active role. The army did form some black combat units, usually led by white officers, as well as a black air corps unit. By mid-1942 black officers were being trained and graduated from integrated officer candidate schools at the rate of 200 a month. More than 80 black pilots won the Distinguished Flying Cross.

For both Mexican Americans and Asian Americans the war offered an opportunity to enter the American mainstream. Putting on a uniform was an essential act of citizenship. Mexican Americans had a higher enlistment rate than the population in general. A California congressional representative observed that "as I read the casualty list from my state, I find that anywhere from one-fourth to one-third of these names are names such as Gonzales and Sanchez." Chinese Americans served at the highest rate of all groups. As Harold Liu of New York's Chinatown recalled, "for the first time Chinese were accepted as being friends. . . . All of a sudden we became part of an American dream." Korean Americans were especially valuable in the Pacific theater because many could translate Japanese.

Like other Asian Americans, Filipinos had a powerful reason to enlist. Service offered an opportunity to fight for the liberation of their homeland from Japanese invaders. And, like other minorities, Filipino Americans realized that in fighting for freedom abroad they were fighting for freedom at home. A Filipino soldier commented that he was doing something he had never before been allowed to do: serve "as an equal with American boys." Such loyalty had its rewards. Filipinos who volunteered became citizens. The California attorney general reinterpreted laws that had once prevented Filipinos from owning land. Now they could buy their own farms. Jobs opened in war factories. The status of other Asian Americans and Mexican Americans improved in similar ways. Minorities who served gained useful experience in dealing with the Anglo world.

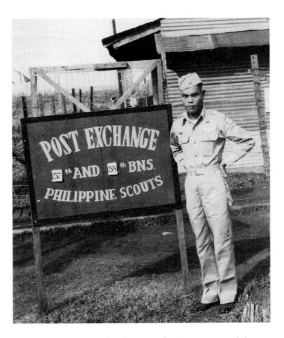

In the face of Japanese occupation, many Filipinos actively supported the American war effort. Valentine Untalan survived capture by the Japanese and went on to serve in the American army's elite Philippine Scouts. Like a growing number of Filipinos, he moved to the United States after the war ended.

After the war, minority veterans would provide new leadership in their communities.

Homosexuals who wished to join the military faced a dilemma. Few Americans of the day had any knowledge of gays in their midst, and fewer had much tolerance for homosexuality. Still, many gays risked exposure. Charles Rowland, from Arizona, recalled that he and other gay friends "were not about to be deprived the privilege of serving our country in a time of great national emergency by virtue of some stupid regulation about being gay." Homosexuals who did pass the screening test found themselves in gender-segregated bases, where life in an overwhelmingly male or female environment allowed many, for the first time in their lives, to meet like-minded gay men and women. Like other servicemen and -women, they served in a host of roles, fighting and dying on the battlefield or doing the unglamorous jobs that kept the army going.

Choices for Homosexuals

Women at War

World War II brought an end to the military as an exclusive male enclave that women entered only as nurses. During the prewar mobilization, Eleanor Roosevelt and other female leaders had campaigned for a regular military organization for women. The War Department came up with a compromise that allowed women to join the Women's Army Auxiliary Corps (WAAC), but only with inferior status and lower pay. By 1943 the "Auxiliary" had dropped out of the title: WAACs became WACs, with full army status, equal ranks, and equal pay. (The navy had a similar force called the WAVEs.)

WACs

Women could look with a mixture of pride and resentment on their wartime military service. Thousands served close to the battlefields, working as technicians, mechanics, radio operators, postal clerks, and secretaries. Although filling a vital need, these jobs were largely traditional female ones that implied a separate and inferior status. Until 1944 women were prevented by law from serving in war zones, even as noncombatants. There were female pilots, but they were restricted to shuttling planes behind the lines. At many posts WAVEs and WACs lived behind barbed wire and could move about only in groups under armed escort.

War Production

When Pearl Harbor brought the United States into the war, Thomas Chinn sold his publishing business and devoted himself full-time to war work. Like many other Chinese Americans, he was working for the first time outside Chinatown. He served

To fight inflation, the Office of Price Administration (OPA) imposed rationing on products in short supply. Consumers received coupons to trade for goods such as meat, shoes, and gasoline. The program was one of the most unpopular of the war.

West Coast War Industries

as a supervisor in the Army Quartermaster Market Center, which was responsible for supplying the armed forces with fresh food as it was harvested across California. Chinn found himself coordinating a host of cold storage warehouses all the way from the Oregon border as far south as Fresno. "At times," he recalled, "in order to catch seasonal goods such as fresh vegetables, as many as 200 or 300 railroad cars would be shuttling in and out" of the warehouses.

Food production and distribution were only two of the many areas that demanded attention from the government. After Pearl Harbor, steel, aluminum, and electric power were all in short supply, creating bottlenecks in production lines. Roosevelt recognized the need for more direct government control of the economy.

Although the conversion from peace to war came slowly at first, the president used a mix of compulsory and voluntary programs to control inflation and guarantee an ever-increasing supply of food, munitions, and equipment. In the end the United States worked a miracle of production that proved every bit as important to victory as any battle fought overseas.

Finding an Industrial Czar

Roosevelt's first attempt at coordinating the production effort was to set up a War Production Board (WPB) under the direction of former Sears, Roebuck president Donald M. Nelson. On paper, Nelson's powers were impressive. The WPB had authority to allocate resources and organize factories in whatever way promoted national defense. In one of its first acts, the WPB ordered an end to all civilian car and truck production. The American people would have no new cars until the war ended.

In practice, Nelson was hindered by other federal agencies with their own czars in control of petroleum, rubber, and labor resources. To end the bottlenecks once and for all, the president in 1943 installed Supreme Court Justice James F. Byrnes as director of the new Office of War Mobilization (OWM). A canny political facilitator, Byrnes became the dictator the economy needed. By assuming control over vital materials such as steel, aluminum, and copper, the OWM made the bottlenecks disappear. Such centralized planning helped ease the conversion to war production of industries both large and small. While the "Big Three" automakers—Ford, General Motors, and Chrysler—generated some 20 percent of all war goods, small business also played a vital role. A manufacturer of model trains, for example, made bomb fuses.

The aircraft industry transformed the industrial landscape of the West Coast. When production of aircraft factories peaked in 1944, the industry had 2.1 million workers. Most of the new factories were located around Los Angeles, San Diego, and Seattle, where large labor pools, temperate climates, and available land made the locations attractive. The demand for workers opened opportunities for many Asian workers who had been limited to jobs within their own ethnic communities. By 1943, 15 percent of all shipyard workers around San Francisco Bay were Chinese.

As the military relied on large, established firms to turn out planes, ships, and tanks, big corporations increased their dominance over the American economy. Workers in companies with more than 10,000 employees amounted to just 13 percent of the workforce in 1939; by 1944 they made up more than 30 percent. In agriculture a similar move toward bigness occurred, as small farms were consolidated into larger ones. Large commercial farming by corporations rather than individuals (later called "agribusiness") came to dominate agriculture.

Productivity increased for a less tangible but equally important reason: pride in work done for a common cause. Civilians volunteered for civil defense, hospitals, and countless scrap drives. Children became "Uncle Sam's Scrappers" and "Tin-Can

Colonels" as they scoured vacant lots for valuable trash. One teenager in Maywood, Illinois, collected more than 100 tons of paper between Pearl Harbor and D-Day. Backyard "victory" gardens added 8 million tons of food to the harvest in 1943; car pooling conserved millions of tires. Morale ran high because people believed that every contribution, no matter how small, helped defeat the Axis.

Science Goes to War

The striking success of aircraft against ships at Coral Sea and Midway demonstrated how science and technology changed the way war was fought. The air war in Europe spurred the development of a new generation of fighter planes and bombers that could fly faster and farther while carrying more firepower. To combat enemy bombers and submarines, English and American scientists rushed to perfect electronic detection devices such as radar and sonar.

Without sonar the Allies might never have won the submarine war in the North Atlantic. At the same time, improved American submarines crippled Japanese shipping in the western Pacific. By 1944 the home islands faced serious shortages of vital raw materials. Above the water, the newly developed techniques of radar-controlled naval and antiaircraft gunnery gave American ships a decided edge in crucial sea battles. It became possible to hit targets obscured by darkness, fog, or smoke. One of the most critical technical advances was also one of the best kept secrets of the war, the proximity fuse. By placing a small radio device in a warhead, scientists created a shell that did not need to hit a target to destroy it. Proximity fuses accounted for the success of American antiaircraft guns against Japanese planes and German V-1 bombs.

Scientific advances saved lives as well as destroying them. Insecticides, pesticides, and drugs limited the spread of infectious diseases like malaria and syphilis. Penicillin had its first widespread use in World War II. The health of the nation actually improved during the war. Life expectancy rose by three years overall and by five years for African Americans. Infant mortality was cut by more than a third, and in 1942 the nation recorded its lowest death rate in history. Still, such discoveries sometimes had unforeseen consequences. Although the pesticide DDT helped control malaria and other insect-borne diseases, its harmful effects on the environment became clear only years later.

Scientific Advances

Science made its most dramatic advances in atomic research. In 1938 German scientists discovered the process of **fission,** in which atoms of uranium-235 were split, releasing an enormous amount of energy. Leading European physicists who had come to America to escape the Nazis understood all too well the military potential of the German discovery. In 1939 Enrico Fermi, Albert Einstein, and Leo Szilard warned President Roosevelt "that extremely powerful bombs of a new type may thus be constructed."

Roosevelt initiated what became the largest research and development effort in history, code-named the Manhattan Project. More than 100,000 scientists, engineers, technicians, and support workers from the United States, Canada, and England worked at 37 installations across the country to build an atomic bomb. Yet, even with $2 billion in funding, scientists feared they might not build a bomb before the Germans did.

The Manhattan Project

War Work and Prosperity

Not only did war production end the depression, it revived prosperity. As late as 1940 unemployment stood at almost 7 million. By 1944, it had virtually disappeared. Jeff Davies, president of Hoboes of America, reported in 1942 that 2 million of his members were "off the road." Employers, eager to overcome the labor shortage, welcomed disabled workers. The hearing-impaired found jobs in deafening factories; very short people became aircraft inspectors because they could crawl inside wings and other cramped spaces. By the summer of 1943 nearly 3 million children aged 12 to 17 were working.

Tax Reform

Roosevelt had to find some means to pay the war's enormous cost without undermining prosperity. His approach mixed both conservative and liberal elements. The Treasury Department raised money voluntarily, by selling war bonds through advertising campaigns. To raise more funds, Secretary of the Treasury Henry Morgenthau proposed a tax structure that was highly progressive—that is, it taxed higher income at a higher rate. Conservatives in Congress balked at sweeping tax reforms. After six months of wrangling, Congress passed a compromise, the Revenue Act of 1942, which levied a flat 5 percent tax on all annual incomes over $624. That provision struck hardest at low-income workers: in 1942 almost 50 million citizens paid taxes compared with 13 million the year before.

Organized Labor

Wartime prosperity did not end the tug-of-war between business and labor. In 1941 alone more than 2 million workers walked off their jobs in protest over wages and working conditions. To end labor strife Roosevelt established the War Labor Board (WLB) in 1942. Like the agency Woodrow Wilson had created during World War I, the new WLB had authority to impose arbitration in any labor dispute. Its most far-reaching decision established a compromise between employers and unions that gave workers 15 days to leave the union after a contract was signed. Any worker who remained a member had to pay union dues for the life of the contract. That policy led to an almost 40 percent growth in union membership between 1941 and 1945, when a record 14.75 million workers held union cards.

Despite the efforts of the WLB, strikes did occur. Dissatisfied railroad workers tied up rail lines in a wildcat strike in 1943. General George C. Marshall cursed it as the "damnedest crime ever committed against America." To break the impasse, the government seized the railroads and then granted wage increases. That same year the pugnacious John L. Lewis allowed his United Mine Workers to go on strike. "The coal miners of America are hungry," he charged. "They are ill-fed and undernourished." Roosevelt seized the mines and ran them for a time; he even considered arresting union leaders and drafting striking miners. But as Secretary of the Interior Harold Ickes noted, a "jailed miner produces no more coal than a striking miner." In the end the government negotiated a settlement that gave miners substantial new benefits.

Most Americans were unwilling to forgive Lewis or his miners. A huge coal shortage along the East Coast had left homes dark and cold. "John L. Lewis—Damn your coal black soul," wrote the military newspaper *Stars and Stripes*. In reaction, Congress easily passed the Smith-Connally Act of 1943. It gave the president more authority to seize vital war plants shut by strikes and required union leaders to observe a 30-day "cooling-off" period before striking. Roosevelt vetoed the bill, only to be overridden in both houses.

Despite these incidents, workers remained dedicated to the war effort. Stoppages actually accounted for only about one-tenth of one percent of total work time during the war. When workers did strike, it was usually in defiance of their union leadership, and they left their jobs for just a few days.

In other ways, however, the workforce was transformed by the turmoil of war. In the years after Pearl Harbor, over 15 million civilians changed their addresses. "The war dispersed the reservation people as nothing ever had," recalled Vine DeLoria, an Indian activist. "Every day, it seemed, we would be bidding farewell to families as they headed west to work in defense plants on the coast." So many African Americans left the South that cotton growers began to buy mechanical harvesters to replace their labor. So many Appalachian hill people traveled back and forth from Kentucky to Detroit that the bus company added an express service. Western states that had deported Mexican workers during the Depression now welcomed a contract labor program set up by the Department of Agriculture, which brought in several hundred thousand *braceros,* or farm laborers. Their labor was vital to the war effort.

War Labor Board

Lewis Leads a Coal Strike

John L. Lewis

Women Workers

With as many as 12 million men in uniform, women (especially married women) became the nation's largest untapped source of labor. During the high-unemployment years of the Depression, both government and business had discouraged women from competing with men for jobs. Now, suddenly, magazines and government bulletins began trumpeting "the vast resource of womanpower." The percentage of female workers grew from around a quarter in 1940 to more than a third by 1945. These women were no longer mostly young and single, as female workers of the past had been. A majority were either married or between 55 and 64 years old.

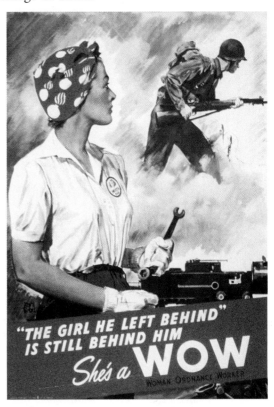

Womanpower Fills
the Labor Shortage

Beyond patriotism, many women preferred the relative freedom of work and wages to the confines of home. With husbands off at war, millions of women needed additional income and had more free time. Black women in particular realized dramatic gains. Once concentrated in low-paying domestic and farm jobs with erratic hours and tedious labor, some 300,000 rushed into factories that offered higher pay and more regular hours. Given the chance to learn skills like welding, aircraft assembly, and electronics, women shattered many stereotypes about their capabilities. The diary of a ship welder in Oregon recorded both amazement and pride at what she accomplished:

> I, who hates heights, climbed stair after stair after stair till I thought I must be close to the sun. I stopped on the [tanker's] top deck. I, who hate confined spaces, went through narrow corridors, stumbling my way over rubber-coated leads. . . . I welded in the poop deck lying on the floor while another welder spattered sparks from the ceiling and chippers like giant woodpeckers shattered our eardrums. . . . I did overhead welding, horizontal, flat, vertical. . . . I made some good welds and some frightful ones. But now a door in the poop deck of an oil tanker is hanging, four feet by six of solid steel, by my welds. Pretty exciting!

*Patriotic appeals encouraged
women to join the labor force.*

Although the demand for labor improved the economic status of women, it did not alter conventional views about gender roles. Most Americans assumed that when the war ended, veterans would pick up their old jobs and women would return to the home. The birthrate, which had fallen during the Depression, began to rise in 1943 as prosperity returned. And other traditional barriers continued to limit women's opportunities, even in wartime. As women flooded into government bureaucracies, factory production lines, and corporate offices, few became managers. Supervision remained men's work. In short, the war inspired a change in economic roles for women without fomenting a revolution in attitudes about gender. That would come later.

A Question of Rights

Franklin Roosevelt had been a government official during World War I. Now, presiding over a bigger world war, he was determined to avoid many of the patriotic excesses he had witnessed then: mobs menacing immigrants, the patriotic appeals to spy on neighbors, the raids on pacifist radicals. Even so, the conflicts arising over race, ethnic background, and class differences could not be avoided. In a society in which immigration laws discriminated against Asians by race, the war with Japan made life difficult for loyal Asian Americans of all backgrounds. Black and Latino workers faced as much discrimination in shipyards and airplane factories as they had in peacetime industries.

Little Italy

Aliens from enemy countries fared far better in World War II than in World War I. When the war began, about 600,000 Italian aliens and 5 million Italian Americans lived in the United States. Most still resided in Italian neighborhoods centered around churches, fraternal organizations, and clubs. Some had been proud of Mussolini and supported *fascismo*. "Mussolini was a hero," recalled one Italian American. "A superhero. He made us feel special." Those attitudes changed abruptly after Pearl Harbor. During the war, Italian Americans pledged their loyalties to the United States.

At first the government treated Italians without citizenship (along with Japanese and Germans) as "aliens of enemy nationality." They could not travel without permission, enter strategic areas, or possess shortwave radios, guns, or maps. By 1942 few Americans believed that German Americans or Italian Americans posed any real danger. Eager to keep the support of Italian voters in the 1942 congressional elections, Roosevelt chose Columbus Day 1942 to lift restrictions on Italian aliens.

Concentration Camps

Americans showed no such tolerance to the 127,000 Japanese living in the United States, whether they were aliens or citizens. Ironically, tensions were least high in Hawaii, where the war with Japan had begun. Local newspapers there expressed confidence in the loyalty of Japanese Americans, who in any case were crucial to Hawaii's economy.

On the mainland, Japanese Americans remained largely separated from the mainstream of American life. State laws and local custom threw up complex barriers to integration. In the western states, where they were concentrated around urban areas, most Japanese could not vote, own land, or live in decent neighborhoods. Approximately 47,000 Japanese aliens, known as **Issei,** were ineligible for citizenship under American law. Only their children could become citizens. Despite such restrictions, some Japanese achieved success in small businesses like landscaping, while many others worked on or owned farms that supplied fruits and vegetables to growing cities.

West Coast politicians pressed the Roosevelt administration to evacuate the Japanese from their communities. It did not seem to matter that about 80,000 were American

Issei

The bleak landscape of the internment camp at Manzanar, California, was typical of the sites to which the government sent Japanese Americans. In such a harsh environment the Japanese had no real opportunity to create productive farm communities, as government officials had promised.

citizens, called **Nisei,** and that no evidence indicated that they posed any threat. "A Jap's a Jap," commented General John De Witt, commander of West Coast defenses. "It makes no difference whether he is an American citizen or not." In response, the War Department in February 1942 drew up Executive Order 9066, which allowed the exclusion of any person from designated military areas. Under De Witt's authority, the order was applied only on the West Coast against Japanese Americans. By late February Roosevelt had agreed that both Issei and Nisei would be evacuated. But where would they go?

The army began to ship the entire Japanese community to "assembly centers." Most Nisei incurred heavy financial losses as they sold property at far below market value. Their distress became a windfall for people who had long resented their economic competition. "We've been charged with wanting to get rid of the Japs for selfish reasons," admitted the Grower-Shipper Vegetable Association. "We might as well be honest. We do. It's a question of whether the white man lives on the Pacific Coast or the brown man." At the assembly centers—racetracks, fairgrounds, and similar temporary locations—the army had not prepared basic sanitation, comfort, or privacy. "We lived in a horse stable," remembered one young girl. "We filled our cheesecloth with straw—for our mattress." The authorities at least had the decency to keep families together.

Most Japanese were interned in 10 camps in remote areas of seven western states. No claim of humane intent could change the reality—these were concentration camps. Internees were held in wire-enclosed compounds by armed guards. Temporary tar-papered barracks housed families or small groups in single rooms. Each room had a few cots, some blankets, and a single light bulb. That was home.

Some Japanese within the camps protested. Especially offensive was a government loyalty questionnaire that asked Nisei if they would be willing to serve in the armed forces. "What do they take us for? Saps?" asked Dunks Oshima, a camp prisoner. "First, they . . . run me out of town, and now they want me to volunteer for a suicide squad so I could get killed for this damn democracy. That's going some, for sheer brass!" Yet thousands of Nisei did enlist, and many distinguished themselves in combat.

Other Japanese Americans challenged the government through the courts. Fred Korematsu in California and Gordon Hirabayashi in Washington State were arrested when they refused to report for relocation. "As an American citizen, I wanted to uphold the principles of the Constitution," recalled Hirabayashi. But the Supreme Court let stand military policies aimed specifically at Japanese Americans. The majority opinion stated that "residents having ethnic affiliations with an invading enemy may be a greater source of danger than those of different ancestry," even though the army had never demonstrated that any danger existed. And in *Korematsu v. United States* (1944), the Court upheld the government's relocation program as a wartime necessity. Three justices dissented, criticizing relocation as the "legalization of racism."

Concentration camps in America did not perpetuate the horror of Nazi death camps, but they were built on racism and fear. Worse, they violated the traditions of civil rights and liberties for which Americans believed they were fighting.

At War with Jim Crow

When World War II began, Americans lived in a society deeply segregated along racial lines. Three quarters of the 12 million black Americans lived in the South. Hispanic Americans, then numbering around one million, resided largely in a belt along the U.S.–Mexican border. Though separated by geography, religion, language, and history, these two groups shared many common experiences. Both were segregated in housing and in public places. Neither had much access to health care, decent educations, or good jobs. Both found employment primarily as low-wage agricultural workers.

Hispanic and black leaders recognized the irony of a war their government fought in the name of freedom. That same government denied them basic civil rights and liberties, including the right to vote. "A jim crow army cannot fight for a free world," the NAACP declared. Several barriers stood in the way of the freedom to seek higher wage work and improved housing. For one, many unions simply refused to allow minorities to join. For another, most employers refused to hire minorities or restricted them to unskilled jobs such as janitor. Finally, residential segregation was deeply embedded in the South by law and throughout the country by common practice.

These inequities A. Phillip Randolph was determined to change. Randolph had developed organizing skills as a leader of the Brotherhood of Sleeping Car Porters, the most powerful black labor organization. Now, he looked to bring down the wall of discrimination that blocked minority workers from skilled jobs in defense industries and segregated them in government agencies, unions, and the armed forces. "The Administration leaders in Washington will never give the Negro justice," Randolph argued, "until they see masses—ten, twenty, fifty thousand Negroes on the White House lawn." To that end he began in 1941 to organize a march on Washington.

A demonstration of racial discontent was something President Roosevelt wished to avoid. He had the power to issue an executive order banning workplace segregation within the government and within companies receiving federal contracts, as Randolph demanded. Fearful of alienating Southerners and union members, Roosevelt refused

to act until confronted by the threat of the march. Only then, in June 1941, did he issue Executive Order 8802 barring discrimination in the hiring of government or defense industry workers. To enforce the order he established the Fair Employment Practices Commission (FEPC).

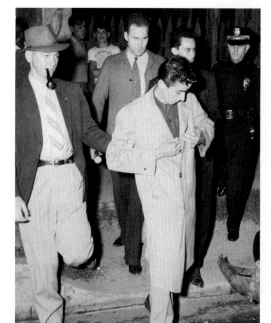

While it never fulfilled Randolph's hopes, the FEPC was in some ways the boldest step toward racial justice since the Era of Reconstruction. The Commission opened jobs in California's shipyards and aircraft factories that had previously refused to hire Hispanics. Thousands of workers migrated to the coast from Texas where job discrimination was the most severe. Facing acute labor shortages, the United States joined with the Mexican government to create a guest worker, or *bracero*, program. It guaranteed laborers from Mexico both better wages and improved working conditions. Despite the need for labor, opposition to the program from nativists in Texas remained severe.

Black Americans encountered similar resistance. More than half of all defense jobs were closed to minorities. In the aircraft industry blacks held just 200 janitorial positions out of over 100,000 new jobs created. The FEPC had the authority to investigate these inequities, but when faced with powerful employers and unions the Commission acted reluctantly if at all. In most sections of the country it honored "whites only" hiring practices. "Hitler has not done anything to the colored people," one worker told the president, "—it's people right here in the United States who are keeping us out of work and keeping us down." In the end labor shortages more than government action

A "zoot suiter" gets escorted by the police.

improved the job situation. By 1944, African Americans, who made up 10 percent of the nation's population, held 8 percent of its jobs.

As blacks and Hispanics moved into urban areas, they also competed with whites for the diminishing supply of housing. The government tried to ease the problem by building new developments. In Detroit, housing authorities picked a site along the edge of a Polish neighborhood. When the first black family moved into the new development, Detroit authorities sent in the National Guard to protect the newcomers from a band of the Ku Klux Klan. As summer approached tensions rose with the heat. Sporadic rioting broke out until, in June 1943, white mobs began beating blacks riding the trolley lines or going to movies. In retaliation, black rioters looted white stores. It took 6,000 regular army soldiers to impose a troubled calm, but not before violence claimed the lives of 24 blacks and 9 whites.

The situation in southern California was no less volatile. There Hispanics were frustrated by the persistence of white racism, job and housing discrimination, and high unemployment even amid a booming economy. Whites, in turn, blamed the rapid growth in the Hispanic population for an increase in crime. Their particular hostility focused on pachucos, or "zoot suiters." These were young Hispanic men and boys who adopted the style of Harlem hipsters: oiled hair swept back into a ducktail; broad-shouldered, long-waisted suit coats; baggy pants pegged at the ankles, the whole outfit polished off with a knee-length, gold chain. For most "zooters" this style expressed a modest form of rebellion; for a few it was the uniform of a criminal culture; for many whites it was a racial affront. The all-white Los Angeles city council even made it a crime to wear a zoot suit.

In June 1943, navy shipmen stationed at the local base invaded Hispanic neighborhoods in search of zooters who had allegedly assaulted their comrades. These self-styled vigilantes grabbed any zooters they saw, ripped their clothes, shaved their heads, and beat their victims. Only when Hispanics retaliated did the Los Angeles police respond, all the while ignoring white violence. The local press added to the hysteria with irresponsible and inaccurate headlines such as "Zooters Threaten L.A. Police." An investigatory commission appointed by California Governor Earl Warren rejected the press charges and placed the blame more properly on white racism and the daily indignities faced by the Hispanic community.

Zoot Suit Riots

Despite their many frustrations, minority leaders recognized the war effort as an opportunity to develop new strategies to confront old grievances. For example, the Congress of Racial Equality (**CORE**) found inspiration in the nonviolent passive resistance adopted by the leader of India's independence movement, Mohandas K. Gandhi. In northern cities CORE used sit-ins, boycotts, and picketing in an effort to desegregate movie theaters, restaurants, and other public places. In 1944 the Supreme Court indicated that it was reconsidering issues of racial inequality when, in *Smith v. Allwright*, it struck down the "all-white" primary used in southern states to disfranchise black voters. In the one-party South, the candidate who won the primary usually ran without major opposition in the general election. Unable to participate in the primaries, black voters had no meaningful influence. In rejecting this practice the Court indicated another way in which wartime experiences had opened new approaches to confronting racial discrimination.

CORE

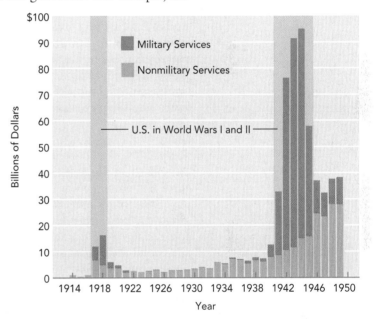

The New Deal in Retreat

After Pearl Harbor Roosevelt told reporters that "Dr. New Deal" had retired so that "Dr. Win-the-War" could get down to business. Political opposition, however, could not be eliminated even during a global conflict. The increasingly powerful anti–New Deal coalition of Republicans and rural Democrats saw in the war an opportunity to attack programs they had long resented. They quickly ended the Civilian Conservation Corps and the National Youth Administration, reduced the powers of the Farm Security Administration, and blocked moves to extend Social Security and unemployment benefits. Seeming to approve such measures, voters in the 1942 elections sent an additional 44 Republicans to the House and another 9 to the Senate. The GOP began eyeing the White House.

By the spring of 1944 no one knew whether Franklin Roosevelt would seek an unprecedented fourth term. The president's health had declined noticeably. Pallid skin, sagging shoulders, and shaking hands seemed open signs that he had aged too much to run. In July, one week before the Democratic convention, Roosevelt announced his decision: "All that is within me cries out to go back to my home on the Hudson River. . . . But as a good soldier . . . I will accept and serve." Conservative Democrats, however, made sure that Roosevelt's liberal vice president, Henry Wallace, would not remain

The Impact of World War II on Government Spending   *As the chart shows, the war spurred government spending more than the New Deal, even on nonmilitary sectors. Note that after both world wars, nonmilitary spending was higher than in the prewar years.*

Roosevelt Wins a Fourth Term

on the ticket. In his place they settled on Harry S. Truman of Missouri, a loyal New Dealer and party stalwart. The Republicans chose the moderate governor of New York, Thomas E. Dewey, to run against Roosevelt, but Dewey never had much of a chance. At the polls, voters gave Roosevelt 25.6 million popular votes to Dewey's 22 million, a clear victory, although the election was tighter than any since 1916. Like its aging leader, the New Deal coalition was showing signs of strain.

Winning the War and the Peace

To impress upon newly arrived officers the vastness of the war theater in the Pacific, General Douglas MacArthur laid out a map of the region. Over it, he placed an outline map of the United States. Running the war from headquarters in Australia, MacArthur pointed out, the distances were about the same as if, in the Western Hemisphere, the center was located in South America. On the same scale, Tokyo would lie far up in northern Canada, Iwo Jima somewhere in Hudson Bay, Singapore in Utah, Manila in North Dakota, and Hawaii off the coast of Scotland.

In a war that stretched from one end of the globe to the other, the Allies had to coordinate their strategies on a grand scale. Which war theaters would receive equipment in short supply? Who would administer conquered territories? Inevitably, the questions of fighting a war slid into discussions of the peace that would follow. What would happen to occupied territories? How would the Axis powers be punished? If a more stable world order could not be created, the cycle of violence might never end. So, as Allied armies struggled mile by mile to defeat the Axis, Allied diplomacy concentrated just as much on winning the peace.

The Fall of the Third Reich

After pushing the Germans out of North Africa in May 1943, Allied forces looked to drive Italy from the war. Late in July, two weeks after a quarter of a million British and American troops had landed on Sicily, Mussolini fled to German-held northern Italy. Although Italy surrendered early in September, Germany continued to pour in reinforcements. It took the Allies almost a year of bloody fighting to reach Rome, and at the end of the campaign they had yet to break German lines. Along the eastern front, Soviet armies steadily pushed the Germans out of Russia and back toward Berlin.

D-Day, 1944 *The final key to defeating the Nazis was the invasion of western Europe at Normandy. D-Day for the invasion was June 6, 1944, and the massive undertaking would not have been possible had the Allies been unable to use England as a base to gather their forces. Stalin supported D-Day with a spring offensive in eastern Europe.*

The Normandy landing involved complex problems of moving troops and matériel. The Rhino ferry allowed the landing forces to improvise docking facilities soon after the invasion forces landed. Sailors described these awkward craft as "ugly as hell, cranky as hell—but efficient as hell."

D-Day

General Dwight D. Eisenhower, fresh from battle in North Africa and the Mediterranean, took command of Allied preparations for Operation Overlord, a massive invasion of Europe striking from across the English Channel. By June 1944 all attention focused on the coast of France, for Hitler, of course, knew the Allies were preparing to invade. He suspected they would hit Calais, the French port city closest to the British Isles. Allied planners did their best to encourage this belief, even deploying fake armaments across the Channel. On the morning of June 6, 1944, the invasion began—not at Calais but on the less fortified beaches of Normandy (see map, page 784). Almost 3 million men, 11,000 aircraft, and more than 2,000 vessels took part in D-Day.

As Allied forces hit the beaches, luck and Eisenhower's meticulous planning favored their cause. Persuaded that the Allies still wanted Calais, Hitler delayed sending in two reserve divisions. His indecision allowed the Allied forces to secure a foothold. Over the next few days more than 1.5 million soldiers landed on the beaches—but they still had to move inland. The Allied advance from Normandy took almost two months, not several weeks as expected. But once Allied tanks broke through German lines their progress was spectacular. In August Paris was liberated, and by mid-September the Allies had driven the Germans from France and Belgium.

All went well until December 1944, when Hitler threw his reserves into a last, desperate gamble. The unexpected German onslaught drove the Allied lines back along a 50-mile bulge. There the Germans trapped the 101st Airborne Division. When asked to surrender, General Tony MacAuliffe sent back a one-word reply: "Nuts!" His troops held, General George Patton raced to the rescue, and the last German offensive collapsed. Little stood between the Allies and Berlin.

Two Roads to Tokyo

In the bleak days of 1942 General Douglas MacArthur—flamboyant and jaunty with his dark sunglasses and corncob pipe—had emerged as America's only military hero. MacArthur believed that the future of America lay in the Far East. The Pacific theater, not the European, should have top priority, he argued. In March 1943 the Combined Chiefs of Staff agreed to his plan for a westward advance along the northern coast of New Guinea toward the Philippines and Tokyo. Naval forces directed by Admiral Chester Nimitz used amphibious warfare to move up the island chains of the Central Pacific (see the map below).

By July 1944 the navy's leapfrogging campaign had reached the Marianas, east of the Philippines. From there B-29 bombers could reach the Japanese home islands. As a result, Admiral Nimitz proposed bypassing the Philippines in favor of a direct attack on Formosa (present-day Taiwan). MacArthur insisted on keeping his promise "to eighteen million Christian Filipinos that the Americans would return." Roosevelt himself came to Hawaii to resolve the impasse, giving MacArthur the green light. Backed by more than 100 ships of the Pacific Fleet, the general splashed ashore on the island of Leyte in October 1944 to announce his return.

The decision to invade the Philippines led to savage fighting until the war ended. As retreating Japanese armies left Manila, they tortured and slaughtered tens of

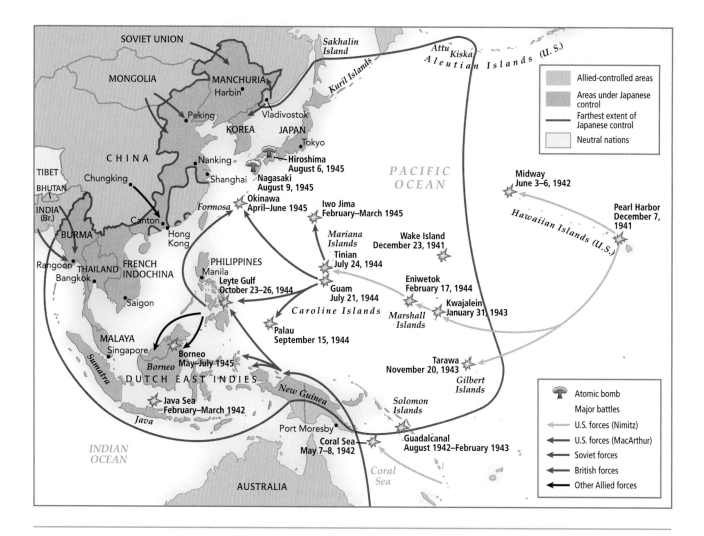

The Pacific Campaigns of World War II   *The extraordinary distances of the Pacific spurred the United States to devise a two-front strategy to defeat Japan. MacArthur's army forces used Australia as a base of operations, aiming for the Philippines and the southeast coast of China. Once those areas were secured, forces could then launch air attacks on Japan. The navy, under command of Admiral Nimitz, set out to destroy the Japanese fleet and to conduct a series of amphibious landings on island chains in the Central Pacific. Meanwhile, British forces launched separate operations in Burma, forces under Chiang Kai-shek occasionally engaged Japanese forces on China's mainland, and in August 1945 Soviet troops attacked northern China.*

thousands of Filipino civilians. The United States suffered 62,000 casualties redeeming MacArthur's pledge. But a spectacular U.S. Navy victory at the Battle of Leyte Gulf spelled the end of the Japanese Imperial Navy as a fighting force. MacArthur and Nimitz prepared to tighten the noose around Japan's home islands.

Battle of Leyte Gulf

Big Three Diplomacy

While the Allies cooperated to gain military victories in both Europe and the Pacific, negotiations over the postwar peace proved knottier. Churchill believed that only a stable European balance of power, not an international agency, could preserve peace. In his view the Soviet Union was the greatest threat to upsetting that balance of power. Premier Joseph Stalin left no doubt that an expansive notion of Russian security defined his war aims. For future protection Stalin expected to annex the Baltic states, once Russian provinces, along with bits of Finland and Romania and about half of prewar Poland. In eastern Europe and other border areas such as Iran, Korea, and Turkey, he wanted "friendly" neighbors. It soon became apparent that "friendly" meant regimes dependent on Moscow.

Early on, Franklin Roosevelt had promoted his own version of an international balance of power, which he called the "Four Policemen." Under its framework, the Soviet Union, Great Britain, the United States, and China would guarantee peace through military cooperation. But by 1944 Roosevelt was seeking an alternative both to this scheme and to Churchill's wish to return to a balance of power that safely hemmed in the Russians. He preferred to bring the Soviet Union into a peacekeeping system based on an international organization similar to the League of Nations. This time, Roosevelt intended that the United States, as well as all the great powers, would participate. Whether Churchill and Stalin—or the American people as a whole—would accept the idea was not yet clear.

The Road to Yalta

The outlines—and the problems—of a postwar settlement became clearer during several summit conferences among the Allied leaders. In November 1943, with Italy's surrender in hand and the war against Germany going well, Churchill and Roosevelt agreed to make a hazardous trip to Teheran, Iran. There, the Big Three leaders met together for the first time and had a chance to take a personal measure of each other. ("Seems very confident," Roosevelt said of Stalin, "very sure of himself, moves slowly— altogether quite impressive.") The president tried to charm the Soviet premier, teasing Churchill for Stalin's benefit, keeping it up "until Stalin was laughing with me, and it was then that I called him 'Uncle Joe.'"

Teheran Conference

Teheran was the high point of cooperation among the Big Three. There Roosevelt and Churchill committed to the D-Day invasion Stalin had so long sought. In return he promised to launch a spring offensive to keep German troops occupied on the eastern front. He also reaffirmed his earlier pledge to declare war against Japan once Germany was beaten.

But thorny disagreements over the postwar peace had not been resolved. That was clear in February 1945, when the Big Three met one last time, at the Russian resort city of Yalta, on the Black Sea. By then, Russian, British, and American troops were closing in on Germany. Roosevelt arrived tired, ashen. At 62, limited by his paralysis, he had visibly aged. He came to Yalta mindful that although Germany was all but beaten, Japan still held out in the Pacific. Under no circumstances did he want Stalin to withdraw his promises to enter the fight against Japan and to join a postwar international organization. Churchill remained profoundly mistrustful of Soviet intentions. As Germany and Japan disintegrated, he saw power vacuums opening up in both Europe and Asia. These the Russians appeared only too eager to fill. Most diplomats in the American State Department and a growing number of military officers and politicians shared Churchill's fears.

Yalta Conference

During World War I, short flying ranges and an inability to carry heavy loads limited what airplanes could do. Between the two wars, however, airframes grew stronger, engines more powerful, and payloads greater. Air-power strategists began to suggest that concerted waves of planes could attack industrial and military targets deep in enemy territory.

During the blitzkriegs against Poland and France in the opening campaigns of the war, Hitler's air attacks terrorized civilian populations and disrupted enemy forces. Air Marshal Hermann Goering predicted that bombers from the German Luftwaffe would soon bring England to its knees. The Battle of Britain, fought during the winter of 1940–1941, signaled the start of the age of modern air warfare. For the first time in history, one nation tried to conquer another from the skies. Goering's boast failed as England continued doggedly to resist.

Despite the Luftwaffe's failure, Allied air-power strategists believed heavy bombers could cripple Germany and Japan. The first test of such "strategic bombing" came in 1942, when more than 1,100 planes of the British Royal Air Force (RAF) destroyed some 20,000 homes, 1,500 stores and offices, and about 60 factories around Cologne, Germany. Horrific as that sounds, the attack did not level the city, as RAF planners had predicted. Indeed, later studies indicated that for all the damage done, Axis productivity actually increased until the last months of the war. Still, strategic bombing disrupted Japanese and German industry, brought the war home to the civilian

The B-29 bombers gave the American air force much greater range, speed, and bomb loads. The Enola Gay (above), named after the pilot's mother, was modified to carry the first atom bomb, dropped on Hiroshima.

Dispute over Poland

Allied differences were most clearly reflected in the disagreements over Poland. For Britain, Hitler's invasion of Poland had been the flashpoint for war. It was fighting, in part, to ensure that Poland survived as an independent nation. For Stalin, Poland was the historic corridor of invasion used by Russia's enemies. After Soviet troops reentered Poland, he insisted that he would recognize only the Communist-controlled government at Lublin. Stalin also demanded that Russia receive territory in eastern Poland, for which the Poles would be compensated with German lands. That was hardly the **self-determination** called for in the Atlantic Charter. Roosevelt proposed a compromise. For the time being, Poland would have a coalition government; after the war, free elections would settle the question of who should rule. The Soviets would also receive the territory they demanded in eastern Poland, and the western boundary would be established later.

Similarly, the Allies remained at odds about Germany's postwar future. Stalin was determined that the Germans would never invade Russia again. Many Americans shared his desire to have Germany punished and its war-making capacity eliminated. At the Teheran Conference, Roosevelt and Stalin had proposed that the Third Reich be drastically dismembered, split into five powerless parts. Churchill was much less eager to bring low the nation that was the most natural barrier to Russian expansion. The era after World War I, he believed, demonstrated that a healthy European economy required an industrialized Germany.

Dividing Germany

Again, the Big Three put off making a firm decision. For the time being, they agreed to divide Germany into separate occupation zones (France would receive a zone carved from British and American territory). These four powers would jointly occupy Berlin, while an Allied Control Council supervised the national government.

When the Big Three turned their attention to the Far East, Stalin held a trump card. Roosevelt believed that only a bloody invasion of Japan itself could force a surrender. He thus secured from Stalin a pledge to enter the Pacific war within three months population, and diverted enemy forces from the front to home defense.

Raids on Dresden and on Tokyo dramatized the horrors of the new technology. Dresden, a charming German city almost untouched by the twentieth century, had largely been ignored until February 1945. The RAF hit it first; then, with fires still raging, the American bombing wave struck. A huge inferno drew all the oxygen out of the center of the city, so that victims who did not burn suffocated. Some 60,000 citizens of Dresden died. In March 340 American bombers hit Tokyo with incendiary bombs. The resulting firestorms, whipped by strong winds, leveled 16 square miles, destroyed 267,000 homes, left 83,000 dead, and injured 41,000. The heat was so intense that the water in canals boiled.

To ensure the success of aerial warfare, aircraft designers on both sides raced to make their planes bigger and faster. The first English raids used the Wellington bomber, a plane 65 feet long with a wing span of 86 feet and a bomb load of 1,500 pounds. In contrast, the American B-29s that bombed Hiroshima and Nagasaki carried up to 10 tons on a plane that was about 50 percent larger. The Wellington flew 255 miles an hour and cruised as high as 12,000 feet, with a range of 2,200 miles, whereas the new B-29s could travel more than 350 miles an hour, at altitudes up to 30,000 feet, with a range of up to 5,000 miles—more than double the Wellington's. German scientists took an even more radical step. To increase the speed and range of their weaponry they produced a new V-1 pilotless "buzz bomb" (named for the sound of its jet engine) and the V-2 rocket, the first true missile used as a weapon. Launched from bases in Europe, V-1s and V-2s easily reached targets in England. For all the terror they inspired, however, they were inaccurate and the Germans nerer launched enough of them to mount a decisive threat.

With the development of long-range air power, the "front line" of traditional war vanished. Every civilian became a potential combatant, every village a potential target in a total war. Although air power was not decisive in the war, the creation of longer-range aircraft with heavier payloads forced Americans to rethink their ties to the world. The nation was now a matter of hours, not days, away from both steadfast friends and potential enemies.

of Germany's defeat. His price was high. Stalin wanted to reclaim territories that Russia had lost in the Russo-Japanese War of 1904–1906, including islands north of Japan as well as control over the Chinese Eastern and South Manchurian railroads.

The agreements reached at Yalta depended on Stalin's willingness to cooperate. In public Roosevelt put the best face on matters. He argued that the new world organization (which Stalin had agreed to support) would "provide the greatest opportunity in all history" to secure a lasting peace. As if to lay to rest the isolationist sentiments that had destroyed Woodrow Wilson's dream, Roosevelt told Congress, "We shall take responsibility for world collaboration, or we shall have to bear the responsibility for another world conflict." Privately the president was less optimistic. He confessed to one friend that he doubted that, "when the chips were down, Stalin would be able to carry out and deliver what he had agreed to."

The Fallen Leader

The Yalta Conference marked one of the last and most controversial chapters of Franklin Roosevelt's presidency. Critics charged that the concessions to Stalin had left American national interests unprotected. Poland had been betrayed; China sold out; the United Nations crippled at birth. Yet Roosevelt gave to Stalin little that Stalin had not liberated with Russian blood and could have taken anyway.

What peace Roosevelt might have achieved can never be known. He returned from Yalta visibly ill. On April 12, 1945, while sitting for his portrait at his vacation home in Warm Springs, Georgia, he complained of a "terrific headache," then suddenly fell unconscious. Two hours later he was dead, the victim of a cerebral hemorrhage. Not since the assassination of Lincoln had the nation so grieved. Under Roosevelt's leadership government had become a protector, the president a father and friend, and the United States the leader in the struggle against Axis tyranny.

Eleanor recalled how many Americans later told her that "they missed the way the President used to talk to them. . . . There was a real dialogue between Franklin and the people."

Truman Becomes President

Harry S. Truman faced the awesome task of replacing Roosevelt. "Who the hell is Harry Truman?" the chief of staff had asked when Truman was nominated for the vice presidency in 1944. In the brief period he served as vice president, Truman had met with Roosevelt fewer than 10 times. He knew almost nothing about the president's postwar plans and promises. When a reporter now addressed him as "Mr. President," he winced. "I wish you didn't have to call me that," he said. Sensing his own inadequacies, Truman adopted a tough pose and made his mind up quickly. People welcomed the new president's decisiveness as a relief from Roosevelt's evasive style. Too often, though, Truman acted before the issues were clear. He at least knew victory in Europe was near as Allied troops swept into Germany.

The Holocaust

The horror of war in no way prepared the invading armies for the liberation of the concentration camps. Hitler, they discovered, had ordered the systematic extermination of all European Jews, as well as Gypsies, homosexuals, and others considered deviant. The SS, Hitler's security force, had constructed six extermination centers in Germany and Poland. By rail from all over Europe the SS shipped Jews to die in the gas chambers.

No issue of World War II more starkly raised questions of human good and evil than what came to be known as the Holocaust. Tragically, the United States could have done more to save some of the 6 million Jews that were killed. Until the autumn of 1941 the Nazis permitted Jews to leave Europe, but few countries would accept them—including the United States. Americans haunted by unemployment feared

In April 1945, at the concentration camp in Buchenwald, Germany, Senator Alben Barkley of Kentucky viewed a grisly reminder of the horrors of the Nazis' "final solution." As vice president under Harry Truman, Barkley urged the administration to support an independent homeland in Israel for Jews.

that a tide of new immigrants would make competition for jobs even worse. Tales of persecution from war refugees had little effect on most citizens: opinion polls showed that more than 70 percent of Americans opposed easing quotas. After 1938 the restrictive provisions of the 1924 Immigration Act were made even tighter.

American Jews wanted to help, especially after 1942, when they learned of the death camps. But they worried that highly visible protests might only aggravate American **anti-Semitism.** They were also split over support for Zionists working to establish a Jewish homeland in Palestine. The British had blocked Jewish emigration to Palestine and, to avoid alienating the Arabs, opposed Zionism. Roosevelt and his advisers ultimately decided that the best way to save Jews was to win the war quickly, but that strategy still does not explain why the Allies did not do more. They could have bombed the rail lines to the camps, sent commando forces, or tried to destroy the death factories.

Anti-Semitism offers a partial answer. Assistant Secretary of State Breckinridge Long, the man responsible for immigration policy, personified a tradition of gentlemanly anti-Semitism. Polite on the surface but deeply bigoted, Long used his authority over visas to place obstacles in the way of desperate Jewish refugees. Worse, Long blocked a plan that both Treasury Secretary Henry Morgenthau and the president had approved to ransom Jews in Romania and 6,000 Jewish children in France. Morgenthau, the only Jewish member of Roosevelt's cabinet, had at first shown little interest in the debate over Palestine and the refugees. Long's actions so disturbed him, however, that he sent Roosevelt a report titled "The Acquiescence of This Government in the Murder of the Jews." The president immediately stripped Long of his authority. He appointed a War Refugee Board charged with saving as many Jews as possible and promised to seek the establishment of a Jewish commonwealth in Palestine. But some 18 precious "long and heartbreaking" months had been lost and with them an untold number of lives.

Influence of Anti-Semitism

A Lasting Peace

After 15 years of depression and then war, the Allies sought a new international framework for cooperation among nations. That system, many believed, needed to be economic as well as political. At a 1944 meeting at Bretton Woods, a resort in New Hampshire, Americans led the way in creating two new economic organizations: the International Monetary Fund (IMF) and the International Bank for Reconstruction and Development, later known as the World Bank. The IMF hoped to promote trade by stabilizing national currencies, and the World Bank was designed to stimulate economic growth by investing in projects worldwide. Later that summer the Allies met at Dumbarton Oaks, a Washington estate, to lay out the structure for the proposed United Nations Organization (UNO, later known simply as the UN). An 11-member Security Council would oversee a General Assembly composed of delegates from all member nations. By the end of the first organizational meeting, held in San Francisco in April 1945, it had become clear that the United Nations would favor the Western powers in most postwar disputes.

Bretton Woods Economic Strategies

Dumbarton Oaks and the UNO

While the United Nations was organizing itself in San Francisco, the Axis powers were collapsing in Europe. As Mussolini attempted to escape to Germany, anti-fascist mobs in Italy captured and slaughtered him like a pig. Adolf Hitler committed suicide in his Berlin bunker on April 30. Two weeks later General Eisenhower accepted the German surrender.

In one final summit meeting, held in July 1945 at Potsdam (just outside Berlin), President Truman met Churchill and Stalin for the first time. Two issues dominated the meeting: Germany's political fate and how much the defeated nation would pay in reparations. The three leaders agreed that Germany should be occupied and demilitarized. Stalin insisted that Russia receive a minimum of $10 billion, regardless of how much it might hurt postwar Germany or the European economy. A complicated compromise allowed Britain and the United States to restrict reparations from

Potsdam Summit

their zones. But in large part Stalin had his way. For the foreseeable future, Germany would remain divided into occupation zones and without a central government of its own.

Atom Diplomacy

The most crucial factor affecting postwar relations never even reached the bargaining table in Potsdam. On July 16, 1945, the first atomic fireball rose from the desert in Alamogordo, New Mexico. Scientists at the Manhattan Project had successfully detonated their first explosive device. On receiving the news, Truman returned to the negotiations a changed man—firmer, more confident. He "told the Russians just where they got on and off and generally bossed the whole meeting," observed Churchill. Several questions loomed. Should the United States now use the bomb? Should it warn Japan before dropping it? And perhaps equally vital, should Truman inform Stalin?

Should the Bomb be Dropped?
A few scientists had recommended not using the bomb or at least attempting to convince Japan to surrender by offering a demonstration of the new weapon's power. A high-level committee of administrators, scientists, and political and military leaders dismissed that idea, though some later regretted they did so. Nor did Truman choose to tell Stalin about the bomb. He only mentioned obliquely that the United States possessed a weapon of "awesome destructiveness." Stalin, whose spies had already informed him of the bomb, showed no surprise. He only remarked casually that he hoped the Americans would use their new weapon to good effect against Japan. Atomic diplomacy had failed its first test. Stalin immediately stepped up the Russian program to build an atom bomb. After Potsdam the nuclear arms race was on.

Finally, Truman and Churchill decided to drop the first bomb with only an implied warning to the Japanese. In an ultimatum issued at Potsdam, they demanded unconditional surrender and threatened Japan with "inevitable and complete destruction" using the "full application of our military power" if it did not comply. Unaware of the warning's full meaning, officials in Tokyo made no formal reply.

The Bomb as a Threat to the Soviets
Truman and Churchill knew Japan was on the verge of defeat. Japan's leaders had even sent peace feelers to the Russians. Why, then, did the Allies insist on unconditional surrender? Some historians have charged that Secretary of State James Byrnes, a staunch anticommunist, wanted a dramatic combat demonstration of the bomb that would serve to persuade Stalin to behave less aggressively in negotiations with the British and Americans. However much Byrnes had Soviet diplomacy on his mind, most evidence indicates that Truman decided to drop the bomb in order to end the war quickly.

Before leaving Potsdam, Truman ordered crews on Tinian Island in the South Pacific to proceed to their first target as soon as weather permitted. On August 6 the *Enola Gay,* a B-29 bomber, dropped a uranium bomb nicknamed "Little Boy" that leveled four square miles of Hiroshima, an industrial and military center. The blast immediately killed nearly 80,000 people (including 20 American prisoners of war). A German priest came upon soldiers who had looked up as the bomb exploded. Their eyeballs had melted from their sockets. Another eyewitness spoke of survivors "so broken and confused that they moved and behaved like automatons." Two days later the Soviet Union declared war on Japan, and on August 9 a second atom bomb (a plutonium weapon nicknamed "Fat Man") exploded over the port of Nagasaki. Another 60,000 people were killed instantly. In both cities many who lived through the horror began to sicken and die as radiation poisoning claimed tens of thousands of additional lives.

The two explosions left the Japanese stunned. Breaking all precedents, the emperor intervened and declared openly for peace. On September 3 a humiliated Japanese delegation boarded the battleship *Missouri* in Tokyo Bay and signed the document of surrender. World War II had ended.

This aerial view of Hiroshima gives stark testimony to the destructive force of the atomic blast. In one of the many bitter ironies, only the shells of the western-style buildings survived.

"World War II changed everything," observed one admiral long after the war. The defeatism of the Depression gave way to the exhilaration of victory. Before the war Americans seldom exerted leadership in international affairs. After, the world looked to the United States to rebuild the economies of Europe and Asia and to maintain peace. World War II had not only shown the global interdependence of economic and political systems; it had also increased that interdependence. Out of the war developed a truly international economy. At home the trends toward bigness and centralization vastly accelerated. Advances in electronics, communications, and aviation brought the world closer to every home. Government grew, too. The size of the national debt alone guaranteed that Washington would continue to dominate the economy. Americans had come to believe in a strong defense, even if that meant a large federal bureaucracy and a generous military budget.

Still, a number of fears loomed, despite the victory parades snaking down the nation's main streets. Would the inevitable cutbacks in spending bring on another depression? Would Soviet ambitions undo the new global peace, much as fascism and economic instability had undone the peace of Versailles? And then there was the shadow of the atom bomb looming over the victorious as well as the defeated. The United States might control atomic technology for the present, but what if the weapon fell into unfriendly hands? With the advent of the atomic age, no one in the world, not even in the United States, was safe anymore.

Significant Events

1929	Stock market crash signals onset of worldwide economic crisis
1931–1932	Japan invades Manchuria
1933	Roosevelt recognizes the Soviet Union

1935	Nye Committee hearings; first Neutrality Act
1936	Second Neutrality Act
1937	Third Neutrality Act (cash-and-carry); Roosevelt's quarantine speech; *Panay* incident
1938	Munich meeting
1939	Fall of Czechoslovakia; Germany signs nonaggression pact with the Soviet Union; World War II begins in Europe
1940	German blitzkrieg against Low Countries and France; destroyers-for-bases deal; Roosevelt wins third term
1941	Lend-Lease Act; Roosevelt creates Fair Employment Practices Commission; Germany invades Soviet Union; Roosevelt and Churchill sign Atlantic Charter; Japan occupies Indochina; Pearl Harbor attacked; Hitler and Mussolini declare war on the United States
1942	War Production Board (WPB) and War Labor Board created; submarine war in the Atlantic; internment of Japanese Americans; Bataan and Corregidor fall; battles of Guadalcanal, Coral Sea, and Midway; American and British troops invade North Africa
1943	British-American forces invade Italy; Smith-Connolly Act; race riot in Detroit; zoot suit riots; Big Three meet at Teheran
1944	D-Day invasion of France; U.S. forces return to Philippines; island-hopping campaign reaches Guam; Battle of the Bulge; Dumbarton Oaks and Bretton Woods meetings; *Smith v. Allwright;* Roosevelt wins fourth term; Allies invade Germany
1945	Yalta Conference; Roosevelt dies; Truman becomes president; first United Nations Organization meeting; Germany surrenders; Potsdam Conference; atom bombs dropped on Japan; World War II ends

Chapter Summary

World War II deepened the global interdependence of nations and left the United States as the greatest economic and military power in the world.

- As fascism spread in Europe and as militarism spread in Asia, Franklin Roosevelt struggled to help America's allies by overcoming domestic political isolation and the fervor for neutrality.

- Despite German aggression against Poland in 1939, France and the Low Countries in 1940, and the Soviet Union in 1941, the United States did not enter the war until the Japanese surprise attack on Pearl Harbor in December 1941.

- The alliance forged among British prime minister Winston Churchill, Soviet premier Joseph Stalin, and President Franklin Roosevelt did not swerve from its decision to subdue Germany first, even though early defeats and America's lack of preparation slowed the war effort until 1943.

- At home America's factories produced enough goods to supply the domestic economy and America's allies.

  - Demands for labor created opportunities for women and minorities.
  - War hysteria aggravated old prejudices and led to the internment of Japanese Americans.
  - New Deal reform ended as "Dr. Win-the-War" replaced "Dr. New Deal."

- Although the successful landings in France on D-Day and the island-hopping campaign in the Pacific made it clear that the Allies would win the war, issues over Poland, Germany, and postwar boundaries raised doubts about the peace.

- The war ended with the atomic bombings of Hiroshima and Nagasaki, but not soon enough to limit the horrors of the Holocaust.

Additional Reading

A comprehensive treatment of the war years is David Kennedy, *The American People in World War II: Freedom from Fear: Part II* (2003). Robert Divine, *The Reluctant Belligerent* (2nd ed., 1979), is still excellent on the prewar diplomacy. Perhaps the most comprehensive single volume on the war is Martin Gilbert, *The Second World War: A Complete History* (2004), although Gerhard Weinberg, *The World at Arms: A Global History of World War II* (revised ed., 2005), captures the vast scale. Richard Lingeman, *Don't You Know There's a War On: The Homefront, 1941–1945* (updated ed., 2003), is a classic study. Emily Yellin, *Our Mother's War: American Women at Home and at the Front During World War II* (2005), explores the many roles women played. Tetsuden Kashmia, *Judgment Without Trial: Japanese American Imprisonment During World War II* (2003), examines the diverse experiences of those in the camps and reveals that planning for internment of the Japanese began well before the war.

The decision to drop two atom bombs on Japan remains one of the most controversial legacies of the war. To better understand the racial dimension, see John Dower, *War without Mercy: Race and Power in the Pacific War* (1986). Richard Rhodes, *The Making of the Atomic Bomb* (1987), re-creates the history of the Manhattan Project. Gar Alperowitz, *The Decision to Use the Atomic Bomb* (1995), extends an interpretation he first advanced in *Atomic Diplomacy* (1965) that the Soviet Union was the planners' real target. Martin Sherwin, *A World Destroyed* (rev. ed., 1985), and J. Samuel Walker, *Prompt and Utter Destruction: Truman and the Use of the Atomic Bomb against Japan* (1997), view the decision more as a way to end the war quickly. David Holloway, *Stalin and the Bomb: The Soviet Union and Atomic Energy 1939–1956* (1994), uses Russian sources to trace the origins of atomic diplomacy. Students who wish to work with some of the original documents should see Michael Stoff et al., *The Manhattan Project: A Documentary Introduction to the Atomic Age* (1991).

For a fuller list of readings, see the Bibliography at www.mhhe.com/davidsonnation6.

Historians Reconstruct the Past

Did the Atomic Bomb Save Lives?

History is littered with countless *what ifs,* especially concerning events of great moment. What if the South had won the Civil War? What if Washington's crossing of the Delaware had failed? What if the Allies had resolved to defeat Japan without dropping two atomic bombs? Historians regularly deal with such counterfactual questions, but they often find it difficult to weigh alternatives or realistically explore the roads not taken. Whether the use of the atomic bomb actually saved lives is one such question, and it was debated almost right from the moment of decision. How do we weigh the alternatives?

When news came that the United States had exploded a powerful new atomic device over Japan, the GIs in the field saw immediately that there would be no need for a massive invasion of Japan. As the lyrics of one popular song put it, "I believe the bomb that struck Hiroshima / was the answer to a fighting boy's prayers." After the war, Winston Churchill made the same point by calling the bomb "a miracle of deliverance." To conquer Japan "yard by yard might well require the loss of a million American lives," he told Congress. President Truman's memoirs put the totals somewhat lower: he referred to military estimates of over a million *casualties,* including half a million American deaths.

To most Americans, such large numbers made sense. Japanese resistance during the Pacific campaigns had been fierce. On the island of Okinawa alone, hand-to-hand fighting

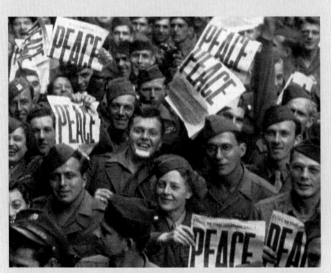

claimed over 12,000 American soldiers, sailors, and marines. American troops used flamethrowers to burn Japanese out of caves and holes. In the half century following World War II, most historians assumed that dropping the bomb saved the United States from mounting a bloody invasion of the Japanese home islands.

But how did Truman, Churchill, and other participants arrive at such casualty figures? The conclusion that the United States dropped the bomb to end the war quickly and to avoid 500,000 American deaths became one of the most controversial of World War II. The debate arose, in part, because of the horror of nuclear weaponry. Critics have suggested that Japan might well have been persuaded to surrender without an atomic attack.

Would Japan Surrender?

That debate—which began in earnest during the 1960s—has analyzed a host of factors affecting Truman's decision (see pages 792). Many navy and air corps officers believed that a naval blockade and conventional bombing were enough to force Japan's surrender without an invasion. The country, after all, was virtually without defense against bombing raids. Later critics have suggested that the Allies should have modified their demand for "unconditional surrender," instead allowing the Japanese to keep their revered institution of the emperor. (As events turned out, Japan surrendered only after such a guarantee was issued.) Others argue that the United States should have arranged for a demonstration of the bomb's power without actually detonating one over Japan.

Yet, as the debates over these alternatives swirled during the 1960s and 1970s, no one challenged the estimates of a million-casualty invasion. That number had been put forward in 1947 by Henry Stimson, the highly respected former secretary of war. In an article for *Harper's* magazine Stimson wrote, "We estimated the major fighting would not end until the latter part of 1946 at the earliest. I was informed that such operations might be expected to cost over a million casualties, to American forces alone."

made use of this newly gained power. If the test should
fail, then it would be even more important to us to bring
about a surrender before we had to make a physical conquest
of Japan.   General Marshall told me that it might cost half
a million American lives to force the enemy's surrender on
his home grounds.

Harry S. Truman, Memoirs, *typescript, page 804: an estimate of half a million deaths. Reprinted by permission of Margaret Truman Daniel.*

Shifting Numbers

Stimson's account cast a long shadow. A few years later Harry Truman provided an air force historian with a significantly lower number. Truman recalled that General George Marshall, the army chief of staff, had told him in July 1945 that in an invasion of Japan one-quarter of a million casualties would be the cost as well as an equal number of Japanese. But when a White House aide checked Truman's memory against Stimson's account, he discovered the discrepancy—one million versus only a quarter million. "The President's casualty figure [should] be changed to conform with that of Secretary Stimson," the aide advised, "because presumably Stimson got his from Gen. Marshall; the size of the casualty figures is very important."

The last phrase is significant. Why were the numbers so important? Obviously, the higher the number of potential casualties, the stronger the case that using the bomb saved lives. So it is worth looking a bit more closely at Stimson's article.

In fact, the idea to write an article was not actually Stimson's. It came from another atomic policy maker, James Conant. Conant, the president of Harvard University, had become increasingly concerned about "the spreading accusation that it was unnecessary to use the atomic bomb at all." He complained privately in 1946 that "This type of sentimentalism . . . is bound to have a great deal of influence on the next generation. The type of person who goes into teaching, particularly school teaching, will be influenced a great deal by this type of argument." Conant believed that Stimson had the prestige to counter such criticisms. One of the nation's most distinguished public servants, he had been twice a secretary of war, an ambassador, and secretary of state.

So Stimson agreed to write an article. But where did he get his casualty

Hiroshima, August 6, 1945

Remains of a wristwatch from the atomic blast site at Hiroshima. The bomb exploded at 8:16 a.m.

estimates? During the war a memo from former president Herbert Hoover had been circulated, warning that an invasion could claim anywhere from half a million to a million American lives. At the time, in June 1945, a successful test of an atomic bomb was still a month away and the possibility of an invasion loomed larger. Stimson was convinced that the war might be ended without an invasion if the Allies would only assure the Japanese that the position of emperor would be protected. Hoover's dire warning about the costs of an invasion reinforced Stimson's argument against invading.

But unlike the aide who later helped Truman with his memoirs, Stimson did not get similarly high casualty estimates from General Marshall. Marshall's staff thought Hoover's estimates were way too high. They estimated that the first-stage invasion (of Kyushu Island) might produce American casualties of perhaps 31,000, including about 7,000 to 8,000 deaths. If the invasion of Japan's main island, Honshu, took place, those numbers would rise to 120,000 casualties and 25,000 deaths. Estimates by General MacArthur were slightly higher, but within the same range. For reasons that remain unclear, however, when Stimson wrote his article after the war, he chose to use the higher estimates.

Thus, intentionally or not, Stimson's article greatly overestimated the number of invasion casualties predicted by the American military. And Conant's private worries show that those who dropped the bomb were more sensitive about their decision than they wished to admit. One of the most telling illustrations of the pressure to keep the estimates high can be seen in the successive drafts of Harry Truman's own memoirs, which were finally published in 1955. The assistants who helped Truman kept revising the figure upward. Truman's recollection, in 1952, mentioned only 250,000 casualties (not deaths); that figure jumped to 500,000 casualties in the first draft; then, in the published version, to a "half-million" *lives* saved.

Weighing Political Calculations

Do the lower figures mean that historians should condemn Truman, Stimson, and others for preferring to use the bomb rather than invade Japan? Not necessarily. After Japan's surprise attack on Pearl Harbor and its fierce resistance in the Pacific islands, American sentiments against the Japanese ran high. The atomic bomb had cost $2 billion to develop, and officials always assumed that if the bomb were successful, it would be used. Why else develop it? Truman (and most Americans) probably believed that even an invasion costing 25,000 lives would have justified using the bomb.

Even so, historians must constantly remind themselves that seemingly "impartial" accounts are influenced by the conditions under which they were created. Stimson set out not simply to tell the facts about the decision to drop the bomb. He wished to justify a decision he believed was necessary and proper. Like Conant, he understood that the record of the past is always shaped by those who do the telling. "History," he wrote in 1948, "is often not what actually happened but what is recorded as such."

Japanese fighting on Okinawa and other Pacific islands produced high casualty and death rates for American forces, reinforcing the notion that an invasion of Japan would claim many American lives.

> THE WHITE HOUSE
> WASHINGTON   Dec. 31, 1952
>
> My dear Professor Cate:—
> Your letter of Dec. 6th 1952 has
> ~~been delivered to~~
>
> ~~with this~~
> I asked Gen. Marshall what it
> would cost in lives to land on
> the Tokio plane and other places
> in Japan. It was his opinion that
> ¼ million casualties would be
> the minimum cost as well
> as an equal number of the enemy.

Earlier letter from Truman to an air force historian. Here, Truman's and Marshall's estimate is a quarter of a million casualties, not deaths.

Bibliography

Stimson's "The Decision to Use the Bomb" appears in the February 1947 issue of *Harper's* magazine. The debate over his casualty estimates and those of Truman and Churchill was launched by Barton J. Bernstein, "A Postwar Myth: 500,000 Lives Saved," *Bulletin of the Atomic Scientists* 42 (June/July 1986), and by Rufus Miles, "Hiroshima: The Strange Myth of Half a Million Lives Saved," *International Security* 10 (Fall 1985). Bernstein provides valuable background on Stimson's 1947 article in "Seizing the Contested Terrain of Nuclear History," *Diplomatic History* 19 (Winter 1993). Also useful is John Ray Skates, *The Invasion of Japan: Alternative to the Bomb* (1994). The debate over the projected invasion, of course, is only one aspect of the larger question of whether atom bombs should have been dropped on Japan. See, for example, Gar Alperovitz, *The Decision to Use the Atomic Bomb* (1995). For other readings on that topic, see the Bibliography for Chapter 26.

CHAPTER 27
Cold War America
1945~1954

Glad to Be Home?

The war had been over for almost five months and still troopships steamed into New York and other ports. Timuel Black was packing his duffel belowdecks when he heard some of the white soldiers shout, "There she is! The Statue of Liberty!" Black felt a little bitter about the war. He'd been drafted in Chicago in 1943, just after race riots ripped the city. His father, a strong supporter of civil rights, was angry. "What the hell are you goin' to fight in Europe for? The fight is here." He wanted his son to go with him to demonstrate in Detroit, except the roads were blocked and the buses and trains screened to prevent more African Americans from coming in.

Instead, Black went off to fight the Nazis, serving in a segregated army. He'd gone ashore during the D-Day invasion, survived the Battle of the Bulge, and marched through one of the German concentration camps. "The first thing you get is the stench," he recalled. "Everybody knows that's human stench. You begin to realize something terrible had happened. There's quietness. You get closer and you begin to see what's happened to these creatures. And you get—I got more passionately angry than I guess I'd ever been." He thought: if it could happen here, to the Germans, it could happen anywhere. It could happen to black folk in America. So when the white soldiers called to come up and see the Statue of Liberty, Black's reaction was, "Hell, I'm not goin' up there. Damn that." But after all, he went up. "All of a sudden, I found myself with tears, cryin' and saying the same thing [the white soldiers] were saying. Glad to be home, proud of my country, as irregular as it is. Determined that it could be better."

At the same time Betty Basye was working across the continent as a nurse in a burn-and-blind center at Menlo Park, California. Her hospital treated soldiers shipped back from the Pacific: "Blind young men. Eyes gone, legs gone. Parts of the face. Burns—you'd land with a firebomb and be up in flames." She'd joke with the men, trying to keep their spirits up, talking about times to come. She liked to take Bill, one of her favorites, for walks downtown. Half of Bill's face was gone, and civilians would stare. It happened to other patients, too. "Nicely dressed women, absolutely staring, just standing there staring." Some people wrote the local paper, wondering why disfigured vets couldn't be kept on their own grounds and off the streets. Such callousness made Basye indignant. The war was over—"and we're still here." After a time, she started dating a soldier back from the South Pacific. "I got busy after the war," she recalled, "getting married and having my four children. That's what you were supposed to do. And getting your house in suburbia."

The Queen Elizabeth *docked in New York harbor on July 20, 1945, with as many of its 14,576 troops as possible crowding the decks or hanging out of portholes in anticipation of the return to home, families, and peacetime.*

Yet as Basye and Black soon discovered, the return to "normal" life was filled with uncertainties. The first truly global war had left a large part of Europe in ruins and the old balance of power shattered. The dramatic events occurring month after month during 1945 and 1946 made it clear that whatever new world order emerged, the United States would have a central role in building it. Isolation seemed neither practical nor desirable in an era in which the power of the Soviet Union and communism seemed on the rise.

Effects of the Cold War

To blunt that threat the United States converted not so much to peace as to a "cold war" against its former Soviet ally. This undeclared war came to affect almost every aspect of American life. Abroad, it justified a far wider military and economic role for the United States in areas like the Middle East and the Pacific Rim nations of Asia, from Korea to Indochina. At home it sent politicians scurrying across the land in a search for Communist spies and "subversives," from the State Department to the movie studios of Hollywood and even into college classrooms.

Preparing for war in times of peace dramatically increased the role of the military-industrial-university complex formed during World War II. A nation that had traditionally followed an isolationist foreign policy now possessed military forces deployed across the globe. A people who had once kept government intrusion into the economy at a minimum now voted to maintain programs that ensured an active federal role. That economy produced prosperity beyond anything Americans had known before.

The Rise of the Cold War

World War II devastated lands and people almost everywhere outside the Western Hemisphere. Once the war ended the world struggled to rebuild. Power that had once been centered in Europe shifted to nations on its periphery. In place of Germany, France, and England, the United States and the Soviet Union emerged as the world's two reigning superpowers—and as enemies. Their rivalry was not altogether an equal one. The United States ended the war with a booming economy, a massive military establishment, and the atomic bomb. In contrast, much of the Soviet Union lay in ruins.

Americans Fear Soviet Intentions

But the defeat of Germany and Japan left no power in Europe or Asia to block the still formidable Soviet army. And many Americans feared that desperate, war-weary peoples would find the appeal of communism irresistible. If Stalin intended to extend the Soviet Union's dominion, only the United States had the economic and military might to block him. Events in the critical years of 1945 and 1946 persuaded most Americans that Stalin did have such a plan. The Truman administration concluded that "the USSR has engaged the United States in a struggle for power, or 'cold war,' in which our national security is at stake and from which we cannot withdraw short of national suicide." What had happened that led Western leaders to such a dire view of their former Soviet allies? How did such a wide breach open between the two nations?

American Suspicions

Roots of the Cold War

Even before postwar events deepened American suspicions of the Soviets, an ideological gulf had separated the two nations. The October Revolution of 1917 shocked most Americans. They had come to view Lenin's Bolshevik revolutionaries with a mixture of fear, suspicion, and loathing. As the Communists grasped power, they had often used violence and terror to achieve their ends. As Marxists they rejected both religion and the notion of private property, two institutions central to the American dream. Furthermore, Soviet propagandists had made no secret that they intended to export revolution throughout the world, including the United States.

Munich Analogy

One event leading to World War II taught Western leaders to resist "appeasement." In 1938 British prime minister Neville Chamberlain's attempt to satisfy Hitler's demands on Czechoslovakia only emboldened the Nazis to expand further. After the war, Secretary of the Navy James Forrestal applied the Munich analogy to the new Europe. Appeasing Russian demands, he believed, would only seem like an attempt "to buy their understanding and sympathy. We tried that once with Hitler. . . . There are no returns on appeasement." To many of Truman's advisers, the Soviet dictator seemed as much bent on conquest as Hitler had been.

Communist Expansion

During the war, Stalin did make numerous demands to control territory along the Soviet borders. And with the coming of peace, he continued to push for greater influence. He asked for a role in controlling the Dardanelles, the narrow straits linking Soviet ports on the Black Sea with the Mediterranean Sea. Soviet forces occupying northern Iran lent support to rebels seeking to break away from the Iranian government. In Greece, local Communists led the fighting to overturn the traditional monarchy.

Asia, too, seemed a target for Communist ambitions. Russian occupation forces in Manchuria were turning over captured Japanese arms to Chinese Communists under Mao Zedong. Russian troops controlled the northern half of Korea. In Vietnam leftist nationalists were fighting against the return of colonial rule.

Despite Russian actions, many historians have argued, American policy makers consistently exaggerated Stalin's ambitions. At war's end, much of the farmland and industry in the Soviet Union lay in ruins. When Stalin looked outward, he saw American occupation forces in Europe and Asia ringing the Soviet Union, their military might backed by a newly developed atomic arsenal. American corporations owned or controlled vast oil fields in the Middle East. Along with the French and the British, the United States was a strong presence in Southeast Asia. Given that situation, many historians have argued, Stalin's actions after the war were primarily defensive, designed to counter what appeared to him a threatening American-European alliance.

More recent evidence from once-secret files of the Soviet Union suggests that despite the ravages of war, Stalin recognized that in 1945 the Soviet Union was emerging as a more powerful state. With Germany and Japan defeated, Soviet borders to the east and west were secure from invasion. Only to the south did Stalin see a problem, along the border with Iran. Further, he recognized that the people of Britain and the United States had tired of fighting. Their leaders were not about to threaten the Soviet Union with war, at least not in the near term. Equally significant, Soviet spies had informed Stalin in 1946 that the United States possessed only a few atom bombs. For the time being, the nuclear threat was more symbolic than real. As a political realist Stalin saw an opportunity to advance the interests of the Soviet state and his own regime—as long as his actions did not risk war.

The tensions arising from the conflicting Soviet and American points of view came to a head in the first months of 1946. Stalin announced in February that the Soviet Union would act vigorously to preserve its national security. In a world dominated by capitalism, he warned, future wars were inevitable. The Russian people had to ensure against "any eventuality" by undertaking a new five-year plan for economic development.

Although some Americans thought Stalin was merely rallying Russian support for his domestic programs, others saw their worst fears confirmed. *Time* magazine, an early voice for a "get tough" policy, called Stalin's speech "the most warlike pronouncement uttered by any top-rank statesman since V-J day." "I'm tired of babying the Soviets," remarked President Truman, who in any case seldom wore kid gloves. Even his mother passed along a message: "Tell Harry to be good, be honest, and behave himself, but I

Churchill, Truman, and Stalin met at Potsdam in July 1945. Their smiles masked serious disagreements about the shape of the postwar world.

The Move to "Get Tough"

think it is now time for him to get tough with someone." In March Winston Churchill warned that the Soviets had dropped an "Iron Curtain" between their satellite nations and the free world. Poland, East Germany, Romania, and Bulgaria lay behind it. Iran, Greece, Turkey, and much of Europe seemed at risk.

A Policy of Containment

As policy makers groped for an effective way to deal with these developments, the State Department received a diplomatic cable, extraordinary for both its length (8,000 words) and its impact in Washington. The author was George Kennan, chargé d'affaires in Moscow and long a student of Soviet conduct. Kennan argued that Russian leaders, including Stalin, were so paranoid that it was impossible to reach any useful accommodations with them. This temperament could best be explained by "the traditional and instinctive Russian sense of insecurity." That insecurity, when combined with Marxist ideology that viewed capitalism as evil, created a potent force for expansion. Soviet power, Kennan explained, "moves inexorably along a prescribed path, like a toy automobile wound up and headed in a given direction, stopping only when it meets some unanswerable force."

George Kennan Defines Containment

The response Kennan recommended was "containment." The United States must apply "unalterable counterforce at every point where [the Soviets] show signs of encroaching upon the interests of a peaceful and stable world." The idea of containment was not particularly novel, but Kennan's historical analysis provided leaders in Washington with a framework for analyzing Soviet behavior. By applying firm diplomatic, economic, and military counterpressure, the United States could block Russian aggression. Truman wholeheartedly adopted the doctrine of containment.

The Truman Doctrine

At first it appeared that Iran, lying along the Soviet Union's southern border, would provide the first test for containment. An independent Iran seemed crucial in protecting rich fields of petroleum in the Persian Gulf region. American oil companies had already taken a major position in the region alongside British fields established earlier in the century. Stalin had pledged to withdraw Russian troops from Iran after the war, but did not, hoping to force Iran to grant the Soviets economic and political concessions. In March 1946 Secretary of State James Byrnes went to the United Nations, determined to force a showdown over continued Soviet occupation of northern Iran. But before he could extract his pound of Russian flesh, the Soviets reached an agreement with Iran to withdraw.

The face-off in Iran only intensified American suspicions. In Europe severe winter storms and a depressed postwar economy threatened to encourage domestic Communist movements. A turning point in the cold war came in early 1947, when Great Britain announced that it could no longer support the governments of Greece and Turkey. Without British aid, the Communists seemed destined to win critical victories. Truman decided that the United States should provide $400 million in military and economic aid. He went before Congress in March, determined to "scare hell out of the country." The world was now divided into two hostile camps, the president warned. To preserve the American way of life, the United States must now step forward and help "free people" threatened by "totalitarian regimes." This rationale for aid to Greece and Turkey soon became known as the Truman Doctrine.

Aid to Greece and Turkey

The Truman Doctrine marked a new level of American commitment to a cold war. Just what responsibility the Soviets had for unrest in Greece and Turkey remained unclear. But Truman had linked communism with rebel movements all around the globe. That committed Americans to a relatively open-ended struggle. In the battle between communism and freedom, the president gained expanded powers to act when unrest threatened. Occasionally Congress would regret giving the executive branch so much

TIME Maps by R.M.Chapin Jr.

As American fears of Soviet intentions increased, journalists often described communism as though it were a disease, an inhuman force, or a savage predator. In April 1946, Time *magazine, a particularly outspoken source of anti-Communist rhetoric, portrayed the spread of "infection" throughout Europe and Asia as the "Red Menace."*

power, but by 1947 anticommunism had become the dominant theme in American policy, both foreign and domestic.

The Marshall Plan

For all its importance, the Truman Doctrine did not address the area of primary concern to Washington, Western Europe. Across Europe desperate people scrounged for food and coal to heat their homes. Streets stood dark at night. National treasuries had neither capital nor credit needed to reopen darkened factories. American diplomats warned that without aid to revive the European economy, Communists would seize power in Germany, Italy, and France.

In June 1947 Secretary of State George C. Marshall stepped before a Harvard commencement audience to announce a recovery plan for Europe. He invited all European nations, East and West, to request assistance to rebuild their economies. Unlike Truman, Marshall did not emphasize the Communist menace. All the same, his massive aid plan was designed to eliminate conditions that produced the discontent Communists often exploited. Humanitarian aid also had its practical benefits. As Europe recovered, so would its ability to buy American goods. The secretary did not rule out Soviet participation, but he gambled that fears of American economic domination would lead the Soviets and their allies to reject his offer.

At first **neo-isolationists** in Congress argued that the United States could not afford such generosity. But when Communists expelled the non-Communists from Czechoslovakia's government, the cold war seemed to spread. Congress then approved the Marshall Plan, as it became known. And as the secretary anticipated, the Soviets blocked the efforts of Czechoslovakia and Poland to participate. The blame for dividing Europe fell, as Marshall guessed it would, on the Soviet Union, not the United States.

Communism in Czechoslovakia

The Fall of Eastern Europe

The intensive American efforts to stabilize Europe and the eastern Mediterranean provoked Stalin to take countermeasures. Most shocking to the Western nations were his steps to consolidate Soviet political and military domination over Eastern Europe. In 1947 he moved against Hungary, run since 1945 by a moderate government chosen under relatively free elections. Soviet forces imposed a Communist regime dependent on Moscow. In February 1948 Communists toppled the duly elected government of Czechoslovakia. Shortly after, news came that the popular Czech foreign minister, Jan Masaryk, had fallen to his death from a small bathroom window. Suicide was the official explanation, but many suspected murder. In response to the Marshall Plan, the Soviet foreign ministry initiated a series of trade agreements tightly linking the Soviet and Eastern European economies. It also established the Cominform, or Communist Information Bureau, to assert greater political control over foreign Communist parties.

The spring of 1948 brought another clash between the Soviets and their former allies, this time over Germany. There, the United States, Great Britain, and France decided to transform their occupation zones into an independent West German state. The Western-controlled sectors of Berlin, however, lay over 100 miles to the east, well within the Soviet zone. On June 24 the Soviets reacted by blockading land access to Berlin. Truman did not hesitate to respond. "We are going to stay, period." But he did say no when General Lucius Clay proposed to shoot his way through the blockade. Instead, the United States began a massive airlift of supplies that lasted almost a year. In May 1949 Stalin lifted the blockade, conceding that he could not prevent the creation of West Germany.

Berlin Airlift

Stalin's aggressive actions accelerated the American effort to use military means to contain Soviet ambitions. By 1949 the United States and Canada had joined with Britain, France, Belgium, the Netherlands, and Luxembourg to establish the North Atlantic Treaty Organization (NATO) as a mutual defense pact. For the first time since George Washington had warned against the practice in his Farewell Address of 1793, the United States during peacetime entered into entangling alliances with European nations.

NATO Formed

Truman's firm handling of the Berlin crisis won him applause from both Democrats and Republicans. They were equally enthusiastic about another bold presidential action. Minutes after the Israelis announced their independence in May 1948, Truman recognized the new state of Israel. He had previously supported the immigration of Jews into Palestine despite the opposition of oil-rich Arab states and diplomats in the State Department. The president sympathized with Jewish aspirations for a homeland. He also faced a tough campaign in 1948 in which Jewish votes would be critical. As British prime minister Clement Attlee observed, "There's no Arab vote in America, but there's a heavy Jewish vote and the Americans are always having elections."

Israel Recognized

The Atomic Shield versus the Iron Curtain

The Berlin crisis forced Truman to consider the possibility of war. If it came, would atomic weapons again be used? That dilemma raised two other difficult questions. Should the decision to use atomic weapons rest in civilian or military hands? And was it possible to find a way to ease the atomic threat by creating an international system to control nuclear power?

On the question of civilian or military control of the bomb, Truman's response was firm. He was not going to have "some dashing lieutenant colonel decide when would be the proper time to drop one." In 1946 Congress seemed to have decided the issue in Truman's favor when it passed the McMahon Act. This bill established the Atomic Energy Commission (AEC), with control of all fissionable materials for both peacetime and military applications. The AEC was a civilian, not a military, agency.

The Atomic Energy Commission

But civilian control was not as complete as Truman had demanded. The wartime head of the Manhattan Project, General Leslie Groves, had been working behind the scenes to give the military a decisive voice in atomic policy. During debate over the bill, Groves had leaked information about a Canadian atomic spy ring delivering secrets to the Soviet Union. That news spread doubts that scientists and civilians could be trusted with key secrets. Thus Groves persuaded Congress to allow the military to review many civilian decisions and even severely limit their actions.

The idea of international control of atomic energy also fell victim to cold war fears. Originally, a high-level government committee proposed to Truman that the mining and use of the world's atomic raw materials be supervised by an agency of the United Nations. The committee argued that in the long run the United States would be more secure under a system of international control than relying on its temporary nuclear monopoly. But Truman chose Bernard Baruch, a staunch cold warrior, to draw up the

Baruch Plan

Cold War Europe   *By 1956 the postwar occupation of Europe had hardened into rigid cold war boundaries. The United States reacted to the presence of Soviet conventional forces in Eastern Europe by rearming West Germany and creating the NATO alliance (1949) for the defense of nations from the North Atlantic through the Mediterranean basin. The U.S.S.R. formed a counteralliance under the Warsaw Pact (1955). Although Bonn became the de facto capital of West Germany, Berlin remained the official capital and into the 1960s the focus of the most severe cold war tensions.*

recommendations to the United Nations in June 1946. Baruch's proposals ensured that the United States would dominate any international atomic agency. The Soviets countered with a plan calling for destruction of all nuclear bombs and a ban on their use. But Baruch had no intention of bargaining. It was either his plan or nothing, he announced. And so it was nothing. The Truman administration never seriously considered giving up the American nuclear monopoly. Stalin, for his part, gave top priority to the Soviet atomic bomb program. Failure at the United Nations thus promoted an arms race, not nuclear supremacy.

As the arms race intensified, American military planners found themselves relying more and more on atomic weapons. The Soviet army had at its command over 260 divisions. In contrast, the United States had reduced its forces by 1947 to little more than a single division. As the cold war heated up, American military planners

Nuclear Deterrence

The Fallout from Fallout

Taking the Pulse of the Nuclear Age

How do you measure fear—or joy—in an entire culture? Taking the emotional measure of a single individual is difficult enough. Yet historians have made efforts to explore the collective mood of the atomic age. Their strategy has been to hunt both high and low for evidence of how political leaders and thinkers as well as ordinary folk reacted to the threat of atomic warfare. Sources have ranged from newspapers, editorials, and magazines to radio shows, song lyrics, movies, letters, advertisements, and comic strips.

Fear was one common response. Newspapers of the era abounded with doomsday scenarios projecting the "final crisis in human history." A typical cartoon pictured an ominous stack of bombs designed to make those dropped on Japan seem puny by comparison. Yet historians have also found curiosity, irreverence, and even marketing hype surrounding the advent of nuclear energy. For just 15 cents and one Kix box top any American kid in 1946 could become the proud owner of an Atomic Bomb Ring. Some three quarters of million youngsters took advantage of the ad's preposterous claim that if they viewed the ring in a darkened room, "WHAM! You'll see frenzied flashes of uncontrollable light . . . caused by the released energy of atoms splitting like crazy. . . ."

Adults discovered their own ways to make peace with the bomb. Some went to the "Atomic Café" to sip atomic cocktails. Hollywood offered up voluptuous starlet Linda Christian as "the anatomic bomb." Whether the mood was one of hope, fear, or cupidity, the atom bomb penetrated deeply into the popular culture. It also led some historians to speculate that these early attempts to make light of the nuclear peril were in reality an attempt to quiet a "paralyzing fear."

Kix Atomic Bomb Ring

As this diagram of a hypothetical bombing of Washington suggests, Americans began to understand that radioactive fallout was a grave danger as well.

were forced to adopt a nuclear strategy in face of the overwhelming superiority of Soviet forces. They would deter any Soviet attack by setting in place a devastating atomic counterattack.

At first, this strategy of nuclear **deterrence** was little more than a makeshift doomsday scenario to incinerate vast areas of the Soviet Union. A 1946 war plan, "Pincher," proposed obliterating 20 Soviet cities if the Soviets attacked Western Europe. But, by 1949, the Joint Chiefs of Staff had fully committed themselves to a policy of nuclear deterrence in an indefinitely extended cold war. Western Europe was on its way to economic recovery, thanks to the Marshall Plan. Soviet pressure on Iran, Greece, and Turkey had abated.

Yet these tentative successes brought little comfort. The Soviet Union was not simply a major power seeking to protect its interests and expand where opportunity permitted. In the eyes of many Americans, the Soviets were determined, if they could, to overthrow the United States from either without or within. This war was being fought not only around the globe but right in America, by unseen agents using subversive means. In this way, the cold war mentality soon came to shape the lives of Americans at home much as it did American policy abroad.

Postwar Prosperity

At war's end, many business leaders feared that a sudden drop in government purchases would bring back the hard times of the 1930s. Instead, despite a rocky year or two adjusting to the peacetime economy, Americans entered into the longest period of prosperity in the nation's history, lasting until the 1970s. Even the fear of communism could not dampen the simple joys of getting and spending.

Two forces drove the postwar economic boom. One was unbridled consumer and business spending that followed 16 years of depression and war. High war wages had piled up in savings accounts and war bonds. Eager consumers set off to find the new cars, appliances, and foods unavailable during the war. Secondly, government expenditures at the local, state, and federal levels provided a boost to prosperity. The three major growth industries in the decades after World War II were health care, education, and government programs. Each of these was spurred by public spending. Equally important, the federal government poured billions of dollars into the military-industrial sector. The defense budget, which fell to $9 billion in 1947, reached $50 billion by the time Truman left office. Over the longer term, these factors promoting economic growth became clearer. In 1946, though, the road from war to peace seemed more uncertain, especially for Americans at the margins of the economy.

Sources of Prosperity

Having lived through twelve years of depression, Americans placed jobs at the top of their postwar domestic agenda. The Employment Act of 1946 shifted responsibility for a full-employment economy from the private sector to the federal government.

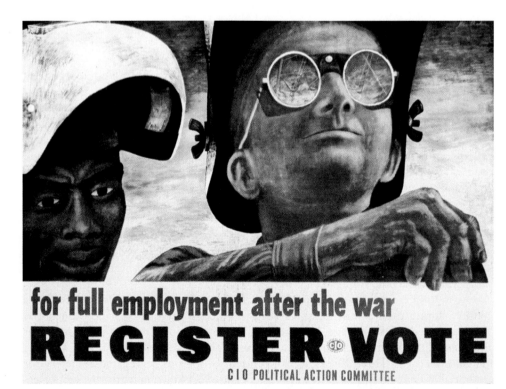

After World War II, Branch Rickey of the Brooklyn Dodgers was determined to break the color line in baseball. For years he had wanted to give black players the opportunity to play in the majors. Equally to the point, he was convinced that this action would improve his team. "The greatest untapped reservoir of raw material in the history of the game is the black race," he explained, adding, "The Negroes will make us winners for years to come."

In the early years of professional baseball, African Americans had played on several major league teams. In 1887, however, as Jim Crow laws spread across the South, the threat of a boycott by some white players caused team owners to adopt an unwritten rule barring black players. That ban stood for 60 years.

World War II created a new climate. The hypocrisy of fighting racism abroad while promoting it at home was becoming harder for team owners to ignore.

"If a black boy can make it on Okinawa and Guadalcanal," Commissioner Albert "Happy" Chandler told reporters in April 1945, "hell, he can make it in baseball."

Jackie Robinson and his teammates celebrating a key win in the 1948 pennant race. Though Robinson had made the Dodgers a much better team, full integration of major league sports took many more years.

Postwar Adjustments

With millions of veterans looking for peacetime jobs, workers on the home front, especially women and minorities, found themselves out of work. As peace came, almost 75 percent of the working women in one survey indicated that they hoped to continue their jobs. But as the troops came home, male social scientists stressed how important it was for women to accept "more than the wife's usual responsibility for her marriage" and offer "lavish—and undemanding—affection" on returning GIs. One marriage counselor urged women to let their husbands know "you are tired of living alone, that you want him now to take charge."

For minorities, the end of the war brought the return of an old labor practice, "last hired, first fired." At the height of the war over 200,000 African Americans and Hispanics had found jobs in shipbuilding. By 1946 that number had dwindled to fewer than 10,000. The influx of Mexican laborers under the bracero program temporarily halted. In the South, where the large majority of black Americans lived, wartime labor shortages had become surpluses, leaving few jobs available.

At the same time, many Hispanic and black veterans who had fought for their country during the war resented returning to a deeply segregated society. Such GIs "have acquired a new courage, have become more vocal in protesting the restrictions and inequalities with which they are confronted," noted one white Texan. When a funeral director in Three Rivers, Texas, refused to open its segregated cemetery for the burial of Felix Longoria, a Mexican American soldier killed in battle, his supporters

Economic factors played a role as well. The African American migration to northern cities during World War II created a new, untapped audience for major league baseball. Growing cold war tensions added another factor. Even a Mississippi newspaper saw blacks in the major leagues as "a good answer to our communist adversaries who say the Negro has no chance in America."

Rickey recognized the enormous hostility that the first black player would face. He found the ideal prospect in Jackie Robinson, a World War II veteran and a remarkable athlete who had lettered in four sports at UCLA. Rickey told Robinson in 1945, "I need a man that will take abuse, insults." Robinson would be carrying "the flag for [his] race."

Robinson was willing. He had risked court-martial during the war to fight segregation. "Nobody's going to separate bullets and label them 'for white troops' and 'for colored troops,'" Robinson told a superior officer. But he assured Rickey, "If you want to take this gamble, I will promise you there will be no incident." Rickey assigned him to Montreal, where he led the Dodgers' farm team to a championship.

When the Dodgers invited Robinson to spring training, several southern-born players circulated a petition stating their opposition to playing with a black man. But manager Leo Durocher bluntly warned them they would be traded if they refused to cooperate. Robinson would make them all rich, Durocher insisted.

On April 15, 1947, Robinson made his debut with the Dodgers at Ebbets Field. A black newspaper, the Boston *Chronicle*, proclaimed, "TRIUMPH OF WHOLE RACE SEEN IN JACKIE'S DEBUT IN MAJOR LEAGUE BALL."

But the abuse heaped on Robinson was worse than Rickey had anticipated. Robinson received death threats, his family was harassed, and some hotels barred him from staying with the team. He secretly wore a protective lining inside his hat in case he was beaned (he was hit a record nine times during the season, 65 times in seven years). Through it all, Robinson kept his temper, though not without difficulty. Once when a Cubs player kicked him, Robinson started to swing, then stopped. "I knew I was kind of an experiment," he recalled; " . . . the whole thing was bigger than me."

In Robinson's first year, the Dodgers won the pennant and he was named Rookie of the Year. Two years later he was named the Most Valuable Player in the National League. After he retired in 1957, the skill and dignity he brought to the game earned him a place in baseball's Hall of Fame.

In the wake of his success, other teams added African Americans. Professional basketball and football followed baseball's lead. Still, the pace of integration was slow, and it was not until 1959 that all major league teams had at least one black member. Thanks to the vision of Branch Rickey and the courage of Jackie Robinson, America's pastime had become truly a national game.

organized. Led by Dr. Hector Garcia, a former army medical officer, the American G.I. Forum was founded in 1948 to campaign for civil rights. Longoria was finally buried in Arlington National Cemetery after the G.I. Forum convinced Congressman Lyndon Baines Johnson to intervene.

Black veterans had a similar impact on the civil rights movement. Angered by violence, frustrated by the slow pace of desegregation, they breathed new energy into civil rights organizations like the NAACP and CORE (the Congress of Racial Equality). Voting rights was one of the issues they pushed. Registration drives in the South had the greatest success in urban centers like Atlanta. Other black leaders pressed for improved education.

Out in the countryside, however, segregationists used economic intimidation, violence, and even murder, to preserve the Jim Crow system. White citizens in rural Georgia lynched several black veterans who had shown the determination to vote. Such instances disturbed President Truman, who saw civil rights as a key ingredient in his reform agenda. The president was especially disturbed when he learned that police in South Carolina had gouged out the eyes of a recently discharged black veteran. Truman responded in December 1946 by appointing a Committee on Civil Rights. A year later the committee published its report, *To Secure These Rights*.

Discovering inequities for minorities, the committee exposed a racial caste system that denied African Americans employment opportunities, equal education, voting rights, and decent housing. But every time Truman appealed to Congress to implement the committee's recommendations, southern senators threatened to filibuster.

The Liga Pro Defensa Escolar, *or Pro Schools Defense League, pushed to abolish segregated schooling, which affected Latinos as well as African Americans. No doubt deliberately, the League's emblem was written in English.*

That opposition forced the president to resort to executive authority to achieve even modest results. In his most direct attack on segregation, he issued an **executive order** in July 1948 banning discrimination in the armed forces. Segregationists predicted disaster, but experience soon demonstrated that integrated units fought well and exhibited minimal racial tension.

Several Supreme Court decisions gave added weight to Truman's civil rights initiatives. In cases that indicated a growing willingness to reconsider the doctrine that black facilities could be "**separate but equal**" (*Plessy v. Ferguson,* 1896), the Court struck down several state education laws clearly designed to create separate but inferior facilities.

Organized Labor

For organized labor, reconversion brought an abrupt drop in hours worked and overtime paid. As wages declined and inflation ate into paychecks, strikes spread. Autoworkers walked off the job in the fall of 1945; steelworkers, in January 1946; miners, in April. In 1946 some 5 million workers struck, a rate triple that of any previous year. Antiunion sentiment soared. The crisis peaked in May 1946 with a national rail strike, which temporarily paralyzed the nation's transportation network. An angry President Truman asked, "What decent American would pull a rail strike at a time like this?"

At first, Truman threatened to seize the railroads and then requested from Congress the power to draft striking workers into the military. The strike was settled before the threat was carried out, but few people, whether conservative or liberal, approved the idea of using the draft to punish political foes. Labor leaders, for their part, became convinced they no longer had a friend at the White House.

Truman under Attack

In September 1945 Harry Truman had boldly claimed his intention to extend the New Deal into the postwar era. He called for legislation to guarantee full employment, subsidized public housing, national health insurance, and a peacetime version of the Fair Employment Practices Commission to fight job discrimination. Instead of promoting his liberal agenda, he found himself fighting a conservative backlash. Labor unrest was just one source of his troubles. The increased demand for consumer goods temporarily in short supply triggered a sharp inflation. For two years prices rose as much as 15 percent annually.

With Truman's political stock falling, conservative Republicans and Democrats blocked the president's attempts to revive and extend the New Deal. All he achieved was a watered-down full-employment bill, which created the Council of Economic Advisers to guide the president's policies. The bill did establish the principle that the government rather than the private sector was responsible for maintaining full employment. As the congressional elections of 1946 neared, Republicans pointed to production shortages, the procession of strikes, the mismanagement of the economy. "To err is Truman," proclaimed the campaign buttons—or, more simply, "Had Enough?" Evidently many voters had. The Republicans gained control of both houses of Congress. Not since 1928 had the Democrats fared so poorly.

Leading the rightward swing was Senator Robert A. Taft of Ohio, son of former president William Howard Taft. Bob Taft not only wanted to halt the spread of the New Deal—he wanted to dismantle it. "We have to get over the corrupting idea we can legislate prosperity, legislate equality, legislate opportunity," he said in dismissing the liberal agenda. Taft especially wished to limit the power of the unions. In 1947 he pushed the

Taft-Hartley Act

Taft-Hartley Act through Congress, over Truman's veto. In the event of a strike, the bill allowed the president to order workers back on the job during a 90-day cooling-off period while collective bargaining continued. It also permitted states to adopt right-to-work laws, which banned the closed shop by eliminating union membership as a prerequisite for many jobs. Union leaders criticized the new law as a slave-labor act but discovered they could live with it, though it did hurt union efforts to organize, especially in the South.

A Welfare Program for GIs

Despite Republican gains, most Americans still supported the New Deal's major accomplishments: Social Security, minimum wages, a more active role for government in reducing unemployment. The administration maintained its commitment to setting a minimum wage, raising it again in 1950, from 45 to 75 cents. Social Security coverage was broadened to cover an additional 10 million workers. Furthermore, a growing list of welfare programs benefited not only the poor but veterans, middle-income families, the elderly, and students. The most striking of these was the GI Bill of 1944, designed to reward soldiers for their service during the war.

The GI Bill

For veterans, the "GI Bill of Rights" created unparalleled opportunity. Those with more than two years of service received all tuition and fees plus living expenses for three years of college education. By 1948 the government was paying the college costs of nearly half of all male students as more than 2 million veterans took advantage of the GI Bill. Increased educational levels encouraged a shift from blue- to white-collar work and self-employment. Veterans also received low-interest loans to start businesses or farms of their own and to buy homes. The GI Bill accelerated trends that would transform American society into a prosperous, heavily middle-class suburban nation.

Less fortunately, the bill did little to help minorities and females. Few women received benefits under the bill. African Americans and Hispanics, even those eligible for veterans' benefits, were hampered by Jim Crow restrictions in segregated universities and in jobs in both the public and private sectors. The Federal Housing Administration even helped draw up "model" restrictive housing covenants. In order to "retain stability," neighborhoods were allowed to use the covenants to segregate according to "social and racial classes."

The Election of 1948

With his domestic program blocked, Harry Truman faced almost certain defeat in the election of 1948. The New Deal coalition that Franklin Roosevelt had held together for so long seemed to be coming apart. On the left Truman was challenged by Henry Wallace, a progressive who had been vice president under Roosevelt and who wanted to pursue New Deal reforms even more vigorously than Truman did. Disaffected liberals bolted the Democratic party to support Wallace on a third-party Progressive ticket.

Henry Wallace and the Progressives

Within the southern conservative wing of the party, archsegregationists resented Truman's moderate civil rights proposals for a voting rights bill and an antilynching law. When the liberal wing of the party passed a civil rights plank as part of the Democratic platform, delegates from several Deep South states stalked out of the convention. They banded together to create the States' Rights or "Dixiecrat" party, with J. Strom Thurmond, the segregationist governor of South Carolina, as their candidate.

Dixiecrats

With the Democrats divided, Republicans smelled victory. They moved toward the political center by rejecting the conservative Taft in favor of the more moderate former New York governor Thomas Dewey. Dewey proved so aloof that he inspired scant enthusiasm. "You have to know Dewey well to really dislike him," quipped one Taft supporter. Still, most observers assumed that Dewey would walk away with the race. Pollster Elmo Roper stopped canvassing the voters two months before the election.

Truman, however, did not roll over and play dead. He launched a stinging attack against the "reactionaries" in Congress: that "bunch of old mossbacks . . . gluttons of privilege . . . all set to do a hatchet job on the New Deal." From the rear platform of his campaign train, he made almost 400 speeches in eight weeks. Over and over he hammered away at the "do-nothing" 80th Congress, which, he told farmers, "had stuck a pitchfork" in their backs. Hours before the polls closed, the archconservative Chicago *Tribune*

Truman Fights Back

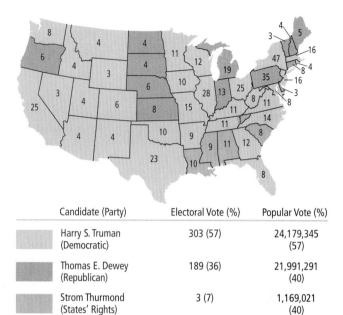

Candidate (Party)	Electoral Vote (%)	Popular Vote (%)
Harry S. Truman (Democratic)	303 (57)	24,179,345 (57)
Thomas E. Dewey (Republican)	189 (36)	21,991,291 (40)
Strom Thurmond (States' Rights)	3 (7)	1,169,021 (40)
Harry A. Wallace (Progressive)		1,157,172 (40)
Other candidates (Communist, Prohibition, Socialist Labor, Liberty)	–	272,713 –

Election of 1948

happily headlined "Dewey Defeats Truman." But the experts were wrong. Not only did the voters return Truman by over 2 million popular votes, but they also gave the Democrats commanding majorities in the House and Senate.

The defection of the liberal and conservative extremes had allowed Truman to hold the New Deal coalition together after all. Jews grateful for his stand on Israel, Catholics loyal to the Democratic party, and ethnics all supported him. He had been the first major presidential candidate to campaign in Harlem. Farmers hurt by falling prices deserted the Republicans. An easing of inflation had reminded middle-income Americans that they had benefited significantly under Democratic leadership. "I have a new car and am much better off than my parents were. Why change?" one suburban voter remarked.

The Fair Deal

As he began his new term, Harry Truman expressed his conviction that all Americans were entitled to a "Fair Deal" from their government. His agenda called for a vigorous revival of New Deal programs such as national health insurance and regional TVA-style projects. Echoing an old Populist idea, Truman hoped to keep his working coalition together by forging stronger links between farmers and labor. But the conservative coalition of Democrats and Republicans in Congress blocked any significant new initiatives. On the domestic front Truman remained largely the conservator of Franklin Roosevelt's legacy.

The Cold War at Home

Bob Raymondi, a mobster serving a prison term in the late 1940s, was no stranger to extortion, racketeering, or gangland killings. In fact, he was so feared that he dominated the inmate population at Dannemora Prison. Raymondi began to make the acquaintance of a group of Communists who had been jailed for advocating the overthrow of the government. He enjoyed talking with people who had some education. When Raymondi's sister learned about his new friends, she was frantic. "My God, Bob," she told him. "You'll get into trouble."

Was something amiss? Most Americans judged it riskier to associate with Communists than with hardened criminals. Out of a population of 150 million, the Communist party in 1950 could claim a membership of only 43,000. (More than a few of those were FBI undercover agents.) But Americans did worry about Communists. In part, conscientious citizens were appalled by party members who excused Stalin's violent crimes against his own people. Millions of Russians had been executed or sent to Siberian labor camps; under those circumstances, most Americans found it outrageous to hear American Communists dismiss civil liberties as "bourgeois."

Conservative Anti-Communism

Conservatives were especially outspoken about the Communist menace. Some honestly feared the New Deal as "creeping socialism." The president's advisers, it seemed to them, were either Communist agents or their unwitting dupes. Leftists, they believed, controlled labor unions, Hollywood, and other interest groups sympathetic to the New Deal. Conservative outrage grew as Stalin extended Soviet control in Eastern Europe and Asia. Many conservatives charged that a conspiracy within Roosevelt's administration had sold out America to its enemies. More cynical conservatives used Red baiting simply to discredit people and ideas they disliked.

The Shocks of 1949

Truman won in 1948 in large part because of his strong leadership in foreign affairs. In 1949 a series of foreign policy shocks allowed Republicans to seize the anti-Communist issue. In August American scientists reported that rains monitored in the Pacific contained traces of hot nuclear waste. Only one conclusion seemed possible: the Soviet Union possessed its own atom bomb. When Truman announced the news, Congress was debating whether to spend $1.5 billion for military aid to the newly formed NATO alliance. The House stopped debating and passed the bill, while Truman decided to accelerate research into a newer, more powerful fusion, or hydrogen, bomb. Senator Arthur Vandenberg, a Republican with wide experience in international affairs, summed up the reaction of many to the end of the American nuclear monopoly: "This is now a different world."

The H-bomb

Then in December came more bad news. The long-embattled Nationalist government of Chiang Kai-shek had fled mainland China to the offshore island of Formosa (present-day Taiwan). By January Communist troops under Mao Zedong were swarming into Beijing, China's capital city. Chiang's defeat came as no surprise to State Department officials, who had long regarded the Nationalists as hopelessly corrupt and inefficient. Despite major American efforts to save Chiang's regime, full-scale civil war had broken out in 1947. Mao's triumph was hardly unexpected.

China Falls to Communists

But Republicans, who had up until 1949 supported the president's foreign policy, now broke

The fall of China to the Communist forces of Mao Zedong was one of two great cold war shocks of 1949. Anti-Communists joined members of the China Lobby in blaming Truman for "losing China."

ranks. For some time, a group of wealthy conservatives and Republican senators had resented the administration's preoccupation with Europe. Time-Life publisher Henry Luce used his magazines to campaign for a greater concern for Asian affairs and especially more aid to defeat Mao Zedong. Luce and his associates, known as the "China Lobby," were supported in part with funds from the Chinese embassy. When Chiang at last collapsed, his American backers charged Democrats with letting the Communists win.

The Hiss Case

Worries that subversives had sold out the country were heightened when former State Department official Alger Hiss was brought to trial in 1949 for perjury. Hiss, an adviser to Roosevelt at the Yalta Conference, had been accused by former Communist Whittaker Chambers of passing secrets to the Soviet Union during the 1930s. Though the evidence in the case was far from conclusive, the jury convicted Hiss for lying about his association with Chambers. And in February 1950 the nation was further shocked to learn that a high-ranking British physicist, Klaus Fuchs, had spied for the Russians while working on the Manhattan Project. Here was clear evidence of conspiracy at work.

The Loyalty Crusade

President Truman sought to blunt Republican accusations that he was "soft" on communism. Ten days after proposing the Truman Doctrine in March 1947, the president signed an executive order establishing a Federal Employee Loyalty Program designed to guard against the possible disloyalty of "Reds, phonies, and 'parlor pinks.'" Since the FBI could hardly find time to examine all of the 2 million government employees, the order required supervisors to review and certify the loyalties of those who worked below them, reporting to a system of federal loyalty review boards.

Loyalty Review Board

The system quickly got out of hand. Seth Richardson, the conservative head of the Loyalty Review Board, argued that the government could "discharge any employee for reasons which seem sufficient to the Government, and without extending to such employee any hearing whatsoever." After several years the difficulty of proving that employees were actually disloyal became clear, and Truman allowed the boards to fire those who were "potentially" disloyal or "bad security risks," such as alcoholics, homosexuals, and debtors. Suspect employees, in other words, were assumed guilty until proven innocent. After some 5 million investigations, the program identified a few hundred employees who, though not Communists, had at one time been associated with suspect groups. Rather than calm public fears, the loyalty program gave credibility to the growing Red scare.

HUAC, Hollywood, and Unions

About the same time Truman established the Loyalty Review Board, the House Committee on Un-American Activities (HUAC) began to investigate Communist influence in the film industry. Hollywood, with its wealth, glamour, and highly visible Jewish and foreign celebrities, had long aroused a mixture of attraction and suspicion among traditional Americans. "Large numbers of moving pictures that come out of Hollywood carry the Communist line," charged committee member John Rankin of Mississippi. Indeed, during the Depression some Hollywood figures had developed ties to the Communist party or had become sympathetic to party causes. To generate support for the Allies during the war, Hollywood (with Roosevelt's blessing) produced films with a positive view of the Soviet Union such as *Mission to Moscow* and *Song of Russia.*

Hollywood Ten

HUAC called a parade of movie stars, screenwriters, and producers to sit in the glare of its public hearings. Some witnesses, such as Gary Cooper and Ronald Reagan, were considered "friendly" because they supplied names of suspected leftists. Others refused to inform on their colleagues. Eventually 10 uncooperative witnesses, known as the "Hollywood Ten," refused on First Amendment grounds to say whether they were or ever had been Communists. They served prison terms for contempt of Congress.

For all its probing, HUAC never offered convincing evidence that filmmakers were in any way subversive. About the most damning evidence presented was that one eager left-leaning extra, when asked to "whistle something" during his walk-on part, hummed a few bars of the Communist anthem the "Internationale." The investigations did, however, inspire nervous Hollywood producers to turn out films such as *I Was a Communist for the FBI* (1950). The studios also adopted a blacklist that prevented admitted or accused Communists from finding work. Because no judicial proceedings were involved, victims of false charges, rumors, or spiteful accusations found it nearly impossible to clear their names.

Blacklisting

Suspicion of aliens and immigrants led finally to the passage, over Truman's veto, of the McCarran Act (1950). It required all Communists to register with the attorney general, forbade the entry of anyone who had belonged to a totalitarian organization, and allowed the Justice Department to detain suspect aliens indefinitely during deportation hearings. That same year a Senate committee began an inquiry designed to root out homosexuals holding government jobs. Even one "sex pervert in a Government agency tends to have a corrosive influence upon his fellow employees," warned the committee. The campaign had effects beyond government offices: the armed forces stepped up their rates of dismissal for sexual orientation, while city police more frequently raided gay bars and social clubs.

McCarran Act

The Ambitions of Senator McCarthy

By 1950 anticommunism had created a climate of fear in which legitimate concerns mixed with irrational hysteria. Joseph R. McCarthy, a Senate nonentity from Wisconsin, saw in that fear an issue with which to rebuild his political fortunes. To an audience in Wheeling, West Virginia, in February 1950 he waved a sheaf of papers in the air and announced that he had a list of 205—or perhaps 81, 57, or "a lot of"—Communists in the State Department. (No one, including the senator, could remember the number, which he continually changed.) In the following months McCarthy leveled charge after charge. He had penetrated the "iron curtain" of the State Department to discover "card-carrying Communists," the "top Russian espionage agent" in the United States, "egg-sucking phony liberals," and "Communists and queers" who wrote "perfumed notes."

It didn't seem to matter that McCarthy never substantiated his charges. When examined, his lists contained names of people who had left the State Department long before or who had been cleared by the FBI. When forced into a corner, McCarthy simply lied and went on to another accusation. No one seemed beyond reach. In the summer of 1950 a Senate committee headed by Millard F. Tydings of Maryland concluded that McCarthy's charges were "a fraud and a hoax." Such candor among those in government did not last long, as "Jolting Joe" (one of McCarthy's favorite macho nicknames) in 1952 helped defeat Tydings and several other Senate critics.

McCarthy served as a blunt instrument that some conservative Republicans used to damage the Democrats. Without this support, McCarthy would have had little credibility. Many of his accusations came from information secretly (and illegally) funneled to him by FBI director J. Edgar Hoover. But McCarthyism was also the bitter fruit Truman and the Democrats reaped from their own attempts to exploit the anti-Communist mood. McCarthy, more than Truman, tapped the fears and hatreds of a broad coalition of Catholic leaders, conservatives, and neo-isolationists who harbored suspicion of things foreign, liberal, internationalist, European, or a touch too intellectual. They saw McCarthy and his allies as the protectors of a deeply felt spirit of Americanism.

Many Hollywood films exploited anti-communist fears.

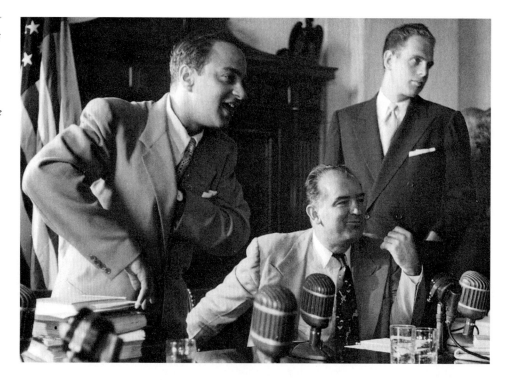

The energetic and opportunistic Roy Cohn (left) served as a key strategist in the inquisition that made Senator Joseph McCarthy a figure to fear. He and fellow staffer David Schine (right) helped McCarthy turn a minor Senate subcommittee into a major power center.

By the time Truman stepped down as president, 32 states had laws requiring teachers to take loyalty oaths, government loyalty boards were asking employees what newspapers they subscribed to or phonograph records they collected. A library in Indiana had banned *Robin Hood* because the idea of stealing from the rich to give to the poor seemed too leftish. As one historian commented, "Opening the valve of anticommunist hysteria was a good deal simpler than closing it."

From Cold War to Hot War and Back

As the cold war heated up in 1949, the Truman administration searched for a more assertive foreign policy—one that went beyond George Kennan's notion of "containment." The new policy was developed by the National Security Council (NSC), an agency created by Congress in 1947 as part of a plan to help the executive branch respond more effectively to cold war crises. Rather than merely "contain" the Soviets, as George Kennan had suggested, the National Security Council wanted the United States to "strive for victory." In April 1950 it sent Truman a document, NSC-68, which came to serve as the framework for American policy over the next 20 years.

NSC-68

NSC-68 called for an immediate increase in defense spending from $13 billion to $50 billion a year, to be paid for with a large tax increase. Most of the funds would go to rebuild conventional forces, but the NSC urged that the hydrogen bomb be developed to offset the Soviet nuclear capacity. Efforts to carry out NSC-68 at first aroused widespread opposition. George Kennan argued that the Soviets had no immediate plans for domination outside the Communist bloc. Thus, NSC-68 was too simplistic and militaristic. Fiscal conservatives, both Democrat and Republican, resisted any proposal for higher taxes. All such reservations were swept away on June 25, 1950. "Korea came along and saved us," Secretary of State Dean Acheson later remarked.

Police Action

In 1950 Korea was about the last place in the world Americans might have imagined themselves fighting a war. Since World War II the country had been divided along the

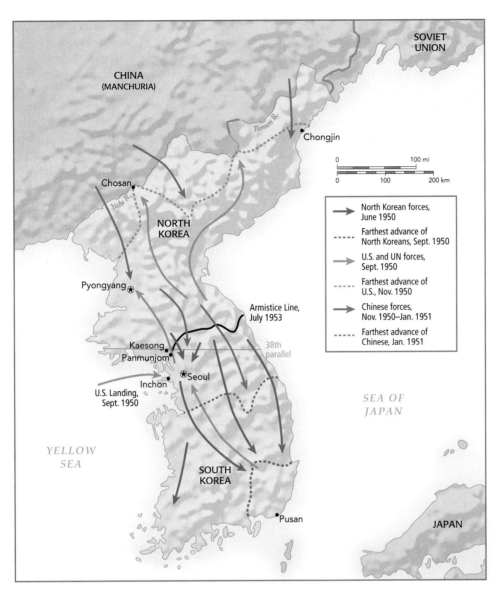

The Korean War   *In their opening offensive, North Korean troops almost pushed South Korean and American forces into the sea at Pusan. After MacArthur rallied UN forces, he commanded a successful landing at Inchon behind North Korean lines and then crossed the 38th parallel into North Korea. Red Chinese troops counterattacked, inflicting one of the most humiliating defeats on U.S. troops in American military history. Fighting continued for another two years.*

38th parallel, the north controlled by the Communist government of Kim Il Sung, the south by the dictatorship of Syngman Rhee. Preoccupied with China and the rebuilding of Japan, the Truman administration's interest had dwindled steadily after the war. When Secretary of State Acheson discussed American policy in Asia before the National Press Club in January 1950, he did not even mention Korea.

On June 24 Harry Truman was enjoying a leisurely break from politics at the family home in Independence, Missouri. In Korea it was already Sunday morning when Acheson called the president. North Korean troops had crossed the 38th parallel, Acheson reported, possibly to fulfill Kim Il Sung's proclaimed intention to "liberate" the South. Soon Acheson confirmed that a full-scale invasion was in progress. The United Nations, meeting in emergency session, had ordered a cease-fire, which the North Koreans were ignoring. With that, Truman flew back to Washington, convinced that Stalin and his Chinese Communist allies had ordered the invasion. Kim, Truman reasoned, would hardly have acted on his own. The threat of a third world war, this one atomic, seemed agonizingly real. Truman and his advisers wanted to respond firmly enough to deter aggression but without provoking a larger war with the Soviet Union or China.

Truman did not hesitate; American troops would fight the North Koreans, though the United States would not declare war. The fighting in Korea would be a "police action" supervised by the United Nations. On June 27 the Security Council passed a U.S.

North Korean Invasion

resolution to send United Nations forces to Korea. That move succeeded only because the Soviet delegate, who possessed veto power, had walked out six months earlier in protest over the council's refusal to seat mainland China. Stalin had secretly approved North Korea's attack, but he promised only supplies. Neither Russian troops nor prestige would be involved, he warned Kim.

Truman's forceful response won immediate approval across America. Congress quickly voted the huge increase in defense funds needed to carry out the recommendations of NSC-68. American allies were less committed to the action. Though 16 nations contributed to the war effort, the United States provided half of the ground troops, 86 percent of the naval units, and 93 percent of the air force. By the time the UN forces could be marshaled, North Korean forces had pinned the South Koreans within a small defensive perimeter centered on Pusan. Then Douglas MacArthur, commander of the UN forces, launched a daring amphibious attack behind North Korean lines at Inchon, near the western end of the 38th parallel. Fighting eastward, MacArthur's troops threatened to trap the invaders, who fled back to the North.

The Chinese Intervene

MacArthur's success led Truman to a fateful decision. With the South liberated, he gave MacArthur permission to cross the 38th parallel, drive the Communists from the North, and reunite the country under Syngman Rhee. With Senator Joe McCarthy on the attack at home, the 1950 elections nearing, and the McCarran Act just passed, Truman was glad enough for the chance to vanquish the North Koreans. By Thanksgiving American troops had roundly defeated northern forces and were advancing on several fronts toward the frozen Yalu River, the boundary between Korea and China. MacArthur, emboldened by success, promised that the boys would be home by Christmas.

Throughout the fall offensive, however, Chinese Premier Zhou Enlai warned that his country would not tolerate an American presence on its border. Washington officials

Marines in North Korea wait at a roadblock on December 1, 1950. American forces retreated after the Chinese crossed the Yalu. The harsh weather added to the casualties.

belittled the warning. Mao Zedong, they assumed, was a Soviet puppet, and Stalin had declared the Korean conflict to be merely a "civil war" and off-limits. But after MacArthur launched his end-the-war offensive, some 400,000 Chinese troops poured across the Yalu, smashing through lightly defended UN lines. At Chosan they trapped 20,000 American and South Korean troops, inflicting one of the worst defeats in American military history. Within three weeks they had driven UN forces back behind the 38th parallel. So total was the rout that Truman wondered publicly about using the atom bomb. That remark sent a frightened British prime minister Clement Attlee flying to Washington to dissuade the president. He readily agreed that the war must remain limited and withdrew his nuclear threat.

Truman versus MacArthur

The military stalemate in Korea brought into the open a simmering feud between MacArthur and Truman. The general had made no secret of his political ambitions or of his differences with Truman over American policy in Asia. He was eager to bomb Chinese and Russian supply bases across the Korean border, to blockade China's coast, and to "unleash" Chiang Kai-shek on mainland China. On March 23 he issued a personal ultimatum to Chinese military commanders demanding total surrender. To his Republican congressional supporters he sent a letter declaring, "We must win. There is no substitute for victory."

To Truman, MacArthur's insubordination threatened the tradition that military policy remained under clear civilian control. Equally alarming, MacArthur's strategy appeared to be an open invitation to another world war. Despite the general's enormous popularity, Truman made plans to discipline him. When General Omar Bradley reported that MacArthur threatened to resign before Truman could act, the irate Truman replied, "The son of a bitch isn't going to resign on me. I want him fired!" Military leaders agreed that MacArthur had to go. On April 11 a stunned nation learned that the celebrated military commander had been relieved of his duties. On his return to the States, cheering crowds gave MacArthur one of the largest ticker-tape parades in New York City's history. Truman's move seemed one of the great political mistakes of his career.

The Global Implications of the Cold War

Behind the scenes, however, Truman was winning this personal clash. At stake was not simply the issue of whether he or MacArthur would prevail. Rather, the outcome would determine the future direction of American foreign policy. The cold war crisis forced American leaders to think globally. Where in the world did the nation's interests lie? What region was most critical to the future? MacArthur believed that the Pacific basin would "determine the course of history in the next ten thousand years." To avoid being swept aside, the United States should make an all-out effort, not just to contain the Communist onslaught in Korea, but to play a major role throughout Asia. "What I advocate is that we defend every place, and I say that we have the capacity to do it," insisted MacArthur. Many conservative Republicans and groups like the China Lobby shared MacArthur's view.

Truman and his advisers continued to see Europe as the key to American foreign policy. Western Europe in particular, they believed, remained the center of the world's economic and military power. Political scientist Hans Morgenthau argued that "he who controls Europe is well on his way toward controlling the whole world." Further, Eurocentric Americans felt that the cultural differences between the United States and Asia were so great that the battle for Asia could not be won by military might. As theologian Reinhold Niebuhr put it, using American cold war weapons against the ideology of communism would be "like the spears of the knights when gunpowder challenged their reign."

Europe, Not Asia, First

With the rise of a cold war between the United States and the Soviet Union, the fears of an atomic war that might leave the world in ashes became a part of everyday life—and of popular culture. This poster advertising Invasion U.S.A., a film first released in 1953, conjured up a New York City in ruins. Hollywood studios made a number of such low-budget movies that reflected American fears of the Communist menace.

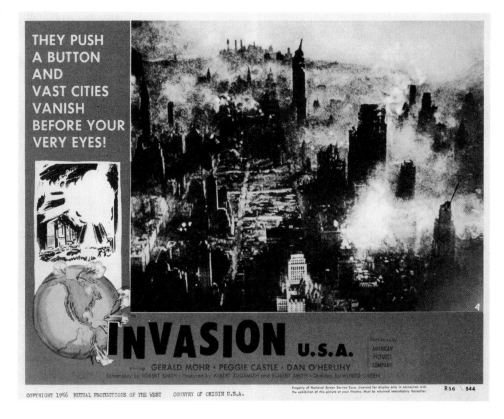

Secretary of State Acheson agreed with the Eurocentrists. Korea was to Acheson but a small link in a global "collective security system." The wider war in Asia that MacArthur favored would threaten American interests in Europe because American resources would be stretched too thinly. Or, as General Bradley told Congress, a war in Asia would lead to "the wrong war, at the wrong place, at the wrong time, and with the wrong enemy." In this debate the Eurocentric faction prevailed. Congressional leaders agreed with Truman that the war in Korea should remain limited and that American resources should go to rebuilding Europe's defenses.

Meanwhile, the war in Korea bogged down in stalemate. As peace negotiators argued over how to reunify Korea, the United States suffered another 32,000 casualties in an ugly war of attrition. By March 1952 Truman's popularity had sunk so low that he lost the New Hampshire presidential primary to Senator Estes Kefauver of Tennessee. With that defeat, he announced he would not run for reelection in 1952.

The Election of 1952

With Truman out of the race, the war in stalemate, and the Fair Deal agenda blunted by anticommunist crusades, the Republicans were determined to triumph in the 1952 elections. Rather than choose Senator Robert Taft from the party's conservative wing, they tapped General Dwight Eisenhower, a World War II hero. Eisenhower was less ideological: in fact, no one even knew whether he was a Republican or Democrat until he announced he was joining the Republican party. Although the Democratic candidate, Senator Adlai Stevenson of Illinois, was an eloquent speaker, he lacked Eisenhower's common touch. "I like Ike!" proclaimed his campaign posters. Furthermore, the general pledged that if elected, he would go to Korea personally to help end the conflict.

The Eisenhower bandwagon hit a speed bump, however, when newspapers reported that a group of wealthy Californians had provided Ike's running mate, the staunch anticommunist Richard Nixon, with an $18,000 "slush fund" to help cover personal expenses.

With his place on the ticket in peril, Nixon made an impassioned television appeal, portraying himself and his wife, Pat, as ordinary folks with a mortgage to pay. And yes, his daughter Tricia had received a cocker spaniel puppy named Checkers, but no matter what his enemies might say, his family was going to keep the dog. Sympathetic viewers deluged GOP headquarters with messages of support. Nixon's survival demonstrated the power of television to influence public opinion.

The election outcome was never much in doubt. Eisenhower's broad smile and confident manner won him more than 55 percent of the vote. "The great problem of America today," Eisenhower had said during the campaign, "is to take that straight road down the middle." Most Americans who voted for him were comforted to think that was just where they were headed.

Even before taking office, Eisenhower traveled to Korea to appraise the situation firsthand. Once in office, he renewed negotiations but warned that unless the talks made speedy progress, the United States might retaliate "under circumstances of our choosing." The carrot-and-stick approach worked. On July 27, 1953, the Communists and the UN forces signed an armistice ending a "police action" in which 54,000 Americans had died. Korea remained divided, almost as it had been in 1950. Communism had been "contained," but at a high price in human lives.

Nixon's Checkers Speech

Eisenhower and Korea

The Fall of McCarthy

It was less clear, however, whether domestic anticommunism could be contained. Eisenhower boasted that he was a "modern" Republican, distinguishing himself from what he called the more "hidebound" members of the GOP. Their continuing anti-Communist campaigns caused him increasing embarrassment. Senator McCarthy's reckless antics, at first directed at Democrats, began to hit Republican targets as well.

By the summer of 1953 the senator was on a rampage. He dispatched two young staff members, Roy Cohn and David Schine, to investigate the State Department's overseas information agency and the Voice of America radio stations. Behaving more like college pranksters, the two conducted a whirlwind 18-day witch-hunt through Western Europe, condemning government libraries for possessing "subversive" books, including volumes by John Dewey and Foster Rhea Dulles, a conservative historian and cousin of Eisenhower's secretary of state. Some librarians, fearing for their careers, burned a number of books. That action drove President Eisenhower to denounce "book burners," though soon afterward he reassured McCarthy's supporters that he did not advocate free speech for Communists.

The administration's own behavior contributed to the hysteria on which McCarthy thrived. The president launched a loyalty campaign, which he claimed resulted in 3,000 firings and 5,000 resignations of government employees. It was a godsend to McCarthyites: What further proof was needed that subversives were lurking in the federal bureaucracy? Furthermore, a well-publicized spy trial had led to the conviction of Ethel and Julius Rosenberg, a couple accused of passing atomic secrets to the Soviets. Although the evidence was not conclusive, the judge sentenced both Rosenbergs to the electric chair, an unusually harsh punishment even in cases of espionage. When asked to commute the death sentence to life imprisonment, Eisenhower refused, and the Rosenbergs were executed in June 1953.

In such a climate—where Democrats remained silent for fear of being called leftists and Eisenhower cautiously refused to "get in the gutter with *that* guy"—McCarthy lost all sense of proportion. When the army denied his aide David Schine a commission, McCarthy decided to investigate communism in the army. The new American Broadcasting Company network, eager to fill its afternoon program slots, televised the hearings. For three weeks, the public had an opportunity to see McCarthy badger witnesses and make a mockery of Senate procedures. Soon after, his popularity began to slide,

The Rosenbergs Executed

McCarthy versus the Army

and the anti-Communist hysteria ebbed as well. In 1954 the Senate finally moved to censure him. He died three years later, destroyed by alcohol and the habit of throwing so many reckless punches.

With the Democrats out of the White House for the first time since the Depression and with right-wing McCarthyites in retreat, Eisenhower did indeed seem to be leading the nation on a course "right down the middle." Still, it is worth noting how much that sense of "middle" had changed.

Both the Great Depression and World War II made most Americans realize that the nation's economy was firmly tied to the international order. The crash in 1929, with its worldwide effects, illustrated the closeness of the links. The New Deal demonstrated that Americans were willing to give the federal government power to influence American society in major new ways. And the war led the government to intervene in the economy even more actively.

So when peace came in 1945, it became clear that the "middle road" did not mean a return to the laissez-faire economics of the 1920s or the isolationist politics of the 1930s. Supporters of the Marshall Plan recognized that the economic recovery of Europe should be an American priority for reasons of self-interest as much as of charity. Gone were the policies of the 1920s, under which the United States sternly demanded repayment of European war debts. ("They hired the money, didn't they?" President Coolidge allegedly complained in 1926.) Encompassing the liberal theories of John Maynard Keynes, the Marshall Plan assumed that American intervention in the world economy would promote not only prosperity but also international security. At home "modern Republicans" supported social welfare programs such as Social Security and granted that the federal government had the power to lower unemployment, control inflation, and manage the economy in a variety of ways.

Finally, the shift from war to peace demonstrated that it was no longer possible to make global war without making a global peace. Under the new balance of power in the postwar world, the United States and the Soviet Union stood alone as superpowers, with the potential capability to annihilate each other and the rest of the world.

Significant Events

1945	Iran Crisis; civil war in Greece
1946	Labor unrest; Kennan's "long telegram"; Stalin and Churchill "cold war" speeches; Republican congressional victories; McMahon Bill creates Atomic Energy Commission; Baruch plan fails at United Nations
1947	Truman Doctrine; Taft-Hartley Act; federal loyalty oath; HUAC investigates Hollywood; Truman's Committee on Civil Rights issues *To Secure These Rights*
1948	Marshall Plan adopted; Berlin blockade; Truman upsets Dewey; Truman recognizes Israel

1949	Soviet atom bomb test; China falls to the Communists; NATO established
1950	McCarthy's Wheeling, West Virginia, speech; Korean War begins; McCarran Act; NSC-68 adopted; Alger Hiss convicted
1951	Truman fires MacArthur; peace talks in Korea
1952	Eisenhower defeats Stevenson
1953	UN armistice ends police action in Korea; Rosenbergs executed
1954	Army-McCarthy hearings; McCarthy censured

Chapter Summary

In the postwar period, the cold war between the Soviet Union and the United States affected every aspect of American domestic and foreign policy and overshadowed American life.

- The cold war had roots in American suspicions of Soviet communism dating back to World War I, but Stalin's aggressive posture toward Eastern Europe and the Persian Gulf region raised new fears among American policy makers.

- In response, the Truman administration applied a policy of containment through the Truman Doctrine, the Marshall Plan, and NSC-68.

- Despite a brief period of inflation, labor unrest, and shortages of goods and housing, the transition from war to peace launched the longest period of prosperity in the nation's history.

- Domestic fear of Communist subversion led the Truman administration to devise a government loyalty program and inspired the witch-hunts of Senator Joseph McCarthy.

- The Soviet detonation of an atomic bomb and the fall of China to the Communists, followed one year later by the Korean War, undermined the popularity of Harry Truman and the Democrats, opening the way for Dwight Eisenhower's victory in the 1952 presidential election.

Additional Reading

A good place to begin reading on the cold war is Walter LaFeber, *America, Russia, and the Cold War* (10th ed., 2006). For the science and politics of the H-bomb see Gregg Herken, *Brotherhood of the Bomb: The Tangled Lives and Loyalties of Robert Oppenheimer, Ernest Lawrence, and Edward Teller* (2003), and Kai Bird and Martin Sherwin, *American Prometheus: The Triumph and Tragedy of J. Robert Oppenheimer* (2006). On the domestic cold war see David Halberstam, *The Fifties* (1994), and Stephen Whitfield, *The Culture of the Cold War* (1991). Robert Sklar, *Movie Made America: A Cultural History of American Movies* (rev. ed., 1994), offers insight into how the cold war affected Hollywood.

Brian Burnes, *Harry S Truman: His Life and Times* (2003), is a lively account of a president who became more popular with the passage of time. Elizabeth Edwards Spalding, *The First Cold Warrior: Harry Truman, Containment and the Remaking of Liberal Internationalism* (2006), measures Truman as an architect of the postwar world order. The best account of the man who gave his name to the red scare is David Oshinsky, *A Conspiracy So Immense: The World of Joe McCarthy* (2005). Two historians have shown how cold war politics and the civil rights movement intersected: Thomas Borstelmann, *The Cold War and the Color Line: American Race Relations in the Global Arena* (2003), and Mary Dudziak, *Cold War Civil Rights: Race and the Image of American Democracy* (2002).

For a fuller list of readings, see the Bibliography at www.mhhe.com/davidsonnation6.

CHAPTER 28
The Suburban Era
1945~1963

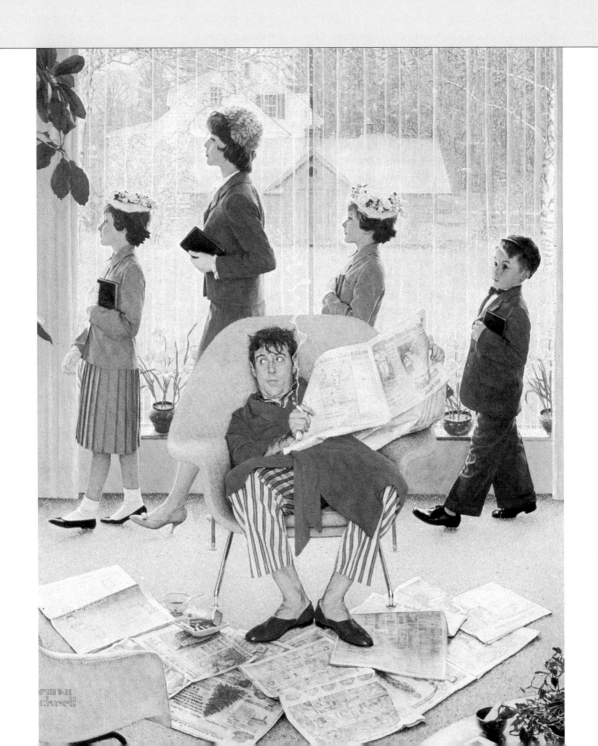

Dynamic Obsolescence (The Wonderful World of Harley Earl)

No company epitomized the corporate culture of the 1950s more than General Motors. GM executives sought to blend in rather than to stand out. They chose their suits in drab colors—dark blue, dark gray, or light gray—to increase their anonymity. Not head car designer Harley Earl. Earl brought a touch of Hollywood into the world of corporate bureaucrats. He had a closet filled with colorful suits. His staff would marvel as he headed off to a board meeting dressed in white linen with a dark blue shirt and *blue suede shoes,* the same shoes that Elvis Presley sang so protectively about.

Mr. Earl—no one who worked for him ever called him Harley—could afford to be a maverick. He created the cars that brought customers into GM showrooms across the country. Before he came to Detroit, engineering sold cars. Advertising stressed the mechanical virtues of reliable brakes or power steering. Earl made style the distinctive feature. Unlike the boxy look other designers favored, an Earl car was low and sleek, suggesting motion even when the car stood still. No feature stood out more distinctively than the fins he first put on the 1948 Cadillac. By the mid-1950s jet planes inspired Earl to design ever more outrageous fins, complemented by huge, shiny chrome grills and ornaments. Critics dismissed the designs as jukeboxes on wheels.

To Earl and GM the criticism hardly mattered. Design sold cars. "It gave [customers] an extra receipt for their money in the form of visible prestige marking for an expensive car," Earl said. The "Big Three" auto manufacturers—General Motors, Ford, and Chrysler—raced one another to redesign their annual models. Earl once joked, "I'd put smokestacks right in the middle of the sons of bitches if I thought I could sell more cars." In the lingo of the Detroit stylists, these designs were "gasaroony," an adjective *Popular Mechanics* magazine translated as "terrific, overpowering, weird." The goal was not a better car but what Earl called "dynamic obsolescence" or change for change's sake. Even a successful style had to go within a year. "We would design a car to make a man unhappy with his 1957 Ford 'long about the end of 1958." Even though the mechanics of cars changed little from year to year, dynamic obsolescence persuaded Americans in the 1950s to buy new cars in record numbers.

In Easter Morning, *Norman Rockwell satirized the contrasting conformities of suburban life. The sheepish father, no doubt forced to wear suits all week, prefers a shocking red bathrobe, a cigarette, and the Sunday paper to the gray flannel lockstep of his churchbound family.*

827

Fins, roadside motels, "gaseterias," drive-in burger huts, interstate highways, shopping centers, and, of course, suburbs—all these were part of a culture of mobility in the 1950s. Americans continued their exodus from rural areas to cities and from the cities to the suburbs. African Americans left the South, heading for industrial centers in the Northeast, Midwest, and West Coast. Mexican Americans concentrated in southwestern cities, while Puerto Ricans came largely to New York. And for Americans in the Snow Belt, the climate of the West and South (at least when civilized by air-conditioning) made the Sun Belt irresistible to ever-larger numbers.

Consensus in the 1950s

The mobility was social, too. As the economy continued to expand, the size of the American middle class grew. In an era of prosperity and peace, some commentators began to speak of a **"consensus"**—a general agreement in American culture, based on values of the broad middle class. In a positive light, consensus reflected the agreement among most Americans about fundamental democratic values. Most citizens embraced the material benefits of prosperity as evidence of the virtue of "the American way." And they opposed the spread of communism abroad.

But consensus had its dark side. Critics worried that it bred a mindless **conformity.** Were Americans becoming too homogenized? Was there a depressing sameness in the material goods they owned, in the places they lived, and in the values they held? Besides, wasn't any notion of consensus hollow as long as racism and segregation prevented African Americans and other minorities from fully sharing in American life?

The baby boomers born into this era seldom agonized over such issues. In the White House President Eisenhower radiated a comforting sense that the affairs of the nation and the world were in capable hands. That left teenagers free to worry about what really mattered: a first date, a first kiss, a first job, a first choice for college, and whether or not to "go all the way" in the back seat of one of Harley Earl's fin-swept Buicks.

The Rise of the Suburbs

Suburban growth accelerated sharply at the end of World War II. During the 1950s suburbs grew 40 times faster than cities, so that by 1960 half the American people lived in them. The return of prosperity brought a baby boom and a need for new housing. Automobiles made the suburbs accessible. But the spurt in suburban growth took its toll on the cities, which suffered as the middle class fled urban areas.

A Boom in Babies and in Housing

The Depression forced many couples to delay beginning a family. In the 1930s birthrates had reached the low point of American history, about 18 to 19 per thousand. As prosperity returned during the war, birthrates began to rise. In 1946 Americans married in record numbers, twice as many as in 1932. The new brides were also younger, most in their peak years of fertility. In a 10-year period the American population increased by 30 million, giving the United States a rate of growth comparable to that of India. By 1952 the birthrate passed 25 live births per thousand, and it did not peak until 1957. Ten years later it had dropped to under 18.

The Boom Worldwide

Historians and demographers have been hard-pressed to explain this extraordinary population bulge. It was not limited to the United States. In several other industrialized nations fertility rates also soared, Australia, New Zealand, Britain, and West Germany prime among them. Yet as the chart on the facing page indicates, the long-term trend in American fertility rates was downward, as it was in other industrialized nations. Fertility rates peaked in Australia and New Zealand in 1961, and three years later, in Great Britain and West Germany. Hence the baby boom stands as an anomaly, one that remains hard to explain.

Perhaps Americans were indeed "making up for lost time" after the war. Rising income allowed more people to afford marriage and children. But Americans should have caught up by the early 1950s, whereas the baby boom continued. Furthermore, rising standards of living do not always or even regularly go hand in hand with a baby boom. Worldwide, urbanization and higher living standards are linked to lower birthrates. In

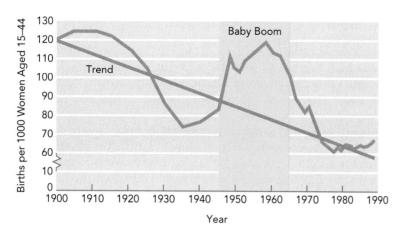

The United States Birthrate, 1900–1989 *Despite periods of rapid rise and fall, the nation's birthrate has shown a steady downward trend. The Depression years showed an even sharper decline as financially strapped couples deferred child rearing. Younger marriages and postwar prosperity triggered the baby boom, but in general, affluence encourages lower birthrates.*

1950 the most industrialized and urban nations had a birthrate of 21.8 per thousand, while in less developed and less densely settled sub-Saharan Africa the rate was 49.8. In South Asia it was 44.8.

Whatever factors contributed to the baby boom, it had both immediate and long-term consequences for American society. For one, the boom in marriages and families increased demand for housing. At war's end, five million American families were eagerly searching for housing, tired of living in doubled-up conditions with other families, in basements, or even in coal cellars. With the help of the GI Bill and the rising prosperity, the chance to own a house rather than rent became a reality for over half of American families. And it was the suburbs that offered the residence most idealized in American culture: a detached single-family house with a lawn and garden.

After World War II inexpensive, suburban housing became synonymous with the name of William Levitt. From building houses for war workers, Levitt learned how to use mass production techniques. In 1947 he began construction of a 17,000-house community in the New York City suburb of Hempstead. All the materials for a Levittown house were precut and assembled at a factory, then moved to the site for assembly. If all went according to schedule, a new house was erected on a cement slab every 16 minutes. Buoyed by his success in Hempstead, Levitt later built developments in Bucks County, Pennsylvania, and Willingboro, New Jersey.

The typical early Levitt house, a "Cape Codder," had a living room, kitchen, bath, and two bedrooms on the ground floor and an expansion attic, all for $7,990. None had custom features, insulation, or any amenities that complicated construction. "The reason we have it so good in this country," Levitt said, "is that we can produce lots of things at low prices through mass production." Uniformity in house style extended to behavior as well. Levitt discouraged owners from changing colors or adding distinctive features to the house or yard. Buyers promised to cut the grass each week of the summer and not to hang out wash on weekends. African Americans were expressly excluded. Other suburban communities excluded Jews and ethnic Americans through restrictive covenants that dictated who could take up residence.

In California, a state with three cars registered for every four residents, suburbs bloomed across the landscape. By 1962 it had become the nation's most populous state. Growth was greatest around Los Angeles. In 1940 city planners began building a freeway system to lure shoppers into downtown Los Angeles. Instead, white Angelinos saw the road network as an opportunity to migrate to the suburbs. Eventually one-third of the Los Angeles area was covered by highways, parking lots, and interchanges, increasing to two-thirds in the downtown areas.

Levittown, U.S.A.

William Levitt and his "Cape Codder" tract homes

Cities and Suburbs Transformed

Single-family houses on their own plots of land required plenty of open land, unlike the row houses built side by side in earlier suburban developments. That meant Levitt and other builders chose vacant areas outside major urban areas. With the new houses farther away from factories, offices, and jobs, the automobile became more indispensible than ever.

As the population shifted to suburbs, traffic choked old country roads. To ease this congestion, the Eisenhower administration proposed a 20-year plan to build a massive interstate highway system of some 41,000 miles. Eisenhower addressed cold war fears to build support, arguing that the new system would ease evacuation of cities in case of nuclear attack. In 1956 Congress passed the Interstate Highway Act, setting in motion the largest public works project in history. The federal government picked up 90 percent of the cost through a Highway Trust Fund, financed by special taxes on cars, gas, tires, lubricants, and auto parts.

Interstate Highway Act of 1956

The Interstate Highway Act had an enormous impact on American life. Average annual driving increased by 400 percent. Shopping centers, linked by the new roads, sprang up to provide suburbanites with an alternative to the longer trip downtown. Almost every community had at least one highway strip dotted with drive-in movies, stores, bowling alleys, gas stations, and fast-food joints.

For cities, the interstates created other problems. The new highway system featured beltways—ring roads around major urban areas. Instead of leading traffic downtown, the beltways allowed motorists to avoid the center city altogether. As people took to their cars, intercity rail service and mass transit declined. Seventy-five percent of all government transportation dollars went to subsidize travel by car and truck; only one percent was earmarked for urban mass transit. At the same time that middle-class homeowners were moving to the suburbs, many low-paying, unskilled jobs disappeared from the cities. These trends forced the urban poor into reverse commuting, from city

Declining Cities

Like a freak of evolution run riot, automotive tailfins metamorphosed from the modest stubs of a 1948 Cadillac into the monstrous protrusions of the 1959 Cadillac. With a return of prosperity, the suburban era celebrated a culture of mobility.

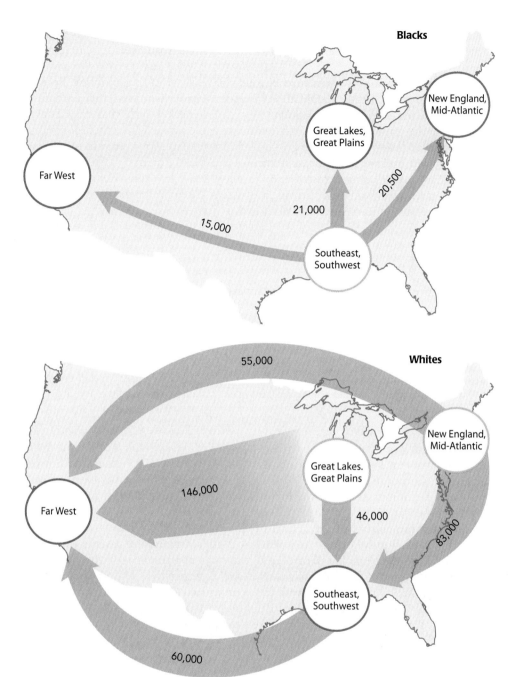

Blacks

Whites

Average Annual Regional Migration, 1947–1960 *In this period, African Americans were moving in significant numbers to urban centers in the Northeast, the Midwest, and the Far West. Whites were being drawn to the increasingly diversified economy of the South as well as to the new industries, stimulated by the war, in the Far West. By the 1970s, the trend had become known as the "Sun Belt" phenomenon.*

to suburb. All these trends made cities less attractive places to live or do business. With fewer well-to-do taxpayers to draw on, city governments lacked the tax base to finance public services. A vicious cycle ensued that proved most damaging to the urban poor, who had few means of escape.

Much of the white population that left cities for suburbs was replaced by African Americans and Hispanics. They were part of larger migrations, especially of millions of black families leaving the South to search for work in urban centers. Most headed for the Middle Atlantic, Northeast, and Upper Midwest regions. While central cities lost 3.6 million white residents, they gained 4.5 million African Americans. Indeed, by 1960 half of all black Americans were living in central cities.

Earlier waves of European immigrants had been absorbed by the expanding urban economy. During the 1950s, however, the flight of jobs and middle-class taxpayers to the suburbs made it difficult for African Americans and Hispanics to follow the same path. In the cities fewer jobs awaited them, while declining school systems made it harder for newcomers to acculturate. In the hardest-hit urban areas, unemployment rose to over 40 percent.

Minorities and Suburbs

In contrast, the suburbs remained beyond the reach of most minorities. Because few black or Hispanic families could afford the cost of suburban living, they accounted for less than 5 percent of the population there. The few black suburbs that existed dated from before the war and had little in common with the newer white "bedroom communities." Black suburbanites were poorer, held lower-status jobs, lived in more ramshackle housing, and had less education than urban African Americans. Even minorities who could afford the suburbs discovered that most real estate agents refused to show them houses; bankers would not provide mortgages. The developers of Levittown did not sell directly to African Americans until 1960.

The Culture of Suburbia

In suburban tracts across America, a new appetizer began appearing at trendy dinner parties. Named the California Dip, it was the brainchild of the Lipton Company, which was searching for new ways to market its dehydrated onion soup. Homemakers simply mixed Lipton's soup powder with sour cream and served it up with chips. As one commentator has noted:

> Using potato chips as little shovels, you gathered up the deliciously salty but drip-prone liquid and popped it, potato chip and all, into your mouth as quickly and gracefully as possible. There was anxiety in all this—particularly the fear that a great glop of the stuff would land on your tie or the rug—but also immense satisfaction.

As much genius, perhaps, went into the naming of the dip as into the recipe. Sour cream had been a mainstay in ethnic dishes such as blintzes (thin Jewish pancakes) and borscht (an Eastern European beet soup). With the all-American name of "California Dip," sour cream's ethnic associations were left behind. The ingredient went mainstream—into the consensus.

The evolving culture of the suburbs reflected a similar process, a shucking off of ethnic associations. In many city neighborhoods, immigrant parents or grandparents lived on the same block or even in the same apartment with their children. In the suburbs, single-family dwellers often left their relatives and in-laws behind, which meant that ethnic lifestyles were less pronounced. The restrictive immigration policies of the 1920s had also reduced the number of newly arrived foreign-born Americans. Thus suburban culture reflected the tastes of the broad, mostly assimilated middle classes.

Suburbs and Social Class

Class distinctions were more pronounced between suburban communities than within them. The upper middle class clustered in older developments, which often revolved around country clubs. Working-class suburbs sprouted on the outskirts of large manufacturing centers, where blue-collar families eagerly escaped the city. Within suburbs a more homogeneous suburban culture evolved. "We see eye to eye on most things," commented one Levittown resident, "about raising kids, doing things together with your husband . . . we have practically the same identical background."

American Civil Religion

If suburban residents retained less of their ethnic heritages, most held on to their religious beliefs. Religion continued to be a distinctive and segregating factor during the 1950s. Catholics, Protestants, and Jews generally married within their own faiths, and in the suburbs they kept their social distance as well.

The Religious Division

Communities that showed no obvious class distinctions were sometimes deeply divided along religious lines. Catholics attended parochial rather than public schools, formed their own clubs, and generally did not socialize with their Protestant neighbors.

Protestant and Catholic members of the same country club usually did not play golf or tennis in the same foursomes. As for Jews, social historian Richard Polenberg has remarked that whereas a gulf divided many Catholics and Protestants, Jews and Gentiles "seem to have lived on the opposite sides of a religious Grand Canyon." Even superficial signs of friendliness masked the persistence of old stereotypes.

Although such religious boundaries remained distinct, religion was central to American life. Church membership rose to more than 50 percent for the first time in the twentieth century, and by 1957 the Census Bureau reported that 96 percent of the American people cited a specific affiliation when asked "What is your religion?" The religious upswing was supported in part by the prevailing cold war mood, because Communists were avowedly atheists. Cold war fervor led Congress in 1954 to add the phrase "under God" to the Pledge of Allegiance.

Patriotic and anticommunist themes were strong in the preaching of clergy who pioneered the use of television. Billy Graham, a Baptist revival preacher, first attracted national attention at a tent meeting in Los Angeles in 1949. Following in the tradition of nineteenth-century revivalists like Charles Finney and Dwight Moody, he soon achieved an even wider impact by televising his meetings. Though no revivalist, the Roman Catholic bishop Fulton J. Sheen became a popular television celebrity. In his weekly program he extolled traditional values and attacked communism.

The growing consensus among Americans was that *any* religious belief was better than none. President Eisenhower made the point quite clear. "Our government makes no sense unless it is founded on a deeply religious faith," he proclaimed, "—and I don't care what it is." Children got the message too. Every Friday afternoon kids watching *The Howdy Doody Show* were exhorted by Buffalo Bob to worship "at the church or synagogue of your choice."

Baptist Billy Graham led the revival of evangelical religion in American culture. While his message emphasized the traditional Fundamentalist themes of sin, redemption, and the Second Coming of Christ, his up-to-date methods took advantage of television, advertising, radio, and paperback books to reach the widest possible audience.

"Homemaking" Women in the Workaday World

The growth of a suburban culture revealed a contradiction in the lives of middle-class women. Never before were their traditional roles as housewives and mothers so central to American society. Yet never before did more women join the workforce outside the home.

Most housewives found that suburban homes and growing families required increasing time and energy. With relatives and grandparents less likely to live nearby, mothering became full-time work. Dependence on automobiles made many a suburban housewife the chauffeur for her family. In the 1920s grocers or milkmen had commonly delivered their goods from door to door; by the 1950s delivery services were being replaced by housewives doing "errands."

Yet between 1940 and 1960 the percentage of wives working outside the home doubled, from 15 to 30 percent. Although some women took jobs simply to help make ends meet, often more than financial necessity was involved. Middle-class married women went to work as often as lower-class wives, and women with college degrees were the most likely to get a job. Two-income families were able to spend far more on extras: gifts, education, recreation, and household appliances. In addition, women found status and self-fulfillment in their jobs, as well as a chance for increased social contacts.

Working Women

More women were going to college, too, but that increased education did not translate into economic equality. The percentage of women holding professional jobs actually dropped between 1950 and 1960. And the gap between men's and women's wages was greater than in any other industrial nation. In the United States, the median wage for women was less than half that for men.

When World War II ended, many Americans were happy to find housing of any kind. But prosperity in the 1950s brought a demand for houses that, like automobiles, reflected the status of their owners. No longer would William Levitt's 900-square-foot Cape Cod saltbox satisfy popular demand.

The most renowned of all suburban architectural features, the picture window, traced its roots to architect Frank Lloyd Wright. Wright's turn-of-the-century innovations combined open interior space, wide windows for natural lighting, and a horizontal, single-story layout. California architects translated Wright's ideas into the ranch house, where rooms flowed into each other and indoor spaces opened to the outdoors to take advantage of the mild climate. Houses with fewer walls and defined spaces discouraged formality and even privacy.

Developers across the country seized on the California "fantasy" style to conjure up dreams of glamorous informal living. The use of picture windows allowed them to make small houses seem more spacious. Critics of suburban living suggested that the picture window was a means to ensure conformity. Why, after all, was the window most often placed looking onto the front yard, except to afford homeowners a means to keep an eye on neighbors who were watching them through their own picture windows? In truth, it made sense to have a picture window look onto the street in order to keep an eye on children.

By 1955, surveys showed that three-quarters of all would-be buyers wanted a single-story house. But with soaring land prices and new zoning codes, builders could not fit enough

floor space onto typical lots. To build a two-story house without seeming to, they hit upon the split-level, or "raised ranch": something, as one critic wryly noted, that "looked like a ranch-style house that had fallen out of the air and landed on something else." The basic construction, two simple boxes side by side, was cheap to build. By placing half the living space—either the kitchen, dining, and family rooms or the bedrooms—in what would otherwise be a basement, the split level created more habitable living space at little additional cost.

Most of all, homeowners in the 1950s wanted family rooms and "live-in kitchens." One magazine described the family room as "the newest room in the house, but also the oldest," for the concept originated in the middle-class Victorian front parlor. Like it, the 1950s

Media Images of Women

Despite women's wider roles in society, the media most often portrayed women either as sex objects or as domesticated housewives and mothers. A typical article appearing in *Redbook* in 1957 made a heroine of Junior, a "little freckle-faced brunette" who had given up work. As the story closed, Junior nursed her baby at two in the morning, crooning "I'm glad, glad, glad I'm just a housewife." In 1950 Lynn White, the president of Mills College for women, advocated a curriculum that displaced traditional academic subjects with those that were "distinctly feminine," such as crafts and home economics.

To housewife and mother, many suburban women of the 1950s added the role of chauffeur. Husbands who once walked to work and children who walked to school now needed to be delivered and picked up. The average suburban woman spent one full working day each week driving and doing errands.

In the wake of the baby boom and a demand for new homes, mass-produced houses soon filled suburban developments all across the United States. By varying styles only slightly, developers were able to construct houses quickly at prices many young couples could afford.

pine paneling and furniture designed for comfort and durability, with the television as the focus of the room.

The new, larger live-in kitchens of the suburbs were designed, one advertiser claimed, to make "mother a member of the family again." Everyone could gather while mom cooked. The same space would also hold appliances such as dishwashers, dual ovens, and televisions, which became common kitchen features.

Clearly, suburban houses were more than "Little boxes on the hillside / Little boxes all the same," as one folk-singing critic of the 1960s complained. To the people who flocked to suburbia, their homes represented a compromise between fantasy and practicality.

living room acquired more elegant furnishings for use during holidays or special entertaining. That led to the conversion of what often had been a basement "rumpus" room for the kids into a family room. Here, families sought a cozier feel with

A Revolution in Sexuality?

Among both women and men, the suburbs encouraged a change in sexual attitudes, especially among the middle classes who lived there. Throughout the twentieth century, a trend had been under way deemphasizing the tradition that sex within marriage was primarily for the procreation of children—a duty (especially for women) to be endured rather than enjoyed. During the 1920s reformer Ben Lindsey promoted the idea of "companionate marriage," stressing personal happiness and satisfaction as primary goals. Such a marriage included the enjoyment of sex for both wife and husband. The suburban home of the 1950s encouraged such ideals, symbolizing as it did a place of relaxation and enjoyment. Unlike city apartments, where extended families often lived in crowded conditions, the suburban single-family houses provided greater privacy and more space for intimacy.

The increased willingness to see sexual pleasure as an integral part of marriage received additional attention in 1948 with the publication of an apparently dry scientific study, *Sexual Behavior in the Human Male*. Its author, Professor Alfred Kinsey, hardly expected the storm of publicity received by that study or its companion, *Sexual Behavior in the Human Female* (1953). Kinsey began his research career as a zoologist with a zest for classifying data. During the 1940s he turned to collecting information on sexual behavior. Based on more than 10,000 interviews, Kinsey reached conclusions that were unorthodox and even startling for his day. Masturbation and premarital petting, he reported, were widespread. Women did not just endure sex as a wifely duty; they enjoyed it in much the same way men did. Extramarital sex was common for both husbands and wives. About 10 percent of the population was homosexual.

Publicly, Kinsey maintained a posture of scientific objectivity. He argued that he had only published a report "on what people do" and wasn't concerned with "what they should do." But biographers of Kinsey have revealed that, in fact, he was as much

The Kinsey Report

interested in social change as in scientific research, believing that many acts treated as deviant should be placed within a normal range of sexual behavior. His personal attitudes influenced that conclusion, for sexual obsessions were central to Kinsey's private life. (He practiced masochism; and he, his wife, and members of his staff filmed themselves engaging in group sex.) Though the public remained unaware of his private life, Kinsey provoked intense controversy. Social scientists objected that Kinsey's sample was too narrow to produce valid norms, and his most severe critics called him "a menace to society." According to opinion polls, most Americans disagreed. The large majority took comfort (as he had hoped) that behaviors once condemned as sinful or perverse were widely practiced.

The Flickering Gray Screen

In the glow of postwar prosperity, most Americans found themselves with more leisure time and more income. In the suburbs, a yard to tend and a young family to raise determined that much of that free time would be spent around the house. The new medium of television fit perfectly into suburban lifestyles. It provided an ideal way to entertain families at home as well as to sell them consumer goods.

Television viewership boomed after World War II. By 1949 Americans had bought a million sets; by 1960 that number had jumped to 46 million, and by then more Americans had television sets than had bathrooms. Home viewing transformed American entertainment habits, cutting sharply into pastimes like movies and professional sports. In cities around the country more than 4,000 neighborhood theaters closed. Many were replaced in the suburbs by popular drive-ins, which allowed whole families to enjoy movies in the comfort of their cars.

Television and Politics

In 1948 television began its involvement in politics, covering both the Democratic and the Republican conventions. Two years later, it combined entertainment, politics, and news by televising a series of hearings on organized crime chaired by Senator Estes Kefauver. Some 30 million viewers watched senators grill mobster Frank Costello about his criminal organization and its ties to city governments. Millions more watched Senator Joseph McCarthy's ill-fated crusade against the army in 1954. Clearly, television demonstrated the potential to shape the political life of the nation. By the mid-1950s, however, controversy over news coverage of issues like McCarthyism led the networks to downgrade public affairs programs. As an alternative, the networks turned to Hollywood film studios, which provided them with telefilm series. By selling time to advertisers, the networks, rather than the sponsors, gained ultimate control over program content. By 1959 live television was virtually a thing of the past.

The Politics of Calm

In presiding over these changes in American society, President Dwight David Eisenhower projected an aura of paternal calm. Pursuing "modern Republicanism," the new president sought consensus, not confrontation. No longer would die-hard conservatives like Herbert Hoover and Robert Taft dictate the Republican agenda. Eisenhower declared that he was "conservative when it comes to money and liberal when it comes to human beings."

Eisenhower's Modern Republicanism

Eisenhower had been raised in a large Kansas farm family. His parents, though poor, offered him a warm, caring home steeped in religious faith. In an era of organization men, Eisenhower succeeded by mastering the military's bureaucratic politics. A graduate of West Point, "Ike" was neither a scholar nor an aggressive general like George Patton. Yet these genial ways could not hide his ambition or his ability to judge character shrewdly. It took a gifted organizer to coordinate the D-Day invasion and to hold together the egocentric generals who pushed east to Berlin. Eisenhower was so widely respected that both parties had considered running him in the 1948 presidential race.

In pursuing his pragmatic course, Eisenhower resisted conservative demands to dismantle New Deal programs. He even agreed to increases in Social Security, unemployment insurance, and the minimum wage. He accepted a small public housing program and a modest federally supported medical insurance plan for the needy. But as a conservative, Eisenhower remained uncomfortable with big government. Thus he rejected more far-reaching liberal proposals on housing and universal health care through the Social Security system.

To make modern Republicanism successful, Eisenhower had to woo the newly prosperous Democratic voters joining the middle class. Success in that effort hinged on how well the administration managed the economy. The Democrats of the New Deal had established a tradition of activism. When the economy faltered, deficit spending and tax cuts were used to stimulate it. Eisenhower, in contrast, wanted to reduce federal spending and the government's role in the economy. When a recession struck in 1953–1954, the administration was concerned more with balancing the budget and holding inflation in line than with reducing unemployment through government spending.

Eisenhower was similarly pragmatic in other areas. When major projects called for federal leadership, as with the Highway Act, he supported the policy. In 1954 he signed the St. Lawrence Seaway Act, which joined the United States and Canada in an ambitious engineering project to open the Great Lakes to ocean shipping. Like the highway program, the Seaway was fiscally acceptable because the funding came from user tolls and taxes rather than from general revenues.

Despite a recession in 1953–1954, Eisenhower remained popular. Even after he suffered a major heart attack in 1955, voters gladly reelected him over Adlai Stevenson in 1956. But poor economic performance took its toll on the Republican party. In 1958, when recession again dragged down the economy, the Democrats took a commanding 68-seat majority in the House and a 12-vote advantage in the Senate. Modern Republicanism did not put down deep roots outside Eisenhower's White House.

Eisenhower Reelected

The Conglomerate World

Large corporations welcomed the administration's probusiness attitudes as well as the era's general prosperity. Wages for the average worker rose over 35 percent between 1950 and 1960. At the same time, the economic distress of the 1930s had led corporate executives to devise new ways to minimize the danger of economic downturns. Each of the approaches expanded the size of corporations in various ways in order to minimize shocks in specific markets.

One expansion strategy took the form of diversification. In the 1930s, a giant like General Electric had concentrated largely in one industrial area: equipment for generating electric power and light. When the Depression struck, GE found its markets evaporating. The company responded by entering markets for appliances, X-ray machines, and elevators—all products developed or enhanced by the company's research labs. In the postwar era General Electric diversified even further to become a **conglomerate,** expanding into nuclear power, jet engines, and television. Diversification was most practical for large industrial firms, whose size allowed them to support extensive research and development.

Diversification

Conglomeration often turned small companies into giants. Unlike earlier horizontal and vertical combinations, conglomerate mergers could join companies with seemingly unrelated products. Over a 20-year period International Telephone and Telegraph branched out from its basic communications business into baking, hotels and motels, car rental, home building, and insurance. Corporations also became multinational by expanding their overseas operations or buying out potential foreign competitors. Large integrated oil companies like Mobil and Standard Oil of New Jersey (Exxon) developed huge oil fields in the Middle East and markets around the free world.

One aid to managing these modern corporate giants was the advent of electronic data processing. In the early 1950s computers were virtually unknown in private industry. But banks and insurance companies saw these calculating machines as an answer to their need to manipulate huge quantities of records and statistical data. Manufacturers, especially in the petroleum, chemical, automotive, and electronics industries, began to use computers to monitor their production lines, quality control, and inventory.

Cracks in the Consensus

As corporations merged in order to increase their reach, power, and stability, they saw themselves as a part of the emerging consensus over the American way. ("What's good for the country is good for General Motors.") Yet there were distinct cracks in the consensus. Intellectuals and social critics spoke out against the stifling features of a conformist corporate culture. At the fringes of American society, the beatniks rejected conformity, while the more mainstream rock and roll movement broadcast its own brand of youthful rebellion.

Critics of Mass Culture

In Levittown, New Jersey, a woman who had invited her neighbors to a cocktail party eagerly awaited them dressed in newly fashionable Capri pants—a tight-fitting calf-length style. Alas, one early-arriving couple glimpsed the woman through a window. What on earth was the hostess wearing? *Pajamas?* Who in their right mind would entertain in pajamas? The couple sneaked home, afraid they had made a mistake about the day of the party.

Finally, they mustered enough courage to attend the party. But when the hostess later learned of their misunderstanding, she put her Capri pants in the closet for good. Levittown was not ready for such a change in fashion.

Suburban Conformity

Was America turning into a vast suburban wasteland, where the neighbors' worries over Capri pants would stifle all individuality? Many intellectuals worried openly about the homogenized lifestyle created by mass consumption, conformity, and **mass media.** Critics such as Dwight Macdonald sarcastically attacked the culture of the suburban middle classes: *Reader's Digest* Condensed Books, uplifting film spectacles such as *The Ten Commandments,* television dramas that pretended to be high art but in reality were little more than simplistic pontificating. "Midcult," Macdonald called it, which was his shorthand for middlebrow culture.

Other critics charged that the skyscrapers and factories of giant conglomerates housed an all-too-impersonal world. In large, increasingly automated workplaces, skilled laborers seemed little more than caretakers of machines. Large corporations required middle-level executives to submerge their personal goals in the processes and work routines of a large bureaucracy. David Riesman, a sociologist, condemned stifling conformity in *The Lonely Crowd* (1950). In nineteenth-century America, Riesman argued, Americans had been "inner directed." It was their own consciences that formed their values and drove them to seek success. In contrast, modern workers had developed a personality shaped not so much by inner convictions as by the opinions of their peers. The new "other-directed" society of suburbia preferred security to success. "Go along to get along" was its motto.

David Riesman's The Lonely Crowd

William Whyte's The Organization Man

William Whyte carried Riesman's critique from the workplace to the suburb in *The Organization Man* (1956). Here he found rootless families, shifted from town to town by the demands of corporations. (IBM, according to one standard joke, stood for "I've Been Moved.") The typical organization man was sociable but not terribly ambitious. He sought primarily to keep up with the Joneses and the number of consumer goods they owned. He lived in a suburban "split-level trap," as one critic put it, one among

A Man's Man on the Silver Screen

Reconstructing Gender

All societies construct idealized images of men and women—creations that reveal the expectations and norms of a culture. During the twentieth century the mass medium of film trafficked constantly in such constructions, and historians have analyzed these gender ideals every bit as much as they have studied politics, economics, and social trends.

For the generation that lived through the Depression and World War II, John Wayne defined manliness—tough, emotionally remote, a man's man given to straight talk, not small talk. Wayne was "the Duke," known for his roles as a cowboy and a war hero.

James Dean in Rebel Without a Cause. *Dean was just 24 when he died in a car crash in 1955.*

By contrast, James Dean was slight of build, almost feminine in his good looks, a man who needed mothering to face a hostile world. Wayne made almost 200 movies; Dean appeared in just three. Yet during the 1950s, while Wayne continued to turn out sturdy performances, it was Dean who captured the hearts and imagination of the young movie-going audience.

Historians who study gender have suggested that the popular response to Dean marked a significant shift in American definitions of masculinity. Dean's world was defined not by stoicism and patriotism forged during the Depression's hard times and a world war but by his sensitivity and rebellion against a society that never seemed to understand the emotional turmoil he felt within, despite a world of prosperity and abundance. One historian described Dean as "the most inward of actors: his performances were always about the beautiful chaos of his own soul." Had Dean been a lone rebel, out of sync with the culture, historians might not have seen his screen persona as part of a trend. But Dean shared the screen with other rebellious stars such as Marlon Brando and Elvis Presley. As the 1960s would soon prove, Dean anticipated a new era of youthful rebellion.

millions of "haggard" men, "tense and anxious" women, and "the gimme kids," who, like the cartoon character Dennis the Menace, looked up from the litter under the Christmas tree to ask, "Is that all?"

No doubt such portraits were overdrawn. (Where, after all, did Riesman's nineteenth-century inner-directed Americans get their values, if not from the society around them?) But such critiques indicated the problems of adjustment faced by people working within large bureaucratic organizations and living in suburbs that were decentralized and self-contained.

The Rebellion of Young America

Young Americans were among suburbia's sharpest critics. Dance crazes, outlandish clothing, strange jargon, rebelliousness toward parents, and sexual precociousness—all these behaviors challenged middle-class respectability. More than a few parents and public figures warned that America had spawned a generation of rebellious juvenile

Juvenile Delinquency

delinquents. Psychologist Frederic Wertheim told a group of doctors, "You cannot understand present-day juvenile delinquency if you do not take into account the pathogenic and pathoplastic [infectious] influence of comic books." Others laid the blame on films and the lyrics of popular music.

The center of the new teen culture was the high school. Whether in consolidated rural school districts, new suburban schools, or city systems, the large, comprehensive high schools of the 1950s were often miniature melting pots in which middle-class students were exposed to, and often adopted, the style of the lower classes. Alarmed school administrators complained of juvenile delinquents who wore jeans and T-shirts, challenged authority, and defiantly smoked cigarettes, much like the motorcycle gang leader portrayed by Marlon Brando in the film *The Wild One* (1954).

In many ways the argument about juvenile delinquency was an argument about social class and, to a lesser degree, race. Adults who complained that delinquent teenagers dressed poorly, lacked ambition, and were irresponsible and sexually promiscuous were voicing the same arguments traditionally used to denigrate other outsiders—immigrants, the poor, and African Americans. Nowhere were these racial and class undertones more evident than in the hue and cry greeting the arrival of rock and roll.

The Rise of Rock and Roll

Before 1954 popular music had been divided into three major categories: pop, country and western, and rhythm and blues. A handful of major record companies with almost exclusively white singers dominated the pop charts. On one fringe of the popular field was country and western, often split into cowboy musicians such as Roy Rogers and Gene Autry and the hillbilly style associated with Nashville. The music industry generally treated rhythm and blues as "race music," whose performers and audience were largely black. Each of these musical traditions grew out of regional cultures. As the West and the South merged into the national culture, so too were these musical subcultures gradually integrated into the national mainstream.

By the mid-1950s the distinctiveness of the three styles began to blur. Singers on the white pop charts recorded a few songs from country and from rhythm and blues. The popularity of crossover songs such as "Sh-boom," "Tutti-Frutti," and "Earth Angel" indicated that a major shift in taste and market was under way. Lyrics still reflected the pop field's preoccupation with young love, marriage, and happiness, but the music now vibrated with the rawer, earthier style of rhythm and blues. Country and western singer Bill Haley brought the new blend to the fore in 1954 with "Shake, Rattle, and Roll," the first rock song to reach the top ten on the pop charts.

And then—calamity! Millions of middle-class roofs nearly blew off with the appearance in 1955 of the rhythmic and raucous Elvis Presley. By background, Elvis was a country boy whose musical style combined elements of gospel, country, and blues. But it was his hip-swinging, pelvis-plunging performances that electrified teenagers. To more conservative adults, Presley's long hair, sideburns, and tight jeans seemed menacingly delinquent, an expression of hostile rebellion. What they often resented but rarely admitted was that Elvis looked lower class, sounded black, and really could sing.

The King, Elvis Presley

The Beat Generation

Beyond the frenetic rhythms of rock and roll, and even farther beyond the pale of suburban culture, flourished a subculture known as the beat generation. In run-down urban neighborhoods and college towns this motley collection of artists, intellectuals, musicians, and middle-class students dropped out of mainstream society. In dress and behavior the beatniks self-consciously rejected what they viewed as the excessive spiritual bankruptcy of America's middle-class culture. Cool urban hipsters—especially African American jazz musicians like John Coltrane and Sonny Rollins—were their models. They read poetry, listened to jazz, explored Oriental philosophy, and experimented openly with drugs, mystical religions, and sex.

The "beats" viewed themselves as being driven to the margins of society, rejecting the culture of abundance, materialism, and conformity. "I saw the best minds of my generation destroyed by madness, starving hysterical naked," wrote Allen Ginsberg in his 1955 poem *Howl.* They had become "angelheaded hipsters . . . who in poverty and tatters and hollow-eyed and high sat up smoking in the supernatural darkness of cold-water flats floating across the tops of cities contemplating jazz." Jack Kerouac tapped the frenzied energy beneath the beatniks' cool facade in *On the Road* (1957), a novel based on his travels across the country with his friend Neal Cassady. Kerouac finished the novel in one frenetic three-week binge, feeding a 120-foot roll of paper through his typewriter and spilling out tales of pot, jazz, crazy sex, and all-night raps undertaken in a search for "IT"—the ultimate transcendental moment when mind and experience mesh.

Nationalism in an Age of Superpowers

Try as they might, the beats could not ignore the atomic menace that overshadowed American society at midcentury. Along the Iron Curtain of Eastern Europe and across the battle lines of northern Asia, Soviet-American rivalry had settled into a stalemate. The American public shared with most foreign policy makers a view of the globe as divided between the "free world" nations and the "communist bloc." Thus the Eisenhower administration sought ways to contain the Soviets: setting up security and trade agreements, employing covert action to install governments favorable to the United States, and using the threat of nuclear war, if need be.

To the Brink?

Eisenhower (left) and his Secretary of State John Foster Dulles.

John Foster Dulles

As a general who had fought in a global war and as commander of NATO, Eisenhower was no stranger to world politics. Still, he shared the conduct of foreign policy with his secretary of state, John Foster Dulles. Dulles approached his job with a somber enthusiasm. Coming from a family of missionaries and diplomats, he had within him a touch of both. He viewed the Soviet-American struggle in almost religious terms: a fight of good against evil between two irreconcilable superpowers. Admirers praised his global vision; detractors saw him as "the wooliest type of pontificating American." Certainly Dulles did not lack confidence. "With my understanding of the intricate relationship between the peoples of the world," he told Eisenhower, "and your sensitiveness to the political considerations, we will make the most successful team in history."

The administration was determined to make Truman's containment strategy more forceful. Dulles, the more confrontational of the two men, wanted the United States to aid in liberating the "captive peoples" of Eastern Europe and other Communist nations. On the other hand, Eisenhower was equally determined to cut back military spending and troop levels in order to keep the budget balanced. The president, who understood well how the military services and their allies in defense industries competed for government money, was irked at the "fantastic programs" the Pentagon kept proposing. "If we demand too much in taxes in order to build planes and ships," he argued, "we will tend to dry up the accumulations of capital that are necessary to provide jobs for the million or more new workers that we must absorb each year."

So Eisenhower and Dulles hit on a more economical strategy. Rather than rely on conventional forces, they would contain Soviet aggression by using the threat of massive nuclear retaliation. Dulles insisted that Americans should not shrink from the threat of nuclear war: "If you are scared to go to the brink, you are lost." As Treasury Secretary George Humphrey put it, a nuclear strategy was much cheaper—"a bigger bang for the buck." Henceforth American foreign policy would have an aggressive "New Look." Behind the more militant rhetoric, however, lay an ongoing commitment to containment.

The New Look in Foreign Policy

Brinkmanship in Asia

Moving from talk of **brinksmanship** to concrete action did not prove easy. When Dulles announced American intentions to "unleash" Chiang Kai-shek to attack mainland

Taiwan and Mainland China

Asian Trouble Spots   *After the Geneva Accords divided Indochina into North and South Vietnam, Secretary of State Dulles organized the Southeast Asia Treaty Organization (SEATO) to resist Communist aggression in Southeast Asia. In addition to the conflict in Vietnam, tensions were fueled by the mutual hostility between mainland Communist China and Chiang Kai-shek's Taiwan as well as the offshore islands of Quemoy and Matsu.*

China from his outpost on Taiwan (formerly Formosa), China threatened to invade Taiwan. At that, Eisenhower ordered the Seventh Fleet into the area to protect rather than unleash Chiang. If the Communists attacked, he warned bluntly in 1955, "we'll have to use atomic weapons."

Nuclear weapons also figured in the American response to a crisis in Southeast Asia. There, Vietnamese forces led by Ho Chi Minh were fighting the French, who had returned to reestablish their own colonial rule. Between 1950 and 1954, the United States provided France with more than $1 billion in military aid in Vietnam. Eisenhower worried that if Vietnam fell to a Communist revolutionary like Ho, other nations of Southeast Asia would soon follow. "You have a row of dominoes set up," the president warned, "you knock over the first one. . . . You could have the beginning of a disintegration that would have the most profound influences."

Vietnamese Victory at Dien Bien Phu

The French in 1954 tried to force a final showdown with Ho's forces at Dien Bien Phu. With Vietnamese and Chinese Communist troops holding the surrounding hilltops, the French garrison of 12,000 could not have chosen a worse place to do battle. Desperate, the French government pleaded for more American aid and the Joint Chiefs of Staff responded by volunteering to relieve the besieged French forces with a massive American air raid—including the use of tactical nuclear weapons, if necessary. Instead, Eisenhower pulled back. After Korea, the idea of American involvement in another Asian war aroused opposition from both allies and domestic political leaders.

Collapsing under the siege, the garrison at Dien Bien Phu surrendered in May 1954. At a peace conference held in Geneva, Switzerland, Ho Chi Minh agreed to withdraw his forces north of the 17th parallel, temporarily dividing the nation into

North and South Vietnam. Because of Ho's widespread popularity, he could count on an easy victory in the elections that the peace conference agreed would be held within two years. Dulles, however, viewed any Communist victory as unacceptable, even if the election was democratic. He convinced Eisenhower to support a South Vietnamese government under Ngo Dinh Diem. Diem, Dulles insisted, was not bound by the agreement signed in Geneva to hold any election. The United States became further involved by sending a military mission to train an army to keep Diem in power.

United States Backs Diem

The Covert Side of the New Look

In pursuing their aggressive New Look in foreign policy, Dulles and Eisenhower sometimes authorized the Central Intelligence Agency (CIA) to use **covert operations** against those they saw as sympathetic to Moscow. For example, in Iran in 1951 a nationalist government under Mohammed Mossadeq seized the assets of a giant British oil company. With the United States boycotting Iranian oil, Dulles worried that Mossadeq would turn to the neighboring Soviet Union for aid. Eisenhower approved a secret CIA operation to topple the Mossadeq government. Led by Teddy Roosevelt's grandson, Kermit Roosevelt, Operation Ajax ousted Mossadeq and returned Iran's monarch, Shah Mohammad Reza Pahlavi, to his throne in August 1953.

Overthrowing Mossadeq

Dulles looked for similar results in Guatemala. Unlike Iran, however, Guatemala had an elected democratic government under Colonel Jacobo Arbenz Guzmán. Arbenz was determined to reduce the poverty in his country by confiscating the idle farmland of rich landowners and giving it to the peasants. Guatemala's richest landowner was the Boston-based United Fruit Company. When the Guatemalan government seized 400,000 acres from United Fruit, the company's agents branded Arbenz a Communist. Arbenz was no communist, but as the American ambassador later explained "the man thought like a communist and talked like a communist, and if not actually one, would do until one came along." A week after a CIA-trained band of Latin American mercenaries entered the country, supported by American planes, the leader of the Guatemalan rebels replaced the Arbenz democracy with a military dictatorship that quickly returned the expropriated lands to United Fruit.

Intervention in Guatemala

Success in Iran and Guatemala gave American policy makers a misplaced faith that covert operations could achieve dramatic results at low cost. But in overthrowing

The CIA secretly helped overthrow the Guatemalan government in 1954. One plan, apparently never carried out, called for the assassination of 58 Guatemalan officials. But the CIA's chilling "Conference Room Technique" survived, a four-step plan showing how "a room containing as many as a dozen subjects can be 'purified' in about 20 seconds" by two assassins. Step 4 was to "leave propaganda," making it seem as if Communists had carried out the massacre.

popular governments or defending unpopular ones, the United States gained a reputation in many Third World countries as a foe of national liberation, popular democracy, and social reform. In 1958 the depth of anti-American feeling became obvious when angry crowds in several Latin American countries attacked Vice President Richard Nixon's car, spat at him, and pelted him with eggs and stones.

Rising Nationalism

Korea, Indochina, Iran, Guatemala—to Dulles and Eisenhower, the crises in all these countries could be traced back to the Soviet dictatorship. Yet American policy could not be simply anti-Communist. World War II had disrupted Europe's longstanding imperial relationships. As nationalists in the Middle East, Africa, and Southeast Asia fought to gain independence from their colonial masters, new nations like India proclaimed themselves "nonaligned," independent of the Soviet Union and the United States. As the two superpowers competed for the allegiance of emerging nations, the United States sought to counter the moves of the dynamic Soviet leader who had replaced Joseph Stalin.

Nikita Khrushchev

Stalin had died in March 1953 after becoming increasingly isolated, arbitrary, vengeful, and perhaps simply mad. Nikita Khrushchev, a party stalwart with a formidable intellect and peasant origins in the farm country of the Ukraine soon gained power. In some ways Khrushchev resembled another farm-belt politician, Harry Truman. Both were unsophisticated yet shrewd, earthy in their sense of humor, energetic, short-tempered, and largely inexperienced in international affairs. Khrushchev kept American diplomats off balance: at times genial and conciliatory, he would suddenly become demanding and boastful.

At home Khrushchev established a more moderate regime, gradually shifting the economy toward production of consumer goods. Internationally, he sought to ease tensions and reduce forces in Europe, hoping to make Western Europeans less dependent on the United States. Yet the growing tide of nationalism made it difficult for either superpower to pursue more conciliatory policies.

Nikita Khrushchev was by turns bombastic and somber, threatening and conciliatory—a style that both captivated and alarmed Americans.

When Khrushchev began to ease Stalin's iron ways, nationalists in Soviet-controlled Eastern Europe pushed for greater independence. Riots erupted in Poland, while in Hungary students took to the streets. When the rioting spread, Moscow accepted the new Hungarian government and began to remove Soviet tanks. But Hungary's decision to withdraw from the Warsaw Pact proved too threatening. In October 1956 Soviet tanks rolled back into Budapest and crushed the uprising. The U.S. State Department issued formal protests but did nothing to help liberate the "captive nations." For all Dulles's tough talk, the New Look foreign policy recognized that the Soviets possessed a sphere of influence in which the United States would not intervene.

Eastern Europe was not the only nationalist crisis Eisenhower faced in 1956. In Egypt, the nationalist Colonel Gamal Abdel Nasser was attempting to modernize his country and rebuild his army. Dulles hoped to win Nasser's friendship by offering American aid to build the Aswan Dam, a massive power project on the Nile River. But when Nasser formed an Arab alliance against the young state of Israel and continued to pursue economic ties with the Warsaw bloc, Dulles decided to teach the Egyptian leader a lesson. He withdrew the American pledge on Aswan. Nasser angrily upped the ante by seizing the Suez Canal, through which tankers carried most of Europe's oil.

Events moved quickly. Israel, alarmed at Nasser's Arab alliance, invaded Egypt's Sinai peninsula on October 29—the same day Hungary announced it was leaving the Warsaw Pact. Three days later French and

British forces seized the canal in an attempt to restore their own interests and prestige. Eisenhower saw it as colonialism reborn and joined the Soviet Union in supporting a UN resolution condemning Britain, France, and Israel. The two superpowers demanded an immediate cease-fire. By December American pressures forced Britain and France to remove their forces.

Given the unstable situation in the Middle East, Eisenhower convinced Congress to grant him the authority to use force against any Communist attack in that region. What became known as the Eisenhower Doctrine in effect allowed the president in times of crisis to preempt Congress's power to declare war. In 1958 he used that power to send U.S. marines into Lebanon, a small nation that claimed to have been infiltrated by Nasser's supporters. Since no fighting had yet occurred, sunbathers on the beaches of Beirut, Lebanon's capital, were startled as 5,000 combat-clad marines stormed ashore. In the end the crisis blew over and the American forces withdrew.

The Eisenhower Doctrine

Nationalist forces were also in ferment in Latin American countries, where only 2 percent of the people controlled 75 percent of the land. Repressive dictatorships exercised power, and foreign interests—especially American—dominated Latin American economies. Given the unequal distribution of wealth and a rapidly growing population, social tensions were rising. Cuba, only 90 miles south of American shores, was typical.

The United States owned many Cuban economic resources, including 80 percent of its utilities, and operated a naval base at Guantánamo Bay. Cuban dictator Fulgencio Batista had close ties both to the American government and to major crime figures who operated gambling, prostitution, and drug rings in Havana. A disgruntled middle-class lawyer, Fidel Castro, gained the support of impoverished peasants in Cuba's mountains and in January 1959 drove Batista from power.

Castro's Revolution in Cuba

At first many Americans applauded the revolution and welcomed Castro when he visited the United States. But President Eisenhower was distinctly cool to the cigar-smoking Cuban. By summer Castro had filled key positions with Communists, launched a sweeping agricultural reform, and confiscated American properties. In retaliation Eisenhower placed an embargo on Cuban sugar and mobilized opposition to Castro in other Latin American countries. Cut off from American markets and aid, Castro turned to the Soviet Union.

The Response to *Sputnik*

Castro's turn to the Soviets seemed all the more dangerous because the Soviet Union in 1957 stunned America by launching the first space satellite, dubbed *Sputnik*. By 1959, the Soviets had crash-landed a much larger payload on the moon. If the Russians could target the moon, surely they could launch nuclear missiles against America. In contrast, the American space program suffered so many delays and mishaps that rockets exploding on launch were nicknamed "flopniks" and "kaputniks."

How had the Soviets managed to catch up with American technology so quickly? Some analysts blamed U.S. schools, especially weak programs in science and math. In 1958 Eisenhower joined with Congress to enact a National Defense Education Act, designed to strengthen graduate education and the teaching of science, math, and foreign languages. At the same time, crash programs were undertaken to build basement fallout shelters to protect Americans in case of a nuclear attack. Democrats charged that the administration had allowed the United States to face an unacceptable "missile gap" (an accusation that was not borne out).

A Missile Gap?

Thaws and Freezes

Throughout this series of crises, each superpower found it difficult to interpret the other's motives. The Russians exploited nationalist revolutions where they could—less successfully in Egypt, more so in Cuba. "We will bury you," Khrushchev admonished

Even before the launch of Sputnik in 1957, Americans had begun devising fallout shelters for protection from the effects of a nuclear attack. This one was exhibited in 1955.

Americans, though it was unclear whether he meant through peaceful competition or military confrontation.

Rather than adopt a more belligerent course, Eisenhower determined to use the final 18 months of his presidency to improve Soviet-American relations. The shift in policy was made easier because the president knew from American intelligence (but could not admit publicly) that the missile gap was not real. Eisenhower chose to invite Khrushchev to visit the United States in September 1959. The Soviet premier undertook a picturesque tour across America, swapping comments about manure with Iowa farmers, reacting puritanically to movie cancan dancers, and grousing when his visit to the new capitalist marvel, Disneyland, was canceled for security reasons.

The U-2 Incident

Eisenhower's plans for a return visit to the Soviet Union were abruptly canceled in 1960 after the Russians shot down a high-altitude U-2 American spy plane over Soviet territory. At first Eisenhower claimed that the plane had strayed off course while doing weather research, but Khrushchev sprang his trap: the CIA pilot, Gary Powers, had been captured alive. The president then admitted that for reasons of national security he had personally authorized the U-2 overflights.

That episode ended Eisenhower's hopes that his personal diplomacy might thaw cold war tensions. Yet a less mature president might have led the United States into more severe conflict or even war. Eisenhower was not readily impressed by the promises of new weapons systems or overheated talk about a missile gap between the United States and the Soviet Union. He left office with a warning that too much military spending would lead to "an unwarranted influence, whether sought or unsought" by the **military-industrial complex** at the expense of democratic institutions.

The Cold War along a New Frontier

The 1960 election promised to bring the winds of change to Washington. The opponents— Vice President Richard Nixon and Senator John F. Kennedy of Massachusetts—were the first major presidential candidates born in the twentieth century. At the age of 43, Kennedy would be the youngest person ever elected to the presidency, and Nixon was only four years older. The nation needed to find new challenges and "new frontiers,"

Kennedy proclaimed. His rhetoric was noble, but the direction in which he would take the nation was far from clear.

The Election of 1960

The Catholic Issue

Jack Kennedy's biggest hurdle to election was social as much as political. He was a Roman Catholic out of Irish Boston, and no Catholic had ever been elected president. Conservative Protestants, many concentrated in the heavily Democratic South, were convinced that a Catholic president would never be "free to exercise his own judgment" if the pope ordered otherwise. Kennedy chose to confront the issue head-on. In September he entered the lions' den, addressing an association of hostile Protestant ministers in Houston. The speech was the best of his campaign. "I believe in an America where the separation of church and state is absolute," he said, "—where no Catholic prelate would tell the President (should he be Catholic) how to act, and no Protestant minister would tell his parishioners how to vote." House Speaker Sam Rayburn, an old Texas pol, was astonished by Kennedy's bravura performance. "My God! . . . He's eating them blood raw."

Both candidates stressed cold war themes. Kennedy lamented the apparent "missile gap" and attacked Eisenhower and Nixon for not better managing tensions between Communist China and the nationalists on Formosa (Taiwan). Vice President Richard Nixon ran on his record as an experienced leader and staunch anti-Communist, but his campaign faltered in October as unemployment rose. Nixon agreed to a series of debates with Kennedy—the first to be televised nationally. Image proved more telling than issues. According to one poll, radio listeners believed Nixon won the debate; but television viewers saw a fatigued candidate with "five o'clock shadow," because Nixon had refused to use television makeup. A relaxed Kennedy convinced many viewers that he could handle the job.

Televised Presidential Debates

In the end religion, ethnicity, and race played decisive roles in Kennedy's triumph. One voter was asked if he voted for Kennedy because he was a Catholic. "No, because *I* am," he answered; and in key states Catholic support made a difference. "Hyphenated" Americans—Hispanic, Jewish, Irish, Italian, Polish, and German—voted Democratic in record numbers, while much of the black vote that had gone to Eisenhower in 1956 returned to the Democratic fold. Indeed, when civil rights leader Martin Luther King was imprisoned during a protest in Georgia, Kennedy attracted the support of black Americans by telephoning his sympathy to Dr. King's wife. Interest in the election ran so high that 64 percent of voters turned out, the largest percentage in 50 years. Out of 68.8 million ballots cast, Kennedy won by a margin of just 119,000.

The Hard-Nosed Idealists of Camelot

Many observers compared the Kennedy White House to Camelot, King Arthur's magical court. A popular musical of 1960 pictured Camelot as a land where skies were fair, men brave, women pretty, and the days full of challenge and excitement. With similar vigor, Kennedy brought into his administration bright, energetic advisers. He and his stylish wife, Jacqueline, invited artists, musicians, and intellectuals to the White House. Impromptu touch football games on the White House lawn displayed a rough-and-tumble playfulness, akin to Arthur's jousting tournaments of old.

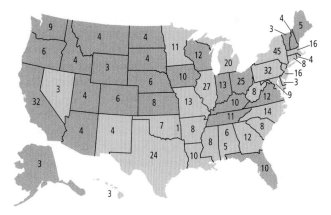

Candidate (Party)	Electoral Vote (%)	Popular Vote (%)
John F. Kennedy (Democratic)	303 (56)	34,226,731 (49.7)
Richard M. Nixon (Republican)	219 (41)	34,108,157 (49.6)
Robert Byrd (Independent)	15 (3)	501,643 (0.7)

Election of 1960

The urbane and energetic John F. Kennedy (center) was associated with both King Arthur (left, played by Richard Burton in the 1960 musical) and the spy James Bond (played by Sean Connery, right). Kennedy and his advisers prided themselves on their pragmatic, hard-nosed idealism. But whereas Bond used advanced technology and covert operations to save the world, in real life such approaches had their downside, as the growing civil war in Vietnam would demonstrate.

In truth, Kennedy was not a liberal by temperament. Handsome and intelligent, he possessed an ironic, self-deprecating humor. In Congress he had led an undistinguished career, supported Senator Joe McCarthy, and earned a reputation as a playboy. Once Kennedy set his sights on the White House, however, he revealed an astonishing capacity for political maneuvering and organization. To woo the liberals in his party, he surrounded himself with a distinguished group of intellectuals and academics.

Robert McNamara

Robert Strange McNamara typified the pragmatic, liberal bent of the new Kennedy team. Steely and brilliant, McNamara was one of the postwar breed of young executives known as the "whiz kids." As a Harvard Business School professor and later as president of Ford Motor Company, he specialized in using quantitative tools to streamline business. As the new secretary of defense, McNamara intended to find more flexible and efficient ways of conducting the cold war.

Kennedy liked men such as McNamara—witty, bright, intellectual—because they seemed comfortable with power and were not afraid to use it. The president's leisure reading reflected a similar adventurous taste: the popular James Bond spy novels. Agent 007, with his license to kill, was sophisticated, a cool womanizer (as Kennedy himself continued to be), and ready to use the latest technology to deal with Communist villains. Ironically, Bond demonstrated that there could be plenty of glamour in being hard-nosed and pragmatic. That illicit pleasure was the underside, perhaps, of Camelot's high ideals.

The (Somewhat) New Frontier at Home

Despite bold campaign promises, the president's domestic legislative achievements were modest. Once in the White House, Kennedy found himself hemmed in by a Democratic Congress dominated by conservatives. He convinced Congress to raise the minimum wage to $1.25. But on key issues, including aid to education and medical health insurance, Kennedy made no headway.

He wavered too on how to manage the economy. The president's liberal economic advisers favored increased government spending to reduce unemployment, even if that spending meant a budget deficit. Similarly, they argued that tax cuts could be used to increase consumer spending and so stimulate the economy. Kennedy toyed with both remedies, but conservatives continued to push for a balanced budget. Only in 1963 did he send a tax proposal to Congress, which passed it the following year.

Always pragmatic, Kennedy hoped to work with, not against, the leaders of big business to promote growth for the whole nation. But he did believe that the government should be able to limit wages and prices for large corporations and unions. If not, an inflationary spiral might result. Wage increases would be followed by price increases followed by even higher wage demands.

To prevent that, the Council of Economic Advisors proposed to stabilize prices by tying wage increases to improved productivity. In April 1962 the United Steel Workers, like most other major unions, agreed to a contract that followed those guidelines. The large steel corporations, however, broke their part of the informal bargain by raising steel prices substantially. Incensed, Kennedy called for investigations into price fixing, mounted antitrust proceedings, and shifted Pentagon purchases to smaller steel companies that had not raised prices. The pressure caused the big companies to drop the price hikes but soured relations between Kennedy and the business community.

Showdown with Big Steel

Kennedy's Cold War

During the 1960 race for the White House, Kennedy had pledged to fight the cold war with new vigor. Once elected, the new president was determined not to be seen as soft on communism, the charge Republicans had so often hurled against the Democrats. The cold war contest, Kennedy argued, had shifted from the traditional struggle over Europe to the developing nations in Asia, Africa, and Latin America. The United States should be armed with a more flexible range of military and economic options.

The "Alliance for Progress," announced in the spring of 1961, indicated the course Kennedy would follow. He promised $20 billion in foreign aid to Latin America over 10 years—four times what Truman and Eisenhower had provided. In return, Latin American nations would agree to reform unfair tax policies and begin agricultural land reforms. If successful, the alliance would discourage future Castro-style revolutions. With similar fanfare, the administration set up the Peace Corps. This program sent idealistic young men and women to Third World nations to provide technical, educational, and public health services. Under the alliance, a majority of Peace Corps volunteers were assigned to Latin America.

Alliance for Progress and Peace Corps

To give economic programs some military muscle, the Pentagon created jungle warfare schools in North Carolina and the Canal Zone. These schools trained Latin American police and paramilitary groups to fight guerrilla wars. They also trained American special forces such as the Green Berets in the arts of jungle warfare. If the Soviets or their allies promoted "wars of liberation," United States commandos would be ready to fight back.

Kennedy believed, too, that the Soviets had made space the final frontier of the cold war. Only a few months after the president's inauguration, a Russian cosmonaut orbited the world for the first time. In response, Kennedy challenged Congress to authorize a manned space mission to the moon that would land by the end of the decade. In February 1962 John Glenn circled the earth three times in a "fireball of a ride." The race to the moon was on.

Space Program

Cold War Frustrations

In more down-to-earth ways, high ideals did not translate easily into practical results. Instability remained a problem throughout Latin America. In the first five years of the alliance, nine Latin American governments were overthrown by military coups. The Peace Corps, for its part, proved a tremendous public relations success and helped thousands of Third World farmers on a people-to-people basis. But individual Peace Corps workers could do little to change corrupt policies on a national level.

Nor did Kennedy succeed in countering revolutionary "wars of liberation." His prime target was Fidel Castro's Communist regime in Cuba. After breaking diplomatic relations in 1960, the Eisenhower administration had secretly authorized the CIA to

Bay of Pigs Invasion

The World of the Superpowers   *This map shows the extent of the cold war Soviet and American military buildup. The United States established a worldwide network of bases and alliances surrounding Soviet bloc nations that extended from Japan and South Korea, South Vietnam, Pakistan, and Turkey in Asia to the nations of the NATO alliance in Europe. Soviet efforts to expand its influence in the Third World led to the creation of an outpost in Cuba. Around these strategic perimeters, hot spots and centers of crisis continued to simmer.*

organize an invasion of that nation. The CIA assured Kennedy that its 1,400-member army of Cuban exiles could inspire their compatriots in Cuba to overthrow Castro. Eager to establish his own cold war credentials, the president approved an attack. But the invasion in April 1961 turned into a disaster. The poorly equipped rebel forces landed at the swampy Bay of Pigs with no protective cover for miles. Within two days Castro's army had rounded them up. Taking responsibility for the fiasco, Kennedy suffered a bitter humiliation whose sting goaded the administration to undertake further covert operations. The CIA secretly hatched plans to destabilize the Cuban government or even murder Castro.

Kennedy's advisers took a similar covert approach in South Vietnam. There, a civil war with religious overtones was under way. The unpopular dictator Ngo Dinh Diem remained in power. South Vietnamese Communists, known as the Vietcong, waged a guerrilla war against Diem with support from North Vietnam. Buddhist elements also backed the rebellion against Diem, who was a Catholic. In May 1961, a month after the Bay of Pigs invasion, Kennedy secretly ordered 500 Green Berets and military advisers to Vietnam to help Diem. By 1963 the number of "military advisers" had risen to more than 16,000 soldiers. Increasingly, they were being drawn into combat with the Vietcong.

Kennedy and Vietnam

Diem's corruption, police state tactics, and ruthless campaign against his Buddhist opposition increasingly isolated the regime. As the Kennedy administration lost faith in Diem, it tacitly encouraged a military coup by South Vietnamese military officers. To the surprise of American officials, the coup plotters not only captured Diem but shot him in November 1963. Despite Kennedy's policy of pragmatic idealism, the United States found itself mired in a Vietnamese civil war, which it had no clear strategy for winning.

Diem Falls

Confronting Khrushchev

Vietnam and Cuba were just two areas in the Third World where Kennedy sought to battle Communist forces. But the conflict between the United States and the Soviet Union soon overshadowed developments in Asia, Africa, and Latin America.

June 1961 was the president's first chance to take the measure of Nikita Khrushchev, at a summit meeting held in Vienna. For two long days, Khrushchev was brash and belligerent. East and West Germany must be reunited, he demanded. In the divided capital of Berlin, located deep within East Germany (see map, page 807), citizens from all across East Germany were crossing from the eastern sector of Berlin into the free western zone as a way of escaping Communist rule. This "problem" must be settled within six months, Khrushchev insisted. Kennedy tried to stand up to Khrushchev's bullying, but he left Vienna worried that the Soviet leader perceived him as weak and inexperienced. By August events in Berlin confirmed his fears. Under cover of night, the Soviets threw up a wall sealing off any entry into West Berlin. Despite American protests, the heavily guarded Berlin Wall stayed up.

The Berlin Wall

Tensions with the Soviet Union led the administration to rethink American nuclear strategy. Under the Dulles doctrine of massive retaliation, almost any incident threatened to trigger a launch of the full arsenal of nuclear missiles. Kennedy and McNamara sought to replace the policy of **mutually assured destruction (MAD)** with a "flexible response doctrine." By limiting the level of a first nuclear strike, they would leave room for negotiation. In that case, however, conventional forces in Europe would have to be built up so that they could better deter aggression. McNamara proposed equipping them with smaller tactical nuclear weapons.

A Flexible Nuclear Response

But what if the Soviets were tempted to launch a first-strike attack to knock out American missiles? McNamara's flexible response policy required that enough American missiles survive in order to retaliate. If the Soviets knew the United States could survive a first strike, they would then be less likely to launch a surprise attack. So McNamara began a program to place missile sites underground and to develop submarine-launched missiles. The new flexible response policies resulted in a 15 percent increase in the 1961 military budget, compared with only 2 percent increases during the last two years of Eisenhower's term. Under Kennedy, the military-industrial complex thrived.

The Missiles of October

The peril of nuclear confrontation became dramatically clear in the Cuban missile crisis of October 1962. President Kennedy had emphasized repeatedly that the United States would treat any attempt to place offensive weapons in Cuba as an unacceptable

The discovery of Soviet offensive missile sites in Cuba, revealed by low-level American reconnaissance flights, led to the first nuclear showdown of the cold war. For several tense days in October 1962, President Kennedy met with his National Security Council to debate the proper course of action.

threat. Khrushchev promised that the Soviet Union had no such intention but bristled privately at what he perceived as a gross inequality in the cold war. "The Americans had surrounded our country with military bases and threatened us with nuclear weapons," he told high Soviet officials in May 1962. In that month he convinced them to begin building a secret nuclear base in Cuba. "Now [the Americans] would learn just what it feels like to have enemy missiles pointing at you."

Throughout the summer the buildup went undetected by Americans. But by October 14, overflights of Cuba by U-2 spy planes had uncovered the offensive missile sites. Kennedy was outraged.

For a week, American security advisers met in secret strategy sessions. Hawkish advisers urged air strikes against the missile sites, and at first Kennedy agreed. "We're certainly going to . . . take out these . . . missiles," he said. But others pointed out that the U-2 flights had not photographed all of Cuba. What if there were more concealed bases with missiles ready to fire? The Soviets could then launch an atomic attack on the United States despite the air strikes. Furthermore, if the United States attacked Cuba with no advance warning, the act would appear to the world uncomfortably like the Japanese surprise attack on Pearl Harbor in World War II.

A Naval Blockade

Although the Joint Chiefs of Staff continued to press for a large air attack, Kennedy finally chose the more restrained option, a naval blockade to intercept "all offensive military equipment under shipment to Cuba." On October 22, word of the confrontation began to leak out. "CAPITAL CRISIS AIR HINTS AT DEVELOPMENTS ON CUBA; KENNEDY TV TALK IS LIKELY," ran the *New York Times* headline. Americans were stunned that evening by the president's television address.

Over the next few days, tensions mounted as a Soviet submarine approached the line of American ships. On October 25 the navy stopped an oil tanker. Several Soviet ships reversed course. In Cuba, Soviet general Issa Pliyev felt that he had to assume the worst—that despite all the talk of a blockade, an American invasion of Cuba was being prepared. Pliyev sent a coded message to Moscow that "in the opinion of the Cuban friends [i.e., the Castro government] the U.S. air strike on our installations in Cuba will occur in the night between October 26 and October 27 or at dawn on October 27."

Equally ominously, he added, "We have taken measures to disperse 'techniki' [the nuclear warheads] in the zone of operations." In other words, Pliyev was making his nuclear missiles operational.

The morning of October 27, alarmed Soviet technicians detected a U-2 plane flying over Cuba. Was this the beginning of the expected attack? General Pliyev had issued strict instructions not to use force without his authorization, but when the air defense command looked to consult him, he could not be found. Soviet officers went ahead and shot it down, killing its pilot.

Meanwhile, Kennedy was making strenuous efforts to resolve the crisis through diplomatic channels. On October 26 he had received a rambling message from Khrushchev agreeing to remove the missiles in return for an American promise not to invade Cuba. The following day a second, more troubling message arrived with a new condition, that the United States must also dismantle its missile bases in Turkey, which bordered on the Soviet Union. Then word came of the downed U-2, further heightening tension. If the Soviets launched an attack from their Cuban bases, stated policy called for U.S. retaliation. Worried that events might spiral out of control, the president put off that decision until the following morning.

Kennedy decided to ignore Khrushchev's second letter and accept the offer in the first: removal of Soviet missiles if the Americans pledged not to invade Cuba. He also gave private assurances that the missiles in Turkey would come out within half a year. In Moscow, Khrushchev agreed reluctantly to the deal, telling his advisers somberly that there were times to advance and times to retreat; and this time, "we found ourselves face to face with the danger of war and of nuclear catastrophe, with the possible result of destroying the human race." Thus the face-off ended on terms that saved either side from overt humiliation.

The nuclear showdown prompted Kennedy and his advisers to seek ways to control the nuclear arms race. "We all inhabit this small planet," he warned in June 1963. "We all breathe the same air. We all cherish our children's future. And we are all mortal." The administration negotiated a nuclear test ban with the Soviets, prohibiting all above-ground nuclear tests. Growing concern over radioactive fallout increased public support for the treaty. A telephone hot line was also installed, providing a direct communications link between the White House and the Kremlin for use in times of crisis. At the same time Kennedy's prestige soared for "standing up" to the Soviets.

Nuclear Test Ban Treaty

The Cuban missile crisis was the closest the world had come to "destroying the human race," in Khrushchev's words, and it sobered both superpowers. It did not end the cold war, however; indeed, both nations endured long, drawn-out regional wars before scaling back their ambitions—the United States in Vietnam and the Soviet Union in Afghanistan. Yet the intensity of confrontation—with Eisenhower and Dulles's brinkmanship, Khrushchev's provocations, and Kennedy's cold war rhetoric—began to ease. The nuclear anxieties of the 1950s, so much a part of the suburban era, yielded to different concerns in the 1960s.

In large part, that change came about because the supposed consensus of the 1950s masked a profound *lack* of consensus concerning the state of equality in America. While the suburbs flourished, urban areas decayed. While more white Americans went to college, more African Americans found themselves out of work on southern farms or desperate for jobs in northern ghettos, and still in segregated schools. As Mexican American migrant workers picked crops in California or followed the harvest north from Texas, they saw their employers resist every attempt to unionize and improve their wages. To all these Americans, the often-proclaimed "consensus" about opportunity in American life was no longer acceptable. The 1950s sparked a movement pursued by ordinary Americans who acted, despite the reluctance of their leaders, to bring about a civil rights revolution.

Significant Events

1947	Levittown construction begins
1950	David Reisman's *The Lonely Crowd* published
1952	Fertility rate in the United States reaches new high
1953	Mossadeq overthrown in Iran
1954	CIA overthrows Arbenz in Guatemala
1955	Elvis Presley ignites rock and roll
1956	Interstate Highway Act; Eisenhower reelected; Suez crisis
1957	*Sputnik* launched; Eisenhower Doctrine
1958	Marines sent into Lebanon; NASA established
1959	Castro seizes power in Cuba; Khrushchev visits United States; Soviet probe hits moon
1960	U-2 incident; Kennedy-Nixon debates; Kennedy elected president
1961	Eisenhower warns of military-industrial complex; Alliance for Progress; Peace Corps begun; Bay of Pigs invasion; Kennedy steps up U.S. role in Vietnam; Berlin Wall built
1962	Cuban missile crisis
1963	Diem assassinated in Vietnam

Chapter Summary

At midcentury, during an era of peace and prosperity, the United States began to build a new social and political agenda.

- Automobiles and the culture of the highways helped bind Americans to one another in a "consensus" about what it meant to be an American.

  —Highways made possible rapid suburban growth.
  —Suburbs proved popular with the growing white-collar middle class.
  —Consensus in suburbs blurred class distinctions and promoted the notion of "civil religion."
  —Suburban life nurtured the ideal of the woman who found fulfillment as a homemaker and a mother, even though more women began to work outside the home.

- President Eisenhower resisted the demands of conservatives to dismantle the New Deal and of liberals to extend it, in favor of moderate, or "middle of the road," Republicanism.

- Cracks in consensus appeared among discontented intellectuals and among teenagers who, through Elvis Presley and new teen idols, discovered the power of rock and roll.

- Efforts to more vigorously contain the U.S.S.R. and Communist China, through a policy of "brinkmanship," proved difficult to apply because of growing Third World nationalism.

  —Eisenhower held back from using tactical nuclear weapons during crises in Vietnam and Taiwan.
  —Successful CIA operations in Iran and Guatemala encouraged American policy makers to use covert operations more frequently.
  —Post-colonial nationalism contributed to crises in Hungary, Egypt, and Cuba, where President Kennedy was embarrassed by the failure of an invasion attempt to overthrow Fidel Castro.

- Relations between the two superpowers thawed gradually but not without recurring confrontations between the United States and the Soviet Union.

- —Under Eisenhower, the Soviet success with *Sputnik* increased fears that the United States was vulnerable to missile attacks, while the U-2 spy plane incident worsened relations.

- —John F. Kennedy proved willing to use covert operations as well as diplomatic and economic initiatives like the Peace Corps and the Alliance for Progress.
- —The construction of Soviet missile bases 90 miles from American shores triggered the Cuban missile crisis of 1962, the closest the United States and the Soviet Union ever came to nuclear war.

Additional Reading

David Halberstam profiles suburban America engagingly in *The Fifties* (1994); using suburban Orange County, California, as her focus, Lisa McGirr, *Suburban Warriors: The Origins of the New American Right* (2001), explores how conservatives organized at the political grassroots level. An interesting source linking suburbia to a new environmental consciousness is Adam Rome, *The Bulldozer in the Countryside; Suburban Sprawl and the Rise of American Environmentalism* (2001). Karal Ann Marling, *As Seen on TV: The Visual Culture of Everyday Life in the 1950s* (1998), gives insight into the popular aesthetics of the era. Glenn Altschuler, *All Shook Up: How Rock and Roll Changed America* (2003), shows how rock music reshaped American culture. As a corrective response to the view of women in the 1950s popularized by Betty Friedan, *The Feminine Mystique* (1963), see the provocative essays in Joanne Meyerowitz, ed., *Not June Cleaver: Women and Gender in Postwar America* (1994).

Fred Greenstein, *The Hidden Hand Presidency: Eisenhower as Leader* (rev. ed., 1994), contradicted the view of Ike as a bumbling president. Just as historians have refurbished Eisenhower's image, they have also removed some of the tarnish from Kennedy. See, for example, Graham Allison, *The Essence of Decision: Explaining the Cuban Missile Crisis* (2nd ed., 1999), and Warren Bass, *Support Any Friend: Kennedy, the Middle East, and the Making of the U.S.-Israel Alliance* (2003). To do some judging on your own, look at Ernest R. May and Philip Zelikow, eds., *The Kennedy Tapes: Inside the White House During the Cuban Missile Crisis* (1997). Two fine books on Kennedy and Vietnam are Fredrik Logevall, *Choosing War: The Lost Chance for Peace and the Escalation of War in Vietnam* (2003), and David Kaiser, *American Tragedy: Kennedy, Johnson, and the Origins of the Vietnam War* (2002).

For a fuller list of readings, see the Bibliography at www.mhhe.com/davidsonnation6.

CHAPTER 29
Civil Rights & Uncivil Liberties
1947~1969

Two Roads to Integration

Six-year-old Ruby knew the lessons. She was to look straight ahead—not to one side or the other—and especially not at *them*. She was to keep walking. Above all, she was not to look back once she'd passed, because that would encourage them. Ruby's parents had instructed her carefully, but she still struggled to keep her eyes straight. The first day of school, federal marshals were there along with her parents. So were hundreds of nasty white people who came near enough to yell things like "You little nigger, we'll get you and kill you." Then she was within the building's quiet halls and alone with her teacher. She was the only person in class: none of the white students had come. As the days went by during that autumn of 1960, the marshals stopped walking with her but the hecklers still waited. And once in a while Ruby couldn't help looking back, trying to see if she recognized the face of one woman in particular.

Ruby's parents were not social activists. They signed their daughter up for the white school because "we thought it was for all the colored to do, and we never thought Ruby would be alone." Her father's white employer fired him; letters and phone calls threatened the family's lives and home. Ruby seemed to take it all in stride, though her parents worried that she was not eating the way she used to. Often she left her school lunch untouched or refused anything other than packaged food such as potato chips. It was only after a time that the problem was traced to the hecklers. "They tells me I'm going to die, and that it'll be soon. And that one lady tells me every morning I'm getting poisoned soon, when she can fix it." Ruby was convinced that the woman owned the variety store nearby and would carry out her threat by poisoning the family's food.

Over the course of a year, white students gradually returned to class and life settled into a new routine. By the time Ruby was 10, she had developed a remarkably clear perception of herself. "Maybe because of all the trouble going to school in the beginning I learned more about my people. Maybe I would have anyway; because when you get older you see yourself and the white kids; and you find out the difference. You try to forget it, and say there is none; and if there is you won't say what it be. Then you say it's my own people, and so I can be proud of them instead of ashamed."

On August 28, 1963, more than 250,000 demonstrators joined the great civil rights march on Washington. Although the day belonged to the Reverend Martin Luther King, Jr., the movement's most prominent leader, ordinary Americans both black and white played key roles in initiating the civil rights crusade.

If the new ways were hard for Ruby, they were not easy for white southerners either—even those who saw the need for change. One woman, for years a dedicated teacher in Atlanta, vividly recalled a traumatic summer 10 years earlier, when she went north to New York City to take courses in education. There were black students living in the dormitory, an integrated situation she was not used to. One day as she stepped from her shower, so did a black student from the nearby stall. "When I saw her I didn't know what to do," the woman recalled. "I felt sick all over, and frightened. What I remember—I'll never forget it—is that horrible feeling of being caught in a terrible trap, and not knowing what to do about it. I thought of running out of the room and screaming, or screaming at the woman to get out, or running back into the shower. . . . My sense of propriety was with me, though—miraculously—and I didn't want to hurt the woman. It wasn't *her* that was upsetting me. I knew that, even in that moment of sickness and panic." So she ducked back into the shower until the other woman left.

Summer was almost over before she felt comfortable eating with black students at the same table. And when she returned home, she told no one about her experiences. "At that time people would have thought one of two things: I was crazy (for being so upset and ashamed) or a fool who in a summer had become a dangerous 'race mixer.'" She continued to love the South and to speak up for its traditions of dignity, neighborliness, and honor, but she saw the need for change. And so in 1961 she volunteered to teach one of the first integrated high school classes in Atlanta, even though she had her doubts. By the end of two years she concluded that she had never spent a more exciting time teaching. "I've never felt so useful, so constantly useful, not just to the children but to our whole society. American as well as Southern. Those children, all of them, have given me more than I've given them."

When Ruby drew pictures for psychologist Robert Coles, her true feelings came out. Her white children had all their features carefully sketched. The black children had body parts missing. "When I draw a white girl, I know she'll be okay," Ruby explained, "but with the colored it's not okay."

For Americans in all walks of life, the upheavals that swept America in the 1960s were wrenching. From the schoolrooms and lunch counters of the South to the college campuses of the North, from eastern slums to western migrant labor camps, American society was in ferment.

On the face of it, such agitation seemed to be a dramatic reversal of the placid 1950s. Turbulence and change had overturned stability and consensus. Yet the events of the 1960s grew naturally out of the social conditions that preceded those years. The civil rights movement was brought about not by a group of farsighted leaders in government but by ordinary folk who sought change, often despite the reluctance or even fierce opposition of people in power. After World War II, grassroots organizations like the NAACP for blacks and the American GI Forum for Latinos acted with a new determination to achieve the equality of opportunity promised by the American creed.

Thus the 1950s were a seedbed for the more turbulent revolutions of the 1960s. The booming postwar economy held out the possibility of better lives for minorities; yet systematic discrimination and racism, long embedded in American life by custom and law, prevented prosperity from spreading equally. Time and again, activists challenged the political system to deal with what the 1950s had done—and what had been left undone. As one friend of Martin Luther King predicted in 1958, "If the young people are aroused from their lethargy through this fight, it will affect broad circles throughout the country." And, he might have added, around the world, because a similar spirit of reform existed on a global scale.

The Civil Rights Movement

The struggle of African Americans for equality during the postwar era is filled with ironies. By the time barriers to legal segregation in the South began to fall, millions of black families were leaving for regions where discrimination was less easily challenged in court. The South they left behind was in the early stages of an economic boom. The cities to which many migrated to had entered a period of decline. Yet, as if to close a circle, the rise of large black voting blocs in major cities created political pressures that helped force the nation to dismantle the worst legal and institutional barriers to racial equality.

The Changing South and African Americans

After World War II the southern economy began to grow significantly faster than the national economy. The remarkable about-face began during the New Deal with federal programs like the Tennessee Valley Authority. World War II brought even more federal dollars to build and maintain military bases and defense plants. And the South attracted new business because it offered a "clean slate." In contrast to the Northeast and Upper Midwest, the South had few unions, little regulation and bureaucracy, and low wages and taxes. Finally, there was the matter of climate, which later caused the region to be nicknamed the **Sun Belt.** Especially with improvements in air-conditioning, the South grew more attractive to skilled professionals, corporate managers, and affluent retirees.

Before World War II, 80 percent of African Americans lived in the South. Most raised cotton as sharecroppers and tenant farmers. But the war created a labor shortage at home, as millions of workers went off to fight and others went to armament factories. This shortage gave cotton growers an incentive to mechanize cotton picking. In 1950 only 5 percent of the crop was picked mechanically; by 1960 at least half was. Farmers began to consolidate land into larger holdings. Tenant farmers, sharecroppers, and hired labor of both races, no longer in short supply, left the countryside for the city.

Mechanized Cotton Farming

The national level of wages also profoundly affected southern labor. When federal minimum wage laws forced lumber or textile mills to raise their pay scales, the mills no longer expanded. In addition, steel and other industries with strong national unions and manufacturers with plants around the country set wages by national standards. Those changes brought southern wages close to the national average by the 1960s. As the southern economy grew, what had for many years been a distinct regional economy became more diversified and more integrated into the national economy.

As wages rose and unskilled work disappeared, job opportunities for black southerners declined. Outside cotton farming, the lumber industry had provided the largest number of jobs for young black men. There, the number of black teenagers hired by lumber mills dropped 74 percent between 1950 and 1960. New high-wage jobs were reserved for white southerners, because outside industries arriving in the South made no effort to change local patterns of discrimination. So the ultimate irony arose. As per capita income rose and industrialization brought in new jobs, black laborers poured out of the region in search of work. They arrived in cities that showed scant tolerance for racial differences and little willingness or ability to hire unskilled black labor.

The NAACP and Civil Rights

In the postwar era the NAACP decided it would use the judicial system to attack Jim Crow laws. That stepped-up attack reflected the increased national political influence that African Americans achieved as they migrated in great numbers out of the South. No longer could northern politicians readily ignore the demands black leaders made for greater equality. Presidents Roosevelt and Truman had taken small but significant steps to address the worst forms of legal and economic discrimination. And across the South black churches and colleges became centers for organized resistance to segregation.

Thurgood Marshall

Thurgood Marshall emerged as the NAACP's leading attorney. Marshall had attended law school in the 1930s at Howard University in Washington. There, the law school's dean, Charles Houston, was in the midst of revamping the school and turning out sharp, dedicated lawyers. Marshall not only was sharp but had the common touch. "Before he came along," one observer noted,

> the principal black leaders—men like Du Bois and James Weldon Johnson and Charles Houston—didn't talk the language of the people. They were upper-class and upper-

Overton Park Zoo in Memphis, Tennessee, was segregated like thousands of other public facilities throughout the South in the late 1950s. In the case of the zoo, Tuesdays were "colored" days, the only time when blacks could attend—except if the Fourth of July fell on a Tuesday. Then "colored" day was moved to Thursday.

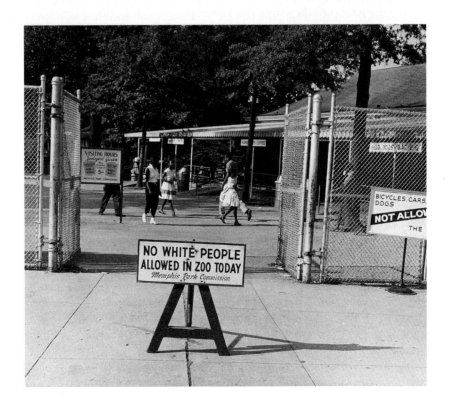

middle-class Negroes. Thurgood Marshall was *of* the people. . . . Out in Texas or Oklahoma or down the street here in Washington at the Baptist church, he would make these rousing speeches that would have 'em all jumping out of their seats. . . . "We ain't gettin' what we should," was what it came down to, and he made them see that.

During the late 1930s and early 1940s Marshall toured the South (in "a little old beat-up '29 Ford"), typing out legal briefs in the back seat, trying to get teachers to sue for equal pay, and defending blacks accused of murder in a Klan-infested county in Florida. He was friendly with whites, not shy, and black citizens who had never even considered the possibility that a member of their race might win a legal battle "would come for miles, some of them on muleback or horseback, to see 'the nigger lawyer' who stood up in white men's courtrooms."

For years NAACP lawyers had worked hard to organize local chapters, to support members of the community willing to risk their jobs, property, and lives in order to challenge segregation. But they waged a moderate, pragmatic campaign. They chose not to attack head-on the Supreme Court decision (*Plessy v. Ferguson,* 1896) that permitted "separate but equal" segregated facilities. They simply demonstrated that a black college or school might be separate, but it was hardly equal if it lacked a law school or even indoor plumbing.

The *Brown* Decision

In 1950 the NAACP determined to convince the Supreme Court to overturn the separate but equal doctrine itself. Oliver Brown was one of the people who provided a way. Brown was dissatisfied that his daughter Linda had to walk past an all-white school on her way to catch the bus to her segregated black school in Topeka, Kansas. A three-judge federal panel rejected Brown's suit because the schools in Topeka, while segregated, did meet the court's test of equality. But after two years of arguments the NAACP convinced the Supreme Court to overturn the lower court ruling in *Brown v. Board of Education of Topeka* (1954).

Marshall and his colleagues succeeded in part because of a change in the Court itself. The year before, President Eisenhower had appointed Earl Warren, a liberal Republican from California, as chief justice. Warren, a forceful advocate, managed to persuade the last of his reluctant colleagues that segregation as defined in *Plessy* perpetuated racial supremacy. The Court ruled unanimously that separate facilities were inherently unequal. To keep black children segregated by race, it ruled, "generates a feeling of inferiority as to their status in the community that may affect their hearts and minds in a way unlikely ever to be undone."

Overturning Plessy

At the time of the *Brown* decision, 21 states and the District of Columbia operated segregated school systems. All of them had to decide, in some way, how to comply with the new ruling. The Court allowed a certain amount of leeway, handing down a second ruling in 1955 that required that desegregation be carried out "with all deliberate speed." Some border states reluctantly decided to comply, but in the Deep South, many citizens called for die-hard defiance. In 1956, 19 U.S. senators and 81 representatives issued a "Southern Manifesto," which "declared their intent to use "all lawful means" to reestablish legal segregation.

Latino Civil Rights

Mexican Americans also considered school desegregation as central to their campaign for civil rights. At the end of World War II, only 1 percent of children of Mexican descent in Texas graduated from high school. Both the American GI Forum (see pages 810–811) and the League of United Latin American Citizens (LULAC; page 728) supported legal challenges to the system.

In a 1947 case, *Mendez et al. v. Westminster School District of Orange County,* the courts had ordered several California school districts to integrate. LULAC saw a way to apply that ruling in Texas. The superintendent in the town of Bastrop had refused a

Delgado and Segregated Schools

request to enroll first-grader Minerva Delgado in a nearby all-white school. Civil rights lawyer and activist Gus Garcia, a legal adviser to both LULAC and the GI Forum, helped bring a case on Minerva's behalf against the school district. Before *Delgado et al. v. Bastrop et al.* went to trial, a Texas judge ordered an end to segregated schools beyond the first grade (based on the assumption that the youngest Mexican American children needed special classes to learn English). *Delgado* served notice that Mexicans would no longer accept second-class citizenship. It also served as a precedent in *Brown v. Board of Education* in 1954.

Unlike African Americans, Latinos did not face a Jim Crow system of laws imposing segregation. Throughout the Southwest the states recognized just two races: black and white. That dividing line left Mexican Americans in legal limbo. Though legally grouped with whites, they were by long-standing social custom barred from many public places, they could not serve on juries, and they faced widespread job discrimination. To remedy the situation, Mexican Americans had to establish themselves in the courts as a distinct class of people.

Hernández and Desegregation

An opportunity arose in the case of Pete Hernández, who had been convicted of murder by an all-white jury in Jackson County, Texas. Indeed, as Mexican American lawyer Gus Garcia realized, no Mexican American had served on a Jackson jury in the previous 25 years. Garcia, one of the leaders of the American GI Forum, saw in the tactics of Thurgood Marshall and the NAACP a way to use the Hernández case to extend to Mexicans the benefits of the Fourteenth Amendment's equal protection clause.

The key to the case was ingenious but direct. The state argued that because Mexicans were white, a jury without Mexicans was still a jury of peers. Yet the courthouse in which Hernández was tried had two men's rooms. One said simply, "MEN." The other, labeled with a crudely hand-lettered sign, said "COLORED MEN" and below that, in Spanish, "HOMBRES AQUI [MEN HERE]." As one of Gus Garcia's colleagues recalled, "In the jury pool, Mexicans may have been white, but when it came to nature's functions they were not." This and similar examples of discrimination persuaded the Supreme Court, in *Hernández v. Texas,* to throw out the state's argument. Latinos in south Texas, like African Americans across the South, were held to be a discrete group whose members deserved equal protection under the law. "The Fourteenth Amendment is not directed solely against discrimination due to a 'two-class theory,' that is, based upon differences between 'white' and Negro," ruled Chief Justice Earl Warren. Warren's reasoning made it possible for Latinos to seek redress as a group rather than as individuals. After *Hernández,* the Mexican American community had both the legal basis and the leadership to broaden its attack against discrimination.

Attorney Gus Garcia (left) was one of the key leaders of the American GI Forum, founded by Mexican American veterans to pursue their civil rights. He and his colleagues successfully appealed the conviction of Pete Hernández (center) before the Supreme Court in 1954.

A New Civil Rights Strategy

Neither the *Brown* nor the *Hernández* decision ended segregation, but they combined with political and economic forces to usher in a new era of southern race relations. In December 1955 Rosa Parks, a 43-year-old black civil rights activist, was riding the bus home in Montgomery, Alabama. When the driver ordered her to give up her seat for a white man, as Alabama Jim Crow laws required, she refused. Police took her to jail and eventually fined her $14.

Rosa Parks

Determined to overturn the law, a number of women from the NAACP, friends of Parks, met secretly at midnight to draft a letter of protest.

> Another Negro woman has been arrested and thrown into jail because she refused to get up out of her seat on the bus and give it to a white person. . . . Until we do something to stop these arrests, they will continue. The next time it may be you, or you or you. This woman's case will come up Monday. We are, therefore, asking every Negro to stay off the buses on Monday in protest of the arrest and trial.

Thousands of copies of the letter were distributed, and the Monday **boycott** was such a success it was extended indefinitely. Buses wheeled around the city virtually empty, losing over 30,000 fares a day. The white community, in an effort to halt the unprecedented black challenge, resorted to various forms of legal and physical intimidation. No local agent would insure cars used to carpool black workers. A bomb exploded in the house of the Reverend Martin Luther King Jr., the key boycott leader. And when that failed to provoke the violence that whites could use to justify harsh reprisals, 90 black leaders were arrested for organizing an illegal boycott. Still, the campaign continued until November 23, 1956, when the Supreme Court ruled that bus segregation was illegal.

The triumph was especially sweet for Martin Luther King Jr., whose leadership in Montgomery brought him national fame. Before becoming a minister at the Dexter Street Baptist Church, King had little personal contact with the worst forms of white racism. He had grown up in the relatively affluent middle-class black community of Atlanta, Georgia, the son of one of the city's most prominent black ministers. He attended Morehouse College, an academically respected black school in Atlanta, and Crozer Theological Seminary in Philadelphia before entering the doctoral program in theology at Boston University. As a graduate student, King embraced the pacifism and nonviolence of the Indian leader Mohandas Gandhi and the activism of Christian reformers of the progressive era. King heeded the call to Dexter Street in 1954 with the idea of becoming a theologian after he served his active ministry and finished his dissertation.

Martin Luther King Jr.

As boycott leader it was King's responsibility to rally black support without triggering violence. Because local officials were all too eager for any excuse to use force, King's nonviolent approach was the ideal strategy. King offered his audience two visions. First, he reminded them of the many injustices they had been forced to endure. The boycott, he asserted, was a good way to seek redress. Then he counseled his followers to avoid the actions of their oppressors: "In our protest there will be no cross burnings. No white person will be taken from his home by a hooded Negro mob and brutally murdered." And he evoked the Christian and republican ideals that would become the themes of his civil rights crusade. "If we protest courageously, and yet with dignity and Christian love," he said, "when the future history books are written, somebody will have to say, 'There lived a race of people, of black people, of people who had the moral courage to stand up for their rights. And thereby they injected a new meaning into the history of civilization.'"

Nonviolence as a Strategy

Indeed, the African Americans of Montgomery did set an example of moral courage that rewrote the pages of American race relations. Their firm stand caught the attention of the national news media. King and his colleagues were developing the tactics needed to launch a more aggressive phase of the civil rights movement.

Little Rock and the White Backlash

The civil rights spotlight moved the following year to Little Rock, Arkansas. White officials there had reluctantly adopted a plan to integrate the schools with a most

Angry white students, opposed to integration, menace black students during a recess at Little Rock's Central High. This civil rights crisis was the first covered by television. For weeks NBC correspondent John Chancellor took a chartered plane daily from Little Rock to Oklahoma City to deliver film footage for the nightly news program. Such national attention made people outside the South more sensitive to civil rights issues.

deliberate lack of speed. Nine black students were scheduled to enroll in September 1957 at the all-white Central High School. Instead, the school board urged them to stay home. Governor Orval Faubus, generally a moderate on race relations, called out the Arkansas National Guard on the excuse of maintaining order. President Eisenhower tacitly supported Faubus in his defiance of court-ordered integration by remarking that "you cannot change people's hearts merely by laws."

Still, the Justice Department could not simply let Faubus defy the federal courts. It won an injunction against the governor, but when the nine blacks returned on September 23 a mob of 1,000 abusive whites greeted them. So great was national attention that President Eisenhower felt compelled to send in federal troops and take control of the National Guard. For a year the Guard preserved order until Faubus, in a last-ditch maneuver, closed the schools. Only in 1959, under pressure of another federal court ruling, did Little Rock schools reopen and resume the plan for gradual integration.

The skirmishes of Montgomery and Little Rock were a beginning, not an end. In fact, segregationist resistance increased in the wake of King's Montgomery success. From 1955 to 1959 civil rights protesters endured over 200 acts of violence in the South. Legislatures and city councils passed scores of laws attempting either to outlaw the NAACP or prevent it from functioning. Black leaders were unable to achieve momentum on a national scale until 1960. Then, a series of spontaneous demonstrations by young people changed everything.

A Movement Becomes a Crusade

On January 31, 1960, Joseph McNeill got off the bus in Greensboro, North Carolina, a freshman on the way back to college. When he looked for something to eat at the lunch counter, the waitress gave the familiar reply. "We don't serve Negroes here."

It was a refrain repeated countless times and in countless places. Yet for some reason this rebuke particularly offended McNeill. He and his roommates had read a pamphlet describing the 1955 bus boycott in Montgomery, Alabama. They decided it was time to make their own protest against segregation. Proceeding the next day to the "whites only" lunch counter at a local store, they sat politely waiting for service. "The waitress looked at me as if I were from outer space," recalled one of the protesters. Rather than serve them, the manager closed the counter. Word of the action spread. A day later—Tuesday—the four students were joined by 27 more. Wednesday, the number jumped to 63, Thursday, to over 300. Come the weekend, 1,600 students rallied to plan further action.

On Monday, February 8, **sit-ins** began in nearby Durham and Winston-Salem. Tuesday it was Charlotte. Thursday, High Point and Portsmouth, Virginia. A news broadcast reassured white residents in Raleigh that black students there would not follow Greensboro's example. In response, angry black students launched massive sit-ins at variety stores in Raleigh. By Lincoln's birthday, the demonstrations had spread to Tennessee and Florida; by April, to 78 different southern and border communities. By September at least 70,000 African Americans as well as whites had participated. Thousands had been arrested and jailed.

The campaign for black civil rights gained momentum not so much by the power of national movements as through a host of individual decisions by local groups, churches, and citizens. When New Orleans schools were desegregated in 1960, young Ruby's parents had not intended to make a social statement. But once involved, they refused to back down. The students at Greensboro had not been approached by the NAACP, but acted on their own initiative.

Riding to Freedom

Of course, organizations channeled these discontents and aspirations. But the new generation of younger activists also shaped and altered the organizations. Beginning in the 1960s, the push for desegregation moved from court actions launched by the NAACP and the Urban League to newer groups determined to take direct action. Since organizing the Montgomery boycott, Martin Luther King and his Southern Christian Leadership Conference (SCLC) had continued to advocate nonviolent protest: "To resist without bitterness; to be cursed and not reply; to be beaten and not hit back." A second key organization, the Congress of Racial Equality (CORE), was more willing than the SCLC to force confrontations with the segregationist system. Another group, the Student Non-Violent Coordinating Committee (SNCC, pronounced "Snick"), grew out of the Greensboro sit-in. SNCC represented the more militant, younger generation of black activists who grew increasingly impatient with the slow pace of reform.

Newer Civil Rights Organizations

In May 1961 CORE director James Farmer led a group of black and white "freedom riders" on a bus trip into the heart of the South. They hoped their trip from Washington to New Orleans would focus national attention on the inequality of segregated facilities. Violent southern mobs gave them the kind of attention they feared. In South Carolina, thugs beat divinity student John Lewis as he tried to enter an all-white waiting room. Mobs in Anniston and Birmingham, Alabama, assaulted the freedom riders as police ignored the violence. One of the buses was burned.

President Kennedy had sought to avoid forceful federal intervention in the South. When the freedom riders persisted in their plans, he tried to convince Alabama officials to protect the demonstrators so that he would not have to send federal forces. His hopes were dashed. From a phone booth outside the bus terminal, John Doar, a Justice Department official in Montgomery, relayed the horror to Attorney General Robert Kennedy, the president's brother:

> Now the passengers are coming off. They're standing on a corner of the platform. Oh, there are fists, punching! A bunch of men led by a guy with a bleeding face are beating them. There are no cops. It's terrible! It's terrible! There's not a cop in sight. People are yelling, "There those niggers are! Get 'em, get 'em!" It's awful.

Appalled, Robert Kennedy ordered in 400 federal marshals, who barely managed to hold off the crowd. Martin Luther King, addressing a meeting in town, phoned the

Freedom Riders Attacked

In May 1961, a mob in Montgomery, Alabama surrounded the Negro First Baptist Church where Martin Luther King, Jr., was leading an all-night vigil. King put in a call to Attorney General Robert Kennedy, who sent 400 federal marshals to keep order.

attorney general to say that their church had been surrounded by an angry mob of several thousand—jeering, throwing rocks, and carrying firebombs. As Kennedy later recalled, "I said that we were doing the best that we could and that he'd be as dead as Kelsey's nuts if it hadn't been for the marshals and the efforts that we made."

Both Kennedys understood that civil rights was the most divisive issue the administration faced. For liberals, civil rights measured Kennedy's credentials as a reformer. Kennedy needed black and liberal votes to win reelection. Yet an active federal role threatened to drive white southerners from the Democratic party. It was for that reason that Kennedy had hedged on his promise to introduce major civil rights legislation. Through executive orders, he assured black leaders, he could eliminate discrimination in the government civil service and in businesses filling government contracts. He appointed several African Americans to high administrative positions and five, including Thurgood Marshall, to the federal courts. The Justice Department beefed up its civil rights enforcement procedures. But the freedom riders, by their bold actions, forced the Kennedys to do more.

Civil Rights at High Tide

By the fall of 1961 Attorney General Robert Kennedy had persuaded SNCC to shift tactics to voter registration, which he assumed would stir less violence. Voting booths, Kennedy noted, were not like schools, where people would protest, "We don't want our little blond daughter going to school with a Negro."

As SNCC and CORE workers arrived in southern towns in the spring of 1962, they discovered that voting rights was not a peaceful issue. Over two years in Mississippi they registered only 4,000 out of 394,000 black adults. Angry racists attacked with legal harassment, jailings, beatings, bombings, and murders. Terrorized workers who called for protection found it woefully lacking. FBI agents often stood by taking notes while SNCC workers were assaulted. Undaunted, SNCC workers made it clear that they intended to stay. They fanned out across the countryside to speak with farmers who had never before dared to ask for a vote.

James Meredith

Confrontation increased when a federal court ordered the segregated University of Mississippi to admit James Meredith, a black applicant. When Governor Ross Barnett personally blocked Meredith's registration in September 1962, Kennedy faced the same crisis that had confronted Eisenhower at Little Rock in 1957. The president

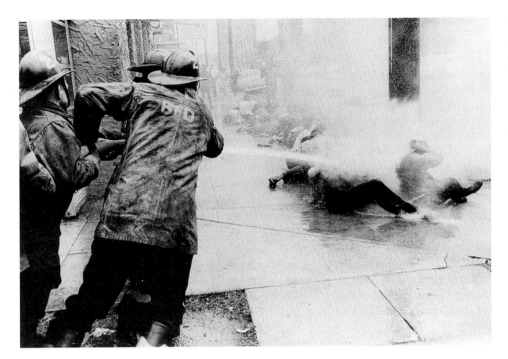

In Birmingham, Alabama, firefighters used high-pressure hoses to disperse civil rights demonstrators. The force of the hoses was powerful enough to tear bark off trees. Pictures like this one aroused widespread sympathy for the civil rights movement.

ordered several hundred federal marshals to escort Meredith into a university dormitory. Kennedy then announced on national television that the university had been integrated and asked students to follow the law of the land. Instead, a mob moved on campus, shooting out streetlights, commandeering a bulldozer, and throwing rocks and bottles. To save the marshals, Kennedy finally sent in federal troops, but not before 2 people were killed and 375 wounded.

In Mississippi, President Kennedy had begun to lose control of the civil rights issue. The House of Representatives, influenced by television coverage of the violence, introduced a number of civil rights measures. And Martin Luther King led a group to Birmingham, Alabama, to force a showdown against segregation. From a prison cell there, he produced one of the most eloquent documents of the civil rights movement, his "Letter from Birmingham Jail." Addressed to local ministers who had counseled an end to confrontation, King defended the use of civil disobedience. The choice, he warned, was not between obeying the law and nonviolently breaking it to bring about change; it was between his way and streets "flowing with blood," as restive black citizens turned toward more militant ideologies.

"Letter from Birmingham Jail"

Once freed, King led new demonstrations. Television cameras were on hand that May as Birmingham police chief "Bull" Connor, a man with a short fuse, unleashed attack dogs, club-wielding police, and fire hoses powerful enough to peel the bark off trees. When segregationist bombs went off in African American neighborhoods, black mobs retaliated with their own riot, burning a number of shops and businesses owned by whites. In the following 10 weeks, more than 750 riots erupted in 186 cities and towns, both North and South. King's warning of streets "flowing with blood" no longer seemed far-fetched.

Kennedy sensed that he could no longer compromise on civil rights. In phrases that, like King's, drew heavily on Christian and republican rhetoric, he asked the nation, "If [an American with dark skin] cannot enjoy the full and free life all of us want, then who among us would be content to have the color of his skin changed and stand in his place? Who among us would then be content with counsels of patience and delay?" The president threw his support behind a strong civil rights bill to end segregation and protect black voters. When King announced a massive march on Washington for August 1963, Kennedy objected that it would undermine support for his bill. "I have never engaged in any direct action movement which did not seem ill-timed," King replied.

On August 28 some 250,000 people gathered at the Lincoln Memorial to march and sing in support of civil rights and racial harmony. Appropriately, the day belonged

The March on Washington

to King. In the powerful tones of a southern preacher, he reminded the crowd that the Declaration of Independence was a promise that applied to all people, black and white. "I have a dream," he told them, that one day "all of God's children, black men and white men, Jews and Gentiles, Protestants and Catholics, will be able to join hands and sing in the words of the old Negro spiritual, 'Free at last! Free at last! Thank God Almighty, we are free at last!'" Congress began deliberation of the civil rights bill, which was reported out of the Judiciary Committee on October 23.

The Fire Next Time

While liberals applauded Kennedy's stand on civil rights and appreciative African Americans rejoined the Democratic party, substantial numbers of southern whites and northern ethnics deserted. The president scheduled a trip to Texas to recoup some southern support. On November 22, 1963, the people of Dallas lined the streets for his motorcade. Suddenly, a sniper's rifle fired several times. Kennedy slumped into his wife's arms, fatally wounded. His assassin, Lee Harvey Oswald, was caught several hours later. Oswald seemed a mysterious figure: emotionally unstable, he had spent several years in the Soviet Union. But his actions were never fully explained, because only two days after his arrest—in full view of television cameras—he was gunned down by a disgruntled nightclub operator named Jack Ruby.

Tragedy in Dallas

In the face of the violence surrounding the civil rights campaign as well as the assassination of the president, many Americans came to doubt that programs of gradual reform could hold the nation together. A few black radicals believed that the Kennedy assassination was a payback to a system that had tolerated its own racial violence—the "chickens coming home to roost," as separatist Malcolm X put it. Many younger black leaders observed that civil rights received the greatest national coverage when white, not black, demonstrators were killed. They wondered, too, how Lyndon Johnson, a consummate southern politician, would approach the civil rights programs.

The new president, however, saw the need for action. Just as the Catholic issue had tested Kennedy's ability to lead, Johnson knew that without strong leadership on civil rights, "I'd be dead before I could ever begin." On November 23, his first day in office, he promised civil rights leaders that he would pass Kennedy's bill. Despite a southern filibuster in the Senate, the Civil Rights Act of 1964 became law the following summer. The bill marked one of the great moments in the history of American reform. It barred discrimination in public accommodations such as lunch counters, bus stations, and hotels; it authorized the attorney general to bring suit to desegregate schools, museums, and other public facilities; it outlawed discrimination in employment by race, color, religion, sex, or national origin.

LBJ and the Civil Rights Act of 1964

Still, the Civil Rights Act did not bar the techniques that southern registrars routinely used to prevent black citizens from voting. A coalition of idealistic young black and white protesters had continued the Mississippi voting drive in what they called "Freedom Summer." In 1965 Martin Luther King led a series of demonstrations, climaxed by a 54-mile walk from Selma to Montgomery, Alabama. As pressure mounted, Johnson sent Congress a strong Voting Rights Act, which was passed in August 1965. The act suspended literacy tests and authorized federal officials to supervise elections in many southern districts. With some justice Johnson called the act "one of the most monumental laws in the entire history of American freedom." Within a five-year period black registration in the South jumped from 35 to 65 percent.

Voting Rights Act of 1965

Black Power

The civil rights laws did not strike at the **de facto segregation** found outside the South. This segregation was not codified in law but practiced through unwritten custom. In large areas of America, African Americans were locked out of suburbs, kept out of decent schools, barred from exclusive clubs, and denied all but the most menial jobs. Nor did the Voting Rights Act deal with the sources of urban black poverty.

The median income for urban black residents was approximately half that for white residents.

In such an atmosphere, militants sharply questioned the liberal goal of integration. Since the 1930s, the Nation of Islam, dedicated to complete separation from white society, had attracted as many as 100,000 members, mostly young men. During the early 1960s the sect drew even wider attention through the energetic efforts of Malcolm X. This charismatic leader had learned the language of the downtrodden from his own experience as a former hustler, gambler, and prison inmate. His militancy alarmed whites, though by 1965 Malcolm was in fact moving toward a more moderate position. He accepted integration but emphasized black community action. After he broke with Elijah Muhammed, leader of the Black Muslims, Malcolm was gunned down by rivals.

But by 1965–1966, even CORE and SNCC had begun to give up working for nonviolent change. If black Americans were to liberate themselves fully, militants argued, they could not merely accept rights "given" to them by whites—they had to claim them. Some members began carrying guns to defend themselves. In 1966 Stokely Carmichael of SNCC gave the militants a slogan—"Black Power"—and the defiant symbol of a gloved fist raised in the air. In its moderate form, the black power movement encouraged African Americans to recover their cultural roots, their African heritage, and a new sense of identity. African clothes and natural hairstyles became popular. On college campuses black students pressed universities to hire black faculty, create black studies programs, and provide segregated social and residential space.

For more militant factions, the Black Panther party of Oakland called on the black community to arm. Because California law forbade carrying concealed weapons, Panther leader Huey Newton and his followers openly brandished shotguns and rifles as they patrolled the streets protecting blacks from police harassment. In February 1967 Newton found the showdown he had been looking for. "O.K., you big fat racist pig, draw your gun," he shouted while waving a shotgun. A gun battle with police left Newton wounded and in jail.

Eldridge Cleaver, who assumed leadership of the party, attracted the attention of whites with his searing autobiography, *Soul on Ice*. But even at the height of the Black Panthers' power, the group never counted more than 2,000 members nationwide.

Violence in the Streets

No ideology shaped the reservoir of frustration and despair that existed in the ghettos. Often, a seemingly minor incident such as an arrest or an argument on the streets triggered violence. A mob would gather, and police cars and white-owned stores would be firebombed or looted. Riots broke out in Harlem and Rochester, New York, in 1964, the Watts area of Los Angeles in 1965, Chicago in 1966, and Newark and Detroit in 1967. In the riot at Watts, more than $200 million in property was destroyed and 34 people died, all of them black. It took nearly 5,000 troops to end the bloodiest rioting in Detroit, where 40 died, 2,000 were injured, and 5,000 were left homeless.

To most whites the violence was unfathomable and inexcusable. Lyndon Johnson spoke for many when he argued that "neither old wrongs nor new fears can justify arson and murder." Martin Luther King, still pursuing the tactics of nonviolence, came to understand the anger behind it. Touring Watts only days after the riots, he was approached by a band of young blacks. "We won," they told him proudly. "How can you say you won," King countered, "when thirty-four Negroes are dead, your community

Nation of Islam

Malcolm X

Black Panthers

A National Guardsman watches as flames consume large areas of the Watts section of Los Angeles during the 1965 riot. Often, a seemingly trivial event set off such scenes of violence, revealing the depth of explosive rage harbored within urban ghettos.

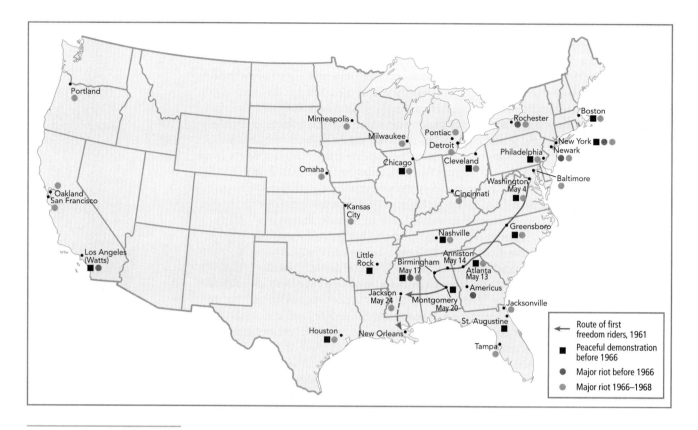

Civil Rights: Patterns of Protest and Unrest *The first phase of the civil rights movement was confined largely to the South, where the freedom riders of 1961 dramatized the issue of segregation. Beginning in the summer of 1964, urban riots brought the issue of race and politics home to the entire nation. Severe rioting followed the murder of Martin Luther King Jr. in 1968, after which the worst violence subsided.*

is destroyed, and whites are using the riot as an excuse for inaction?" The youngsters were unmoved. "We won because we made them pay attention to us."

For Johnson, ghetto violence and black militance mocked his efforts to achieve racial progress. The Civil Rights and Voting Rights acts were essential parts of the Great Society he hoped to build. In that effort he had achieved a legislative record virtually unequaled by any other president in the nation's history. What Kennedy had promised, Johnson delivered. But the growing white backlash and the anger exploding in the nation's cities exposed serious flaws in the theory and practice of liberal reform.

Lyndon Johnson and the Great Society

Like the state he hailed from, Lyndon Baines Johnson was in all things bigger than life. His gifts were greater, his flaws more glaring. Insecurity was his Achilles heel and the engine that drove him. If Kennedy had been good as president, Johnson would be "the greatest of them all, the whole bunch of them." If FDR won in a landslide in 1936, Johnson would produce an even larger margin in 1964. And to anyone who displeased him, he could be ruthlessly cruel. His scatological language and preoccupation with barnyard sex amused few and offended many. Yet Johnson could not understand why so few people genuinely liked him; one courageous diplomat, when pressed, found the nerve to respond, "Because, Mr. President, you are not a very likable man."

Johnson was born in Stonewall, Texas, in the hill country outside Austin, where the dry climate and rough terrain only grudgingly yielded up a living. He arrived in Washington in 1932 as an ardent New Dealer who loved the political game. When he became majority leader of the Senate in 1954, he cultivated an image as a moderate conservative who knew what strings to pull or levers to jog to get the job done. On an important bill, he latched onto the undecided votes until they succumbed to the famous "Johnson treatment," a combination of arguments, threats, emotional or patriotic appeals, and enticing rewards. Florida senator George Smathers likened Johnson to "a great overpowering thunderstorm that consumed you as it closed around you."

Despite his compulsion to control every person and situation, Johnson possessed certain bedrock strengths. No one was better at hammering out compromises among competing interest groups. To those who served him well he could be loyal and generous. As president, he cared sincerely about society's underdogs. His support for civil rights, aid to the poor, education, and the welfare of the elderly came from genuine conviction. Like Franklin Roosevelt, whom he deeply admired, Johnson shared the liberal belief that the government should play an active role in managing the economy in order to soften the boom-and-bust swings of capitalism. Like progressives from the turn of the century, liberals looked to improve society by applying the intelligence of "experts." Liberals had confidence, at times bordering on arrogance, that poverty could be eliminated and the good society achieved. That faith might prove naive, but during the 1960s such optimism was both infectious and energizing.

Johnson's Liberal Faith

The Origins of the Great Society

In the first months after the assassination, Johnson acted as the conservator of the Kennedy legacy. "Let us continue," he told a grief-stricken nation. Liberals who had dismissed Johnson as an unprincipled power broker grudgingly came to respect the energy he showed in steering the Civil Rights Act and tax cut legislation through Congress. Kennedy's advisers believed tax cuts would create economic growth beneficial to the poor. Under Johnson, they did.

Kennedy had come to recognize that prosperity alone would not ease the plight of America's poor. In 1962 Michael Harrington's book *The Other America* brought attention to the widespread persistence of poverty despite the nation's affluence. Harrington focused attention on the hills of Appalachia that stretched from western Pennsylvania south to Alabama. In some counties a quarter of the population survived on a diet of flour and dried-milk paste supplied by federal surplus food programs. Under Kennedy, Congress had passed a new food stamp program as well as laws designed to revive the economies of poor areas, replacing urban slums with newer housing and retraining the unemployed. Robert Kennedy also headed a presidential committee to fight juvenile delinquency in urban slums by involving the poor in **community action** programs. Direct participation, they hoped, would overcome "a sense of resignation and fatalism" that sociologist Oscar Lewis had found while studying the Puerto Rican community of New York City.

Discovering Poverty

It fell to Lyndon Johnson to fight Kennedy's "war on poverty." By August 1964 this master politician had driven through Congress the most sweeping social welfare bill since the New Deal. The Economic Opportunity Act addressed almost every major cause of poverty. It included training programs such as the Job Corps, granted loans to rural families and urban small businesses as well as aid to migrant workers, and launched a domestic version of the Peace Corps, known as VISTA (Volunteers in Service to America). The price tag for these programs was high. Johnson committed almost $1 billion to Sargent Shriver, a Kennedy brother-in-law, who directed the new Office of Economic Opportunity (OEO).

The speed Johnson demanded led inevitably to confusion, conflict, and waste. Officials at OEO often found themselves in conflict with other cabinet departments as well as with state and local officials. For example, OEO workers organized voter registration drives in order to oust corrupt city officials. Others led rent strikes to force improvements in public housing. The director of city housing in Syracuse, New York, reacted typically: "We are experiencing a class struggle in the traditional Karl Marx style in Syracuse, and I do not like it." Such battles for power and bureaucratic turf undermined federal poverty programs.

The Election of 1964

In 1964, however, these controversies had not yet surfaced. Johnson's political stock remained high. To an audience at the University of Michigan in May, he announced his ambition to forge a "Great Society," in which poverty and racial injustice no longer

Lyndon Johnson applied the "Johnson treatment" (as shown here, in 1957, to Senator Theodore Green) whenever he wanted people to see things his way. Few could say no, as he leaned in and reminded them who dominated the situation.

existed. The chance to fulfill his dreams seemed open to him, for the Republicans nominated Senator Barry Goldwater of Arizona as their presidential candidate. Ruggedly handsome, Goldwater was a true son of the West who held a narrow view of what government should do, for he was at heart a **libertarian.** Government, he argued, should not dispense welfare, subsidize farmers, tax incomes on a progressive basis, or aid public education. At the same time, Goldwater was so anti-Communist that he championed a large defense establishment.

Goldwater's extreme views allowed Johnson to portray himself as a moderate. He chose Minnesota's liberal Senator Hubert Humphrey to give regional balance to the ticket. Only the candidacy of Governor George Wallace of Alabama marred Johnson's election prospects. In Democratic primaries, Wallace's segregationist appeal won nearly a third or more of the votes in Wisconsin, Indiana, and Maryland—hardly the Deep South. He was persuaded, however, to drop out of the race.

The election produced the landslide Johnson craved. Carrying every state except Arizona and four in the Deep South, he received 61 percent of the vote. Democrats gained better than two-to-one majorities in the Senate and House. Many observers saw the election as a repudiation of Goldwater and his conservative values. In reality, his defeat opened the way for grass-roots conservatives to gain control of the Republican party.

The Great Society

In January 1965 Johnson announced a legislative vision that would extend welfare programs on a scale beyond Franklin Roosevelt's New Deal. By the end of 1965, 50 bills had been passed, many of them major pieces of legislation, with more on the agenda for the following year.

Programs in Education

As a former teacher, Johnson made education the cornerstone of his Great Society. Stronger schools would compensate the poor for their disadvantaged homes, he believed. Under the Elementary and Secondary School Act, students in low-income school districts were to receive educational equipment, money for books, and enrichment programs like Project Head Start for nursery-school-age children.

Johnson also pushed through the Medicare Act to provide the elderly with hospital health insurance. Medicare targeted the elderly, because older people used hospitals three times more than other Americans and generally had incomes only half as large. Because Medicare made no provision for the poor who were not elderly, Congress also passed a program called Medicaid. Participating states received federal matching grants to pay the medical expenses of those on welfare or too poor to afford medical care.

The Great Society reformed immigration policy, in ways that reflected the drastic changes in global economics and culture since the last major immigration legislation was passed in 1924. Then, the National Origins Act (see pages 707–708) reflected the deeply Eurocentric orientation of American society and its prejudices against people of color. Virtually all the annual admissions quota of 154,000 went to Northern Europeans. Asians were barred almost entirely. By the 1960s American attitudes were changing, in terms of both race and region. American soldiers, after all, had fought wars to defend Korea, the Philippines, Vietnam, Taiwan, Japan, and other Asian nations. How could it justify discriminating against citizens from those countries?

By 1965, with Asian economies growing, the war in Vietnam expanding, and civil rights sentiments at a peak, the need for reform took on special urgency. The Immigration Act of 1965 abolished the national origins system. It increased annual admissions to 170,000 people and put a cap of 20,000 on immigrants from any single nation. The law gave marked preference to reuniting families of those immigrants already in the United States—so much so that some observers nicknamed it the "brothers and sisters act." Asians and Eastern Europeans were among its prime beneficiaries.

The act's liberalization was offset, however, by prejudice toward Central Americans, especially Mexicans. The National Origins Act of 1924 had placed no limit on immigrants from the Americas. But by the 1960s many in Congress feared a massive influx of workers from south of the border. Widespread poverty in Latin American nations had left thousands unemployed and desperate to find work. Hence the new act capped arrivals from the Western Hemisphere at 120,000 annually. In that way immigration reform reflected the shifting balance of the global economy.

Booming economies took an increasing toll on the environment. By the mid-1960s many Americans had become increasingly concerned about acrid smog from factories and automobiles; about lakes and rivers polluted by detergents, pesticides, and industrial wastes; and about the disappearance of wildlife. In 1962 Rachel Carson in *Silent Spring* warned the nation of the destructive impact of DDT and other insecticides. Congress in 1964 passed the National Wilderness Preservation System Act to set aside 9.1 million acres of wilderness as "forever wild." Lady Bird Johnson, the president's wife, campaigned to eliminate the garish billboards and junkyards along many of the nation's roads. Congress first established pollution standards for interstate waterways and a year later provided funds for sewage treatment and water purification. Legislation also tightened standards on air pollution. Environmental reform provoked opposition from groups like mining companies, cattle-grazers, and the timber industry, who wanted to continue using the public domain for their own purposes. But the public accepted the benefits of the new regulation.

For all he had done, Johnson wanted to do more. In 1966 he pushed through bills to raise the minimum wage, improve auto safety, aid mass transit, and develop "model cities." But opposition mounted. "Doesn't matter what kind of majority you come in with," Johnson predicted early on. "You've got just one year when they treat you right, and before they start worrying about themselves." Yet as late as 1968 Johnson pushed major legislation through Congress to ban discrimination in housing (Fair Housing Act), to build public housing, to protect consumers from unfair credit practices (Truth-in-Lending Act), and to protect scenic rivers and expand the national park system.

Historians have difficulty measuring the Great Society's impact. It produced more legislation and more reforms than the New Deal. However, economic statistics suggested

Medicare and Medicaid

Immigration Reform

The Environment

Evaluating the Great Society

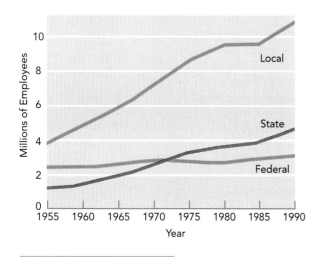

Growth of Government, 1955–1990 *Government has been a major growth industry since World War II. Most people think of "big government" as federal government. But even during the Great Society, far more people worked in state and local government.*

that general prosperity, accelerated by the tax cut bill, did more to fight poverty than all the OEO programs. And the inevitable scandals began to surface.

Despite such problems the Great Society established the high-water mark of interventionist government, a trend that began in the progressive era and flourished during the Great Depression and in World War II. Although Americans continued to pay lip service to the notion that government should remain small and interfere little in citizens' lives, no strong movement emerged to eliminate Medicare or Medicaid. Few Americans disputed the right of the government to regulate industrial pollution, or to manage the economy, and provide citizens with a safety net of benefits in sickness and in old age. In this sense, the tradition of liberalism prevailed, whatever Johnson's failings.

The Reforms of the Warren Court

Although Lyndon Johnson and the Congress left the stamp of liberalism on federal power during the decade, the third branch of government played a role that, in the long run, proved equally significant. Supreme Court chief justice Earl Warren turned what was traditionally the least activist branch of government into a center of liberal reform. His political skills, compassion, and tact had been instrumental in bringing his colleagues to a unanimous ruling on school desegregation in *Brown v. Board of Education.* Warren continued to use these skills, until his retirement in 1969, to forge a liberal coalition of justices who handed down a series of landmark decisions in broad areas of civil liberties and civil rights.

In 1960 the rights of citizens accused of a crime but not yet convicted were often unclear. Those too poor to afford lawyers frequently faced trial without representation. The police and the courts seldom informed those accused of a crime of their rights under the Constitution. In a series of decisions, the Court ruled that the Fourteenth Amendment provided broad guarantees of **due process** under the law. *Gideon v. Wainwright* (1963), an appeal launched by a Florida prisoner, made it clear that all

Protecting Due Process

citizens were entitled to legal counsel in any case involving a possible jail sentence. In *Escobedo v. Illinois* (1964) and *Miranda v. Arizona* (1966) the Court declared that individuals detained for a crime must be informed of the charges against them, of their right to remain silent, and of their right to have an attorney present during questioning. Though these decisions applied to all citizens, they were primarily intended to benefit the poor, who were most likely to be in trouble with the law and least likely to understand their rights.

Banning School Prayer

In *Engel v. Vitale* (1962), the Court issued a ruling that especially troubled conservative religious groups. The case involved a nonsectarian prayer written by the New York State Board of Regents that public school students were required to recite. Even if dissenting children could be excused, the Court ruled, they faced indirect pressure to recite the prayer. That violated the constitutional separation of church and state. The following year the Court extended the ban on school prayer to cover the reading of the Bible and the Lord's Prayer.

Other decisions promoted a more liberal social climate. In *Griswold v. Connecticut* (1964) the Warren Court overturned a nineteenth-century law banning the sale of contraceptives or providing medical advice about their use. The Court demonstrated its distaste for censorship by greatly narrowing the legal definition of obscenity. A book had to be "utterly without redeeming social value" to permit censorship. The combination of decisions reforming criminal rights, prayer, free speech, and morality angered conservatives of almost all social and political backgrounds. These issues would again become a political battleground in the 1980s and beyond.

I was sentenced to the State Penitentiary
by The Circuit Court of Bay County, State of
Florida. The present proceeding was commenced
on a writ or petition for a Writ of Habeus Corpus
To The Supreme Court of The State of
Florida to vacate The sentence, on the
grounds that I was made to stand
Trial without the aid of counsel, and, at all
times of my incarseretion. The said Court
refused To appoint counsel and therefore
deprived me of Due process of law, and violate
my rights in The Bill of Rights and the
constitution of the United States.
　　　　　　　　　　　　　　Clarence Earl Gideon
5th day of Jan 1962 Petitioner
Lawrence C Jugga
NoTaRy PubliC

Gideon's Letter to the Supreme Court
John F. Davis, Clerk, Supreme Court of the United States

Clarence Earl Gideon (right) used this handwritten letter to bring his appeal to the
attention of the Supreme Court. In the Gideon case the court ruled that even poor
defendants have the right to legal counsel. Such incidents, while rare, restore faith in
the idea of a government for the people.

The Court's most far-reaching decision was probably one of its least controversial, though politically most sensitive. As cities and suburbs grew, few states redrew their legislative districts to reflect the change. Rural (and generally conservative) elements continued to dominate state legislatures. In *Baker v. Carr* (1962) and a series of later cases the Court ruled that the states must apportion seats not by "land or trees or pastures," but as closely as possible by the principle of "one person, one vote."

One Person, One Vote

The Counterculture

In 1964 some 800 students from Berkeley, Oberlin, and other colleges met in western Ohio to be trained for the voter registration campaign in the South. Middle-class students who had grown up in peaceful white suburbs found themselves being instructed for this "Mississippi Freedom Summer" by protest-hardened SNCC coordinators. The lessons were sobering. When beaten by police, the SNCC staff advised, assume the fetal position—hands protecting the neck, elbows covering the temples. That minimized injuries from nightsticks. A few days later, grimmer news arrived. A volunteer who had left for Mississippi two days earlier had already been arrested by local police. Now he and two others were reported "missing." Six weeks later, their mangled bodies were found, bulldozed into the earthworks of a freshly finished dam. That did not stop other sobered volunteers from heading to Mississippi.

By the mid-1960s conservatives, civil rights groups, and the poor were not alone in rejecting liberal solutions. Dissatisfied members of the middle class—and especially the young—joined a revolt against the conventions of society and politics as usual. The students who returned to campus from the voter registration campaign that summer of 1964 were the shock troops of a much larger movement.

Activists on the New Left and Right

More than a few students had become disillusioned with the slow pace of reform. Since the "establishment"—whether it was liberal or conservative—blocked meaningful change, why not overthrow it? Tom Hayden, raised in a working-class family outside Detroit, went to college at the University of Michigan, then traveled to Berkeley, and soon joined civil rights workers in Mississippi. Hayden, along with Al Haber, another student at the University of Michigan, was a driving force in forming the radical Students for a Democratic Society (SDS). SDS had little sympathy with an "old left" generation of radicals who grew up in the 1930s and still debated the merits of Marxism. Action was the route to change, Hayden argued: through sit-ins, protest marches, and direct confrontation. At a meeting in Port Huron, Michigan, in 1962 the group condemned the modern bureaucratic society exemplified by the organization man of the 1950s. The Port Huron Statement called for "participatory democracy," in which large organizations run by bureaucrats would be decentralized and turned into face-to-face communities in which individual participation mattered.

SDS and Port Huron

The Free Speech Movement at the University of California, Berkeley, was a case in point. To most liberals, Berkeley seemed the gem of the California state university system. Like so many other universities, it had educated a generation of GIs following World War II. But to people like Tom Hayden and the SDS, Berkeley was a bureaucratic monster, enrolling more than 30,000 students and marching them into impersonal classrooms to hear lectures from remote professors. In the fall of 1964, Berkeley declared off-limits the one small area in which political organizations had been allowed to advertise their causes. When university police tried to remove a recruiter for CORE, thousands of angry students surrounded the police car for 32 hours. They were led by a student named Mario Savio.

The Free Speech Movement

Before traveling south to Freedom Summer in 1964, Savio had been an undistinguished graduate student in philosophy. Mississippi changed him. And not just Savio. Twelve of the 21 Freedom Summer veterans at Berkeley were arrested during the protest. "In our free-speech fight," Savio proclaimed, "we have come up against what may emerge as the greatest problem of our nation—depersonalized, unresponsive bureaucracy." When the university's president, Clark Kerr, threatened to expel Savio, 6,000

Edie Black from Smith College was one of hundreds of middle-class students who volunteered during Freedom Summer of 1964. Here she teaches in a school at Mileston, Mississippi. Many students returned to their campuses in the fall radicalized, ready to convince others to join them in finding alternatives to "the system."

students took control of the administration building, stopped classes with a strike, and convinced many faculty members to join them. Kerr backed down, placing no limits on free speech on campus except those that applied to society at large. But the rebellious spirit spread to other major universities, such as Michigan, Yale, and Columbia, and then to campuses across the nation.

Not all students were radicalized on college campuses. To the conservative members of Young Americans for Freedom (YAF), those behind the Free Speech Movement at Berkeley were a motley crowd of beatniks, liberals, and Communists. YAF had a larger (though probably less visible) membership than leftist groups like SNCC or Students for a Democratic Society (SDS). These clean-cut young Americans seldom marched or demonstrated. They wanted instead to limit the power of the federal government that they believed threatened true freedom and liberty. Both Eisenhower's "middle of the road Republicanism" and Kennedy's liberalism, they charged, sapped the "moral and physical strength of the nation." YAF denounced the Peace Corps as "a grand exercise in self-denial and altruism, paid for by the American taxpayers and administered by the United Nations." Barry Goldwater embodied for YAF members the values they cherished. Although Goldwater went down to defeat, the ranks of the YAF would supply a new generation of conservative activists in the 1980s.

Young Americans for Freedom

Vatican II and American Catholics

Many conservatives feared that the secular trends of modern life threatened the Christian faith as well. They worried that even the traditions of the Roman Catholic church seemed under siege when Pope John XXIII summoned church leaders to an ecumenical council, popularly known as Vatican II. It assembled in October 1962.

Racing against the cancer that would soon fell him, Pope John bade the council deal with issues of social change engaging the world in the 1960s, including poverty, nuclear war, atheism, and birth control. He wished, as well, to bring the church hierarchy more closely in touch with lay members and with the modern world around it. By the time the council concluded in 1965 Pope John had died, having been succeeded by Pope Paul VI, and the acts of the council had transformed the church. At a superficial level, many changes seemed small, though they affected the everyday lives of American Catholics. No longer was it a requirement to go without meat on "fish Fridays" or to say confession on Saturdays. More significant, during services American priests would now face the congregation rather than the altar and conduct the mass in English rather than Latin. Lay members would also have a greater role in implementing the faith. In addition, Vatican II encouraged a spirit of **ecumenism**, in which Catholics would seek greater understanding with other Christians.

Ecumenism

The changes of Vatican II energized many Catholics and led them to embrace further reform within and without the church. Priests like Fathers Daniel and Philip Berrigan were active in the antipoverty and antiwar movements of the era. Many female Catholics sought a larger role for women in religious life. Yet even those who did not take to the streets or the pulpit felt the effects of Vatican II.

The Rise of the Counterculture

Spiritual matters also aroused more secular rebels, who found their culture too materialistic and shallow. These alienated students, often from conservative backgrounds, began to grope toward spiritual, nonmaterial goals. "Turn on to the scene, tune in to what is happening, and drop out of high school, college, grad school, junior executive," advised Timothy Leary, a Harvard psychology professor who dropped out himself. People who heeded Leary's call to spiritual renewal rejected politics for a lifestyle of experimentation with music, sex, and drugs. Observers labeled their movement a "counterculture."

Madison Avenue Hippies?

Reconsidering the Sources of the Counterculture

Most Americans identify the ferment of the 1960s with the counterculture, when young rebels taught the country to be "hip." Historians looking at advertising of the early 1960s discovered that, in fact, the advertising industry in many ways had anticipated and even shaped some themes of youthful rebellion. This advertisement for the VW Beetle defied every convention of automobile selling. Whereas most 1950s automobile ads sold status wrapped up in idealized views of American life, black and white images of the VW touted "a better car" sold for "less money."

The strategy of "planned obsolescence" especially disturbed critics of the American auto industry. Each year Detroit made cosmetic changes to cars' appearances to seduce consumers into buying new, but seldom improved, models. Here, Volkswagen mocks the annual restyling frenzy. It changed the Beetle "not to make it look different," but "to make it work better." Nor did VW talk down to its customers. As historians discovered, the VW advertisers respected the audience's intelligence: "Call a spade a spade. And a suspension a suspension. Not something like "orbital cushioning."

Never.

We'd no sooner make an over-chromed, two-toned Volkswagen than we'd change the classic beetle shape.

It's not that the chromed version looks so bad; it just doesn't make the car work any better.

That's the rule of thumb we go by; we change the VW only to improve it, not to make last year's model look obsolete.

In 1961, for example, we were able to get more horsepower from our air-cooled engine without making it any bigger or less economical.

(One thing did get bigger this year: the tail lights.)

Everything on the VW happens for a reason; nothing is for show.

We don't even have a chrome piece that spells out our name.

We do have a little round emblem with our initials on it, though.

After all, we can't let 600,000 Americans go riding around in unidentified cars.

The counterculture of the 1960s had much in common with earlier religious revival and utopian movements. It admired the quirky individualism of Henry David Thoreau, and like Thoreau, it turned to Zen Buddhism and other Oriental philosophies. Like Brook Farm and other nineteenth-century utopian communities, the new hippie communes sought perfection along the fringes of society. Communards built geodesic domes based on the designs of architect Buckminster Fuller; they "learned how to scrounge materials, tear down abandoned buildings, use the unusable," as one member of the Drop City commune put it. The introduction of the birth control pill in 1962 ushered in an era of increased sexual freedom. Young rebels embraced the new freedoms as a means to liberate them from the repressive inhibitions that distorted the lives of their "uptight" parents. Drugs appeared to open the inner mind to a higher state of consciousness or pleasure. No longer would people be bound by conventional relationships and the goals of a liberal, bourgeois society.

The early threads of the 1960s counterculture led back to the 1950s and the subculture of the beat generation (see pages 840–841). For the beats, unconventional drugs had long been a part of the scene, but now their use expanded dramatically. Professor Timothy Leary began experimenting with hallucinogenic mushrooms in Mexico and

Communes

soon moved on to LSD. The drug "blew his mind," as he put it, and he became so outspoken in making converts that Harvard blew him straight out of its hallowed doors.

Whereas Leary's approach to LSD was cool and contemplative, novelist Ken Kesey (*One Flew over the Cuckoo's Nest*) embraced it with antic frenzy. His ragtag company of druggies and freaks formed the "Merry Pranksters" at Kesey's home outside San Francisco. Writer Tom Wolfe chronicled their outrageous style in *The Electric Kool-Aid Acid Test*, a book that pioneered the "New Journalism." Wolfe dropped the rules of reporting that demanded objectivity and distance by taking himself and his readers on a **psychedelic** tour with Kesey and his fellow Pranksters. Their example inspired others to drop out.

The Rock Revolution

In the 1950s rock and roll defined a teen culture preoccupied with young love, cars, and adult pressures. One exception was the Kingston Trio, which in 1958 popularized folk music that appealed to young adult and college audiences. As the interest in folk music grew, the lyrics increasingly focused on social or political issues. Joan Baez helped define the folk style by dressing simply, wearing no makeup, and rejecting the commercialism of popular music. She joined folksinger Bob Dylan in the civil rights march on Wash ington in 1963, singing "We Shall Overcome" and "Blowin' in the Wind." Such folksingers reflected the activist side of the counterculture as they sought to provoke their audiences to political commitment.

In 1964 a new sound from England exploded on the American scene. Within a year the Beatles, four musicians from Liverpool, were giving concerts and appearances on television that drove teen audiences into frenzies as the mod crooners sang "I Want to Hold Your Hand." With hair that was considered long in the 1960s, modish English clothes, fresh faces, and irreverent wit, they looked and sounded like nothing young Americans had experienced before. Their boyish enthusiasm captured the Dionysian spirit of the new counterculture. But the Beatles' enormous commercial success also reflected the creativity of their music. Along with other English groups such as the Rolling Stones, the Beatles reconnected white American audiences with the rhythm-and-blues roots of rock and roll.

Until 1965 Bob Dylan was the quintessential folk artist, writing about nuclear weapons, pollution, and racism. He appeared at concerts with longish frizzy hair, working-class clothes, an unamplified guitar, and a harmonica suspended on a wire support. But then Dylan shocked his fans by donning a black leather jacket and shifting to a "folk-rock" style featuring an electric guitar. His new songs seemed to suggest that the old America was almost beyond redemption. The Beatles, too, transformed themselves. After a pilgrimage to India to study transcendental meditation, they returned to produce *Sergeant Pepper's Lonely Hearts Club Band,* possibly the most influential album of the decade. It blended sound effects with music, alluded to trips taken with "Lucy in the Sky with Diamonds" (LSD), and concluded, "I'd love to turn you on." Out in San Francisco, bands such as the Grateful Dead pioneered "acid rock" with long pieces aimed at echoing drug-induced states of mind.

The debt of white rock musicians to rhythm and blues led to increased integration in the music world. Before the 1960s black rhythm-and-blues bands had played primarily to black audiences, in segregated clubs, or over black radio stations. The civil rights movement and a rising black social and political consciousness gave rise to "soul" music. One black disc jockey described soul as "the last to be hired, first to be fired, brown all year round, sit-in-the-back-of-the-bus feeling." Soul was the quality that expressed black pride and separatism. Out of Detroit came the "Motown sound," which combined elements of gospel, blues, and big band jazz. Diana Ross and the Supremes, the Temptations, Stevie Wonder, and other groups under contract to Berry Gordy's Motown Record Company appealed to

LSD inspired the genre of psychedelic art that adorned this Grateful Dead phonograph album cover, with its freaked-out lettering that seemed to dazzle and dance even if the viewer had not inhaled or ingested hallucinogens. (The album is title American Beauty Rose.*)*

The Beatles

Dylan

Soul Music

Three-piece suits, fur coats, berets, Grateful Dead T-shirts—clothing has always made a statement about the values of the wearer. In the 1950s that statement was conformity. The khaki slacks and brush-cut hair popular with middle-class boys hinted at military regimentation. Rock-and-rollers, lower-class kids, and farm boys often wore dungarees and T-shirts, perhaps with a cigarette pack tucked in the rolled-up sleeve. Beatniks advertised their nonconformity by adopting an exotic look: long hair, goatees, turtlenecks, and sandals.

During the 1960s nonconformity became the norm. The revolution began in earnest with the coming of the Beatles, four British rockers from working-class

The Beatles had a major impact on men's style as well as on popular music. This 1963 photo shows their "mod" look popular first in England. Later they adopted a hippie look.

Liverpool. John, Paul, George, and Ringo hit the United States like a cultural tidal wave. Their longish hair, mod clothes, and

zaniness defined a new masculine style. It was youthful rather than macho, irreverent without being overtly rebellious.

black and white audiences alike. Yet, although soul music promoted black consciousness, it offered little by way of social commentary. It evoked the traditional blues themes of workday woes, unhappy marriages, and the troubles between men and women.

The West Coast Scene

For all its themes of alienation, rebellion, and utopian quest, the counterculture also signaled the increasing importance of the West Coast in American popular culture. In the 1950s the shift of television production from the stages of New York to the film lots of Hollywood helped establish Los Angeles as a communications center. San Francisco became notorious as a home of the beat movement. And then in 1958 the unthinkable happened. The Brooklyn Dodgers and the New York Giants baseball teams fled the Big Apple for Los Angeles and San Francisco. By 1963 the "surfing sound" of West Coast rock groups like the Beach Boys and Jan and Dean had made southern California's preoccupation with surfing and cars into a national fad.

The First Be-In
Before 1967 Americans were only vaguely aware of another West Coast phenomenon, the hippies. But in January a loose coalition of drug freaks, Zen cultists, and political activists banded together to hold the first well-publicized Be-In. The beat poet Allen Ginsberg was on hand to offer spiritual guidance. The Grateful Dead and Jefferson Airplane, acid rock groups based in San Francisco, provided entertainment. A mysterious group called the Diggers somehow managed to supply free food and drink, while the notorious Hell's Angels motorcycle gang policed the occasion. Drugs of all kinds were plentiful. And a crowd attired in a bizarre mix of Native American, circus, Oriental, army surplus, and other costumes came to enjoy it all.

The West Coast had long been a magnet for Americans seeking opportunity, escape, and alternative lifestyles; now the San Francisco Bay Area staked its claim as the spiritual center of the counterculture. Politically conscious dropouts gravitated toward Berkeley; the apolitical "flower children" moved into Haight-Ashbury, a run-down San Fran-

The ambiguity of this androgynous image, especially the long hair, disturbed many Americans. While traditional men thought long hair was effeminate, rock stars saw it as sexy. And in the 1960s rock stars displaced movie stars as the public figures who most defined the male image. Mick Jagger of the Rolling Stones rejected the idea that "being masculine means looking clean, close-cropped, and ugly."

New fashions represented a desire to break social constraints in favor of greater sensuality and freedom of expression. Nowhere was that more evident than in the costuming of the counterculture. Middle-class students began to let their hair grow. African American men and women found an alternative way to make long hair into a cultural statement. They gave up wavy processing or short cuts that mirrored Anglo hair and let their hair grow into full Afros. Many whites with naturally curly hair imitated the Afro look.

Fashion had become a function of politics and rebellion. Traditional Americans saw beads, long hair, sandals, drugs, radical politics, and rock and roll as elements of a revolution. To them, hippies and radicals were equally threatening. To restore order, they tried to censor and even outlaw the trappings of the counterculture. Schools expelled boys when their hair was too long and girls when their skirts were too short. It became indecent to desecrate the flag by sewing patches of red, white, and blue on torn blue jeans. Short-haired blue-collar workers harassed long-haired hippies and antiwar protesters. The personal fashions of the youth rebellion came to symbolize a "generation gap" between the young and their elders.

In time, however, that gap narrowed. Men especially broke with past tradition. Sideburns lengthened and mustaches and beards flourished as they had not since the nineteenth century. Men began to wear jewelry, furs, perfume, and shoulder-length hair. Subdued tweeds and narrow lapels gave way to bell-bottoms, broad floral ties, and wide-collared, sometimes psychedelic, shirts. By the early 1970s, commercial success, not legal repression, had signaled an end to the revolution in fashion. As formerly hostile blue-collar workers and GIs began to sport long hair and hip clothes, fashion no longer made such clear distinctions. Even middle-aged men and women donned boots, let their hair grow a bit fuller, and slipped into modified bell-bottoms. The democratic and eclectic spirit of the 1960s persisted. Informality provided Americans of both sexes with a wider choice in fashions.

cisco neighborhood of apartments, Victorian houses, and "head shops" selling drug paraphernalia, wall posters, Indian bedspreads, and other eccentric accessories. Similar dropout communities and communes sprang up across the country. Colleges became centers of hip culture, offering alternative courses, eliminating strict requirements, and tolerating the new sexual mores of their students.

In the summer of 1969 all the positive forces of the counterculture converged on Bethel, New York, in the Catskill Mountains resort area, to celebrate the promise of peace, love, and freedom. The Woodstock Music Festival attracted 400,000 people to the largest rock concert ever organized. For one long weekend the audience and performers joined to form an ephemeral community based on sex, drugs, and rock and roll. But even then, the counterculture was dying. Violence intruded on the laid-back urban communities that hippies had formed. Organized crime and drug pushers muscled in on the lucrative trade in LSD, amphetamines, and marijuana. Bad drugs and addiction took their toll. Urban slum dwellers turned hostile to the strange middle-class dropouts who, in ways the poor could not fathom, found poverty ennobling. Free sex often became an excuse for rape, exploitation, and loveless gratification.

Much that had once seemed outrageous in the hippie world was readily absorbed into the marketplace. Advertisers were in the forefront of promoting a "hip" style. Rock groups became big business enterprises commanding huge fees. Slick concerts with expensive tickets replaced communal dances with psychedelic light shows. Yogurt, granola, and herbal teas appeared on supermarket shelves. Ironically, much of the world that hippies forged was co-opted by the society they had rejected.

By the late 1960s most dreams of human betterment seemed shattered—whether those dreams emanated from the promise of the march on Washington, Lyndon Johnson's Great Society, or the communal society of the hippie counterculture. Recession and inflation brought an end to the easy affluence that made liberal reform programs and alternative lifestyles seem so easily affordable. Poverty and unemployment menaced even middle-class youth who had found havens in communes, colleges, and graduate schools. Racial tensions divided black militants and the white liberals of the civil rights movement into sometimes hostile camps.

But the civil rights movement changed the United States in fundamental ways. Although de facto segregation and racism remained entwined in American life, segregation as a legal system had been overturned. No longer was it enshrined by the decisions of the highest court in the land, as it had been in *Plessy v. Ferguson.* And the rise of black power—in both its moderate and radical forms—reflected a political and cultural current that was international as well as national. In Africa, the drive for civil rights revolved around the effort to overthrow the imperial powers of Europe. In colony after colony, African nationalists fought for their independence, with Ghana leading the way in 1957. Too often the new governments devolved into dictatorships; while in South Africa the white regime maintained a system of *apartheid* that strictly segregated the races and smothered black political and economic progress. But colonial empires continued to fall across the globe.

The United States granted independence to its principal Asian colony, the Philippines, in 1946. Yet Americans too found themselves ensnared by the conflicts of colonialism. More than any other single factor, a growing war in France's former colony, Vietnam, destroyed the promise of Lyndon Johnson's Great Society and distracted from the campaign for civil rights. After 1965 the nation divided sharply as the American military role in Southeast Asia grew. Radicals on the left looked to rid America of a capitalist system that promoted race and class conflict at home and imperialism and military adventurism abroad. Conservatives who supported the war called for a return to more traditional values like law and order. Both the left and the right attacked the liberal center. Their combined opposition helped undermine the consensus Lyndon Johnson had worked so hard to build.

Significant Events

1947	*Delgado et al. v. Bastrop et al.* (desegregation case)
1954	*Hernández v. Texas; Brown v. Board of Education* (desegregation case)
1955	Montgomery bus boycott begins
1956	"Southern Manifesto"
1957	Little Rock crisis
1960	Greensboro sit-ins
1961	CORE freedom rides begin
1962	James Meredith desegregates University of Mississippi; *Engel v. Vitale; Baker v. Carr;* SDS Port Huron Statement
1963	March on Washington; *Gideon v. Wainwright;* Kennedy assassinated
1964	*Escobedo v. Illinois; Griswold v. Connecticut;* Civil Rights Act passed; SNCC Freedom Summer; Johnson enacts Kennedy tax cuts; Economic Opportunity Act; VISTA established; Wilderness Preservation System Act; Johnson defeats Goldwater; Berkeley "Free Speech" Movement; Beatles introduce British rock

1965	Johnson launches the Great Society; King's Selma protest; Voting Rights Act; Watts riots; Malcolm X assassinated; Medicare and Medicaid acts; Immigration Act; escalation in Vietnam
1966	*Miranda v. Arizona;* Stokely Carmichael of SNCC coins "Black Power" slogan; Model Cities Act; minimum wage raised
1967	Black Panthers battle Oakland, California, police; first "Be-In"
1968	Fair Housing Act
1969	Woodstock Music Festival

Chapter Summary

Largely excluded from the prosperity of the 1950s, African Americans and Latinos undertook a series of grassroots efforts to gain the legal and social freedoms denied them by racism and, in the South, by an entrenched system of segregation.

- Early postwar campaigns focused on legal challenges to the system, culminating with victories in the Supreme Court decisions of *Brown v. Board of Education* and *Hernández v. Texas.*

- Later in the 1950s, Martin Luther King and other civil rights activists used new techniques of protest, such as the boycott, to desegregate the bus system in Montgomery, Alabama.

- Continued resistance by white southerners sparked a school integration dispute in Little Rock, Arkansas.

- Beginning in 1960, widespread grassroots efforts from African American churches, students, and political groups across the South accelerated the drive for an end to segregation.

- Violence against sit-ins, freedom rides, voter registration drives, and other forms of nonviolent protest made the nation sympathetic to the civil rights cause.

- In the wake of the assassination of President Kennedy, Lyndon Johnson persuaded Congress to adopt the Civil Rights Act of 1964 and the Voting Rights Act of 1965.

- The Supreme Court under Chief Justice Earl Warren expanded civil rights and liberties through its *Gideon, Escobedo,* and *Miranda* decisions, while also easing censorship, banning school prayer, and increasing voting rights.

- Lyndon Johnson delivered on the liberal promise of his Great Society through his 1964 tax cut, aid to education, Medicare and Medicaid, wilderness preservation, and urban redevelopment, and through the many programs of his war on poverty.

- Johnson's liberal reforms did not satisfy student radicals, minority dissidents, gays, and the counterculture whose members sought to transform America into a more just and less materialistic society.

Additional Reading

Steven Lawson, Charles Payne, and James Patterson provide an excellent overview in *Debating the Civil Rights Movement, 1945–1968* (2006). An older, still effective survey is Robert Weisbrot, *Freedom Bound: A History of America's Civil Rights Movement* (1990). Though exhaustive in detail (nearly 3,000 pages in all), Taylor Branch's three-volume biography of Martin Luther King Jr. is superb: *Parting the Waters, America in the King Years, 1954–63* (1988); *Pillar of Fire: America in the King Years, 1963–65* (1998); and *At the Edge of Canaan: America in the King Years, 1965–68* (2006). Given the importance of leaders such as King, the prominent role of women is sometimes underrepresented. As a corrective, see Bettye Collier-Thomas and V. P. Franklin, eds., *Sisters in the Struggle: African-American Women in the Civil Rights–Black Power Movements* (2001). Latino civil rights movements are covered in Henry A. J. Ramos, *American G.I. Forum* (1998), and F. Arturo Rosales, *Chicano! The History of the Mexican-American Civil Rights Movement* (1997).

Todd Gitlin, *The Sixties* (1987), set the early tone for books that are part history and part memoir. Terry Anderson, *The Movement and the Sixties* (1995), offers a view that is both politically engaged and scholarly. For a narrative history of the era see Mark Hamilton Lytle, *America's Uncivil Wars: The Sixties Era from Elvis to the Fall of Richard Nixon* (2006). Robert Dallek, *An Unfinished Life: John F. Kennedy, 1917–1963* (2003), draws a portrait that balances Kennedy's virtues and vices. The best recent biography of Lyndon Johnson is Randall Woods, *LBJ: Architect of Ambition* (2006).

For a fuller list of readings, see the Bibliography at www.mhhe.com/davidsonnation6.

CHAPTER 30
Vietnam and the End
of the Liberal Era

1963~1976

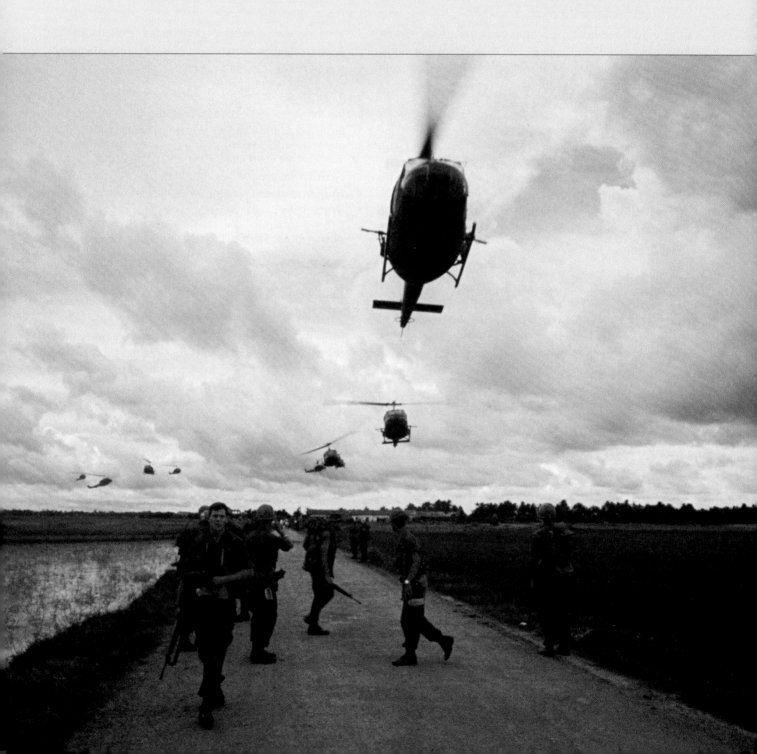

Who Is the Enemy?

Vietnam from afar: it looked almost like an emerald paradise. "I remember getting up on the flight deck and seeing one of the most beautiful visions I've ever seen in my life," recalled Thomas Bird, an army rifleman sent there in 1965: "A beautiful white beach with thick jungle background. The only thing missing was naked women running down the beach, waving and shouting 'Hello, hello, hello.'" Upon landing, Bird and his buddies were each issued a "Nine-Rule" card outlining proper behavior toward the Vietnamese. "Treat the women with respect, we are guests in this country and here to help these people."

But who were they helping and who were they fighting? When American troops sought to engage Vietcong forces, the VC generally disappeared into the jungle beyond the villages and rice fields. John Muir, a marine rifleman, walked into a typical hamlet with a Korean lieutenant. To Muir the place looked ordinary, but the Korean had been in Vietnam a while. "We have a little old lady and a little old man and two very small children," he pointed out. "According to them, the rest of the family has been spirited away . . . either been drafted into one army or the other. So there's only four of them and they have a pot of rice that's big enough to feed fifty people. And rice, once it's cooked, will not keep. They gotta be feeding the VC." Muir, whose only experience with rice till then had been Minute Rice or Uncle Ben's, watched as the lieutenant set the house on fire. The roof "started cooking off ammunition because all through the thatch they had ammunition stored."

GIs soon learned to walk down jungle trails with a cautious shuffle, looking for a wire or a piece of vine that seemed too straight. "We took more casualties from booby traps than we did from actual combat," recalled David Ross, a medic. "It was very frustrating because how do you fight back against a booby trap? You're just walking along and all of a sudden your buddy doesn't have a leg. Or you don't have a leg." Yet somehow the villagers would walk the same paths and never get hurt. Who was the enemy and who the friend?

The same question was being asked half a globe away, on the campus of Kent State University in May 1970. By then the Vietnam War had dragged on for more than five years and had driven President Lyndon Johnson from office. And it had embroiled his successor, Richard Nixon, in controversy when he expanded the war into Cambodia. Kent State, just east of

In Vietnam, helicopters gave infantry unusual mobility—a critical element in a war with no real front line, because troops could be quickly carried from one battle to another. These soldiers await a pick up amid rice paddies south of Saigon.

Death at Kent State: who was the enemy, who was the friend?

Akron, Ohio, was one of the many campuses that flourished in the 1950s and 1960s to accommodate the children of the baby boom. Opposition to the war had become so intense in this normally apolitical community that 300 students had torn the Constitution from a history text and, in a formal ceremony, buried it. "President Nixon has murdered it," they charged. That evening demonstrators spilled into the nearby town, smashed shop windows, and returned to campus to burn down an old army ROTC building. The panicked mayor declared a state of emergency, and Governor James Rhodes ordered in 750 of the National Guard. Student dissidents were the "worst type of people we harbor in America," he announced. "We are going to eradicate the problem."

When demonstrators assembled for a rally on the college commons, the National Guard ordered them to disperse, though the troops' legal right to break up a peaceful demonstration was debatable. The protesters stood their ground. Then the guardsmen advanced, wearing full battle gear and armed with M-1 rifles, whose high-velocity bullets had a horizontal range of almost two miles. Some students scattered; a few picked up rocks and threw them. The guardsmen suddenly fired into the crowd, many of whom were students passing back and forth from classes. Incredulous, a young woman knelt over Jeffrey Miller; he was dead. By the time calm was restored, three other students had been killed and nine more wounded, some caught innocently in the Guard's indiscriminate fire.

News of the killings swept the nation. At Jackson State, a black college in Mississippi, antiwar protesters seized a women's dormitory. On May 14 state police surrounding the building opened fire without provocation, killing two more students and wounding a dozen. In both incidents the demonstrators had been unarmed. The events at Kent State and Jackson State turned sporadic protests against the American invasion of Cambodia into a nationwide student strike. Many students believed the ideals of the United States had been betrayed by those forces of law and order sworn to protect them.

Who was the friend and who the enemy? Time and again the war in Vietnam led Americans to ask that question. Not since the Civil War had the nation been so deeply divided. As the war dragged on, debate moved off college campuses and into the homes of middle Americans, where sons went off to fight and the war came home each night on the evening news. As no other war had, Vietnam seemed to stand the nation on its head. When American soldiers shot at Vietnamese "hostiles" who could not always be distinguished from "friendlies," or when National Guardsmen fired on their neighbors across a college green, who were the enemies and who were the friends?

The Road to Vietnam

For several thousand years Vietnam had struggled periodically to fight off foreign invasions. Buddhist culture penetrated eastward from India. More often Indochina faced invasion and rule by the Chinese from the north. After 1856 the French entered as a colonial power, bringing with them a strong Catholic tradition.

Ho Chi Minh was one Vietnamese who hoped to throw off French influence as well as that of the Chinese. Ho was in France at the end of World War I, when President Wilson came to Versailles calling for self-determination for small nations. He bought a formal pinstriped suit at a secondhand store and attended the peace conference to petition for Vietnam. When the delegates ignored his plea, he became a Communist, taking the recent Russian Revolution as his model. Visits to Moscow followed, after which he returned to the Indochina region to organize revolutionary activity.

Ho Chi Minh

Once Japan was defeated in 1945, Ho seized the opportunity to unite Vietnam under a nationalist government. But as France moved to recover control of its old colony, Ho and his forces waged eight years of guerrilla war against the French, which led to victory at Dien Bien Phu in 1954 (see page 842). Ho's dream of an independent Vietnam seemed at hand. He agreed at the Geneva peace conference to withdraw his forces north of the 17th parallel in return for a promise to hold free elections in both the North and the South.

The United States, however, was determined to thwart Ho. Having supported the French in what they saw as a fight to contain communism, President Eisenhower helped install Ngo Dinh Diem and then supported Diem's decision not to hold elections. Frustrated South Vietnamese Communists—the Vietcong—began their guerrilla war once again. "I think the Americans greatly underestimate the determination of the Vietnamese people," Ho remarked in 1962, as President Kennedy was committing more American advisers to South Vietnam.

Ngo Dinh Diem

Lyndon Johnson's War

For Kennedy, Vietnam had been just one of many anti-Communist skirmishes his activist advisers wanted to fight. As attention focused increasingly on Vietnam, Kennedy accepted President Eisenhower's "domino theory": if the pro-Western Catholic government fell to the Communists, all the other nations of Southeast Asia would collapse in a row. Such an event would discredit Kennedy's effort to use counterinsurgency to fight the cold war with new vigor. But even 16,000 American "advisers" had been unable to help the unpopular Diem, who was overthrown by the military in November 1963. When Kennedy was assassinated in the same month as Diem, the problem of Vietnam was left to Lyndon Johnson.

The Domino Theory

Johnson's political instincts told him to keep the Vietnam War at arm's length. He felt like a catfish, he remarked, who had "just grabbed a big juicy worm with a right sharp hook in the middle of it." Johnson's heart was in his Great Society programs. Yet fear of the political costs of defeat in Vietnam led him steadily toward deeper American involvement.

Nguyen Ai Quoc, who became Ho Chi Minh, once worked at London's posh Carlton Hotel in the pastry kitchen of the renowned French chef Escoffier. But he was soon swept up in socialist and nationalist politics, appearing at the Versailles Peace Conference (left) to plead for an independent Vietnam. By the time the United States was increasing its involvement in Vietnam, Ho had accumulated a lifetime of anticolonialist and revolutionary activity and become a revered leader of his people. He died in 1969, six years before his dream of a united Vietnam became a reality.

Until August 1964 American advisers had focused on South Vietnam itself: guiding the South Vietnamese army in its struggle against the Vietcong. North Vietnam, for its part, had been infiltrating modest amounts of men and supplies along the Ho Chi Minh Trail, a primitive network of jungle routes threading through Laos and Cambodia into the highlands of South Vietnam. In the summer of 1964 North Vietnam began to modernize the trail. At the time American officials were unaware of the change, but they realized all too well that the Vietcong already controlled some 40 percent of South Vietnam. Johnson strategists decided to relieve the South by increasing pressure on North Vietnam itself.

Tonkin Gulf Incident

American ships in the Gulf of Tonkin began to patrol the North Vietnamese coast and provide cover for secret South Vietnamese raids. On August 2, three North Vietnamese patrol boats exchanged fire with the American destroyer *Maddox*—neither side hurting the other—and then the Vietnamese boats fled. Two nights later, in inky blackness and a heavy thunderstorm, radar operators on the *C. Turner Joy* reported a torpedo attack. But a follow-up investigation could not establish whether enemy ships had even been near the scene. The president was not pleased. "For all I know our navy might have been shooting at whales out there," he remarked privately.

Whatever his doubts, President Johnson called the incidents "open aggression on the high sea" and ordered retaliatory air raids on North Vietnam. He did not disclose that the navy and South Vietnamese forces had been conducting secret military operations in the Gulf of Tonkin at the time. Citing the confrontation, Johnson asked Congress for authority to take "all necessary measures" to "repel any armed attack" on American forces and to "prevent future aggression." Congress overwhelmingly passed what became known as the Tonkin Gulf resolution.

Senator Ernest Gruening of Alaska, one of the two lawmakers to object, sensed danger. The resolution gave the president "a blank check" to declare war, a power the Constitution specifically reserved to Congress. Johnson insisted—no doubt sincerely at the time—that he had no such intention. But as pressure for an American victory increased, the president exploited the powers the resolution gave him.

Rolling Thunder

In January 1965 Johnson received a disturbing memorandum from McGeorge Bundy and Robert McNamara. "Both of us are now pretty well convinced that our present policy can lead only to disastrous defeat," they said. The United States should either increase its attack—*escalate* was the term used in 1965—or simply withdraw. In theory **escalation** would increase military pressure to the point at which further resistance cost more than the enemy was willing to bear. By taking gradual steps, the United States would demonstrate its resolve to win while leaving the door open to negotiations.

Escalation

The theory that made so much sense in Washington did not work well in Vietnam. Each stage of American escalation only hardened the resolve of the Vietcong and North

The War in Vietnam   *North Vietnam established the Ho Chi Minh Trail (red arrows) through central Laos in order to supply South Vietnam's Vietcong forces. In the earlier stages of the war, supplies were transported by foot, but by 1964 the North Vietnamese were building roads and bridges that could handle heavy trucks.*

Vietnamese. When a Vietcong mortar attack in February killed seven Marines stationed at Pleiku airbase, Johnson ordered U.S. planes to begin bombing North Vietnam. The following month Operation Rolling Thunder was launched, a systematic bombing campaign aimed at bolstering confidence in South Vietnam and cutting the flow of supplies from the North.

But Rolling Thunder achieved none of its goals. American pilots could seldom spot the Ho Chi Minh Trail under its dense jungle canopy. Even when bombs hit, North Vietnamese crews kept the supplies moving by quickly filling the bomb craters or improvising pontoon bridges from woven bamboo stalks. Equally discouraging, South Vietnamese leaders spent their energy on political intrigue. One military government after another proved equally inept. And Ho Chi Minh refused to negotiate unless the bombing stopped and American troops went home.

Once the Americans established bases from which to launch the new air strikes, these, too, became targets for guerrilla attacks. When General William Westmoreland, the chief of American military operations in Vietnam, requested combat troops to defend the bases, Johnson sent in 3,500 marines, almost without considering the implication of his decision. Until then, only military "advisers" to the South Vietnamese had been sent. Once the crucial decision to commit combat troops had been taken, the urge to shore up and protect those already there became strong. Another 40,000 soldiers arrived in May and 50,000 more by July.

Johnson deliberately downplayed the escalation because he feared a political backlash. By the end of 1965 almost 185,000 American troops had landed—and still the call for more continued. In 1968, at the height of the war, 536,000 American troops were being supported with helicopters, jet aircraft, and other advanced military technologies. This conflict was "escalation" with a vengeance.

Social Consequences of the War

The impact of the war, naturally enough, fell hardest on the baby-boom generation of the 1950s. As these young people came of age, draft calls for the armed services were rising. At the same time, the civil rights movement and the growing counterculture were encouraging students to question the goals of establishment America. Whether they fought in Vietnam or protested at home, supported the government or demonstrated against it, eventually these baby boomers—as well as Americans of all ages—were forced to take a stand on Vietnam.

The Soldiers' War

The social structure determining which Americans would be required to fight and which would remain civilian was the draft. The system in place generally favored the middle and upper classes because college students and graduate students at first received deferments. Thus the Vietnam War increased male enrollment in colleges. As the war escalated, the draft was changed so that some students were called up through a lottery system. Still, those who knew the medical requirements might be able to produce a doctor's affidavit certifying a weak knee, flat feet, or bad eyes—all grounds for flunking the physical. About half the potential draftees flunked—two to three times the rejection rate of those called up by the NATO allies. Of the 1,200 men in Harvard's class of 1970, only 56 served in the military, and only 2 of them in Vietnam.

The poorest and least educated were also likely to escape service, because the Armed Forces Qualification Test and the physical often screened them out. Thus the sons of blue-collar America were most likely to accept Uncle Sam's letter of induction, as were the sons of Latino and black Americans, who, having fewer skills, were more often assigned to combat duty. The draft also made it a relatively young man's

The Vietcong often fought in small groups, using the dense vegetation to cover their movements. These suspects faced an arduous interrogation as U.S. soldiers tried to learn more about the location of Vietcong units.

war. The average soldier serving in Vietnam was 19, compared with 26 years old for World War II.

Most American soldiers came to Vietnam well trained and with high morale. But the physical and psychological hardships inevitably took their toll. In a war of continual small skirmishes, booby traps, and search-and-destroy missions, it was hard to relax. An American force would fight its way into a Communist-controlled hamlet, clear and burn it, and move on—only to be ordered back days or weeks later because the enemy had moved in again. Because success could not be measured in territory gained, the measure became the "body count": the number of Vietcong killed. Unable to tell who was friendly and who was hostile, GIs sometimes took out their frustrations on innocent civilians. Their deaths helped inflate the numbers used to prove that the Americans were winning.

Body Counts

No matter where they were, ground forces could count on air strikes to strafe or bomb suspected enemy positions. Because the Vietcong routinely mixed with the civilian population, the chances for deadly error increased. Bombs of napalm (jellied gasoline) and white phosphorus rained liquid fire from the skies, coating everything from village huts to the flesh of fleeing humans. Cluster bombs, designed to explode hundreds of pellets in midair, sprayed the enemy with high-velocity shrapnel. To clear jungle canopies and expose Vietcong camps and roads, American planes spread more than 100 million pounds of defoliants such as Agent Orange. ("Only You Can Prevent Forests" was the sardonic motto of one unit assigned to the task.) The destroyed forests totaled more than one-third of South Vietnam's timberlands—an area approximately the size of the state of Rhode Island. In many ways the ecological devastation was more severe than the military destruction.

The Air War and Agent Orange

By 1967 the war costs exceeded more than $2 billion a month. The United States dropped more bombs on Vietnam than it had dropped during all of World War II. After one air attack on a Communist-held provincial capital, American troops walked into the remains, now mostly ruined buildings and rubble. "We had to destroy the town in order to save it," an officer explained. As the human and material costs of the war increased, that statement stuck in the minds of many observers. What sense was there in a war that saved people by burning their homes?

The War at Home

As the war dragged on, such questions provoked anguished debate among Americans, especially on college campuses. Faculty members held "teach-ins" to explain the issues to concerned students. Scholars familiar with Southeast Asia questioned every major assumption the president used to justify escalation. The United States and South Vietnam had brought on the war, they charged, by violating the Geneva Accords of 1954. Moreover, the Vietcong were an indigenous rebel force with legitimate grievances against Saigon's corrupt government. The war was a civil war among the Vietnamese, not an effort by Soviet or Chinese Communists to conquer Southeast Asia, as Eisenhower, Kennedy, and Johnson had claimed.

Hawks and Doves

By 1966 national leaders had similarly divided into opposing camps of **"hawks"** and **"doves."** The hawks argued that America must win in Vietnam to save Southeast Asia from communism, to preserve the nation's prestige, and to protect the lives of American soldiers fighting the war. A large majority of the American people supported those views. The doves were a prominent minority. African Americans as a group were far less likely than white Americans to support the war. Some resented the diversion of Great Society resources from the cities to the war effort. The heightened sense of racial consciousness of many black Americans led them to identify with the Vietnamese people. Martin Luther King, SNCC, and CORE all opposed the war.

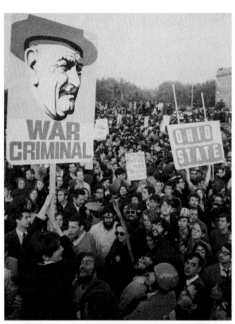

Despite the liberal achievements of the Great Society, antiwar protestors vilified Lyndon Johnson as a war criminal.

By 1967 college students and faculty turned out in crowds of thousands to express their outrage: "Hey, hey, LBJ, how many kids have you killed today?" More than 300,000 people attended the demonstration organized in April 1967 in New York City. Sixty college protesters organized by SDS leaders from Cornell University burned their draft cards in defiance of federal law. In the fall more violent protests erupted as antiwar radicals stormed a draft induction center in Oakland, California. The next day 55,000 protesters, including some prominent writers and artists, ringed the Pentagon in Washington. Mass arrests followed.

Student protests forced policy makers and citizens to take a sobering look at the justice of the war. But the guerrilla tactics of more radical elements alienated many. It would be hard to exaggerate the shock that university communities felt when radicals shut down Columbia University and clashed with police for a week in 1968. The following year black militant students—bandoliers draped across their shoulders, shotguns at their sides—seized the student union at Cornell. Even more shocking, a graduate student at the University of Wisconsin was killed in his lab when a bomb exploded there. The device had been planted by radicals protesting government-sponsored defense research.

McNamara Loses Faith

On the other hand, key moderates both within and outside the government were convinced that the United States could not win the war. Senator William Fulbright of Arkansas was among them. Having helped President Johnson push the Tonkin Gulf resolution through the Senate, Fulbright now held hearings sharply critical of American policy. Defense Secretary McNamara became the most dramatic defector. For years the statistically minded secretary had struggled to quantify the success of the war effort. General Westmoreland duly provided body counts, number of bombs dropped, and pacification reports. But by 1967 McNamara had become skeptical. "The picture of the world's greatest superpower killing or seriously injuring 1,000 non-combatants a week, while trying to pound a tiny, backward nation into submission on an issue whose merits are hotly disputed, is not a pretty one," he advised. By the end of the year, he had resigned.

Inflation

As the war dragged on, it had one severe economic consequence: inflation. By 1967 the cost of the war had soared to more than $50 billion a year. Medicare, education, housing, and other Great Society programs raised the domestic budget sharply, too. Through it all Johnson refused to raise taxes, for fear of losing support for his domestic programs. From 1950 to 1960 the average rate of inflation hovered at about 2 percent a year. From 1965 to 1970, as the war escalated, it jumped to around 4 percent. The economy was headed for trouble.

The Unraveling

Almost all the forces dividing America seemed to converge in 1968. Until January of that year, most Americans had reason to believe General Westmoreland's estimate that the United States was winning the war. Johnson and his advisers, whatever their private doubts, in public painted an optimistic picture. With such optimism radiating from Washington, few Americans were prepared for the events of the night of January 30, 1968.

Tet Offensive

As the South Vietnamese began their celebration of Tet, the Vietnamese lunar new year, Vietcong guerrillas launched a series of concerted attacks. Assault targets included Saigon's major airport, the South Vietnamese presidential palace, and Hue, the ancient Vietnamese imperial capital. Perhaps most unnerving to Americans, 19 crack Vietcong commandos blasted a hole in the wall of the American embassy compound in Saigon and stormed in. They fought in the courtyard until all 19 lay dead.

Tet must rank as one of the great American intelligence failures, on a par with Pearl Harbor or China's intervention in Korea. For nearly half a year the North Vietnamese had lured American troops into pitched battles at remote outposts like Khe Sanh, Con Thien, Song Be, and Dak To. As American forces dispersed, the Vietcong infiltrated major population areas of Saigon and the delta region. A few audacious VC, disguised as South Vietnamese soldiers, even hitched rides on American jeeps and trucks.

Though surprised by the Tet offensive, American and South Vietnamese troops counterattacked, repulsing most of the assaults. Appearing before the American press, General Westmoreland announced that the Vietcong had "very deceitfully" taken advantage of the Vietnamese holiday "to create maximum consternation" and that their "well-laid plans went afoul." In a narrow military sense, Westmoreland was right. The enemy had been driven back, sustaining perhaps 40,000 deaths. Only 1,100 American and 2,300 South Vietnamese soldiers had been killed—a ratio of more than 10 to 1 (though 12,500 civilians died).

Military Success

But Americans at home received quite another message. Tet created a "credibility gap" between the administration's promises and the harsh reality. Westmoreland, Johnson, and other officials had repeatedly claimed that the Vietcong were on their last legs. Yet as Ho Chi Minh had coolly informed the French after World War II, "You can kill ten of my men for every one I kill of yours . . . even at those odds, you will lose and I will win." Highly respected CBS news anchor Walter Cronkite drew a gloomy lesson of Tet for his national audience: "To say that we are mired in stalemate seems the only realistic, yet unsatisfactory, conclusion."

Stalemate

Two months later, American forces remained edgy about Vietcong attacks. At the remote hamlet of My Lai, American troops under Lieutenant William Calley swept in, rounded up the villagers, and slaughtered more than 200 men, women, and children. The dead of My Lai would have been just more figures in the "body count," except that an army photographer had taken pictures and a helicopter pilot intervened. If returning veterans were to be believed, there had been hundreds of similar incidents, though perhaps few as bloody. On the Communist side, vengeance was at times even more severe. Before Hue could be retaken, the Vietcong had shot, clubbed to death, or buried alive perhaps 3,000 civilians.

My Lai

The Tet offensive sobered Lyndon Johnson as well as his new secretary of defense, Clark Clifford. Clifford was a stalwart believer in the war. But as he reviewed the American position in Vietnam, he could get no satisfactory answers from the Joint Chiefs of Staff, who had requested an additional 206,000 troops. "How long would it

Levels of U.S. Troops in Vietnam (at Year End)
This graph suggests one reason why protest against the war increased after 1964, peaked by 1968, and largely ended after 1972.

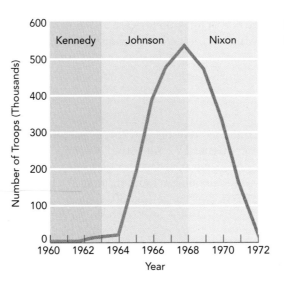

Clifford recalled asking them.

They didn't know. How many more troops would it take? They couldn't say. Were two hundred thousand the answer? They weren't sure. Might they need more? Yes, they might need more. Could the enemy build up [their own troop strength] in exchange? Probably. So what was the plan to win the war? Well, the only plan was that attrition would wear out the Communists, and they would have had enough. Was there any indication that we've reached that point? No, there wasn't.

Clifford decided to build a case for deescalation. To review policy, he formed a panel of "wise men," respected pillars of the cold war establishment. The war could not be won, the panel advised. Johnson should seek a negotiated settlement.

Meanwhile, the antiwar forces had found a political champion in Senator Eugene McCarthy from Minnesota, a whimsical maverick who wrote poetry in his spare time. McCarthy announced that no matter what the odds, he would challenge Johnson in the 1968 Democratic primaries. Idealistic college students got haircuts and shaves in order to look "clean for Gene." Thus transformed, they canvassed New Hampshire voters. Johnson had not formally entered the 1968 presidential race, but his supporters sponsored a write-in campaign, confident of a decisive win in this opening primary. When the votes were counted, McCarthy had lost by only 300 out of 50,000 votes cast. For the president, so slim a victory was a stunning defeat. To the outrage of McCarthy supporters, Robert Kennedy, John Kennedy's younger brother, now announced his own antiwar candidacy.

"Clean for Gene"

"I've got to get me a peace proposal," the president told Clifford. The White House speechwriters finally put together an announcement that bombing raids against North Vietnam would be halted, at least partially, in hopes that peace talks could begin. They were still trying to write an ending when Johnson told them, "Don't worry; I may have a little ending of my own." On March 31 he supplied it, announcing: "I have concluded that I should not permit the presidency to become involved in the partisan divisions that are developing in this political year. . . . Accordingly I shall not seek, and I will not accept, the nomination of my party for another term as your president."

LBJ Withdraws

The Vietnam War had pulled down one of the savviest, most effective politicians of the modern era. North Vietnam, for its part, responded to the speech by sending delegates to a peace conference in Paris, where negotiations bogged down. American attention focused on the situation at home, where all the turbulence, discontent, and violence of the 1960s seemed to be coming together.

The Shocks of 1968

The King and Kennedy Assassinations

On April 4 Martin Luther King Jr. traveled to Memphis to support striking sanitation workers. He was relaxing on the balcony of his motel when James Earl Ray, an escaped convict, fatally shot him. King's campaign of nonviolence was overshadowed by the frustration and anger that greeted news of his death. Riots broke out that evening in ghetto areas of the nation's capital; by the end of the week, disturbances had rocked 125 more neighborhoods across the country. Almost before Americans could recover, a disgruntled Arab nationalist, Sirhan Sirhan, assassinated Robert Kennedy on the evening of June 5. Running in opposition to the war, Kennedy had just won a crucial primary victory in California.

The deaths of King and Kennedy pained Americans deeply. In their own ways, both men exemplified the liberal tradition, which reached its high-water mark in the 1960s. King had retained his faith in a Christian theology of nonviolence. He sought change without resorting to the language of the fist and the gun. In the final years of his life, his campaign broadened to include the poor of all races. Robert Kennedy had begun his career as a pragmatic politician who, like his brother John, had not hesitated to use power ruthlessly. But Kennedy, like King, had come to reject the war his brother had supported, and he seemed genuinely to sympathize with the poor and minorities. At the same time, he was popular among traditional white ethnics and blue-collar workers. Would the liberal political tradition have flourished longer if these two charismatic figures had survived the turbulence of the 1960s?

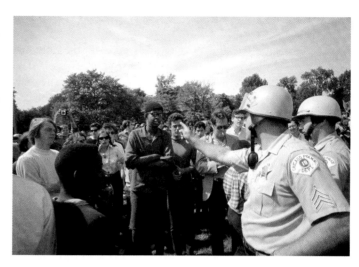

Chicago police confront protesters during the 1968 Democratic convention. With provocation on both sides, violence inevitably erupted.

Chicago

Once violence had claimed the clearest liberal voices, it became obvious that the Democrats would choose Hubert Humphrey when their convention met at Chicago in August. Humphrey had begun his career as a progressive and a strong supporter of civil rights. But as Johnson's loyal vice president he was intimately associated with the war and the old-style liberal reforms that could never satisfy radicals. Humphrey's impending nomination meant, too, that no major candidate would speak for Americans disillusioned with the war or the status quo.

Chicago, where the Democrats met, was the fiefdom of Mayor Richard Daley, long the symbol of machine politics. Daley was determined that the radicals who poured into Chicago would not disrupt "his" Democratic convention. The radicals were equally determined that they would. For a week the police skirmished with demonstrators: police clubs, riot gear, and tear gas versus the demonstrators' eggs, rocks, and balloons filled with paint and urine. Finally, with the mayor's blessing, the police turned on the crowd in what a federal commission later labeled a police riot. In one pitched battle, many officers took off their badges and waded into the crowd, nightsticks swinging, chanting, "Kill, kill, kill." Reporters, medics, and other innocent bystanders were injured. Theodore White, a veteran journalist covering the assemblage, scribbled his verdict in a notebook as police chased hippies down Michigan Avenue. "The Democrats are finished," he wrote.

Convention Mayhem

The clashes in Chicago reflected a growing willingness among students worldwide to use violence to press their revolutionary causes. In 1966 Chinese students were in the vanguard of Mao Zedong's Red Guards, formed to enforce a Cultural Revolution that was purging China of all bourgeois middle-class culture. Although that revolution persecuted millions among the educated classes and left China in economic shambles, Mao became a hero to student activists in Europe and America, who also lionized other armed revolutionaries: Fidel Castro and Che Guevara of Cuba and Ho Chi Minh.

Revolutionary Clashes Worldwide

Revolutionary targets varied. In Italy students denounced the official Marxism of the Soviet Union and the Italian Communist party. French students at the Sorbonne in Paris rebelled against the university's efforts to discipline student activists and protested their decrepit classrooms and dormitories. Students in Czechoslovakia launched a full-scale rebellion in the Prague Spring of 1968, which the Soviets eventually crushed. Although radical agendas varied from region to region, students showed remarkable unanimity in condemning one event on the world stage: the American war in Vietnam.

Whose Silent Majority?

George Wallace

Radicals were not the only Americans alienated from the political system in 1968. Governor George Wallace of Alabama sensed the frustration among the "average man on the street, this man in the textile mill, this man in the steel mill, this barber, this beautician, the policeman on the beat." In running for president, Wallace sought the support of blue-collar workers and the lower middle classes.

Wallace had first come to national attention as he stood at the door barring integration of the University of Alabama. In 1968 he formed his own American Independent party with the hawkish General Curtis LeMay as his running mate. (LeMay spoke belligerently of bombing North Vietnam "back to the stone age.") Wallace did not simply appeal to law and order, militarism, and white backlash; he was too sharp for that. With roots in southern Populism, he called for federal job-training programs, stronger unemployment benefits, national health insurance, a higher minimum wage, and a further extension of union rights. Polls in September revealed that many Robert Kennedy voters had shifted to Wallace. A quarter of all union members backed him.

Nixon's "Silent Majority"

As their candidate, the Republicans had chosen Richard Nixon, a traditional anti-Communist (now reborn as the "new," more moderate Nixon). Nixon also sought to attract away from Wallace into the Republican party, traditionally Democratic voters, especially southern Democrats. Nixon himself had modest roots. His parents owned a general store in Whittier, California, where he had worked to help the family out. He won a scholarship to Harvard, but fearing the cost of traveling east, he turned it down in favor of nearby Whittier College. At Duke Law School he was so pinched for funds that he lived in an abandoned toolshed. If ever there had been a candidate who could claim to be self-made, it was Nixon; and he believed himself a representative of the **silent majority,** as he later described it, not a vocal minority of protesters and demonstrators.

Nixon set two fundamental requirements for his campaign: to distance himself from President Johnson on Vietnam and to turn Wallace's "average Americans" into a Republican "silent majority." The Vietnam issue was delicate. He told his aide Richard Whalen, "I've come to the conclusion that there's no way to win the war. But we can't say that, of course. In fact, we have to seem to say the opposite." For most of his campaign he hinted that he had a secret plan to end the war but steadfastly refused to disclose it. He pledged only to find an honorable solution, at the same time promising to promote "law and order" while cracking down on "pot, pornography, protest, and permissiveness."

Despite a late surge from Hubert Humphrey, Nixon captured 43.4 percent of the popular vote to 42.7 percent for Humphrey and 13.5 percent for Wallace. More important, Nixon's "southern strategy" paid off; he and Wallace carried the entire southern tier of states except Texas. Some voters had punished the Democrats not just for the war but also for supporting civil rights. The majority of the American electorate seemed to have turned their backs on liberal reform and the idea of an activist government.

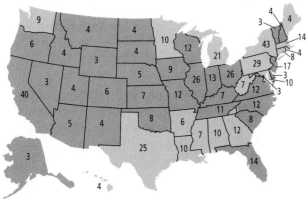

Candidate (Party)	Electoral Vote (%)	Popular Vote (%)
Richard M. Nixon (Republican)	301 (56)	31,785,480 (44)
Hubert H. Humphrey (Democratic)	191 (36)	31,275,166 (43)
George C. Wallace (American Independence)	46 (8)	9,906,473 (13)

Election of 1968

The Election of 1968

Nixon's War

In Richard Nixon, Americans had elected two men to the presidency. On the public side, he appeared as the traditional small-town, middle-class conservative who cherished individual initiative, chamber-of-commerce capitalism, Fourth of July patriotism, and Victorian mores. The private Nixon was a troubled man. His language among intimates was caustic and profane. He waxed bitter toward those he saw as enemies. Never a natural public speaker, he was physically rather awkward—a White House aide once found toothmarks on a "childproof" aspirin cap the president had been unable to pry open. But Nixon seemed to search out challenges—"crises" to face and conquer.

The new president viewed ending the war as his most pressing challenge. In meeting it, he found a congenial ally in National Security Adviser Henry Kissinger. Kissinger, like Nixon, had a global vision of foreign affairs. Like Nixon, he had a tendency to pursue his ends secretly, skirting the traditional channels of government such as the Department of State.

Henry Kissinger

Vietnamization—and Cambodia

Nixon promised a "peace with honor," which boiled down to preserving a pro-American South Vietnamese government. The strategy Nixon adopted was "Vietnamization," which involved a carrot and a stick. On its own initiative, the United States began gradually withdrawing troops as a way to advance the peace talks in Paris. The burden of fighting would shift to the South Vietnamese army, equipped now with massive amounts of American supplies.

Using the stick, President Nixon hoped to drive the North Vietnamese into negotiating peace on American terms. Quite consciously, he traded on his reputation as a cold warrior who would stop at nothing. As he explained to his chief of staff, Robert Haldeman,

> I call it the Madman Theory, Bob. I want the North Vietnamese to believe that I've reached the point where I might do anything to stop the war. We'll just slip the word to them that, "for God's sake, you know Nixon is obsessed about Communists. We can't restrain him when he's angry—and he has his hand on the nuclear button"—and Ho Chi Minh himself will be in Paris in two days begging for peace.

To underline his point, Nixon in the spring of 1969 began bombing North Vietnamese supply depots inside neighboring Cambodia. Johnson had refused to widen the war in this manner, fearing domestic reaction. Nixon simply kept the raids secret.

The North Vietnamese refused to cave in, and Ho Chi Minh's death in 1969 changed nothing. His successors continued to reject any offer that did not end with complete American withdrawal. Once again Nixon decided to turn up the heat. Over the opposition of his secretaries of defense and state, he ordered American troops into Cambodia to wipe out North Vietnamese bases there. This action was, to be sure, Johnson's old policy of escalation—precisely the opposite of the withdrawal Nixon had promised. But the Joint Chiefs argued that such an attack would buy time to strengthen the South Vietnamese army.

Invading Cambodia

Nixon recognized that a storm of protest would arise. (The administration was "going to get unshirted hell for doing this," he noted.) On April 30, 1970, he announced the "incursion" of American troops into Cambodia, proclaiming that he would not allow "the world's most powerful nation" to act "like a pitiful helpless giant." The wave of protests that followed included the Kent State tragedy as well as another march on Washington by 100,000 protesters. Even Congress was upset enough to repeal the Tonkin Gulf resolution, a symbolic rejection of Nixon's invasion. After two months American troops left Cambodia, having achieved little.

Bombing a Path toward Peace

For a time, Vietnamization seemed to be working. As more American troops went home, the South Vietnamese forces improved modestly. But for American GIs still in the country, morale became a serious problem. Obviously the United States was gradually pulling out its forces. After Tet, it was clear there would be no victory. So why were the "grunts" in the field still being asked to put their lives on the line? The anger surfaced increasingly in incidents known as "fragging," in which GIs threw fragmentation grenades at officers who pursued the war too aggressively.

The problem with morale only underlined the dilemma facing President Nixon. As the troops became restive, domestic opposition to the war grew. By repealing the Gulf of Tonkin resolution, Congress itself had put the president on notice that he would have to negotiate a settlement soon. Yet, at peace talks in Paris, the North Vietnamese refused to agree to a settlement until all American forces had left Vietnam. And, if American troops left, South Vietnamese resistance would very likely collapse, for Vietnamization had not worked well. Unwilling to commit more American troops on the ground, President Nixon in May 1972 ordered a sustained bombing campaign as well as the mining and blockade of Haiphong harbor. When that pressure failed, a frustrated president ordered an even more intense bombing campaign in December. American planes dropped more explosives on North Vietnam in 12 days than they had in the previous two years.

Once again Henry Kissinger returned to Paris determined to end the war. He promised aid to the North Vietnamese for rebuilding their country and made a secret pledge to South Vietnam to send American troops if they were needed to save the government. By January 1973 the negotiators finally agreed to terms. The United States would recognize North Vietnam's government and withdraw all its forces from Vietnam, Laos, and Cambodia. North Vietnam agreed to release its prisoners of war. The American phase of the war—one that had lasted for nearly 30 years—was finally over. But the final act in the drama remained to be played out, for the peace between North and South Vietnam remained uneasy at best.

Before and after: the devastating impact of American bombing and use of defoliants such as Agent Orange on the Vietnamese countryside.

The Move toward Détente

Despite Nixon's insistence on "peace with honor," Vietnam was not a war he had chosen to fight. Both Kissinger and Nixon recognized that the United States no longer had the strength to exercise unchallenged dominance across the globe. The Soviet Union, not Vietnam, remained their prime concern. Ever since Khrushchev had backed down at the Cuban missile crisis in 1962, the Soviets had steadily expanded their nuclear arsenal. Continued instability in Southeast Asia, the Middle East, and other Third World areas threatened the strength of the non-Communist bloc. Thus Vietnam diverted valuable military and economic resources from more critical areas.

In what the White House labeled the new "Nixon Doctrine," the United States announced it would no longer expect to fight every battle, win every war, or draw every line to keep the global peace. Instead, Americans would shift some of the military burden for containment to such allies as Japan in the Pacific, the shah of Iran in the Middle East, Zaire in central Africa, and the apartheid government in South Africa. Over the next six years American foreign military sales jumped from $1.8 billion to $15.2 billion. At the same time, Nixon and Kissinger looked for new ways to contain Soviet power not simply by the traditional threat of arms but through negotiations to ease tensions. This policy was named, from the French, **détente.**

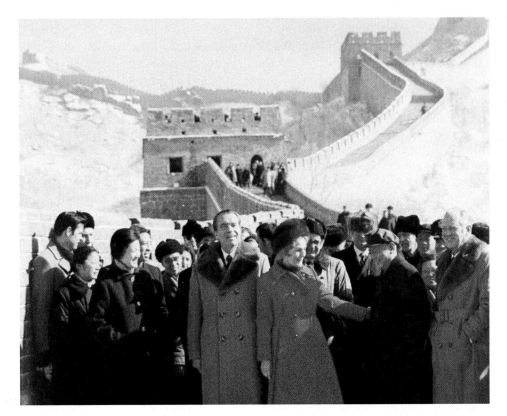

On seeing China's Great Wall, an ebullient Richard Nixon pronounced it a "great wall, built by a great people." Perhaps precisely because he had been so staunch an anti-Communist, Nixon appreciated the enormous departure his trip marked in Sino-American relations.

To pursue détente Kissinger and Nixon used "linkages," a system of making progress on one issue by connecting it with another. They recognized, for example, how much the cold war arms race burdened the Soviet economy. To ease that push, they would make concessions to the Soviets on nuclear arms. The Soviets in return would have to limit their arms buildup and, in a linked concession, pressure North Vietnam to negotiate an end to the war. To add pressure, Nixon and Kissinger developed a "China card." The United States would stop treating Mao Zedong as an archenemy and, instead, would open diplomatic relations with the Chinese. Fearful of a more powerful China, the Soviets would be more conciliatory toward the United States.

It took a shrewd diplomatist to sense an opportunity to shift traditional cold war policy. Conservative Republicans in particular had denounced the idea of ever recognizing Mao's government, even after 20 years. Now Richard Nixon, the man who had built a career fighting communism, sent Henry Kissinger to China on a secret mission (he was nursing a stomachache, his aides assured the press) to arrange a week-long trip to China for the president. During that visit in early 1972, Nixon pledged to normalize relations, a move the public enthusiastically welcomed. Only Nixon's impeccable anti-Communist credentials had allowed him to reverse the direction of America's China policy.

A new overture to the Soviet Union followed the China trip. Eager to acquire American grain and technology, Soviet premier Leonid Brezhnev invited Nixon to visit Moscow in May 1972. The two leaders struck a major wheat deal, but the most important benefit of the meeting was the signing of the first Strategic Arms Limitation Treaty (SALT I). In the agreement, both sides pledged not to develop a new system of antiballistic missiles, which would have accelerated the costly arms race. And they agreed to limit the number of intercontinental ballistic missiles each side would deploy. But it was not clear that the linkages achieved in Moscow and Beijing would help extricate the United States from Vietnam.

SALT I

In campaigning for the presidency in 1960 John F. Kennedy charged the Republicans with creating a missile gap. While the American space program limped along, the Soviet Union had launched *Sputnik*. Only a few months after Kennedy's inauguration, Russian cosmonaut Yuri Gagarin orbited the world in a five-ton spacecraft. The first American space flight on May 6, 1961, succeeded only in carrying Commander Alan Shepard into a suborbital flight of 300 miles. Kennedy feared that if it lost the space race, the United States might lose the cold war as well.

Thus Kennedy ordered his science advisers "to shift our efforts in space from low to high gear." He announced on national television that the United States would do something truly dramatic: land a man on the moon and bring him back alive "before the decade is out." No matter how great the cost, Kennedy believed the investment was sound. "We must go into space because whatever mankind must undertake, free men must fully share," he proclaimed.

There were skeptics, such as former President Eisenhower, who thought anyone was "nuts" to spend billions for a space spectacular that promised little in the way of scientific discoveries. To many members of Congress, however, the space program was a huge pork barrel, so they voted to fund Kennedy's "great new American enterprise." From then on the space program achieved a string of triumphs. In February 1962 Colonel John Glenn successfully circled the earth three times in "a fireball of a ride"; an unmanned satellite passed Venus later that year; and a Telstar communications satellite began relaying television broadcasts, launching an era of truly global mass communications.

One after another, the space spectaculars continued, much to the public's delight. In March 1965 American astronauts first maneuvered their capsule; in May Edward White took America's first space walk; the following year two vehicles met and docked for the first time. By Christmas eve 1968 the *Apollo 8* mission was circling the moon. It seemed a "vast, lonely and forbidding sight," one astronaut remarked to hundreds of millions in a live telecast.

On July 20, 1969, the lunar module of *Apollo 11* at last touched down on the earth's closest neighbor. Commander Neil Armstrong, moving awkwardly in his bulky space suit, worked his way down a ladder to the white, chalky surface. He was not alone. Besides Edwin Aldrin, who followed him,

The New Identity Politics

The liberal tradition had long embraced a belief in the common humanity shared by all Americans. The nation's ideals should be colorblind, liberals reasoned, because under the skin, all people—men and women, young and old, black, white, brown, yellow, and red—were the same. As Lyndon Johnson expressed the idea (updating Shakespeare's Shylock with a Texas twang), "They cry the same tears, they feel hungry the same, they bleed the same." Whatever differences existed came not from race or gender but from cultural circumstances and historical experiences. In that belief civil rights advocates and liberal feminists committed themselves to an integrated America. All people should have the same rights and opportunities.

Pluralism versus Assimilation

Identity politics, in contrast, substituted a model of **pluralism** for the unified one sought by integrationists. Traditionally, Latino civil rights groups such as LULAC and World War II veterans in the American GI Forum had sought assimilation into American society. Now minorities began to forge identities in opposition to the prevailing culture. By 1970 black nationalists had abandoned the politics of integration for the politics of black pride. To these activists the qualities that distinguished black Americans were what made them distinct—their music, clothing, hairstyles, and religion. In similar ways radical feminists, Latinos, Native Americans, and gays demanded that the nation respect and protect their essential differences. The United States should rejoice in being a plural and diverse nation.

To some degree the Supreme Court had already granted that point in both the *Brown* and *Hernandez* decisions of 1954 (see pages 861–862). In each case the Court declared that Latinos and African Americans had suffered not simply as individuals but as groups. To correct past injustices, identity politics called for positive steps—what the Johnson Administration called **affirmative action**—to repair the damage done by past injustices. In 1971, in the case of *Griggs v. Duke Power Company* the Supreme

Affirmative Action

Landing on the moon may have been one small step for a man, but NASA spent $25 billion on the project, over $2 billion for each of the 12 astronauts who took lunar walks.

and Michael Collins, orbiting in the command module, Armstrong brought along a quarter of the world's population, who monitored the moment live on television. "That's one small step for a man, one giant leap for mankind," he proclaimed.

Apollo 11 marked the climax of a phase of exploration, not a beginning. After *Apollo 17* and $25 billion in costs, Richard Nixon predicted "this may be the last time in this century men will walk on the moon." Space travel since then has belonged largely to the space shuttles and to unmanned missions around the solar system and space telescopes to penetrate distant galaxies.

Court asserted that employers could use affirmative action to hire more minorities and women. But no matter whether the practitioners of identity politics pursued advancement through the courts or on the street, in the marketplace or in corporate boardrooms, they affirmed a pluralistic America that celebrated cultural diversity over unity.

Latino Activism

Part of the increased visibility of minorities resulted from a new wave of immigration from Mexico and Puerto Rico after World War II. That wave was augmented by Cubans, after the 1959 revolution that brought Fidel Castro to power. Historical, cultural, ethnic, and geographic differences made it difficult to develop a common political agenda among Latinos. Still, some activists sought greater unity among Latino groups.

After World War II a weak island economy and the lure of prosperity on the mainland brought more than a million Puerto Ricans into New York City. As citizens of the United States, they could move freely to the mainland and back home again. That dual consciousness, however, discouraged many from establishing deep roots stateside. Equally important, the newcomers were startled to discover that, whatever their status at home, on the mainland they were subject to racial discrimination and most often segregated into urban slums. In 1964 approximately half of all recent immigrants lived below the poverty level, according to the Puerto Rican Forum. Unemployment was three times greater for Puerto Ricans than for whites and 50 percent higher than for blacks. Light-skinned inmigrants were able to escape those conditions by blending into the middle class as "Latin Americans." As a result, the Puerto Rican community lost some of the leadership necessary to push for civil and political rights in the United States.

Still, a shared island orientation preserved a strong group identity. By the 1960s the urban barrios had gained greater political consciousness, as groups such as Aspira

Puerto Ricans and Cubans

adopted the strategies of civil rights activists and as organizations such as the Black and Puerto Rican Caucus linked with other minority groups. The Cubans who arrived in the United States after 1959—some 350,000 over the course of the decade—forged fewer ties with other Latinos. Most settled around Miami. An unusually large number came from Cuba's professional, business, and government class and were racially white and politically conservative.

Mexican Americans, on the other hand, constituted the largest segment of Latinos. Until the 1940s most were farmers and farm laborers in Texas, New Mexico, and California. But during the 1950s, the process of mechanization had affected them just as it had southern blacks. By 1969 about 85 percent of Mexican Americans had settled in cities. With urbanization came a slow improvement of the range and quality of jobs they held. A body of skilled workers, middle-class professionals, and entrepreneurs emerged.

Cesar Chavez and the UFW

Yet Mexican agricultural workers continued to face low wages and harsh working conditions. Previous attempts to unionize them had failed partly because workers migrated from job to job and strikebreakers were easily imported. In 1963 a soft-spoken but determined farmworker, Cesar Chavez, recruited fellow organizers Gil Padilla and Dolores Huerta to make another attempt. Their efforts over the next several years led to the formation of the United Farm Workers (UFW) labor union.

Chavez, like Martin Luther King, proclaimed an ethic of nonviolence. Also like King, he was guided by a deep religious faith (Roman Catholicism in the case of Chavez and most Mexican American farmworkers). When the union's meager financial resources made it difficult to sustain a strike of Mexican and Filipino grape workers that began in the summer of 1966, Chavez rallied supporters for a 250-mile march on Sacramento. "Dr. King had been very successful" with such marches, he noted. Seeking additional leverage, the union looked to use consumers as an economic weapon by organizing a boycott of grapes in supermarkets across the nation. Combined with a 24-day hunger strike by Chavez—a technique borrowed from Gandhi—the boycott forced growers to negotiate contracts with the UFW beginning in 1970.

Chicano Activists

Chavez's movement was rooted in the traditional issues of labor organizing. But just as Martin Luther King had found his nonviolent approach challenged by more radical activists, a new generation of Mexican Americans forged a more aggressive brand of identity politics. Many began calling themselves Chicanos. Like blacks, Chicanos saw themselves as a people whose culture had been taken from them. Their heritage had been rejected, their labor exploited, and their opportunity for advancement denied. Of Chavez's generation, Reies Lopez Tijerina attracted wide attention as a charismatic leader. His movement in northern New Mexico ("La Alianza") organized armed bands to occupy federal lands that Hispanos in the region had once used for grazing livestock. In Denver, Rodolfo "Corky" Gonzales laid out a blueprint for a separatist Chicano society, with public housing set aside for Chicanos and the development of economically independent barrios in which a new cultural pride could flourish. "We are a Bronze People with a Bronze Culture," declared Gonzales. "We are a Nation. We are a union of free pueblos. We are Aztlán."

Most Mexican American migrant workers were devout Catholics. This farmworker's altar combines both religious symbols (the Crucifixion) and the UFW's red-and-black Aztec eagle (surrounded by the arms of workers of different races, showing solidarity) into designs signifying the strike and national grape boycott.

Recruits to the new activism came from both college and high school students. Like other members of the baby boom generation, Mexican Americans attended college in increasing numbers. In addition, Lyndon Johnson's Educational Opportunity Programs, part of his war on poverty, brought thousands more Latinos onto college campuses, especially in California. As for high schools, in Los Angeles in 1968 thousands of Chicano high school students walked out to protest substandard educational conditions. Two years later the new ethnic militancy led to the formation of La Raza Unida (The Race United). This third-party movement sought to gain power in communities in which Chicanos were a majority and to extract concessions from the Democrats and Republicans. The more militant "Brown Berets" adopted the paramilitary tactics and radical rhetoric of the Black Panthers.

La Raza Unida

The Choices of American Indians

Like African Americans and Latinos, Indians began to protest, yet the unique situation of Native Americans (as many had begun to call themselves) set them apart from other minorities. A largely hostile white culture had in past centuries sought either to exterminate or to assimilate American Indians. Ironically, the growing strength of the civil rights movement created another threat to Indian tribal identities. Liberals came to see the reservations not as oases of Indian culture but as rural ghettos. During the 1950s liberals joined conservatives (eager to repeal the New Deal) and western state politicians (eyeing tribal resources) in adopting a policy of "termination." The Bureau of Indian Affairs would reduce federal services, gradually sell off tribal lands, and push Indians into the "mainstream" of American life.

Termination

Although most full-blooded Indians objected to the policy, some mixed bloods and Indians already assimilated into white society supported the move. The resulting relocation of approximately 35,000 Indians accelerated a shift from rural areas to cities. The urban Indian population, which had been barely 30,000 in 1940, reached more than 300,000 by the 1970s.

The social activism of the 1960s inspired Indian leaders to shape a new political agenda. In 1968 urban activists in Minneapolis created AIM, the American Indian Movement. A year later like-minded Indians living around San Francisco Bay formed Indians of All Tribes. Because the Bureau of Indian Affairs refused to address the

American Indian Movement

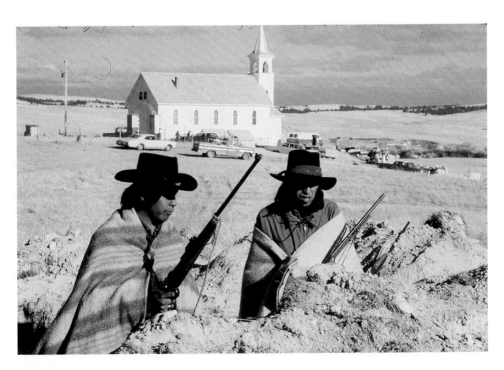

In 1890 the U.S. cavalry killed 146 Indians at Wounded Knee, South Dakota. In 1973 members of the American Indian Movement (pictured at left) seized the hamlet of Wounded Knee, making it once again a symbol of conflict.

problems of urban Indians, more militant members of AIM dramatized their dissatisfaction by seizing the abandoned federal prison on Alcatraz Island in San Francisco Bay. The Alcatraz protest was not "a movement to liberate the island, but to liberate ourselves," explained one member. The action sparked a national Pan-Indian rights movement. Then, in 1973, AIM organizers Russell Means and Dennis Banks led a dramatic takeover of a trading post at Wounded Knee, on a Sioux reservation in South Dakota. Ever since white cavalry had gunned down over a hundred Sioux in 1890 (see page 516), Wounded Knee had symbolized for Indians the betrayal of white promises and the bankruptcy of reservation policy. Even more, Wounded Knee now demonstrated the problems that Indian activists faced. When federal officers surrounded the trading post, militants discovered that other Indians did not support their tactics, and they were forced to leave. A Pan-Indian movement was difficult to achieve when so many tribes were determined to go their own ways as distinct, self-regulating communities. During the 1970s more than 100 different organizations were formed to unite various tribes pursuing political and legal agendas at the local, state, and federal levels.

Asian Americans

In removing quotas that had discriminated against immigration from non-European nations (page 873), the 1965 Immigration Act removed one of the major affronts to Asian Americans. Further, it spurred a rapid increase in immigration from Asia to the United States. Asians, who in 1960 constituted just 1 percent of the American population (about a million people), were by 1985 2 percent (about five million). This new wave included many middle-class professionals, a lower percentage of Japanese, and far more newcomers from Southeast and South Asia. Civil rights reforms had already swept away legal barriers to full citizenship.

Many Americans treated these new immigrants as "model minorities." They brought skills in high demand, worked hard, were often Christians, and seldom protested. The 1970 census showed Japanese and Chinese Americans with incomes substantially above the median for white Americans. Such statistics hid significant fault lines within communities. Although many professionals assimilated into the American mainstream, agricultural laborers and sweatshop workers remained trapped in poverty. And no matter how much Anglos praised their industry, the distinguishing appearance of Asian Americans still amounted to what one sociologist defined as a "racial uniform." They were nonwhites in a white society.

Few Americans were aware of Asian involvement in identity politics. That was in part because the large majority of Asian Americans lived in just three states—Hawaii, California, and New York. Further, Asian Americans were less likely to join in the era's most vocal protests. As the Asian population increased, so too would the demands of Asian Americans for recognition of their place in a multicultural society.

Gay Rights

In 1972, Black Panther leader Huey Newton observed that homosexuals "might be the most oppressed people" in American society. Certainly Newton was qualified to recognize oppression when he saw it. But by then a growing number of homosexuals had publicly declared their sexual identity. Growing political activism placed them among minorities demanding equal rights.

Even during the "conformist" 1950s, gay men founded the Mattachine Society (1951) to fight antihomosexual attacks and to press for a wider public acceptance of their lifestyle. Lesbians formed a similar organization, the Daughters of Bilitis, in 1955. Beginning in the mid-1960s, more radical gay and lesbian groups began organizing to raise individual consciousness and to establish a gay culture in which they felt free. One group called for "acceptance as full equals . . . basic rights and equality as citizens; our human dignity; . . . [our] right to love whom we wish."

The movement's defining moment came on Friday June 27, 1969, when New York City police raided the Stonewall Inn, a Greenwich Village bar. Such raids were common enough: gay bars were regularly harassed by the police in an attempt to control urban "vice." This time the patrons fought back, first with taunts and jeers, then with paving stones and parking meters. Increasingly, gay activists called on homosexuals to "come out of the closet" and publicly affirm their sexuality. In 1974 gays achieved a major symbolic victory when the American Psychiatric Association removed homosexuality from its list of mental disorders.

Stonewall Incident

Feminism

The movement for women's rights and equality in the United States was not, of course, a creation of the 1960s. It began well before the Civil War, and the sustained political efforts of its supporters had won women the vote in 1920. But the women's movement of the 1960s and 1970s began to push for equality in broader, deeper ways.

Writer Betty Friedan was one of the first women to voice dissatisfaction with the cultural attitudes prevalent at midcentury. Even though more women were entering the job market, the media routinely glorified housewives and home-makers while discouraging those women who aspired to independent careers. In *The Feminine Mystique* (1963) Friedan protested that "our culture does not permit women to accept or gratify their basic need to grow and fulfill their potentialities as human beings."

The Feminine Mystique

Ms. magazine, edited by feminist Gloria Steinem, gave the women's movement a means to reach a broader audience. The cover of the first issue, published in 1972, uses the image of a many-armed Hindu goddess to satirize the multiple roles of the modern housewife.

The Feminine Mystique gave birth to a new women's rights movement. The Commission on the Status of Women appointed by President Kennedy proposed the 1963 Equal Pay Act and helped add gender to the forms of discrimination outlawed by the 1964 Civil Rights Act. Women also assumed an important role in both the civil rights and antiwar movements. They accounted for half the students who went south for the Freedom Summers in 1964 and 1965. Living with violence and assuming heavy responsibilities, these women discovered new freedom and self-confidence.

Movement women also realized that they were themselves victims of systematic discrimination. Male reformers often limited them to behind-the-scenes services such as cooking, laundry, and fulfilling sexual needs. Casey Hayden, a veteran of SDS and SNCC, confronted the male leadership. The "assumptions of male superiority are as widespread . . . and every bit as crippling to the woman as the assumptions of white superiority are to the Negro," she wrote. By 1966 activist women were less willing to see their grievances eclipsed by other political constituencies.

National Organization
for Women

Friedan joined a group of 24 women and 2 men who formed the National Organization for Women (NOW). The new feminists sought to force the Johnson administration to enforce the gender equality provisions of the Civil Rights Act of 1964. When feminists argued that "sexism" was not qualitatively different from racism, Johnson accepted the argument and in 1967 included women as well as African Americans, Hispanics, and other minorities as groups covered by federal affirmative action programs.

Social Trends Supporting
Feminism

Broader social trends established a receptive climate for feminism. After 1957 the birthrate began a rapid decline; improved methods of contraception, such as the birth control pill, permitted more sexual freedom and smaller family size. By 1970 more than 40 percent of all women, an unprecedented number, were employed outside the home. Education also spurred the shift from home to the job market and increased consciousness of women's issues. Higher educational levels allowed women to enter an economy oriented increasingly to white-collar service industries rather than blue-collar manufacturing.

By 1970 feminists had captured the media's attention. Fifty thousand women participated in NOW's Strike for Equality Parade down New York's Fifth Avenue. Television cameras zeroed in on signs with such slogans as "Don't Cook Dinner—Starve a Rat Today." Some newscasters reported that marchers had burned their bras to protest sexual stereotyping. "Bra burners" became the media's condescending phrase used to deny credibility to militant feminists such as Kate Millett, whose *Sexual Politics* (1970) condemned a male-dominated "patriarchal" society.

Equal Rights and Abortion

With its influence growing, the feminist movement sought to translate women's grievances into a political agenda. NOW members could agree in 1967 to a "Bill of Rights" that called for maternity leave for working mothers, federally supported daycare facilities, child care tax deductions, and equal education and job training. But they divided on two other issues: the passage of an Equal Rights Amendment to the Constitution and a repeal of all state antiabortion laws.

At first, support seemed strong for an Equal Rights Amendment that would forbid all discrimination on the basis of gender. In 1972 both the House and the Senate passed the Equal Rights Amendment (ERA) virtually without opposition. Within a year 28 of the necessary 38 states had approved the ERA.

Roe v. Wade

Many participants in the women's movement also applauded the Supreme Court's decision, in *Roe v. Wade* (1973), to strike down 46 state laws restricting a woman's access to abortion. In his opinion for the majority, Justice Harry Blackmun observed that a woman in the nineteenth century had "enjoyed a substantially broader right to terminate a pregnancy than she does in most states today." As legal abortion in the first three months of pregnancy became more readily available, the rate of maternal deaths from illegal operations, especially among minorities, declined.

But the early success of the ERA and the feminist triumph in *Roe v. Wade* masked underlying divisions among women's groups. *Roe v. Wade* triggered a sharp backlash from many Catholics, Protestant Fundamentalists, and socially conservative women. Their opposition inspired a crusade for a "right to life" amendment to the Constitution. A similar conservative reaction breathed new life into the "STOP ERA" crusade of Phyllis Schlafly, an Illinois political organizer. Although Schlafly was a professional working woman herself, she believed that women should embrace their traditional role as homemakers subordinate to their husbands. "Every change [that the ERA] requires will deprive women of a right, benefit, or exemption that they now enjoy," she argued. In the end the campaign for ERA failed, also because many women (and a considerable number of men) wanted to use the political system, rather than a constitutional amendment, to correct the most glaring inequalities between the sexes.

Value Politics: The Consumer and Environmental Movements

Among those seeking to reform America were leaders of movements defined by their ideas and values rather than by personal identity. Where many participants in identity politics viewed themselves as outsiders, consumer advocates and environmentalists generally came from the social mainstream. Still, they shared with the counterculture a worry that excessive materialism wasted resources and generated pollution, while too many corporations exploited the public through misleading advertising and shoddy, even dangerous, products.

Technology and Unbridled Growth

As early as 1962, marine biologist Rachel Carson had warned in *Silent Spring* against the wanton use of chemical pesticides, especially DDT. Though chemical companies sought to discredit her work as shrill, hysterical, and unreliable, a presidential commission vindicated her conclusions. Pesticides were only one aspect of what environmentalists considered misguided technology. A report issued in 1965 indicated that just one river near an urban area in the United States (the St. Croix near St. Paul, Minnesota) was not significantly polluted. Certainly, anyone with a sense of irony could not help marveling that the industrially fouled Cuyahoga River running through Cleveland, Ohio, burst into flames in 1969. Smog, radioactive fallout, lethal pesticides, and polluted rivers were the by-products of a society wedded to technology and unbridled economic growth.

Rachel Carson and the Environment

To consumer advocates, growing fatality rates on American highways were a symptom of another kind of corporate failure. Besides contributing to smog and other forms of pollution, automobiles were inherently dangerous to their occupants. That was a conclusion announced by an intense young consumer reformer, Ralph Nader, in his 1965 exposé *Unsafe at Any Speed: The Designed-In Dangers of the American Automobile*. Nader's particular target was the rear-engine Chevrolet Corvair introduced by General Motors to compete with foreign imports. GM's internal studies confirmed crash data that the Corvair tended to flip over during turns or skidded uncontrollably. Though the company fixed the problem, it also hired private investigators to try to discredit Nader.

Convinced that pesticides such as DDT posed no threat to humans, public health and agriculture officials sprayed people and land with a reckless abandon that compelled Rachel Carson to begin efforts to curb pesticide use.

The Fire That Wasn't There—Or Was It?

Judging a Story Whose Time Had (Finally) Come

"Some River! Chocolate-brown, oily, bubbling with subsurface gases, it oozes rather than flows." So *Time* magazine described the Cuyahoga River, running through Cleveland, Ohio, after the river itself caught fire during the summer of 1969. *Time's* story featured the photograph (below) of a fire whose billowing smoke nearly blotted out the sky. What better way to dramatize the problem of environmental pollution? Over the years thousands of books and articles have referred to the incident—including this textbook.

Then Mark Lytle, one of the authors of this text, began writing a book about Rachel Carson, investigated the fire, and discovered a more complicated history. By the time journalists reached the scene in 1969, the fire department had already put out the blaze. The *Cleveland Plain Dealer* covered the story briefly, only in its back pages. There was no photograph to be had. Indeed, before the fire ever broke out, Cleveland had already established a commission to begin cleaning up the river and set aside $100 million to do the job.

Was the environmental concern over the incident overblown? The photograph a hoax? Not exactly. *Time,* stuck without a picture, scrambled and found a photo from a different fire on the river, in 1952. In fact, the Cuyahoga was no stranger to hot times. Fires had broken out on its oily waters in 1868, 1883, 1887, 1912, 1922, 1936, 1941, 1948 and—most devastating of all—in 1952. Nor was Cleveland the only city with a burning river. Pollutants fueled river fires in Baltimore, Buffalo, and Detroit. Thus, in some ways, the story was even worse than when first painted. It simply had received less national attention over the years. Growing environmental awareness, not the magnitude of this particular event, made the Cuyahoga fire of 1969 a symbol of industrial abuses.

The company picked the wrong target. Nader was the son of immigrant Lebanese parents who supported their son's success at Princeton and Harvard Law School. He lived simply and had no vices. And when he discovered GM's campaign against him, he successfully sued the company. GM's embarrassed president publicly apologized, but by then Nader had become a counterculture hero and *Unsafe at Any Speed* a bestseller. In 1966, Congress passed the National Traffic and Motor Vehicle Safety Act and the Highway Safety Act. For the first time the government required seatbelts and set safety standards for cars, tires, and roads.

With the money from his lawsuit, Nader founded a consumer advocacy organization in 1969, the Center for the Study of Responsive Law. His staff of low-paid but eager lawyers, student interns, and volunteers investigated a wide range of consumer and environmental issues. "Nader's Raiders" as his staff was called, shared their leader's view that it was time for corporations "to stop stealing, stop deceiving, stop corrupting politicians with money, stop monopolizing, stop poisoning the earth, air and water, stop selling dangerous products, stop exposing workers to cruel hazards." In the tradition of progressive reform Nader looked to an active, interventionist government and informed citizen-consumers to regulate corporate behavior.

Nader's Raiders

Many environmentalists, too, had links to the progressive era and the idea that government action could police corporate irresponsibility, limit the waste of nonrenewable natural resources, and preserve scenic and natural wonders for the benefit of future generations. What made modern environmentalism distinct from the consumer movement and its own progressive roots was a growing focus on the field of ecology. Since the early twentieth century, this biological science had demonstrated how closely life processes throughout nature depended on one another. All living things were interconnected, including human beings. In condemning the abuse of pesticides, Rachel Carson had called for a **biocentric** approach to nature rather than an anthropocentric, or human-centered one.

Focus on Ecology

Barry Commoner, a politically active biologist, argued in his book *The Closing Circle* (1971) that modern society courted disaster by trying to "improve on nature." American farmers, for example, greatly increased their crop yields by switching from animal manures to artificial fertilizers. But the change consumed large quantities of energy, raised costs, often left soils sterile, and polluted nearby water. By the 1970s chemical discharges had virtually killed Lake Erie. Technology might prove profitable in the short run, Commoner argued, but in the long run modern methods were bankrupting the environment.

Barry Commoner

Ralph Nader's dogged, ascetic style forced corporations like General Motors to more seriously examine public safety issues. Nader's organization, Public Citizen, expanded its efforts on behalf of consumers to a wide range of issues.

Political Action

While he was no friend of liberal reform, President Nixon sensed that these value movements had broad popular appeal. His administration supported the passage of the National Environmental Policy Act of 1969, which required environmental impact statements for all major public projects and charged the government to uphold the public interest. In an effort to unify the many government agencies dealing with environmental policy, Nixon in 1970 established the Environmental Protection Agency (EPA). The agency's first major regulatory action recognized Rachel Carson's campaign by banning most domestic uses of DDT, despite opposition from chemical companies and agricultural interests. The president also signed a bill establishing an Occupational

Environmental Protection Agency

Safety and Health Agency (OSHA) to enforce health and safety standards in the workplace, and Clean Water and Clean Air Acts.

On April 22, 1970, millions of Americans demonstrated their commitment to a healthy environment as they celebrated the first Earth Day. For a few hours, pedestrians strolled city streets closed to motor vehicles, school children planted trees and picked up litter, college students demonstrated, and Congress adjourned. The enthusiasm reflected the movement's dual appeal: it was both practical in seeking to improve the quality of air, water, and earth and spiritual in celebrating the unity of living things. But Senator Gaylord Nelson of Wisconsin, who helped bring Earth Day about, appreciated the occasion's more radical implications. "The Establishment sees this as a great big antilitter campaign. Wait until they find out what it really means . . . to clean up our earth."

Earth Day (margin note)

The Legacy of Identity and Value Politics

Earth Day did not signal a consensus on an environmental ethic. Nor could Ralph Nader persuade Congress that the country needed a new agency to represent the interests of consumers. President Nixon, for one, was not willing to impose regulations that stifled growth, especially when facing a troubled economy. Radical activists "aren't really one damn bit interested in safety or clean air," he commented to one industry group. "What they are interested in is destroying the system." If he faced "a flat choice between jobs and smoke," nature would be the loser.

Nixon's political instincts were shrewd. Both the 1968 and 1972 presidential elections revealed a shift in political power toward the southern and western rims of the United States where traditional values flourished and where whites, in the wake of the civil rights revolution, were deserting the Democrats in droves. These were the voters Nixon courted, in what he sometimes referred to as his "southern strategy" to replace the old New Deal coalition with a new Republican majority. To many of the president's supporters it seemed as if the consensus of the 1950s was being ripped apart. By the early 1970s his silent majority had wearied of the demands of angry minorities and protestors. Like the president, they worried more about job security than clean air and water. As one bumper sticker declared, "Out of work? Hungry? Eat an environmentalist."

Nixon's "Southern Strategy" (margin note)

The president sought to channel a similar backlash against identity politics. Conservatives opposed many of the remedies proposed by the movement, such as the Equal Rights Amendment, integration of private clubs, and use of quotas for hiring and college admissions. They argued that merit, not race or gender, should determine an individual's opportunities. Furthermore, white males and ethnic groups such as Italian and Polish Americans resented government programs for minorities that worked to their disadvantage. Quotas to hire black police, for example, took jobs away from qualified whites. Ethnic identity organizations such as the Italian American Civil Rights League spoke out against affirmative action for minorities.

Even critics could not deny that political and social activists had brought a sense of empowerment to people who had long seen themselves as "other." The reforms of the 1960s opened doors to jobs, careers, and avenues of success previously closed to all but white males. But a pluralistic approach to equality also tended to fragment rather than unify the nation. It divided liberals from activists further to the left and signaled that reform had reached its high-water mark, even as white men continued to earn more than women or minorities. The road to equality—whether in the workplace, schools, or even the bedroom—remained a fault line along which the nation would divide.

Pragmatic Conservatism

In August 1969, 4,000 angry white union workers marched on city hall in Pittsburgh, Pennsylvania. Suddenly, a confrontation with police turned violent, leaving 50 protestors injured and 200 under arrest. A month later the scene repeated itself in Chicago, where hundreds of construction workers "slugged it out with 400

Philadelphia Plan

policemen," according to the *Chicago Tribune*. In both cases the issue was the "Philadelphia Plan" for affirmative action. Under it, the Nixon administration adopted the rule set forth in 1967 by the Johnson administration that government funding would be provided only if contractors' bids had "the result of producing minority group representations in all trades and in all phases of the construction project." The building trades unions wanted to know why they had been singled out when so many other industries did not meet those goals. Race played a role as well. "Why should these guys be given special consideration, just because they happen to be black?" one angry worker asked.

By 1969 affirmative action had become a political hot potato and Richard Nixon knew it. Over the course of his first term the president charted a pragmatic course, preserving and even expanding popular entitlements such as social security, seeking a middle ground on civil rights and affirmative action, while following the liberal tides in areas such as environmental protection.

The New Federalism

The president recognized the rightward flow of the political winds. To attack the image of a federal government grown too big and too intrusive, Nixon adopted what he called the New Federalism. "After a third of a century of power flowing from the people to Washington," he explained, "it is time now for a New Federalism in which power, funds, and responsibility all flow from Washington to the people." Under the old system Washington allocated money to states and localities to fund specific projects—a highway, a sewer system, or a welfare program. Nixon proposed giving block grants that would allow states and localities to determine both the problems and the best way to fix them.

The economy posed a problem of another kind. By 1970 the nation had entered its first recession in a decade. Despite economists' expectations that unemployment would rise and prices and demand would fall, the opposite seemed to occur. Unemployment did rise, but so did wages and prices. Americans were getting the worst of two worlds: a stagnant economy combined with rising prices—"stagflation," economists termed it. Stagflation Hostile Democrats preferred "Nixonomics," but in truth, the problems were not of Nixon's making. Lyndon Johnson had brought on inflation by refusing to raise taxes to pay for the war in Vietnam and his Great Society programs. Most contracts for government and union workers had automatic cost-of-living adjustments so that wages kept pace with inflation even as businesses reduced employment.

Mindful that his own silent majority were the people most pinched by the slower economy, Nixon decided that unemployment posed a greater threat than inflation. Stunning conservatives, he adopted a deficit budget designed to stimulate job growth and in August 1971 proclaimed a freeze in wages and prices for 90 days to try to cool the inflationary cycle. For a Republican to institute wage and price controls was near heresy—almost as startling as Nixon's overtures to China in the diplomatic arena. Union leaders applauded, however, and the president maintained wage and price controls for more than a year. His strategy to form a new majority was taking shape.

Social Policies and the Courts

Affirmative action, school prayer, contraception, criminal rights, obscenity, and school busing were all issues on which Supreme Court decisions offended the silent majority. By and large the liberal Court placed rights and liberties ahead of traditional values and law enforcement. The justices recognized, for example, that 15 years after its *Brown v. Board of Education* decision, most school districts remained segregated. Their determination to achieve desegregation led them to support busing, a policy that many School Busing whites opposed. Black parents, though concerned that white hostility might threaten their children, generally supported busing as a means to a better education. In 1969, when the state of Mississippi asked the Court to delay a desegregation plan, the justices refused. They ruled, in *United States v. Jefferson County Board of Education,* that states had an obligation to "terminate dual systems at once and operate now and hereafter only unitary schools." Two years later, in *Swann v. Charlotte-Mecklenburg Board of Education* (1971), the Court further ruled that busing, balancing ratios, and redrawing school district lines were all constitutional means of achieving integration.

The Nixon Court

Under both Presidents Kennedy and Johnson, the Justice Department normally supported affirmative action and desegregation. Nixon reversed those priorities. His administration backed Mississippi's request for a delay and filed a brief against busing. As the president told his staff, "What we need now is not just speaking out against busing, we need action to stop it." Nixon thus looked to create a court more in line with his conservative agenda. The retirement in 1969 of Earl Warren, the liberal chief justice, allowed the president to appoint Warren Burger, a jurist who highly valued court precedents and traditions but had no ambition to break new ground. A second vacancy allowed Nixon to push his southern strategy. He nominated two southern conservatives, both of whom the Senate rejected. Besides lacking significant accomplishments or relevant qualifications, the two had each shown themselves hostile to civil rights and organized labor. Nixon finally chose the moderate Harry Blackmun from Minnesota.

In 1971 the president finally realized his hope to reshape the Court when he appointed Lewis Powell, a highly regarded Virginia lawyer, and William Rehnquist, a staunch conservative from Arizona. Under Chief Justice Burger the Court would no longer lead the fight for minority rights, but neither would it reverse the achievements of the Warren Court.

A Victory Too Far?

McGovern and the Democrat's Liberal Faction

As the election of 1972 approached, the president seemed on course to create his new Republican majority, especially after the Democrats nominated a strongly antiwar candidate, Senator George McGovern of South Dakota. Nixon's victory over Hubert Humphrey in 1968 led frustrated Democrats (including McGovern) to rewrite the party's nominating rules to ensure that minorities, women, and young people received proportional representation in the delegations to the national convention. No longer would the city machines, labor leaders, and southern courthouse politicos choose the presidential nominee. McGovern's ardent opposition to the war and his support for feminism won him the support of the party liberals. The party platform embraced all the issues the silent majority resented—immediate withdrawal from Vietnam, an end to the draft, amnesty for war protestors, and a minimum guaranteed income for the poor. McGovern even supported the legalization of marijuana and abortion rights for women. As one observer remarked, the Democrats "demonstrated little concern for middle class anxiety over busing, law and order, and affirmative action."

By November of 1972 one question remained: how big would Richard Nixon's majority be? On election day, only Massachusetts and the heavily black District of Columbia voted Democratic. Nixon received an overwhelming 61 percent of the popular vote.

Given that landslide, the passing of a liberal era of reform might have seemed inevitable. Indeed, the newly reelected president called for a revolution that would "give expression to the more conservative values of the New Majority." In his inaugural speech Nixon reminded his supporters, "America was not built on government, but by people; not by welfare, but by work."

But the liberal era did not end cleanly or logically, for Nixon did not always act logically or pursue his own best political interests. The president's electoral triumph did little to quiet his sense of grievance toward those he considered his enemies. Among them were antiwar protestors, hippies, and black nationalists as well as figures in the mainstream media, intellectuals, and Jews. Nixon aimed to settle some scores. "We haven't used the Bureau [FBI] and we haven't used the Justice Department, but things are going to change now . . . and they're going to get it, right?" he remarked to his chief of staff H. R. Haldeman after his reelection.

At the direction of the president, members of Nixon's staff began to compile an "enemies list" that included television news commentators, celebrity antiwar activists, and other prominent citizens. Some on the list became the targets of special tax audits by the Internal Revenue Service. The president, mistrustful of aging FBI director J. Edgar Hoover, had earlier authorized his assistant John Ehrlichman to form a White House team called "the plumbers," to find and plug leaks of sensitive information. One of their first targets was Daniel Ellsberg, a disillusioned official who in 1971 leaked to the press a secret report on the escalation of the war in Vietnam. Dubbed the *Pentagon Papers,* the report covered only the Johnson years, but Nixon feared that the leak would make the White House appear weak. He insisted on prosecuting Ellsberg and, in hopes of gaining evidence against him, ordered the Plumbers to burglarize the office of Ellsberg's psychiatrist.

The Plumbers and the *Pentagon Papers*

Nixon also took his battle to Congress. When a bill passed that he opposed, he simply refused to spend the appropriated money. Some members of Congress claimed that this practice, called impoundment, violated the president's constitutional responsibility to uphold the law. By 1973 the president had impounded some $15 billion out of more than 100 federal programs. Eventually, the Supreme Court ruled that impoundment was unconstitutional, but Nixon's political fall would come through a clash with Congress and the Court—as well as the press.

The Watergate Break-In

One of the names on Nixon's enemies list was Lawrence O'Brien, chairman of the Democratic National Committee. In June 1972 five burglars entered Democratic headquarters in the Watergate Hotel complex, only to be caught by Washington police. These were clearly not ordinary thieves. They carried walkie-talkies, bugging devices, and over $2,000 in crisp new 100-dollar bills. One of the men had previously worked for the CIA; another carried an address book that included an entry for E. Howard Hunt at the "W. House."

Nixon's press secretary dismissed the break-in as a "third rate burglary attempt" and warned that "certain elements may try to stretch this beyond what it is." In August the president himself announced that White House counsel John Dean's own thorough investigation had concluded that "no one on the White House staff . . . was involved in this bizarre incident. What really hurts in matters of this sort is not the fact that they occur. What really hurts is if you try to cover up."

Matters were not so easily settled, however. *Washington Post* reporters Bob Woodward and Carl Bernstein traced some of the burglars' money back to the president's reelection campaign, which had a secret "slush fund" to pay for projects to harass the Democrats. The dirty tricks that were paid for included forged letters, false news stories, paid demonstrators, and espionage. When the burglars themselves pleaded guilty in January 1973, along with two White House aides, the judge in the case threatened the defendants with long sentences if they refused to reveal who had paid them. "These 100-dollar bills were floating around like coupons," he complained.

Woodward and Bernstein

One burglar finally confessed that the group had been bribed to plead guilty and perjure themselves to protect administration officials. The White House then announced that all previous statements on Watergate were "inoperative." By April Nixon staff members had begun to "lawyer up." Soon after, President Nixon accepted the resignation of his two closest aides, John Ehrlichman and H. R. Haldeman. He also fired White House counsel John Dean, who had agreed to cooperate with prosecutors. In hearings conducted by Senator Sam Ervin of North Carolina, Dean explained in meticulous detail that the president had personally taken part in a cover-up designed to disguise White House links to the Watergate break-in. Still, it remained Dean's word against the president's—until a Senate investigator discovered that Nixon had been secretly taping conversations in the Oval Office. The tapes could reveal just who was telling the truth.

Ervin Hearings

Authority to subpoena the tapes rested with Archibald Cox, a Harvard law professor, appointed as a special prosecutor to investigate Watergate. When Cox asked for the

Under the leadership of North Carolina senator Sam Ervin (left), the Senate Committee investigating the Watergate scandal attracted a large television audience. John Dean (seated), the former White House legal counsel, provided the most damning testimony linking President Nixon to the cover-up. But only when the existence of secretly recorded White House tapes became known was his account corroborated.

tapes, the president refused, citing executive privilege and matters of national security. As the battle over the tapes raged, the public was astonished to discover that Vice President Spiro Agnew had been soliciting bribes both as governor of Maryland and as vice president. To avoid jail, he agreed to resign his office and plead no contest to a single charge of income tax evasion. Under the provisions of the Twenty-fifth Amendment, Nixon appointed Representative Gerald R. Ford of Michigan to replace Agnew.

Vice President Agnew Resigns

The Resignation of a President

Impeachment seemed ever more possible, as Cox and Nixon deadlocked over the tapes. Nixon offered written transcripts instead of the tapes, but Cox had no reason to trust the president's motives and rejected the offer. With that, on Saturday October 20, Nixon ordered his special prosecutor fired. The public response to what was soon called the "Saturday Night Massacre" included 150,000 angry telegrams sent to Washington. By the following Tuesday 84 House members had filed 16 different bills of impeachment.

White House Tapes

Cox's successor, Leon Jaworski, continued to pursue the recorded evidence. In April 1974 the White House turned over 1,200 pages of tape transcripts. Even the edited versions damaged the president's case. They revealed Nixon in private as profane, cynical, and ruthless. At one point he outlined for John Dean one method of how to "take care of those jackasses in jail." When Dean estimated their silence might cost a million dollars, Nixon replied, "We could get that . . . You could get a million dollars. And you could get it in cash." When Dean raised the issue of perjury, Nixon advised, "You can say 'I don't remember.' You can say 'I don't recall.'"

Even those revelations did not produce the "smoking gun" demanded by the president's defenders. Special Prosecutor Jaworski thus petitioned the Supreme Court for additional tapes. In *United States v. Nixon* the Court ruled unanimously that the president had to turn them over. The new evidence revealed that on June 23, 1972, only days after the break-in, Nixon knew that the burglars were tied to the White House and knew that his own attorney general, John Mitchell, had been involved in the plans.

The House of Representatives adopted three articles of impeachment charging the president with obstruction of justice, using federal agencies to harass private citizens, and hindering the Senate committee's efforts to investigate the cover-up. Not willing to be the first president convicted in a Senate impeachment trial, Richard Nixon resigned his office on August 8, 1974. The following day Gerald Ford was sworn in as president. "The Constitution works," Ford assured the nation. "Our long national nightmare is over."

Had the system worked? In one sense, yes. For the first time a president had been forced to leave office for breaking the law. Four cabinet officers, including Attorney General Mitchell, the highest law officer in the nation, were convicted of crimes, and 25 Nixon aides eventually served prison terms. Yet the larger issue involved what one historian called an "imperial presidency," in which power shifted increasingly into the Oval Office and into executive agencies, officials often acted illegally and with little congressional oversight. Nixon's misdeeds also involved the misuse of campaign funds, impoundment, and other actions that weakened the checks and balances among the branches of government. Future presidents would extend the reach of the office in similar ways, citing the demands of national security. The system works, as the Founders understood, only when informed citizens and dedicated officials apply the power of government to the pursuit of the general good.

The Road's End for Vietnam and Liberalism

For those Americans with a growing mistrust of government, Watergate confirmed their worst suspicions. Ironically, the attempt by Republican Richard Nixon to enlarge the powers of the presidency had brought this result. Yet the cynicism of Watergate hurt the liberal vision of an active government as much as Nixon's dreams of unfettered power. John Kennedy's early belief that he and his "whiz kid" cabinet could counter Soviet guerilla wars seemed hopelessly optimistic at a time when the United States was in full retreat from Vietnam. Lyndon Johnson's confident war on poverty had given way to pessimistic reports of urban blight and the twin scourges of inflation and recession.

Gerald Ford inherited an office almost crippled by the stench of scandal. As an unelected president, he had no popular mandate. His colleagues in the House from both parties liked and respected him, but they saw little that was presidential in his manner. Perhaps appropriately, Ford's goals were modest. He wished mainly to continue Nixon's policy of cautious détente with the Soviet Union and to preside over a domestic program built on budgetary restraint. "If I am remembered, it will be for healing the land," he wrote in his memoirs.

A Post-Imperial President

Healing did not come easily to a land scarred by the upheavals of the 1960s. The unpretentious Ford made himself readily available to the media. But only one month into office and without any warning, he granted Richard Nixon a full pardon for any crimes he might have committed. Ford hoped to put Watergate behind the nation rather than look backward in recrimination. But the pardon succeeded only in deepening the nation's cynicism. It meant that Nixon would never face prosecution nor assume responsibility for his crimes. Worse, the president showed no similar charity for Vietnam War draft resisters. He offered them conditional **amnesty** only after a review by a government panel.

For its part, a democratically controlled Congress was determined to rein in the imperial presidency. The War Powers Act of 1973 required that henceforth, the president must consult Congress whenever possible before committing troops to the

War Powers Act

battlefield, report to Congress within two days of taking action, and withdraw troops after 60 days unless Congress voted to retain them.

Reports of widespread abuses by the nation's intelligence services strengthened congressional resolve to control the executive branch. Hearings revealed that the CIA had routinely violated its charter forbidding it to spy on Americans at home. Abroad, the agency had attempted to assassinate foreign leaders in Cuba, the Congo, South Vietnam, and the Dominican Republic. The FBI had also used illegal means to infiltrate and disrupt domestic dissidents. J. Edgar Hoover had authorized an operation to drive Martin Luther King to suicide. Determined to eliminate abuses of executive authority, the Senate established committees to oversee intelligence operations.

The Search for Stability

Influence of Kissinger

Hemmed in by a newly assertive Congress, Ford relied on Henry Kissinger's guidance on foreign policy matters. Kissinger already played a major role during the final years of Nixon's administration, as Watergate consumed the president's attention. The secretary of state perceived himself as a realist, who could not avoid offending idealists on the political left and right. Quoting the German writer Goethe, Kissinger explained, "If I had to choose between justice and disorder, on the one hand, and injustice and order, on the other, I would always choose the latter."

Kissinger followed that maxim, certainly (with Nixon's blessing), by ordering the CIA to finance a military coup in Chile in 1973. The coup overthrew the democratically elected socialist leader, Salvador Allende Gossens. Allende died in the coup and the new government quickly became a brutally oppressive military regime. Kissinger argued that the United States had the right to limit democratic disorder in Latin America, in order to guard against the evils of Communism.

Energy and the Middle East

Kissinger also looked to manage the effects of an energy crisis brought to a head by events in the Middle East. The United States and its allies had long depended on Middle Eastern oil and, as the United States' energy appetite grew, so did its dependence on foreign sources. Indeed, the modern American economy was built in large part on access to cheap energy, both foreign and domestic. Low oil prices discouraged conservation or alternative energy sources. Prime among the nation's foreign suppliers were the 13 nations making up the Organization of Petroleum Exporting Countries (OPEC)—including seven Arab states and Iran.

The importance of that supply became clear in the autumn of 1973, when on Yom Kippur, the holiest day of the Jewish year, troops from Egypt and Syria launched a surprise attack on Israel. The seven Arab members of OPEC supported Egypt and Syria by imposing a boycott on oil exports to countries seen as friendly to the Israelis. Lasting from October 1973 to March 1974, the boycott staggered the economies of western nations and Japan. The price of crude oil had been rising steadily in any case, from under $2 a barrel in 1972 to over $12 by 1976. And, as the price of petroleum soared, so did the cost of carbon-based plastics used in a huge range of products from phonograph records to raincoats to tires. Inflation rose to an annual rate of 14 percent. Meanwhile, with gasoline suddenly scarce, motorists found themselves waiting in line for hours at the pump, in hopes of purchasing a few gallons.

The energy crisis struck hardest at what became known as the Rust Belt, the older industrial region stretching from New England and the mid-Atlantic states across the upper Mid-West to Wisconsin. Because the Rust Belt imported most of its energy, it was especially vulnerable to rising prices. Much of its transportation, housing, and industry was built without regard for energy efficiency. With tax bases and revenues shrinking, factories no longer competitive, and social service costs rising,

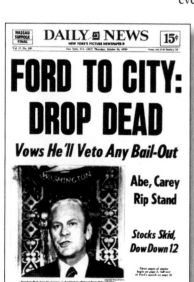

As the energy crisis contributed to New York City's near-bankruptcy, Gerald Ford at first opposed federal assistance. New Yorkers were not amused.

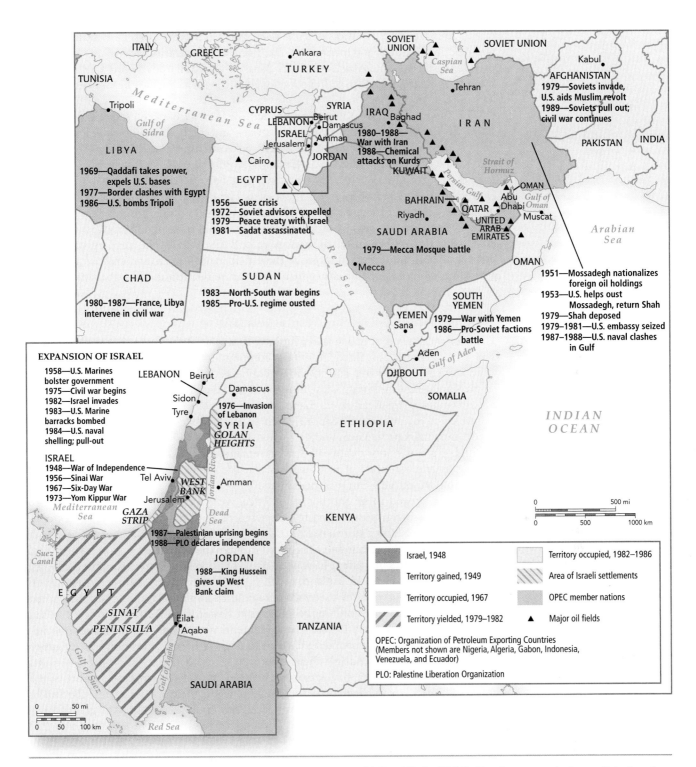

Oil and Conflict in the Middle East, 1948–1988   *After World War II, the Middle East became a vital geopolitical region beset by big-power rivalry and complicated by local tribal, ethnic, and religious divisions and political instability. Much of the world's known oil reserves lie along the Persian Gulf. Proximity to the former Soviet Union and vital trade routes like the Suez Canal have defined the region's geographic importance. Revolutions in Iran and Afghanistan, intermittent warfare between Arabs and Jews, the unresolved questions of Israel's borders and a Palestinian homeland, the disintegration of Lebanon, and a long, bloody war between Iran and Iraq were among the conflicts that unsettled the region.*

many cities faced financial disaster. In October 1975 New York City announced it was near bankruptcy and petitioned the Ford administration for relief. When the president refused, the *New York Daily News* headline blared, "Ford to City: Drop Dead." The administration did eventually extend a loan, but not before the political damage had been done.

To mitigate the crisis Kissinger mediated the conflict between Israel and the Arab states. From January to April 1974 he flew back and forth so often between Jerusalem in Israel and Cairo in Egypt that observers nicknamed his plane the "Yo-Yo express" and Kissinger's efforts "shuttle diplomacy." Eventually, the secretary persuaded the Israelis to withdraw their troops from the west bank of the Suez Canal and to disengage from Syrian troops along the Golan Heights, which overlooked Israel. An uncertain peace returned, and OPEC lifted its boycott. The following year Congress addressed the energy crisis by ordering electric utilities to switch from expensive oil to more abundant and cheaper (though more polluting) coal. The new legislation also ordered the auto industry to improve the efficiency of its cars and created a strategic petroleum reserve as one means of managing future disruptions on a short-term basis.

Limits Across the Globe

Global Competition from Pacific Rim Nations

The energy crisis was only one factor limiting American ambitions at home and abroad. The United States also faced mounting competition from more efficient and lower wage industries in Europe and in the emerging economies of the Pacific rim (Japan, South Korea, Taiwan, Hong Kong, Singapore, and the Philippines). Those lower wages convinced many American-based manufacturers to move high-wage jobs overseas. Key industries of the American economy such as automobiles and consumer electronics steadily lost markets to Japan and Germany. The AFL-CIO complained that as skilled and high-pay union jobs disappeared, what remained would be "a nation of hamburger stands, a country stripped of its industrial capacity . . . a nation of citizens busily buying and selling hamburgers and root beer floats."

Détente proved to be another way to deal with American limits. President Ford and Henry Kissinger both looked to ease tensions (and military budgets) by extending agreements Nixon had reached with Russian leader Leonid Brezhnev. The Soviet economy, like the American one, was mired in stagnation made even worse by the cost of aid to client states in Eastern Europe and the Third World. In two summit meetings, the second held at Helsinki, Finland, in 1975, the United States and the Soviet Union established the framework for a second strategic arms limitation treaty. They also agreed to recognize formally the cold war boundaries in Eastern and Western Europe that had been in place since the late 1940s. The agreements were hardly earthshaking, but neither superpower felt itself confident enough to negotiate from a position of strength or to move more boldly on nuclear disarmament.

For the United States, one reason for caution lay halfway across the globe, where in January 1975 North Vietnamese forces had renewed their offense against the South. Fearing that final defeat was at hand, President Ford implored Congress to grant $1 billion in aid to South Vietnam, Laos, and Cambodia. He sounded the same warning that earlier presidents had issued during the 1950s and the 1960s: if Vietnam fell, nations all over the world would doubt American commitments. This time, few at home bought the argument that Vietnam was the first in a long row of dominos. "My God, we're all tired of it, we're sick to death of it," exclaimed one citizen in Oregon. "55,000 dead and $100 billion spent and for what?" The only funds Congress would appropriate were $300 million to evacuate Americans and ease the withdrawal of refugees. In April 1975 Saigon fell, amid scenes of desperate Americans and South Vietnamese fighting to squeeze onto evacuation helicopters.

"The enemy must fight his battles far from his home base for a long time," a Vietnamese strategist wrote. "We must further weaken him by drawing him into protracted campaigns.

Once his initial dash is broken, it will be easier to destroy him." The enemy in question was not the Americans, nor the French, but Mongol invaders of 1284 C.E. The strategy of resistance and attrition that kept the Chinese at bay for centuries also defeated the United States. Between 1961 and 1973 the war cost uncounted billions in national treasure, killed some 57,000 soldiers, and left over 300,000 wounded. The cost to Southeast Asia was almost incalculable. Much of the land lay devastated, and some 6.5 million South Vietnamese had become refugees along with 3 million Laotians and Cambodians. In excess of 3 million Vietnamese soldiers and civilians died during the war.

Harry S. Truman may have started the United States down the road to war in Vietnam when he agreed to support French colonial rule as a way to contain Communism in Southeast Asia. Certainly presidents Eisenhower and Kennedy increased American involvement and Richard Nixon ended it. But fairly or not, Vietnam is remembered as Lyndon Johnson's war. He committed both the material and human resources that escalated the violence with such devastating results.

In that sense, Vietnam marked the end of liberalism triumphant as well as the end of the United States as an unequaled superpower. For the war destroyed the consensus that unified Americans in the decades after World War II. That consensus assumed that the prosperity generated by America's capitalist economy made it possible to fight communism abroad, at the same time solving social problems at home. Americans would have both guns and butter, Johnson insisted. That liberal dream died in the rice paddies of Vietnam, on tear gas-filled university campuses, and in riot-torn streets. No longer did most Americans believe that the world could be remade in their image with the help of brilliant intellectuals or well-intended government social programs. If Richard Nixon had not overreached, he might have replaced the liberal creed with a new conservative approach to government. But Nixon had exceeded the limits of presidential power in his desire for mastery, just as liberalism exceeded its limits in the quagmire of Lyndon Johnson's war. The rise of a new conservative tide would have to wait until the end of the 1970s.

Significant Events

1945	Ho Chi Minh unifies Vietnam
1954	French defeated at Dien Bien Phu; Geneva accords signed
1963	Diem assassinated; United States has 16,000 "advisers" in Vietnam
1964	Tonkin Gulf incident
1965	Rolling Thunder begins bombing of North Vietnam; Ralph Nader's *Unsafe at Any Speed* published
1966	Cesar Chavez campaign on behalf of farm workers; National Organizations of Women established
1967	March on the Pentagon; Johnson's advisers oppose war

1968   U.S. troop levels in Vietnam peak at 536,000; Tet offensive; McCarthy challenges Johnson in New Hampshire primary; Johnson withdraws from race; Martin Luther King Jr. assassinated; Robert Kennedy assassinated; riots at Democratic Convention; George Wallace candidacy; Nixon wins election

1969   National Environmental Policy Act; secret bombing of Cambodia; *Apollo 11* moon mission; "Vietnamization" policy adopted; Stonewall incident, Greenwich Village

1970   First Earth Day; U.S. troops invade Cambodia; killings at Kent State and Jackson State; march on Washington; NOW organizes Strike for Equality; Environmental Protection Agency created; Clean Air and Water acts; creation of OSHA; repeal of Tonkin Gulf resolution; recession creates stagflation

1971   Nixon adopts wage and price controls; *Swann v. Charlotte-Mecklenburg Board of Education;* Pentagon Papers published

1972   Nixon trip to China; détente with Soviet Union SALT I; Watergate burglary; Nixon reelected; mining of Haiphong Harbor; Christmas bombings of North Vietnam

1973   Vietnam peace treaty; *Roe v. Wade;* AIM supporters occupy Wounded Knee; Saturday Night Massacre; War Powers Act; OPEC oil boycott triggers U.S. recession

1974   House adopts articles of impeachment; Nixon resigns; Ford becomes president; Kissinger Arab-Israeli diplomacy; Ford pardons Nixon

1975   Thieu government falls in South Vietnam; Helsinki Summit

Chapter Summary

Though presidents from Truman to Nixon sent American forces to Indochina, Vietnam was Lyndon Johnson's war, and the political divisions it caused ended both his presidency and the consensus on liberal reform.

- To force the North Vietnamese to negotiate, Johnson escalated the American war effort. By 1966 American soldiers were doing most of the fighting. American warplanes subjected North Vietnam to heavy bombing.

- As the nation divided into prowar hawks and antiwar doves, the Vietcong's Tet offensive shocked Americans. Johnson almost lost the New Hampshire presidential primary to senator Eugene McCarthy, leading the president to abandon his reelection campaign.

- In the wake of the assassinations of Martin Luther King and Robert Kennedy, Hubert Humphrey became the Democrats' presidential nominee. But riots at the Chicago convention so damaged Humphrey's candidacy that Richard Nixon won the election, promising a "peace with honor" in Vietnam.

- A wide range of minorities—Latinos, Indians, Asian Americans, gays, and feminists—adopted identity politics as a way to claim their full rights and opportunities as Americans.

  - Mexican American migrant workers led by Cesar Chavez successfully established a farmworkers' union, the UFW, while a rising generation of Latino students adopted more militant techniques for establishing a Chicano identity.
  - Though often divided by tribal diversity, militant Native Americans called attention to the discrimination faced by Indians in urban settings as well as on reservations.
  - Feminists campaigned for civil and political equality as well as to change deep-seated cultural attitudes of a "patriarchal" society.
  - In addition to reform movements based on identity, the value politics of environmentalists and consumer advocates extended the spirit of reform.

- White House involvement in the Watergate break-in and the president's subsequent cover-up led to the first resignation of an American president.

- President Gerald Ford inherited an office weakened by scandal, an economy in recession, and Congressional determination to rein in an "imperial presidency."

- An energy crisis brought on by Arab-Israeli conflict and an oil boycott by the OPEC nations worsened an already ailing American economy.

- Secretary of State Henry Kissinger used shuttle diplomacy to bring an uneasy peace to the Middle East. He and President Ford sought to preserve American power and ease diplomatic tensions by pursuing détente with the Soviet Union.

- The fall of Vietnam after three decades of debilitating war left liberal ideals in disarray, though Nixon's overreaching in the White House temporarily forestalled a resurgence of conservatism in the United States.

Additional Reading

Two books—David Kaiser, *American Tragedy: Kennedy, Johnson, and the Origins of the Vietnam War* (2000), and Fred Logevall, *Choosing War: The Last Chance for Peace and the Escalation of War in Vietnam* (1999)—trace the road by which the United States escalated its military commitments in Vietnam. Among those who lay the blame with Lyndon Johnson see Michael Hunt, *Lyndon Johnson's Cold War Crusade in Vietnam, 1945–1968* (1997), and Lloyd Gardner, *Pay Any Price: Lyndon Johnson and the Wars for Vietnam* (1997). H. W. Brands, *The Foreign Policies of Lyndon Johnson: Beyond Vietnam* (1999), reminds us that the president faced other issues. For the soldiers' experience, look at the classic by Michael Herr, *Dispatches* (1977), and David Maraniss, *They Marched Into Sunlight: War and Peace, Vietnam and America, October 1967* (2004). Maraniss looks simultaneously at soldiers on the battlefront, protest that tore apart the University of Wisconsin, and policymaking in Washington.

Keith Olsen, *Watergate: The Presidential Scandal That Shook America* (2003), is a lively brief account of Nixon's fall, while Stanley Kutler, *The Wars of Watergate: The Last Crisis of Richard Nixon* (1992), provides more detail. For a look at the politics of division and emergence of identity and value political movements that divided the nation see Mark Lytle, *America's Uncivil Wars* (2006), and for an argument that the 1970s were more significant than the 1960s see Bruce Shulman, *The Seventies: The Great Shift in American Culture, Society, and Politics* (2002). Gender politics are widely explored in Ruth Rosen, *The World Split Open: How the Modern Women's Movement Changed America* (2001). Excellent on the environmental movement is Robert Gottlieb, *Forcing the Spring: The Transformation of the American Environmental Movement* (1996). Mark H. Lytle, *The Gentle Subversive: Rachel Carson, Silent Spring, and the Rise of the Environmental Movement* (2007), provides a brief biographical approach to the topic.

For a fresh, nonpartisan look at Richard Nixon see Melvin Small, *The Presidency of Richard Nixon* (2003), or Richard Reeves, *President Nixon: Alone in the White House* (2002). A dissenter from the camp of Kissinger admirers is Jussi Hanhimaki, *The Flawed Architect: Henry Kissinger and American Foreign Policy* (2004).

For a fuller list of readings, see the Bibliography at www.mhhe.com/davidsonnation6.

Historians Reconstruct the Past

The Contested Ground of Collective Memory

Perhaps the nation's most cherished commemorative space lies along the mall in Washington, D.C. As the mall makes clear, a culture defines itself by the history it elevates in public places. Such markers are hardly limited to Washington. Town squares boast statues; post office murals portray the deeds of forebears; even sports arenas hang honored jerseys from the rafters. As scholars of commemoration point out, all societies find visible ways to affirm their collective values. But the *history* of how a monument came to exist can be as revealing as the monument itself. Historians have studied such histories to discover why hallowed ground is so often contested ground. How does the building of a simple monument reveal the fault lines of an entire culture?

A Simple V in the Ground

For the historian, the array of monuments along the Washington mall presents an intriguing puzzle. Today the most frequently visited and publicly acclaimed site also happens to be the least epic. Unlike Washington's 555-foot obelisk, this memorial does not soar. Unlike Lincoln's Greek temple, there are no columns evoking classical grandeur. In fact, at any reasonable distance the memorial cannot even be seen. It is simply a V of highly polished black granite incised into the ground—a V whose wide arms, each 247 feet long, converge 10 feet below the surface of the boulevard. This site is the Vietnam Veterans Memorial. Amid considerable controversy, the memorial was built in the wake of what was not only the nation's longest war but a divisive one that the United States lost.

Why, in a mall that takes special care to burnish the nation's proudest memories, has this memorial moved so many Americans?

That question intrigues historians, who have been drawn in recent years to the study of collective memories. Their interest is not the traditional concern over whether this or that recollection is accurate. At issue instead is the *process* of memory making: "how people together searched for common memories to meet present needs, how they first recognized such a memory and then agreed, disagreed, or negotiated over its meaning." At first, the definition seems unnecessarily complex. But the process of forging a collective memory *is* complex and can take years or even decades.

Civil War Memories

For example, most people today take for granted commemorative statues honoring two sworn enemies, Ulysses S. Grant and Robert E. Lee. Yet the tradition that allows us to venerate *both* generals is possible only because of a collective memory that emphasizes the heroism of all Americans who fought. That memory began to take form in the 1880s, when northern and southern veterans started to hold joint reunions.

But for African Americans of that era, Confederate leaders such as Lee symbolized slavery, making this emerging collective memory difficult to endorse. Frederick Douglass, a former slave and prominent Republican, warned that monuments honoring Lee would only "reawaken the confederacy." He argued that emancipation, not martial valor, deserved the most emphasis. To that end, he supported efforts of African Americans to erect the Freedmen's Memorial Monument in Washington. The nation may "shut its eyes to the past . . . ," he warned, "but the colored people of this country are bound to keep the past in lively memory till justice shall be done them." Even today the collective memories of the Civil War remain contested ground.

The same can be said for the war in Vietnam. By the 1980s the vast majority of Americans, whether they had opposed or defended American involvement in Vietnam, agreed that the war had been a mistake. How, then, would a nation used to celebrating success find a way to remember failure?

How to Remember a Disputed War?

Vietnam veteran Jan Scruggs took an approach that was consciously apolitical. Rather than celebrate the war, Scruggs proposed a monument honoring the veterans themselves. From 1959 to 1975 over three million American men and women had served in Vietnam, of whom 75,000 returned home permanently disabled. Yet many felt their sacrifices had been lost amid the debate over the war. To promote reconciliation Congress in 1980 set aside a two-acre site on the mall, almost equidistant from the Washington and Lincoln memorials.

In the competition to select a design for the memorial, over 1,400 entries were submitted, all judged anonymously. The panel's unanimous choice came as a surprise: the entry of Maya Ying Lin, a Chinese American student at Yale University's School of Arts and Architecture. The idea for the design had occurred to her when she visited the projected site. "I thought about what death is . . . ," Lin recalled, "a sharp pain that lessens with time, but can never heal over. A scar. Take a knife and cut open the earth, and with time the grass would heal it."

To view the monument a visitor descends a gentle incline. Because there are no steps, the handicapped have easy access. The memorial's polished black granite sets a somber tone, yet the open sky and reflection of the sun dispel any sense that this is a tomb or mausoleum. A person beginning the descent at first sees only a few names carved into the granite, but as the wall deepens, so does the procession of names. Altogether, 70 panels enumerate over 54,000 Americans who died in Vietnam. As Lin insisted, "you cannot ever forget that war is not just a victory or loss. It's really about individual lives."

Objections and Competing Visions

The design immediately aroused controversy. Some critics resented Lin's relative youth, her ethnicity, and the fact that she was a woman. Others objected to the memorial's abstract and decidedly unheroic character. Lin had rejected a traditional approach in favor of a more feminine and non-Western sensibility. "I didn't set out to conquer the earth, or to overpower it the way Western man usually does," she acknowledged. Ross Perot, a major financial supporter and later a presidential candidate, called the memorial a slap in the face to

Maya Lin

veterans. Others less politely described it as a public urinal. To them the black granite seemed a mark of shame and the descent below ground level an admission of wrongdoing.

So loud were these objections that in 1982 the secretary of the interior refused a construction permit until the memorial's sponsors agreed to add to the site a realistic sculpture by Frederick Hart. Hart, one of Lin's most outspoken critics, created three soldiers with an American flag, installed in 1984. This memorial provoked a female Vietnam veteran, Diane Carlson Evans, to lead a campaign for one additional monument, to honor the women of Vietnam. This third sculptural piece (also realistic) portrays three nurses, one holding a wounded soldier.

Despite his personal dislike of the statue (because the slave was kneeling rather than proudly standing) Frederick Douglass helped dedicate the Freedmen's Memorial Monument to Abraham Lincoln in 1876. Douglass believed emancipation was central to remembering the Civil War.

Who captured the contested terrain of Vietnam commemoration? For the historian, the evidence lies in the crowds who flock to Maya Lin's memorial. Often, visitors seek out the name of someone they knew and make a rubbing of it to take with them. So many have left flowers, flags, and personal objects, along with messages and poems, that the Park Service has created a museum for them. The messages vary wildly, from the hopeful and resolute to the sorrowful and disgusted:

> Thank you for having the courage to fight . . .
> You never would listen to anyone and you
>   finally screwed up . . .
> I am sorry Frankie, I know we left you,
>   I hope you did not suffer too much . . .

Given such diverse reactions, Lin's choice of polished black marble was inspired. "The point," she said, "is to see yourself reflected in the names."

For the historian who passes by—even a century from now—the site will always bear witness to Vietnam's contested ground. As on a real battlefield, the opposing sides stand arrayed: heroic, realistic figures on one side, challenged and ultimately outflanked by the wide embrace of that silent granite V. In aesthetic terms, traditional realism wars with abstract modernity. But that contrast only reflects a deeper cultural divide over the way we choose to remember war. Maya Lin's commemoration would have been unthinkable in 1946, when a triumphant United States was emerging as one of the world's superpowers. In an age of limits, when even superpowers falter, the gleam of black marble reflects faces that are less certain that martial valor can guarantee a nation's immortality.

Bibliography   A useful introduction to the concept of collective memory is *Memory and American History* (1990), edited by David Thelen. Suzanne Vromen summarizes the controversy over Maya Lin's memorial in "The Vietnam Veterans Memorial, Washington, D.C.: Commemorating Ambivalence," *Focaal*, 25 (1995), 95–102. For more detail see Jan

C. Scruggs and Joel T. Swerdlow, *To Heal a Nation* (1985); Brent Ashabranner, *Always to Remember: The Story of the Vietnam Veterans Memorial* (1988); and James Mayo's more interpretive *War Memorials as Political Landscapes* (1988). For Maya Ying Lin, see Peter Tauber, "Monument Maker," *New York Times Sunday Magazine,* February 24, 1991: 49–55, and a fine documentary film, *Maya Lin: A Strong, Clear Vision* (1995).

CHAPTER 31
The Conservative Challenge
1976~1992

The New American Commons

In the early 1970s San Diego city officials looked out at a downtown that was growing seedier each year as stores and shoppers fled to the suburban malls that ringed the city. Nor was San Diego an exception. Across the nation many once-thriving downtown retail centers became virtual ghost towns at the close of the business day. But San Diego found a way to bounce back. The city launched a $3 billion redevelopment plan calling for a convention center, a marina, hotels, and apartment complexes.

At the core of the redevelopment plan was Horton Plaza, a mall with the look of an Italian hill town. Stores with stucco facades fronted twisting pedestrian thoroughfares where Renaissance arches lured customers to upscale stores like Banana Republic, to jewelers, and to sporting goods shops. Jugglers and clowns wandered the streets, while guitarists serenaded passersby. Horton Plaza soon ranked just behind the zoo and Sea World as San Diego's prime tourist attraction. By 1986 it drew more than 12 million shoppers and tourists.

For all its extravagance, Horton Plaza was hardly an innovation. The first enclosed mall, Southdale Center, had been completed nearly 20 years earlier in Edina, Minnesota, near Minneapolis. Edina had good reason for enclosure: with chilling winters and 100 days a year of rain, shopping conditions were hardly ideal for outdoor strollers. The mall's planners had approached Victor Gruen, an architect seeking ways to reclaim urban downtowns from what he saw as the tyranny of the automobile. Gruen contrasted the pedestrian-dominated streets and fountain-filled squares of European villages with the acres of sterile parking lots surrounding suburban shopping centers. As he noted in his manifesto, *The Tired Heart of Our Cities,* automobiles added pollution and congestion to the urban environment. Southdale provided an alternative: a climate-controlled marketplace where shoppers could browse or get a bite to eat at a café without dodging cars or inhaling exhaust fumes.

At first retailers feared that customers who couldn't drive by their stores or park in front wouldn't stop and shop. Success dispelled those fears. By 1985, when Horton Plaza opened, Southdale had expanded to a three-level, 144-store complex, spreading over 1.1 million square feet. Nationwide, there were more shopping centers (25,000) than either school districts or hospitals. Some 2,800 were enclosed, like Southdale.

Completed in 1980, the year former California governor Ronald Reagan was elected president, the Crystal Cathedral in Orange County, California, symbolized the rising influence of conservatives and evangelical Christians in American life and politics. Though the church's theology was traditional, it used the most modern techniques of the mass media to spread its message.

With their soaring atriums, lavish food courts, and splashing fountains, malls became the cathedrals of American material culture. Shopping on Sunday rivaled churchgoing as the weekly family ritual. Whereas American youth culture centered on the high school in the 1950s and on college campuses in the 1960s, in the 1970s and 1980s it gravitated toward mall fast-food stores and video amusement arcades. For single men and women, malls became a place to find a date. Older people in search of moderate exercise discovered that the controlled climate was ideal for "mall walking." Malls even had their counterculture—"mall rats" who hung out and often diverted themselves by shoplifting.

Malls as Symbols of an Age

Malls as cathedrals of consumption reflected a society turning away from social protest and crusades to more private paths of personal fulfillment. Some individuals adopted a consumerist or material path. Others chose a more spiritual direction. Evangelical religion offered them redemption in the prospect of being "born again." Still others extolled the virtues of traditional family values. Through private charity and volunteerism they proposed to replace the intrusive social policies of the modern welfare state. Along less orthodox paths, the "human potential movement" taught techniques such as yoga, Transcendental Meditation, and "biogenics" as means to find inner fulfillment. The search for moral meaning spread out, much as a mall did, along many corridors and past a host of spiritual boutiques, all nestled among the ever-present food courts and the acres of parking arrayed around the new American commons.

Because of the twin calamities of Watergate and Vietnam, it was not surprising that political leaders addressed what they saw as a spiritual hunger and discontent among Americans. On the eve of the nation's bicentennial, opinion polls showed that some 70 percent of those surveyed believed "over the last 10 years, this country's leaders have consistently lied to the people." Jimmy Carter, the president who followed Gerald Ford into the White House—and the first president elected from the deep South—saw the problem as a "crisis of confidence." It struck, he said, "at the very heart and soul and spirit of our national will. We can see this crisis in the growing doubt about the meaning of our own lives and in the loss of a unity of purpose for our nation." In 1981 Carter's successor, Ronald Reagan, sought to reverse that widespread pessimism and restore national confidence. He evoked a vision of the United States as a "city upon a hill" that would inspire the rest of the world through its actions and virtues. In doing so Reagan deliberately echoed language Puritan leader John Winthrop used to describe the seventeenth-century Massachusetts Bay colony.

City on a Hill

Carter and Reagan's rhetoric carried strong religious overtones. The Puritans, after all, strove to create a Christian commonwealth that was both well ordered and moral. Where Carter evoked a sense of decline and uncertainty (living in a time of "declension," the Puritans would have said), Reagan's vision was more uplifting. It drew on the nineteenth-century idea of manifest destiny, that the United States should spread across the continent and become preeminent on the world's stage. The nation should "stand tall" as the world's number-one military power, Reagan insisted. But while Carter and Reagan both reflected a move to the right, the nation was still very much split in its orientation. After 1975 Americans gravitated between the born-again conservative revolution and a more secular, centrist politics. Despite the efforts of religious conservatives to elevate their vision of public morality, popular culture continued to reflect the trends of the 1960s, when sex and violence became standard media fare, tolerance for alternative lifestyles grew, and diversity became a rationale for extending affirmative action to women and minorities. Liberal activists continued to see government, not the private sector, as the best way to clean up the environment, improve schools, reduce urban violence, and solve public health issues such as the AIDS epidemic.

The conservative rebellion thus fed off this secular and liberal vision of society—not simply by opposing it but often by harnessing its techniques in the service of more conservative causes. In doing so, the long-brewing rebellion gained the momentum to become a revolution, leaving behind the half-measures of Jimmy Carter and sweeping Ronald Reagan into power.

The Conservative Rebellion

In California, Howard Jarvis, a retired Mormon businessman, had for years promoted tax-cutting referenda on the state ballot. While those measures failed to attract widespread support, Jarvis's efforts to reduce property taxes did. In the case of property taxes, the issue was equity, not simply lower taxes. Small homeowners often paid taxes at much higher rates than large property owners and businesses that received breaks from friendly and often corrupt tax assessors. Hence, the extremely conservative Jarvis began to frame his antigovernment agenda in populist terms: his supporters, he claimed, were the small interests and individuals: teachers, blue-collar workers, and "a great number of Negroes." His group, the United Organizations of Taxpayers (UOT) received no money from oil companies, bankers, land speculators, or insurance companies.

Tax Revolt

By the late 1970s California was ripe for the Jarvis rebellion. Inflation imposed a crushing burden on middle and lower class homeowners. At the same time their taxes rose steadily. One woman complained to California Governor Jerry Brown that her hopes to live in a house mortgage free were not possible, "because our government won't let this happen." An old radical and union organizer described state politicians and bureaucrats as "those leeches who must have more and more taxes." Such mounting anger helped UOT collect 1.25 million signatures to place Proposition 13 on the ballot in 1978. Opponents warned that the loss of revenue would force school closings, job losses, and reduced police and fire protection.

Proposition 13

Proposition 13 succeeded because it offered homeowners immediate relief. It cut property taxes 57 percent and made it difficult for the state and local legislatures to raise taxes in the future. Significantly, the proposition gained support from voters of all income levels and from liberals and conservatives. Only African Americans and public employees opposed the measure, since both those groups depended heavily on public sector jobs. Californians, who paid 50 percent more in property taxes in 1978 than did citizens of any other state, only a year later paid taxes 35 percent below the national average.

The tax rebellion quickly spread across the nation. The *New York Times* likened it to "a modern Boston Tea Party." Over the next four years 12 states passed similar resolutions, while many legislatures cut public spending and taxes, hoping to avoid the voters' wrath. Even in Massachusetts, where government programs were generally popular, voters capped local property taxes and prevented future increases of more than 2½ percent, no matter how much inflation rose or the population grew. The only state to support the liberal George McGovern in 1972 voted narrowly for Ronald Reagan in 1980. After 1975, Americans no longer embraced the liberal consensus that professional expertise in the service of government could solve the nation's problems and promote progress.

The Diverse Evangelical World

But the conservative rebellion was not merely the child of a faltering economy, stagnating wages, and a resistance to paying taxes. The social ferment of the 1960s had taken its toll on spiritual life and on the churches. During that decade mainline Protestant churches struggled over how their religious beliefs should engage with civil rights, the war in Vietnam, issues of sex and gender, and more liberated lifestyles. As congregations moved to embrace more liberal definitions of faith, many Protestants found themselves yearning for a more traditional religious experience. Protestants moved in large numbers from long established denominations such as Presbyterians and Congregationalists to evangelical churches. By the mid-1980s, some 36 percent of Americans described themselves as "born again." Similar trends occurred among Catholics and Jews, many of whom also resisted the liberalization of their faith.

Fundamentalists

The growing evangelical movement encompassed a diverse range of religious practices and beliefs. Fundamentalists rejected the liberal Protestant move toward interpreting scripture figuratively and in light of rigorous historical scholarship. Their showdown with the teaching of evolution during the 1925 Scopes trial (see pages 709–711) made clear fundamentalists' unwillingness to accept a secular view of the world. In the decades following Scopes, many of these believers retreated from a society that they viewed as both corrupt and corrupting, waiting for the imminent return of Christ.

Pentecostals and Charismatics

Where fundamentalists found the spirit of Christ alive in the Bible but faint in the modern world, pentecostals believed that modern worshippers still had access to Christ's spiritual gifts. The presence of the Holy Spirit within marked a holy Christian, a presence often revealed by glossolalia, or speaking in tongues. The laying on of hands or faith healing was another spiritual gift. Charismatics shared with Pentecostals the faith in spiritual gifts, but they usually associated themselves with non-Pentecostal churches.

Even though sects such as the Southern Baptists and Assemblies of God attracted large national memberships, the real focus among evangelicals was local, centered in church communities. Such congregations insisted that salvation came through a spiritual rebirth (being "born again") after a person had acknowledged sinfulness and embraced Christ's atonement. Evangelical tradition encouraged proselytizing by the faithful, often in the form of revivals and spiritual awakenings. Finally, most evangelicals anticipated the rapture, when Christ would return to transport true believers into his Father's kingdom. These shared beliefs, when combined with a commitment to piety, put evangelicals squarely at odds with modern society. They imposed a strict personal morality, often insisted on the central role of fathers in the family, and in some churches forbade such worldly evils as dancing, cosmetics, movies, gambling, and premarital sex.

Pat Robertson

Though evangelicals condemned much of modern culture, many preachers advocated a "prosperity theology" that encouraged economic success. They also used the media to spread the word, none more effectively than did Virginia-based Pat Robertson, the son of a Virginia politician. Robertson, a magnetic Southern Baptist, used cable and satellite broadcasts to expand the Christian Broadcast Network into a media empire. His *700 Club* reached an audience of millions and inspired his colleague Jim Bakker to launch the even more popular *Praise the Lord Club*—PTL for short. Although the content featured gospel singing, fervent preaching, faith healing, and speaking in tongues, the format mirrored that of major network talk shows, opening with a Christian monologue, conversations with celebrity guests, and musical entertainment.

The Catholic Conscience

American Catholics faced their own decisions about the lines between religion and politics. In the 1960s a social activist movement had arisen out of the church council known as Vatican II (1962–1965). Convened by Pope John XXIII and continued by his successor, Pope Paul VI, the council sought to revitalize the church and to reappraise its role in the modern world (see page 877). The reforms of Vatican II reduced the amount of Latin in the mass, invited greater participation by ordinary church members, and encouraged closer ties to other Christians and to Jews.

Pope John Paul II

Disturbed by these currents, Catholic conservatives found support for their views when the magnetic John Paul II assumed the papacy in 1979. Pope John Paul reined in the modern trends inspired by Vatican II. He ruled against a wider role for women in the church hierarchy and stiffened church policy against birth control. These edicts put him at odds with a majority of American Catholics. The American church also faced a crisis as fewer young men and women chose celibate lives as priests and nuns.

Though conservative Catholics and Protestant evangelicals were sometimes wary of one another, they shared certain views. Both groups lobbied for the government to provide federal aid to parochial schools and Fundamentalist academies. But it was the issue of abortion that attracted the greatest mutual support. Pope John Paul reaffirmed the church's teaching that all life begins at conception and that abortion amounts to murder of the unborn. Evangelicals, long skeptical of the power of secular technology and science, attacked abortion as another instance in which science had upset the natural moral order of life.

Moving Religion into Politics

Since many evangelicals believed that the apocalypse—the end times of the world—were imminent, before the 1970s they saw little reason to reform society. Many refused even to vote. Gradually that apolitical stance weakened. A number of Supreme Court decisions, beginning with the ban on school prayer in *Engle v. Vitale*, (1962) struck conservatives as an attack on their faith, but none more so than *Roe v. Wade*. If an unborn fetus was fully human, was it not necessarily endowed with both a soul and with human rights? Abortion constituted "the slaughter of the innocents." Here was a case where it seemed that the government posed a threat to faith and family. So also did the inclusion of such subjects as Darwinian evolution and sex education in school curricula.

Some conservative parents countered by establishing Christian academies, many of which were racially as well as religiously segregated. The Internal Revenue Service proposed in 1978 to deny tax-exempt status for schools that failed to meet its standards of racial integration. Reacting strongly, conservatives bombarded the IRS, their Congressional representatives, and the White House with protests. By 1979 the IRS dropped its desegregation initiative.

Having crossed the line into politics, evangelicals began to organize their efforts. In 1977 the Reverend Jerry Falwell from Lynchburg, Virginia, joined his fellow Baptist

*Conservatives and
Roe V. Wade*

*Jerry Falwell and
the LaHayes*

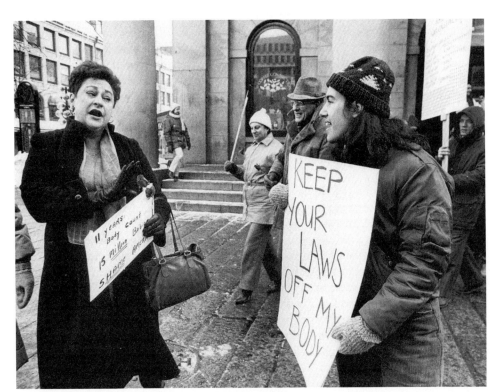

During the late 1970s and the 1980s conservatives increasingly spoke out against abortion and in favor of the right to life for an unborn fetus. Adopting the tactics of protest and civil disobedience once common to radicals in the 1960s, in this photograph they clash with pro-choice demonstrators outside Faneuil Hall in Boston.

preacher, Tim LaHaye of San Diego to fight for the repeal of a gay rights ordinance in Miami, Florida. LaHaye and his wife Beverly, a writer, had formed the Concerned Women of America (CWA), a "pro-family" organization that by the 1980s claimed more members than the National Organization of Women. The LaHayes were outspoken opponents of homosexuality and pornography. Under their leadership, CWA crusaded against abortion, no-fault divorce laws, and the Equal Rights Amendment.

Jerry Falwell

Their ally, the Reverend Falwell, epitomized the entrepreneurial gifts of many preachers of prosperity theology. His daily radio broadcasts and Sunday television

The Reverend Jerry Falwell's Moral Majority actively supported Ronald Reagan as well as other political candidates who shared the Moral Majority's social agenda.

show, the *Old Time Gospel Hour,* reached an audience of over a million. His home church ran multiple Sunday services to accommodate a congregation of 17,000. In addition, Falwell founded a school, a facility for alcoholics, a summer camp, and Liberty University. And when he and LaHaye defeated the gay rights ordinance in Miami, they went on to form the Moral Majority, a political action organization, which Falwell described as "pro-life, pro-family, pro-morality, and pro-American." The Moral Majority also shared the conservative opposition to labor unions, environmental reform, and most government-based social welfare programs.

The Media as Battleground

Both evangelicals and political conservatives believed the mass media played a central role in corrupting family values. Its permissive, even positive portrayal of unmarried women, premarital sex and drug use, profanity, homosexuality, nudity, and violence offended their moral sensibilities. The conservative determination to censor media content clashed with a liberal commitment to free speech and toleration for diversity in lifestyles.

Hollywood movies had long pushed the boundaries of acceptable content, but by the 1970s television began to introduce more controversial and politicized programming. In 1971 producer Norman Lear introduced *All in the Family,* whose main character, Archie Bunker, embodied the blue-collar backlash against liberal and permissive values. The ultimate male chauvinist, Archie treated his wife Edith like a servant, clashed with his modestly rebellious daughter Gloria, and heaped verbal abuse on his leftist Polish-American son-in-law. All things liberal or cosmopolitan—"Hebes," "Spics," and "Commie Crapola"—became targets for Archie's coarse insults. Although the show was watched by millions, it was attacked from both the left and the right. Many conservatives who shared Archie's values found the language offensive, while some minority leaders charged that the show legitimized the prejudices it attacked.

The most popular sitcom of the 1970s, *M*A*S*H,* was also the most liberal. Set in a hospital unit during the Korean War, the show criticized the politicians who mired the United States in Vietnam. As the show evolved over ten years, it reflected changing liberal sensibilities. "Hawkeye" Pierce and his fellow surgeons began the series as hard-drinking, womanizing foes of war and the military. Ten years later they still hated the army and war, but they had become more vulnerable and in touch with their emotions. And head nurse Margaret "Hot Lips" Houlihan was transformed from a flag-waving martinet into a woman seeking a career and respect in a man's world. The irreverence central to the show's appeal angered conservatives, who argued that *M*A*S*H* demonstrated how secular liberal values dominated the media. A similar bias, they believed, warped movies, newspapers, and popular music.

Yet the media was criticized by liberals as well. Feminists and minorities complained that popular culture too often treated them as stereotypes, if it bothered to portray them at all. Then, in January 1977 an audience of some 130 million Americans, at

Archie Bunker

M*A*S*H

that time the largest ever, watched the ABC television miniseries *Roots*. Based loosely on African American novelist Alex Haley's family history, *Roots* told of the proud West African Kunta Kinte, his captivity into slavery, and his ultimate emancipation with the coming of the Civil War. Some people saw the popularity of the series as proof that Americans had developed a new sympathy for African Americans and their history. Haley took a different view of the matter. Americans, he suspected, embraced the story because of its elemental concern with family, ancestry, and personal identity. In tracing his family's history, Haley offered a route to self-discovery as well.

Roots

Perhaps inevitably, the wars for the soul of prime time entertainment spilled into the political arena. Fearful that the Moral Majority's political pressure would lead television producers to censor themselves, the creator of Archie Bunker, Norman Lear, formed People for the American Way. The organization self-consciously opposed the agenda set by LaHaye and Falwell. People for the American Way campaigned for diversity and tolerance. In turn, conservatives, particularly the religious right, became more determined to advance their pro-life and pro-family agenda.

Jimmy Carter: Restoring the Faith

In the escalating war between liberal and conservative forces, James Earl "Jimmy" Carter succeeded in his quest for the presidency because he did not fit neatly into either camp. Carter represented a new breed of Southern governors—they came from the Sun Belt, not the Cotton Belt; they were economic progressives, not segregationists. At the same time, Carter had credentials conservatives could appreciate. He was a former Navy man and nuclear engineer, a peanut farmer from the humble town of Plains, Georgia, and had served as Georgia's governor. More unusual still, Carter openly declared his faith as a "born again" Christian, a term largely unused outside evangelical circles.

Over its eleven years, the cast of M.A.S.H. introduced many new characters. Among the few in the original cast who appeared in all eleven years were Loretta Swit ("Hot Lips" Houlihan), Alan Alda (Hawkeye/Pierce seated), Jamie Farr (the cross-dressing Maxwell Q. Klinger/upper right) and William Christoper (Father Mulcahy/upper left).

When he began campaigning, only two percent of Americans had heard of him outside his home state. Carter turned his outsider's status to advantage by bringing honesty and openness to Washington. "I will not lie to you," he assured voters. President Ford, for his part, had to fight off a challenge from his party's right wing, led by Ronald Reagan, a former California governor, movie actor, and television host. Reagan grew up as a New Deal Democrat, but deeply held concerns with high income taxes and communism had turned him toward conservative causes. Only because Ford controlled the party's nominating process was he able to defeat Reagan at the Republican convention. In the election Carter eked out a slim victory.

The Search for Direction

On Inauguration Day Jimmy Carter redeemed his pledge to bring simplicity and directness to Washington politics. Rather than the usual limousine ride down Pennsylvania Avenue, the new president and his family walked. The imperial presidency, he made clear, was a thing of the past. But Congress was equally determined to rein in the executive branch in its own way. To succeed in governing, Carter and his brash Georgia outsiders would have to prove they could swim among the political sharks.

Carter brought to the office a mastery of detail, disciplined work habits, and a wealth of plans to address the energy crisis, economic stagnation, the financial woes facing the nation's cities, and a host of foreign policy issues. What he and his advisors had not decided was how to set priorities. Veteran politicians warned not to try too much too soon, but Carter admitted, "it's almost impossible for me to delay something that I see needs to be done."

True to form, Carter jumped into the political fray almost immediately, by calling for the elimination of 19 expensive pork barrel water projects as financially wasteful and environmentally destructive. The move stunned even Democrats, who liked bringing home funds to their communities. They promptly threatened to bury his other legislative proposals unless he backed down, which he was forced to do.

Energy and the Environment

Regardless of Carter's skills as a politician, the times demanded that he address two related issues: the environment and skyrocketing energy prices. Those issues were in constant tension, since satisfying energy needs required the use of natural resources, just at the time when the need to protect them had become more evident.

Carter did make progress on a number of environmental fronts. He strengthened the Environmental Protection Agency as well as the clean air and water regulations the EPA enforced. And he championed legislation to create a Superfund that could spend $1 billion a year to clean up toxic waste sites.

Oil shortages in the 1970s increased American dependence on nuclear power as an alternative energy source. The danger became evident in 1979 when an accident closed a nuclear power plant at Three Mile Island near Harrisburg, Pennsylvania. The large towers pictured on this Time magazine cover are part of the cooling system in which the accident occurred.

Problems arose, however, when environmental and energy policies clashed. The exceptionally harsh winter that greeted the new administration drove the price of heating oil even higher and pushed Carter to promise a comprehensive new energy policy. His preferred strategy for increasing fuel supplies was the most environmentally friendly: conservation. Americans, after all, were consuming more energy in 1977 than they had been before the OPEC oil boycott spawned gas lines during the Nixon years. But the energy industry lobbied for the opposite solution. Instead of cutting back on the demand for energy, they looked to increase the supply, by deregulating the price of natural gas and oil to encourage new production.

Carter's National Energy Program was certainly comprehensive (it contained 113 separate recommendations), but it was also complicated. "Gas guzzler" taxes promoted conservation. So did new efficiency standards for buildings and appliances. Solar tax credits encouraged alternative energy. And an almost incomprehensible plan to use deregulation to give energy "its true value" targeted oil and gas interests. Citing the need to "act quickly," Carter described the fight for a comprehensive plan as "the moral equivalent of war." Unfortunately few areas of public policy were more subject to the pressure of special interests, and after 18 months of debate Congress managed to approve only deregulation, some energy conservation tax credits, and a new cabinet-level Department of Energy. No comprehensive policy ever emerged.

Environmentalists and energy advocates clashed again over the issue of nuclear power. Many utility companies viewed that resource as a nonpolluting way to reduce dependency on foreign oil. Most environmentalists fervently opposed nuclear plants, especially because no solution existed to deal with radioactive wastes created by the power plants. Environmentalists' worst fears were realized in March 1979 when a plume of radioactive steam spewed from a nuclear reactor at Three Mile Island in central Pennsylvania. Local authorities evacuated 100,000 panicked residents from nearby communities. Whatever support existed for nuclear energy evaporated along with the steam from the overheated reactor. While existing plants continued to operate, no new ones were built in the decades to come.

The Sagging Economy

Throughout the 1970s wages stagnated, unemployment rose, and so did inflation, spurred upward by rising energy costs, falling industrial productivity, and foreign competition. President Carter at first proposed stimulating the economy with a series of popular tax rebates. And he did win the approval of progressive politicians by finding new funding for federal programs such as food stamps, Social Security, Medicare, and Medicaid. But these attempts to cushion the blow of hard times were countered by the president's fiscal conservatism. Confronted by the large deficit from the Nixon and Ford years, Carter canceled his proposed tax rebates.

Furthermore, Carter favored increased competition by deregulating a variety of large industries, just as he had deregulated oil and gas interests. Supporters likened deregulation to removing the "dead hand" of government and freeing the quick-footed and competitive corporations. Deregulation produced lower fares in the airline industry, and similar legislation deregulated the trucking and telecommunications industries. "Government cannot solve our problems," Carter insisted. It could not "eliminate poverty, or provide a bountiful economy, or reduce inflation, or save our cities, or cure illiteracy or provide energy." That sentiment, spoken by a Democrat, indicated how successful conservatives had been in promoting their ideas.

Deregulation

Foreign Policy: Principled or Pragmatic?

In foreign policy, Jimmy Carter again gravitated between conservative and liberal impulses, between being practical and being idealistic. Like Nixon and Kissinger, Carter recognized that the United States had neither the strength nor the resources to impose its will in a postcolonial world. But unlike his conservative critics, Carter viewed the threat of Soviet strength with greater skepticism. Too often, he believed, a knee-jerk fear of Soviet power led Americans to support right-wing dictators, no matter how brutal or corrupt, simply because they professed to be anticommunist.

Given these assumptions, Carter insisted that the United States should take a moral posture by giving human rights a higher priority. He spoke out publicly on behalf of political prisoners and reduced foreign aid to some dictatorships (though strategic allies such as the Philippines under the autocratic Ferdinand Marcos were largely spared). Argentinean Nobel Peace Prize winner Adolfo Pérez Esquivel claimed he owed his life to Carter's policies. Hundreds of other journalists and dissidents, who routinely faced imprisonment, torture, and even murder, benefited as well.

Human Rights

Carter also eased decades of animosity against Yankee imperialism by negotiating a treaty to turn over to Panama control of the Canal Zone, a 10-mile-wide strip that the United States administered under a perpetual lease. For many conservatives, Carter's initiative offered further evidence of declining American power. Presidential hopeful Ronald Reagan condemned the proposed treaty as "appeasement," while Senator S. I. Hayakawa of California quipped, "It's ours; we stole it fair and square." Despite such criticisms the Senate ratified the final agreement in 1978.

Panama Canal Treaties

For conservatives, however, the real test of Carter's mettle would come in relations with the Soviet Union. There, the president's first impulse was to continue the policy of détente scorned so long by the right wing. Soviet premier Leonid Brezhnev accepted Carter's overtures to negotiate, as his nation had been struggling with an economy saddled by inefficient industries and obligations to poor client states such as Cuba, Vietnam, and East Germany. The Soviets became even more willing to negotiate after the Carter administration offered diplomatic recognition to communist China—playing "the China card" as Kissinger and Nixon once had. At a summit meeting held in Vienna in 1979 Carter and Brezhnev followed through on the strategic arms limitation agreement set in motion by President Ford. The agreement, SALT II, was seriously flawed because neither side would agree to scrap major weapon systems. But even Carter's minor concessions were hotly attacked by conservatives, who blocked ratification of the treaty in the Senate.

AFTER THE FACT in Brief

Unstapling the Truth

A Look at Eyewitness Testimony

In June 1978, Jimmy Carter gave a speech strongly criticizing Soviet behavior in Africa and condemning abuses of human rights. Yet much in the speech seemed to be reaching out to the Soviet Union in a fashion that was downright friendly. The *Washington Post* called it "Two Different Speeches." "What [Carter] did, and this is a literal fact," wrote journalist James Fallows, "is staple together a memo from [Secretary of State Cyrus] Vance to one from [National Security Advisor Zbigniew] Brzezinski and that was his speech." Fallows did not simply report what someone told him; he claimed he actually saw Carter staple the memos together.

Historians have widely repeated that "staple" story, using it to explain how Carter failed to reconcile conflicting advice into a consistent foreign policy. Brzezinski was well known to harbor distinctly hawkish views, while Secretary of State Vance routinely preferred negotiation and dialogue. "In essence stapling the different papers together, the president gave an address marked by glaring contradiction between toughness and conciliation, between the mailed fist and the dove's coo," explained one diplomatic history textbook. The story is false, however. Examining handwritten memos and notes in the Carter Library, historian Robert Strong found no staple marks. In his speech, Carter had in fact melded the ideas of numerous advisors, including Vance and Brzezinski.

Why then has this widely repeated legend continued to echo? Strong concluded that Fallows's story became folklore "because it made sense to political observers who were accustomed to expect very little from Carter's oratory" and who already viewed his foreign policy as muddled.

The Middle East: Hope and Hostages

Throughout the cold war, instability in the oil-rich Middle East continually threatened to set off a larger conflict. Secular dictators in Iran, Egypt, Syria, and Iraq vied with autocratic monarchies in Saudi Arabia, Kuwait, Jordan, and the Arab emirates. Vast inequality existed between oil-rich sheiks and impoverished peasants and nomadic tribes. Tensions simmered between rival Islamic religious sects, the Sunnis and Shi'ites, while at the same time all the Arab nations were united in their hostility toward Israel.

American policy for the region was pulled in two different directions. On the one hand the United States wanted to insure the free flow of Middle Eastern oil to the industrial world; on the other, it was committed to the survival of Israel. The energy crises of the 1970s heightened the tensions within these goals, as did Israel's decision to refuse Palestinian demands for a homeland in the West Bank. The diplomatic impasse eased somewhat when Egyptian president Anwar Sadat traveled to Israel to meet Israeli president Menachem Begin. Sensing an opportunity to promote peace, Carter invited the two leaders to Camp David in September of 1978.

Camp David Accords

For 13 days the two antagonists argued, while Carter kept them at the table. Each feared the consequence of giving the other side too much. Finally, they struck a limited compromise: Sadat would recognize Israel; Israel would return the Sinai Peninsula to Egypt. On the question of a Palestinian state in the West Bank and Gaza, Begin would not yield. Even so, the discussions had been historic. Begin and Sadat shared the Nobel Peace Prize for their courageous diplomacy, but it could just as well have gone to Carter, who brokered the peace.

Iranian Revolution

Amid the turmoil of the Middle East, the Shah of Iran had long seemed a stabilizing force. From the American point of view, a strong Iran limited Soviet access to the

It was at Camp David, in private talks sponsored by President Jimmy Carter (center), that Egyptian president Anwar el-Sadat (left) and Israeli prime minister Menachem Begin (right) hammered out a "Framework for Peace in the Middle East" as a first step toward ending decades of war and mutual distrust.

Persian Gulf. But in the autumn of 1978 Shi'ite fundamentalists rebelled against the Shah. Long dismayed by the increasing westernization of their society, they found the presence of tens of thousands of non-Muslim American military advisers particularly offensive. When the shah's regime collapsed in February 1979, the religious leader Ayatollah Ruhollah Khomeini established an Islamic republic. Later that year the United States admitted the ailing Shah to an American hospital for medical treatment, upon which several hundred Iranian students stormed the U.S. embassy in Tehran and took 53 Americans hostage. Though this act violated every convention of western diplomacy, the United States was helpless to respond.

A President Held Hostage

At first, American policymakers worried that the Soviet Union might take advantage of the new Khomeini regime. In truth, the Soviets were fearful themselves that Islamic fundamentalists might spread unrest among the Muslim populations living within Soviet borders. In December 1979, the Soviet Union invaded neighboring Afghanistan, where Islamic rebels had toppled a pro-Soviet regime. President Carter condemned the invasion, but in practical terms there was little he could do to counter it. As a symbolic gesture, he announced that the United States would boycott the 1980 Olympics in Moscow.

Soviets Invade Afghanistan

Once again, the problems of energy dependence and the economic instability interacted to create a political crisis. Nightly newscasts aired the spectacle of "America Held Hostage" in Iran. And the turbulence in the Middle East set off another round of OPEC increases in the price of oil. Soaring energy costs soon drove up inflation to near 14 percent and some interest rates above 20 percent. Chrysler Corporation, the nation's third leading car manufacturer, teetered on the edge of bankruptcy and was saved only by a federally guaranteed loan.

Hyperinflation

With polls giving Carter a negative rating of 77 percent, the president once again moved right. He revived the cold war rhetoric of the 1950s and accelerated the development of new classes of nuclear weapons. But whereas the CIA in 1953 had successfully overthrown an Iranian government, an airborne mission launched in April 1980 to rescue the hostages ended in disaster. Eight marines died when two helicopters and a plane collided in Iran's central desert in the midst of a blinding sandstorm. Carter's secretary of state, Cyrus Vance, who had opposed the mission, resigned in protest. The United States, as even the president admitted, was mired in "a crisis of confidence."

The administration's mistakes had no doubt contributed to it. Yet the obstacles to projecting American power internationally were not simply a result of Carter's mismanagement. Vietnam had demonstrated the clear limits of what U.S. forces could accomplish in distant lands; the long lines for expensive gas rose from an energy crisis decades in the making. The problems in the Middle East had proved intractable over many centuries. Finally, Carter could not be blamed for the reluctance of Americans to sacrifice personal comforts for the general good. American culture had long defined wealth as having more, not wanting less. In 1980 the discouraged electorate discovered in Ronald Reagan a political leader who shared that faith.

Prime Time with Ronald Reagan

Since the late nineteenth century, the United States has experienced three major shifts in party alignment. During the 1880s and 1890s thin margins separated the Democratic and Republican parties at the polls. William McKinley's victory over Democrat-Populist candidate William Jennings Bryan in 1896 ushered in an era of Republican dominance. That collapsed only after Herbert Hoover failed to ease the widespread distress of the Great Depression and Franklin Roosevelt and his New Deal shaped a new majority coalition. For the next 40 years Democratic presidents and Congresses were the rule rather than the exception.

The recession of the 1970s and the accompanying runaway inflation similarly brought on a new political order. Republicans undermined the Democrats' New Deal coalition and established a conservative majority that would dominate American politics for at least three decades. In the 1980 presidential campaign, Ronald Reagan asked Americans, "Are you better off now than you were four years ago?" Many thought not, as Reagan swept the election with an unexpectedly large majority. The fight against inflation and high taxes would be the cornerstone of his administration and would replace unemployment as the determining issues in federal economic policy.

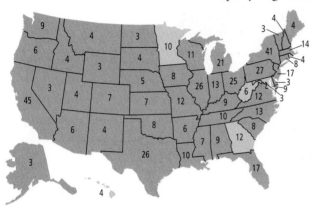

Candidate (Party)	Electoral Vote (%)	Popular Vote (%)
Ronald Reagan (Republican)	489 (91)	43,904,153 (51)
Jimmy Carter (Democratic)	49 (9)	35,483,883 (41)
John B. Anderson (Independent)	–	5,719,437 (7)
Minor parties	–	1,395,558 (1)

Election of 1980

The Great Communicator

Reagan Revolution

Reagan's message was clear. "It is time to reawaken the industrial giant, to get government back within its means, and to lighten the punitive tax burden." To both liberals and conservatives this signaled the onset of what came to be called "the Reagan Revolution." Liberals feared—and conservatives hoped—that the revolution meant a harder line on cold war issues and an assault on a wide range of social programs and regulations at home. What both groups ignored in the early days of the administration were the moderating forces at work. As governor of California, Reagan had showed a willingness to accommodate his ideas to political realities. At times he increased both spending and taxes. As president, he appointed to his administration advisors with diverging ideas about how to fix the economy and build American prestige. The *Washington Post* commented that Reagan was not someone to allow rigid ideas to prevent flexible policies. Equally important, noted the *Post*, almost anyone who met him thought he was "a nice guy, a happy secure person who likes himself and most other people."

In other ways Reagan contradicted expectations. With his jaunty wave and jutting jaw, he projected an aura of physical vitality and movie star good looks. Yet at 69 he was the oldest person to become president, and no one since Calvin Coolidge slept as soundly or as much. Such serenity marked his refusal to become bogged down in the details of his job. Outsiders applauded his "hands-off" style after four years under Jimmy Carter, whose obsession with policy details led critics to say he missed the forest for the trees. Reagan set the tone and direction of his administration, leaving the rest to his advisors. Sometimes that left Reagan in the dark about major programs. Donald Regan, his first Treasury Secretary, once noted, "The Presidential mind was not cluttered with facts."

Ronald Reagan's image as a plainspoken westerner helped build his reputation as "the great communicator."

The effectiveness of Reagan's message was no accident. The president had honed his public speaking skills as an actor, as a spokesperson for General Electric, and as a politician. His communications staff planned everything from the president's words to a speech's location and camera angles down to the lighting. But the elaborate preparation also depended on Reagan's discipline as a performer. The president understood as well as his staff how to use a battlefield, a classroom, or the flag to communicate a hopeful message.

Luck played a role as well. Problems that handcuffed Carter seemed to ease on Reagan's watch. The day he took office Iran announced it would release the American hostages after 444 days of captivity. Three aging Russian leaders, beginning with Leonid Brezhnev in 1982, died suddenly, thereby greatly reducing the influence of the Soviet Union. And when a disturbed gunman shot Reagan in the chest two months after his inauguration the wounds were not life threatening. Even Reagan's critics admired his courage in the face of death.

The Reagan Agenda

In addition to luck, however, Reagan viewed the economic downturn as an excellent reason to push for his revolution in government. His agenda called for massive tax cuts, deregulation of the economy, and a reduction in spending for social programs. Only the military would be spared the budget cutters' axe, because Reagan planned a forceful foreign policy to contain Soviet power.

A commitment to **supply-side economics** became the cornerstone of the Reagan revolution. Supply-side advocates argued that high taxes and government regulation stifled business. The key to revival lay in a large tax cut—a politically popular proposal, though economically controversial. Lower tax revenues would not increase the massive and growing federal budget deficits, insisted supply-side economist Arthur Laffer. His calculations suggested that lower tax rates would stimulate the economy so greatly, that tax revenues would actually grow, thanks to higher profits and a renewed prosperity. Broad cuts in social programs would further reduce deficits.

After little more than half a year in office, Congress handed the president most of the cuts he requested. The Economic Recovery Tax Act (ERTA) lowered income tax rates over the following three years by 25 percent, capital gains by 40 percent, and investment income rates by 28 percent. Taxpayers in the highest brackets were far and away the biggest winners. At the same time Reagan signed the Omnibus Budget Reconciliation Act, which slashed some $35 billion in spending from government programs. *The Wall Street Journal* hailed the two measures as a "spectacular tax victory," and news commentators suggested that Reagan had ended 50 years of liberal government.

Liberal government relied on the support of big labor. Here, too, Reagan struck a decisive blow. In 1981, members of PATCO, the air controllers union, struck against what they claimed were dangerous and debilitating working conditions. PATCO workers were, however, both highly paid and public service employees. Reagan declared their strike illegal and, without addressing the issues they raised, summarily fired them.

Large corporations seized on the antiunion climate to wrest significant concessions on wages and work rules.

Environmental Deregulation

Environmental regulations were a special target of conservative revolutionaries. **"Sagebrush rebels,"** as many westerners called themselves, encouraged logging in national forests; easing restrictions on mining, oil drilling, and real estate development; and opening western lands to cattle grazing. As his Secretary of Interior, Reagan chose James Watt, an outspoken sagebrush rebel and Christian fundamentalist. Watt, in turn, opened public lands for development. He even denied the Beach Boys a concert permit because he considered their California surf music immoral. Watt's outrageous comments forced his resignation in 1983, but the administration continued to attack environmental regulation. Reagan personally rejected the conclusion of scientists that acid rain from coal-fired Ohio Valley utilities was responsible for dying lakes and forests in Eastern Canada and New England.

A Halfway Revolution

Despite Reagan's tax cut victories in the political arena, continued recession, rising interest rates, and crippling federal deficits sent the stock market into a tailspin. At first the president refused to compromise his commitment to lower taxes. Still, the evidence was clear that supply-side predictions of booming tax revenues were not materializing, especially in the economic downturn. So Reagan reversed course and accepted the Tax Equity and Fiscal Responsibility Act of 1982, a measure including $98 billion in tax increases disguised as "revenue enhancements." A year later Social Security reform led to further tax increases. In both cases Regan allowed pragmatism to trump ideology.

"Revenue Enhancements"

After the reversal on tax cuts, the economy began a strong upturn that extended through both of the president's terms in office. Labor productivity improved, inflation subsided to 4.3 percent, unemployment fell, and the stock markets rose sharply. Falling energy costs played a major role as OPEC members exceeded their production quotas. Having sold for as much as $30 per barrel, crude prices fell as low as $10.

Economic Inequality

The benefits of an improved economy were distributed unevenly across economic classes and regions. For the wealthiest Americans the 1980s were the best of times. The top 1 percent commanded a greater share of wealth (37 percent) than at any time since 1929. Their earnings per year were 25 times greater than the 40 percent of Americans

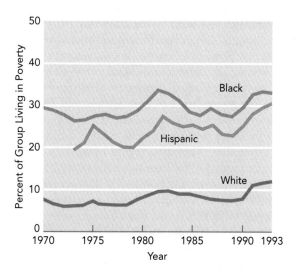

Poverty in America, 1970–1993 *Social Security and other income supplements to older Americans reduced their rate of poverty. For all other traditionally impoverished groups the prosperity of the Reagan-Bush years left them slightly worse off than in 1980. The charts also indicate that poverty was most severe for unwed or divorced mothers and their children, and people of color.*

at the bottom of the economic ladder. Still, good times meant new jobs—over 14.5 million of them. Three million of these were concentrated in unskilled, minimum wage areas such as hotels, fast-food restaurants, and retail stores. High paying jobs in financial services, real estate, insurance, and law went largely (70 percent) to white males. Only 2 percent went to African Americans.

The 1980s also saw an acceleration of the trend toward **outsourcing** high-wage industrial jobs to areas such as Mexico and Asia, which offered low-wage workers and no unions. Given its commitment to free markets and free trade, the Reagan administration resisted pressure to develop plans to keep jobs at home. Thus, even as the economy grew and inflation dropped below 2 percent, unemployment hovered above 6 percent, and poverty levels ranged from 11 to 15 percent. Cuts in programs such as food stamps, Medicaid, and school lunches increased the burden on the poor. The decision to classify ketchup as a vegetable and thereby meet government nutritional standards for a well-balanced diet symbolized for liberals the administration's indifference to those in need.

Outsourcing

The Contours of Science and the Landscape of Technoburbs

New technologies and an increasingly global economy accounted for changes in Americans' work and wealth distribution as much as Reagan's tax and spending cuts. During the 1980s sales of such new electronic goods as VCRs, cell phones, fax machines, compact disc players, and, above all, computers soared. In the 1970s Steve Jobs and Steve Wozniak, two technophiles from California, founded Apple Computer and introduced an affordable and user-friendly home computer. A few years later IBM entered the market with the PC and adopted a rival operating system, MS-DOS, designed by two software programmers, Paul Allen and Bill Gates. Success in marketing computers transformed the ways in which Americans moved, managed, and stored information.

The PC Revolution

Computer-assisted technologies were part of a larger revolution in medical technologies that was changing American lives. The CAT scan (Computed Axial Tomography) generated three-dimensional images of the body from flat (that is, two-dimensional) X-ray pictures. Magnetic Resonance Imaging and Proton Emission Tomography (MRIs and PET scans) used different techniques to probe the human body. Neurochemistry made discoveries about brain functions that resulted in a new generation of psychotropic drugs, which modified moods and emotions. **Biogenetic engineering** was yet another dynamic technology. In 1977 Genentech Corporation used recombinant DNA research to produce a synthetic protein. Five years later, the company created a synthetic version of insulin, the first genetically engineered drug to win approval from the FDA. The health care industry in the 1980s was by far the biggest producer of new jobs.

Medical Technologies

As these technologies began to change lives, they also changed the landscape—literally. Unlike manufacturing industries of old, high-tech companies did not depend on transportation networks to move raw materials or ship finished products to market. They could set up shop where the quality of life was high and office rents were low or near university centers that generated new ideas, researchers, and entrepreneurs. The 1980s saw an explosion of edge cities or "technoburbs" along interstate highways where office and industrial parks housed technology companies, pharmaceutical concerns, professional services, and back office operations for banks, credit cards, and other providers of financial services. As developers turned open meadows and farmlands into office parks, the string of technoburbs stretching between San Francisco and San Jose came to be known as Silicon Valley—so named because of the miniature silicon wafers at the heart of microprocessor technology.

Winners and Losers in the Labor Market

Several characteristics distinguished workers in the new technology industries from those in older industrial sectors. In general they were much younger and better educated. Further, unlike the stuffy corporate culture of the 1950s, which stressed the idea of "go along to get along," the new businesses were far more informal. Casual clothing replaced

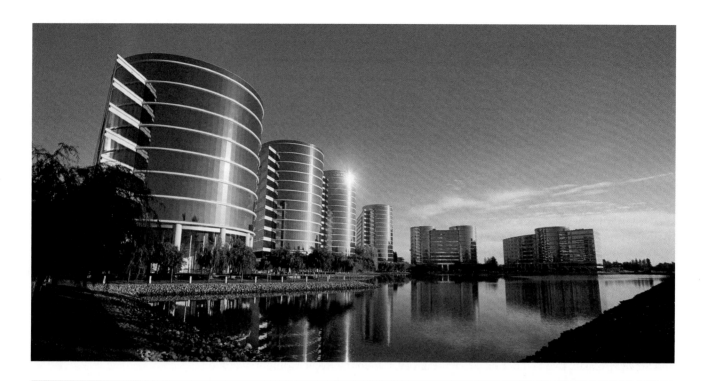

Many high technology companies build headquarter complexes much like college campuses. Oracle, a business software systems company, built this gleaming complex in Redwood, California, part of what has come to be known as Silicon Valley.

the grey flannel suits; individualism and creativity marked the road to success, and those who flaunted authority were welcomed. The media began referring to young, upwardly mobile, urban professionals as Yuppies—part of the younger generation that repudiated the antimaterialistic values of their Hippie forebears.

Yuppies

Access to computers marked a generational divide. To Gen-Xers, those born after 1963 (the end of the baby boom), computers and other electronic devices were second nature. Computerization and information technologies streamlined the work place so that the time and cost of new product development and production fell sharply. Increased productivity also reduced the demand for low-skill workers. By contrast, demand for workers with education and technical skills rose (as did wages) and thereby increased the income gap between those at the top and bottom of the labor market.

Women: High-Wage vs. Low-Wage Jobs

In an economy in which brains displaced brawn, educated women were among the big winners. Not only did they find more jobs in high tech areas and computerized offices, but they greatly increased their presence in law, medicine, business, and other professional schools. Still, many women continued to flow into lower-paying jobs in health care, education, social services, and government. The net result was that well-educated women gained far more economic independence and a more substantial political voice, while women with fewer skills and less education saw their earnings eroded. Single mothers with children, many who worked in low-wage jobs, were the nation's most impoverished group.

Job displacement in the 1980s had a devastating impact on two other groups, African American men and organized labor. Beginning in the 1970s black males lost much of the gains they had made over the previous three decades. The decline in manufacturing industries such as steel and autos struck hardest at the older industrial cities where blacks had gained a foothold in the economy. Often lacking the education required in the technology sector, black men had difficulty finding new jobs and many simply dropped out of the labor market. Sociologists began to describe an underclass, trapped in poverty, while middle class blacks escaped devastated urban neighborhoods.

Union Decline

As manufacturing declined so, too, did membership in unions. Labor organized 27 percent of all workers in 1953, 20 percent in 1980, 16 percent in 1990. Only the increase in the number of unionized government workers helped offset the shrinkage in the industrial sector. Deregulation made matters worse. With increased competition in the airlines, trucking, and telecommunications industries (all areas where membership had been strong), unions were forced to make concessions on wages and benefits. A two-tier system emerged where younger workers received lower pay and hence had less incentive to join unions. Smaller numbers reduced labor's political clout, weakened the Democratic Party, and spurred the conservative revolution.

Standing Tall in a Chaotic World

Ronald Reagan's view of world affairs was primal. "The Soviet Union underlies all the unrest in the world," he stated in his 1980 campaign. Thus he made the defeat of the communist menace a central mission of his administration. To that end he believed Americans must put Vietnam behind them and once again stand tall in the world. Although he was pleased to see the Soviet threat dissolving by the end of his years in office, the president also discovered that firmness and military force alone were not sufficient to calm regional crises across the world.

The Military Buildup

Reagan described the Soviet Union as the "evil empire." His plan to defeat that enemy centered on a massive buildup of the American military. Whereas Richard Nixon had thought the United States needed enough force to fight one and one-half wars at any time, Reagan pushed for enough to fight three and one-half around the globe. That required expenditures of over $1.6 trillion in his first five years (Carter had planned for $1.2 trillion). The combination of massive defense spending and tax cuts created huge deficits, despite supply-side claims that tax revenues would rise sharply.

Deficits

Deficits drove up interest rates and thus the value of the dollar. The strong dollar slowed exports as the cost of American goods rose on world markets. Lower prices gave imports such as Japanese autos a large competitive advantage over American producers. The United States deficit of payments (the value of imports over exports) soared. From the end of World War I until the Reagan years, the United States had been the world's leading creditor nation. By 1986 it had become the world's largest debtor.

Debt was only one of the liabilities of the massive military buildup. Huge cost overruns and wasteful spending became widespread. Exposés of $600 toilet seats and $7,000 coffee pots symbolized spending run amok. Worse yet were the multibillion-dollar weapons systems that either were unneeded or ran into huge cost overruns. Air Force planners, for example, persuaded Congress to fund the B-2 bomber, a plane costing $2 billion each and designed to penetrate Soviet air defenses. Only later did investigators determine that those Soviet air defenses did not exist. In general, advocates of the defense buildup exaggerated Soviet capabilities in order to pressure Congress to appropriate vast sums of money.

Talk of "standing tall" also spread fear. Reagan and his tough-talking defense planners spoke out about winning any nuclear exchange with the Soviet Union. Author Jonathan Schell debunked those claims in his book *Nuclear Winter*. In it, Schell described a war no one would win, in which debris in the atmosphere would create conditions fatal to all life on earth. Such warnings revived the antinuclear movement across East Asia, Europe, and America. Bishops of the American Catholic Church felt moved to announce their opposition to nuclear war.

Disaster in the Middle East

The Middle East continued to be a flashpoint of U.S–Soviet tensions when in 1982 Israel invaded neighboring Lebanon to destroy missiles supplied by Syria, a Soviet client state. Israeli General Ariel Sharon also used the invasion to strike a decisive blow

Lebanon

against forces of the Palestine Liberation Organization (PLO) that were camped in Lebanon. As the Israeli offensive bogged down, however, international outrage over the massacre of Palestinians in Israeli-controlled camps forced Sharon to withdraw his troops.

Reagan then decided to send American troops to Beirut, Lebanon's capital, to protect the Palestinians and keep the peace between warring Christian and Muslim factions. Unfamiliar with the terrain or the politics, the Americans were drawn into supporting Christian militias. Muslim radicals responded first by bombing the American Embassy and then, in October 1983, a U.S. marine barracks. Some 239 troops died. Confronting a chorus of criticism from the media, Congress, and his own Defense Department, Reagan withdrew American troops from Lebanon.

Terrorist Attacks The president also searched with little success for a response to terrorist attacks and hostage-taking by Islamic fundamentalists. In 1982 agents of Libya's Muammar al-Qadhafi exploded a bomb on an American airliner flying over Lockerbie, Scotland. Three years later terrorists took hostages in Lebanon, hijacked American airline flights, killed an American hostage on a Mediterranean cruise ship, and bombed a West German nightclub popular with American troops. In response to such provocations, the president was always forceful and uncompromising: "Let terrorists beware: . . . our policy will be one of swift and effective retribution."

But against whom should the United States seek retribution? American intelligence agencies had only sketchy profiles of the many terrorist factions and their political allies. In 1986 the president launched an attack against Libya, which sponsored terrorism. But so too did Syria and Iran, against whom the administration did nothing.

Frustrations in Central America

At first, Reagan found he could stand tall closer to home. On the pretext of protecting American medical students studying on the Caribbean island of Grenada, American troops crushed a band of pro-Cuban rebels and evacuated the students, who were hardly at risk. But the action in Grenada was largely symbolic.

More challenging was Reagan's campaign to overthrow the left-wing Sandinista government in Nicaragua. The president justified arming the anti-Sandinista "Contras," as "freedom fighters" battling in the spirit of America's Founding Fathers. True, the Contras included a few democrats and disillusioned Sandinistas, but the majority had served in the brutal and corrupt dictatorship of Anastasio Somoza, which the Sandinistas overthrew in 1979.

Contras Reagan had no desire to broker a settlement between the opposing forces. Instead, he allowed the CIA to help the Contras mine Nicaragua's harbor, in hopes of destabilizing the Sandinistas. When the mines damaged foreign ships—a violation of international law—conservatives and liberals alike condemned the president's actions. Congress adopted the Boland Amendment, which explicitly forbade the CIA or "any other agency or entity involved in intelligence activities" to spend money to support the Contras "directly or indirectly." Reagan reluctantly signed the measure, though he remained determined to overthrow the Sandinistas.

Neither mushrooming deficits nor frustrations in the Middle East and Central America dented Ronald Reagan's popularity. The booming economy kept his poll ratings high. In the 1984 election he easily won a second term, winning 59 percent of the popular vote against Walter Mondale of Minnesota. Only Mondale's choice of Geraldine Ferraro of New York as the first female running mate in a presidential campaign, added a note of interest. Reagan and his advisers entered his second term determined to force solutions to some of his most stubborn foreign policy problems. It was a decision that led to scandal and threatened the Constitutional system of checks and balances.

The Iran-Contra Connection

By mid-1985 Reagan policy makers felt two major frustrations. First, Congress had forbidden any support of the Contras in Central America, and second, Iranian-backed improvement in Soviet-American relations. By the 1980s the Soviet Union was far weaker than American experts, including the CIA, had ever recognized. The Soviet economy stagnated; the Communist party was mired in corruption. The war in Afghanistan had become a Russian Vietnam. By accelerating the arms race, Reagan placed additional pressure on the Russians.

In 1985 a fresh spirit entered the Kremlin. Unlike the aged leaders who preceded him, Mikhail Gorbachev was young and saw the need for reform within the Soviet Union. Gorbachev's fundamental restructuring, or perestroika, set about improving relations with the United States. He reduced military commitments and adopted a policy of openness (glasnost) about problems in the Soviet Union. In October, the two leaders held their second summit in Reykjavík, Iceland. Gorbachev dangled the possibility of abolishing all nuclear weapons. Reagan seemed receptive to the idea, but in the end he and his advisors backed away from such a radical proposal. A summit in Moscow two years later eliminated an entire class of nuclear missiles with ranges of 600 to 3,400 miles. Both sides agreed to allow on-site inspections of missile bases and the facilities where missiles would be destroyed.

Thus, as the election of 1988 approached, the president could claim credit for improved relations with the Soviet Union. Loyalty to Ronald Reagan made Vice President George H. W. Bush the Republican heir apparent. The Democratic challenger, Governor Michael Dukakis of Massachusetts, pointed out that poor and even many middle-class Americans had lost ground during the 1980s. But Bush put the lackluster Dukakis on the defensive. With the economy reasonably robust, Bush won by a comfortable margin. The Reagan agenda remained on track.

Mikhail Gorbachev

An End to the Cold War

President George Herbert Walker Bush was born to both privilege and politics. The son of a Connecticut senator, he attended an exclusive boarding school and then the Ivy League Yale University. That background made him part of the East Coast establishment often scorned by more populist Republicans. Yet once the oil business lured Bush to Texas, he moved to the right, becoming a Goldwater Republican when he ran unsuccessfully for the Senate in 1964. Foreign policy interested him far more than domestic politics. But in the end, inattention to domestic issues proved his undoing as the economy slid into recession.

A Post–Cold War Foreign Policy

To the astonishment of most Western observers, Mikhail Gorbachev's reform policies led not only to the collapse of the Soviet empire but also to the breakup of the Soviet Union itself. In December 1988, Gorbachev spoke in the United Nations of a "new world order." To that end he began liquidating the Soviet cold war legacy, as the last Russian troops began leaving Afghanistan and then Eastern Europe.

Throughout 1989 Eastern Europeans began to test their newfound freedom. In Poland, Hungary, Bulgaria, Czechoslovakia, and, most violently, Romania, Communist dictators fell from power. Nothing more inspired the world than the stream of celebrating East Germans pouring through the Berlin Wall in November 1989. Within a year the wall, a symbol of Communist oppression, had been torn down and Germany reunified. Although Gorbachev struggled to keep together the 15 republics that made up the U.S.S.R., the forces of nationalism and reform pulled the Soviet Union apart. The Baltic republics—Lithuania, Latvia, and Estonia—declared their independence in 1991. Then, in December, the Slavic republics of Ukraine, Belarus, and Russia formed a new Commonwealth of Independent States. By the end of December eight more of the former Soviet republics had joined the loose federation. Boris Yeltsin, the charismatic president of Russia, became the Commonwealth's dominant figure. With no Soviet Union left to preside over, Gorbachev resigned as president.

The Fall of Communism

The Berlin Wall had stood since August 1961 as a symbol of cold war tensions. Thus, Americans joined these Germans in celebrating the wall's destruction. At long last, the cold war seemed to be at an end.

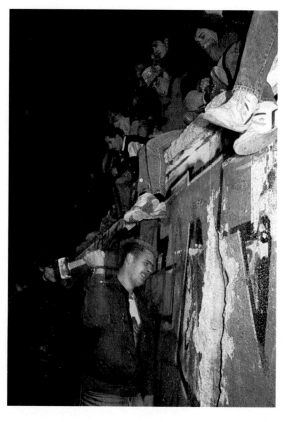

Although President Bush increasingly supported Gorbachev's reforms, he did so with caution. Even if he had wished to aid Eastern Europe and the new Commonwealth states, soaring deficits at home limited his options. The administration seemed to support the status quo in Communist China, too. When in June 1989 China's aging leadership crushed students rallying for democratic reform in Beijing's Tiananmen Square, Bush muted American protests.

The fall of the Soviet Union signaled the end of a cold war that, more than once, had threatened a nuclear end to human history. At a series of summits with Russian leaders, the United States and its former rivals agreed to sharp reductions in their stockpiles of nuclear weapons. The Strategic Arms Reduction Treaty (or START), concluded in July 1991, far surpassed the limits negotiated in earlier SALT talks. By June 1992 Bush and Yeltsin had agreed to even sharper cuts.

The Gulf War

With two superpowers no longer facing off against each other, what would the "new world order" look like? If anything, regional crises loomed larger. Instability in the Middle East produced the greatest foreign policy challenge. From 1980 to 1988 Iran and Iraq had battered each other in a debilitating war. During those years the Reagan administration assisted Iraq with weapons and intelligence, until at last it won a narrow victory over Iran's fundamentalists. But Iraq's ruthless dictator, Saddam Hussein, had run up enormous debts. To ease his financial crisis, Hussein cast a covetous eye on his neighbor, the small oil-rich sheikdom of Kuwait. In August 1990, 120,000 Iraqi troops invaded and occupied Kuwait, catching the Bush administration off guard. Would Hussein stop there?

Saddam Hussein

"We committed a boner with regard to Iraq and our close friendship with Iraq," admitted Ronald Reagan. Embarrassed by having supported the pro-Iraqi policy, Bush was determined to thwart Hussein's invasion of Kuwait. The president successfully coordinated a United Nations–backed economic boycott. Increasing the pressure further, he deployed half a million American troops in Saudi Arabia and the Persian Gulf. By November Bush had won a resolution from the Security Council permitting the use of military force if Hussein did not withdraw.

Operation Desert Storm

On January 17, 1991, planes from France, Italy, Britain, Saudi Arabia, and the United States began bombing Baghdad and Iraqi bases. Operation Desert Storm had begun. After weeks of merciless pounding from the air, ground operations shattered Hussein's vaunted Republican Guards in less than 100 hours. In an act of spite, Hussein resorted to ecoterrorism. His forces set Kuwait's oil fields ablaze and dumped huge quantities of crude oil into the rich Persian Gulf ecosystem. It did him no good: by the end of February Kuwait was liberated, and nothing stood between Allied forces and Iraq's capital, Baghdad. Bush was unwilling to advance that far—and most other

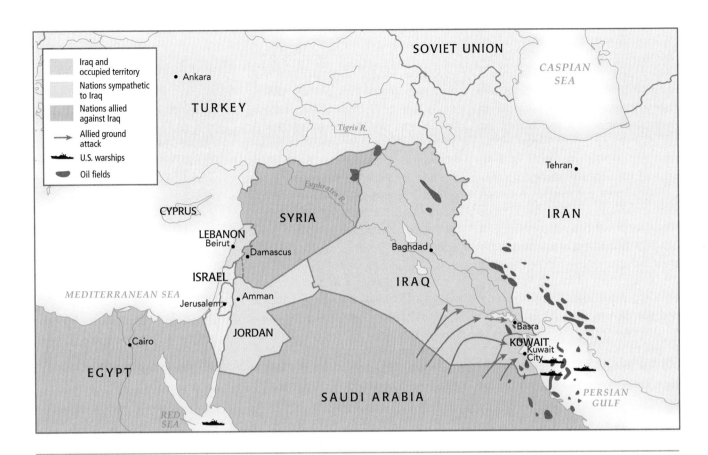

War with Iraq: Operation Desert Storm   *When Saddam Hussein invaded oil-rich Kuwait on August 2, 1990, the United States formed a coalition to force out the Iraqis. (Although Turkey was not a formal member, it allowed its airfields to be used. Israel remained uninvolved to avoid antagonizing Arab coalition members.) The coalition launched Operation Desert Storm in January 1991; land forces invaded on February 24 (Operation Desert Saber), routing Iraqi troops, who left Kuwait in ruin and its oil fields aflame.*

nations in the coalition agreed. If Hussein were toppled, it was not clear who in Iraq would fill the vacuum of power.

Domestic Doldrums

Victory in the Gulf War boosted the president's popularity so high that aides brushed aside the need for any bold domestic program. "Frankly, this president doesn't need another single piece of legislation, unless it's absolutely right," asserted John Sununu, his cocky chief of staff. "In fact, if Congress wants to come together, adjourn, and leave, it's all right with us." That attitude suggested a lack of direction that proved fatal to Bush's reelection hopes.

At first, Bush envisioned a domestic program that would soften the harsher edges of the Reagan revolution. He promised to create a "kinder, gentler" nation. Yet pressures from conservative Republicans kept the new president from straying too far in the direction of reform. When delegates from 178 nations met at an "Earth Summit" in Rio de Janeiro in 1992, the president opposed efforts to draft stricter rules to lessen the threat of global warming. Bush did sign into law the sweeping Clean Air Act passed by Congress in 1990. But soon after, Vice President Dan Quayle established a "Council on Competitiveness" to rewrite regulations that corporations found burdensome.

Similarly, the president called for reform of an educational system whose quality had declined through the 1980s. But, while he convened a well-publicized "Education Summit" in 1989, the delegates issued a modest set of goals only after the president was urged to do so by his cochair at the summit, Governor Bill Clinton of Arkansas.

Environmental Issues

During the 1880s Jacob Riis "discovered" a class of people he described as invisible. They were "individuals who have lost connection with home life, or never had any, or whose homes had ceased to be sufficiently separated, decent, and desirable to afford what are regarded as ordinary wholesome influences of home and family." A century later investigators for the *Chicago Tribune* discovered in American cities "a lost society dwelling in enclaves of despair and chaos that infect and threaten the communities at large." This ghetto world of dilapidated housing, poverty, and despair was home to as many as 5 million Americans. Yet while many of its spaces and avenues were public, it too was invisible, except when its private behavior became so violent or criminal that the news forced the broad middle class to pay attention.

Like Riis the *Tribune* reporters portrayed this urban blight through the story of individual lives. Dorothy Sands was one. In 1957 Dorothy, her mother, Ora Streeter, and the rest of her family lived in a one-room shack in rural Mississippi. To escape the South, her job, and her abusive husband, Ora took six small children to Chicago, where her mother lived. For her daughter Dorothy, "It was something like going to a new world."

Life in Chicago imposed disappointments and cruelties of its own. For several years Streeter struggled to make a decent life for her family. Arthritis finally prevented her from working and forced her to sign up for public assistance. Dorothy, the oldest child, assumed responsibility for the household. With what little time she had for herself, she reached the ninth grade.

The bleak spaces of public housing in the "Chicago projects" and in other decaying urban areas made life difficult for residents.

The Conservative Court

Although Presidents Reagan and Bush both spoke out against abortion, affirmative action, the banning of prayer in public schools, and other conservative social issues, neither made

In 1991 Justice Clarence Thomas survived a bitter Senate battle during his Supreme Court confirmation hearings. Here, he is sworn in by Chief Justice William Rehnquist as Thomas's wife and President George H. W. Bush and Barbara Bush look on. Thomas's conservative views on abortion and affirmative action were later confirmed by the votes he cast as a justice.

But at age 15 her dream of a nursing career ended when she discovered she was pregnant. In 1965, after her mother died, Dorothy began a relationship with Carra Little, a man who promised he could not get her pregnant. Within a year, Dorothy had her second child. She asked the doctors to sterilize her, but they refused. And the children kept arriving—four more. "When you are young, you don't really think about the future," Dorothy recalled.

After Little died suddenly of a heart attack in 1976, the household disintegrated. Dorothy's oldest daughter, Barbara, like her mother and grandmother before her, became pregnant at age 15. By 1985 Dorothy was a 37-year-old grandmother living in a three-room apartment with five of her six children, her daughter LaWanda's new boyfriend, two grandchildren ages 7 and 2, and two teenage runaways. In 20 years, the family had never been off welfare and no one in the household had held a regular job.

With public assistance money Dorothy could afford only rooms in a dilapidated three-story building on Chicago's West Side. Each evening people pried open the building's front door to do "crack" or drink grain alcohol. Sometime in 1985 the family stopped bathing because every time they turned on the water, plaster fell into the tub. The building manager reneged on his promise to make repairs. So the children just stood over the sink and washed their clothes by hand. Meals were irregular affairs, because money was scarce and no one liked to cook. For two weeks each month the family splurged on eggs for breakfast and Spam for dinner. More often they got by on hot dogs, rice, and beans.

Of the neighborhood's 61,500 people, more than half received some form of welfare. People lucky enough to find work quickly moved away. One government official described "a caste of people almost totally dependent on the state, with little hope of breaking free."

For the rest of the American people, more fortunate in their circumstances, a question persisted: how could the problems of the largely invisible underclass be solved before the violence and desperation of their private world overwhelmed the city streets?

action a legislative priority. Even so, both presidents shaped social policy through their appointments to the Supreme Court. Reagan placed three members on the bench, including in 1981 Sandra Day O'Connor, the first woman to sit on the high court. Bush nominated two justices. As more liberal members of the Court retired (including William Brennan and Thurgood Marshall), the decisions handed down became distinctly more conservative. The appointment of Antonin Scalia gave the Court its most outspoken conservative.

In 1991 the Senate hotly debated President Bush's nomination of Clarence Thomas, an outspoken black conservative and former member of the Reagan administration. The confirmation hearings became even more contentious when Anita Hill, an attorney who had worked for Thomas, testified that he had sexually harassed her. Women's groups blasted the all-male Judiciary Committee for keeping Hill's allegations private until reporters uncovered the story. Thomas and his defenders accused his opponents of using a disgruntled woman to help conduct a latter-day lynching. In the end the Senate narrowly voted to confirm, and Thomas joined Scalia as one of the Court's most conservative members.

The Clarence Thomas Hearings

Evidence of the Court's changing stance came most clearly in its attitude toward affirmative action—those laws that gave preferred treatment to minority groups in order to remedy past discrimination. State and federal courts and legislatures had used techniques such as busing and the setting of quotas to overturn past injustices. As early as 1978, however, the Court began to set limits on affirmative action. In *Bakke v. Regents of the University of California* (1978), the majority ruled that college admissions staffs could not set fixed quotas, although they could still use race as a guiding factor in trying to create a more diverse student body. Increasingly, the Court made it easier for white citizens to challenge affirmative action programs. At the same time it set higher standards for those who wished to put forward a claim of discrimination. "An amorphous claim that there has been past discrimination in a particular industry cannot justify the use of an unyielding racial quota," wrote Justice O'Connor in 1989.

Disillusionment and Anger

Ronald Reagan had given a sunny face to conservatism. He had assured voters that if taxes were cut, the economy would revive and deficits would fall. He promised that if "big government" could be scaled back, there would be a new "morning in America." Yet a decade of hands-off conservative leadership left the deficit ballooning and state and local governments larger than ever. A growing number of Americans felt that the institutions of government had come seriously off track. Indeed, such cynicism was fueled by the attacks on big government by Reagan and Bush.

S&L Crisis   A series of longer-term crises contributed to this sense of disillusionment. One of the most threatening centered on the nation's savings and loan institutions. By the end of the decade these thrifts were failing at the highest rate since the Great Depression. To help increase bank profits, the Carter administration and Congress had agreed to cut back federal regulations. That move allowed savings and loan institutions to invest their funds more speculatively. Few depositors noticed or cared, because their money was insured by the Federal Savings and Loan Insurance Corporation. The government, however, had to pay depositors if these banks failed. Reagan's advisers as well as members of Congress ignored the warnings that fraud and mismanagement were increasing sharply. Only during the Bush administration did it become clear that the cost of rebuilding the savings banks and paying off huge debts might run into hundreds of billions of dollars.

The late 1980s also brought a public health crisis. Americans were spending a higher percentage of their resources on medical care than were citizens in other nations, yet they were no healthier. As medical costs soared, more than 30 million Americans had no health insurance. The crisis was worsened by a fatal disorder that physicians began diagnosing in the early 1980s: acquired immunodeficiency syndrome, or AIDS. With no cure available, the disease threatened to take on epidemic proportions not only in the United States but around the globe. Yet because the illness at first struck hardest at the male homosexual community and intravenous drug users, many groups in American society were reluctant to address the problem.

Bank failures, skyrocketing health costs, anger over poverty and discrimination—none of these problems by themselves had the power to derail the conservative revolution. Still, the various crises demonstrated how pivotal government had become in providing social services and limiting the abuses of powerful private interests in a highly industrialized society.

As the AIDS epidemic spread in the 1980s, quilts such as these expressed sorrow for lost friends and loved ones. The quilts also served to raise public awareness of the need for a more effective policy to aid the afflicted and fight the disease.

The Election of 1992

In the end, George Bush's inability to rein in soaring government deficits proved most damaging to his reelection prospects. "Read my lips! No new taxes," he pledged to campaign audiences in 1988. But the president and Congress were at loggerheads over how to reach the holy grail of so many conservatives: a balanced budget. In 1985 Congress had passed the Gramm-Rudman Act, establishing a set of steadily increasing limits on federal spending. These limits were meant to force Congress and the president to make hard choices needed to reach a balanced budget. If they did not, automatic

Gramm-Rudman Act

across-the-board cuts would go into effect. By 1990 the law's automatic procedures were threatening programs such as Medicare, which Republicans and Democrats alike supported. Facing such unpopular cuts, Bush agreed to a package of new taxes along with budget cuts. Conservatives felt betrayed, and in the end, the deficit grew larger all the same.

As the election of 1992 approached, unemployment stood at more than 8 percent, penetrating to areas of the economy not affected by most recessions. Statistics showed that wages for middle-class families had not increased since the early 1970s and had actually declined during Bush's presidency. Many Reagan Democrats seemed ready to return to the party of Franklin Roosevelt, who had mobilized an activist government in a time of economic depression.

White-Collar Unemployment

Meanwhile, the Democrats gave their nomination to Governor Bill Clinton of Arkansas. Clinton had personal hurdles to surmount: he was dogged by reports of marital infidelity, by his weak admission that he had tried marijuana while a student (but had not inhaled), and by his youthful opposition to the war in Vietnam. Still, he gained ground by hammering away at Bush for failing to revive the economy. "It's the economy, stupid!" read the sign tacked up at his election headquarters to remind Clinton workers of the campaign's central theme. Clinton painted himself as a new kind of Democrat: moderate, willing to work with business, and not a creature of liberal interest groups.

"It's The Economy . . ."

At the voting booth, middle-of-the-road voters turned to Clinton and, in smaller numbers, to third-party challenger H. Ross Perot. Clinton captured 43 percent of the popular vote (to Bush's 38 and Perot's 19) in the largest turnout—55 percent—in 20 years. The election of four women to the Senate, including the first African American woman, Carol Moseley Braun, indicated that gender had become an electoral factor.

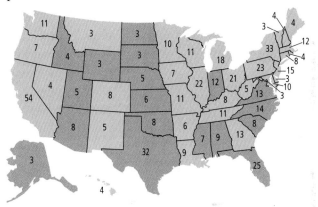

Candidate (Party)	Electoral Vote (%)	Popular Vote (%)
Bill Clinton (Democratic)	370 (69)	44,908,254 (43)
George H. W. Bush (Republican)	168 (31)	39,102,343 (38)
Ross Perot (Independent)	–	19,725,433 (19)

Election of 1992

The 1992 election left the fate of the conservative revolution unresolved. Under Reagan and Bush the economy had grown and inflation had subsided. Yet prosperity benefited mostly those at the upper end of the income scale. The majority of Americans saw their financial situation stagnate or grow worse. Reagan and Bush both had supported a conservative social agenda that sought to restrict abortion rights, return prayer to the schools, and end affirmative action, but neither had done much to put that agenda into action. Both presidents significantly weakened the capacity of the federal government to implement social programs. No longer did Americans expect Washington to solve all the issues of the day. How, then, would the nation meet the future needs of the increasing numbers of poor, minority, elderly, and immigrant Americans?

Reagan and Bush had also presided over the end of the cold war. Despite a growing isolationist sentiment among Democrats and Republicans, both presidents had shown a willingness to assert American power—in Libya, in Lebanon, in Nicaragua, in Panama, in Somalia, in the Persian Gulf—though these were situations in which no major conflict threatened. What role would the United States play in the post–cold war era, when it stood as the lone superpower in the world arena? That was a question for William Jefferson Clinton as he sought to lead the United States into the twenty-first century.

Significant Events

1976	Carter defeats Ford
1978	Panama Canal treaties ratified; revolution in Iran; Camp David meetings on the Middle East; *Bakke v. Regents of the University of California*
1979	Moral Majority established
1980	Reagan defeats Carter
1981	Reagan breaks air traffic controllers' strike; recession sets in; Economic Recovery Tax Act; United States begins aiding Nicaraguan Contras
1982	Attack on U.S. Marine barracks in Lebanon
1983	Invasion of Grenada
1984	Boland Amendment passed; Reagan defeats Mondale
1985	Gramm-Rudman Act sets in motion a plan to balance budget; United States begins secret arms-for-hostage negotiations with Iran
1986	Reykjavík summit; Iran-Contra scandal breaks
1988	Bush elected president
1989	Eastern Europe nations break with Soviet Union; China crushes revolt in Tiananmen Square; Berlin Wall taken down
1990	Iraq invades Kuwait; Clean Air Act; Bush agrees to higher taxes in budget agreement with Congress
1991	Operation Desert Storm launched; Strategic Arms Reduction Treaty (START) concluded; Clarence Thomas hearings; 11 former republics of the Soviet Union become the Commonwealth of Independent States
1992	Clinton defeats Bush and Perot

Chapter Summary

During the years of the Carter, Reagan, and Bush administrations, the nation's political and social agenda was increasingly determined by a conservative movement, including newly politicized evangelical Christians, that sought to restore traditional religious and family values, patriotism, and a more limited role for government.

- Jimmy Carter, unable to end the recession at home, pursued success abroad with a human rights policy and the negotiation of the Camp David Accords between Israel and Egypt—only to have the Soviet invasion of Afghanistan and the Iranian hostage crisis undermine his foreign policy.

- Ronald Reagan led the conservative tide with a program to limit the power of labor unions, reduce government regulation, lower taxes, and sharply increase spending on the military.

- Despite a revived economy, Reaganomics had two undesirable outcomes: huge government budget deficits and a growing gap in income between the rich and poor.

- Conservative appointments to the federal judiciary and the Supreme Court led to decisions increasing limits on government intervention in the areas of civil rights, affirmative action, abortion rights, and the separation of church and state.

- Reagan's efforts to "stand tall" in foreign policy led to the Iran-Contra scandal, which revealed a broad pattern of illegal arms shipments to right-wing rebels in Nicaragua and the trading of arms to Iran in an unsuccessful attempt to win the release of hostages in Lebanon—actions for which the president was sharply criticized but not impeached.

- Both Reagan and George Bush welcomed reforms set in motion by Mikhail Gorbachev that led by 1991 to the breakup of the Soviet Union, reductions in nuclear arms, and an end to the cold war.

- In the post–cold war era, regional conflicts proved more troublesome as Iraq's invasion of Kuwait led Bush to form a UN coalition that routed the forces of Saddam Hussein in Operation Desert Storm.

- For George Bush, a continuing recession, high budget deficits, and high unemployment undermined his bid for reelection.

Additional Reading

Bruce Shulman, *The Seventies* (2002), follows the transition from the 1960s to the Reagan era. An intriguing new look at the same subject is Philip Jenkins, *Decade of Nightmares: The End of the Sixties and the Making of Eighties America* (2006). An even-handed treatment of Jimmy Carter is Robert A. Strong, *Working in the World: Jimmy Carter and the Making of American Foreign Policy* (2000). Two books that do justice to Ronald Reagan and the politics of the right are John Ehrman, *The Eighties: America in the Age of Reagan* (2006), and Gil Troy, *Morning in America: How Ronald Reagan Invented the 1980s* (2005). Considering the transformation into the digital world is Fred Turner, *From Counterculture to Cyberculture: Stewart Brand,* The Whole Earth Catalogue, *and the Rise of Digital Utopianism* (2006).

Randall Balmer, *Mine Eyes Have Seen the Glory: A Journey Into the Evangelical Subculture in America* (2006), offers the perspectives of someone raised in the evangelical tradition. The issue of income inequality is well explained in Frank Levy, *The New Dollars and Dreams: American Incomes and Economic Change* (1999). Racial currents of the era are powerfully conveyed in Nicholas Lemann, *The Promised Land* (1995). The reasonably friendly treatment of George H. W. Bush by Ryan Barilleaux and Mark Rozell, *Power and Prudence: The Presidency of George H. W. Bush* (2004), can moderate the often insightful Kevin Phillips, *American Dynasty: Aristocracy, Fortune, and the Politics of Deceit* (2004). On the first Gulf War see Alberto Bin, Richard Hill, and Archer Jones, *Desert Storm: A Forgotten War* (1998).

For a fuller list of readings, see the Bibliography at www.mhhe.com/davidsonnation6.

CHAPTER 32

Nation of Nations in a Global Community

1980–2007

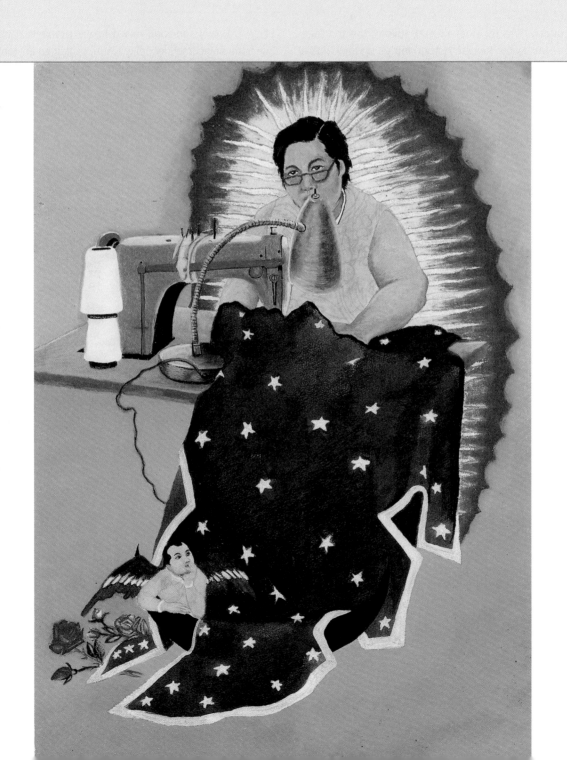

Of Grocery Chains and Migration Chains

Juan Chanax had never been far from San Cristobal, a small village in the Guatemalan highlands. In that region, some 2,000 years earlier, his Mayan ancestors had created one of the world's great civilizations. By the late 1970s, however, the local economy of San Cristobal had come to depend on low-wage work at an American textile factory. Chanax made barely enough to live on and could not afford treatment for his son's illness. He decided to go north to the United States where he could improve himself—to *"superarme"* as he put it—where *"people could work and make their own lives."* So began a journey that changed the destiny of Chanax, San Cristobal, and the multicultural community in America.

Getting safely across the U.S. border was an ordeal. Chanax survived encounters with thieves and hostile border guards before arriving three months later in Houston, Texas. He carried little more than a letter introducing him to several Guatemalans. They suggested he apply at Randall's, an upscale Houston supermarket chain. High oil prices during the energy crisis had sparked an economic boom in the city, and Randall's was eager to expand. The grocery chain did not want just any low-wage workers. It specialized in high-priced goods in fancy suburban stores. Its upscale customers received valet parking, hassle-free shopping, and service from uniformed employees. Shortly before Chanax began working at Randall's, one of its managers had a falling out with several African American employees. When the manager criticized their work, they argued heatedly, until one employee finally threw a mop at the manager and quit.

That incident proved to be an opportunity, for Chanax was happy to do any job without complaint. Even on his minimum-wage salary, he could wire money home to his family. And when the manager said Randall's would soon need more workers, Chanax arranged for his brother-in-law and an uncle to come north. Over time Randall's began to hire Guatemalans exclusively. Shortly before a new store opened, the managers would tell Chanax how many maintenance people they needed. He would then recruit more Mayas from San Cristobal.

As the newcomers arrived, Chanax and the experienced Mayas prepared them for the job. Preparation meant more than learning to clean and stack. The recruits were also told to arrive on time, work hard, disrespect no one, and use proper

By the mid 1990s over a quarter of a million laborers worked in Southern California's garment industry, many of them recently arrived immigrants from Mexico and Central America. "Very often we work until eight or nine at night the six days and then work a half day Sunday," commented one. Chicano artist Yolanda López celebrates the virtues of a hardworking seamstress by portraying her as the Virgin of Guadalupe, the traditional patron saint of Mexico.

manners. If a problem arose, they were to go not to a Randall's manager but to another Guatemalan. "That way," as Chanax observed, "if there was any problem, if a man was sick or had to leave work early or anything, we would solve it ourselves."

Migration Chain   Within five years after Chanax reached Houston, over a thousand Mayas from San Cristobal were working at Randall's. A single person had created what scholars call a migration chain. Through Chanax, Randall's had found access to a minimum-wage workforce who would perform willingly—in the company's words—as "cheerful servants." The Mayas, in turn, found opportunities unavailable in Guatemala. In the process Chanax and other early immigrants had become department managers and supervising assistants; their wives often worked as maids and servants in the homes of Houston's rapidly growing upper-income communities.

In many ways, Juan Chanax and his fellow Guatemalans mirrored the classic tale of immigrants realizing the American dream. In suburban Houston they formed their own community in an area that came to be known as Las Americas. There, various Central American immigrant groups established churches and social clubs amid some 90 apartment complexes that a decade or two earlier had housed mostly young, single office workers. On weekends and evenings rival soccer teams played in the nearby park. (Juan, also the soccer league's president, helped new teams fill out the forms required by the parks department to use its fields.) The growth of Las Americas in the late twentieth century echoed the pattern of immigrants who had come to the United States at the century's opening.

Changes in the Patterns of Global Immigration   Yet those patterns had changed in important ways, too. Although cities remained the mecca of most immigrants, Juan and many newcomers of the 1980s and 1990s settled in suburban areas, particularly in the West and Southwest. Industrial factories provided the lion's share of work in the 1890s, but a century later the service industries—grocery stores, fast-food chains, janitorial companies—absorbed many more of the new arrivals. Even the faces had changed, as European immigrants found themselves outnumbered by Latinos from Mexico and Central America as well as by Asians from the Philippines, China, Korea, Southeast Asia, and the Indian subcontinent, not to mention increasing numbers of Arabs from the Middle East and Africans. This broad geographic range reflected perhaps the most important shift in immigration: its truly global character. Transportation and communications networks tied immigrants to their home countries more strongly than in the past, allowing newcomers like Juan to keep regularly in touch with their former neighbors and relatives by phone as well as mail. Immigrants continued to participate in home-country politics more easily; they could wire money instantly to relatives and even build homes thousands of miles away where one day they planned to retire.

The global nature of immigration was only one aspect of American society more tightly linked to the world community. The effects of a recession or financial collapse in Russia or Thailand could spread to the United States in a matter of weeks or months. A communications revolution in the 1990s created a World Wide Web—the *www* in Internet addresses—that tied together correspondents, consumers, manufacturers, and information systems. Politics too became both global and local. Representatives of Arab and Afghan guerilla fighters regularly visited Arab-American communities in the United States during their war in Afghanistan against the Soviet Union, looking to raise money for their cause. In 1993, just three months after terrorists placed a bomb in the garage of the World Trade Center in New York City, Ayman al-Zawahiri, an Egyptian doctor, came seeking funds. Posing as Dr. Abdul Mu'iz of the Kuwaiti Red Crescent (a relief organization parallel to the Red Cross), Zawahiri visited mosques across the United States. In 33 cities he opened branches of an organization dedicated to supporting the new **jihad,** or holy war. One leader of the crusade was a tall, lanky Saudi radical named Osama bin Laden.

The New Immigration

The Immigration Act of 1965 (see page 873) altered the face of American life. The law-makers who passed the act did not expect such far-reaching consequences, because they assumed that Europeans would continue to predominate among newcomers. Yet reform of the old quota system opened the way for a wave of immigrants unequaled since the beginning of the century.

Turmoil abroad pushed many immigrants toward the United States, beginning in the 1960s with Fidel Castro's revolution in Cuba and unrest in the Dominican Republic. The war in Vietnam and its aftermath produced more than 500,000 refugees in the 15 years after 1975. Revolutionary conflicts in Central America during the 1980s launched new streams. Yet economic factors played as great a role as the terrors of war. Although some Filipinos fled the repressive regime of Ferdinand Marcos, many more came to the United States in a more straightforward search for economic prosperity. When Mexico suffered an economic downturn in the 1980s, emigration there rose sharply.

In all, about 13 million immigrants arrived in the United States between 1990 and 2005. The nation's foreign-born population rose to 11.7 percent, the highest proportion since World War II. In the 1990s, the Latino population increased by over 35 percent to about 30.3 mil-lion. The Asian American population grew at an even faster rate, to about 10.8 million. Through the decade a steadily expanding economy made immigrants a welcome source of new labor. Prosper-ity, in turn, reduced—though it did not eliminate—conflict among long-standing residents, new immigrants, and people on the mar-gin of the labor market.

Economic and Political Causes of Immigration

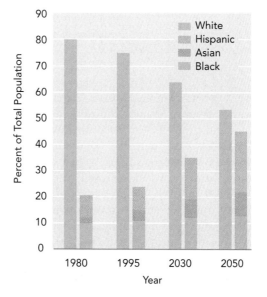

Projected Population Shifts, 1980–2050 *The 6.5 million immigrants who arrived between 1990 and 1998 accounted for 32 percent of the increase in the total U.S. population. Census figures project an increasing racial and ethnic diversity. White population is projected to drop from 80 percent in 1980 to about 53 percent in 2050, with the nation's Latino population rising most sharply.*

The New Look of America—Asian Americans

In 1970, 96 percent of Asian Americans were Japanese, Chinese, or Filipino. By the year 2000, those same three groups constituted only about half of all Asian Americans. As the diversity of Asian immigration increased, Asian Indians, Koreans, and Vietnamese came to outnumber Japanese Americans. The newcomers also varied dramatically in economic background, crowding both ends of the economic spectrum.

The higher end included many Chinese students who, beginning in the 1960s, sought out the United States for a college education, then found a job and stayed, even-tually bringing in their families. "My brother-in-law left his wife in Taiwan and came here as a student to get his Ph.D. in engineering," explained Subi Lin Felipe. "After he received his degree, he got a job in San Jose. Then he brought in a sister and his wife, who brought over one of her brothers and me. And my brother's wife then came." Asian Indians were even more acculturated upon arrival because about two-thirds entered the United States speaking English and with college degrees already in hand. Indian engi-neers played a vital role in the computer and software industries. Similarly, Korean and Filipino professionals took skilled jobs, particularly in medical fields.

Prosperous Newcomers

Yet Asian immigrants also included those on the lower rungs of the economic ladder. Among the new wave of Chinese immigrants, or *San Yi Man,* many blue-collar

Blue-Collar Asians

The Hmong people from Cambodia were among the many refugees fleeing Southeast Asia in the wake of the Vietnam War. While Chue and Nhia Thao Cha stayed in a refugee camp in Thailand, they stitched a traditional Hmong story cloth that, in this detail, shows refugees boarding a plane to come to the United States.

workers settled in the nation's Chinatowns, where they worked in restaurants or sewed in sweatshops. Without education and language skills, often in debt to labor contractors, most remained trapped in Chinatown's ethnic economy. Refugees from war and revolution in Southeast Asia often made harrowing journeys. Vietnamese families crowded into barely seaworthy boats, sometimes only to be terrorized by pirates, other times nearly drowned in storms before reaching poorly equipped Thai refugee camps. By 1990 almost a million refugees had arrived in the United States, three-quarters of them from Vietnam, most of the others from Laos or Cambodia. Thus the profile of Asian immigration resembled an hourglass, with the most newcomers either relatively affluent or extremely poor. Even so, such statistics could be misleading. More than half of all Asian American families lived in just five metropolitan areas—Honolulu, Los Angeles, San Francisco, Chicago, and New York—where the cost of living ranked among the nation's highest. High prices meant real earnings were lower. Within professions like dentistry, nursing, and health technology where Asians found work, they often held lower-paying positions. Those Asians who worked in sales were more often retail clerks than insurance agents or stockbrokers.

Asian Downward Mobility   Finally, Asian Americans experienced two forms of downward mobility. First, highly educated Asian immigrants often found it difficult or impossible to land jobs in their professions. To American observers, Korean shopkeepers seemed examples of success, when in fact such owners often enough had been former professionals forced into the risky small-business world. One Filipino doctor noted that strict state licensing standards prevented him from opening up his own medical practice. Instead, he found himself working as a restaurant meat cutter for employers who had no idea about his medical background. "They thought I was very good at separating meat from the bone," he commented ironically. Second, schools reported significant numbers of Asian American students who were failing. This "lost generation" were most often the children of families who entered the United States with little education and few job skills.

The New Look of America—Latinos

Like Asian Americans, Latinos in the United States constituted a diverse mosaic, reflecting dozens of immigrant streams. Although the groups shared a language, they usually settled in distinct urban and suburban barrios across the United States. Such enclave communities provided support to newcomers and an economic foothold for newly established businesses. Money circulated within a community; the workers and owners of an ethnic grocery, for example, spent their wages at neighboring stores, whose profits fueled other immigrant businesses in a chain reaction.

Washington Heights, at the northern tip of New York City, followed that path as nearly a quarter of a million Dominicans settled there during the 1970s and 1980s. A hundred blocks to the south, Manhattan's downtown skyscrapers seemed distant; shopkeepers' stereos along the major thoroughfares boomed music of trumpets and congas, while peddlers pushed heavily loaded shopping carts through busy streets, crying "¡A peso! ¡A peso!" ("For a dollar!"). In addition, Dominican social clubs planned dances or hosted political discussions. Sports clubs competed actively. Similarly, in Miami and elsewhere in South Florida, Cuban Americans created their own self-sustaining enclaves. A large professional class and strong community leadership brought them prosperity and political influence.

The Dominicans of Washington Heights

Along the West Coast, Los Angeles was the urban magnet for many Latino (and Asian) immigrants. Mexican immigrants had long flocked to East Los Angeles, which in the 1990s continued to allow access to the jobs in factories, warehouses, and railroad yards across the river. Many Mexican Americans now owned their own businesses and homes. But beginning in the mid-1980s and 1990s the neighborhood of MacArthur Park became the focal point for the newest immigrants from Mexico and Central America. MacArthur Park was less developed as a community, and many of its residents were transient, passing quickly to other neighborhoods or jobs.

East Los Angeles

As more factories and service industries became decentralized, locating themselves beyond urban downtowns, the barrios followed as well. Las Americas near Houston, where Juan Chanax lived, was one example; but suburban barrios could be found dotted all across the nation, from Rockville, Maryland, to Pacoima, California, near Burbank. Pacoima's well-kept bungalows housed working-class Mexican Americans who had lived in California for decades. But the front lawns of many residences were often paved over to hold the cars of additional workers or families, and the garages were converted to dormitories with a sink and toilet, where four or five newcomers from Central America could rent a spot to lay a bedroll on the cement floor.

Illegal Immigration

Because Mexico and the United States share such a long common border—and an equally long history of intermingling of peoples and cultures—many Mexicans entered the United States illegally. But the number of illegal immigrants increased during the 1980s as Central Americans joined the northward flow, along with Mexicans escaping a sharp economic downturn in their own country. By 1985, the number of illegal immigrants in the United States was estimated at anywhere from 2 to 12 million.

Congress attempted to stem that flow by passing the Immigration and Control Act of 1986. Tightened border security was coupled with a new requirement that American employers bear the responsibility of certifying their workers as legal residents of the United States. At the same time, those illegal immigrants who had arrived before 1986 were granted amnesty and allowed to become legal residents. In the end, however, the terms of the law failed to create the clean slate Congress had hoped for. California's fruit and vegetable growers, who worried that they would not have enough laborers under the new rules, lobbied for exceptions to the rules, which allowed over 1.7 million additional illegal immigrants to gain amnesty. Furthermore, the many immigrants who suddenly became legal under the terms of the law quickly sought to reunite their families, bringing in wives and children illegally. Thus legal immigrants continued to be intertwined with illegals in a host of different ways: as relatives helping loved ones make the transition to living in the United States, as landlords boarding newcomers until they could get on their feet, as links with communities in the home country—just as Juan Chanax continued to be after he received amnesty from the act in 1986.

Immigration and Control Act of 1986

For Americans who traveled by car in the 1950s, the end of the day meant a stop at a motel. These motels were mostly mom-and-pop businesses in rural towns or along highways into the nation's cities. Because the motel industry had no standards, a motorist never knew what to expect. A flashy sign might lure the unsuspecting tourist into a rattrap. Still, the majority provided clean sheets, a decent bed, and a hot shower at an affordable price.

In the 1960s, the newly completed interstate highway system brought drivers to major exchanges. There, large chains like Ramada, Sheraton, and Holiday Inn were ready to provide travelers with accommodations that were familiar whether they were in California or Maine. Holiday Inn's slogan was "At Holiday Inn the best surprise is no surprise." The rise of the major motel chains spelled financial disaster for the mom-and-pop operations, which were often built in older, less desirable locations that by the 1970s were showing signs of decay.

For reasons that remain far from clear, immigrants from India began to go into the lodging business. One Indian motel

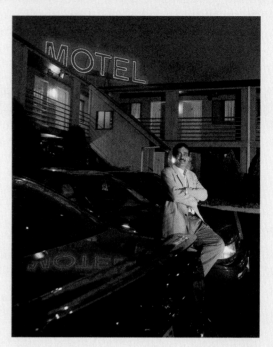

Dinu Patel, the owner of a motel in Branford, Connecticut. By 1999 a little over 50 percent of all American non-chain motels were owned by people of Indian origin.

Links with the Home Country

Because systems of communication and transportation drew the world closer, the new immigrants found it easier to maintain links with their points of origin and wire money back to relatives. Pacoima, the suburban barrio outside Burbank, California, boasted only a small town center. But along that half-mile stretch, 13 different currency exchanges were open for business to handle immigrant funds. By 1992, the amount of funds sent worldwide was so great that it was surpassed in volume only by the currency flows of the global oil trade.

And not just money traveled these routes. An immigrant entering La Curaçao, a furniture store in Los Angeles's MacArthur Park, could sign up to buy a bedroom suite on the installment plan. When the payments were completed, the furniture was released—not in Los Angeles but at a branch warehouse in El Salvador, where relatives could pick up the purchase. Cultural ties remained strong as well. Young Mexican immigrants flocked on Saturday night to popular dance halls such as the Lido in Los Angeles to hear a variety of music known as *banda*. Women wore tight tank tops and jeans or skirts, while the men's cowboy outfits were distinguished by their *cuarta*, a small riding whip at the belt, and by a kerchief hanging from the right hip pocket, with the name of the wearer's native Mexican state embroidered proudly for all to see.

Banda Music

Religious Diversity

The global nature of the new immigration also reshaped the religious faiths of America. During the 1950s, most Americans' sense of religious diversity encompassed the mainline Protestant churches, Roman Catholicism, and Judaism. But immigrants brought with them not only their own brands of Christianity and Judaism but also Buddhist, Hindu, and Islamic beliefs. By 2001 there were perhaps a million Buddhists and a owner cited an ancient Sanskrit phrase, *Atithi devo bhava*—the guest is God. "Hospitality is in our culture," he concluded. But there were other reasons, more practical. After the Immigration Reform Act of 1965 Indians, along with other Asians, came to the United States in large numbers. Newcomers of modest means saw motels as an attractive opportunity. Because many of the new Indians were professionals who did not "like working for other people," as one owner recalled, motels supplied an independent business. They also provided housing without the need to tie up capital in a home. Prejudice played a role too. More affluent Indians who approached the large chains learned quickly that "the big brands didn't really want us."

By the mid-1980s Indians owned 50 percent of all the nonchain motels in the country. A closer look at the motel phenomenon makes the story a bit less unusual. Sociologists have defined such occupational clustering as a "nonlinear ethnic niche." After the early pioneers from a group discover the opportunities in a particular enterprise or profession, they attract fellow ethnics to it. What Indians did with motels, Arabs in greater Detroit did with gas stations, Koreans with groceries, and Vietnamese in Los Angeles with fingernail salons.

Once an ethnic group achieved dominance in a niche, other groups found it difficult to move in. Indians kept close track of any motel properties that came up for sale. Hotel brokers, in turn, learned that they were among the most reliable prospects. "If it's a motel with less than 60 rooms," one broker commented, "the likely buyers will be Indians 98 times out of 100. And why not? They run them better than anyone else." All that was needed, one owner recalled, was financing, which relatives and other Indians generally provided, and "the will to work long hours."

By the late 1990s Indian motels employed over 800,000 people and had property valued at close to $40 billion. In fact, Indians provided 37 percent of all the hotel rooms in America. Twenty five years ago, "the hotel establishment . . . didn't want to know about us," one owner remarked. "But now we are the establishment."

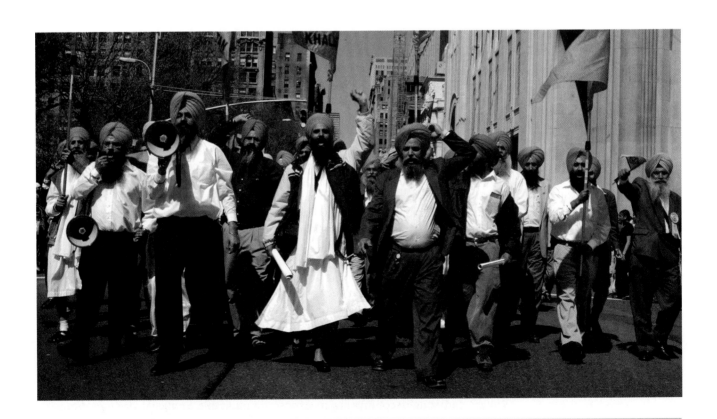

Sikhs—seen marching here in the New York City annual Sikh Day Parade in 2003—trace their origins to India's Punjab region. Because the men generally wear turbans and beards, Americans and other westerners often mistake them for Arabs.

million Hindus living in the United States and anywhere from 2 to 6 million Muslims. (Precise figures are difficult to obtain.) The largest number of Muslims came from Pakistan and South Asia, but close to a million were from the Arab world, especially Lebanon, Egypt, and Syria. Mosques became common around New York, Los Angeles, and Detroit.

Mainline Protestants and Catholics changed as well. The Presbyterian Church (U.S.A.) increased its Korean-speaking congregations from about 20 in 1970 to over 350. In New York City, Episcopalian services were held in 14 different languages. And Catholic churches increasingly found themselves celebrating mass in both English and Spanish. Such arrangements took place not only in urban congregations such as the Church of the Nativity in South Central Los Angeles (where Latinos alternated services with African Americans) but increasingly even in rural areas like Columbus Junction, Iowa, whose Catholic church was energized by Mexican Americans working in a nearby meat-processing plant.

The Clinton Presidency: Managing a New Global Order

In 1993 William Jefferson Clinton became the first baby boomer to occupy the White House. His wife, Hillary Rodham Clinton, would be the most politically involved presidential wife since Eleanor Roosevelt. Like so many couples of their generation, the Clintons were a two-career family. Both trained as lawyers at Yale University during the tumultuous 1960s. Bill chose politics as his career, while Hillary mixed private practice with public service. Their marriage had not been easy. Revelations of Clinton's sexual affairs as governor of Arkansas almost ruined his campaign for the presidency. The first couple seemed, however, more intent on making public policy than in defending their private lives.

Meeting President John Kennedy had inspired Clinton to enter politics. Like Kennedy, Clinton envisioned himself as an activist president, not a detached leader like Reagan. But Clinton's desire for major legislative initiatives ran up against the election results of 1992. He had received just 43 percent of the popular vote, while the Republicans had narrowed the Democratic majorities in Congress. Still, Clinton believed that an activist executive could achieve much. He pledged to revive the economy and rein in the federal deficit that had grown so enormously during the Reagan years. Beyond that, he called for systematic reform of the welfare and health care systems.

As one of his first presidential acts, the new president attempted to eliminate a rule that banned homosexuals from serving in the military, fulfilling a campaign pledge to the gay community. Resistance from conservatives and the military led Clinton to *Don't Ask; Don't Tell* accept a compromise position satisfactory to no one: "Don't ask; don't tell." As long as gay soldiers kept their sexual orientation private, they could serve their country.

Such early missteps could be set down partly to the stumbles of a newcomer learning his way around the office. But larger issues of character could not be dismissed. One observer shrewdly noted that there were two Bill Clintons—the idealistic young man from Hope, Arkansas (his hometown), and the boy from Hot Springs (his mother's home). The latter was a resort town associated with the seamier side of Arkansas high life. With increasing frequency, the leadership mustered by the idealistic politician from Hope seemed to be undermined by the character flaws of the boy from Hot Springs.

Although Clinton's conservative opponents disliked his politics, it was the president's moral lapses that they most deeply resented. Critics nicknamed him "Slick Willie" and sought continually to expose discreditable or illegal dealings from his past. Accusations were published that, when Clinton was governor in the early 1980s, both he and his wife had received special treatment from a failed real estate venture *Whitewater* known as Whitewater. An air of mystery deepened when Vince Foster, a White House adviser and close friend of Hillary Clinton's from Arkansas, committed suicide. (The Clintons' most vocal critics suggested that the verdict of suicide was merely a murder cover-up, although the best evidence suggested depression as a cause.) Rumors also abounded about Clinton's womanizing, fanned in 1994 when a former Arkansas state employee, Paula Jones, filed a sexual harassment suit against the president. Under pressure from congressional conservatives, Attorney General Janet Reno appointed former judge Kenneth Starr as a special prosecutor to investigate Whitewater. But during Clinton's first term, investigations by Starr as well as two Senate committees produced no evidence that the Clintons had acted illegally.

The New World Disorder

Determined to focus on domestic issues, Clinton hoped to pay less attention to foreign affairs. He discovered that the "new world order," hailed by both Mikhail Gorbachev and George Bush, seemed more like a world of regional disorders. The United States depended heavily on Russian president Boris Yeltsin to bring order out of chaos, yet market reforms failed to revive Russia's stagnant economy. Elsewhere in the world, rampant ethnic and nationalist movements provoked a number of regional crises. By using American power in a limited way, Clinton gained considerable public support.

Boris Yeltsin

In sub-Saharan Africa, corruption and one-party rule severely weakened most economies, tribal violence mounted, and AIDS became epidemic. Brutal civil wars broke out in both Somalia and Rwanda. As a presidential candidate, Clinton had supported President Bush's decision in December 1992 to send troops to aid famine-relief efforts in Somalia. But attempts to install a stable government proved difficult. Tragically, the United States as well as European nations failed to intervene in Rwanda before over a million people were massacred in 1994. By contrast, the United States joined a multinational effort in Haiti in 1994 that sustained an uneasy peace.

Yugoslavian Turmoil

Europe's most intractable trouble spot proved to be Yugoslavia, a nation divided by ethnic rivalries between Serbs and Croats within a number of provinces, including Serbia, Croatia, and Bosnia. After Bosnia became independent in 1992 both sides, but especially the Serbs, resorted to what was euphemistically referred to as "ethnic cleansing"—the massacre of

Conflicts in Bosnia and Croatia

rival populations—to secure control. Serbs even set up rape camps where they brutalized Muslim women. The United States initially viewed the civil war in Yugoslavia as Europe's problem. But as the civilian death toll mounted to a quarter of a million, Nobel Peace Prize winner and Holocaust survivor Elie Wiesel beseeched President Clinton, "Stop the bloodshed. . . . Something, anything, must be done." Still, the ghosts of Vietnam loomed. Many members of Congress feared the prospect of American troops bogged down in a distant civil war. By 1995 Clinton had committed the United States to support NATO bombing of Serb forces,

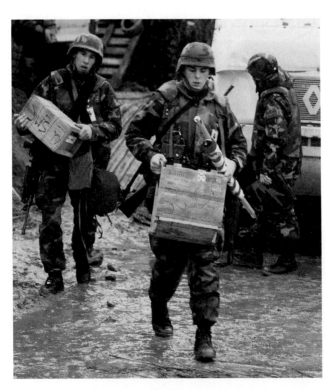

American troops were part of the NATO peacekeeping force sent to Bosnia after the Dayton Accords of 1995. These marines were among the first arrivals, who encountered chilly, wet weather.

and when Bosnian and Croatian forces began to win back territory, the Serbs agreed to peace talks at a meeting in Dayton, Ohio. The Dayton Accords created separate Croatian, Bosnian, and Serbian nations. Some 60,000 NATO troops, including 20,000 Americans, moved into Bosnia to enforce the peace.

Dayton Accords

Intervention in Kosovo

Having lost Croatia and Bosnia, Serbia was determined not to lose Kosovo, a province in which the Serb minority ruled over a mostly Albanian population. In fighting Albanian rebels Serbian police and militia groups committed widespread atrocities against civilians. Hundreds of thousands of Albanian refugees poured into the surrounding countries. In the spring of 1999 Clinton committed U.S. forces to a NATO bombing campaign that forced Serbia to agree to a NATO occupation of Kosovo. Once again, American troops entered as peacekeepers.

Middle East Peace

Steps forward in Haiti and the Balkans could not quiet fears of a new Middle East crisis. Sporadic protests and rioting by Palestinians in the Israeli-occupied territories of Gaza and the West Bank gave way in the 1990s to negotiations. At a ceremony hosted by President Clinton in 1993, Palestinian leader Yasir Arafat and Israeli prime minister Itzak Rabin signed a peace agreement permitting self-rule for Palestinians in the Gaza Strip and in Jericho on the West Bank. In 1995 Arafat became head of the West Bank Palestinian National Authority.

Middle East Peace Negotiations

Still, a full settlement remained elusive. As Clinton pursued negotiations, he found he had limited leverage to broker a lasting peace. The assassination of Prime Minister Rabin in 1995, by an angry Orthodox Jew, began a period of increased suspicion on both sides as extremists sought to derail the peace process. Clinton engaged in two marathon negotiating sessions with the two sides, in 1998 and in 2000 at Camp David, in hopes of hammering out an agreement that would allow for a separate Palestinian state alongside Israel. But the negotiations ended without agreement, and positions on both sides hardened. Whether in the Middle East, Eastern Europe, Africa, or the Caribbean, such regional crises demonstrated that a new global "world order" would be difficult to maintain.

The Clinton Presidency on Trial

Throughout Clinton's presidency the nation experienced a powerful economic expansion. Despite low unemployment, there was little inflation. Prosperity allowed the president to eliminate the budget deficits that had soared during the 1980s. But increased government revenues did not persuade Congress to support Clinton's reform agenda.

Recovery without Reform

Clinton Program

In his first speech to Congress, Clinton proposed a program that began reducing the deficit as well as providing investments to stimulate the economy and repair the nation's decaying public infrastructure. In contrast, Presidents Reagan and Bush had cut funds to rebuild schools, roads, dams, bridges, and other public structures. In August 1993 a compromise budget bill passed by only a single vote in the Senate, with Republicans blocking the stimulus portion of Clinton's program. Still, deficit reduction was a significant achievement.

NAFTA

The victory in the budget battle gave Clinton momentum. In the fall he hammered together a bipartisan coalition to pass NAFTA, the North American Free Trade Agreement. With the promise of greater trade and more jobs, the pact linked the United States economy more closely with those of Canada and Mexico. The president also helped supporters of gun control overcome the powerful opposition of the National Rifle Association to pass the Brady Bill, which required a five-day waiting period on gun purchases.

President Clinton's most ambitious attempt at reform was to overhaul the nation's health care system to provide all Americans with basic health care (along with a card to guarantee it). But medical interest groups defeated the proposal, arguing it would create yet another huge and inefficient bureaucracy. In 1996 Congress passed a more modest medical reform bill that made it easier for workers to retain health insurance if they lost or changed jobs.

Health care reform topped Clinton's legislative agenda. A task force led by Hillary Clinton developed a plan to provide health coverage for all Americans, including the 37 million who in 1994 remained uninsured. The plan rejected a more sweeping single-payer system, in which the government would act as the central agency reimbursing medical expenses. At the same time, it proposed more far-reaching changes than did a Republican plan merely to reform insurance laws in order to make private medical coverage more readily available. But a host of interest groups attacked the proposal, especially small businesses that worried they would bear the brunt of the system's financing. Even a compromise bill lacked the votes needed to win approval.

Health Care Reform

If the Clintons' plan had passed, the president and the Democratic majority in Congress might have staked their claim to a government that was actively responding to some of the long-term problems facing American society. But the failure of health care reform heightened the perception of an ill-organized administration and an entrenched Congress content with the status quo. Republicans, sensing the level of public frustration, stepped up their opposition to other Democratic legislation. The 1994 midterm elections confirmed the public's anger over political gridlock, as Republicans captured majorities in both the House and the Senate.

The Conservative Revolution Revived

The combative new Speaker of the House, Newt Gingrich of Georgia, proclaimed himself a "genuine revolutionary" and vowed to complete what Ronald Reagan had begun. Gingrich used the first hundred days of the new Congress to bring to a vote ten proposals from his campaign document "The Contract with America." The contract proposed a balanced budget amendment, tax cuts, and term limits for all members of Congress. To promote family values, its anticrime package included a broader death penalty and welfare restrictions aimed at reducing teen pregnancy. Although the term limits proposal did not survive, the other nine proposals were passed by the House.

The Contract with America

The whirlwind performance was impressive. "When you look back five years from now," enthused Republican governor Tommy Thompson of Wisconsin, "you're going to say 'they came, they, saw, they conquered.'" But the Senate was less eager to enact the House proposals. And as Republicans assembled a more comprehensive budget, it became clear that the public was increasingly worried about the Gingrich revolution.

"I am a genuine revolutionary," House Speaker Newt Gingrich proclaimed, and the newly elected Republican freshmen in Congress led the charge to complete the Reagan revolution. By clothing Newt's followers as stiff-armed, flag-waving militarists, illustrator Anita Kunz recalls Mussolini's overzealous Brown Shirts. Enough of the public agreed, forcing the Republicans to backpedal.

Fiscally, the Republicans set out to balance the federal budget by scaling back Medicare expenditures and allowing Medicare premiums to double. Republicans also sought reduced protection for endangered species, relaxed pollution controls set up by the Clean Water Act, and gave mining, ranching, and logging interests greater freedom to develop public lands.

Government Shutdown

When President Clinton threatened to veto the Republican budget, Republicans twice forced the federal government to shut down. The result was a disaster for the self-proclaimed revolutionaries. Most of the public viewed their stance as intransigent, and the Congress was forced to back down. At the same time, President Clinton moved steadily to preempt the Republican agenda. By 1995, he was proposing his own route toward a balanced budget by 2002. Similarly, in 1996 the president signed into law a sweeping reform of welfare. For the first time in 60 years, the social welfare policies of the liberal democratic state were being substantially reversed. The bill ended guarantees of federal aid to poor children, turning over such programs to the states. Food stamp spending was cut, and the law placed a five-year limit on payments to any family. Most adults receiving payments were required to find work within two years.

Welfare Reform

Thus as the election of 1996 approached, the Republican revolution had been either dampened or co-opted by the president. The Republicans nominated former senator Bob Dole, a party loyalist, to run for president. But with the economy robust, Bill Clinton became the first Democrat since Franklin Roosevelt to win a second term in the White House.

Women's Issues in the Clinton Years

"Building up women does not diminish men," Bill Clinton had insisted during the 1992 election campaign. In that spirit he appointed Ruth Bader Ginsburg to the Supreme Court and three women to his Cabinet, including Janet Reno as his attorney general. Giving his wife Hillary Clinton a prominent role in the administration also underscored Clinton's interest in advancing the goals of feminists.

Both Clintons supported a woman's right to control decisions on reproduction, on which conservatives challenged them. With the Supreme Court still unwilling to overturn *Roe v. Wade,* prolife advocates sought to limit the decision's application as much as possible. They proposed to make illegal a late-term procedure known as "partial birth" abortion. Doctors seldom performed the procedure and did so only to save a mother's life. Twice President Clinton vetoed bills that would criminalize the procedure.

UAW v. Johnson Controls

More problematic for feminists was the legacy of the Supreme Court decision in the 1991 case of *UAW v. Johnson Controls.* Since *Muller v. Oregon* in 1908 (see page 636), the Court had declared laws constitutional that gave women special protection based on their biological differences from men. Using this standard, Johnson Controls had established a policy of not hiring women workers to manufacture batteries, because the lead fumes in the workplace might damage a pregnant woman's unborn fetus. The workers' union challenged the policy, noting that fertile men who faced reproductive risks in the workplace were not restricted. The Court agreed with the union, ruling that the emphasis on biological differences denied women an "equal employment opportunity." Justice Harry Blackmun wrote that a woman's decision as to whether her "reproductive role is more important to herself and her family than her economic role" was one she could make on her own.

Many feminists hailed the decision as a step toward workplace equality. Others saw it as more ambiguous. Should laws recognize biological difference, or should they uphold equality? Was it "equal treatment" to order women into a workplace that had been designed by and for men, with little regard for safety standards or a woman's health? Feminists continued to debate how to balance gender neutrality with gender justice. "For some, feminism necessarily means the promotion of equality between men and women," historian Elizabeth Fox Genovese wrote. "For others, it just as necessarily means the celebration of differences between women and men." *Contrasting Views of Feminism*

Scandal

Almost every two-term president has faced some crisis in his second term. Franklin Roosevelt upended a hornet's nest with his plan to pack the Supreme Court. Watergate brought down Richard Nixon, whereas the Iran-Contra controversy tarnished Reagan. Bill Clinton's scandal was more personal, yet it confronted him with the American political system's ultimate sanction: impeachment, conviction, and removal from office.

Four years into the Whitewater investigation, Special Prosecutor Kenneth Starr had spent $30 million and produced only the convictions of several of the president's former business partners. (The Watergate investigation during the Nixon years, in contrast, lasted only about two years.) Starr dismissed the grand jury in Arkansas without filing charges against either of the Clintons on Whitewater. Then in January 1998, Starr hit what looked like the jackpot. A disgruntled federal employee with links to the Bush administration, produced audiotapes of phone conversations in which a 21-year-old White House intern, Monica Lewinsky, talked of an intimate relationship with the president. *The Lewinsky Affair*

Starr succeeded in preventing Clinton from learning of the tapes before the president and Lewinsky testified in depositions that they had not had "sexual relations." When word of the tapes leaked out several days later, the news media predicted ominously that the president must resign or face **impeachment**—if not for his personal conduct, at the very least for lying under oath. That summer Starr subpoenaed the president to appear before a Washington grand jury. Four hours of testimony was taken on videotape, and in September Starr recommended that the president be impeached on the grounds of perjury, obstruction of justice, and witness tampering.

To the astonishment of the news media, the public did not support Republican calls for impeachment. Although Clinton had clearly engaged in behavior most Americans found inappropriate or even repugnant, they seemed to draw a line between public and private actions. Furthermore, Starr's report went into such lurid detail that many questioned the special prosecutor's motives. Nonetheless, along strict party lines, a majority in the House voted three articles of impeachment for lying to the grand jury, suborning perjury, and orchestrating a cover-up. In January 1999 the matter went to the Senate for trial. *Impeachment*

Unlike the Watergate scandals, in which Richard Nixon resigned because a bipartisan consensus determined that impeachment was necessary, the accusers and defenders of Bill Clinton divided along strongly partisan lines. The Senate voted to acquit, with five Republicans joining all 45 Senate Democrats in the decision. *Acquittal*

The Politics of Surplus

The impeachment controversy left the president weakened, but hardly powerless. Throughout the political tempest the nation's economy had continued to grow. By 1999 the rate of unemployment had dropped to 4.1 percent, the lowest in nearly 30 years, while the stock market reached new highs. Furthermore, as the economy expanded, federal tax receipts grew with it. By 1998 Bill Clinton faced a situation that would have seemed improbable a few years previous—a budget surplus. By balancing the budget the president had appropriated a key Republican issue. Political debate shifted to what to do with the surplus.

Social Security Crisis

Clinton sought to revive much of his initial agenda: aiding education, paying down the national debt, and protecting Social Security and Medicare funds from predicted future deficits. The deficits seemed sure to arise because an entire generation of graying baby boomers was heading toward retirement beginning around the year 2010. During the 1990s six workers paid taxes for each retiree collecting benefits; by around 2030, only three workers would be paying taxes for each person collecting benefits. That ratio threatened fiscal disaster. Clinton thus argued that the budget surplus could best be used to ensure the solvency of Social Security and Medicare.

Hanging By a Chad: The Election of 2000

No shortage of issues faced voters in the 2000 presidential election. Budget surpluses, social security reform, and tax cuts topped the list. Vice President Al Gore, running for the Democrats, had served in Vietnam and the Senate, written a book on the global environmental crisis, supported the development of the Internet, and was especially active as vice president. Despite these strengths, he often seemed awkward campaigning for the presidency.

By contrast, the affable Texas governor George W. Bush (son of the 41st president) had little interest in world affairs. He once asked a Saudi diplomat why people expected him to know so much about a puny country such as North Korea. "I don't have the foggiest idea about what I think about international, foreign policy," he confessed. Bush's previous record in business was mixed at best, and as governor he served in a state where the office holder wielded little power. But Bush made character the central issue of his campaign—not his or Gore's, but Bill Clinton's. By making Clinton the issue, Bush deprived Gore of a vital campaign asset, because the president remained popular with voters.

Hanging Chads

The outcome of the election came down to just one state—Florida, where Bush led by just 300 votes. Nationwide, Gore had a 500,000 edge in the popular vote, but without Florida's 25 electoral votes neither candidate had a majority in the Electoral

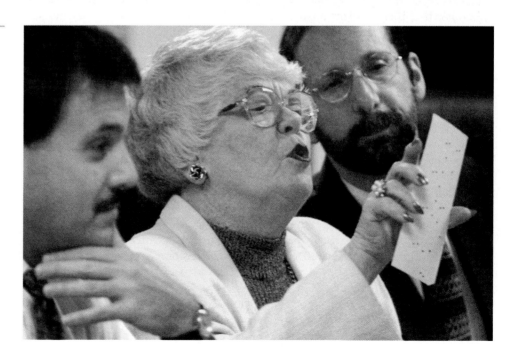

Election officials in Broward County, Florida, examine a ballot for chads, punched paper from holes, in the hotly contested presidential election of 2000.

College. Evidence immediately surfaced of widespread voting irregularities. Some Florida counties used ballots with complicated layouts that led voters to choose the wrong candidate. Other counties used punch-card machines so old that they routinely failed to perforate the ballot or left partial holes that popularly became known as "hanging chads." More serious were allegations that the state had actively suppressed voting in heavily black counties. Those accusations were especially troubling since George Bush's brother, Jeb, was Florida's governor.

Florida Punch Card Ballot

After weeks of legal wrangling, the Florida state supreme court granted a Democratic request that the contested votes could be manually recounted. When the Republicans appealed, the issue came before the United States Supreme Court. Normally, it left such decisions up to the state courts, because the Constitution gave the states control over election laws. But this Court, dominated by Reagan and Bush appointees, agreed to hear the case of *Bush v. Gore*. On December 12, 2000, the Court ruled 5-4 that the recount must end. The majority argued that because the recount applied to only three counties, it valued some votes more than others. Regardless of who had the better argument, in *Bush v. Gore,* the Supreme Court, not the American voters, made George W. Bush the 43rd president of the United States.

Bush v. Gore

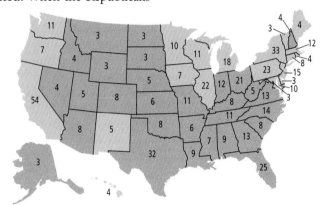

	Candidate (Party)	Electoral Vote (%)	Popular Vote (%)
	George W. Bush (Republican)	271 (50.4)	50,456,062 (47.9)
	Al Gore (Democrat)	266 (49.5)	50,996,582 (48.4)
	Ralph Nader (Green)	–	3,949,201 (3.8)

Election of 2000

The United States in a Networked World

In 1988 economist Lawrence Summers was working on the presidential campaign of Michael Dukakis. At a meeting in Chicago, the staff assigned him a car with a telephone. Summers was so impressed, he recalled, that "I used it to call my wife to tell her I was in a car with a phone." A decade later as deputy treasury secretary in the Clinton administration, he visited the Ivory Coast in Africa to help launch an American-supported health project. One village on his itinerary could be reached only by dugout canoe. As Summers stepped into the canoe for his return trip, an aide handed him a cell phone. "Washington has a question for you," the aide said. The same man who once marveled at a phone in his car in Chicago ten years later expected one in his dugout canoe in the interior of Africa.

The Internet Revolution

Like Lawrence Summers, most Americans by the beginning of the twenty-first century were linked to a global communications network. Computers, cell phones, BlackBerries, MP3 players, and other electronic devices provided almost instant contact with a wider world. Since the 1950s miniaturization of electronics through microchip technology had made that connectivity possible.

Although the Internet communications revolution gained global momentum only after 1995, its roots could be traced to the early 1960s. In 1962 J. C. R. Licklider of the Massachusetts Institute of Technology wrote a series of memos laying out the concept of what he grandly termed a "Galactic Network": computers all across the world connected in order to share data and programs. But the technology for sending data efficiently along phone lines was still primitive. Computer technicians cobbled together a network between four host computers in 1969. Known as the ARPANET, it allowed university and Department of Defense researchers to share computer capacity more efficiently as well as to create a communications system that could survive a nuclear attack. Managers discovered that many of the researchers with access to the network used it to send personal messages. E-mail had been born.

The Galactic Network and ARPANET

The Personal Computer

A second phase of the revolution began in the 1970s when entrepreneurs such as Steve Jobs and Bill Gates helped write software to operate personal computers (see page 941). At the same time, the Internet (successor to the ARPANET) was growing too. By 1985 it linked about 1,000 host computers. To help users connect, sites were given domain names instead of a faceless string of numbers. Taking the next step in the evolutionary process, British-born physicist Tim Berners-Lee wrote software that created the World Wide Web as a facet of the Internet. Berners-Lee saw the possibility for a universal system with access to anything that was information. He applied the hypertext link (**http://**) that allowed users to move freely from one site to sites of related interest, each with its own Web address, or URL (uniform resource locator).

The World Wide Web

Berners-Lee shared the democratic vision common among software programmers and Internet pioneers. They saw the Web as open and free to all. Users could communicate without restriction and find access to any form of information. Such openness was the bane of authoritarian governments, which found it difficult to control public opinion in a world in which information flowed freely. The unregulated format of the Web raised substantial legal, moral, and political questions in the United States as well. By 1999 five million Web sites were in operation—among them sites promoting pornography, hate speech, and even instructions on how to build atomic bombs. A number of politicians and civic groups called for the censorship of the more extreme Web content. Others argued that the greater danger lay in allowing the Internet to become dominated by large telecommunications companies. These advocates called for legislation protecting "Net neutrality."

E-Commerce

Business spending on technology jumped from 3 percent in the 1960s to 45 percent by the mid-1990s, fueled by the recognition that the Web's interconnectivity gave it enormous commercial potential. Businesses could now interact with their customers without respect to physical location or time zone. E-commerce practitioners began using the Internet to disseminate company or product information, generate leads, take orders, and build customer databases. Business-to-business sales went from $40 billion in 1998 to some $1.1 trillion by 2007, while retail sales approached $400 billion.

Equally impressive was the emergence of a new virtual culture. When people wanted to know where to find something on the Web, they had only to use the Google search engine. By 2006 Google was fast emerging as the site that would link browsers to all the possibilities of the Internet. And through Internet browsers and other software, individuals could chat, find a job, download music, and even locate potential mates.

Use of the Internet broadened sharply after 1995. As of 2000, the number of pieces of mail handled daily by the U.S. Postal Service was 668 million. The average number of e-mails sent daily was 10 billion. This graphic by Stephen G. Eick, of Bell Laboratories, plotted worldwide Internet traffic.

American Workers in a Two-Tiered Economy

The benefits of prosperity were not evenly distributed, however. Economists described the United States in the 1990s as a two-tiered labor market in which most increases in earning went to people at the top of the wage scale. Thus despite the computer revolution and the decade's prosperity, the median income of American families was barely higher in 1996 than in 1973. Indeed, the earnings of the average white male worker actually fell. Only because so many women entered the job market did the family standard of living remain the same. In the early 1970s some 37 percent of women worked outside the home; in 1999 about 57 percent did.

Education was a critical factor in determining winners in the computer economy. Families with college-educated parents were three times more likely to have home access to the Web than were those families in which parents' education ended with high school. Because average education levels were relatively lower among African Americans and Latinos (and relatively higher among Asian Americans), the computer divide took on a racial cast as well. But the implications went beyond mere access to the Web. More important, the high-wage sector of the computer economy required educated workers, and the demand for them drove up those workers' salaries.

In contrast, most semiskilled and unskilled workers saw little growth in earnings despite full employment. The choices facing the nation's half-million long-haul truck drivers was a case in point. Typically, drivers piloting these eighteen-wheel rigs—on the road for two to three weeks at a time—made as much as $35,000 a year in the mid-1990s, about the same as they had in the 1970s. The hours were long and the conditions grueling. But most truckers had no appealing alternative. The highest-paid unskilled workers in the United States averaged 2,000 hours per year at about $14 per hour, or $28,000 a year—an effective pay cut of $7,000. "So there [was] a lot of movement between companies," one executive observed, but few drivers were willing to quit. Unlike computer programmers or corporate executives who were in high demand, low-skill workers like the truckers were not able to increase their earnings simply by switching jobs. Some economists concluded that "the most important economic division is not between races, or genders, or economic sectors, but between the college-educated and the noncollege-educated."

The prosperity of the late 1990s produced an interesting dilemma. On the one hand, it eased many social tensions that had long divided the nation. Inner-city crime rates fell; the poor began to experience a marked improvement in their economic situation; consumer confidence reached an all-time high. But over the longer term, the boom's statistics were not encouraging. Despite the decline in the poverty rate, it remained above the rate for any year in the 1970s. If the strongest economy in 30 years left the poverty rate higher than during the inflation-plagued years of the 1970s, what would happen if the economy faltered?

Wage Stagnation

Multiculturalism and Contested American Identity

No state more fully represented the multicultural and global complexion of late-twentieth-century America than California. More of the nation's recently arrived immigrants from Asia, Central America, and Mexico settled there than in any other state. By 1990, fully 33 percent of the residents of Los Angeles County were foreign-born, a figure rivaling the high-water mark of 40 percent set by New York City in 1910. Predictably, then, it was California that so often led the national debate over multiculturalism.

African Americans and the Persistence of the Racial Divide

In the 1990s the highest-paid celebrity in the world was an African American—Michael Jordan. Oprah Winfrey, also an African American, was the highest-paid woman in America. Both political parties eyed former general Colin Powell as a possible presidential

The Los Angeles riots of 1992 revealed divisions in the city's multicultural communities of African Americans, Latinos, and Asian Americans.

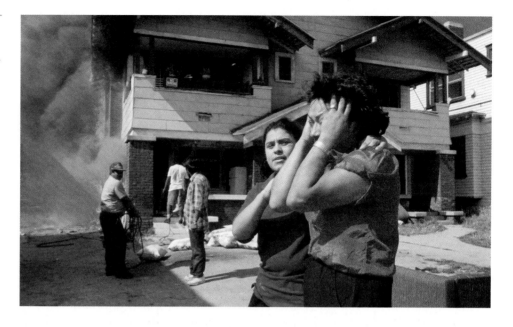

candidate. Although the situation of African Americans had improved vastly compared with their position in the 1950s, race still mattered—as the case of Rodney King, a black motorist, showed.

Rodney King and the Los Angeles Riots

In 1991 Los Angeles police arrested King for speeding and drunken driving. As he lay on the ground, the four white officers proceeded to beat him with nightsticks more than 50 times. When blacks complained about such brutality at the hands of largely white police, public officials often dismissed their complaints. This case was different. A man in a nearby apartment videotaped the beating, which the news media repeatedly broadcast to the entire nation. But the following year, an all-white suburban jury acquitted the officers, concluding that King had been threatening and that the officers had acted within their authority.

The verdict enraged the African American community in Los Angeles, where widespread riots erupted for three days, making the violence the worst civil disturbance in Los Angeles history. By the time police and the National Guard restored order, nearly 2,000 people had been injured, 40 people had died, over 4,500 fires burned, and $500 million of property had been looted, damaged, or destroyed.

Complexity of the Riots

At first glance the riot appeared to be much like the one that had decimated Watts, a poor area of Los Angeles, in 1965 (see pages 869–870). Poor African Americans had lashed out in frustration at white racism. In fact, the 1992 riots were multiracial in character, exposing divisions in Los Angeles's multicultural communities. Rioters, both black and Latino, damaged over 2,000 small groceries, liquor stores, and other businesses run by Korean American immigrants. African Americans also attacked Latinos; and after the first day, Latinos also joined in the disturbances. But there was a revealing pattern. In the more established Latino communities of East Los Angeles, where families had more to lose, residents remained quiet or worked actively to maintain the peace. In contrast, fires and looting destroyed many businesses in the MacArthur Park area, where the newest Latino immigrants lived. "Everybody said, 'How can they destroy their neighborhoods, their jobs . . . ?'" commented a Latino demographer from UCLA. "Well, my answer is that they did not consider it to be their own." Thus the 1992 riots exposed tension and competition among ethnic groups.

African Americans in a Full-Employment Economy

In 1966 the African American community of North Lawndale, on Chicago's West Side, was one of the worst slums in America. At the time, Martin Luther King Jr. rented an apartment there, hoping to draw attention to its plight. When he was assassinated two years later, rioters burned down much of the neighborhood. Over the next 20 years half the population moved away from the crime, drug addiction, and violent gangs.

By the late 1990s North Lawndale had undergone a rebirth. African American professionals had returned to the neighborhood. Homes that once stood deserted now sold for over $250,000. What happened in North Lawndale reflected new circumstances for many African Americans across the country during a decade of economic expansion. Home ownership reached 46 percent and employment increased from around 87 percent in 1980 to nearly 92 percent in 1998. African Americans in increasing numbers rose up the ladder in corporate America. Many started their own businesses. Test scores for reading and math proficiency also improved, and more African Americans, though fewer males, attended college.

Inner-City Renewal

Economic success brought new hope to the nation's inner cities. Crime and poverty decreased significantly, especially rates of murder and violence. Births to unwed mothers reached a postwar low. Fewer blacks lived below the poverty level and fewer were on welfare. The most hard-core block of the unemployed—males between 16 and 24—found many more jobs. The gap between wages for whites and blacks narrowed as well. Life expectancy increased substantially—from 63.8 years for African American males in 1980 to 66.1 in 1996 (compared with 70.7 and 73.8 for white males).

Yet many African Americans were reserved in their reaction to such statistics. "To the extent that you proclaim your success," one community leader remarked, "people forget about you." Furthermore, an economic downturn might reverse those gains, especially if employers resorted to the traditional practice of "last hired, first fired."

Civil rights leaders were most concerned about the continued assault on affirmative action. In 1996 California voters passed a ballot initiative, Proposition 209, that eliminated racial and gender preferences in hiring and college admissions. Ironically, the leading advocate for Proposition 209 was a conservative black leader, Ward Connerly. Connerly argued that racial preferences demeaned black and other minority students by setting up a double standard that patronizingly assumed minorities could not compete on an equal basis. In any case, Proposition 209 had a striking effect. Enrollments of Latinos and blacks at the elite California university campuses and professional schools dropped sharply: down 57 percent for black students at Berkeley and 34 percent for Latinos. What remained was a student body that was only 3 percent black and 9 percent Latino, in a state in which African Americans constituted 7 percent and Latinos 29 percent of the population. Major state universities in Washington, Texas, and Michigan also experienced declines after passing similar laws.

Proposition 209 Against Affirmative Action

Also in 1996 a federal circuit court had gone so far as to claim, in *Hopwood v. State of Texas et al.,* that race could not be used as a factor in college admissions. The Supreme Court did not fully address that issue until 2003, in the case of *Gratz v. Bollinger,* when the Bush administration pressed the Court to strike down the use of any racial preference in the admissions programs of the University of Michigan. Leading universities, retired military officers, and some corporate leaders supported Michigan's position. They argued that by encouraging diversity, affirmative action benefited their institutions. In deciding the case the justices did strike down a point system used by Michigan giving minorities preference in undergraduate admissions. However the Court approved, 5 to 4, a separate program used by the university's law school, which gave race some influence in the admissions process. Affirmative action had been reduced in scope but not abolished.

Global Pressures in a Multicultural America

Clearly the enormous changes wrought by immigration and the new global economy gave the United States a more multicultural flavor. Salsa rhythms became part of the pop-cultural mainstream, and Latino foods competed with Indian curries, Japanese sushi, and Thai takeout for the consumer dollars of two-career American families with little time to prepare a home-cooked meal. Baseball, the national pastime, became truly All-American as major league rosters filled with stars from the Dominican Republic, Mexico, Cuba, Panama, and Venezuela.

But the mix of cultures did not occur without friction. Throughout American history, the dominant culture has reacted defensively when immigrant flows increased from new sources or when jobs were hard to find. Following waves of Irish immigration, the Know-Nothings of the 1850s demanded, "Americans should rule America." In 1916 Madison Grant warned, in *The Passing of the Great Race,* that unrestricted immigration might lead to racial suicide. Soon after, nativists in Congress put in place tight new immigration restrictions. After reforming their immigration laws in the 1960s, Americans once again debated how diverse the United States could become without losing its traditional identity.

Proposition 187

Libertad by *Ester Hernandez*

In 1990, Lawrence Auster echoed Madison Grant, with *The Path to National Suicide,* in which he warned of the "browning of America." Four years later opponents of immigration in California put forward Proposition 187, a state ballot initiative that denied health, education, and welfare benefits to illegal aliens. Despite the opposition of most major religious, ethnic, and educational organizations, the measure passed with a lopsided 59 percent majority. In the end, however, Proposition 187 never went into effect because a federal judge ruled unconstitutional the provision denying education to the children of illegal aliens.

A movement to make English the official language of the United States received even broader support. While willing to grant that speaking a native tongue was acceptable in the privacy of the home, one leader of the English-only movement declared, "English is the 'glue' that helps keep American culture vibrant and dynamic." In 1986, 73 percent of Californians voted to make English the state's official language. Similarly, as a new wave of Cuban immigrants flooded southern Florida during the 1980s, voters of Dade County adopted an initiative making English the county's official language. In 1993 Florida voters approved an English-only referendum for the state. By 1996 23 states had adopted either resolutions or laws declaring English their official language.

Traditionally, nativist conflicts pit the dominant majority culture against the minority cultures of more recent arrivals. But in a multicultural society, such polar opposites often break down. In 1998 yet another ballot initiative passed in California (Proposition 227), mandating that schools phase out all their bilingual education programs. Students would be granted only one year of English-language immersion courses before receiving all instruction in English. In this instance both white and Latino voters approved the proposition by nearly the same margin, within one or two points of 62 percent. And the measure itself had been proposed after a group of Spanish-speaking parents boycotted their elementary school until it agreed to teach their children to read and write in English.

In 2006, immigration and especially the status of the approximately 11 million illegal aliens became a hotly debated issue. On the one hand, immigrant groups organized a day of marches and demonstrations in major cities across the country, proclaiming their loyalty to the United States and asking Congress to make it possible for them to become citizens. On the other hand, advocates of a more restrictive policy insisted that illegal immigration imposed a heavy burden on wages and government services. Since aliens earned less than natives, these workers were also more likely to need means-tested government benefits such as Medicaid and food stamps. Thirty-one percent of Mexican households received some form of public assistance in 1999, compared with only 17 percent of non-Mexican immigrants and 14 percent of natives.

The debate revealed a split particularly among Republicans. President Bush and many in the business community hoped to keep open the flow of low-wage labor and supported a guest worker program along with a plan to legalize the status of millions of illegal aliens. Other Republicans, especially in states with high immigrant populations, campaigned to close the borders and oust those who had entered the country illegally. All the two camps could agree on was a plan to build a 700-mile fence along the Mexican border. (In the end, though, Congress did not appropriate money to build it.) Hispanics voiced their displeasure in the 2006 elections. Some 70 percent of them voted for Democrats who tended to side with the president on the immigration debate.

The question of how the United States will manage its borders remains unresolved. Even the idea of a "nation" takes on new meaning in a global economy in which jobs, people, and goods move wherever markets for them exist. As the communications superhighway speeds information to all corners of the globe and international migrations bring new people to America's shores, the American political system will continue to evolve ways of encompassing a diversity that now reflects the entire world.

Terrorism in a Global Age

Along the northeast coast of the United States September 11, 2001, dawned bright and clear. In the World Trade Center, Francis Ledesma was sitting in his office on the sixty-fourth floor of the South Tower when a friend suggested they go for coffee. Francis seldom took breaks that early, but he decided to make an exception. In the cafeteria he heard and felt a muffled explosion: a boiler exploding, he thought. But then he saw bricks and glass falling by the window. When he started to head back to his office for a nine o'clock meeting, his friend insisted they leave immediately. Out on the street Francis saw the smoke and gaping hole where American Airlines Flight 11 had hit the North Tower. At that moment a huge fireball erupted as United Airlines Flight 175 hit their own South Tower. "We kept looking back," Francis recalled as they escaped the area, "and then all of a sudden our building, Tower 2, collapsed. I really thought that it was a mirage."

That was only the beginning of the horror. Shortly after takeoff from Dulles Airport American Airlines Flight 77 veered from its path and crashed into the Pentagon. Several passengers on United Airlines Flight 93 from Newark to San Francisco heard the news over their cell phones before hijackers seized that plane. Rather than allow another attack, passengers stormed the cockpit. Moments later the plane crashed into a wooded area of western Pennsylvania.

From a secure area at Barksdale Air Force Base in Louisiana, President George W. Bush addressed a shaken nation. He called the crashes a "national tragedy" and condemned those responsible. "Freedom itself was attacked this morning by a faceless coward, and freedom will be defended," he assured the American people.

In an age of instant global communications, the entire world watched as the tragedy unfolded. Three minutes after the first plane hit the World Trade Center, ABC News announced that an explosion had rocked the towers. British television was already covering the fire when the second plane reached its target at 9:03 A.M. Japanese networks were on the air with coverage of the Pentagon crash about an hour later, around midnight their time. TV Azteca in Mexico carried President Bush's statement from Barksdale Air Force Base, and China Central Television was not far behind. This was, indeed, an international tragedy. The aptly named World Trade Center was a hub for global trade and finance. Citizens of more than 50 nations had died in the attack.

As for the United States, not since Pearl Harbor had the nation experienced such a devastating attack on its homeland. Most directly the tragedy claimed approximately 3,000 lives. More than 20,000 residents living in lower Manhattan had to evacuate their homes. The attack had broader economic consequences as well. Before September 11 the booming economy of the 1990s was already showing serious signs of strain, as many overextended Internet companies retrenched or went out of business. The World Trade Center attack pushed the nation into a recession. Added to those economic worries were new fears for security. The attacks were not the work of enemy nations but of an Arab terrorist group known as al Qaeda, led by a shadowy figure, Saudi national Osama bin Laden. How many of al Qaeda's terrorist cells were still

Global Dimensions of the Attack

Economic Downturn

The cold war of the 1950s had imagined a Manhattan like this: debris everywhere, buildings in ruin, the city shrouded in smoke and ash (see the movie poster on page 822). On September 11, 2001, however, disaster on such a large scale came not from confrontation with another superpower but through the actions of international terrorists. The attack made clear that in a post–cold war world, global threats could come from small groups as well as powerful nations.

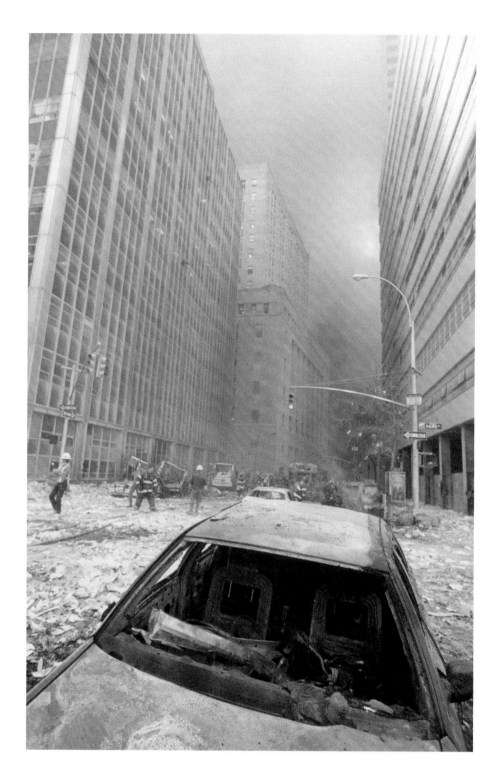

undetected within the United States? After the World Trade Center attack, nations were no longer the only threat to national security. Smaller groups—subnational or international—possessed the capability of using weapons of mass destruction to make war against the most powerful nation in the world.

A Conservative Agenda at Home

The crisis of September 11, 2001, energized George W Bush. Before the attacks, his administration seemed to lack direction. Bush's claim to leadership was shaky partly because when he took office in January 2001, a majority of the electorate had voted for his opponent, Al Gore.

Although the new president's inaugural address promised a moderate course, the actions of the new administration showed that it was taking a more conservative path. Whereas Bill Clinton had pushed the Democrats to the center of the political spectrum during his years in office, Karl Rove, the new president's trusted political adviser, urged Bush to govern from his base on the right. A tight group of advisers led by Rove, Vice President Dick Cheney, Defense Secretary Donald Rumsfeld, and lobbyist Grover Norquist steered the president's conservative program. Although the president appointed women and minorities to his cabinet, he also placed evangelicals such as Attorney General John Ashcroft in key positions. Majorities in both Houses of Congress and opportunities to appoint two justices to the Supreme Court gave the Republicans control over all three branches of government.

The partisan tone of the administration became quickly apparent. When Vice President Cheney convened leaders of the energy industry to recommend new policies, he included no one from the environmental community. Rather than promote conservation, the gathering stressed ways to increase production: drilling in environmentally sensitive coastal areas and the Alaska National Wildlife Refuge.

Energy Policy

To improve education, the administration pressed to make schools more accountable through the use of standardized tests. Liberals such as Senator Ted Kennedy joined the president in January 2002 when he signed into law the "No Child Left Behind" initiative. Yet while the bill allowed for $18 billion in funding, the administration asked for only $12 billion, leaving much of the burden of implementing the ambitious new program to financially strapped state and local governments. Evangelical Christians were pleased with the president's proposal for "faith-based initiatives" that would provide public funds to churches involved in education and social work. Critics complained that such aid blurred the line separating church and state.

Education

Tax cuts formed the cornerstone of the Bush agenda. Many conservatives wanted lower taxes in order to limit the government's ability to initiate new policies—a strategy referred to as "starving the beast." With the threat of recession looming, Bush defended his proposals as a means to boost the economy and create more jobs. Congress supported the proposed cuts, passing first the Economic Growth and Tax Reform Reconciliation Act of 2001 (EGTRRA) and then the Job Creation and Workers Assistance Act of 2002 (JCWA). Size alone did not make these tax bills controversial. Critics objected that the cuts did little for job creation and that those in high income brackets received most of the benefits. Citizens for Tax Justice claimed that by 2010, when (and if) the Bush tax reductions were fully in place, 52 percent of the total tax relief would be going to the richest 1 percent of Americans. Further, tax cuts turned the federal budget surpluses of the late 1990s into massive deficits.

Tax Cuts

The Bush administration reversed a number of environment rulings put in place during the Clinton era, including a gradual ban of snowmobiles in Yellowstone and Grand Teton National Parks. In general the new administration was more receptive to deregulation and voluntary standards as ways of addressing environmental problems.

Unilateralism in Foreign Affairs

Even before the events of September 11, the president rejected the multilateralism in foreign affairs that since World War II had guided American presidents, including his father. President Bush was determined that the United States would play a global role, but largely on its own terms.

Kyoto Protocol Rejected

    The administration's unilateral approach was made clear when it rejected the 1997 Kyoto Protocol on global warming to which 178 other nations had subscribed. "We have no interest in implementing that treaty," announced Christie Whitman, head of the Environmental Protection Agency, arguing that compliance would add an unfair burden on American energy producers. Environmentalists around the globe protested the decision. With only 4 percent of the world's population, the United States produced about 25 percent of the Earth's greenhouse gas emissions.

    After seven months in office George Bush's conservative agenda at home and his unilateralism abroad had not stirred widespread enthusiasm. But September 11 changed perspectives around the world. "This is not only an attack on the United States but an attack on the civilized world," insisted German chancellor Gerhard Schroeder. Even normally hostile nations such as Cuba and Libya conveyed shock and regrets. At home the president was careful to distinguish between the majority of "peace-loving" Muslims and "evil-doers" such as Osama bin Laden. But he made it clear that "our enemy is a radical network of terrorists" and that governments around the world had a simple choice: "Either you are with us or you are with the terrorists."

    In a war with so many shadowy opponents, it was not easy to agree on which radical groups most threatened American security. The "radical network of terrorists" worked underground, spread across dozens of nations. Even the states most hospitable to al Qaeda proved hard to single out. Afghanistan was an obvious target. It was the seat of the Taliban, the extreme Islamic fundamentalists who ruled the country, and the haven of bin Laden. Yet 15 of the 19 hijackers in the World Trade Center attacks hailed from Saudi Arabia, long an ally of the United States.

The Roots of Terror

Before September 11 few Americans had paid much attention to terrorist movements. Indeed, few American radicals had resorted to terrorist tactics. During the Red scare following World War I anarchists had exploded bombs, including one detonated on Wall Street in New York City. During the 1960s radical groups such as the Weathermen and the Symbionese Liberation Army had planted bombs and robbed banks. In 1995 Timothy McVeigh, a right-wing terrorist, exploded a bomb that killed 161 people in the federal building in Oklahoma City. Yet those events were shocking precisely because, in the United States, they were relatively rare.

    Most terrorists resort to violence not because they are strong, but because they are weak. By creating widespread fear they hope to undermine the legitimacy of governments or force their enemies to recognize their grievances. In both Northern Ireland and Israel, two centers of recent terrorist activities, the ruling governments possessed far more power than the insurgents.

Pressures in Saudi Arabia

    In the Middle East, conditions that fostered terrorist movements increased during the 1980s and 1990s, especially in Saudi Arabia. By 2000 that nation's population had nearly tripled, to 19 million, since 1980. Per capita income fell from around $19,000 to $7,300. Much of the Saudi population was young and educated and possessed little hope for the future. These discontented young Saudis received their education in schools run by Wahabbi clerics, a sect of radical Islamic fundamentalists. The Wahabbis viewed the United States and its secular Western values as the greatest threat to Islam.

    The mass unemployment in Saudi Arabia afflicted other Islamic nations as well. But while social conditions in the Middle East fostered terrorist movements, ironically it was the cold war—and, indirectly, the United States—that provided terrorists with

For most of the twentieth century, Americans were accustomed to thinking of terrorism as a problem encountered abroad, as in Northern Ireland, where this IRA mural was painted on a wall (left) or in Israel, where Palestinian terrorists used bombings to campaign for their own independent state (center). In 1995 terrorism at home shocked Americans, when Timothy McVeigh (right) was arrested for bombing a federal building in Oklahoma City.

training and weapons. During the early 1980s the Soviet Union was bogged down in its war in Afghanistan. The CIA, with help from Pakistan, Saudi Arabia, and the United Kingdom, encouraged Muslims from all over the world to join the Afghan rebels. Between 1982 and 1992, approximately 35,000 Muslim radicals traveled to Afghanistan from over 40 Islamic nations in the Middle East, Africa, Central Asia, and the Far East. U.S. policy makers were delighted with the alliance they had helped forge. "What was more important in the world view of history?" asked Zbigniew Brzezinski, national security adviser during the Carter administration. "A few stirred-up Muslims or the liberation of Central Europe and the end of the Cold War?"

One of the militants who had journeyed to Afghanistan was Osama bin Laden, a lanky Saudi who during the 1980s founded al Qaeda to forge a broad-based alliance of Arab rebels. When Iraq invaded Kuwait in 1991, bin Laden called upon Saudi Arabia to help repel the invasion. To his dismay, the Saudis allowed the United States to use its lands to invade Iraq—not at all the kind of holy war bin Laden imagined. From his network of hidden camps in Afghanistan he began directing a worldwide terror network, including operatives in the United States.

Osama bin Laden

Bin Laden's organization differed from previous movements. As historian Walter LaFeber has noted, earlier attacks came from nation-based groups, with nationalist objectives. The Irish Republican Army wanted a unified Ireland. Palestinians wanted an independent state of their own. Al Qaeda, in contrast, had no national home. It was born out of the global alliance of radical Muslims who gathered in Afghanistan in the 1980s, its primary motivation was religious rather than nationalist.

A Global Terrorist Strategy

Al Qaeda's campaign against the United States began with the 1993 bombing of the World Trade Center. That attack killed six people but did only minimal damage to the building. Further attacks occurred in places far from the United States. Twice the Clinton administration retaliated against al Qaeda with missile attacks; once it narrowly missed killing bin Laden himself in one of his Afghan camps.

The War on Terror: First Phase

The military offensive against terrorism began in early October 2001. Despite intense American pressure to deliver bin Laden "dead or alive," the Taliban rulers of Afghanistan

Afghanistan

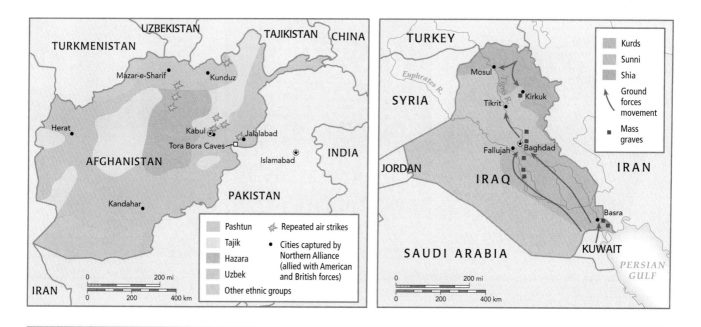

The War on Terror: Afghanistan And Iraq *In Afghanistan al Qaeda forces were concentrated in the mountainous region along the border with Pakistan. Ethnic and religious divisions influenced allegiances in both wars. In Iraq the most severe resistance to American occupation occurred from around Baghdad to Fallujah in the west and Tikrit to the north. In this "Sunni triangle," Sunni Muslims had prospered more under Saddam Hussein than had Shi'ite Muslims to the south.*

refused to expel him or al Qaeda. The United States then launched air attacks followed by an invasion, which quickly brought down the Taliban. The United States established a coalition government in Kabul to help in the slow and uncertain process of rebuilding Afghanistan.

Although it became clear months later that bin Laden had managed to escape the bombing campaign, this first stage of the war on terrorism went well. Many Afghans celebrated the end of Taliban rule, particularly women, whose rights had been severely restricted by the regime.

Domestically the war on terrorism faced a daunting task. The United States was an open society, where citizens expected to travel freely and valued their privacy. How aggressively should the government act to prevent terrorist incidents? A month after the World Trade Center attacks the vulnerability of American society was further exposed by the deaths of five people from letters tainted with anthrax virus sent through the postal system. Evidence eventually pointed to a domestic rather than foreign source of the virus, but widespread fears led the administration to propose the USA Patriot Act. Congress passed it so quickly, some members did not even read the bill before voting for it. The act broadly expanded government powers to use electronic surveillance, monitor bank transactions (to fight money laundering), and investigate suspected terrorists.

With these expanded powers the Justice Department detained hundreds of aliens—mostly Muslims and Arabs. By May 2003 some 5,000 aliens were being held. Of those, only four had been charged with any terrorist activity, two of whom were acquitted. Critics argued that these detentions, as well as the broad powers of the Patriot Act, threatened the constitutional rights of Americans as well as the natural rights of aliens. In July 2004 a near-unanimous Supreme Court rejected the Bush administration's claim that in fighting terrorism the president could jail indefinitely American citizens deemed to be "enemy combatants."

Beyond locating and arresting terrorists, an effort was set in motion to secure vital systems of transportation, communication, and energy production. To coordinate new measures, Bush created the cabinet-level Department of Homeland Security.

Anthrax Virus

USA Patriot Act

The War on Iraq

With the war in Afghanistan ended, the president's focus shifted from Osama bin Laden to Iraq's brutal dictator, Saddam Hussein. Indeed, a decision to overthrow Hussein had been made in the first weekend after the September 11 attacks. The only question, Deputy Defense Secretary Paul Wolfowitz acknowledged, "was whether [invading Iraq] should be in the immediate response or whether [the president] should concentrate simply on Afghanistan first."

Among the leaders of the major powers, only Prime Minister Tony Blair (left) of the United Kingdom unreservedly supported President Bush's war in Iraq. The two leaders met in the Azores several days before the invasion of Iraq with the prime ministers of Spain and Portugal.

In September 2002 the president appeared before the UN General Assembly, challenging it to enforce its inspection program in Iraq for weapons of mass destruction (WMD). Beginning in 1998 Iraq had refused to allow UN inspectors to verify the destruction of its WMDs. "All the world now faces a test," concluded the president, "and the United Nations a difficult and defining moment. Are Security Council resolutions to be honored and enforced, or cast aside without consequence?"

The speech proved effective. Under renewed pressure from the United Nations, Hussein allowed inspections to resume, but Bush grew impatient. "If we know Saddam Hussein has dangerous weapons today—and we do—," he proclaimed, "does it make any sense for the world to wait . . . for the final proof, the smoking gun that could come in the form of a mushroom cloud?" The president had already laid the groundwork for a policy of not waiting, by asserting that the United States would be "ready for preemptive action when necessary to defend our liberty and to defend our lives."

This **doctrine of preemption**—announcing that the United States might attack before it was itself attacked—was a major departure from the cold war policy of containment. "A preventive war, to my mind, is an impossibility," President Eisenhower declared in 1954. But Bush argued that, in an era in which terrorist enemies struck without warning, containment would no longer work. With midterm elections looming in October 2002 the president persuaded Congress to pass a joint resolution giving him full authority to take military action against Iraq if he deemed it necessary.

Preemption Versus Containment

UN weapons inspectors, however, reported that they could find no evidence of WMDs or programs to build them. The Security Council refused to support an American resolution giving the United States the authority to lead a UN-sponsored invasion. Only the United Kingdom, Spain, and Italy, among the major powers, were willing to join the United States. France and Germany balked, as did Russia.

On March 19, 2003, without a UN mandate, a "coalition of the willing" (30 nations, though the actual troops were virtually all American and British) attacked Iraq. The invasion was accomplished with amazing speed and precision. Within days U.S. forces were halfway to Baghdad. On May 1 Bush announced an end to major combat operations. Coalition casualties (135 dead and 1,511 wounded) were remarkably low.

A Messy Aftermath

The swift execution of the war at first blinded Americans to the difficulty of the occupation that would follow. Vice President Dick Cheney predicted that coalition forces "would be greeted as liberators" by the Iraqis. Instead an insurgency, led by disgruntled supporters of the deposed Saddam Hussein, began a steady campaign of violence against the occupying troops. Without Saddam's iron hand, the country's religious and ethnic sects began to turn on one another. The Kurds maintained relative peace in areas under their control in northern Iraq, but in other regions the majority **Shi'ite** and minority **Sunni** Muslims fell into sectarian violence. Most major nations refused to send aid or peacekeeping forces to support an occupation they had not approved.

Failed Occupation

The war—and then the growing insurgency—destroyed roads, bridges, power plants, water works, and public services. Sabotage prevented oil production from reaching its prewar levels, which the administration had counted on to help pay for the war. President Bush appointed L. Paul Bremer to act as civil administrator coordinating the reconstruction efforts. But Bremer ignored the advice of his military predecessor and ordered the disbanding of Hussein's army and police forces. Many displaced and disillusioned Iraqi officers joined the insurgency. Furthermore, American weapons inspectors could find no evidence that Saddam Hussein had ever possessed weapons of mass destruction or even the means to build them.

Democratization became the new rationale for the war in Iraq. In June of 2004 the United States turned over formal control of the country to a provisional Iraqi government. Elections held in January 2005 established a permanent government, but significantly, while most Kurds and Shi'ites voted, few Sunnis participated. Home rule did nothing to ease the insurgency. By the spring of 2005 over 1,200 American and coalition soldiers had died—more than six times as many as in the war to topple Saddam. Iraqi civilian deaths numbered in the tens of thousands. American spending on the war exceeded $150 billion at a time when the annual federal deficit had ballooned to over $550 billion.

Abu Ghraib Prison

The cost of war to the United States could not be measured solely in terms of dollars spent or lives lost. In the spring of 2004, the world was shocked to learn that American soldiers guarding Iraqi prisoners at Abu Ghraib prison had systematically abused and tortured them. The Bush administration blamed a few "bad apples." Investigations revealed, however, that officials not only condoned but also authorized torture to encourage "successful exploitation of detainees." Similar conditions existed in the prison established at the American base at Guantanamo Bay in Cuba, where hundreds of terror suspects were held without the right to legal defense or trial. The Justice Department's Office of Legal Council defended the behavior on the grounds that in some cases cruel, inhuman, or degrading acts could not be classified as torture.

Governing from the Right

Energizing the Base

Bush's political fortunes remained promising through the 2004 presidential election. Facing his Democratic challenger Senator John Kerry from Massachusetts, the president made the war on terror the centerpiece of the election while also energizing his conservative base by invoking traditional religious values. (Republicans were careful to place referenda on same-sex marriages on the ballots of several key states, to bring out conservative voters.) Kerry opposed the war but was tarred with "flip-flopping" on the issue (he voted for one funding request, he noted, before he voted against it). Once again, the election's outcome came down to a single state—this time Ohio. Had 60,000 out of 5.6 million Ohio voters switched to Kerry he would have won an electoral majority but not the popular vote.

Reforming Social Security

With Republican control of all three branches of government, the moment seemed opportune to promote long sought conservative goals. Bush began a politically risky campaign to reform Social Security, long a conservative goal. With the baby-boom generation closing in on retirement, the federal retirement system faced insolvency if steps were not taken to fix it, he warned. But he met stiff opposition, even from some in his own party, to his proposal to **privatize** the system by creating individual retirement accounts. Critics worried that individuals risked losing their nest eggs if they chose unwisely, whereas the existing system guaranteed a return, even if it was less spectacular.

The president pressed what proved to be a second losing issue—tax cuts. In particular, he called for the cuts scheduled to end in 2010 to be made permanent and the estate tax to be eliminated. Yet the issue that had worked for Republicans so well and so long seemed finally to be running out of steam. Critics pointed out that not since the Gilded Age had Americans experienced such income inequality. With deficits soaring and no end to the Iraq War in sight, even the Republican Congress would not deliver for Bush.

Arguing that the election had demonstrated renewed support for the conservative moral agenda, the president supported not only legislation barring partial birth abortion but also opposition to medical research performed on embryonic stem cells, another sensitive issue for many evangelicals. In another case involving medical ethics, Bush spoke out in favor of prolonging the life of a woman, Terri Schiavo, who had lain in a persistent vegetative state for 15 years. But the president exerted the most significant impact on conservative values by appointing two new justices to the Supreme Court, John Roberts and Samuel Alito. In 2007 the Court issued a number of decisions indicating a move to the right. By a 5–4 majority, the Court weakened the campaign finance law, limited free speech in schools, and protected religious groups offering publicly financed social programs.

Moral Issues

Disasters Domestic and Foreign

Bush's early second-term failures on Social Security and tax cuts proved to be no more than a headwind to his popularity—at least when compared to the gale from Hurricane Katrina, which slammed into the Gulf Coast in September 2005. New

Hurricane Katrina and New Orleans Flooding

Orleans escaped the worst until its levees broke and the city was inundated. Most of the city's well-to-do escaped before the storm, but no one had made adequate provision to evacuate the elderly, disabled, and poor, most of whom were African American. For days desperate survivors hung to rooftops. Thousands died, while tens of thousands huddled in the damaged Superdome sports arena.

The president at first did no more than fly over the site of the disaster, and he seemed disengaged from the crisis. The official he had appointed to head the Federal Emergency Management Agency (FEMA) had little experience, and the agency floundered in trying to respond. Much of the nation looked on in disbelief and anger at what appeared to be the administration's callous indifference. Over two years later, residents of New Orleans still waited for a Federal plan to rebuild their city. Katrina reminded Americans that there are some problems that only effective government can solve.

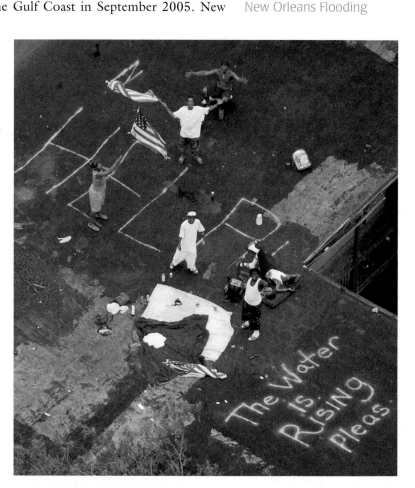

Halfway across the globe the president faced another growing crisis, a deteriorating situation in Iraq. American and Iraqi casualties continued to mount, and the insurgency turned into a near civil war. Even the president's own military commanders began take issue with the administration's assertions

A plea from New Orleans residents threatened by Hurricane Katrina.

that progress was being made. *Washington Post* reporter Bob Woodward, who at first had written laudatory accounts of Bush's response to September 11 and his handling of the Iraq War, began portraying an administration out of touch with reality and with no plan to end the war.

The Time and Tides of the World's Longest Mural

The Collective Process and History

We have seen historians at work over these past chapters interpreting maps, analyzing diaries, and weighing the social significance of starched collars, gramophones, and atomic blaster rings. Most often the detective work involved was initiated by a curious scholar working alone. Yet history is a collective endeavor too. Scholars are helpless without the research of others. And as a nation we depend on museums, survey courses, and even textbooks to reconstruct and reimagine the past.

Some remarkable collective history remains on view today along a concrete wall of Tujungo Wash, a flood drainage canal in the San Fernando Valley near Los Angeles. For a full half mile the world's longest mural sets forth in bold images a history of ethnic California, beginning in prehistory and ending in the 1950s. The project, "the Great Wall," was begun in 1974 and took more than five summers to complete. It employed over 400 youth and their families, from diverse social and economic backgrounds, who worked with artists, oral historians, ethnologists, scholars, and hundreds of community members. Led by artist Judith Baca the mural's creators looked to voice histories that had been ignored by the mainstream culture before the tumultuous identity politics of the 1960s and 1970s.

Like all histories, this one has changed—in this case because of the sun beating down on the paint, occasional floods submerging the mural, and chemical damage from lawn fertilizer runoff. In the twenty-first century, a restoration project has gotten underway to refurbish the paintings and add new ones, bringing the history up to the year 2000. The quest for immortality has gone virtual as well: a three-dimensional fly-by rendering of the wall is now available on the Web at www.sparcmurals.org.

History is much like the Great Wall murals. Built by many collaborators, subject to misfortune and chance, dependent on the dedication of those determined to remember. Always, without fail, under construction.

FOREBEARERS OF CIVIL RIGHTS   THE ORIGINS OF GAY RIGHTS

A section of the "Great Wall" painted along the flood drainage canal of Tujunga Wash.

Civil War in Iraq   By the fall of 2006 voters were ready to voice their displeasure—not only with the war but with a culture of corruption in Congress where lobbyists routinely traded cash contributions and gifts for legislative favors. A number of representatives left Congress in disgrace for their financial and sexual improprieties. What only a year earlier seemed impregnable Republican majorities in both houses collapsed. In the midterm elections the Democrats retook both the House and the Senate.

In 1952 the stalemate in Korea killed Harry Truman's desire for another term as president. Vietnam destroyed Lyndon Johnson and helped lead Richard Nixon into the Watergate scandal. So, too, by 2006 the war in Iraq threatened whatever hopes George W. Bush harbored for a conservative revolution at home and for "ending tyranny in the world," as he had proclaimed in his second inaugural address. Forty years earlier, as Bush came of age politically, John Kennedy warned against overreaching the nation's power. With only 6 percent of the world's people, Kennedy observed, the United States could not impose its will on the other 94 percent. Nor could it "right every wrong or reverse every adversity." In a world drawn closer by the Internet, global flows of goods and people, and international terror networks, only time would tell whether a nation of nations had the maturity and wisdom needed to police an uncertain world.

Significant Events

1965	Immigration Reform Act
1969	ARPANET created
1986	Immigration and Control Act; Proposition 63
1992	Rodney King verdict; Los Angeles riots; Bill Clinton elected
1993	NAFTA passed; peace agreement between Israel and Palestinians; Clinton's deficit reduction budget adopted
1994	Health care reform fails; Kenneth Starr appointed special prosecutor; Rwanda massacres; Republicans win control of Congress; California's Proposition 187 denies benefits to illegal aliens
1995	Dayton Accords; GOP government shutdowns; U.S. troops in Bosnia
1996	Welfare reform adopted; Clinton defeats Dole; California passes Proposition 209 against affirmative action
1998	Lewinsky scandal; federal budget surplus
1999	Senate acquits Clinton of impeachment charges; NATO planes bomb Serbia; American troops enter Kosovo as NATO peacekeepers
2000	George W. Bush wins election in *Gore v. Bush*
2001	United States withdraws from the Kyoto Protocol on global warming; Economic Growth and Tax Reform Reconciliation Act (EGTRRA) enacted; Terrorists destroy the World Trade Center; Patriot Act passed; United States deposes Afghanistan's Taliban regime
2002	No Child Left Behind Act signed; President Bush asserts a doctrine of preemptive war
2003	*Gratz v. Bollinger* preserves limited use of affirmative action; Department of Homeland Security created; United States and allies invade Iraq
2004	Abu Ghraib prison scandal; Bush reelected
2005	Elections establish Iraqi government under a new constitution; Hurricane Katrina devastates New Orleans; sectarian violence in Iraq degenerates into civil war
2006	Democrats win control of Congress
2007	Supreme Court under Chief Justice Roberts becomes more conservative

Chapter Summary

By the twenty-first century the United States had become increasingly tied to a worldwide network of economic, financial, and demographic relationships that increased both the nation's diversity and its interdependence.

- The Immigration Act of 1965 opened the United States to a global wave of immigration in the 1980s and 1990s.

  - Immigrants from Asia—hailing from South and Southeast Asia as much as from China, Japan, and the Philippines—crowded both ends of the economic spectrum in an hourglass profile.
  - Legal and illegal immigrants from Mexico, Cuba, and Central America settled in both urban and suburban barrios.

- During the Clinton presidency, regional conflicts replaced cold war rivalries as the central challenge of foreign policy.

- President Clinton's domestic agenda included rebuilding the nation's infrastructure, improving education, and reforming the health care system.

  - A divided and (after the elections of 1994) increasingly hostile Congress limited the president's legislative program.
  - The campaign of Republican conservatives to impeach the president ended when the Senate failed to convict.
  - The closely contested election of 2000 was settled when the Supreme Court ruled against a recount of disputed Florida ballots, giving George W. Bush the victory.

- The growth of the Internet, the World Wide Web, and e-commerce was part of a revolution in communications and information management. But those advances also threatened to create a two-tiered economy divided by levels of education and literacy.

- The political battles of the 1990s over race, immigration, and multiculturalism suggest that identities shaped by race, ethnicity, social class, and religion will continue to be a source of both strength and political conflict.

- President George W. Bush proposed a conservative agenda of lower taxes, education reform, and promotion of private energy development.

  - Major tax cuts favoring high-income Americans marked the Bush administration's major domestic accomplishment in its first year.

- The attacks of Arab terrorists on the U.S. World Trade towers, on September 11, 2001, led the president to declare a global war on terrorism.

  - In October 2001 a U.S. attack on Afghanistan toppled the Taliban, although Osama bin Laden escaped.
  - The new Homeland Security Department and USA Patriot Act limited civil rights and liberties in an effort to combat domestic terrorist threats.

- In March 2003 President Bush launched a preemptive invasion of Iraq to prevent Saddam Hussein from using weapons of mass destruction against the United States.

  - No weapons of mass destruction were found and reconstruction of Iraq proved more difficult than predicted.
  - In 2004 the United States turned over control of Iraq to a coalition government, which was unable to prevent a civil war breaking out between rival Sunni and Shi'ite factions.

- George Bush won reelection in 2004 but in his second term ran into increasing opposition.

  - The president failed to privatize Social Security and to make his tax cuts permanent. But he did appoint two conservative justices to the Supreme Court.
  - The slow federal response to Hurricane Katrina, increasing political corruption scandals, and growing disillusionment with the war in Iraq allowed the Democrats to regain control of Congress in 2007.

Additional Reading

Accounts of the most recent past often reflect the partisan spirit of those engaged in ongoing controversies. Sidney Blumenthal, *The Clinton Wars* (2003), is an insider's unabashed defense of the Clintons. In *Madam Secretary* (2003), Madeline Albright reveals much about her road to political prominence. Richard Posner, a federal judge, takes on two judicial controversies—impeachment in *An Affair of State: The Investigation and Trial*

of President Clinton (1999) and the Gore-Bush controversy in *Breaking the Deadlock: The 2000 Election, the Constitution, and the Courts* (2003).

Joseph Stiglitz, *The Roaring Nineties: A New History of the World's Most Prosperous Decade* (2004), offers a liberal perspective on economic inequalities. Some of Thomas Friedman's ideas about globalization, in *The World is Flat* (2006) and *The Lexus and the Olive Tree* (1999), are challenged in Jack Goldsmith and Tim Wu, *Who Controls the Internet: Illusions of a Borderless World* (2006). On multiculturalism and the prospects for democracy, see Alan Wolf, *One Nation, After All* (1998) and *Does American Democracy Still Work?* (2006). A look at social disintegration is Robert Putnam, *Bowling Alone: The Collapse and Revival of American Community* (2000). Richard Alba and Victor Nee, *Remaking America: Assimilation and Contemporary Immigration* (2003), argues that today's immigrants are following a path similar to those who arrived in the early twentieth century. Roberto Suro examines Latino cultures in the 1990s in *Strangers Among Us: How Latino Immigration is Transforming America* (1998).

The fortunes of the presidency of George W. Bush are traced by *Washington Post* insider Bob Woodward—admiringly in the first two volumes *Bush at War* (2002) and *Plan of Attack* (2004).

Two years later, in *State of Denial: Bush at War, Part III* (2006), Woodward responds to the evidence of failure in Iraq. A book that captures both the success and the danger of the Rove political machine is Jacob Hacker and Paul Pierson, *Off Center: The Republican Right and the Erosion of American Democracy* (rev. ed. 2006). As for the Iraq War, Lawrence Wright, *The Looming Tower: Al-Qaeda and the Road to 9/11* (2006), makes the case that Osama bin Laden purposely drew George Bush into a trap. Ron Suskind, *The One Percent Doctrine* (2006), uses CIA sources to follow the war on terror. Thomas Ricks, *Fiasco: The American Adventure in Iraq* (2006), mines military sources to reveal the incompetence behind the American failure to plan for reconstruction in Iraq.

For a fuller list of readings, see the Bibliography at www.mhhe.com/davidsonnation6.

The Declaration of Independence

In Congress, July 4, 1776,

THE UNANIMOUS DECLARATION OF THE THIRTEEN UNITED STATES OF AMERICA

When, in the course of human events, it becomes necessary for one people to dissolve the political bands which have connected them with another, and to assume, among the powers of the earth, the separate and equal station to which the laws of nature and of nature's God entitle them, a decent respect to the opinions of mankind requires that they should declare the causes which impel them to the separation.

We hold these truths to be self-evident, that all men are created equal; that they are endowed by their Creator with certain unalienable rights; that among these, are life, liberty, and the pursuit of happiness. That, to secure these rights, governments are instituted among men, deriving their just powers from the consent of the governed; that, whenever any form of government becomes destructive of these ends, it is the right of the people to alter or to abolish it, and to institute a new government, laying its foundation on such principles, and organizing its powers in such form, as to them shall seem most likely to effect their safety and happiness. Prudence, indeed, will dictate that governments long established, should not be changed for light and transient causes; and, accordingly, all experience hath shown, that mankind are more disposed to suffer, while evils are sufferable, than to right themselves by abolishing the forms to which they are accustomed. But, when a long train of abuses and usurpations, pursuing invariably the same object, evinces a design to reduce them under absolute despotism, it is their right, it is their duty, to throw off such government and to provide new guards for their future security. Such has been the patient sufferance of these colonies, and such is now the necessity which constrains them to alter their former systems of government. The history of the present King of Great Britain is a history of repeated injuries and usurpations, all having, in direct object, the establishment of an absolute tyranny over these States. To prove this, let facts be submitted to a candid world:

He has refused his assent to laws the most wholesome and necessary for the public good.

He has forbidden his governors to pass laws of immediate and pressing importance, unless suspended in their operation till his assent should be obtained; and, when so suspended, he has utterly neglected to attend to them.

He has refused to pass other laws for the accommodation of large districts of people, unless those people would relinquish the right of representation in the legislature; a right inestimable to them, and formidable to tyrants only.

He has called together legislative bodies at places unusual, uncomfortable, and distant from the depository of their public records, for the sole purpose of fatiguing them into compliance with his measures.

He has dissolved representative houses repeatedly for opposing, with manly firmness, his invasions on the rights of the people.

He has refused, for a long time after such dissolutions, to cause others to be elected; whereby the legislative powers, incapable of annihilation, have returned to the people at large for their exercise; the state remaining, in the meantime, exposed to all the danger of invasion from without, and convulsions within.

He has endeavored to prevent the population of these States; for that purpose, obstructing the laws for naturalization of foreigners, refusing to pass others to encourage their migration hither, and raising the conditions of new appropriations of lands.

He had obstructed the administration of justice, by refusing his assent to laws for establishing judiciary powers.

He has made judges dependent on his will alone, for the tenure of their offices, and the amount and payment of their salaries.

He has erected a multitude of new offices, and sent hither swarms of officers to harass our people, and eat out their substance.

He has kept among us, in time of peace, standing armies, without the consent of our legislatures.

He has affected to render the military independent of, and superior to, the civil power.

He has combined, with others, to subject us to a jurisdiction foreign to our Constitution, and unacknowledged by our laws; giving his assent to their acts of pretended legislation:

For quartering large bodies of armed troops among us:

For protecting them by a mock trial, from punishment, for any murders which they should commit on the inhabitants of these States:

For cutting off our trade with all parts of the world:

For imposing taxes on us without our consent:

For depriving us, in many cases, of the benefit of trial by jury:

For transporting us beyond seas to be tried for pretended offences:

For abolishing the free system of English laws in a neighboring province, establishing therein an arbitrary government, and enlarging its boundaries, so as to render it at once an example and fit instrument for introducing the same absolute rule into these colonies:

For taking away our charters, abolishing our most valuable laws, and altering, fundamentally, the powers of our governments:

For suspending our own legislatures, and declaring themselves invested with power to legislate for us in all cases whatsoever.

He has abdicated government here, by declaring us out of his protection, and waging war against us.

He has plundered our seas, ravaged our coasts, burnt our towns, and destroyed the lives of our people.

He is, at this time, transporting large armies of foreign mercenaries to complete the works of death, desolation, and tyranny, already begun, with circumstances of cruelty and perfidy scarcely paralleled in the most barbarous ages, and totally unworthy the head of a civilized nation.

He has constrained our fellow citizens, taken captive on the high seas, to bear arms against their country, to become the executioners of their friends, and brethren, or to fall themselves by their hands.

He has excited domestic insurrections amongst us, and has endeavored to bring on the inhabitants of our frontiers, the merciless Indian savages, whose known rule of warfare is an undistinguished destruction of all ages, sexes, and conditions.

In every stage of these oppressions, we have petitioned for redress, in the most humble terms; our repeated petitions have been answered only by repeated injury. A prince, whose character is thus marked by every act which may define a tyrant, is unfit to be the ruler of a free people.

Nor have we been wanting in attention to our British brethren. We have warned them, from time to time, of attempts made by their legislature to extend an unwarrantable jurisdiction over us. We have reminded them of the circumstances of our emigration and settlement here. We have appealed to their native justice and magnanimity, and we have conjured them, by the ties of our common kindred, to disavow these usurpations, which would inevitably interrupt our connections and correspondence. They, too, have been deaf to the voice of justice and consanguinity. We must, therefore, acquiesce in the necessity which denounces our separation, and hold them as we hold the rest of mankind, enemies in war, in peace, friends.

We, therefore, the representatives of the United States of America, in general Congress assembled, appealing to the Supreme Judge of the world for the rectitude of our intentions, do, in the name, and by the authority of the good people of these colonies, solemnly publish and declare, that these united colonies are, and of right ought to be, free and independent states: that they are absolved from all allegiance to the British Crown, and that all political connection between them and the state of Great Britain is, and ought to be, totally dissolved; and that, as free and independent states, they have full power to levy war, conclude peace, contract alliances, establish commerce, and to do all other acts and things which independent states may of right do. And, for the support of this declaration, with a firm reliance on the protection of Divine Providence, we mutually pledge to each other our lives, our fortunes, and our sacred honor.

The foregoing Declaration was, by order of Congress, engrossed, and signed by the following members:

JOHN HANCOCK

New Hampshire	**New York**	**Delaware**	**North Carolina**
Josiah Bartlett	William Floyd	Caesar Rodney	William Hooper
William Whipple	Philip Livingston	George Read	Joseph Hewes
Matthew Thornton	Francis Lewis	Thomas M'Kean	John Penn
	Lewis Morris		
Massachusetts Bay	**New Jersey**	**Maryland**	**South Carolina**
Samuel Adams	Richard Stockton	Samuel Chase	Edward Rutledge
John Adams	John Witherspoon	William Paca	Thomas Heyward, Jr.
Robert Treat Paine	Francis Hopkinson	Thomas Stone	Thomas Lynch, Jr.
Elbridge Gerry	John Hart	Charles Carroll, of Carrollton	Arthur Middleton
	Abraham Clark		

Rhode Island
Stephen Hopkins
William Ellery

Connecticut
Roger Sherman
Samuel Huntington
William Williams
Oliver Wolcott

Pennsylvania
Robert Morris
Benjamin Rush
Benjamin Franklin
John Morton
George Clymer
James Smith
George Taylor
James Wilson
George Ross

Virginia
George Wythe
Richard Henry Lee
Thomas Jefferson
Benjamin Harrison
Thomas Nelson, Jr.
Francis Lightfoot Lee
Carter Braxton

Georgia
Button Gwinnett
Lyman Hall
George Walton

Resolved, That copies of the Declaration be sent to the several assemblies, conventions, and committees, or councils of safety, and to the several commanding officers of the continental troops; that it be proclaimed in each of the United States, at the head of the army.

The Constitution of the United States of America[1]

We the People of the United States, in Order to form a more perfect Union, establish Justice, insure domestic Tranquility, provide for the common defence, promote the general Welfare, and secure the Blessings of Liberty to ourselves and our Posterity, do ordain and establish this CONSTITUTION for the United States of America.

ARTICLE I

Section 1. All legislative Powers herein granted shall be vested in a Congress of the United States, which shall consist of a Senate and House of Representatives.

Section 2. The House of Representatives shall be composed of Members chosen every second Year by the People of the several States, and the Electors in each State shall have the Qualifications requisite for Electors of the most numerous Branch of the State Legislature.

No Person shall be a Representative who shall not have attained to the Age of twenty-five Years, and been seven Years a Citizen of the United States, and who shall not, when elected, be an Inhabitant of that State in which he shall be chosen.

[Representatives and direct Taxes[2] shall be apportioned among the several States which may be included within this Union, according to their respective Numbers, which shall be determined by adding to the whole Number of free Persons, including those bound to Service for a Term of Years, and excluding Indians not taxed, three fifths of all other Persons.][3] The actual Enumeration shall be made within three Years after the first Meeting of the Congress of the United States, and within every subsequent Term of ten Years, in such Manner as they shall by Law direct. The Number of Representatives shall not exceed one for every thirty Thousand, but each State shall have at Least one Representative; and until such enumeration shall be made, the State of New Hampshire shall be entitled to chuse three, Massachusetts eight, Rhode-Island and Providence Plantations one, Connecticut five, New York six, New Jersey four, Pennsylvania eight, Delaware one, Maryland six, Virginia ten, North Carolina five, South Carolina five, and Georgia three.

When vacancies happen in the Representation from any State, the Executive Authority thereof shall issue Writs of Election to fill such Vacancies.

The House of Representatives shall chuse their Speaker and other Officers; and shall have the sole Power of Impeachment.

Section 3. The Senate of the United States shall be composed of two Senators from each State, chosen by the Legislature thereof, for six Years; and each Senator shall have one Vote.

Immediately after they shall be assembled in Consequence of the first Election, they shall be divided as equally as may be into three Classes. The Seats of the Senators of the first Class shall be vacated at the Expiration of the second Year, of the second Class at the Expiration of the fourth Year, and of the third Class at the Expiration of the sixth Year, so that one-third may be chosen every second Year; and if Vacancies happen by Resignation, or otherwise, during the Recess of the Legislature of any State, the Executive thereof may make temporary Appointments until the next Meeting of the Legislature, which shall then fill such Vacancies.

No Person shall be a Senator who shall not have attained to the Age of thirty Years, and been nine Years a Citizen of the United States, and who shall not, when elected, be an Inhabitant of that State for which he shall be chosen.

The Vice President of the United States shall be President of the Senate, but shall have no vote, unless they be equally divided.

The Senate shall chuse their other Officers, and also a President pro tempore, in the absence of the Vice President, or when he shall exercise the Office of President of the United States.

The Senate shall have the sole Power to try all Impeachments. When sitting for that purpose they shall be on Oath or Affirmation. When the President of the United States is tried, the Chief Justice shall preside: And no person shall be convicted without the Concurrence of two thirds of the Members present.

Judgment in Cases of Impeachment shall not extend further than to removal from Office, and disqualification to hold and enjoy any Office of honor, Trust, or Profit

---

[1]This version follows the original Constitution in capitalization and spelling. It is adapted from the text published by the United States Department of the Interior, Office of Education.
[2]Altered by the Sixteenth Amendment.
[3]Negated by the Fourteenth Amendment.

under the United States: but the Party convicted shall nevertheless be liable and subject to Indictment, Trial, Judgment, and Punishment, according to Law.

Section 4. The Times, Places and Manner of holding Elections for Senators and Representatives, shall be prescribed in each State by the Legislature thereof; but the Congress may at any time by Law make or alter such Regulations, except as to the Places of Chusing Senators.

The Congress shall assemble at least once in every Year, and such Meeting shall be on the first Monday in December, unless they shall by Law appoint a different Day.

Section 5. Each House shall be the Judge of the Elections, Returns and Qualifications of its own Members, and a Majority of each shall constitute a Quorum to do Business; but a smaller number may adjourn from day to day, and may be authorized to compel the Attendance of absent Members, in such Manner, and under such Penalties, as each House may provide.

Each House may determine the Rules of its Proceedings, punish its Members for disorderly Behaviour, and, with the Concurrence of two thirds, expel a Member.

Each House shall keep a Journal of its Proceedings, and from time to time publish the same, excepting such Parts as may in their Judgment require Secrecy; and the Yeas and Nays of the Members of either House on any question shall, at the Desire of one fifth of those Present, be entered on the Journal.

Neither House, during the Session of Congress, shall, without the Consent of the other, adjourn for more than three days, nor to any other Place than that in which the two Houses shall be sitting.

Section 6. The Senators and Representatives shall receive a Compensation for their Services, to be ascertained by Law, and paid out of the Treasury of the United States. They shall in all Cases, except Treason, Felony, and Breach of the Peace, be privileged from Arrest during their Attendance at the Session of their respective Houses, and in going to and returning from the same; and for any Speech or Debate in either House, they shall not be questioned in any other Place.

No Senator or Representative shall, during the Time for which he was elected, be appointed to any civil Office under the Authority of the United States, which shall have been created, or the Emoluments whereof shall have been increased, during such time; and no Person holding any Office under the United States shall be a Member of either House during his continuance in Office.

Section 7. All Bills for raising Revenue shall originate in the House of Representatives; but the Senate may propose or concur with Amendments as on other bills.

Every Bill which shall have passed the House of Representatives and the Senate, shall, before it become a Law, be presented to the President of the United States; If he approve he shall sign it, but if not he shall return it, with his Objections, to that House in which it shall have originated, who shall enter the Objections at large on their Journal, and proceed to reconsider it. If after such Reconsideration two thirds of that House shall agree to pass the bill, it shall be sent, together with the objections, to the other House, by which it shall likewise be reconsidered, and if approved by two thirds of that House, it shall become a Law. But in all such Cases the Votes of both Houses shall be determined by Yeas and Nays, and the Names of the Persons voting for and against the Bill shall be entered on the Journal of each House respectively. If any Bill shall not be returned by the President within ten Days (Sundays excepted) after it shall have been presented to him, the Same shall be a Law, in like Manner as if he had signed it, unless the Congress by their Adjournment prevent its Return, in which Case it shall not be a Law.

Every Order, Resolution, or Vote to which the Concurrence of the Senate and House of Representatives may be necessary (except on a question of Adjournment) shall be presented to the President of the United States; and before the Same shall take Effect, shall be approved by him, or being disapproved by him, shall be repassed by two thirds of the Senate and House of Representatives, according to the Rules and Limitations prescribed in the Case of a Bill.

Section 8. The Congress shall have Power To lay and collect Taxes, Duties, Imposts and Excises, to pay the Debts and provide for the common Defence and general Welfare of the United States; but all Duties, Imposts and Excises shall be uniform throughout the United States;

To borrow money on the credit of the United States;

To regulate Commerce with foreign Nations, and among the several States, and with the Indian Tribes;

To establish an uniform rule of Naturalization, and uniform Laws on the subject of Bankruptcies throughout the United States;

To coin Money, regulate the Value thereof, and of foreign Coin, and fix the Standard of Weights and Measures;

To provide for the Punishment of counterfeiting the Securities and current Coin of the United States;

To establish Post Offices and post Roads;

To promote the Progress of Science and useful Arts, by securing for limited Times to Authors and Inventors the exclusive Right to their respective Writings and Discoveries;

To constitute Tribunals inferior to the Supreme Court;

To define and punish Piracies and Felonies committed on the high Seas, and Offenses against the Law of Nations;

To declare War, grant Letters of Marque and Reprisal, and make Rules concerning Captures on Land and Water;

To raise and support Armies, but no Appropriation of Money to that Use shall be for a longer Term than two Years;

To provide and maintain a Navy;

To make Rules for the Government and Regulation of the land and naval forces;

To provide for calling forth the Militia to execute the Laws of the Union, suppress Insurrections and repel Invasions;

To provide for organizing, arming, and disciplining the Militia, and for government such Part of them as may be employed in the Service of the United States, reserving to the States respectively, the Appointment of the Officers, and the Authority of training the Militia according to the discipline prescribed by Congress;

To exercise exclusive Legislation in all Cases whatsoever, over such District (not exceeding ten Miles square) as may, by Cession of particular States, and the acceptance of Congress, become the Seat of the Government of the United States, and to exercise like Authority over all Places purchased by the Consent of the Legislature of the State in which the Same shall be, for the Erection of Forts, Magazines, Arsenals, Dock-yards, and other needful Buildings;—And

To make all Laws which shall be necessary and proper for carrying into Execution the foregoing Powers, and all other Powers vested by this Constitution in the Government of the United States, or in any Department or Officer thereof.

Section 9. The Migration or Importation of such Persons as any of the States now existing shall think proper to admit, shall not be prohibited by the Congress prior to the Year one thousand eight hundred and eight, but a tax or duty may be imposed on such Importation, not exceeding ten dollars for each Person.

The privilege of the Writ of Habeas Corpus shall not be suspended, unless when in Cases of Rebellion or Invasion the public Safety may require it.

No bill of Attainder or ex post facto Law shall be passed.

No capitation, or other direct, Tax shall be laid unless in Proportion to the Census or Enumeration herein before directed to be taken.

No Tax or Duty shall be laid on Articles exported from any State.

No Preference shall be given by any Regulation of Commerce or Revenue to the Ports of one State over those of another: nor shall Vessels bound to, or from, one State, be obliged to enter, clear, or pay Duties in another.

No Money shall be drawn from the Treasury, but in Consequence of Appropriations made by Law; and a regular Statement and Account of the Receipts and Expenditures of all public Money shall be published from time to time.

No Title of Nobility shall be granted by the United States: And no Person holding any Office of Profit or Trust under them, shall, without the Consent of the Congress, accept of any present, Emolument, Office, or Title, of any kind whatever, from any King, Prince, or foreign State.

Section 10. No State shall enter into any Treaty, Alliance, or Confederation; grant Letters of Marque and Reprisal; coin Money; emit Bills of Credit; make any Thing but gold and silver Coin a Tender in Payment of Debts; pass any Bill of Attainder, ex post facto Law, or Law impairing the Obligation of Contracts, or grant any Title of Nobility.

No State shall, without the Consent of the Congress, lay any Imposts or Duties on Imports or Exports, except what may be absolutely necessary for executing its inspection Laws; and the net Produce of all Duties and Imposts, laid by any State on Imports or Exports, shall be for the use of the Treasury of the United States; and all such Laws shall be subject to the Revision and Control of the Congress.

No state shall, without the Consent of Congress, lay any duty of Tonnage, keep Troops, or Ships of War in time of Peace, enter into any Agreement or Compact with another State, or with a foreign Power, or engage in War, unless actually invaded, or in such imminent Danger as will not admit of delay.

ARTICLE II

Section 1. The executive Power shall be vested in a President of the United States of America. He shall hold his Office during the Term of four years, and, together with the Vice President, chosen for the same Term, be elected, as follows:

Each State shall appoint, in such Manner as the Legislature thereof may direct, a Number of Electors, equal to the whole Number of Senators and Representatives to which the State may be entitled in the Congress: but no Senator or Representative, or Person holding an Office of Trust or Profit under the United States, shall be appointed an Elector.

[The Electors shall meet in their respective States, and vote by Ballot for two persons, of whom one at least shall not be an Inhabitant of the same State with themselves. And they shall make a List of all the Persons voted for, and of the Number of Votes for each; which List they shall sign and certify, and transmit sealed to the Seat of the Government of the United States, directed to the President of the Senate. The President of the Senate shall, in the Presence of the Senate and House of Representatives, open all the Certificates, and the Votes shall then be counted. The Person having the greatest Number of Votes shall be the President, if such Number be a Majority of the whole Number of Electors appointed; and if there be more than one who have such Majority, and have an equal Number of Votes, then the House of Representatives shall immediately chuse by Ballot one of them for President; and if no Person have a Majority, then from the five highest on the List the said House shall in like Manner chuse the President. But in chusing the President, the Votes shall be taken by States, the Representation from each State having one Vote; a quorum for this Purpose shall consist of a Member or Members from two-thirds of the States, and a Majority of all the States shall be necessary to a Choice. In every Case, after the Choice of the President, the Person having the greatest Number of Votes of the Electors shall be the Vice President. But if there should remain two or more who have equal votes, the Senate shall chuse from them by Ballot the Vice President.]⁴

The Congress may determine the Time of chusing the Electors, and the Day on which they shall give their Votes; which Day shall be the same throughout the United States.

No person except a natural-born Citizen, or a Citizen of the United States, at the time of the Adoption of this Constitution, shall be eligible to the Office of President; neither shall any Person be eligible to that Office who shall not have attained to the Age of thirty-five years, and been fourteen Years a Resident within the United States.

In Case of the Removal of the President from Office, or of his Death, Resignation, or Inability to discharge the Powers and Duties of the said Office, the same shall devolve on the Vice President, and the Congress may by Law provide for the Case of Removal, Death, Resignation, or Inability, both of the President and Vice President, declaring what Officer shall then act as President, and such Officer shall act accordingly, until the disability be removed, or a President shall be elected.

The President shall, at stated Times, receive for his Services a Compensation, which shall neither be increased nor diminished during the Period for which he shall have been elected, and he shall not receive within that Period any other Emolument from the United States, or any of them.

Before he enter on the execution of his Office, he shall take the following Oath or Affirmation:—"I do solemnly swear (or affirm) that I will faithfully execute the Office of President of the United States, and will, to the best of my Ability, preserve, protect, and defend the Constitution of the United States."

Section 2. The President shall be Commander in Chief of the Army and Navy of the United States, and of the

⁴Revised by the Twelfth Amendment.

Militia of the several States, when called into the actual Service of the United States; he may require the Opinion, in writing, of the principal Officer in each of the executive Departments, upon any subject relating to the Duties of their respective Offices, and he shall have Power to Grant Reprieves and Pardons for Offenses against the United States, except in Cases of Impeachment.

He shall have Power, by and with the Advice and Consent of the Senate, to make Treaties, provided two-thirds of the Senators present concur; and he shall nominate, and by and with the Advice and Consent of the Senate, shall appoint Ambassadors, other public Ministers and Consuls, Judges of the supreme Court, and all other Officers of the United States, whose Appointments are not herein otherwise provided for, and which shall be established by Law: but the Congress may by Law vest the Appointment of such inferior Officers, as they think proper, in the President alone, in the Courts of Law, or in the Heads of Departments.

The President shall have Power to fill up all Vacancies that may happen during the Recess of the Senate, by granting Commissions which shall expire at the End of their next Session.

Section 3. He shall from time to time give to the Congress Information of the State of the Union, and recommend to their Consideration such Measures as he shall judge necessary and expedient; he may, on extraordinary occasions, convene both Houses, or either of them, and in Case of Disagreement between them, with respect to the Time of Adjournment, he may adjourn them to such Time as he shall think proper; he shall receive Ambassadors and other public Ministers; he shall take care that the Laws be faithfully executed, and shall Commission all the Officers of the United States.

Section 4. The President, Vice President and all civil Officers of the United States, shall be removed from Office on Impeachment for, and Conviction of, Treason, Bribery, or other high Crimes and Misdemeanors.

ARTICLE III

Section 1. The judicial Power of the United States, shall be vested in one supreme Court, and in such inferior Courts as the Congress may from time to time ordain and establish. The Judges, both of the supreme and inferior Courts, shall hold their Offices during good Behaviour, and shall, at stated Times, receive for their Services, a Compensation, which shall not be diminished during their Continuance in Office.

Section 2. The judicial Power shall extend to all Cases, in Law and Equity, arising under this Constitution, the Laws of the United States, and Treaties made, or which shall be made, under their Authority;—to all

Cases affecting ambassadors, other public ministers and consuls;—to all cases of admiralty and maritime Jurisdiction;—to Controversies to which the United States shall be a Party;—to Controversies between two or more States;—between a State and Citizens of another State;[5]—between Citizens of different States—between Citizens of the same State claiming Lands under Grants of different States, and between a State, or the Citizens thereof, and foreign States, Citizens, or Subjects.

In all Cases affecting Ambassadors, other public Ministers and Consuls, and those in which a State shall be Party, the supreme Court shall have original Jurisdiction. In all the other Cases before mentioned, the supreme Court shall have appellate Jurisdiction, both as to Law and Fact, with such Exceptions, and under such Regulations as the Congress shall make.

The trial of all Crimes, except in Cases of Impeachment, shall be by Jury; and such Trial shall be held in the State where the said Crimes shall have been committed; but when not committed within any State, the Trial shall be at such Place or Places as the Congress may by Law have directed.

Section 3. Treason against the United States, shall consist only in levying War against them, or in adhering to their Enemies, giving them Aid and Comfort. No Person shall be convicted of Treason unless on the Testimony of two Witnesses to the same overt Act, or on Confession in open Court.

The Congress shall have power to declare the Punishment of Treason, but no Attainder of Treason shall work Corruption of Blood, or Forfeiture except during the Life of the Person attainted.

ARTICLE IV

Section 1. Full Faith and Credit shall be given in each State to the public Acts, Records, and judicial Proceedings of every other State. And the Congress may by general Laws prescribe the Manner in which such Acts, Records and Proceedings shall be proved, and the Effect thereof.

Section 2. The Citizens of each State shall be entitled to all Privileges and Immunities of Citizens in the several States.

A Person charged in any State with Treason, Felony, or other Crime, who shall flee from Justice, and be found in another State, shall on demand of the executive Authority of the State from which he fled, be delivered up, to be removed to the State having Jurisdiction of the crime.

No Person held to Service or Labour in one State, under the Laws thereof, escaping into another, shall, in

Consequence of any Law or Regulation therein, be discharged from such Service or Labour, but shall be delivered up on Claim of the Party to whom such Service or Labour may be due.

Section 3. New States may be admitted by the Congress into this Union; but no new State shall be formed or erected within the Jurisdiction of any other State; nor any State be formed by the Junction of two or more States, or parts of States, without the Consent of the Legislatures of the States concerned as well as of the Congress.

The Congress shall have Power to dispose of and make all needful Rules and Regulations respecting the Territory or other Property belonging to the United States; and nothing in this Constitution shall be so construed as to Prejudice any Claims of the United States, or of any particular State.

Section 4. The United States shall guarantee to every State in this Union a Republican Form of Government, and shall protect each of them against Invasion; and on Application of the Legislature, or of the Executive (when the Legislature cannot be convened) against domestic Violence.

ARTICLE V

The Congress, whenever two-thirds of both Houses shall deem it necessary, shall propose Amendments to this Constitution, or, on the Application of the Legislatures of two-thirds of the several States, shall call a Convention for proposing Amendments, which, in either Case, shall be valid to all Intents and Purposes, as part of this Constitution, when ratified by the Legislatures of three-fourths of the several States, or by Conventions in three-fourths thereof, as the one or the other Mode of Ratification may be proposed by the Congress; Provided that no Amendment which may be made prior to the Year One thousand eight hundred and eight shall in any Manner affect the first and fourth Clauses in the Ninth Section of the first Article; and that no State, without its Consent, shall be deprived of its equal Suffrage in the Senate.

ARTICLE VI

All Debts contracted and Engagements entered into, before the Adoption of this Constitution, shall be as valid against the United States under this Constitution, as under the Confederation.

This Constitution, and the Laws of the United States which shall be made in Pursuance thereof; and all Treaties made, or which shall be made, under the Authority of the United States, shall be the supreme Law of the Land; and the Judges in every State shall be bound thereby, any Thing in the Constitution or Laws of any State to the Contrary notwithstanding.

---

[5]Qualified by the Eleventh Amendment.

The Senators and Representatives before mentioned, and the Members of the several State Legislatures, and all executive and judicial Officers, both of the United States and of the several States, shall be bound by Oath or Affirmation to support this Constitution; but no religious Tests shall ever be required as a qualification to any Office or public Trust under the United States.

ARTICLE VII

The Ratification of the Conventions of nine States shall be sufficient for the Establishment of this Constitution between the States so ratifying the same.

Done in Convention by the Unanimous Consent of the States present the Seventeenth Day of September in the Year of our Lord one thousand seven hundred and Eighty seven, and of the Independence of the United States of America the Twelfth. In Witness whereof We have hereunto subscribed our Names.[6]

GEORGE WASHINGTON
PRESIDENT AND DEPUTY FROM VIRGINIA

New Hampshire
John Langdon
Nicholas Gilman

Massachusetts
Nathaniel Gorham
Rufus King

Connecticut
William Samuel Johnson
Roger Sherman

New York
Alexander Hamilton

New Jersey
William Livingston
David Brearley
William Paterson
Jonathan Dayton

Pennsylvania
Benjamin Franklin
Thomas Mifflin
Robert Morris
George Clymer
Thomas FitzSimons
Jared Ingersoll
James Wilson
Gouverneur Morris

Delaware
George Read
Gunning Bedford, Jr.
John Dickinson
Richard Bassett
Jacob Broom

Maryland
James McHenry
Daniel of St. Thomas Jenifer
Daniel Carroll

Virginia
John Blair
James Madison, Jr.

North Carolina
William Blount
Richard Dobbs Spaight
Hugh Williamson

South Carolina
John Rutledge
Charles Cotesworth Pinckney
Charles Pinckney
Pierce Butler

Georgia
William Few
Abraham Baldwin

Articles in Addition to, and Amendment of, the Constitution of the United States of America, Proposed by Congress, and Ratified by the Legislatures of the Several States, Pursuant to the Fifth Article of the Original Constitution[7]

[AMENDMENT I]
Congress shall make no law respecting an establishment of religion, or prohibiting the free exercise thereof; or abridging the freedom of speech, or of the press; or the right of the people peaceably to assemble, and to petition the Government for a redress of grievances.

[AMENDMENT II]
A well regulated Militia, being necessary to the security of a free State, the right of the people to keep and bear Arms shall not be infringed.

[AMENDMENT III]
No Soldier shall, in time of peace, be quartered in any house, without the consent of the Owner, nor in time of war, but in a manner to be prescribed by law.

[AMENDMENT IV]
The right of the people to be secure in their persons, houses, papers, and effects, against unreasonable searches and seizures, shall not be violated, and no Warrants shall issue, but upon probable cause, supported by Oath or affirmation, and particularly describing the place to be searched, and the persons or things to be seized.

[AMENDMENT V]
No person shall be held to answer for a capital or otherwise infamous crime, unless on a presentment or indictment of

---

[6]These are the full names of the signers, which in some cases are not the signatures on the document.
[7]This heading appears only in the joint resolution submitting the first ten amendments, known as the Bill of Rights.

a Grand Jury, except in cases arising in the land or naval forces, or in the Militia, when in actual service in time of War or public danger; nor shall any person be subject for the same offence to be twice put in jeopardy of life or limb; nor shall be compelled in any criminal case to be a witness against himself, nor be deprived of life, liberty, or property, without due process of law; nor shall private property be taken for public use, without just compensation.

[AMENDMENT VI]

In all criminal prosecutions, the accused shall enjoy the right to a speedy and public trial, by an impartial jury of the State and district wherein the crime shall have been committed, which district shall have been previously ascertained by law, and to be informed of the nature and cause of the accusation; to be confronted with the witnesses against him; to have compulsory process for obtaining witnesses in his favour, and to have the Assistance of Counsel for his defence.

[AMENDMENT VII]

In suits at common law, where the value in controversy shall exceed twenty dollars, the right of trial by jury shall be preserved, and no fact tried by a jury, shall be otherwise reexamined in any Court of the United States, than according to the rules of the common law.

[AMENDMENT VIII]

Excessive bail shall not be required, nor excessive fines imposed, nor cruel and unusual punishments inflicted.

[AMENDMENT IX]

The enumeration of the Constitution, of certain rights, shall not be construed to deny or disparage others retained by the people.

[AMENDMENT X]

The powers not delegated to the United States by the Constitution, nor prohibited by it to the States, are reserved to the States respectively, or to the people. [Amendments I-X, in force 1791.]

[AMENDMENT XI][8]

The Judicial power of the United States shall not be construed to extend to any suit in law or equity, commenced or prosecuted against one of the United States by Citizens of another State, or by Citizens or Subjects of any Foreign State.

[AMENDMENT XII][9]

The Electors shall meet in their respective States and vote by ballot for President and Vice-President, one of whom, at least, shall not be an inhabitant of the same State with themselves; they shall name in their ballots the person voted for as President, and in distinct ballots the person voted for as Vice-President, and they shall make distinct lists of all persons voted for as President, and of all persons voted for as Vice-President, and of the number of votes for each, which lists they shall sign and certify, and transmit sealed to the seat of the government of the United States, directed to the President of the Senate;—The President of the Senate shall, in the presence of the Senate and House of Representatives, open all the certificates and the votes shall then be counted;—The person having the greatest number of votes for President, shall be the President, if such number be a majority of the whole number of Electors appointed; and if no person have such majority, then from the persons having the highest numbers not exceeding three on the list of those voted for as President, the House of Representatives shall choose immediately, by ballot, the President. But in choosing the President, the votes shall be taken by states, the representation from each state having one vote; a quorum for this purpose shall consist of a member or members from two-thirds of the states, and a majority of all the states shall be necessary to a choice. And if the House of Representatives shall not choose a President whenever the right of choice shall devolve upon them, before the fourth day of March next following, then the Vice-President shall act as President, as in the case of the death or other constitutional disability of the President.—The person having the greatest number of votes as Vice-President, shall be the Vice-President, if such number be a majority of the whole number of Electors appointed, and if no person have a majority, then from the two highest numbers on the list, the Senate shall choose the Vice-President; a quorum for the purpose shall consist of two-thirds of the whole number of Senators, and a majority of the whole number shall be necessary to a choice. But no person constitutionally ineligible to the office of President shall be eligible to that of Vice-President of the United States.

[AMENDMENT XIII][10]

Section 1. Neither slavery nor involuntary servitude, except as a punishment for crime whereof the party shall have been duly convicted, shall exist within the United States, or any place subject to their jurisdiction.

Section 2. Congress shall have power to enforce this article by appropriate legislation.

[AMENDMENT XIV][11]

Section 1. All persons born or naturalized in the United States, and subject to the jurisdiction thereof, are

---

[8]Adopted in 1798.
[9]Adopted in 1804.

[10]Adopted in 1865.
[11]Adopted in 1868.

citizens of the United States and of the State wherein they reside. No State shall abridge the privileges or immunities of citizens of the United States; nor shall any State deprive any person of life, liberty, or property, without due process of law; nor deny to any person within its jurisdiction the equal protection of the laws.

Section 2. Representatives shall be apportioned among the several States according to their respective numbers, counting the whole number of persons in each State, excluding Indians not taxed. But when the right to vote at any election for the choice of electors for President and Vice-President of the United States, Representatives in Congress, the Executive and Judicial officers of a State, or the members of the Legislature thereof, is denied to any of the male inhabitants of such State, being twenty-one years of age, and citizens of the United States, or in any way abridged, except for participation in rebellion, or other crime, the basis of representation therein shall be reduced in the proportion which the number of such male citizens shall bear to the whole number of male citizens twenty-one years of age in such State.

Section 3. No person shall be a Senator or Representative in Congress, or elector of President and Vice-President, or hold any office, civil or military, under the United States, or under any State, who, having previously taken an oath, as a member of Congress, or as an officer of the United States, or as a member of any State legislature, or as an executive or judicial officer of any State, to support the Constitution of the United States, shall have engaged in insurrection or rebellion against the same, or given aid or comfort to the enemies thereof. But Congress may by a vote of two-thirds of each House, remove such disability.

Section 4. The validity of the public debt of the United States, authorized by law, including debts incurred for payment of pensions and bounties for services in suppressing insurrection or rebellion, shall not be questioned. But neither the United States nor any State shall assume or pay any debts or obligation incurred in aid of insurrection or rebellion against the United States, or any claim for the loss or emancipation of any slave; but all such debts, obligations, and claims shall be held illegal and void.

Section 5. The Congress shall have the power to enforce, by appropriate legislation, the provisions of this article.

[AMENDMENT XV][12]

Section 1. The right of citizens of the United States to vote shall not be denied or abridged by the United States or by any State on account of race, color, or previous condition of servitude—

---

[12]Adopted in 1870.

Section 2. The Congress shall have power to enforce this article by appropriate legislation.

[AMENDMENT XVI][13]

The Congress shall have power to lay and collect taxes on incomes, from whatever source derived, without apportionment among the several States, and without regard to any census or enumeration.

[AMENDMENT XVII][14]

The Senate of the United States shall be composed of two Senators from each State, elected by the people thereof, for six years; and each Senator shall have one vote. The electors in each State shall have the qualifications requisite for electors of the most numerous branch of the State legislatures.

When vacancies happen in the representation of any State in the Senate, the executive authority of such State shall issue writs of election to fill such vacancies: Provided, That the legislature of any State may empower the executive thereof to make temporary appointments until the people fill the vacancies by election as the legislature may direct.

This amendment shall not be so construed as to affect the election or term of any Senator chosen before it becomes valid as part of the Constitution.

[AMENDMENT XVIII][15]

Section 1. After one year from the ratification of this article the manufacture, sale, or transportation of intoxicating liquors within, the importation thereof into, or the exportation thereof from the United States and all territory subject to the jurisdiction thereof for beverage purposes is hereby prohibited.

Section 2. The Congress and the several States shall have concurrent power to enforce this article by appropriate legislation.

Section 3. This article shall be inoperative unless it shall have been ratified as an amendment to the Constitution by the legislatures of the several States, as provided in the Constitution, within seven years from the date of the submission hereof to the States by the Congress.

[AMENDMENT XIX][16]

The right of citizens of the United States to vote shall not be denied or abridged by the United States or by any State on account of sex.

Congress shall have power to enforce this article by appropriate legislation.

---

[13]Adopted in 1913.
[14]Adopted in 1913.
[15]Adopted in 1918.
[16]Adopted in 1920.

[AMENDMENT XX][17]

Section 1. The terms of the President and Vice-President shall end at noon on the 20th day of January, and the terms of Senators and Representatives at noon on the 3d day of January, of the years in which such terms would have ended if this article had not been ratified; and the terms of their successors shall then begin.

Section 2. The Congress shall assemble at least once in every year, and such meeting shall begin at noon on the 3d day of January, unless they shall by law appoint a different day.

Section 3. If, at the time fixed for the beginning of the term of the President, the President elect shall have died, the Vice-President elect shall become President. If a President shall not have been chosen before the time fixed for the beginning of his term or if the President elect shall have failed to qualify, then the Vice-President elect shall act as President until a President shall have qualified; and the Congress may by law provide for the case wherein neither a President elect nor a Vice-President elect shall have qualified, declaring who shall then act as President, or the manner in which one who is to act shall be selected, and such person shall act accordingly until a President or Vice-President shall have qualified.

Section 4. The Congress may by law provide for the case of the death of any of the persons from whom the House of Representatives may choose a President whenever the right of choice shall have devolved upon them, and for the case of the death of any of the persons from whom the Senate may choose a Vice-President whenever the right of choice shall have devolved upon them.

Section 5. Sections 1 and 2 shall take effect on the 15th day of October following the ratification of this article.

Section 6. This article shall be inoperative unless it shall have been ratified as an amendment to the Constitution by the legislatures of three-fourths of the several States within seven years from the date of its submission.

[AMENDMENT XXI][18]

Section 1. The eighteenth article of amendment to the Constitution of the United States is hereby repealed.

Section 2. The transportation or importation into any State, Territory, or possession of the United States for delivery or use therein of intoxicating liquors, in violation of the laws thereof, is hereby prohibited.

Section 3. This article shall be inoperative unless it shall have been ratified as an amendment to the Constitution by conventions in the several States, as provided in the Constitution, within seven years from the date of the submission hereof to the States by the Congress.

[AMENDMENT XXII][19]

No person shall be elected to the office of the President more than twice, and no person who has held the office of President, or acted as President, for more than two years of a term to which some other person was elected President shall be elected to the office of the President more than once.

But this Article shall not apply to any person holding the office of President when this Article was proposed by the Congress, and shall not prevent any person who may be holding the office of President, or acting as President, during the term within which this Article becomes operative from holding the office of President or acting as President during the remainder of such term.

This article shall be inoperative unless it shall have been ratified as an amendment to the Constitution by the legislatures of three-fourths of the several states within seven years from the date of its submission to the states by the Congress.

[AMENDMENT XXIII][20]

Section 1. The District constituting the seat of Government of the United States shall appoint in such manner as the Congress may direct:

A number of electors of President and Vice-President equal to the whole number of Senators and Representatives in Congress to which the District would be entitled if it were a State, but in no event more than the least populous State; they shall be in addition to those appointed by the States, but they shall be considered, for the purpose of the election of President and Vice-President, to be electors appointed by a State; and they shall meet in the District and perform such duties as provided by the twelfth article of amendment.

Section 2. The Congress shall have power to enforce this article by appropriate legislation.

[AMENDMENT XXIV][21]

Section 1. The right of citizens of the United States to vote in any primary or other election for President or Vice-President, for electors for President or Vice-President, or for Senator or Representative in Congress, shall not be

---

[17]Adopted in 1933.
[18]Adopted in 1933.

[19]Adopted in 1951.
[20]Adopted in 1961.
[21]Adopted in 1964.

denied or abridged by the United States or any state by reason of failure to pay any poll tax or other tax.

Section 2. The Congress shall have the power to enforce this article by appropriate legislation.

[AMENDMENT XXV][22]

Section 1. In case of the removal of the President from office or of his death or resignation, the Vice-President shall become President.

Section 2. Whenever there is a vacancy in the office of the Vice President, the President shall nominate a Vice President who shall take office upon confirmation by a majority vote of both Houses of Congress.

Section 3. Whenever the President transmits to the President Pro Tempore of the Senate and the Speaker of the House of Representatives his written declaration that he is unable to discharge the powers and duties of his office, and until he transmits to them a written declaration to the contrary, such powers and duties shall be discharged by the Vice-President as Acting President.

Section 4. Whenever the Vice-President and a majority of either the principal officers of the executive departments or of such other body as Congress may by law provide, transmit to the President Pro Tempore of the Senate and the Speaker of the House of Representatives their written declaration that the President is unable to discharge the powers and duties of his office, the Vice President shall immediately assume the powers and duties of the office as Acting President.

Thereafter, when the President transmits to the President Pro Tempore of the Senate and the Speaker of the House of Representatives his written declaration that no inability exists, he shall resume the powers and duties of his office unless the Vice President and a majority of either the principal officers of the executive departments or of such other body as Congress may by law provide, transmit within four days to the President Pro Tempore of the Senate and the Speaker of the House of Representatives their written declaration that the President is unable to discharge the powers and duties of his office. Thereupon Congress shall decide the issue, assembling within forty-eight hours for that purpose if not in session. If the Congress, within twenty-one days after receipt of the latter written declaration, or, if Congress is not in session, within twenty-one days after Congress is required to assemble, determines by two-thirds vote of both Houses that the President is unable to discharge the powers and duties of his office, the Vice President shall continue to discharge the same as Acting President; otherwise, the President shall resume the powers and duties of his office.

[AMENDMENT XXVI][23]

Section 1. The right of citizens of the United States, who are eighteen years of age or older, to vote shall not be denied or abridged by the United States or by any State on account of age.

Section 2. The Congress shall have power to enforce this article by appropriate legislation.

[AMENDMENT XXVII][24]

No law, varying the compensation for the services of the Senators and Representatives, shall take effect, until an election of Representatives shall have intervened.

---

[22]Adopted in 1967.

[23]Adopted in 1971.

[24]Adopted in 1992.

Presidential Elections

Year	Candidates	Parties	Popular Vote	% of Popular Vote	Electoral Vote	% Voter Participation
1789	**George Washington**				69	
	John Adams				34	
	Other candidates				35	
1792	**George Washington**				132	
	John Adams				77	
	George Clinton				50	
	Other candidates				5	
1796	**John Adams**	Federalist			71	
	Thomas Jefferson	Dem.-Rep.			68	
	Thomas Pinckney	Federalist			59	
	Aaron Burr	Dem.-Rep.			30	
	Other candidates				48	
1800	**Thomas Jefferson**	Dem.-Rep.			73	
	Aaron Burr	Dem.-Rep.			73	
	John Adams	Federalist			65	
	Charles C. Pinckney	Federalist			64	
	John Jay	Federalist			1	
1804	**Thomas Jefferson**	Dem.-Rep.			162	
	Charles C. Pinckney	Federalist			14	
1808	**James Madison**	Dem.-Rep.			122	
	Charles C. Pinckney	Federalist			47	
	George Clinton	Dem.-Rep.			6	
1812	**James Madison**	Dem.-Rep.			128	
	DeWitt Clinton	Federalist			89	
1816	**James Monroe**	Dem.-Rep.			183	
	Rufus King	Federalist			34	
1820	**James Monroe**	Dem.-Rep.			231	
	John Quincy Adams	Indep.-Rep.			1	
1824	**John Quincy Adams**	Dem.-Rep.	113,122	31.0	84	26.9
	Andrew Jackson	Dem.-Rep.	151,271	43.0	99	
	Henry Clay	Dem.-Rep.	47,136	13.0	37	
	William H. Crawford	Dem.-Rep.	46,618	13.0	41	
1828	**Andrew Jackson**	Democratic	642,553	56.0	178	57.6
	John Quincy Adams	National Republican	500,897	44.0	83	
1832	**Andrew Jackson**	Democratic	701,780	54.5	219	55.4
	Henry Clay	National Republican	484,205	37.5	49	
	William Wirt	Anti-Masonic ⎞		8.0	7	
	John Floyd	Democratic ⎠	101,051		11	
1836	**Martin Van Buren**	Democratic	764,176	50.9	170	57.8
	William H. Harrison	Whig	550,816	49.1	73	
	Hugh L. White	Whig			26	
	Daniel Webster	Whig			14	
	W. P. Mangum	Whig			11	
1840	**William H. Harrison**	Whig	1,275,390	53.0	234	80.2
	Martin Van Buren	Democratic	1,128,854	47.0	60	

Year	Candidates	Parties	Popular Vote	% of Popular Vote	Electoral Vote	% Voter Participation
1844	**James K. Polk**	Democratic	1,339,494	49.6	170	78.9
	Henry Clay	Whig	1,300,004	48.1	105	
	James G. Birney	Liberty	62,300	2.3		
1848	**Zachary Taylor**	Whig	1,361,393	47.4	163	72.7
	Lewis Cass	Democratic	1,223,460	42.5	127	
	Martin Van Buren	Free Soil	291,263	10.1		
1852	**Franklin Pierce**	Democratic	1,607,510	50.9	254	69.6
	Winfield Scott	Whig	1,386,942	44.1	42	
	John P. Hale	Free Soil	155,825	5.0		
1856	**James Buchanan**	Democratic	1,836,072	45.3	174	78.9
	John C. Fremont	Republican	1,342,345	33.1	114	
	Millard Fillmore	American	871,731	21.6	8	
1860	**Abraham Lincoln**	Republican	1,865,908	39.8	180	81.2
	Stephen A. Douglas	Democratic	1,375,157	29.5	12	
	John C. Breckinridge	Democratic	848,019	18.1	72	
	John Bell	Constitutional Union	590,631	12.6	39	
1864	**Abraham Lincoln**	Republican	2,218,388	55.0	212	73.8
	George B. McClellan	Democratic	1,812,807	45.0	21	
1868	**Ulysses S. Grant**	Republican	3,013,650	52.7	214	78.1
	Horatio Seymour	Democratic	2,708,744	47.3	80	
1872	**Ulysses S. Grant**	Republican	3,598,235	55.6	286	71.3
	Horace Greeley	Democratic	2,834,761	43.9	66	
1876	**Rutherford B. Hayes**	Republican	4,034,311	48.0	185	81.8
	Samuel J. Tilden	Democratic	4,288,546	51.0	184	
1880	**James A. Garfield**	Republican	4,446,158	48.5	214	79.4
	Winfield S. Hancock	Democratic	4,444,260	48.1	155	
	James B. Weaver	Greenback-Labor	308,578	3.4		
1884	**Grover Cleveland**	Democratic	4,874,621	48.5	219	77.5
	James G. Blaine	Republican	4,848,936	48.2	182	
	Benjamin F. Butler	Greenback-Labor	175,370	1.8		
	John P. St. John	Prohibition	150,369	1.5		
1888	**Benjamin Harrison**	Republican	5,443,892	47.9	233	79.3
	Grover Cleveland	Democratic	5,534,488	48.6	168	
	Clinton B. Fisk	Prohibition	249,506	2.2		
	Anson J. Streeter	Union Labor	146,935	1.3		
1892	**Grover Cleveland**	Democratic	5,551,883	46.1	277	74.7
	Benjamin Harrison	Republican	5,179,244	43.0	145	
	James B. Weaver	People's	1,029,846	8.5	22	
	John Bidwell	Prohibition	264,133	2.2		
1896	**William McKinley**	Republican	7,108,480	52.0	271	79.3
	William J. Bryan	Democratic	6,511,495	48.0	176	
1900	**William McKinley**	Republican	7,218,039	51.7	292	73.2
	William J. Bryan	Democratic; Populist	6,358,345	45.5	155	
	John C. Wooley	Prohibition	208,914	1.5		
1904	**Theodore Roosevelt**	Republican	7,626,593	57.4	336	65.2
	Alton B. Parker	Democratic	5,082,898	37.6	140	
	Eugene V. Debs	Socialist	402,283	3.0		
	Silas C. Swallow	Prohibition	258,536	1.9		
1908	**William H. Taft**	Republican	7,676,258	51.6	321	65.4
	William J. Bryan	Democratic	6,406,801	43.1	162	
	Eugene V. Debs	Socialist	420,793	2.8		
	Eugene W. Chafin	Prohibition	253,840	1.7		

Year	Candidates	Parties	Popular Vote	% of Popular Vote	Electoral Vote	% Voter Participation
1912	**Woodrow Wilson**	Democratic	6,293,152	42.0	435	58.8
	Theodore Roosevelt	Progressive	4,119,207	28.0	88	
	William H. Taft	Republican	3,484,980	24.0	8	
	Eugene V. Debs	Socialist	900,672	6.0		
	Eugene W. Chafin	Prohibition	206,275	1.4		
1916	**Woodrow Wilson**	Democratic	9,126,300	49.4	277	61.6
	Charles E. Hughes	Republican	8,546,789	46.2	254	
	A. L. Benson	Socialist	585,113	3.2		
	J. Frank Hanly	Prohibition	220,506	1.2		
1920	**Warren G. Harding**	Republican	16,153,115	60.4	404	49.2
	James M. Cox	Democratic	9,133,092	34.2	127	
	Eugene V. Debs	Socialist	919,799	3.4		
	P. P. Christensen	Farmer-Labor	265,411	1.0		
1924	**Calvin Coolidge**	Republican	15,719,921	54.0	382	48.9
	John W. Davis	Democratic	8,386,704	28.8	136	
	Robert M. La Follette	Progressive	4,831,289	16.6	13	
1928	**Herbert C. Hoover**	Republican	21,437,277	58.2	444	56.9
	Alfred E. Smith	Democratic	15,007,698	40.9	87	
1932	**Franklin D. Roosevelt**	Democratic	22,829,501	57.4	472	56.9
	Herbert C. Hoover	Republican	15,760,684	39.7	59	
	Norman Thomas	Socialist	881,951	2.2		
1936	**Franklin D. Roosevelt**	Democratic	27,757,333	60.8	523	61.0
	Alfred M. Landon	Republican	16,684,231	36.5	8	
	William Lemke	Union	882,479	1.9		
1940	**Franklin D. Roosevelt**	Democratic	27,313,041	54.8	449	62.5
	Wendell L. Wilkie	Republican	22,348,480	44.8	82	
1944	**Franklin D. Roosevelt**	Democratic	25,612,610	53.5	432	55.9
	Thomas E. Dewey	Republican	22,117,617	46.0	99	
1948	**Harry S Truman**	Democratic	24,179,345	50.0	303	53.0
	Thomas E. Dewey	Republican	21,991,291	46.0	189	
	J. Strom Thurmond	States' Rights	1,169,021	2.0	39	
	Henry A. Wallace	Progressive	1,157,172	2.0		
1952	**Dwight D. Eisenhower**	Republican	33,936,234	55.1	442	63.3
	Adlai E. Stevenson	Democratic	27,314,992	44.4	89	
1956	**Dwight D. Eisenhower**	Republican	35,590,472	57.6	457	60.6
	Adlai E. Stevenson	Democratic	26,022,752	42.1	73	
1960	**John F. Kennedy**	Democratic	34,226,731	49.7	303	62.8
	Richard M. Nixon	Republican	34,108,157	49.6	219	
	Harry F. Byrd	Independent	501,643		15	
1964	**Lyndon B. Johnson**	Democratic	43,129,566	61.1	486	61.7
	Barry M. Goldwater	Republican	27,178,188	38.5	52	
1968	**Richard M. Nixon**	Republican	31,785,480	44.0	301	60.6
	Hubert H. Humphrey	Democratic	31,275,166	42.7	191	
	George C. Wallace	American Independent	9,906,473	13.5	46	
1972	**Richard M. Nixon**	Republican	47,169,911	60.7	520	55.2
	George S. McGovern	Democratic	29,170,383	37.5	17	
	John G. Schmitz	American	1,099,482	1.4		
1976	**Jimmy Carter**	Democratic	40,830,763	50.1	297	53.5
	Gerald R. Ford	Republican	39,147,793	48.0	240	

Year	Candidates	Parties	Popular Vote	% of Popular Vote	Electoral Vote	% Voter Participation
1980	**Ronald Reagan**	Republican	43,904,153	51.0	489	52.6
	Jimmy Carter	Democratic	35,483,883	41.0	49	
	John B. Anderson	Independent	5,719,437	7.0	0	
	Ed Clark	Libertarian	920,859	1.0	0	
1984	**Ronald Reagan**	Republican	54,455,075	58.8	525	53.3
	Walter Mondale	Democratic	37,577,185	40.5	13	
1988	**George Bush**	Republican	48,886,097	53.9	426	48.6
	Michael Dukakis	Democratic	41,809,074	46.1	111	
1992	**William J. Clinton**	Democratic	44,908,254	43.0	370	55.9
	George H. Bush	Republican	39,102,343	37.4	168	
	H. Ross Perot	Independent	19,741,065	18.9	0	
1996	**William J. Clinton**	Democratic	45,590,703	49.3	379	49
	Robert Dole	Republican	37,816,307	40.7	159	
	H. Ross Perot	Reform	8,085,294	8.4	0	
2000	**George W. Bush**	Republican	50,456,062	47.9	271	51.2
	Al Gore	Democratic	50,996,582	48.4	266	
	Ralph Nader	Green	2,858,843	2.7	0	
2004	**George W. Bush**	Republican	62,048,610	50.7	286	60.7
	John F. Kerry	Democrat	59,028,444	48.3	251	
	Ralph Nader	Independent	465,650	0.4	0	

Presidential Administrations

The Washington Administration (1789–1797)

Vice President	John Adams	1789–1797
Secretary of State	Thomas Jefferson	1789–1793
	Edmund Randolph	1794–1795
	Timothy Pickering	1795–1797
Secretary of Treasury	Alexander Hamilton	1789–1795
	Oliver Wolcott	1795–1797
Secretary of War	Henry Knox	1789–1794
	Timothy Pickering	1795–1796
	James McHenry	1796–1797
Attorney General	Edmund Randolph	1789–1793
	William Bradford	1794–1795
	Charles Lee	1795–1797
Postmaster General	Samuel Osgood	1789–1791
	Timothy Pickering	1791–1794
	Joseph Habersham	1795–1797

The John Adams Administration (1797–1801)

Vice President	Thomas Jefferson	1797–1801
Secretary of State	Timothy Pickering	1797–1800
	John Marshall	1800–1801
Secretary of Treasury	Oliver Wolcott	1797–1800
	Samuel Dexter	1800–1801
Secretary of War	James McHenry	1797–1800
	Samuel Dexter	1800–1801
Attorney General	Charles Lee	1797–1801
Postmaster General	Joseph Habersham	1797–1801
Secretary of Navy	Benjamin Stoddert	1798–1801

The Jefferson Administration (1801–1809)

Vice President	Aaron Burr	1801–1805
	George Clinton	1805–1809
Secretary of State	James Madison	1801–1809
Secretary of Treasury	Samuel Dexter	1801
	Albert Gallatin	1801–1809
Secretary of War	Henry Dearborn	1801–1809
Attorney General	Levi Lincoln	1801–1805
	Robert Smith	1805
	John Breckinridge	1805–1806
	Caesar Rodney	1807–1809
Postmaster General	Joseph Habersham	1801
	Gideon Granger	1801–1809
Secretary of Navy	Robert Smith	1801–1809

The Madison Administration (1809–1817)

Vice President	George Clinton	1809–1813
	Elbridge Gerry	1813–1817
Secretary of State	Robert Smith	1809–1811
	James Monroe	1811–1817
Secretary of Treasury	Albert Gallatin	1809–1813
	George Campbell	1814
	Alexander Dallas	1814–1816
	William Crawford	1816–1817
Secretary of War	William Eustis	1809–1812
	John Armstrong	1813–1814
	James Monroe	1814–1815
	William Crawford	1815–1817
Attorney General	Caesar Rodney	1809–1811
	William Pinkney	1811–1814
	Richard Rush	1814–1817
Postmaster General	Gideon Granger	1809–1814
	Return Meigs	1814–1817
Secretary of Navy	Paul Hamilton	1809–1813
	William Jones	1813–1814
	Benjamin Crowninshield	1814–1817

The Monroe Administration (1817–1825)

Vice President	Daniel Tompkins	1817–1825
Secretary of State	John Quincy Adams	1817–1825
Secretary of Treasury	William Crawford	1817–1825
Secretary of War	George Graham	1817
	John C. Calhoun	1817–1825
Attorney General	Richard Rush	1817
	William Wirt	1817–1825
Postmaster General	Return Meigs	1817–1823
	John McLean	1823–1825
Secretary of Navy	Benjamin Crowninshield	1817–1818
	Smith Thompson	1818–1823
	Samuel Southard	1823–1825

The John Quincy Adams Administration (1825–1829)

Vice President	John C. Calhoun	1825–1829
Secretary of State	Henry Clay	1825–1829
Secretary of Treasury	Richard Rush	1825–1829
Secretary of War	James Barbour	1825–1828
	Peter Porter	1828–1829
Attorney General	William Wirt	1825–1829
Postmaster General	John McLean	1825–1829
Secretary of Navy	Samuel Southard	1825–1829

The Jackson Administration (1829–1837)

Vice President	John C. Calhoun	1829–1833
	Martin Van Buren	1833–1837
Secretary of State	Martin Van Buren	1829–1831
	Edward Livingston	1831–1833
	Louis McLane	1833–1834
	John Forsyth	1834–1837
Secretary of Treasury	Samuel Ingham	1829–1831
	Louis McLane	1831–1833
	William Duane	1833
	Roger B. Taney	1833–1834
	Levi Woodbury	1834–1837
Secretary of War	John H. Eaton	1829–1831
	Lewis Cass	1831–1837
	Benjamin Butler	1837
Attorney General	John M. Berrien	1829–1831
	Roger B. Taney	1831–1833
	Benjamin Butler	1833–1837
Postmaster General	William Barry	1829–1835
	Amos Kendall	1835–1837
Secretary of Navy	John Branch	1829–1831
	Levi Woodbury	1831–1834
	Mahlon Dickerson	1834–1837

The Van Buren Administration (1837–1841)

Vice President	Richard M. Johnson	1837–1841
Secretary of State	John Forsyth	1837–1841
Secretary of Treasury	Levi Woodbury	1837–1841
Secretary of War	Joel Poinsett	1837–1841
Attorney General	Benjamin Butler	1837–1838
	Felix Grundy	1838–1840
	Henry D. Gilpin	1840–1841
Postmaster General	Amos Kendall	1837–1840
	John M. Niles	1840–1841
Secretary of Navy	Mahlon Dickerson	1837–1838
	James Paulding	1838–1841

The William Harrison Administration (1841)

Vice President	John Tyler	1841
Secretary of State	Daniel Webster	1841
Secretary of Treasury	Thomas Ewing	1841
Secretary of War	John Bell	1841
Attorney General	John J. Crittenden	1841
Postmaster General	Francis Granger	1841
Secretary of Navy	George Badger	1841

The Tyler Administration (1841–1845)

Vice President	None	
Secretary of State	Daniel Webster	1841–1843
	Hugh S. Legaré	1843
	Abel P. Upshur	1843–1844
	John C. Calhoun	1844–1845
Secretary of Treasury	Thomas Ewing	1841
	Walter Forward	1841–1843
	John C. Spencer	1843–1844
	George Bibb	1844–1845
Secretary of War	John Bell	1841
	John C. Spencer	1841–1843
	James M. Porter	1843–1844
	William Wilkins	1844–1845
Attorney General	John J. Crittenden	1841
	Hugh S. Legaré	1841–1843
	John Nelson	1843–1845
Postmaster General	Francis Granger	1841
	Charles Wickliffe	1841–1845
Secretary of Navy	George Badger	1841
	Abel P. Upshur	1841
	David Henshaw	1843–1844
	Thomas Gilmer	1844
	John Y. Mason	1844–1845

The Polk Administration (1845–1849)

Vice President	George M. Dallas	1845–1849
Secretary of State	James Buchanan	1845–1849
Secretary of Treasury	Robert J. Walker	1845–1849
Secretary of War	William L. Marcy	1845–1849
Attorney General	John Y. Mason	1845–1846
	Nathan Clifford	1846–1848
	Isaac Toucey	1848–1849
Postmaster General	Cave Johnson	1845–1849
Secretary of Navy	George Bancroft	1845–1846
	John Y. Mason	1846–1849

The Taylor Administration (1849–1850)

Vice President	Millard Fillmore	1849–1850
Secretary of State	John M. Clayton	1849–1850
Secretary of Treasury	William Meredith	1849–1850
Secretary of War	George Crawford	1849–1850
Attorney General	Reverdy Johnson	1849–1850
Postmaster General	Jacob Collamer	1849–1850
Secretary of Navy	William Preston	1849–1850
Secretary of Interior	Thomas Ewing	1849–1850

The Fillmore Administration (1850–1853)

Vice President	None	
Secretary of State	Daniel Webster	1850–1852
	Edward Everett	1852–1853
Secretary of Treasury	Thomas Corwin	1850–1853
Secretary of War	Charles Conrad	1850–1853
Attorney General	John J. Crittenden	1850–1853
Postmaster General	Nathan Hall	1850–1852
	Sam D. Hubbard	1852–1853

Secretary of Navy	William A. Graham	1850–1852
	John P. Kennedy	1852–1853
Secretary of Interior	Thomas McKennan	1850
	Alexander Stuart	1850–1853

The Pierce Administration (1853–1857)

Vice President	William R. King	1853–1857
Secretary of State	William L. Marcy	1853–1857
Secretary of Treasury	James Guthrie	1853–1857
Secretary of War	Jefferson Davis	1853–1857
Attorney General	Caleb Cushing	1853–1857
Postmaster General	James Campbell	1853–1857
Secretary of Navy	James C. Dobbin	1853–1857
Secretary of Interior	Robert McClelland	1853–1857

The Buchanan Administration (1857–1861)

Vice President	John C. Breckinridge	1857–1861
Secretary of State	Lewis Cass	1857–1860
	Jeremiah S. Black	1860–1861
Secretary of Treasury	Howell Cobb	1857–1860
	Philip Thomas	1860–1861
	John A. Dix	1861
Secretary of War	John B. Floyd	1857–1861
	Joseph Holt	1861
Attorney General	Jeremiah S. Black	1857–1860
	Edwin M. Stanton	1860–1861
Postmaster General	Aaron V. Brown	1857–1859
	Joseph Holt	1859–1861
	Horatio King	1861
Secretary of Navy	Isaac Toucey	1857–1861
Secretary of Interior	Jacob Thompson	1857–1861

The Lincoln Administration (1861–1865)

Vice President	Hannibal Hamlin	1861–1865
	Andrew Johnson	1865
Secretary of State	William H. Seward	1861–1865
Secretary of Treasury	Samuel P. Chase	1861–1864
	William P. Fessenden	1864–1865
	Hugh McCulloch	1865
Secretary of War	Simon Cameron	1861–1862
	Edwin M. Stanton	1862–1865
Attorney General	Edward Bates	1861–1864
	James Speed	1864–1865
Postmaster General	Horatio King	1861
	Montgomery Blair	1861–1864
	William Dennison	1864–1865
Secretary of Navy	Gideon Welles	1861–1865
Secretary of Interior	Caleb B. Smith	1861–1863
	John P. Usher	1863–1865

The Andrew Johnson Administration (1865–1869)

Vice President	None	
Secretary of State	William H. Seward	1865–1869
Secretary of Treasury	Hugh McCulloch	1865–1869
Secretary of War	Edwin M. Stanton	1865–1867
	Ulysses S. Grant	1867–1868
	Lorenzo Thomas	1868
	John M. Schofield	1868–1869
Attorney General	James Speed	1865–1866
	Henry Stanbery	1866–1868
	William M. Evarts	1868–1869
Postmaster General	William Dennison	1865–1866
	Alexander Randall	1866–1869
Secretary of Navy	Gideon Welles	1865–1869
Secretary of Interior	John P. Usher	1865
	James Harlan	1865–1866
	Orville H. Browning	1866–1869

The Grant Administration (1869–1877)

Vice President	Schuyler Colfax	1869–1873
	Henry Wilson	1873–1877
Secretary of State	Elihu B. Washburne	1869
	Hamilton Fish	1869–1877
Secretary of Treasury	George S. Boutwell	1869–1873
	William Richardson	1873–1874
	Benjamin Bristow	1874–1876
	Lot M. Morrill	1876–1877
Secretary of War	John A. Rawlins	1869
	William T. Sherman	1869
	William W. Belknap	1869–1876
	Alphonso Taft	1876
	James D. Cameron	1876–1877
Attorney General	Ebenezer Hoar	1869–1870
	Amos T. Ackerman	1870–1871
	G. H. Williams	1871–1875
	Edwards Pierrepont	1875–1876
	Alphonso Taft	1876–1877
Postmaster General	John A. J. Creswell	1869–1874
	James W. Marshall	1874
	Marshall Jewell	1874–1876
	James N. Tyner	1876–1877
Secretary of Navy	Adolph E. Borie	1869
	George M. Robeson	1869–1877
Secretary of Interior	Jacob D. Cox	1869–1870
	Columbus Delano	1870–1875
	Zachariah Chandler	1875–1877

The Hayes Administration (1877–1881)

Vice President	William A. Wheeler	1877–1881
Secretary of State	William M. Evarts	1877–1881
Secretary of Treasury	John Sherman	1877–1881

Secretary of War	George W. McCrary	1877–1879
	Alex Ramsey	1879–1881
Attorney General	Charles Devens	1877–1881
Postmaster General	David M. Key	1877–1880
	Horace Maynard	1880–1881
Secretary of Navy	Richard W. Thompson	1877–1880
	Nathan Goff Jr.	1881
Secretary of Interior	Carl Schurz	1877–1881

The Garfield Administration (1881)

Vice President	Chester A. Arthur	1881
Secretary of State	James G. Blaine	1881
Secretary of Treasury	William Windom	1881
Secretary of War	Robert T. Lincoln	1881
Attorney General	Wayne MacVeagh	1881
Postmaster General	Thomas L. James	1881
Secretary of Navy	William H. Hunt	1881
Secretary of Interior	Samuel J. Kirkwood	1881

The Arthur Administration (1881–1885)

Vice President	None	
Secretary of State	F. T. Frelinghuysen	1881–1885
Secretary of Treasury	Charles J. Folger	1881–1884
	Walter Q. Gresham	1884
	Hugh McCulloch	1884–1885
Secretary of War	Robert T. Lincoln	1881–1885
Attorney General	Benjamin H. Brewster	1881–1885
Postmaster General	Timothy O. Howe	1881–1883
	Walter Q. Gresham	1883–1884
	Frank Hatton	1884–1885
Secretary of Navy	William H. Hunt	1881–1882
	William E. Chandler	1882–1885
Secretary of Interior	Samuel J. Kirkwood	1881–1882
	Henry M. Teller	1882–1885

The Cleveland Administration (1885–1889)

Vice President	Thomas A. Hendricks	1885–1889
Secretary of State	Thomas F. Bayard	1885–1889
Secretary of Treasury	Daniel Manning	1885–1887
	Charles S. Fairchild	1887–1889
Secretary of War	William C. Endicott	1885–1889
Attorney General	Augustus H. Garland	1885–1889
Postmaster General	William F. Vilas	1885–1888
	Don M. Dickinson	1888–1889
Secretary of Navy	William C. Whitney	1885–1889
Secretary of Interior	Lucius Q. C. Lamar	1885–1888
	William F. Vilas	1888–1889
Secretary of Agriculture	Norman J. Colman	1889

The Benjamin Harrison Administration (1889–1893)

Vice President	Levi P. Morton	1889–1893
Secretary of State	James G. Blaine	1889–1892
	John W. Foster	1892–1893
Secretary of Treasury	William Windom	1889–1891
	Charles Foster	1891–1893
Secretary of War	Redfield Proctor	1889–1891
	Stephen B. Elkins	1891–1893
Attorney General	William H. H. Miller	1889–1893
Postmaster General	John Wanamaker	1889–1893
Secretary of Navy	Benjamin F. Tracy	1889–1893
Secretary of Interior	John W. Noble	1889–1893
Secretary of Agriculture	Jeremiah M. Rusk	1889–1893

The Cleveland Administration (1893–1897)

Vice President	Adlai E. Stevenson	1893–1897
Secretary of State	Walter Q. Gresham	1893–1895
	Richard Olney	1895–1897
Secretary of Treasury	John G. Carlisle	1893–1897
Secretary of War	Daniel S. Lamont	1893–1897
Attorney General	Richard Olney	1893–1895
	James Harmon	1895–1897
Postmaster General	Wilson S. Bissell	1893–1895
	William L. Wilson	1895–1897
Secretary of Navy	Hilary A. Herbert	1893–1897
Secretary of Interior	Hoke Smith	1893–1896
	David R. Francis	1896–1897
Secretary of Agriculture	Julius S. Morton	1893–1897

The McKinley Administration (1897–1901)

Vice President	Garret A. Hobart	1897–1901
	Theodore Roosevelt	1901
Secretary of State	John Sherman	1897–1898
	William R. Day	1898
	John Hay	1898–1901
Secretary of Treasury	Lyman J. Gage	1897–1901
Secretary of War	Russell A. Alger	1897–1899
	Elihu Root	1899–1901
Attorney General	Joseph McKenna	1897–1898
	John W. Griggs	1898–1901
	Philander C. Knox	1901
Postmaster General	James A. Gary	1897–1898
	Charles E. Smith	1898–1901
Secretary of Navy	John D. Long	1897–1901
Secretary of Interior	Cornelius N. Bliss	1897–1899
	Ethan A. Hitchcock	1899–1901
Secretary of Agriculture	James Wilson	1897–1901

The Theodore Roosevelt Administration (1901–1909)

Vice President	Charles Fairbanks	1905–1909
Secretary of State	John Hay	1901–1905
	Elihu Root	1905–1909
	Robert Bacon	1909
Secretary of Treasury	Lyman J. Gage	1901–1902
	Leslie M. Shaw	1902–1907

	George B. Cortelyou	1907–1909
Secretary of War	Elihu Root	1901–1904
	William H. Taft	1904–1908
	Luke E. Wright	1908–1909
Attorney General	Philander C. Knox	1901–1904
	William H. Moody	1904–1906
	Charles J. Bonaparte	1906–1909
Postmaster General	Charles E. Smith	1901–1902
	Henry C. Payne	1902–1904
	Robert J. Wynne	1904–1905
	George B. Cortelyou	1905–1907
	George von L. Meyer	1907–1909
Secretary of Navy	John D. Long	1901–1902
	William H. Moody	1902–1904
	Paul Morton	1904–1905
	Charles J. Bonaparte	1905–1906
	Victor H. Metcalf	1906–1908
	Truman H. Newberry	1908–1909
Secretary of Interior	Ethan A. Hitchcock	1901–1907
	James R. Garfield	1907–1909
Secretary of Agriculture	James Wilson	1901–1909
Secretary of Labor and Commerce	George B. Cortelyou	1903–1904
	Victor H. Metcalf	1904–1906
	Oscar S. Straus	1906–1909
	Charles Nagel	1909

The Taft Administration (1909–1913)

Vice President	James S. Sherman	1909–1913
Secretary of State	Philander C. Knox	1909–1913
Secretary of Treasury	Franklin MacVeagh	1909–1913
Secretary of War	Jacob M. Dickinson	1909–1911
	Henry L. Stimson	1911–1913
Attorney General	George W. Wickersham	1909–1913
Postmaster General	Frank H. Hitchcock	1909–1913
Secretary of Navy	George von L. Meyer	1909–1913
Secretary of Interior	Richard A. Ballinger	1909–1911
	Walter L. Fisher	1911–1913
Secretary of Agriculture	James Wilson	1909–1913
Secretary of Labor and Commerce	Charles Nagel	1909–1913

The Wilson Administration (1913–1921)

Vice President	Thomas R. Marshall	1913–1921
Secretary of State	William J. Bryan	1913–1915
	Robert Lansing	1915–1920
	Bainbridge Colby	1920–1921
Secretary of Treasury	William G. McAdoo	1913–1918
	Carter Glass	1918–1920
	David F. Houston	1920–1921
Secretary of War	Lindley M. Garrison	1913–1916
	Newton D. Baker	1916–1921
Attorney General	James C. McReynolds	1913–1914
	Thomas W. Gregory	1914–1919
	A. Mitchell Palmer	1919–1921
Postmaster General	Albert S. Burleson	1913–1921
Secretary of Navy	Josephus Daniels	1913–1921
Secretary of Interior	Franklin K. Lane	1913–1920
	John B. Payne	1920–1921
Secretary of Agriculture	David F. Houston	1913–1920
	Edwin T. Meredith	1920–1921
Secretary of Commerce	William C. Redfield	1913–1919
	Joshua W. Alexander	1919–1921
Secretary of Labor	William B. Wilson	1913–1921

The Harding Administration (1921–1923)

Vice President	Calvin Coolidge	1921–1923
Secretary of State	Charles E. Hughes	1921–1923
Secretary of Treasury	Andrew Mellon	1921–1923
Secretary of War	John W. Weeks	1921–1923
Attorney General	Harry M. Daugherty	1921–1923
Postmaster General	Will H. Hays	1921–1922
	Hubert Work	1922–1923
	Harry S. New	1923
Secretary of Navy	Edwin Denby	1921–1923
Secretary of Interior	Albert B. Fall	1921–1923
	Hubert Work	1923
Secretary of Agriculture	Henry C. Wallace	1921–1923
Secretary of Commerce	Herbert C. Hoover	1921–1923
Secretary of Labor	James J. Davis	1921–1923

The Coolidge Administration (1923–1929)

Vice President	Charles G. Dawes	1925–1929
Secretary of State	Charles E. Hughes	1923–1925
	Frank B. Kellogg	1925–1929
Secretary of Treasury	Andrew Mellon	1923–1929
Secretary of War	John W. Weeks	1923–1925
	Dwight F. Davis	1925–1929
Attorney General	Henry M. Daugherty	1923–1924
	Harlan F. Stone	1924–1925
	John G. Sargent	1925–1929
Postmaster General	Harry S. New	1923–1929
Secretary of Navy	Edwin Derby	1923–1924
	Curtis D. Wilbur	1924–1929
Secretary of Interior	Hubert Work	1923–1928
	Roy O. West	1928–1929
Secretary of Agriculture	Henry C. Wallace	1923–1924
	Howard M. Gore	1924–1925
	William M. Jardine	1925–1929
Secretary of Commerce	Herbert C. Hoover	1923–1928
	William F. Whiting	1928–1929
Secretary of Labor	James J. Davis	1923–1929

The Hoover Administration (1929–1933)

Vice President	Charles Curtis	1929–1933
Secretary of State	Henry L. Stimson	1929–1933
Secretary of Treasury	Andrew Mellon	1929–1932
	Ogden L. Mills	1932–1933
Secretary of War	James W. Good	1929
	Patrick J. Hurley	1929–1933
Attorney General	William D. Mitchell	1929–1933
Postmaster General	Walter F. Brown	1929–1933
Secretary of Navy	Charles F. Adams	1929–1933
Secretary of Interior	Ray L. Wilbur	1929–1933
Secretary of Agriculture	Arthur M. Hyde	1929–1933
Secretary of Commerce	Robert P. Lamont	1929–1932
	Roy D. Chapin	1932–1933
Secretary of Labor	James J. Davis	1929–1930
	William N. Doak	1930–1933

The Franklin D. Roosevelt Administration (1933–1945)

Vice President	John Nance Garner	1933–1941
	Henry A. Wallace	1941–1945
	Harry S Truman	1945
Secretary of State	Cordell Hull	1933–1944
	Edward R. Stettinius Jr.	1944–1945
Secretary of Treasury	William H. Woodin	1933–1934
	Henry Morgenthau Jr.	1934–1945
Secretary of War	George H. Dern	1933–1936
	Henry A. Woodring	1936–1940
	Henry L. Stimson	1940–1945
Attorney General	Homer S. Cummings	1933–1939
	Frank Murphy	1939–1940
	Robert H. Jackson	1940–1941
	Francis Biddle	1941–1945
Postmaster General	James A. Farley	1933–1940
	Frank C. Walker	1940–1945
Secretary of Navy	Claude A. Swanson	1933–1940
	Charles Edison	1940
	Frank Knox	1940–1944
	James V. Forrestal	1944–1945
Secretary of Interior	Harold L. Ickes	1933–1945
Secretary of Agriculture	Henry A. Wallace	1933–1940
	Claude R. Wickard	1940–1945
Secretary of Commerce	Daniel C. Roper	1933–1939
	Harry L. Hopkins	1939–1940
	Jesse Jones	1940–1945
	Henry A. Wallace	1945
Secretary of Labor	Frances Perkins	1933–1945

The Truman Administration (1945–1953)

Vice President	Alben W. Barkley	1949–1953
Secretary of State	Edward R. Stettinius Jr.	1945
	James F. Byrnes	1945–1947
	George C. Marshall	1947–1949
	Dean G. Acheson	1949–1953
Secretary of Treasury	Fred M. Vinson	1945–1946
	John W. Snyder	1946–1953
Secretary of War	Robert P. Patterson	1945–1947
	Kenneth C. Royall	1947
Attorney General	Tom C. Clark	1945–1949
	J. Howard McGrath	1949–1952
	James P. McGranery	1952–1953
Postmaster General	Frank C. Walker	1945
	Robert E. Hannegan	1945–1947
	Jesse M. Donaldson	1947–1953
Secretary of Navy	James V. Forrestal	1945–1947
Secretary of Interior	Harold L. Ickes	1945–1946
	Julius A. Krug	1946–1949
	Oscar L. Chapman	1949–1953
Secretary of Agriculture	Clinton P. Anderson	1945–1948
	Charles F. Brannan	1948–1953
Secretary of Commerce	Henry A. Wallace	1945–1946
	W. Averell Harriman	1946–1948
	Charles W. Sawyer	1948–1953
Secretary of Labor	Lewis B. Schwellenbach	1945–1948
	Maurice J. Tobin	1948–1953
Secretary of Defense	James V. Forrestal	1947–1949
	Louis A. Johnson	1949–1950
	George C. Marshall	1950–1951
	Robert A. Lovett	1951–1953

The Eisenhower Administration (1953–1961)

Vice President	Richard M. Nixon	1953–1961
Secretary of State	John Foster Dulles	1953–1959
	Christian A. Herter	1959–1961
Secretary of Treasury	George M. Humphrey	1953–1957
	Robert B. Anderson	1957–1961
Attorney General	Herbert Brownell Jr.	1953–1958
	William P. Rogers	1958–1961
Postmaster General	Arthur E. Summerfield	1953–1961
Secretary of Interior	Douglas McKay	1953–1956
	Fred A. Seaton	1956–1961
Secretary of Agriculture	Ezra T. Benson	1953–1961
Secretary of Commerce	Sinclair Weeks	1953–1958
	Lewis L. Strauss	1958–1959
	Frederick H. Mueller	1959–1961
Secretary of Labor	Martin P. Durkin	1953
	James P. Mitchell	1953–1961
Secretary of Defense	Charles E. Wilson	1953–1957
	Neil H. McElroy	1957–1959
	Thomas S. Gates Jr.	1959–1961
Secretary of Health, Education, and Welfare	Oveta Culp Hobby	1953–1955
	Marion B. Folsom	1955–1958
	Arthur S. Flemming	1958–1961

The Kennedy Administration (1961–1963)

Vice President	Lyndon B. Johnson	1961–1963
Secretary of State	Dean Rusk	1961–1963
Secretary of Treasury	C. Douglas Dillon	1961–1963
Attorney General	Robert F. Kennedy	1961–1963
Postmaster General	J. Edward Day	1961–1963
	John A. Gronouski	1963
Secretary of Interior	Stewart L. Udall	1961–1963
Secretary of Agriculture	Orville L. Freeman	1961–1963
Secretary of Commerce	Luther H. Hodges	1961–1963
Secretary of Labor	Arthur J. Goldberg	1961–1962
	W. Willard Wirtz	1962–1963
Secretary of Defense	Robert S. McNamara	1961–1963
Secretary of Health, Education, and Welfare	Abraham A. Ribicoff Anthony J. Celebrezze	1961–1962 1962–1963

The Lyndon Johnson Administration (1963–1969)

Vice President	Hubert H. Humphrey	1965–1969
Secretary of State	Dean Rusk	1963–1969
Secretary of Treasury	C. Douglas Dillon	1963–1965
	Henry H. Fowler	1965–1969
Attorney General	Robert F. Kennedy	1963–1964
	Nicholas Katzenbach	1965–1966
	Ramsey Clark	1967–1969
Postmaster General	John A. Gronouski	1963–1965
	Lawrence F. O'Brien	1965–1968
	Marvin Watson	1968–1969
Secretary of Interior	Stewart L. Udall	1963–1969
Secretary of Agriculture	Orville L. Freeman	1963–1969
Secretary of Commerce	Luther H. Hodges	1963–1964
	John T. Connor	1964–1967
	Alexander B. Trowbridge	1967–1968
	Cyrus R. Smith	1968–1969
Secretary of Labor	W. Willard Wirtz	1963–1969
Secretary of Defense	Robert F. McNamara	1963–1968
	Clark Clifford	1968–1969
Secretary of Health, Education, and Welfare	Anthony J. Celebrezze John W. Gardner Wilbur J. Cohen	1963–1965 1965–1968 1968–1969
Secretary of Housing and Urban Development	Robert C. Weaver Robert C. Wood	1966–1969 1969
Secretary of Transportation	Alan S. Boyd	1967–1969

The Nixon Administration (1969–1974)

Vice President	Spiro T. Agnew	1969–1973
	Gerald R. Ford	1973–1974
Secretary of State	William P. Rogers	1969–1973
	Henry A. Kissinger	1973–1974
Secretary of Treasury	David M. Kennedy	1969–1970
	John B. Connally	1971–1972
	George P. Shultz	1972–1974
	William E. Simon	1974
Attorney General	John N. Mitchell	1969–1972
	Richard G. Kleindienst	1972–1973
	Elliot L. Richardson	1973
	William B. Saxbe	1973–1974
Postmaster General	Winton M. Blount	1969–1971
Secretary of Interior	Walter J. Hickel	1969–1970
	Rogers Morton	1971–1974
Secretary of Agriculture	Clifford M. Hardin	1969–1971
	Earl L. Butz	1971–1974
Secretary of Commerce	Maurice H. Stans	1969–1972
	Peter G. Peterson	1972–1973
	Frederick B. Dent	1973–1974
Secretary of Labor	George P. Shultz	1969–1970
	James D. Hodgson	1970–1973
	Peter J. Brennan	1973–1974
Secretary of Defense	Melvin R. Laird	1969–1973
	Elliot L. Richardson	1973
	James R. Schlesinger	1973–1974
Secretary of Health, Education, and Welfare	Robert H. Finch Elliot L. Richardson Caspar W. Weinberger	1969–1970 1970–1973 1973–1974
Secretary of Housing and Urban Development	George Romney James T. Lynn	1969–1973 1973–1974
Secretary of Transportation	John A. Volpe	1969–1973
	Claude S. Brinegar	1973–1974

The Ford Administration (1974–1977)

Vice President	Nelson A. Rockefeller	1974–1977
Secretary of State	Henry A. Kissinger	1974–1977
Secretary of Treasury	William E. Simon	1974–1977
Attorney General	William Saxbe	1974–1975
	Edward Levi	1975–1977
Secretary of Interior	Rogers Morton	1974–1975
	Stanley K. Hathaway	1975
	Thomas Kleppe	1975–1977
Secretary of Agriculture	Earl L. Butz	1974–1976
	John A. Knebel	1976–1977
Secretary of Commerce	Frederick B. Dent	1975–1976
	Rogers Morton	1975–1976
	Elliot L. Richardson	1976–1977
Secretary of Labor	Peter J. Brennan	1974–1975
	John T. Dunlop	1975–1976
	W. J. Usery	1976–1977
Secretary of Defense	James R. Schlesinger	1974–1975
	Donald Rumsfeld	1975–1977

Secretary of Health, Education, and Welfare	Caspar Weinberger	1974–1975
	Forrest D. Mathews	1975–1977
Secretary of Housing and Urban Development	James T. Lynn	1974–1975
	Carla A. Hills	1975–1977
Secretary of Transportation	Claude Brinegar	1974–1975
	William T. Coleman	1975–1977

The Carter Administration (1977–1981)

Vice President	Walter F. Mondale	1977–1981
Secretary of State	Cyrus R. Vance	1977–1980
	Edmund Muskie	1980–1981
Secretary of Treasury	W. Michael Blumenthal	1977–1979
	G. William Miller	1979–1981
Attorney General	Griffin Bell	1977–1979
	Benjamin R. Civiletti	1979–1981
Secretary of Interior	Cecil D. Andrus	1977–1981
Secretary of Agriculture	Robert Bergland	1977–1981
Secretary of Commerce	Juanita M. Kreps	1977–1979
	Philip M. Klutznick	1979–1981
Secretary of Labor	F. Ray Marshall	1977–1981
Secretary of Defense	Harold Brown	1977–1981
Secretary of Health, Education, and Welfare	Joseph A. Califano	1977–1979
	Patricia R. Harris	1979
Secretary of Health and Human Services	Patricia R. Harris	1979–1981
Secretary of Education	Shirley M. Hufstedler	1979–1981
Secretary of Housing and Urban Development	Patricia R. Harris	1977–1979
	Moon Landrieu	1979–1981
Secretary of Transportation	Brock Adams	1977–1979
	Neil E. Goldschmidt	1979–1981
Secretary of Energy	James R. Schlesinger	1977–1979
	Charles W. Duncan	1979–1981

The Reagan Administration (1981–1989)

Vice President	George Bush	1981–1989
Secretary of State	Alexander M. Haig	1981–1982
	George P. Shultz	1982–1989
Secretary of Treasury	Donald Regan	1981–1985
	James A. Baker III	1985–1988
	Nicholas Brady	1988–1989
Attorney General	William F. Smith	1981–1985
	Edwin A. Meese III	1985–1988
	Richard Thornburgh	1988–1989
Secretary of Interior	James Watt	1981–1983
	William P. Clark Jr.	1983–1985
	Donald P. Hodel	1985–1989
Secretary of Agriculture	John Block	1981–1986
	Richard E. Lyng	1986–1989
Secretary of Commerce	Malcolm Baldrige	1981–1987
	C. William Verity Jr.	1987–1989

Secretary of Labor	Raymond Donovan	1981–1985
	William E. Brock	1985–1987
	Ann D. McLaughlin	1987–1989
Secretary of Defense	Caspar Weinberger	1981–1987
	Frank Carlucci	1987–1989
Secretary of Health and Human Services	Richard Schweiker	1981–1983
	Margaret Heckler	1983–1985
	Otis R. Bowen	1985–1989
Secretary of Education	Terrel H. Bell	1981–1985
	William J. Bennett	1985–1988
	Lauro F. Cavazos	1988–1989
Secretary of Housing and Urban Development	Samuel Pierce	1981–1989
Secretary of Transportation	Drew Lewis	1981–1983
	Elizabeth Dole	1983–1987
	James H. Burnley	1987–1989
Secretary of Energy	James Edwards	1981–1982
	Donald P. Hodel	1982–1985
	John S. Herrington	1985–1989

The George H. W. Bush Administration (1989–1993)

Vice President	J. Danforth Quayle	1989–1993
Secretary of State	James A. Baker III	1989–1992
Secretary of Treasury	Nicholas Brady	1989–1993
Attorney General	Richard Thornburgh	1989–1991
	William P. Barr	1991–1993
Secretary of Interior	Manuel Lujan	1989–1993
Secretary of Agriculture	Clayton K. Yeutter	1989–1991
	Edward Madigan	1991–1993
Secretary of Commerce	Robert Mosbacher	1989–1992
	Barbara Franklin	1992–1993
Secretary of Labor	Elizabeth Dole	1989–1991
	Lynn Martin	1991–1993
Secretary of Defense	Richard Cheney	1989–1993
Secretary of Health and Human Services	Louis W. Sullivan	1989–1993
Secretary of Education	Lauro F. Cavazos	1989–1991
	Lamar Alexander	1991–1993
Secretary of Housing and Urban Development	Jack F. Kemp	1989–1993
Secretary of Transportation	Samuel K. Skinner	1989–1992
	Andrew H. Card Jr.	1992–1993
Secretary of Energy	James D. Watkins	1989–1993
Secretary of Veterans Affairs	Edward J. Derwinski	1989–1993

The Clinton Administration (1993–2001)

Vice President	Albert Gore	1993–2001
Secretary of State	Warren Christopher	1993–1997
	Madeleine Albright	1997–2001
Secretary of Treasury	Lloyd Bentsen	1993–1995
	Robert E. Rubin	1995–1999

	Lawrence H. Summers	1999–2001
Attorney General	Janet Reno	1993–2001
Secretary of Interior	Bruce Babbitt	1993–2001
Secretary of Agriculture	Michael Espy	1993–1995
	Dan Glickman	1995–2001
Secretary of Commerce	Ronald Brown	1993–1996
	Mickey Kantor	1996
	William Daley	1997
	Norman Mineta	1997–2001
Secretary of Labor	Robert B. Reich	1993–1997
	Alexis Herman	1997–2001
Secretary of Defense	Les Aspin	1993–1994
	William J. Perry	1994–1997
	William Cohen	1997–2001
Secretary of Health and Human Services	Donna Shalala	1993–2001
Secretary of Housing and Urban Development	Henry G. Cisneros	1993–1997
	Andrew Cuomo	1997–2001
Secretary of Education	Richard W. Riley	1993–2001
Secretary of Transportation	Federico Peña	1993–1997
	Rodney Slater	1997–2001
Secretary of Energy	Hazel R. O'Leary	1993–1997
	Federico Peña	1997
	Bill Richardson	1998–2001
Secretary of Veterans Affairs	Jesse Brown	1993–1998
	Togo D. West Jr.	1998–2001

The George W. Bush Administration (2001–)

Vice President	Richard B. Cheney	2001–
Secretary of State	Colin Powell	2001–2005
	Condoleezza Rice	2005–
Secretary of Treasury	Paul H. O'Neill	2001–2002
	John Snow	2003–2006
	Henry M. Paulson, Jr.,	2006–
Attorney General	John Ashcroft	2001–2005
	Alberto Gonzales	2005–2007
Secretary of Interior	Gale Norton	2001–2006
	Dirk Kempthorne	2006–
Secretary of Agriculture	Ann M. Veneman	2001–2005
	Mike Johanns	2005–
Secretary of Commerce	Don Evans	2001–2005
	Carlos Gutierrez	2005–
Secretary of Labor	Elaine Chao	2001–
Secretary of Defense	Donald Rumsfeld	2001–2006
	Robert M. Gates	2006–
Secretary of Health and Human Services	Tommy G. Thompson	2001–2005
	Michael O. Leavitt	2005–
Secretary of Housing and Urban Development	Melquiades Rafael Martinez	2001–2004
	Alphonso Jackson	2004–
Secretary of Education	Roderick Paige	2001–2005
	Margaret Spellings	2005–
Secretary of Transportation	Norman Y. Mineta	2001–2006
	Mary E. Peters	2006–
Secretary of Energy	Spencer Abraham	2001–2005
	Samuel W. Bodman	2005–
Secretary of Veterans Affairs	Anthony J. Principi	2001–2005
	Jim Nicholson	2005–
Secretary of Homeland Security	Tom Ridge	2001–2005
	Michael Chertoff	2005–

Justices of the Supreme Court

	Term of Service	Years of Service	Life Span
John Jay	1789–1795	5	1745–1829
John Rutledge	1789–1791	1	1739–1800
William Cushing	1789–1810	20	1732–1810
James Wilson	1789–1798	8	1742–1798
John Blair	1789–1796	6	1732–1800
Robert H. Harrison	1789–1790	–	1745–1790
James Iredell	1790–1799	9	1751–1799
Thomas Johnson	1791–1793	1	1732–1819
William Paterson	1793–1806	13	1745–1806
*John Rutledge**	1795	–	1739–1800
Samuel Chase	1796–1811	15	1741–1811
Oliver Ellsworth	1796–1800	4	1745–1807
Bushrod Washington	1798–1829	31	1762–1829
Alfred Moore	1799–1804	4	1755–1810
John Marshall	1801–1835	34	1755–1835
William Johnson	1804–1834	30	1771–1834
H. Brockholst Livingston	1806–1823	16	1757–1823
Thomas Todd	1807–1826	18	1765–1826
Joseph Story	1811–1845	33	1779–1845
Gabriel Duval	1811–1835	24	1752–1844
Smith Thompson	1823–1843	20	1768–1843
Robert Trimble	1826–1828	2	1777–1828
John McLean	1829–1861	32	1785–1861
Henry Baldwin	1830–1844	14	1780–1844
James M. Wayne	1835–1867	32	1790–1867
Roger B. Taney	1836–1864	28	1777–1864
Philip P. Barbour	1836–1841	4	1783–1841
John Catron	1837–1865	28	1786–1865
John McKinley	1837–1852	15	1780–1852
Peter V. Daniel	1841–1860	19	1784–1860
Samuel Nelson	1845–1872	27	1792–1873
Levi Woodbury	1845–1851	5	1789–1851
Robert C. Grier	1846–1870	23	1794–1870
Benjamin R. Curtis	1851–1857	6	1809–1874
John A. Campbell	1853–1861	8	1811–1889
Nathan Clifford	1858–1881	23	1803–1881
Noah H. Swayne	1862–1881	18	1804–1884
Samuel F. Miller	1862–1890	28	1816–1890
David Davis	1862–1877	14	1815–1886

*Appointed and served one term, but not confirmed by the Senate.

Note: Chief justices are in italics

	Term of Service	Years of Service	Life Span
Stephen J. Field	1863–1897	34	1816–1899
Salmon P. Chase	1864–1873	8	1808–1873
William Strong	1870–1880	10	1808–1895
Joseph P. Bradley	1870–1892	22	1813–1892
Ward Hunt	1873–1882	9	1810–1886
Morrison R. Waite	1874–1888	14	1816–1888
John M. Harlan	1877–1911	34	1833–1911
William B. Woods	1880–1887	7	1824–1887
Stanley Matthews	1881–1889	7	1824–1889
Horace Gray	1882–1902	20	1828–1902
Samuel Blatchford	1882–1893	11	1820–1893
Lucius Q. C. Lamar	1888–1893	5	1825–1893
Melville W. Fuller	1888–1910	21	1833–1910
David J. Brewer	1890–1910	20	1837–1910
Henry B. Brown	1890–1906	16	1836–1913
George Shiras Jr.	1892–1903	10	1832–1924
Howell E. Jackson	1893–1895	2	1832–1895
Edward D. White	1894–1910	16	1845–1921
Rufus W. Peckham	1895–1909	14	1838–1909
Joseph McKenna	1898–1925	26	1843–1926
Oliver W. Holmes	1902–1932	30	1841–1935
William R. Day	1903–1922	19	1849–1923
William H. Moody	1906–1910	3	1853–1917
Horace H. Lurton	1909–1914	4	1844–1914
Charles E. Hughes	1910–1916	5	1862–1948
Edward D. White	1910–1921	11	1845–1921
Willis Van Devanter	1911–1937	26	1859–1941
Joseph R. Lamar	1911–1916	5	1857–1916
Mahlon Pitney	1912–1922	10	1858–1924
James C. McReynolds	1914–1941	26	1862–1946
Louis D. Brandeis	1916–1939	22	1856–1941
John H. Clarke	1916–1922	6	1857–1945
William H. Taft	1921–1930	8	1857–1930
George Sutherland	1922–1938	15	1862–1942
Pierce Butler	1922–1939	16	1866–1939
Edward T. Sanford	1923–1930	7	1865–1930
Harlan F. Stone	1925–1941	16	1872–1946
Charles E. Hughes	1930–1941	11	1862–1948
Owen J. Roberts	1930–1945	15	1875–1955
Benjamin N. Cardozo	1932–1938	6	1870–1938
Hugo L. Black	1937–1971	34	1886–1971
Stanley F. Reed	1938–1957	19	1884–1980
Felix Frankfurter	1939–1962	23	1882–1965

	Term of Service	Years of Service	Life Span
William O. Douglas	1939–1975	36	1898–1980
Frank Murphy	1940–1949	9	1890–1949
Harlan F. Stone	1941–1946	5	1872–1946
James F. Byrnes	1941–1942	1	1879–1972
Robert H. Jackson	1941–1954	13	1892–1954
Wiley B. Rutledge	1943–1949	6	1894–1949
Harold H. Burton	1945–1958	13	1888–1964
Fred M. Vinson	1946–1953	7	1890–1953
Tom C. Clark	1949–1967	18	1899–1977
Sherman Minton	1949–1956	7	1890–1965
Earl Warren	1953–1969	16	1891–1974
John Marshall Harlan	1955–1971	16	1899–1971
William J. Brennan Jr.	1956–1990	33	1906–1997
Charles E. Whittaker	1957–1962	5	1901–1973
Potter Stewart	1958–1981	23	1915–1985
Bryon R. White	1962–1993	31	1917–2002
Arthur J. Goldberg	1962–1965	3	1908–1990

	Term of Service	Years of Service	Life Span
Abe Fortas	1965–1969	4	1910–1982
Thurgood Marshall	1967–1991	24	1908–1992
Warren C. Burger	1969–1986	17	1907–1995
Harry A. Blackmun	1970–1994	24	1908–1999
Lewis F. Powell Jr.	1972–1987	15	1907–1998
William H. Rehnquist	1972–1986	14	1924–
John P. Stevens III	1975–	–	1920–
Sandra Day O'Connor	1981–2006	24	1930–
William H. Rehnquist	1986–2005	18	1924–2005
Antonin Scalia	1986–	–	1936–
Anthony M. Kennedy	1988–	–	1936–
David H. Souter	1990–	–	1939–
Clarence Thomas	1991–	–	1948–
Ruth Bader Ginsburg	1993–	–	1933–
Stephen Breyer	1994–	–	1938–
John G. Roberts, Jr,	2005–	–	1955–
Samuel A. Alito, Jr.	2006–	–	1950–

A Social Profile of the American Republic

Year	Population	Percent Increase	Population per Square Mile	Population Percent Urban/ Rural	Percent Male/ Female	Percent White/ Nonwhite	Persons per Household	Median Age
1790	3,929,214		4.5	5.1/94.9	NA/NA	80.7/19.3	5.79	NA
1800	5,308,483	35.1	6.1	6.1/93.9	NA/NA	81.1/18.9	NA	NA
1810	7,239,881	36.4	4.3	7.3/92.7	NA/NA	81.0/19.0	NA	NA
1820	9,638,453	33.1	5.5	7.2/92.8	50.8/49.2	81.6/18.4	NA	16.7
1830	12,866,020	33.5	7.4	8.8/91.2	50.8/49.2	81.9/18.1	NA	17.2
1840	17,069,453	32.7	9.8	10.8/89.2	50.9/49.1	83.2/16.8	NA	17.8
1850	23,191,876	35.9	7.9	15.3/84.7	51.0/49.0	84.3/15.7	5.55	18.9
1860	31,443,321	35.6	10.6	19.8/80.2	51.2/48.8	85.6/14.4	5.28	19.4
1870	39,818,449	26.6	13.4	25.7/74.3	50.6/49.4	86.2/13.8	5.09	20.2
1880	50,155,783	26.0	16.9	28.2/71.8	50.9/49.1	86.5/13.5	5.04	20.9
1890	62,947,714	25.5	21.2	35.1/64.9	51.2/48.8	87.5/12.5	4.93	22.0
1900	75,994,575	20.7	25.6	39.6/60.4	51.1/48.9	87.9/12.1	4.76	22.9
1910	91,972,266	21.0	31.0	45.6/54.4	51.5/48.5	88.9/11.1	4.54	24.1
1920	105,710,620	14.9	35.6	51.2/48.8	51.0/49.0	89.7/10.3	4.34	25.3
1930	122,775,046	16.1	41.2	56.1/43.9	50.6/49.4	89.8/10.2	4.11	26.4
1940	131,669,275	7.2	44.2	56.5/43.5	50.2/49.8	89.8/10.2	3.67	29.0
1950	150,697,361	14.5	50.7	64.0/36.0	49.7/50.3	89.5/10.5	3.37	30.2
1960	179,323,175	18.5	50.6	69.9/30.1	49.3/50.7	88.6/11.4	3.33	29.5
1970	203,302,031	13.4	57.4	73.5/26.5	48.7/51.3	87.6/12.4	3.14	28.0
1980	226,545,805	11.4	64.0	73.7/26.3	48.6/51.4	86.0/14.0	2.76	30.0
1990	248,709,873	9.8	70.3	75.2/24.8	48.7/51.3	80.3/19.7	2.63	32.9
2000	281,422,426	13.1	79.6	79.0/21.0	49.0/51.0	81.0/19.0	2.59	35.4

NA = Not available.

Vital Statistics (rates per thousand)						
Year	Births	Year	Births	Deaths*	Marriages*	Divorces*
1800	55.0	1900	32.3	17.2	NA	NA
1810	54.3	1910	30.1	14.7	NA	NA
1820	55.2	1920	27.7	13.0	12.0	1.6
1830	51.4	1930	21.3	11.3	9.2	1.6
1840	51.8	1940	19.4	10.8	12.1	2.0
1850	43.3	1950	24.1	9.6	11.1	2.6
1860	44.3	1960	23.7	9.5	8.5	2.2
1870	38.3	1970	18.4	9.5	10.6	3.5
1880	39.8	1980	15.9	8.8	10.6	5.2
1890	31.5	1990	16.7	8.6	9.8	4.6
		2000	14.7	8.7	8.5	4.2

NA = Not available.
*Data not available before 1900.

| Year | Total Population | Life Expectancy (in years) | | White Males | Nonwhite Males |
		White Females	Nonwhite Females		
1900	47.3	48.7	33.5	46.6	32.5
1910	50.1	52.0	37.5	48.6	33.8
1920	54.1	55.6	45.2	54.4	45.5
1930	59.7	63.5	49.2	59.7	47.3
1940	62.9	66.6	54.9	62.1	51.5
1950	68.2	72.2	62.9	66.5	59.1
1960	69.7	74.1	66.3	67.4	61.1
1970	70.9	75.6	69.4	68.0	61.3
1980	73.7	78.1	73.6	70.7	65.3
1990	75.4	79.3	76.3	72.6	68.4
2000	76.9	80.0	NA	74.8	NA

The Changing Age Structure

Before the twentieth century, the age distribution of Americans could be charted roughly as a pyramid, as seen in the figures for 1870 and 1920. High birthrates create a broad base at the bottom, while mortality rates winnow the population to a small tip of elderly. But by the year 2000, the pyramid has been transformed more nearly into a cylinder. Over the past two centuries fertility rates have undergone a steady decline, pulling in the base of the pyramid, while higher living standards have allowed Americans to live longer, broadening the top. Only the temporary bulge of the baby boom distorts the shape.

		Regional Origin of Immigrants (percent) EUROPE					
Years	Total Number of Immigrants	Total Europe	North and West	East and Central	South and Other	Western Hemisphere	Asia
1821–1830	143,389	69.2	67.1	–	2.1	8.4	–
1831–1840	599,125	82.8	81.8	–	1.0	5.5	–
1841–1850	1,713,251	93.8	92.9	0.1	0.3	3.6	–
1851–1860	2,598,214	94.4	93.6	0.1	0.8	2.9	1.6
1861–1870	2,314,824	89.2	87.8	0.5	0.9	7.2	2.8
1871–1880	2,812,191	80.8	73.6	4.5	2.7	14.4	4.4
1881–1890	5,246,13	90.3	72.0	11.9	6.3	8.1	1.3
1891–1900	3,687,546	96.5	44.5	32.8	19.1	1.1	1.9
1901–1910	8,795,386	92.5	21.7	44.5	6.3	4.1	2.8
1911–1920	5,735,811	76.3	17.4	33.4	25.5	19.9	3.4
1921–1930	4,107,209	60.3	31.7	14.4	14.3	36.9	2.4
1931–1940	528,431	65.9	38.8	11.0	16.1	30.3	2.8
1941–1950	1,035,039	60.1	47.5	4.6	7.9	34.3	3.1
1951–1960	2,515,479	52.8	17.7	24.3	10.8	39.6	6.0
1961–1970	3,321,677	33.8	11.7	9.4	12.9	51.7	12.9
1971–1980	4,493,300	17.8	4.3	5.6	8.4	44.3	35.2
1981–1990	7,338,000	10.4	5.9	4.8	1.1	49.3	37.3
1991–2000	9,095,417	14.9	4.8	8.6	1.6	49.3	30.7

Dash indicates less than 0.1 percent.

	Recent Trends in Immigration (in thousands)				PERCENT		
	1961–1970	1971–1980	1981–1990	1991–2000	1971–1980	1981–1990	1991–2000
All countries	3,321.7	4,493.3	7,338.1	9095.4	100.0	100.0	100.0
Europe	1,123.5	800.4	761.5	1359.7	17.8	10.4	14.9
Austria	20.6	9.5	18.3	15.5	0.2	0.3	0.2
Belgium	9.2	5.3	7.0	7.0	0.1	0.1	0.1
Czechoslovakia	3.3	6.0	7.2	9.8	0.1	0.1	0.1
Denmark	9.2	4.4	5.3	6.0	0.1	0.1	0.1
France	45.2	25.1	22.4	35.8	0.6	1.3	0.4
Germany	190.8	74.4	91.6	92.6	1.7	2.2	1.0
Greece	86.0	92.4	38.3	26.7	2.1	0.4	0.3
Hungary	5.4	6.6	6.5	9.3	0.1	0.1	0.1
Ireland	33.0	11.5	31.9	56.9	0.3	0.9	0.6
Italy	214.1	129.4	67.2	62.7	2.9	0.2	0.7
Netherlands	30.6	10.5	12.2	13.3	0.2	0.1	0.1
Norway	15.5	3.9	4.2	5.1	0.1	1.1	0.5
Poland	53.5	37.2	83.3	163.7	0.8	0.5	1.8
Portugal	76.1	101.7	40.4	22.9	2.3	0.3	0.3
Spain	44.7	39.1	20.4	17.1	0.9	0.2	0.2
Sweden	17.1	6.5	11.0	12.7	0.1	0.1	0.1
Switzerland	18.5	8.2	8.8	11.8	0.2	0.1	0.1
United Kingdom	213.8	137.4	159.2	151.8	3.1	2.2	1.7
USSR	2.5	39.0	57.7	462.8	0.9	0.3	5.1
Yugoslavia	20.4	30.5	18.8	66.5	0.7	0.5	0.7
Other Europe	9.1	18.9	8.2	57.7	0.2	0.0	0.6

Recent Trends in Immigration (in thousands)					PERCENT		
	1961–1970	1971–1980	1981–1990	1991–2000	1971–1980	1981–1990	1991–2000
Asia	427.6	1588.2	2738.1	2795.6	35.2	37.3	30.7
China	34.8	124.3	298.9	419.1	2.8	4.1	4.6
Hong Kong	75.0	113.5	98.2	109.8	2.5	1.3	1.2
India	27.2	164.1	250.7	363.1	3.7	3.4	4.0
Iran	10.3	45.1	116.0	69.0	1.0	1.6	0.8
Israel	29.6	37.7	44.2	39.4	0.8	0.6	0.4
Japan	40.0	49.8	47.0	67.9	1.1	0.6	0.7
Korea	34.5	267.6	333.8	164.2	6.0	4.5	1.8
Philippines	98.4	355.0	548.7	503.9	7.9	7.5	5.5
Turkey	10.1	13.4	23.4	38.2	0.3	0.3	0.4
Vietnam	4.3	172.8	281.0	286.1	3.8	3.8	3.1
Other Asia	36.5	176.1	631.4	735.4	3.8	8.6	8.0
America	1716.4	1982.5	3615.6	4486.8	44.3	49.3	49.3
Argentina	49.7	29.9	27.3	26.6	0.7	0.4	0.3
Canada	413.3	169.9	158.0	192.0	3.8	2.2	2.1
Colombia	72.0	77.3	122.9	128.5	1.7	1.7	1.4
Cuba	208.5	264.9	144.6	169.3	5.9	2.0	1.9
Dominican Rep.	93.3	148.1	252.0	335.3	3.3	3.4	3.7
Ecuador	36.8	50.1	56.2	76.5	1.1	0.8	0.8
El Salvador	15.0	34.4	213.5	215.7	0.8	2.9	2.4
Haiti	34.5	56.3	138.4	179.6	1.3	1.9	2.0
Jamaica	74.9	137.6	208.1	169.2	3.1	2.8	1.9
Mexico	453.9	640.3	1655.7	2249.4	14.3	22.6	24.7
Other America	264.4	373.8	639.3	744.3	8.3	8.7	8.2
Africa	29.0	80.8	176.8	355.0	1.8	2.4	3.9
Oceania	25.1	41.2	45.2	55.8	0.9	0.6	0.6

Figures may not add to total due to rounding.

American Workers and Farmers						
Year	Total Number of Workers (thousands)	Percent of Workers Male/Female	Percent of Female Workers Married	Percent of Workers in Female Population	Percent of Workers in Labor Unions	Farm Population (thousands)	Farm Population as Percent of Total Population
1870	12,506	85/15	NA	NA	NA	NA	NA
1880	17,392	85/15	NA	NA	NA	21,973	43.8
1890	23,318	83/17	13.9	18.9	NA	24,771	42.3
1900	29,073	82/18	15.4	20.6	3	29,875	41.9
1910	38,167	79/21	24.7	25.4	6	32,077	34.9
1920	41,614	79/21	23.0	23.7	12	31,974	30.1
1930	48,830	78/22	28.9	24.8	7	30,529	24.9
1940	53,011	76/24	36.4	27.4	27	30,547	23.2
1950	59,643	72/28	52.1	31.4	25	23,048	15.3
1960	69,877	68/32	59.9	37.7	26	15,635	8.7
1970	82,049	63/37	63.4	43.4	25	9712	4.8
1980	108,544	58/42	59.7	51.5	23	6051	2.7
1990	117,914	55/45	58.4	44.3	16	3871	1.6
2000	135,208	54/46	61.3	45.7	15	3305	1.1

Year	Gross National Product (GNP) (in billions)*	FOREIGN TRADE (in millions)			Federal Budget (in billions)	Federal Surplus/Deficit (in billions)	Federal Debt (in billions)
		Exports	Imports	Balance of Trade			
1790	NA	$20	$23	$−3	$0.004	$+0.00015	$0.076
1800	NA	71	91	−20	0.011	+0.0006	0.083
1810	NA	67	85	−18	0.008	+0.0012	0.053
1820	NA	70	74	−4	0.018	−0.0004	0.091
1830	NA	74	71	+3	0.015	+0.100	0.049
1840	NA	132	107	+25	0.024	−0.005	0.004
1850	NA	152	178	−26	0.040	+0.004	0.064
1860	NA	400	362	−38	0.063	−0.01	0.065
1870	$7.4	451	462	−11	0.310	+0.10	2.4
1880	11.2	853	761	+92	0.268	+0.07	2.1
1890	13.1	910	823	+87	0.318	+0.09	1.2
1900	18.7	1499	930	+569	0.521	+0.05	1.2
1910	35.3	1919	1646	+273	0.694	−0.02	1.1
1920	91.5	8664	5784	+2880	6.357	+0.3	24.3
1930	90.7	4013	3500	+513	3.320	+0.7	16.3
1940	100.0	4030	7433	−3403	9.6	−2.7	43.0
1950	286.5	10,816	9125	+1691	43.1	−2.2	257.4
1960	506.5	19,600	15,046	+4556	92.2	+0.3	286.3
1970	992.7	42,700	40,189	+2511	195.6	−2.8	371.0
1980	2631.7	220,783	244,871	+24,088	590.9	−73.8	907.7
1990	5803.2	394,030	495,042	−101,012	1253.1	−220.5	3206.6
2000	9872.9	1,102,900	1,466,900	−364,000	1788.8	+236.4	5629.0

*For 1990 and after, gross domestic product (GDP) is given.

Glossary

actual representation view that the people can be represented only by a person whom they have actually elected to office; this understanding of representation was the consensus among colonials during the imperial crisis and the basis of their objection to the British claim that Americans were virtually represented in Parliament.

affirmative action practice of actively seeking to increase the number of racial and ethnic minorities, women, persons in a protected age category, persons with disabilities, and disabled veterans in a work place or school. Such measures sometimes include the setting of quotas or percentages in hiring.

amnesty general pardon granted by a government, usually for political crimes. Proposals of amnesty were made, with varying degrees of exception for high Confederate officials, by presidents Lincoln and Johnson as well as by Congress in 1872. President Ford offered conditional amnesty in 1974 to draft evaders at the conclusion of the Vietnam war.

anti-Semitism hatred, prejudice, oppression, or discrimination against Jews or Judaism. *Semite* originally referred to the descendents of Shem, which included both Jews and Muslims in the Middle East. More recently the term has come to refer primarily to Jews.

appeasement policy of making concessions to an aggressor nation, as long as its demands appear reasonable, in order to avoid war. Hitler's full conquest of Czechoslovakia, violating his promises given at the Munich Conference in 1938, gave the term its negative connotation.

armistice mutually agreed-on truce or temporary halt in the fighting of a war so that the combatants may discuss peace.

artisan skilled craftworker, such as a blacksmith, a cooper, a miller, or a tailor. Master artisans constituted a large segment of the middle classes in American cities and towns from the beginnings of colonial settlement through the 1820s; they owned their own shops and employed a number of younger journeyman artisans, who owned only their tools, and trained even younger and less skilled apprentices in a craft.

assimilate to absorb a culturally distinct group into the dominant culture. The debate over the process of assimilation, of immigrants "becoming American," has been a persistent fault line in American politics. The debate revolves around what qualities are American and the degree to which a dominant culture should define them. The debate is extremely difficult in a society in which immigration plays a crucial role—in a "nation of nations," as Walt Whitman described the United States.

autonomy condition of being independent or, in the case of a political structure, the right to self-government

balanced constitution view that England's constitution gave every part of English society some voice in the workings of its government. While the Crown represented the monarchy and the House of Lords the aristocracy, the House of Commons represented the ordinary people of England.

barter economy networks of trade based on the mutual exchange of goods and services with little or no use of coin or currency.

behaviorism school of psychology that measures human behavior, believes it can be shaped, and discounts emotion as subjective. Behaviorism was founded by psychologist John Watson and was first presented in his *Psychology as the Behaviorist Views It* (1913).

benign neglect policy also known as "salutary neglect," pursued by the British empire in governing its American colonies until the end of the Seven Years' War.

biocentric life-centered; also a theory of moral responsibility stating that all forms of life have an inherent right to exist and that humanity is not the center of existence.

biogenetic engineering process of changing the DNA of a plant or an animal to produce desirable characteristics. Examples of desirable characteristics include fast growth and unusually large size. Not everyone agrees that the plants and animals that are genetically designed are safe for humans to eat or safe for the environment.

black codes series of laws passed by southern states in 1865 and 1866, modeled on the slave codes in effect before the Civil War. The codes did grant African Americans some rights not enjoyed by slaves, but their primary purpose was to keep African Americans as propertyless agricultural laborers.

bloody shirt political campaign tactic of "waving the bloody shirt," used by Republicans against Democrats; it invoked the tremendous loss of life and casualties from the Civil War as a reason to vote for Republicans as the party of the Union and not to trust Democrats, who had often opposed the war. The tactic continued to work, with diminishing success, throughout Reconstruction.

bonds certificates of debt issued by a government or corporation promising to repay the buyers of the bonds their original investment, plus interest, by a specified date of maturity. Bonds have been traditionally used by governments as a way to raise money during wartime or for large-scale projects.

boom-bust cycle periods of expansion and recession or depression that an economy goes through. Also referred to as *business cycle*. Major downturns in the cycle have occurred in the United States beginning in 1819, 1837, 1857, 1873, 1893, 1907, and 1929, the start of the Great Depression.

bootlegging illegal transport or sale of goods, in this case alcoholic beverages during the 1920s. The term derived from the practice of hiding a container of alcohol in the upper part of a boot.

boycott tactic used by protestors, workers, and consumers to pressure business organizations through a mass refusal to purchase their products or otherwise do business with them.

brinksmanship policy of pushing a critical situation to the edge of catastrophe by using the implicit threat of nuclear war in order to persuade an opponent to back down. The strategy was developed by Secretary of State John Foster Dulles under President Dwight Eisenhower.

bureaucratic state   government run by administrative bureaus or divisions and staffed by nonelected officials.

business cycle   *see* **boom-bust cycle.**

carpetbagger   white Republicans, originally from the North, who came to live in the South after the Civil War. They received their nickname from hostile Southerners who claimed that the newcomers arrived carrying all that they owned stuffed into a carpetbag and eager to get rich by plundering the South.

cartel   organization of private businesses that join together to control production, distribution, and prices.

caste system   system of social stratification separating individuals by various distinctions, among them hereditary, rank, profession, wealth, and race. Slavery as a caste system not only separated whites from blacks but assigned value to people according to shadings of color.

cede   to give up possession of, usually by treaty.

celibate   abstaining from sexual intercourse; also unmarried. Celibacy is the abstention from intercourse, a state often motivated by religious teachings.

charter   document issued by a sovereign ruler, legislature, or other authority creating a public or private corporation. England's rulers issued charters setting forth the authority of corporations or joint stock companies to colonize sections of the Americas; state legislatures have issued charters to corporations; and the British (including American colonials) traced basic rights of representation to the Magna Carta (Great Charter) granted by King John in 1215 C.E.

checks and balances   mechanism by which each branch of government—executive, legislative, and judicial—keeps the others within the bounds of their constitutional authority; James Madison emphasized this feature of the federal constitution to assure the Anti-Federalists.

Columbian exchange   transition of people, plants, insects, and microbes between the two hemispheres, initiated when Columbus reached the Americas in 1492.

commercial economy   economy in which individuals are involved in a network of markets and commercial transactions. Such economies are often urban, where goods and services are exchanged for money and credit; agricultural areas are also commercial when crops and livestock are sold in markets rather than consumed by those who grew or raised them. Commercial economies are less egalitarian, because wealth can be concentrated in the hands of fewer individuals. *See also* **semisubsistence economy.**

committees of correspondence   strategy devised by Samuel Adams in 1772 to rally popular support among American colonials against British imperial policies. The committees of correspondence drew up statements of American rights and grievances, distributed those documents within and among the colonies, and solicited responses from towns and counties. This committee structure formed a new communications network, one that fostered intercolonial agreement on resistance to British measures and spread the resistance from seaports into rural areas.

community action   programs designed to identify and organize local leaders to take steps to alleviate poverty and crime in their neighborhoods. Sociologist Saul Alinsky from Chicago organized the Industrial Areas Foundation to support community action programs in the 1960s.

conformity   degree to which people adjust their behavior, values, and ideas to fit into a group or society.

conglomerate   corporation whose various branches or subsidiaries are either directly or indirectly spread among a variety of industries, usually unrelated to one another. The purpose of a conglomerate is generally to increase shareholder value and ensure against market cycles by spreading its risk, rather than to improve market share or production efficiency by concentrating on excelling within a single industry.

Congregationalists   members of a Protestant denomination that originated in sixteenth-century Britain as part of the Puritan movement. While some early Congregationalists, known as Separatists, concluded that the Church of England was beyond reformation, most strove to reform English religion and society while remaining within the Church of England. Early modern Congregationalists embraced Calvinist theological beliefs and held that each individual congregation should conduct its own religious affairs, answering to no higher authority. The Separatists founded Plymouth, the first northern colony, and the Non-Separating Congregationalists predominated elsewhere in seventeenth-century New England.

conscription   act of compulsory enrollment for military service, as opposed to a voluntary enlistment.

consensus   point of view generally shared by a group, institution, or even a culture. Scholars have analyzed and debated the institutions that contribute to the construction of a consensus viewpoint, ranging from schools and churches to the media in their various forms.

constitution   framework of government establishing the contract between rulers and ruled. American revolutionaries insisted on written constitutions to protect individual rights and liberties; by contrast, Britons understood the term *constitution* to mean the existing arrangement of government—not an actual document but a collection of parliamentary laws, customs, and precedents.

consumer goods   products such as food and clothing that fill the needs and wants of individuals. *Producer* or *capital goods*, in contrast, are the factory equipment and other machines used to manufacture or transport other goods or services.

Continental Army   main rebel military force, created by the Second Continental Congress in July 1775 and commanded by George Washington. After the 1776 campaign, most enlistments came from the poorest and most desperate in American society, and it was they who shouldered the burden of the fighting. During the harsh winter at Valley Forge in 1778/1779, the army acquired greater discipline and expertise and thereafter scored important military victories in the mid-Atlantic and the South.

contraband   goods seized by a government during wartime, when the goods were being used by an enemy nation or being shipped to an enemy nation by a neutral nation. The term was also applied during the Civil War to escaped slaves who fled behind Union lines.

Copperhead derogatory term used by Republicans to label northern Democrats who opposed the war policies of the Lincoln administration and advocated a negotiated peace.

CORE Congress on Racial Equality, an organization founded in Chicago in 1942. The group's inspiration was Krishnalal Shridharani's book *War Without Violence,* which outlined Mohandas K. Gandhi's nonviolent philosophy for action. CORE believed that African Americans could use nonviolent civil disobedience to challenge racial segregation.

corporation business entity that has been granted a charter granting it legal rights, privileges, and liabilities distinct from the individual members that are a part of it. A corporation therefore may survive the death of the individuals who created and run it.

Counter-Reformation reform movement within the Roman Catholic Church in response to the Protestant Reformation, seeking to reform and reinvigorate the Church. Religious orders played a large role in the Counter-Reformation, particularly the Jesuit order, known formally as the Society of Jesus, and founded in 1534 by Ignatius of Loyola.

covert operations military or political actions carried out in secret to allow the responsible government or party to deny its role. Governments have often relied on such operations when overt military force is impractical or dangerous or when public negotiations are likely to fail.

de facto segregation spatial and social separation of populations brought about by social behavior rather than by laws or legal mechanisms. Segregation (especially in schools) has often existed without being sanctioned by law. When the practice is accomplished through explicit legal means, it is known as *de jure segregation.*

debt peonage paying off a debt through labor when the debtor lacks sufficient cash or other assets.

Deep South South Carolina, Georgia, Florida, Alabama, Mississippi, Louisiana, and Texas.

demographic factors relating to the characteristics of populations. Demography is the study of populations, looking at such aspects as size, growth, density, and age distribution.

depreciated decreased in value owing to market conditions. Depreciation in the value of banknotes can occur when too much paper money is put into circulation or when users doubt the ability of the government to back up the paper currency with reserves of gold or silver.

détente relaxation of strained relations between nations, especially among the United States, the Soviet Union, and China in the 1970s and late 1980s. In seeking détente, once-hostile parties begin to emphasize their common interests and reduce their points of conflict.

deterrence prevention of an action by fear of the consequences; during the cold war, the theory that war could be avoided because each side knew that the other possessed large numbers of nuclear weapons. Thus any nuclear exchange threatened the survival of both sides.

disfranchisement denial of a citizen's right to vote.

doctrine of preemption war undertaken in anticipation of imminent attack or invasion by another nation or in hopes of gaining a strategic advantage when war seems unavoidable. In that sense the Japanese government viewed its attack on Pearl Harbor as preemptive.

domesticity devotion to home life, and a woman's place at the center of that life. The ideal of domesticity became popular during the nineteenth century as industrialization was increasingly separating work and home as individual spheres.

dry farming farming system to conserve water in semi-arid regions receiving less than 15 to 20 inches of rain a year. Methods include leaving some fields fallow or unplanted to reduce water use, keeping soil broken to absorb any water, and growing drought-resistant crops.

due process constitutional concept, embodied in the Fifth and Fourteenth Amendments, that no person shall be deprived of life, liberty, or property without legal safeguards such as being present at a hearing, having an opportunity to be heard in court, having the opportunity to confront hostile witnesses, and being able to present evidence.

ecosystem a community and/or region studied as a system of functioning relationships between organisms and their environments.

ecumenism movement encouraging unity among religions, especially among Christian denominations and between Christians and Jews. Ecumenical movements promote cooperation and better understanding among different religious denominations.

egalitarian exhibiting or asserting a belief in the equality of humans in a social, political, or economic context.

elect in theology, those of the faithful chosen, or "elected" by God for eternal salvation.

elites class of people given special social, economic, or intellectual status within society. The singular noun *elite* can also be used as a plural, as in *the colonial elite.*

embargo government act prohibiting trade with a foreign country or countries, usually to exert economic pressure.

enlightenment intellectual movement that flourished in Europe from the mid-1600s through the eighteenth century and stressed the power of human reason to promote social progress by discovering the laws that governed both nature and society. In the American colonies, the Enlightenment's influence encouraged scientists such as Benjamin Franklin to experiment and discover useful scientific knowledge, and it also persuaded a growing minority to accept more liberal religious views, known as "rational Christianity."

escalation process of steady intensification, rather than a sudden or marked increase, applied to the increasing American military presence in Vietnam. The term derives from an escalator, which gradually lifts its cargo to a higher level. Nuclear theorist Herman Kahn used the term geopolitically in his *On Escalation: Metaphors and Scenarios* (1968).

evangelical term that derives from a Greek word meaning the bringing of good news—in this case, the Gospel. Protestant evangelicals stressed the need for individual conversion and rebirth stemming from an awareness of sinful guilt and Christ's act of atoning, through his death, for their sins.

excise tax   internal tax placed on the production or sale of a commodity, usually a luxury item or nonessential.

executive order   declaration issued by the president or by a governor possessing the force of law. Executive orders are usually based on existing statutory authority and require no action by Congress or the state legislature to take effect.

expatriate   one who leaves the country of one's birth or citizenship to live in another, usually out of a sense of alienation. The term is often applied to the group of writers and artists living in self-imposed exile in Paris during the 1920s and sometimes referred to as the "Lost Generation." That term was coined by the writer Gertrude Lawrence, describing the rootless generation of American expatriates who found life in the United States culturally sterile and promises of postwar freedom and democracy empty.

federalism   governing principle established by the Constitution in which the national government and the states divide power. A stronger commitment to federalism as the basis of a national republic replaced the system established by the Articles of Confederation, which granted virtually sovereign power to individual states.

fission   splitting of a nucleus of an atom into at least two other nuclei, accompanied by the release of a relatively large amount of energy. The splitting of the nucleus of the uranium isotope U-235 or its artificial cousin, plutonium, powered the atomic bomb.

franchise   see **suffrage** and **disenfranchisement.**

Free Soil party   antislavery party formed in 1848 by northern Democrats disillusioned with southern Democratic support for slavery. The party tried to widen its appeal by focusing less on outright abolition than on opposing the spread of slavery into the territories (the need to protect "free soil" and "free labor"). The party never gained strength, however, as the Republican Party in the 1850s attracted the greater number of antislavery voters.

freedmen   former slaves; the term came into use during the Civil War, as greater numbers of slaves fled or were freed under the terms of the Emancipation Proclamation, and continued to be widely used during Reconstruction. More recently historians have also used the more gender-neutral term, *freedpeople.*

graduated income tax   tax based on a percentage of an individual's income, the percentage increasing as total income increases. Under such a system, wealthy individuals are taxed at a higher rate than are poorer individuals.

Great Awakening   term used by some historians to describe periods of intense religious piety and commitment among Americans that fueled the expansion of Protestant churches. The First Great Awakening extended from the 1730s to the American Revolution; the Second Great Awakening includes the period from about 1790 to the 1840s; the Third Great Awakening took place during the late nineteenth and early twentieth centuries; the Fourth Great Awakening spans the latter half of the twentieth century.

habeas corpus   Latin phrase meaning, "you have the body." For centuries, the term referred in English law to the right of individuals to be brought before a court and informed of the crime alleged against them. The right of habeus corpus is meant to ensure that the government cannot arbitrarily arrest and imprison a citizen without giving grounds for doing so.

hawks and doves   nicknames for the two opposing positions in American policy during the war in Vietnam. Hawks supported the escalation of the war and a "peace with honor." Doves, the peace faction, argued that the United States had intervened in a civil war and should withdraw its troops.

Hessians   German soldiers who fought with the British Army during the American Revolution. Some Hessians taken as prisoners of war later served in the Continental Army and settled in the United States after the Revolution.

horizontal combination   strategy of business growth (sometimes referred to as "horizontal integration") that attempts to stifle competition by combining more than one firm involved in the same level of production, transportation, or distribution into a single firm.

http://   HyperText Transfer Protocol; abbreviation refers to the Internet rules governing the transfer of data between a server and a computer as well as for exchanging files (text, graphic images, sound, video, and other multimedia files) on the World Wide Web.

impeachment   under the U.S. Constitution, the process by which members of the House of Representatives bring charges against a high government official for "Treason, Bribery, or other high Crimes and Misdemeanors." Once an individual is impeached, he or she must stand trial before the Senate, where a majority vote is required for conviction. Conviction results in removal from office.

imperialism   acquisition of control over the government and the economy of another nation, usually by conquest. The United States became an imperialistic world power in the late nineteenth century by gaining control over the Hawaiian Islands and, after the Spanish American War (1898), Guam, the Philippines, Cuba, and Puerto Rico.

indemnity   compensation for loss or damage.

indentures   contract signed between two parties, binding one to serve the other for a specified period of time. The term originated because two copies of the agreement were made, both indented in the same way at its edges, so that each party was provided an identical record of the agreement.

inflation   increase in the overall price of goods and services over an extended period of time; or a similar decrease over time of the purchasing power of money. The latter situation can be caused by an increase of the amount of currency and credit available in an economy. In such cases, when the perceived value of paper money declines (as often happens in wars, when the government tries to raise revenues by printing money), sellers raise the prices of their goods to compensate.

injunction   court order requiring individuals or groups to participate in or refrain from a certain action.

interstate commerce   trade in goods that crosses state lines. Regulation of interstate commerce is reserved in the Constitution for the federal government and has become the constitutional basis for much of federal regulation of business.

Iroquois League Indian confederacy, also known as the Five Nations, that exerted enormous influence throughout the region. In 1712, a sixth tribe, the Tuscaroras, joined the confederation.

isolationism belief that the United States should avoid foreign entanglements, alliances, and involvement in foreign wars. The tradition had its roots in President George Washington's farewell address, which warned in 1796, "It is our true policy to steer clear of permanent alliances with any portion of the foreign world. . . ."

Issei *see* **Nisei**

itinerant traveling preacher attached to no settled congregation. Itinerants played an important role in the first Great Awakening, taking their inspiration from George Whitefield, who preached up and down the Atlantic seaboard. In the early nineteenth century, many Protestant denominations—especially the Methodists and the Baptists—made strategic use of itinerants to evangelize settlers on the frontier.

jihad Arabic term meaning striving or struggling in the way of God. Although broadly the term can indicate a spiritual effort on the part of a Muslim believer to come closer to Allah, the expression is also used to denote a Muslim holy war against unbelievers.

joint stock company business in which capital is held in transferable shares of stock by joint owners. The joint stock company was an innovation that allowed investors to share and spread the risks of overseas investment. Instead of only a few individuals owning a ship and its cargo—which might sink and bring ruin to its investors—joint stock allowed for smaller sums to be invested in a variety of different ventures.

journeyman person who has served an apprenticeship in a trade or craft and who is a qualified worker employed by another person.

judicial review doctrine set out by Chief Justice John Marshall in *Marbury v. Madison*. The decision established that the judicial branch of the federal government possesses the power to determine whether the laws of Congress or the actions of the executive branch violate the Constitution.

laissez faire a French term ("allow to do") referring to an economic doctrine that advocates holding government interference in the economy to an absolute minimum and ideally having none at all.

landed states and landless states some of the 13 colonies that became the United States had originally been granted land whose western boundaries were vague or overlapped the land granted to other colonies. During the Confederation period, the so-called "landless" states had boundaries that were firmly drawn on all sides, such as Maryland, New Jersey, and Massachusetts. The so-called "landed" states possessed grants whose western boundaries were not fixed.

libertarian advocate of a minimalist approach to governing, in which the freedom of private individuals to do as they please ranks paramount. A libertarian philosophy contrasts with the outlook of modern liberals, in which government plays a more active role in meeting the needs of citizens or in managing social and economic life for the common good.

lien legal claim against property used to obtain a loan, which must be paid when the property is sold. Developing first in the South after the Civil War, the crop-lien system allowed merchants to claim a portion (or all) of current or future crops as payment for loans to farmers for seed, tools, and fertilizer. Merchants often insisted that indebted farmers raise a single cash crop, frequently cotton. That requirement helped to ensnare farmers in a cycle of debt as the price of such crops fell.

loyalists supporters of the king and Parliament and known to the rebels as "tories." At the outset of the American Revolution, loyalists made up about one-fifth of the white population, but their ranks diminished steadily after about 1777, as the British army alienated many civilians in every region that they occupied.

loyalty oath oath of fidelity to the state or to an organization. Plans for Reconstruction insisted that southerners returning to the Union take a loyalty oath of some sort, whether that they would be loyal henceforth to the United States or a more strict "ironclad oath" that they never had aided the Confederacy. At other times of stress—as during the Revolutionary era or during the cold war of the 1950s, loyalty oaths and loyalty investigations have been used by groups or governments to enforce obedience to the state or to a revolutionary movement.

managed economy economy directed by the government with power over prices, allocation of resources, and marketing of goods.

Manifest Destiny belief, as Democratic editor John L. O'Sullivan put it, that it had become the United States' "manifest destiny to overspread the continent allotted by Providence for the free development of our yearly multiplying millions." The roots of the doctrine were both religious and political. Protestant religious thinkers had long seen American settlement as setting a pious and virtuous example to the rest of the world. The political ideology of the Revolution encouraged the notion that the benefits of democracy would spread along with the political expansion of the nation. Yet Manifest Destiny was also racist in its assumption of the inferiority of other peoples and cultures; and it encompassed a purely economic desire to expand the nation's commerce and power.

"maroon" communities collective attempts at escape typically undertaken by groups of newly arrived African slaves in the American South. Such slaves fled inland, often to the frontiers of colonial settlement, where they attempted to reconstruct the African villages from which they had been taken captive. Because of their size, such communities proved to be short-lived; they were quickly discovered by white slave patrols or by Indian tribes such as the Cherokees, who profited from returning runaways. "Maroon communities" in the Caribbean proved far more enduring and provided the bases for successful slave rebellions during the eighteenth and early nineteenth centuries.

mass media forms of communication designed to reach a vast audience, generally a nation state or larger, without personal contact between the senders and receivers. Examples would include newspapers, movies, magazines, radio, television, and—today—some sites on the Internet.

mercantilism   European economic doctrine calling for strict regulation of the economy in order to ensure a balance of exports over imports and encrease the amount of gold and silver in a nation's treasury.

merchants of death   term popularized in the 1930s to describe American bankers and arms makers whose support for the Allied cause, some historians charged, drew the United States into World War I.

Mesoamerica   the area stretching from present-day central Mexico southward through Honduras and Nicaragua, in which pre-Columbian civilizations developed.

Methodist   denomination that originated as a reform movement within the Church of England during the mid-eighteenth century, much as the Puritans originated as a reform movement within the English church during the mid-sixteenth century. The distinctive features of early Methodism on both sides of the Atlantic included a strict devotional regimen, an ascetic moral discipline, and an emphasis on evangelical conversion. By the Civil War, Methodists had become the largest Protestant denomination in the United States among both whites and African Americans.

military-industrial complex   combination of the U.S. armed forces, arms manufacturers, and associated political and commercial interests, which grew rapidly during the cold war era. It is another term for the mutually supportive relationship of military contractors, the Pentagon, and sympathetic members of Congress, an alliance also known as the "Iron Triangle."

militia   local defense band of civilians comprising men between the ages of 16 and 65 whose military training consisted only of occasional gatherings known as musters. Militias were organized in towns and counties throughout the American colonies from the beginnings of settlement, but they played a crucial role in the war for independence by supporting the Continental Army whenever the fighting moved into their neighborhoods.

millennialism   belief in the thousand-year reign of Christ predicted in the Bible's final book, the Revelation to John. The belief that dedicated Christians could help bring about this reign of holiness by converting the world to Christianity proved to be a powerful impulse to reform.

miscegenation   marriage, cohabitation, or sexual relations between persons of different races. Since race is a socially constructed identifier rather than one with any scientific or genetic basis, *miscegenation* as a term is used only in its historical context.

monoculture   growth of a single crop to the virtual exclusion of all others, either on a farm or more generally within a region.

mutiny   refusal of rank-and-file soldiers to follow the commands of their superior officers. Mutinies plagued the Continental Army between 1779 and 1781 as resentments mounted among soldiers over spoiled food, inadequate clothing, and back pay.

mutually assured destruction (MAD)   national defense strategy in which a nuclear attack by one side would inevitably trigger an equal response leading to the destruction of both the attacker and the defender. Deterrence theory suggested that when both sides possessed the capability to inflict nuclear annihilation, even after being hit by a first strike, neither side would dare use such weapons.

national debt   cumulative total of all previous annual *federal deficits* or budget shortfalls incurred each year and owed by the federal government.

nativism   outlook championing the supremacy of "native" cultural traits and political rights over those of immigrants from different backgrounds. Nativism flourished during the high immigration of the late 1840s and 1850s, evidenced by the rise of the American ("Know-Nothing") party. In the late nineteenth and early twentieth centuries, nativists pressed for the restriction of immigration and won their biggest victories when Congress enacted the National Origins Acts of 1921 and 1924. As immigrant numbers rose again in the late twentieth century and early twenty-first, the nativist debate again emerged.

naturalization   act of granting full citizenship to someone born outside the country.

navalism   theories of warfare and trade that rely on a nation's navy as a principal instrument of policy.

neo-isolationist   term applied to those who after World War II believed the United States should avoid foreign entanglements. Neo-isolationists especially condemned the United Nations and its supporters, whom they contemptuously referred to as "one-worlders."

"new" immigrants   called "new" because they differed substantially from earlier arrivals who had come mostly from Northern and Western Europe; these newcomers came to the United States between 1880 and 1920 from Eastern and Southern Europe. Unlike most earlier immigrants (with the exception of the Irish), these immigrants were non-Protestants: Catholics, Jews, and Russian Orthodox Christians.

Nisei   American-born citizens of Japanese ancestry, contrasted with *Issei*, native-born Japanese who had moved to the United States. At the outbreak of World War II, Nisei referred specifically to Japanese Americans who lived on the West Coast (but not in Hawaii or the East Coast), who were interned during the war because of prejudice and the widespread fear that they sympathized with Japan.

nomad   a member of a group of people who have no fixed home and who move about, usually seasonally, in pursuit of food, water, and other resources.

normal schools   schools that trained teachers, usually for two years and mostly for teaching in the elementary grades.

northwest territory   present-day states of Ohio, Indiana, Illinois, Michigan, and Wisconsin. The incorporation of this territory into the United States through the Northwest Ordinance of 1785 marked the major achievement of the national government under the Articles of Confederation.

Opposition   diverse group of political thinkers and writers in Great Britain, also known as the Country Party and the Commonwealthmen, who elaborated the tradition of classical republicanism from the late seventeenth century through the eighteenth century. They warned that the executive branch of government (the king and his ministers) was conspiring to corrupt and coopt the legislative branch of government (the House of Commons), thereby endangering popular liberties, and they called for political reforms to make Britain's government more representative of and more accountable to the people. Dismissed in England as a disaffected radical minority, the Opposition exerted a decisive influence on the political thinking of an increasing number of American colonials in the decades leading up to the Revolution.

outsourcing   the contracting of goods or services from outside a company or organization in order to maintain flexibility in the size of the organization's work force. Increasingly outsourcing has used suppliers outside the United States in low-wage countries such as Mexico, India, and China.

pandemic   outbreak of disease that spreads across national boundaries or across the world.

partisan warfare   armed clashes among political rivals, typically involving guerilla fighting and the violent intimidation of civilians by militias. Partisan warfare between loyalists and rebels tore apart communities everywhere in the United States during the war for independence, but the fighting was especially fierce and protracted in the South. The success of rebel insurgencies there ultimately convinced many southern whites to support the cause of independence.

patent   legal document issued by the government giving the holder exclusive rights to use, make, and sell a process, product, or device for a specified period of time. The first patents in America were issued by colonial governments as early as 1641. Congress enacted the first patent law in 1790.

paternalism   attitude or policy of treating individuals or groups in a fatherly manner, by providing for their needs without granting them rights of responsibilities. The relation involves both a dominant and a subordinate party. Sometimes the dominance comes from gender, as in a male patriarchy, whereby females are given subordinate roles. But paternalism can also be expressed in relations between colonial and subject peoples, masters and slaves, or culturally different groups.

pays d'en haut   in the seventeenth century, the lands referred to by the French as the "upper country," the land upriver from Montreal as French fur traders passed into the Great Lakes beyond the southern shores of Lake Ontario. The trading lands stretched all the way to the Mississippi River.

peculiar institution   euphemism for slavery, perhaps revealing in its use. The institution was "peculiar" to the South in that it had been abolished in the North (and other parts of the world, increasingly). *Peculiar* also suggests the contradiction with the ideals of the Declaration of Independence, that "all men are created equal."

per capita income   average yearly income per person in a particular population; it provides one statistical measure of the relative wealth of a region.

pluralism   idea that identity cannot be reduced to a single shared essence. Under such a philosophy, distinct ethnic, cultural, and religious groups are tolerated and affirmed within a society. The philosophy contrasts with the belief, in American politics, that citizens should assimilate into a more uniform cultural identity of shared values. Contrasting metaphors portray an assimilationist United States as a melting pot versus a pluralist mixing bowl.

plurality   in elections, a candidate who receives a plurality wins more votes than any other candidate but less than half of all votes cast. Receiving more than half of the votes cast is called a *majority.*

pocket veto   means of vetoing a bill without formally doing so. Normally, if a president does not veto or sign a bill within 10 days of receiving it, the bill automatically becomes law. If it is received, however, within 10 days of Congress's adjournment, the president can simply "pocket" the bill unsigned, until Congress adjourns, and it does not go into effect.

political culture   patterns, habits, institutions, and traits associated with a political system. The political culture of the Jacksonian era, for example, was marked by a number of innovations: political nominating conventions, torchlight parades, campaign songs, badges, and other souvenirs.

political machine   hierarchical political organization developed in the nineteenth century that controlled the activities of a political party and was usually headed by a political boss.

popular sovereignty   doctrine that a territory could decide by vote whether or not to permit slavery within its boundaries. The doctrine was devised by Senator Stephen Douglas of Illinois as a way to placate southerners who wanted slavery permitted within Kansas Territory, forbidden under the Missouri Compromise. Meant as a compromise measure, the doctrine only inflamed the situation, as both sides worked to win a vote over slavery.

Populism   political outlook that supports the rights and powers of the common people in opposition to the interests of the privileged elite. The Populist Party evolved out of the economic distress of the 1890s among farmers and focused its anger against the era's large industrial corporations, railroad monopolies, and banks. But populism as an outlook and philosophy persisted long after the party had dissolved.

pragmatism   philosophical movement, led by philosophers Charles S. Peirce and William James, that stressed the visible, real-world results of ideas. Pragmatism was embraced by many progressives who wanted to promote the possibilities of change by abandoning the old notion that events were predetermined and inevitable.

predestination   basis of Calvinist theology and a belief that holds that God has ordained the outcome of all human history before the beginning of time, including the eternal fate of every human being. Believers in this doctrine found comfort and meaning from its assurance that God was directing the fate of nations, individuals, and all of creation toward his divine purposes.

Presbyterians   members of a Protestant denomination that originated in sixteenth-century Britain as part of the Puritan movement. Like their fellow Puritan reformers, the **Congregationalists,** the Presbyterians embraced Calvinist theology beliefs; but unlike the Congregationalists, Presbyterians favored a more hierarchical form of church governance, a system in which individual congregations were guided by presbyteries and synods comprising both laymen and ministers.

presidio   military garrison; as Spanish colonizers moved north from central Mexico in the sixteenth and seventeenth century, they constructed presidios to consolidate claims over new territory. Presidios often encouraged the growth of nearby towns and ranches and were probably more important as sites of diplomacy with Indians than as centers of military power. Poor funding and political instability led to the decline of the presidios after Mexican independence in 1821.

privatize   transferral of an economic enterprise or public utility from the control of the government into private ownership. The Bush plan for Social Security reform sought to place retirement contributions into investment accounts managed privately, rather than into a fund managed by the Social Security Administration.

producer goods   goods, such as heavy machinery, used to manufacture other goods, often consumer goods.

psychedelic   characterized by or generating shifts in perception and altered states of awareness, often hallucinatory, and usually brought on by drugs such as LSD, mescaline, or psilocybin. Advocates of the psychedelic state spoke of euphoria, mystic visions, and philosophic insights produced. Critical observers pointed to the potential not only of inducing hallucinations but sometimes psychoses.

public works   government-financed construction projects, such as highways and bridges, for use by the public.

Puritans   members of a reform movement within the Church of England that originated in the sixteenth century and that ultimately formed the Congregationalist and Presbyterian churches. Calvinist in their theology, the Puritans strove to reform English religion, society, and politics by restricting church membership to the pious and godly, by according the laity greater power in church governance, and by enlisting the state to enforce a strict moral code that prohibited drunkenness, gambling, swearing, and attending the theater.

Quakers   Protestant sect, also known as the Society of Friends, founded in mid-seventeenth century England. The Quakers believed that the Holy Spirit dwelt within each human being and that religious conviction was the source of their egalitarian social practices, which included allowing women to speak in churches and to preach in public gatherings. Quakers settled the mid-Atlantic colonies in large numbers and founded the colony of Pennsylvania.

racialism   see *racism*.

racism   form of discrimination based on the belief that one race is superior to another. Racism may be expressed individually and consciously, through explicit thoughts, feelings, or acts; it can be codified into a theory that claims scientific backing for its tenets. It can also be expressed socially and unconsciously, through institutions that promote inequality between races. In the early twentieth century, when racism became much more pronounced, the term *racialism* was also coined.

reconquista   military reconquest of the Iberian peninsula from Islamic Moors of Africa by European Christian rulers. The campaign lasted on and off from 718 to 1492 C.E.

Redeemers   southerners who came to power in southern state governments from 1875 to 1877, claiming to have "redeemed" the South from Reconstruction. The Redeemers looked to undo many of the changes wrought by the Civil War. Their goals included minimizing the role of African Americans in government and reducing their economic independence and strengthening the "New South" through industrial development.

red-light district   area in cities reserved for prostitutes. The term, first employed in the United States, resulted from the use of red lights to show that prostitutes were open for business.

repatriation   act of returning people to their nation of origin. The term often refers to the act of returning soldiers or refugees to their birth country.

republican motherhood   redefinition of the role of women promoted by many American reformers in the 1780s and 1790s, who believed that the success of republican government depended on educated and independent-minded mothers who would raise children to become informed and self-reliant citizens. The ideal of republican motherhood fostered improvements in educational opportunities for women and accorded them an important role in civic life, but it also reinforced the notion that women should confine the sphere of their activities to home and family.

republicanism   belief that representative government safeguards popular liberties more reliably than does either monarchy or oligarchy and that all citizens must practice vigilance and self-denying virtue to prevent their rulers from succumbing to the temptations of power and becoming tyrants. This "classical republicanism" profoundly influenced the political views of many Americans from the middle of the eighteenth century to the middle of the nineteenth century.

Romanticism   intellectual and artistic movement that arose in the early nineteenth century out of a rejection of the Enlightenment values of reason and balance. Romanticism emphasized the individual's expression of emotion and intuition.

sagebrush rebels   group of western cattlemen, loggers, miners, developers, and others who argued that federal ownership of huge tracts of land and natural resources violated the principle of states' rights. This group demanded that government transfer control to individual states, in respect of their right to make decisions about the management of both the land and the natural resources.

scalawag   white southerners who supported the Republican party. The derisive nickname was given by their opponents. Perhaps a quarter of all white southerners voted Republican at some time during Reconstruction.

scientific management   system of factory production that stresses efficiency. The system was pioneered by American engineer Frederick Winslow Taylor. In *The Principles of Scientific Management* (1911), his most famous work, he emphasized time-and-motion studies to enhance productivity. The book became the bible of efficiency experts and Taylor the "Father of Scientific Management."

sedition   words or actions that incite revolt against the law or duly constituted government.

segregation   system, imposed through law and custom, of separating people by race; first enacted into law in Tennessee

(1875) with a statute separating blacks from whites on trains, one of the most prevalent public spaces for racial mingling.

self-determination principle in international law that people have a right to determine their own form of government free from outside control. The principle contrasts with colonialism and imperialism, under which people are subject to foreign rulers.

semisubsistence economy economy in which individuals and families produce most of what they need to live on. Such economies are overwhelmingly rural and also egalitarian, in that wealth is distributed fairly broadly. During the colonial period and early republic, much of the American economy was semisubsistence. *See also* **commercial economy.**

separate but equal rationale for a policy of segregation granting equal facilities and services to African American and whites in schools, hospitals, transportation and lodging facilities, and other public places. The Supreme Court upheld such laws in *Plessy v. Ferguson* (1896). In practice such facilities were separate but seldom equal.

separation of Church and State principle that religious institutions and their representatives should exercise no civil or judicial powers and that civil governments should give no official sanction, privileges, or financial support to any religious denomination or organization.

separation of powers principle that each branch of government—the legislature (Congress), the executive (the President), and the judiciary (the Supreme Court)—should wield distinct powers independent from interference or infringement by other branches of government. During the debates of the Constitutional Convention in 1797, James Madison successfully argued that this separation of powers was essential to a balanced republican government.

settlement house social reform effort that used neighborhood centers in which settlement house workers lived and worked among the poor, often in slum neighborhoods. The first settlement house, Toynbee Hall in London, was founded in 1884. The first settlement house in the United States (The Neighborhood Guild, later University Settlement House) was built in 1886 in New York City and was founded by Stanton Coit.

Shi'ite and Sunni two major branches of Islam, a division not unlike the Protestant-Catholic split in Christianity. After the death of the Prophet Muhammad followers disagreed over who should be his successor. Most believers accepted the tradition of having their leader chosen by community consensus (the Sunni branch), but a minority supported the claim of Ali, the Prophet's cousin. Over the years theological differences have separated Shi'ite and Sunni Muslims as well. Today the Shi'ites are dominant largely in Iran and southeastern Iraq.

silent majority phrase coined by President Richard Nixon in a 1969 speech, referring to the large number of Americans who supported his policies but did not express their views publicly.

sit-in form of direct action in which protesters nonviolently occupy and refuse to leave an area. Mahatma Gandhi employed the tactic during the Indian independence movement, and autoworkers used it in Flint, Michigan, in the late 1930s. Student movements around the world widely adopted the tactic in the 1960s.

social mobility movement of individuals from one social class to another. In general, the stronger the barriers of class, race, gender or caste, the less social mobility exhibited by a society.

socialism philosophy of social and economic organization in which the means of producing and distributing goods is owned collectively or by government.

sociological jurisprudence legal theory that emphasizes the importance not merely of precedent but of contemporary social context in interpreting the law.

specie coined money of gold or silver. Also referred to as hard money or hard currency. In contrast, banknotes or notes are paper money or paper currency.

sphere of influence geographic region beyond its border over which a nation exerts political or economic control.

spoils system practice of rewarding loyal party members with jobs in government. Known more formally as "patronage," the practice drew its name from the old saying, "To the victor belong the spoils," in this instance meaning the rewards of election victories.

steerage least expensive accommodation on a passenger ship, located below decks and often used by immigrants for passage to the United States in the late nineteenth and early twentieth centuries.

stock exchange market at which shares of ownership in corporations are bought and sold. The creation of what were markets for investment capital made it easier to raise the large sums of money needed for large industrial projects.

stratified layered; in this case according to class or social station. A highly stratified society has a greater variety of social levels, from the richest or most socially esteemed to the poorest or least socially approved. A society can be stratified according to wealth, race, religion, or a number of other social markers.

subsistence farming see **semisubsistence economy.**

subversive one who seeks the destruction or overthrow of a legally constituted government; also used as an adjective (for example, *subversive conduct*) to refer more generally to behavior undermining the established social order.

suffrage right to vote; also referred to as the franchise. To *disfranchise* is to take away the right to vote.

sun belt areas of the southern and western parts of the United States that experienced significant economic and population growth since World War II. That growth has been a contrast to the relative decline of the *rust belt,* the older industrial area from New England to the mid-Atlantic region across the upper-Middle West.

supply-side economics theory that emphasizes tax cuts and business incentives to encourage economic growth rather than deficit spending to promote demand. Businesses and individuals, the theory assumes, will use their tax savings to create new businesses and expand old businesses, which in turn will increase productivity, employment, and general well-being.

tariff duty on trade, the purpose of which is primarily to regulate the flow of commerce rather than to raise a revenue. The Molasses Act of 1733, for example, imposed a hefty customs duty on molasses imported from non-British Caribbean islands to encourage American distillers to purchase molasses exclusively from the British West Indies.

task system way of organizing slave labor in the South Carolina low country during the eighteenth century. Masters and overseers of rice and indigo plantations assigned individual slaves a daily task, and after its completion, slaves could spend the rest of the day engaged in pursuits of their own choosing. Gang labor, the system practiced in the Chesapeake, afforded slaves less opportunity for freedom within slavery.

taxes duty on trade (known as external taxation) or a duty on items circulating within a nation or a colony (known as internal taxation) intended primarily to raise a revenue rather than to regulate the flow of commerce. The Sugar Act of 1764 was an external tax, whereas the Stamp Act of 1765 was an internal tax.

Tejano Texan of Hispanic descent. In the early stages of the rebellion against Santa Anna, more than a few Tejanos supported the Texan drive for independence. But as Americans continued to arrive in Texas in large numbers, many viewed Tejanos with suspicion and they were marginalized in Texan society.

temperance movement reform movement, begun in the 1820s, to temper or restrain the sale and use of alcohol. It achieved its greatest success when the Eighteenth Amendment took effect in 1920, outlawing the manufacture, sale, transportation, and importation of alcohol. The amendment was repealed in 1933.

tenement building, often in disrepair and usually five or six stories in height, in which cheap apartments were rented to tenants. Such dilapidated housing sprang up in cities across the United States in the late nineteenth and early twentieth centuries to lodge the growing numbers of immigrants, African Americans, and other poor populations moving to urban centers.

theocracy system of government dominated by the clergy.

totalitarian government system in which the state controls all aspects of economic, political, and even social life, usually through some form of dictatorship. Nazi Germany under Adolf Hitler and the Soviet Union under Joseph Stalin are examples of totalitarian regimes.

trade association organization of individuals and firms in a given industry that provides statistical, lobbying, and other services to members.

trust business arrangement in which owners of shares in a business turn over their shares "in trust" to a board with power to control those businesses for the benefit of the trust. Following the example set by John D. Rockefeller and Standard Oil, trusts blossomed in the late nineteenth century as a means of consolidating power over production, marketing, and pricing, often crowding out other competitors."

union organization of workers designed to improve their economic status and working conditions. Such organizations come in two varieties: the horizontal union, in which all members share a common skill or craft, and the vertical union, composed of workers from all across the same industry.

Upper South the border states (Delaware, Maryland, Kentucky, and Missouri) and Virginia, North Carolina, Tennessee, and Arkansas.

vertical integration strategy of business growth that attempts to reduce costs by gaining control of the successive stages of a business operation, incorporating into a single firm several firms involved in all aspects of the manufacture of a product—from exploiting raw materials to manufacturing and distribution.

Victorianism constellation of middle-class values attributed to the proper virtues of Britain's Queen Victoria. Victorianism responded to the instabilities of an industrial age in which factory work dominated the lives of struggling workers and middle-class clerks as well as down-at-the-heels landed gentry. The culture's emphasis on "refinement" and "manners" established a social hierarchy offering some sense of stability.

virgin soil epidemic epidemic in which the populations at risk have had no previous contact with the diseases that strike them and are therefore immunologically almost defenseless.

virtual representation view that representation is not linked to election but rather to common interests; for example, during the imperial crisis the British argued that Americans were virtually represented in Parliament, even though colonials elected none of its members, because each member of Parliament stood for the interests of the whole empire. See also **actual representation.**

"watered" stock stock issued in excess of the assets of a company. The term derived from the practice of some ranchers who made their cattle drink large amounts of water before weighing them for sale.

welfare capitalism business practice of providing welfare—in the form of pension and profit-sharing programs, subsidized housing, personnel management, paid vacations, and other services and benefits—for workers. The practice was pioneered by Henry Ford under the philosophy that businesses in a capitalist economy should act for the common good of their workers. The philosophy, if not the business-wide practice, became popular in the 1920s as a way of reducing high rates of turnover among employees and integrating technological change into the workplace.

Wisconsin idea series of progressive reforms at the state level promoted by Robert LaFollette during his governorship of Wisconsin (1901–1906). They included primary elections, corporate property taxes, regulation of railroads and public utilities, and supervision of public resources in the public interest. A nonpartisan civil service group, recruited mostly from faculty at the University of Wisconsin, provided a cadre of expert bureaucrats to run the new programs.

yellow journalism brand of newspaper reporting that stresses excitement and shock over even-handedness and dull fact. The term "yellow journalism" derived from the color of the ink used to print the first comic strip, which appeared in William Randolph Hearst's *New York Journal* in 1895. Hearst's newspaper specialized in yellow journalism and is often credited with igniting public passions for war with Spain in 1898.

Credits

Page 470 Valentine Richmond History Center; **472** "A Visit from the Old Mistress," by Winslow Homer, 1876. Oil on canvas, 18 × 24 1/8". National Museum of American Art, Smithsonian Institution, Washington, DC, USA. Gift of William T. Evans/Art Resource, NY; **473** Harper's Weekly; **475** The Library of Congress; **476** *Puck*, 1890; **479** "Portrait of Hiram Rhoades Revels," 1870, by Theodor Kaufmann. Oil on millboard, 12" × 10". Courtesy of the Herbert F. Johnson Museum of Art, Cornell University, Ithaca. NY. Transferred from the Olin, (69.170); **481** The Library of Congress; **484 T** The New-York Historical Society, (50475.); **484 B** © Corbis; **487** Sophie Smith Collection, Smith College; **488** The Granger Collection, New York; **489** Collection of David J. and Janice L. Frent; **490** The New York Public Library/Art Resource, NY; **492** The Library of Congress; **496** The Library of Congress; **499** "Cabbages," 1879, by Thomas Anshutz. The Metropolitan Museum of Art, Morris K. Jessup Fund, 1940. Photo © 2005 The Metropolitan Museum of Art, New York. (40.40); **501** The National Archives; **502** T.E. Armitstead Collection, University of South Alabama Archives; **504** Courtesy of the Billy Graham Center Museum; **506-507** LSU in Shreveport, Noel Memorial Library, Archives and Special Collections; **508** © The Metropolitan Museum of Art/Art Resource, NY; **509** The Library of Congress; **512** Southwest Museum, Pasadena, CA; **514** The Montana Historical Society; **519** Idaho State Historical Society, (349); **522** "Old Chisholm Trail," by Clara McDonald Williamson. The Roland P. Murdock Collection, Wichita Art Museum, (M124.54); **525** Photograph of Mr. and Mrs. David Hilton and children. North of Weissert, rural Custer County, Nebraska, c. 1880. Solomon D. Butcher Collection, Nebraska State Historical Society, Lincoln; **526** © Colorado State University Photographic Services; **528 T** Image courtesy of Circus World Museum, Baraboo, Wisconsin; **528 B** The Library of Congress; **532** The Library of Congress; **533** "Hidatsa Buffalo Robe," by Karl Bodmer. Joslyn Art Museum, Omaha, Nebraska, Gift of the Enron Art Foundation; **534 T** "Piegan Blackfeet Man", by Karl Bodmer. Joslyn Art Museum, Omaha, Nebraska, Gift of the Enron Art Foundation; **534 B** From: William M. Harlow, Inside the Wood: Masterpiece of Nature (Washington DC, 1970); **536** © Bettmann/Corbis; **538** Collection of New York Public Library, Astor, Lenox and Tilden Foundations; **540** Culver Pictures, Inc.; **542 L** © Bettmann/Corbis; **542 R** Edison National Historic Site; **543** The Granger Collection, New York; **544** Culver Pictures, Inc.; **547** The Library of Congress; **548** Courtesy of epodunk.com; **552-553** The Library of Congress; **555** Collier's, 1905; **556** Leslie's Illustrated Newspaper, 1888; **557** Brown Brothers; **558 T** Strong National Museum of Play, Rochester, NY; **558 B** The Library of Congress; **559** Courtesy, MetLife Archives; **562** Deutsches Historisches Museum; **563** Historical Society of Schuylkill County; **564** Culver Pictures, Inc.; **568** Yale University Art Gallery/Art Resource, NY; **570** "Cliff Dwellers," 1913 by George Wesley Bellows. Los Angeles County Museum of Art, Los Angeles County Fund. Photograph © 2004 Museum Associates/LACMA; **573 T** The Library of Congress; **573 B** The National Archives; **575** The National Archives; **576** Collection of The New York Public Library, Astor, Lenox and Tilden Foundations; **578** "The Sawdust Trail," 1916, by George Bellows. Milwaukee Art Museum, Layton Art Collection; **581** Reproduced by permission of Chinn Family, San Francisco, CA; **582** Courtesy of The Winterthur Library; **584** "Blackboard," 1877, by Winslow Homer. © 2000 Board of Trustees, National Gallery of Art, Washington, Gift (Partial and Promised) of Jo Ann and Julian Gans, Jr., in honor of the 50th Anniversary of the National Gallery of Art; **586** Harpers New Monthly Magazine,1893; **588** "Sixth Avenue Shoppers," by Everett Shinn. Pastel and watercolor on board, 21 × 26 1/2". Santa Barbara Museum of Art, Gift of Mrs. Sterling Morton for the Preston Morton Collection; **589** Image courtesy of Circus World Museum, Baraboo, Wisconsin with permission from Ringling Bros. and Barnum & Bailey® THE GREATEST SHOW ON EARTH®; **594** Chicago Historical Society, (ICHI-25164); **598** Courtesy of the Colorado Historical Society; **599** Culver Pictures, Inc.; **601** Courtesy of the California History Room, California State Library, Sacramento, California; **602** Courtesy of Cornell University Library, Ithaca, NY; **606-612** The Library of Congress; **615** Philip P. Choy, Professor of Asian American Studies at San Francisco State University; **616** Hawaii State Archives; **617 L** Chicago Historical Society (ICHi-08428); **617 R** Collection of David J. and Janice L. Frent; **618** "Naval Parade," August 20, 1898, by Fred Pansing. Courtesy of the Museum of the City of New York; **620** Huntsville Public Library, Huntsville, AL; **628 T** The Library of Congress; **628 B** Courtesy Frederic Remington Art Museum, Ogdensburg, New York; **630 T** Theodore Roosevelt Collection, Harvard College Library; **630 B** New York World, in Review of Reviews, April 1898. New York Public Library/Art Resource, NY; **631 T** New York Journal, in Review of Reviews, May 1898. New York Public Library/Art Resource, NY; **631 B** New York Tribune, Twinkles supplement, May 15, 1897. New York Public Library/Art Resource, NY; **632** The Library of Congress; **634** Brown Brothers; **635-637** © Bettmann/Corbis; **638** The Library of Congress; **640** Illinois Historical Society, Macon County; **642** Gondolas in Venice Canal, Venice,California, Photograph by Pacific Novelty Co. California Historical Society, San Francisco, (FN-29415); **644** The Library of Congress; **645** Hulton Archive/Getty Images; **646** National Portrait Gallery, Washington, DC/Art Resource, NY; **647** Culver Pictures, Inc.; **648 L** Brown Brothers; **648 R** The Library of Congress; **649** The Library of Congress; **651** From the Collections of the Henry Ford; **652** The Bancroft Library, University of California, Berkeley; **653-656** Culver Pictures, Inc.; **660** "L'Enfer (Hell)," 1916, by Georges Paul Leroux. Imperial War Museum, London, UK/Bridgeman Art Library, NY; **664** "News Runners Rushing in with the Latest," Artist Unknown, Japanese. Late Meiji era. Color lithograph; ink on card stock. Museum of Fine Arts, Boston, Leonard A. Lauder Collection of Japanese Postcards, (2002.1581); **667** Brown Brothers; **668** "Avenue of the Allies, Great Britain," 1918, by Childe Hassam, (1859–1935). Oil on canvas, 36 × 28 3/8 in. (91.4 × 72.1 cm). Bequest of Miss Adelaide Milton de Groot (1876–1967), 1967 (67.187.127). The Metropolitan Museum of Art, New York, NY, U.S.A. Photo Credit: Image copyright © The Metropolitan Museum of Art/Art Resource, NY; **671** The National Archives; **672** Culver Pictures, Inc.; **673** Trustees of the Imperial War Museum, London; **674** Courtesy New Mexico State Records Center & Archives, Santa Fe, NM. Read Collection, Private Papers, Folder 54a, Series II, Ellis & Jenkins, 1892–1920, Box #9, Serial Number 8425, WWI, Felix Sanchez Photo Number 7224; **676** The National Archives; **680** Earl Lonsbury, Battle Engagement. WPA Photo Collection, The National Archives; **681** Cartoon by D.C. Boonzaier in "Die Burger," October 16, 1918; **686** Culver Pictures, Inc.; **690** "Le Tumulte Noire/Dancing Pair with Woman in Orange," 1929, by Paul Colin. National Portrait Gallery, Smithsonian Institution, Washington, DC. Art Resource, NY. ©

2008 Artists Rights Society, ARS, NY; **692** The Bancroft Library; **694** Henry Ford Museum & Greenfield Village; **696** "A Man is Known by the Car He Keeps", Jan. 24, 1925. From, "Saturday Evening Post."; **698** Dover Publications; **699** © Bettmann/Corbis; **700** The Library of Congress; **701** Evening wrap coat. c. 1928. The Metropolitan Museum of Art, NY. Gift of the Fashion Group, Inc., 1975. (1975.295.1) Photo © 2000 The Metropolitan Museum of Art, NY; **703** "The Roxy Theater," by Leif Neandross. Courtesy of the Rambusch Company Archives, NY; **705** "Blues." 1929, by Archibald John Motley, Jr. Photograph ©1993 The Art Institute of Chicago. All Rights Reserved. Lent by Archie Motley and Valerie Gerrard Browne, 41.1988. Reproduced with the permission of the estate of the artist; **708** Dover Publications; **710** Courtesy of Christine Lesiak/NET Televison; **711** Archives and Manuscripts Division of the Oklahoma Historical Society; **714** © Corbis; **717** The Library of Congress; **722** The Library of Congress. © Ben Shahn Estate/Licensed by VAGA, NY; **724** Brown Brothers; **725** MONOPOLY® & 2007 Hasbro, Inc. Used with Permission. Strong National Museum of Play, Rochester, NY; **726** Radio designed by Harold van Doren and J.G. Rideout. Made by Air-King Products CO., Brooklyn, 1930-33. The Brooklyn Museum of Art, purchased with funds donated by The Walter Foundation, [85.9] Photograph, Scott Hyde; **727** The Library of Congress; **729** The Katherine G. Lederer Ozarks African American History Collection, Missouri State University; **730** "Home Relief Station," 1935–36, by Louis Ribak. Collection of Whitney Museum of American Art, NY. Purchase. (36.148.) Photograph © 2000: Whitney Museum of American Art; **731** United States Air Force; **732** "Riot at Union Square," 1947 [date depicted: March 6, 1930] by Peter Hopkins. Oil on canvas. Museum of the City of New York, Gift of the Artist,(66.82); **735** Martin McEvilly/The New York Daily News; **739** © Condé Nast Archive/Corbis; **741** © Corbis; **744** The Library of Congress; **746** "California Industrial Scenes," (detail), 1934, John Langley Howard. Coit Tower, San Francisco. Photograph, Don Beatty; **747** Amy Jones; **748-749** The Bancroft Library, University of California; **750 L** Walter P. Reuther Library, Wayne State University; **750 R** State Archives of Michigan, (#05060); **751** Dorothea Lange/The Library of Congress; **752** The National Archives; **760** The National Archives; **762** AP Images; **764** © 1942 Edward B. Marks Music Company. Copyright renewed. All rights reserved. Photograph courtesy Franklin Delano Roosevelt Library, Hyde Park, New York; **765** © Corbis; **766** Central Press/Getty Images; **768** © Corbis; **769** The National Archives; **774** "Too Many, Too Close, Too Soon," by Donald Dickson. US Army Center of Military History/Army Art Collection; **776** The National Archives; **778-779** © Corbis; **780** The Library of Congress; **782** © Bettmann/Corbis; **785** "D-Day Normandy, The Rhino Ferry," by O.N. Fisher. © Canadian War Museum. Photo: William Kent, (#12468); **788** © Bettmann/Corbis; **790** The National Archives; **793** "Hiroshima," 1945, by Standish Backus Jr. Courtesy of the Navy Art Collection, Naval Historical Center, Washington, DC; **796** The National Archives; **797 BL** The National Archives; **797 BR** © Brian Brake/Photo Researchers, Inc.; **798** The National Archives; **800** Tony Camerano/AP Images; **803** The Truman Presidential Museum & Library; **805** AP Images; **808 T** General Mills Corporation; **808 B** The CONELRAD Collection, www.conelrad.com; **809** "For Full Employment After the War Register to Vote," 1944, Ben Shahn. The Museum of Modern Art, New York. Gift of the CIO Political Action Committee. Photo © 2005, The Museum of Modern Art, NY/Art Resource, NY. © Ben Shahn Estate/Licensed by VAGA, NY; **810** © Corbis; **812** Rare Books and Manuscripts, Benson Latin Ameri-

can Collection, University of Texas, Austin; **815** © Baldwin H. Ward & Kathryn C. Ward/Corbis; **817** © Warner Bros./Photofest; **818** Eve Arnold/Magnum Photos, Inc.; **820** The National Archives; **822** The CONELRAD Collection, www.conelrad.com; **826** Printed by permission of the Norman Rockwell Family Agency. Copyright © 1959 the Norman Rockwell Family Entities. Courtesy Curtis Publishing; **829** TimePix/Getty Images; **830 T** Courtesy Cadillac Motor Cars; **830 B** Michael Melford; **830** Michael Melford; **833** Elliott Erwitt/Magnum Photos, Inc.; **834** "Catching the 8:05," by Thonton Utz. © 1952 SEPS: Licensed by Curtis Publishing, Indianapolis, IN. All Rights Reserved. www.curtispublishing.com; **835** © Corbis; **839** © Warner Bros./Photofest; **840** © Bettmann/CORBIS; **841** Dwight D. Eisenhower Library; **844** © Bettmann/Corbis; **846** AP Images; **848 L** Photofest; **848 C** © Corbis; **848 R** Photofest; **852** © Corbis; **856** © Steve Schapiro/Corbis; **858** Drawing by Ruby. From *Children of Crisis: A Study of Courage and Fear, Volume I,* by Robert Coles, c. 1964-67. By permission of Little, Brown and Company; **860** © Ernest C. Withers; **862** Texas A & M University, Bell Library, Special Collections & Archives, Dr. Hector Garcia Papers, Corpis Christi, TX; **864** Burt Glinn/Magnum Photos, Inc.; **866** © Bettmann/Corbis; **867** Charles Moore/Black Star/Stock Photos; **869 T** AP Images; **869 B** Michael Alexander/Black Star/Stock Photos; **872** George Tames/New York Times, 1957; **875 R:** AP Images; **876** George Tames/New York Times, 1957; **876** Matt Herron/Take Stock; **878** The Advertising Archive; **879** © 1970 Warner Bros. Records, WS1893. Artwork by Kelly-Mouse Studios; **880** © Bettmann/Corbis; **884** © Tim Page/Corbis; **886** ©John Filo/Valley News Dispatch; **888 L:** Agence France-Presse; **888 R:** Bettman/Corbis; **891** © Tim Page/Corbis; **892** UPI/Bettmann/Corbis; **895** Julian Wasser/Time & Life Pictures/Getty Images; **898** AP Images; **899** © Bettmann/Corbis; **901** NASA; **902** "Farm Workers' Altar" 1967, by Emanuel Martinez. Acrylic on wood. 37 1/2 × 53 × 35 1/2 in. UCLA at the Armand Hammer Museum of Art and Cultural Center; **903** © Corbis; **905** Courtesy of MS. Magazine; **907-909** © Bettmann/Corbis; **914** AP Images; **916** New York Daily News; **922** © Sandra Baker/Liaison Agency/Getty Images; **923 T** AP Images; **923 B** Courtesy of The Lincoln Museum, Ft. Wayne, IN [#748]; **924** Frank Fournier/Contact Press Images; **925** © Sandra Baker/Liaison Agency/Getty Images; **926** © JP Laffont/Sygma/Corbis; **931** © Bettmann/Corbis; **932** AP Images; **933** Photofest; **934** © 1979 Time Inc./TimePix/Getty Images; **936** Gene Anderson; **937** Wally McNamee/Woodfin Camp & Associates; **939** © Corbis; **942** © Gerald French/Corbis; **946** AP Images; **948** Patrick Piel/Liaison Agency/Getty Images; **950 T** Leonard Freed/Magnum Photos Inc.; **950 B** © Dirck Halstead/Liaison Agency/Getty Images; **952** © Reuters/Corbis; **956** Yolanda M. Lopez; **960** (Detail) Hmong story cloth by Dia Cha and Chue & Nhia Cha. All Rights Reserved, Image Archives, Denver Museum of Nature & Science; **962** © Diane Cook & Len Jenshel; **963** Jennifer Szymaszek/AP Images; **965** Tom Haley/SIPA Press; **967** © Wally McNamee/Corbis; **968** Illustration by Anita Kunz for the New Yorker Magazine. Anita Kunz Limited. Reproduced by permission of the artist; **970** © Mayer Robert/Corbis Sygma; **972** Stephen G. Eick/Advizor Solutions; **974** © AFP/Corbis; **976** Courtesy of Ester Hernandez; **978** © Mark M. Lawrence/Corbis; **979** David Grubbs/Billings Gazette; **981 L** © Peter Turnley/Corbis; **981 C** © AFP/Corbis; **981 R** © Ralf-Finn Hestoft/Corbis/SABA; **983** © Reuters NewMedia Inc./Corbis; **985** David J. Phillip/AP Images; **986** Judith F. Baca, "Great Wall of Los Angeles," began 1976. © SPARC www.sparcmurals.org.

Index